US Foreign Policy

05/07

UNIVERSITY OF
WOLVERHAMPTON

US Foreign Policy

Edited by

Michael Cox

Professor of International Relations
and Director of IDEAS
London School of Economics and Political Science
London

Doug Stokes

Senior Lecturer in International Relations
University of Kent at Canterbury
Rutherford College
Kent

OXFORD
UNIVERSITY PRESS

OXFORD

UNIVERSITY PRESS

Great Clarendon Street, Oxford ox2 6dp

Oxford University Press is a department of the University of Oxford.
It furthers the University's objective of excellence in research, scholarship,
and education by publishing worldwide in

Oxford New York

Auckland Cape Town Dar es Salaam Hong Kong Karachi
Kuala Lumpur Madrid Melbourne Mexico City Nairobi
New Delhi Shanghai Taipei Toronto

With offices in

Argentina Austria Brazil Chile Czech Republic France Greece
Guatemala Hungary Italy Japan Poland Portugal Singapore
South Korea Switzerland Thailand Turkey Ukraine Vietnam

Oxford is a registered trade mark of Oxford University Press
in the UK and in certain other countries

Published in the United States
by Oxford University Press Inc., New York

British Library Cataloguing in Publication Data

Data available

Library of Congress Cataloging in Publication Data

Data available

Typeset by Laserwords Private Limited, Chennai, India
Printed in Italy
on acid-free paper by
L.E.G.O. S.p.A.

ISBN 978–0–19–922642–9

10 9 8 7 6 5 4 3 2 1

Acknowledgements

The editors would like to thank Ruth Anderson, our editor at OUP. Her input into the project has been steadfast throughout. Individually, we would also wish to express a debt of gratitude to Fiona Stephen, Rebecca Du Rietz, and Erica Du Rietz for their love and support throughout the completion of this project. Finally, we would like to say a special thank you to all our students, both past and present. Their contributions to this project have been invaluable. We hope this volume will provide the next generation with the necessary conceptual tools for understanding US foreign policy well into the twenty-first century.

M.C.

D.S.

Guided tour of textbook features

This text is enriched with a range of learning tools to help you navigate the text material and reinforce your knowledge of US foreign policy. This guided tour shows you how to get the most out of your textbook package.

Key quotes boxes

These boxes include memorable quotes to help bring ideas and concepts to life.

> **❝ KEY QUOTES 1.1:** ...nal Relations
>
> Realism has no place for an e...tition waxes and wanes, great powers fear each
> cies will not fight each other. T...nd always compete with each other for power.
> that peace between democraci...
> explain it theoretically, we bui...
> world with great import for...

(Mearsheimer 2001: 2)

...lp and power politics are institutions, not essential
...res of anarchy. Anarchy is what states make of it.

(Wendt 1992: 396)

systemic fa... ...inter-   sovereign states. The attribute of sovereignty means
nal or domestic... ...e of the key   that each state regards itself as the highest authority
theoretical debates over whether American foreign   and can order its domestic affairs according to how
policy should be understood as shaped primarily   they see fit. A third assumption is that states act on
by the external environment or primarily by the   the basis of self-help, meaning that they each must
internal environment of the United States. Those   take the appropriate steps to ensure their own sur-
that emphasize systemic factors argue that the most   vival in the anarchical international system. Fourth,
important influence on American foreign policy is   because both defensive and offensive realists believe
the international system and specifically the relative   that states must take the necessary steps to ensure
amount of power that the United States possesses.   their own survival, they argue that power is the main
According to this view, which Fared Zakaria (1992)   currency of international politics. While structural
associates with the concept of the *Primat der Aus-*   realists concur that all states must struggle for power,

Major debates and their impact boxes

These boxes identify major debates and the impact that these have had on real-world issues.

range of new bills designed to address the problem.   rations (including General Electric, BP, and Alcoa)
Indeed, a record number of climate change bills have   have a formed a coalition with four major US envi-
been proposed in the new Congress.[7] Significant   ronmental organizations, known as the US Climate

> **📢 MAJOR DEBATES AND THEIR IMP...** PA's authority to regulate emissions:
> no more deferral... ...to the president?
>
> Although George... ...pendent on the oil, coal, or motor
> dioxide as a po... ...ndustries.
> presidential c... ...of the EPA had claimed in 2003
> after coming... h Jr. had promised to regulate carbo... ...y to regulate GHG emissions,
> he would n... ...ave the requisite legal power in
> Authority (... nt under the Clean Air Act during hi... whether to regulate. Among
> sions unde... gn, he reversed this position shortly... ...for declining to act were sci-
> would pur... ...e with the president's foreign
> on technol... ...te in 2001. He also made it clear tha... ...e EPA believed that regulation
> ing GHG em... ...dent's ability to negotiate with
> from the Kyo... e federal Environmental Protecti... ...ns" to reduce emissions'. How-
> scientists, and... ...who presented the majority opin-
> governments wi... late greenhouse gas (GHG) e... rejected the argument and ruled that
> However, on 2 Ap... ...on should be determined on the basis
> *sachusetts v. Environm...* Act and that his administ... ...ments of the Clean Air Act and not the
> (2007) the US Supreme Co... ...e's foreign policy. The president's broad execu-
> to four that the EPA has the po... ...oach to mitig... ...authority was held not to 'extend to the refusal to
> dioxide emissions from new vehicles, along with other   execute domestic laws' (Supreme Court of the United
> greenhouse gases (GHG), as pollutants under the Clean   States 2007).

Controversies boxes

These boxes identify key controversies such as the risks of the USA's oil addiction.

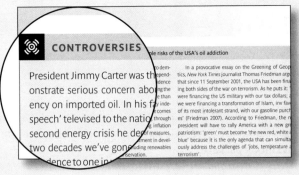

Key points

Chapter sections end with a set of key points that summarizes the most important arguments developed within each chapter topic.

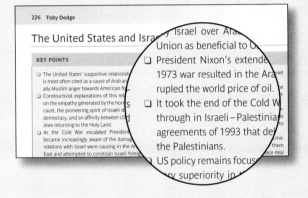

Questions

A set of carefully devised questions has been provided to help you assess your comprehension of core themes, and may also be used as the basis of seminar discussion and coursework.

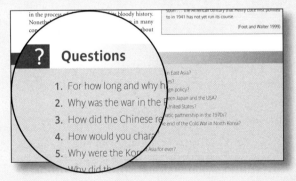

Further reading

To take your learning further, reading lists have been provided as a guide to find out more about the issues raised within each chapter topic and to help you locate the key academic literature in the field.

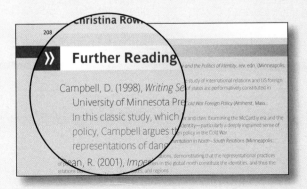

Guided tour of the Online Resource Centre

www.oxfordtextbooks.co.uk/orc/cox_stokes/

The Online Resource Centre that accompanies this book provides students and instructors with a wealth of ready-to-use research, learning, and teaching materials.

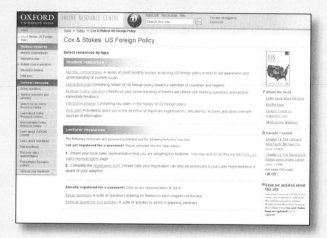

For students

Interactive map

An interactive map is provided with 'hot spots' on seven key regions. To find out more about US foreign policy towards a region, simply click on the area you are interested in.

Interactive timeline

An interactive timeline allows you to find out about the key events in the history of US foreign policy. Click on the date you want and discover what happened that year.

Annotated web links

These web links have been provided to point you in the direction of important organizations, documents, lectures, and other relevant sources of information.

Multiple choice questions

A bank of self-marking multiple choice questions has been provided for each chapter of the text, and includes instant feedback on your answers and cross-references back to the main textbook.

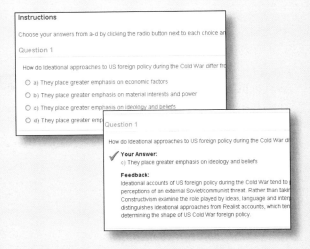

Monthly commentaries

A series of short monthly commentaries will be provided, analysing current and newsworthy events in order to aid your awareness and understanding of US foreign policy.

For lecturers

Essay questions and class activities

A suite of questions and activities that encourage class debate has been provided for use by instructors in tutorials, seminars, and assignments.

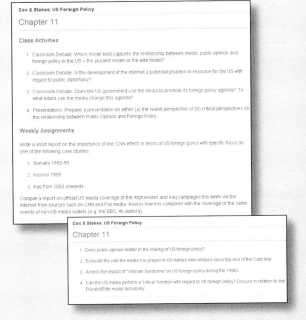

Brief contents

About the editors

 Professor Michael Cox holds a Chair in International Relations at the LSE where he is also Director of IDEAS, a major new Centre of Diplomacy and Strategy. The author and editor of over 20 books, Professor Cox has held several distinguished positions, including Editor of the Review of International Studies, Chair of the European Consortium for Political Research, and Visiting Research Fellow at the Nobel Institute in Oslo and at the Centre for Defence and Strategic Studies in Canberra Australia. Professor Cox formerly taught in the Department of International Politics, the University of Wales Aberystwyth, and The Queen's University of Belfast.

 Dr Doug Stokes is a Senior Lecturer in International Relations at the University of Kent, Canterbury. During his 2004 Economic and Social Research fellowship he authored his first book on US intervention in Colombia and is currently completing a new book on Global Energy Security and US intervention due out in 2009 with Johns Hopkins University Press. He is the editor of Global Society and formerly taught in the Department of International Politics, the University of Wales, Aberystwyth.

Detailed contents

List of boxes

Controversies

Key quotes

Major debates and their impact

About the contributors

Daniel Deudney is Associate Professor of Political Science at Johns Hopkins University. His most recent book is *Bounding Power: Republican Security Theory from the Polis to the Global Village* (2007).

Toby Dodge is a Reader in International Politics in the Politics Department at Queen Mary, University of London. He is also Senior Fellow for the Middle East at the International Institute for Strategic Studies. He is author of *Inventing Iraq: The Failure of Nation Building and a History Denied* (2005) and *Iraq's Future: The Aftermath of Regime Change* (2005). He has co-edited *Iraq at the Crossroads: State and Society in the Shadow of Regime Change* (2003) and *Globalisation and the Middle East: Islam, Economics, Culture and Politics* (2002).

Gregory Dubinsky is a graduate of Wesleyan University and a junior fellow at the Carnegie Endowment for International Peace in Washington, DC.

John Dumbrell is Professor of Government in the School of Government and International Affairs, Durham University. His most recent books are *President Lyndon Johnson and Soviet Communism* (2004: winner of the Richard E. Neustadt book prize for 2005) and *A Special Relationship: Anglo-American Relations from the Cold War to Iraq* (2006). He is currently researching the foreign policy of the presidency of Bill Clinton.

James Dunkerley is Director, Institute for the Study of the Americas, University of London, and author of *Americana: The Americas in the World around 1850* (2000).

Robyn Eckersley is Professor in the School of Political Science, Sociology, and Criminology at the University of Melbourne. She is the author of *The Green State* (2004) and co-editor of *The State and the Global Ecological Crisis* (2005) and *Political Theory and the Ecological Challenge* (2006).

Beth A. Fischer is an assistant professor in the Department of Political Science at the University of Toronto. She is the author of *The Reagan Reversal: Foreign Policy and the End of the Cold War* (1997) and *Triumph? The End of the Cold War and US Foreign Policy Today* (forthcoming) as well as numerous articles on US foreign policy and international security.

G. John Ikenberry is the Albert G. Milbank Professor of Politics and International Affairs at Princeton University. He is the author of *After Victory: Institutions, Strategic Restraint, and the Rebuilding of Order after Major Wars* (2001), which won the 2002 Schroeder-Jervis Award presented by the American Political Science Association for the best book in international history and politics. He is currently writing a book entitled *Liberal Leviathan: The Origins, Crisis, and Transformation of the American System*.

Caroline Kennedy-Pipe is Professor of International Relations at the University of Sheffield. She is currently Chair of the British International Studies Association. She is editor of the journal *Civil Wars* and co-editor of *Minerva*. She is the author of *Russia and the World* (1998) and editor with Clive Jones of *Security in a Global Age* (2000).

Walter LaFeber is the Andrew Tisch and James Tisch University Professor Emeritus, and a Weiss Presidential Teaching Fellow at Cornell University. His recent books include

America, Russia, and the Cold War, 1945–2006, 10th edn. (2007), and *Michael Jordan and the New American Capitalism*, 2nd edn. (2002).

Anatol Lieven is a senior research fellow at the New America Foundation in Washington, DC, and co-author, with John Hulsman, of *Ethical Realism: A Vision for America's Role in the World* (2006). His previous book was *America Right or Wrong: An Anatomy of American Nationalism* (2004). From 1986 to 1998 he was a British journalist in South Asia, the former Soviet Union, and eastern Europe.

Jeffrey W. Meiser is a graduate student in international relations and American politics in the political science department at Johns Hopkins University.

Robert G. Patman is a Professor of Political Studies at the University of Otago, in New Zealand. He is the Director of the Master of International Studies Programme at Otago, and has authored or edited seven books. In addition, he is a co-editor of the new Praeger series on *The Ethics of American Foreign Policy*. He is also a Fulbright Senior Scholar, and provides regular contributions to the national and international media on global issues and events.

Piers Robinson is a lecturer in International Politics at the Department of Politics, University of Manchester. He is author of *The CNN Effect: The Myth of News, Foreign Policy and Intervention* (2002) and is currently writing and researching on media and the 2003 Iraq War.

Paul Rogers is Professor of Peace Studies at Bradford University where he teaches courses on international security, arms control, and political violence. His most recent books are *A War Too Far* and *Into the Long War* (both 2006), *The Political Road to War with Iraq* (with Nick Ritchie, 2006), and *Beyond Terror* (with Chris Abbott and John Sloboda, 2007). A collection of his writings over the past twenty years has just been published in the UK and USA by Routledge under the title of *Global Security and the War on Terror: Elite Power and the Illusion of Control*. His new book *Why We're Losing the War on Terror* was published in November 2007.

Christina Rowley is a lecturer and Ph.D. candidate in the Department of Politics, University of Bristol. She has published articles on the politics of science fiction and on representations of gender in the television show *Firefly* and film *Serenity*. Her doctoral research focuses on representations of gender in Vietnam War films and IR theory.

Peter Rutland is a Professor of Government at Wesleyan University. Recent articles include 'Russia's Economic Role in Asia', in *Strategic Asia 2006* (2006).

Richard Saull is Senior Lecturer in International Politics in the Department of Politics, Queen Mary, University of London. He has written two books on the Cold War, *Rethinking Theory and History in the Cold War* (2001) and *The Cold War and After* (2007).

Brian C. Schmidt is Associate Professor of Political Science at Carleton University. He is the author of *The Political Discourse of Anarchy: A Disciplinary History of International Relations* (1998) and *Imperialism and Internationalism in the Discipline of International Relations* (2006), co-edited with David Long.

Michael Smith is Professor of European Politics and Jean Monnet Chair in the Department of Politics, International Relations, and European Studies at Loughborough University. Among many other books, articles, and chapters, he is the co-author with Steven McGuire of *The European Union and the United States: Competition and Convergence in the World Arena* (2008), and co-edited, with Christopher Hill, *International Relations and the European Union* (2005).

Peter L. Trubowitz is Associate Professor of Government at the University of Texas at Austin and Senior Fellow at the Robert Strauss Center for International Security and Law. He is the author of *Defining the National Interest: Conflict and Consensus in American Foreign Policy* (1998) and numerous articles, chapters, and opinion pieces on world politics, foreign policy, and American politics.

Jutta Weldes is a Reader in International Relations at the University of Bristol. She is the author of *Constructing National Interests: The United States and the Cuban Missile Crisis* (1999), co-editor of *Cultures of Insecurity: State, Communities and the Production of Danger* (1999), editor of *To Seek out New Worlds: Science Fiction and World Politics* (2003), and co-editor of the special issue of the *British Journal of Politics and International Relations* on 'Gender and International Relations' (2007).

Introduction: US foreign policy—past, present, and future

Michael Cox and Doug Stokes

Over the past few years no single topic has been discussed so frequently—and with so much obvious passion—as how to evaluate the sources of America's conduct, the impact its conduct has had on the wider world, and the extent to which its actions have contributed (or not) to global justice and order. Certainly, it is difficult to recall a moment in recent history when the United States and its foreign policy have been the subject of so much anguished reflection both at home and abroad. There are several reasons why.

The first has to do with something that writers had been reflecting on for some years: the fact that the United States not only possessed formidable assets (even the French Foreign Minister in the 1990s referred to America as being a 'hyperpower') but as a result of the collapse of its superpower rival appeared to be in a position that no other nation had ever been in before—of being so dominant that it was inconceivable that any other state could either balance or even think of catching up with it. Few experts had anticipated such a situation; many indeed continued to assume the world would soon return to some kind of equilibrium. However, as one millennium gave way to another, one thing began to look clear: the new century looked as though it might turn out to be just as 'American' as the one that had just passed away. US hegemony was here to stay—or so it seemed—and the sooner other, lesser actors got used to this not entirely acceptable state of affairs, the better.

This radical and apparently permanent transformation in the balance of power was at least one reason why the debate about the role of the United States in the world took on a more intense form. Another was the election of George W. Bush in late 2000 and what looked like a determined effort on the part of his administration to translate this position of strength into a new American foreign policy which not only assumed US primacy, but aimed to enhance it. Indeed, it very soon became evident that the new Bush team was not only prepared to reject established rules whereby the USA tried to work with others to achieve desired outcomes—multilateralism by any other name—but was now ready, willing, and apparently able to employ its formidable assets to bring about the foreign policy outcomes it alone desired. This immediately caused a reaction abroad, one that was rendered all the more intense no doubt because of the character of the President himself, the aggressive image projected by some of his closest confidants (including Vice-President Cheney), and the fact that unlike his Democratic predecessor Bill Clinton—a favourite amongst Europeans in particular—he did not seem at all averse to proclaiming in a most 'American first' way that the United States would no longer be constrained by international institutions, international law, or international opinion.

None of this though would have the impact it did without 11 September 2001 followed in short order by an American attack on Afghanistan and the official declaration by President Bush in January 2002 that there was an 'axis of evil' (comprising North Korea, Iran, and Iraq) whose very existence threatened world order. America he now declared was at 'war' with a global enemy every bit as dangerous as—possibly more so than—those it had previously confronted at different stages during the twentieth century. The notion of what became known as the 'war on terror' did not go uncontested. Some questioned its strategic coherence; a few its implications for relations with the wider Muslim world; and still more the longer-term impact it might have on the health of American democracy itself. But there was little the critics could do to alter the policy path the Bush team had decided to go down. America had been attacked and America had to respond robustly, even ruthlessly. A critical corner had thus been turned. The United States had entered an altogether more dangerous era, similar in broad character—if not necessarily in precise form—to the Cold War of old with its accompanying tensions, stress on national security, and sense that the nation (and the West as a whole) was facing an implacable totalitarian foe whose ultimate purpose was the destruction of the American way of life.

The rapid and unexpected collapse of the post-Cold War era of liberal hope with its underlying assumption that the world could be made safe through the spread of open markets and the promotion of liberal democracy not only reminds us of how deeply unpredictable world politics can be. It also draws our attention to the importance that war has constantly played in America's engagement with the modern world. No doubt America would have emerged onto the international stage—as in fact it had by the beginning of the twentieth century—on the basis of its own enormous resources, strategic isolation, continued territorial unity (made possible by a bloody Civil War of its own), and almost unlimited supply of cheap European labour. But it was global war, and America's victory in all of these after 1914, that was to lay the ground for what some analysts by the end of the twentieth century were referring to as the 'unipolar moment'. The story is normally told in four parts—beginning with the First World War, a human disaster that left a shell-shocked Europe, in Trotsky's telling words, living on borrowed time, shattered dreams, and American loans. The way was further cleared by the time the guns fell silent again in 1945 leaving an all-powerful United States (now controlling 70 per cent of the world's financial resources and most of its advanced military capacity) in sole occupation of Japan and almost complete control of western Europe. America's rise then continued with the Cold War, a multi-layered international competition that effectively transformed the USA into the world's most powerful banker and leading policeman. And it was completed when communism imploded in 1989 and the last remaining obstacle to American primacy in the form of the USSR finally admitted defeat in 1991. This placed the United States in a position that many had previously thought impossible—in the late 1980s some writers were even predicting the nation's decline—and which some (including many Americans) feared on the not unreasonable grounds that a world in which there were two superpowers, each seeking to balance the ambitions of the other, was more likely to a be safer world than one in which there was no balance at all.

Victory in the great struggles of the twentieth century not only had a revolutionary impact on America's position in the international system. It also transformed America economically and militarily while feeding the belief—some would say the hegemonic illusion—that if the past was any guide to the future, there was very little that this most exceptional of nations, blessed both by God and geography, could not do. It was such self-confidence no doubt, born of repeated victories over successive enemies, that probably tempted the Bush administration to risk turning what many had hitherto seen as an imperfectly conducted but legitimate war against Osama bin Laden and radical Islamism into what many increasingly came to view as an illegitimate and unnecessary war against Iraq in 2003. As we now know, military victory in this particular conflict against a much over-hyped 'rogue state' proved to be remarkably easy—possibly too easy, as the short-term joys of liberation very quickly turned into the brute facts of occupation leaving the United States standing between a rock and a hard place, unable to win a war the American people no longer supported, but in a critically important part of the world from which it could not retreat.

One of the more interesting consequences of Iraq was to compel some in the United States to see if there was anything they might learn from the past in order to see how they could extricate themselves from the quagmire in which they now found themselves. But as wiser voices have noted, one should always beware desperate people searching for usable historical analogies, and perhaps no analogy was to be more misused than that which was increasingly drawn between America's various defeats in South-East Asia in the 1970s and the challenges it was now facing in a region home to at least 60 per cent of the world's current oil reserves, two of America's most important allies (Israel and Saudi Arabia), and one of its most important enemies—revolutionary Iran. Admittedly, the USA lost far more troops fighting communism in Vietnam than it was losing fighting insurgents in Iraq. Still, at the end of the day, it did manage to extricate itself from South-East Asia without too much damage being done to its more general position in the world. Indeed, within five years of the communist takeover in Vietnam in 1975 President Reagan was in the White House confidently promising to rebuild American power; within ten the reforming Mikhail Gorbachev had assumed office in the Soviet Union; and in under twenty, Vietnam was already beginning to experiment with capitalism. One had to doubt whether the United States would

be able to recuperate quite so easily or completely following Iraq.

Wars may be appalling things. But one of their more 'positive' consequences from the point of view of the scholar and the student is to increase interest in international affairs; and certainly one of the more beneficial consequences of both the war on terror and America's war in Iraq has been to generate a quite enormous literature ranging from those reflecting in great detail as to how and why the United States went into Iraq in the first place, the role played by various pressure groups in bringing about the war, and, significantly—and possibly of more general interest—whether or not this incursion marked a new imperial turn in American grand strategy. Indeed, one of the richer debates over the past few years in US foreign policy studies has revolved around the issue of imperialism and empire, whether or not the United States is an empire, and if it is, then why do so many Americans seem to deny the fact? This in turn has led to a related discussion about America's future: put simply, will the USA continue to maintain its dominance for the foreseeable future, or, will it, like all other great powers in the past, be overtaken by other states, possibly even be brought down by the adventuristic policies of President Bush himself? It is difficult to come to any firm conclusion. We can certainly agree that the United States is in deep trouble in the Middle East; possibly confronting wider structural challenges (financial deficits, a hollowing out of its industrial base, reduced economic opportunities for the majority) which mean that its ability to influence world politics is likely to diminish over the longer term. But we should be wary of crying wolf. America may be in some distress. But it still retains a formidable array of military and economic assets. It also remains the only global actor with serious international reach. Its enemies meanwhile remain weak (though occasionally deadly) while its allies—even the more irritable of them—show little sign of seeking to build a new world order that does not revolve around the United States. Nor, to provide perspective, should we forget how effective the USA has been over time. Certainly, when judged from the point of view of history, it has been a remarkably successful state, initially as chief architect of a new liberal international order after 1945; then as main protector of the order it had helped construct; and finally as chief driver behind globalization during the 1990s following victory over its main rivals. On the basis of its past record, we should be rather careful not to write America off just yet!

In putting this large and ambitious volume together the editors have called upon a range of expert voices representing a spectrum of opinion drawn from at least three continents—in large part because we have been dissatisfied for some time with other volumes on the subject that have generally tended to be written from only one 'national' point of view, invariably American. The book does not pretend to be exhaustive. Nonetheless, it does manage to touch several intellectual bases; many more, we would guess, than the average textbook on the subject. It also has the added virtue from the point of view of the student and teacher of taking the widest possible look at US foreign policy. Thus it treats the 'outside' just as seriously as it does the 'inside', and, within the 'inside', culture as much as it does economics, and public opinion as much as it does the main sites of organized power. It also brings the story right up to date with three concluding chapters which look in detail at the world after '9/11' and the possible paths that lie ahead for the United States in an increasingly turbulent world. Based on the research of some of the world's leading experts, but made accessible to the general reader, the volume—wide in scope and pluralist in character—we hope sets new standards for discussing contemporary US foreign policy today.

It would be pointless here to summarize what is in the chapters themselves. They will stand or fall on their own obvious academic merits. That said, there are at least five broad themes, narratives if you like, that inform the text.

The first is the importance of the past for understanding the present. History, we need to remind ourselves, is not just some distant place that political scientists ought to visit now and again for chunks of interesting, but not necessarily essential, information, but the very source we need to go back to, to understand how a nation like the United States has arrived at the destination it has and with what baggage on

board. There is a view (associated with the realist school of thought) which argues that the only thing we need to know about a state is the amount of power it has. Its character as such does not matter. This we believe is not merely too abstract; it ignores the specific way in which the United States rose to power in the first place (a subject dealt with in the chapter by LaFeber), the impact this ascent then had upon the United States as an exceptional kind of nation—an issue discussed in some detail by Deudney and his co-author—and how that power in turn was translated into policy in the decades after the United States became a superpower in the 1940s. In the process of deploying its mass assets America was also transformed as a nation, most obviously during the Cold War according to Beth Fischer, when in any average year the nation spent nearly spent nearly 10 per cent of its GNP and 30 per cent of its budget waging global conflict against a perceived communist enemy. Modern students may of course wonder why the volume even bothers with an era now so remote as the Cold War. Our reply quite simply is that unless we understand the Cold War, the way it ended (on largely American terms), and the legacies it left behind (subjects that are analysed in the two chapters by Saull and Dumbrell) we will not be able to grasp what has happened to United States over the last two decades. Furthermore, as at least three of our authors—Ikenberry, Kennedy-Pipe, and Lieven—point out, the past is not just another country but an essential tool for helping us explain where the United States might be heading in the future.

The second large theme—related to the first—concerns the complex relationship between foreign policy understood here as a set of short-term aims and America's longer-term goals and interests. As Weldes and her co-author point out, the notion of interest is a problematic one and cannot be separated from how actors construct identity and how that identity in turn impacts upon perceptions of interest. Still, American foreign policy elites over time have been remarkably consistent in the ways they have tended to think about the world in general and what kind of world would best serve the United States. Naturally, there has been some room for debate and disagreement, but overall policy makers have assumed that the international order that would best advance American interests would be composed in the main of democratic states (in the belief that democracies do not go to war with another), open markets (on the grounds that they raise living standards, foster cooperation, and generate wealth), and self-determining nations (on the assumption that formal empires were not only antithetical to freedom but more likely to exclude American influence). Of course, the United States has not always been able to pursue these goals at all times, or in all places together at the same time. Thus what may have worked in relationship to post-war Europe—a region whose importance to the United States is assessed by Smith—has not always worked when it comes to its complicated, unequal relationship with Latin America, a theme developed by James Dunkerley in his chapter. Nor is it easy to conclude that US relations with Africa (the subject of Patman's chapter) were always motivated by such clearly defined or lofty goals.

That said, there are certain constants in the way America has related to the international system, though as Toby Dodge points out in his contribution, consistency has not always been a feature of the way in which the United States has dealt with the Middle East since it first became seriously involved with the region midway through the twentieth century. Certainly, the Bush goal of promoting democracy will not be easily achieved. Nor, as Rutland and Cox point out in their contributions on Russia and Asia-Pacific respectively, has the United States always achieved all of its ambitious goals in the 'post-communist' world. Still, as Cox shows, the United States has been more successful in managing East Asia since the end of the Cold War than it has in dealing with Russia. Here, it is premature perhaps to talk of a 'new Cold War'. But as Rutland notes, early optimism about a new partnership with Russia has given way to much greater pessimism in Washington.

A third big theme developed here is the central importance of the 'domestic' in shaping US foreign policy choices. Here the book affirms the well-known truth that what the United States does abroad will be determined as much by factors at home—the influence of interest groups, the role of institutions, and the power of ideas—as it will be by external opportunities and threats. It is perhaps too much of a cliché to say that all politics is domestic and that all foreign policy merely a reflection of what happens domestically. But as many of the chapters here reveal, there is no Chinese wall dividing the international from the internal, the global from the specifically local. This is why the book has commissioned a number of original chapters to think about this large problem, one of which (by Michael Foley) deals squarely with the relationship between Congress and the President, a second (by Piers Robinson), that assesses the impact of the media and public opinion on the making of US foreign policy, and yet a third (by Peter Trubowitz), which advances the original claim that if we are to make sense of US foreign policy we should deconstruct the notion of the United States itself and assess its foreign policy as the by-product of shifting regional coalitions and not some eternal notion of what may or may not constitute the American national interest. Furthermore, as Peter Gowan reminds us, foreign policy is not merely a reflection of domestic politics but economic capabilities too, perhaps more so than ever in an increasingly globalized world economic system where power is not only measured in terms of how many weapons one might possess, but also by one's ability to innovate and compete. Foreign policy can never be reduced to economics as some seem to believe. But any study on US foreign policy that ignored material power and economic pressures—which many more conventional texts appear to do—would be seriously incomplete in our view.

This brings us then to the issue of perspective or what is sometimes referred to as 'balance'. As we suggested at the outset, US foreign policy over the past few years has been the subject of intense political debate. Everybody it seems has an opinion on the United States, even, possibly especially, those who have never studied the subject in any great depth. This is not something that can be said about the many expert authors gathered together here. Many, it would be fair to say—Paul Rogers being amongst them—are highly critical of the Bush administration and the way it has defined the war on terror. Some (including Brian Schmidt in his chapter on theory) are also deeply concerned about the impact that Bush's apparent abandonment of realist thinking in favour of dreams of empire will have on the United States and the world over the longer term. None of the authors though seeks either to denounce the United States or cast it in the role of the world's biggest 'rogue state', in spite of its fairly abysmal record in one of the key challenges confronting the international system—global environment (a topic dealt with by Eckersley in her chapter). Still, having strongly held views, as all the authors here most obviously do, does not preclude them from seeking to explore in depth how US foreign policy is made, why policy makers arrive at the decisions they do, and with what consequences. Indeed, it could be argued that only by approaching the subject with sufficient critical distance is it possible to engage in any meaningful—and engaging—way with their respective topics.

Finally, the authors here all accept the self-evident fact that whatever one might think of the United States past, present, or future, it is simply too important to be ignored. Here in large part lies the ultimate rationale for this book. For whether one is a radical critic, a conservative defender, liberal supporter, or of the opinion that American hegemony is a threat to world peace, it is absolutely vital to find out how United States, with its vast national security apparatus, remarkably dynamic economy, complex array of alliances, and highly exportable popular culture, actually impacts on the world. During the seemingly predictable years before 1989, and the somewhat confused ones immediately thereafter, the task was difficult enough. In the altogether different world we live in now with its uncertainties and insecurities, it has become even more so. Thus the need for such a volume on such an important subject in our view. Ideas we are often told matter a great deal. This is true. But material facts like states matter as well— none more so than the United States whose policies in the future (as much as its decisions in the past) are bound to impact on us all, for good or ill, well into the twenty-first century.

1 Theories of US foreign policy

Brian Schmidt

Chapter contents

Introduction

This chapter examines some of the competing theories that have been put forth to explain American foreign policy. In the quest to explain the foreign policy behaviour of the United States, a number of different and competing theories have been developed by International Relations scholars. Some theories focus on the role of the international system in shaping American foreign policy while others argue that various domestic factors inside the United States are the driving force. Still others attempt to combine both external and internal sources. The chapter begins with an introduction to some of the obstacles to constructing a theory of foreign policy. The following section provides a general survey of some of the competing theories of American foreign policy. The next section turns to the theoretical debate over the origins of the Cold War. The chapter concludes by examining the debate over the most appropriate grand strategy that the United States should follow in the post-Cold War era.

The task of explaining American foreign policy is infinitely complex. Part of the difficulty arises from the fact that there are so many diverse factors at play that it is often difficult to determine the underlying reason for a given policy. The United States' decision to invade Iraq in 2003 and overthrow the government of Saddam Hussein clearly reveals a complex array of factors that led to this foreign policy. The problem confronting the foreign policy analyst is which set of factors to focus on in order to explain the external behaviour of the United States. Should one focus on the personality of George W. Bush and the members of his inner circle of advisers? Should one focus on the alleged threat that Iraq posed to the United States and to the distribution of power in the Middle East? Or should one look inside the United States to see how the values of liberty and liberal democracy shape the goals that America attempts to achieve in its external relations with other states in general, and Iraq in particular?

As a result of this complexity, almost all those who have attempted to explain American foreign policy have recognized the centrality of theory. Theory is both necessary and unavoidable when it comes to understanding or explaining international politics. Unavoidable because both policy makers and scholars approach the world from a specific paradigm or world view that in turn generates specific theories. Theories are necessary in that they tell us what to focus on and what to ignore. We need theories to help us organize and make sense of all the information that overwhelms us on a daily basis. While students of foreign policy recognize the centrality of theory, the goal of achieving an overarching theory to explain the foreign policy behaviour of the United States has proven to be illusive. Instead we have a number of competing theories that focus on different levels of analysis to account for the behaviour of the United States.

An early and insightful attempt to develop a theoretical framework for identifying the main sources of a state's foreign policy was developed by the renowned political scientist James N. Rosenau (1971). Rosenau identified five potential sources that influence a state's foreign policy: the external environment of the international system, the domestic, societal environment of a nation-state, the governmental structure that specifies the policy-making process, the bureaucratic roles occupied by individual policy makers, and finally the personal characteristics and idiosyncrasies of individual foreign policy officials and government elites (see Figure 1.1). Each of these five sources can be considered independent variables that either individually or collectively help to explain the foreign policy behaviour of the United States, the dependent variable.

The external or systemic sources of foreign policy draw our attention to the point that the formulation of American foreign policy does not take place in a vacuum, rather the United States, like any other country, must take account of, and respond to, events taking place in the realm of international politics. The terrorist attacks against the United States on 11 September 2001 dramatically illustrate how an event

Independent variables   Dependent variable

External environment (international system) ------→
Societal environment ------------------→
Governmental structure ----------------→   American Foreign Policy
Bureaucratic roles --------------------→
Personalities of individuals -------------→

Fig. 1.1 The multiple sources of American foreign policy

perpetuated by an external actor, in this case by the al-Qaeda terrorist network spearheaded by Osama bin Laden, directly elicits a foreign policy response. The terrorist attacks against the World Trade Center in New York City and the Pentagon in Washington, DC, did not determine the specific course of action that the United States decided to take—the global war on terrorism—but the event itself did necessitate a response. On any given day numerous developments take place in areas outside the United States that American foreign policy officials must respond to even if they were previously preoccupied with a different region or issue area. Moreover, as we will see, the systemic source also highlights the underlying distribution of power in the international system and the effect this has on American foreign policy.

However, many foreign policy analysts insist that the domestic sources of foreign policy are more important than external sources. The societal source accentuates the non-governmental aspects of a country's society that influence its foreign policy behaviour. The national character and value orientation of a country cannot be discounted, as many believe that foreign policy should both reflect and seek to promote the core values and ideology of the domestic political system. Many have observed that this view has been especially strong in the case of the United States as reflected by America's liberal, democratic character and by its desire to promote this political ideology around the world (Smith 1994). Indeed one alleged contributing factor to the decision to wage war against Iraq was the desire by the United States to spread liberty and democracy to Iraq and the Middle East.

In addition to the societal sources of American foreign policy, there is also the particular governmental structure of the United States that plays a key role in the formulation and implementation of foreign policy. The Constitution of the United States establishes an elaborate, and some would argue cumbersome, framework for the formulation of foreign policy. The constitutional separation and division of power between the executive and legislative branches has led to what some refer to as 'an invitation to struggle' over the shaping of American foreign policy. Compared to other political systems, the United States political system allows for a vast array of actors to have a role in the formulation of American foreign policy (see Chapter 6). This includes the President, cabinet officials such as the Secretary of Defense, Secretary of State, and the Secretary of Commerce, advisers to the President such as the National Security Adviser and the Director of the Central Intelligence Agency, members of the United States Congress, lobbyists, both foreign and domestic, and interest groups. In fact this is only a partial list and one can identify a host of additional actors that have a role in the formulation of American foreign policy.

This partial list of actors who have a role in the formulation of foreign policy draws our attention to the role played by large bureaucratic agencies such as the Department of Defense, the State Department, and the Central Intelligence Agency. Those who study the behaviour of bureaucratic organizations often make the point that the individuals who work for a particular agency are socialized to reflect their own agency's interests and needs. In a sense, the characteristics of the bureaucracy are more important than the characteristics and personality of the individuals. Thus even when an individual gains access to the foreign policy-making process, role theory suggests that a person's influence is circumscribed by the policy-making roles they occupy. The basic insight of the role source is captured by the adage 'where you stand depends on where you sit'. Thus the position that a person takes on an issue of foreign policy depends on the bureaucracy that they represent.

The individual source category argues quite simply that individuals—their personality, past experiences, upbringing, personal convictions—matter greatly. Since American foreign policy behaviour follows from decisions made by elites, and often from decisions made by the President of the United States, the individual source prompts us to investigate the characteristics and idiosyncrasies unique to the decision maker. The thesis is that the idiosyncratic characteristics of leaders influence American foreign policy behaviour. For many, it seems impossible to explain the direction of American foreign policy without highlighting the personality traits and beliefs of the current President.

Rosenau's framework is a simplifying device that helps us to identify and isolate the multiple sources of American foreign policy. In this sense it fulfils one of the core functions of theory; it helps us to identify what to focus on in our attempt to explain foreign policy. But Rosenau did not provide a full-blown theory of foreign policy, rather he offered what he termed a 'pre-theory' of foreign policy. Thus he did not specify how each of his five sources directly influences foreign policy behaviour nor did he assess the relative influence of each of the sources. Ideally we want to know which of the sources is most important, because if we needed all five we would not have a parsimonious theory; that is, one that uses the fewest variables but nevertheless offers the most explanatory power. We might have a good description of a state's foreign policy, but we would not really have an explanatory theory. Those who have continued to struggle to construct a theory of foreign policy have engaged in intense debates over the most important sources of a state's external behaviour. We now turn to some of the theories that have been put forth to explain American foreign policy.

Theories of American foreign policy

The previous section made the case that theory is absolutely essential to the task of explaining American foreign policy. Yet even if we agree that theory is necessary, this, by itself, does not establish that it is possible to construct a theory of foreign policy. Kenneth Waltz, one of the leading American scholars of international politics, argues that given the complexity of the foreign policy-making process, and the fact that foreign policy is shaped by both domestic and international factors, it is impossible to construct a theory of foreign policy.[1] According to Waltz, the best that we can hope to achieve is a theory of international politics; that is, one that 'describes the range of likely outcomes of the actions and interactions of states within a given system and shows how the range of expectations varies as systems change' (Waltz 1979: 71).

Many scholars, however, want more than this—they also want to be able to explain the foreign policy behaviour of the United States and other countries. These scholars have ventured to create a theory of foreign policy, one that seeks 'to explain what states try to achieve in the external realm and when they try to achieve it' (Rose 1998: 145).

Compared to a theory of international politics, which is interested in explaining general patterns of behaviour such as the causes of war, a theory of foreign policy seeks to explain why a particular state pursued a specific policy at a certain point in time. A theory of foreign policy is dedicated to answering the question of what causes a state to adopt a specific type of foreign policy. Thus, for example, rather than trying to explain the general, underlying cause of war, a theory of American foreign policy attempts to explain why the United States chose to wage war against Iraq in March 2003.

Systemic theories

As a first cut, we can divide theories of American foreign policy into those that accentuate external or

> **KEY QUOTES 1.1:** Competing theories of International Relations

Realism has no place for an expectation that democracies will not fight each other. To the degree we establish that peace between democracies is a fact, and are able to explain it theoretically, we build an alternative view of the world with great import for expectations and for policy.

(Russett 1993: 24)

The sad fact is that international politics has always been a ruthless and dangerous business, and it is likely to remain that way. Although the intensity of their competition waxes and wanes, great powers fear each other and always compete with each other for power.

(Mearsheimer 2001: 2)

Self-help and power politics are institutions, not essential features of anarchy. Anarchy is what states make of it.

(Wendt 1992: 396)

systemic factors versus those that emphasize internal or domestic factors. Here we have one of the key theoretical debates over whether American foreign policy should be understood as shaped primarily by the external environment or primarily by the internal environment of the United States. Those that emphasize systemic factors argue that the most important influence on American foreign policy is the international system and specifically the relative amount of power that the United States possesses. According to this view, which Fared Zakaria (1992) associates with the concept of the *Primat der Aussenpolitik* (the primacy of foreign policy), a state's foreign policy is a consequence of pressures emanating from the distribution of power in the international system. In other words, the international distribution of power is an autonomous force that has a direct influence on the behaviour of states.

Defensive realism and offensive realism are two prominent theories which argue that systemic pressures play a decisive role in shaping the foreign policy behaviour of the United States. Both theories share a number of similar assumptions about the international system that they believe greatly impact the foreign policy behaviour of all states. First, defensive and offensive realists agree that the international system is anarchic, meaning that there is no higher, centralized authority above states. This follows logically from the second assumption that the most important actors in the international system are

sovereign states. The attribute of sovereignty means that each state regards itself as the highest authority and can order its domestic affairs according to how they see fit. A third assumption is that states act on the basis of self-help, meaning that they each must take the appropriate steps to ensure their own survival in the anarchical international system. Fourth, because both defensive and offensive realists believe that states must take the necessary steps to ensure their own survival, they argue that power is the main currency of international politics. While structural realists concur that all states must struggle for power, the key to understanding a particular state's foreign policy rests with its relative amount of power. The amount of power that the United States possesses at a particular time in history compared to other states in the international system largely determines the character of its foreign policy. For realists it is a truism that capabilities (power) largely determine interests. Thus after the Second World War, as the power of the United States increased relative to that of other states, so did its interests. Many argue that this trend of an expansion of US power and interests continues to this day.

Defensive realism

What effect does the international distribution of power have on the behaviour of a state's foreign policy? According to defensive realists, states are fundamentally security maximizers. The international system, according to defensive realists, only provides incentives for moderate behaviour, and expansionistic policies to achieve security are generally not required because the international system is basically benign. This means that in order to ensure its own survival in the self-help, anarchical environment, a prudent foreign policy for the United States is only to seek an appropriate amount of power. Defensive realists argue that expansionist and aggressive behaviour most often proves to be counterproductive because it triggers other states to form a counterbalancing coalition. As a result of the belief that states are strongly inclined to balance against aggressive powers, they are, in Joseph Grieco's terms, 'defensive positionalists' and 'will only seek the minimum level of power that is needed to attain and to maintain their security and survival' (Grieco 1997: 167). According to many defensive

realists, a direct consequence of the expansionistic foreign policy that the United States has embarked on in the aftermath of 9/11 is that we are beginning to see an active attempt by other states to balance American power. The recent character and extent of balancing behaviour against the United States is further discussed in Controversies 1.1. In addition to balancing inhibiting an excessive power-seeking foreign policy, defensive realists introduce the concept of the offence–defence balance and argue that as a result of variables such geography, technology, and, most importantly, military doctrine, conquest rarely pays and that security can be readily achieved under anarchy.[2]

While the theory of defensive realism predicts that the foreign policy behaviour of the United States should be one of restraint, especially since America, partly owing to geography, enjoys a high degree of

 CONTROVERSIES 1.1: Balancing against the United States?

For realists, the balance of power is an enduring feature of international politics. Although various meanings have been attributed to the concept of the balance of power, the most common definition holds that if the survival of a state or a number of weak states is threatened by a hegemonic state or coalition of stronger states, they each seek to increase their own military capabilities (internal balancing) or join forces, establish a formal alliance (external balancing), and seek to preserve their own independence by checking the power of the opposing side. The mechanism of the balance of power seeks to ensure an equilibrium of power in which case no one state or coalition of states is in a position to dominate all the others.

Today, the controversy is whether the United States is so powerful that the balance of power is no longer an operating principle of international politics. Here the argument is that the United States enjoys such an overwhelming abundance of power relative to all other states that counterbalancing is prohibitively costly (Wohlforth 2002). Apart from the preponderance of American power argument is the liberal claim that the United States is a benign hegemon and that, as a result of a number of institutional constraints, other states do not find American power to

be threatening (Ikenberry 2002). According to these two perspectives, states are not actively seeking to counterbalance the United States.

Other scholars argue that as a result of both unprecedented American power and its recent aggressive unilateral foreign policy behaviour, states are beginning to counterbalance against the United States. The best evidence of this might not be traditional 'hard balancing' in the form of countervailing alliances, but rather in the form of 'soft balancing' that Robert Pape defines as 'nonmilitary tools to delay, frustrate, and undermine aggressive unilateral U.S. military policies' (2005: 10). Some interpret the refusal of the Permanent Members of the Security Council to pass a resolution authorizing the use of force against Iraq as an example of soft balancing. This action did not prevent the United States from invading Iraq, but it did complicate the mission and certainly increased the costs of the war. And while states like China, France, and Russia have so far only adopted institutional and diplomatic strategies to constrain US power, proponents of soft balancing do not rule out the possibility of states turning to hard balancing; especially if the United States unilaterally takes militarily action against additional states.

security, one could argue that the recent history of American foreign policy belies this prediction. Writers such as Noam Chomsky (2004) have argued that the United States has pursued a policy of hegemony and has frequently sought opportunities to increase its power relative to other states. As a fall-back position, defensive realists posit that a variety of domestic pathologies and deformities can prevent a state from conforming to the imperatives of the international system.[3]

Thus when the United States or any other state over-expands or pursues empire, defensive realists argue that the cause of this behaviour is rooted at the domestic level.

Offensive realism

Offensive realists like John Mearsheimer reach a different conclusion about the effect that the distribution of power has on the foreign policy behaviour of states. Rather than security maximizers, offensive realists argue that states are power maximizers, meaning that they are continually searching for opportunities to gain more power relative to other states. Unlike defensive realists, offensive realists do not believe that security in the international system is plentiful. They also do not believe that balancing behaviour is as frequent and efficient as defensive realists contend. According to Mearsheimer, the anarchical structure of the international system, coupled with the deep uncertainty that the United States has about the current and future intentions of other states such as China, compels America to maximize its relative power position. For Mearsheimer, the logic of offensive realism leads states to 'understand that the best way to ensure their survival is to be the most powerful state in the system' (2001: 33).

Global hegemony, according to offensive realism, is the highest goal of every state's foreign policy. Unfortunately, however, Mearsheimer argues that it is impossible because of the 'stopping power of water', which makes it impracticable for any state to project its power over vast distances and to conquer and hold distant territory. While global hegemony is impossible, regional hegemony is not and Mearsheimer argues that

the United States is the only state to ever achieve this esteemed position. In light of the nineteenth-century history of American foreign policy as it expanded across North America and acquired a number of offshore territories in wake of the Spanish–American War (1898), Mearsheimer concludes that the United States is 'well-suited to be poster child for offensive realism' (Mearsheimer 2001: 238). Once America achieved regional hegemony in the western hemisphere, offensive realism predicts that its main foreign policy goal was to prevent the emergence of a hegemon in other regions of the world. A regional hegemon, according to offensive realism, does not like peer competitors. Thus, according to this theory, the United States has actively sought to prevent the emergence of a hegemon in either Europe or Asia. Offensive realists favour an 'offshore balancing' grand strategy and, according to Mearsheimer, this is largely the strategy that the United States has followed since the end of the Second World War. While many realists endorse an offshore balancing grand strategy, it is certainly debatable whether this is the strategy that the United States has followed. For realists and non-realists alike, it is not self-evident that water has stopped the power of the United States from achieving the position of global hegemon (Layne 2006).

Internal, domestic theories

Theories that accentuate internal or domestic factors de-emphasize the utility of system-level theorizing to explain the foreign policy of the United States. These theories follow the tradition of *Innenpolitik* and stress the influence of domestic factors on foreign policy. Rather than an outside-in explanation, these theories reverse the chain of causation to an inside-out explanation. Pressures from within a state determine the character of its foreign policy. Elections, public opinion polls, the condition of the domestic economy, unemployment rates, and the degree of national unity are all factors that foreign policy officials, and especially the President, must take into account when pursuing foreign policy objectives. Rather than the structure of the international system determining the foreign policy of the United States, the political and economic structure of the American polity is argued to be of fundamental importance to explaining America's external behaviour.

Liberalism

Liberalism is one of the most prominent domestic theories of American foreign policy. This should not be very surprising, because the United States is a quintessential liberal state (Hartz 1991). The logic of liberalism dictates that America's foreign policy should reflect and magnify the liberal democratic character of the American polity. According to liberalism, one of the core objectives of American foreign policy is to promote the expansion of individual liberty across the globe. This is argued to be beneficial both to the United States, in that its own security and way of life is enhanced by the presence of a large number of like-minded liberal states, and to the rest of the world as liberalism is a political ideology that enshrines the rights and liberties of all individuals. While liberals agree that American foreign policy should be a reflection of its domestic political values, there is disagreement among liberals on the best way to promote liberty.

For many, liberalism as a theory of foreign policy is most closely associated with President Woodrow Wilson (1913–21). Indeed the association is so close that liberalism and Wilsonianism are almost interchangeable terms. On the eve of the United States belated decision to enter the First World War, Wilson articulated a new vision of the world, and America's role in it, that was imbued with a number of ideas that have come to form the essence of a liberal theory of foreign policy. Most fundamentally, Wilson rejected the so-called timeless principles of realism by arguing that common interests needed to replace the focus on national interests and called for a collective security system to replace the flawed balance of power system. More specifically, Wilson advocated democratic forms of government, free trade, the creation of international institutions to help maintain the peace, and the self-determination of peoples. In order to realize these ideals, liberals from Wilson to the present argue that the United States must take the lead in actively promoting them. This, in turn, is frequently referred to as liberal internationalism whereby the United States, as a liberal democracy, must take on the role of world leadership and actively construct a peaceful liberal order through multilateral cooperation and effective international organizations.

Today, democracy promotion is one of the main elements of a liberal theory of American foreign policy. In addition to the advancement of liberty that liberalism associates with democracy, there is the added benefit that democratic states do not fight other democratic states. Thus liberals argue that it is in the national interest of the United States to promote the spread of democracy. The notion that democratic states do not fight wars with other democracies is what proponents term the democratic peace.[4] If one accepts the empirical finding that democracies do not fight one another, which numerous scholars and American policy makers do embrace, then the issue becomes the best way to encourage democratization so as to enlarge the club of democratic states. Different presidential administrations have been torn between, on the one hand, indirectly promoting democracy through leading by example, foreign aid to support pro-democracy movements, diplomatic encouragement, and, on the other hand, directly promoting democracy by using military force to remove dictators and bring about regime change. Democracy promotion was one of the rationales put forth by the George W. Bush administration to justify the 2003 invasion of Iraq. A democratic Iraq, it was argued, would remove the alleged terrorist threat Saddam Hussein posed to the United States and help jumpstart democratic transitions throughout the Middle East. This is one of the reasons why many liberals supported the Iraq War while realists, who are not only suspicious of the so-called democratic peace but also critical of crusading foreign policies to remake the world in America's image, were generally opposed to the war.

The promotion of free trade and the belief that international institutions help to facilitate international cooperation are two of the other main pillars of a liberal theory of American foreign policy. For a liberal thinker such as G. John Ikenberry, each one of the elements—democracy, free trade, and international institutions—is mutually reinforcing and they simultaneously help to advance American interests and contribute to a pacific world order (Ikenberry 2000). Thus liberals are strong supporters of free trade agreements such as NAFTA as well as membership in international institutions such as the United Nations. We will return to the three cornerstones of liberal internationalism in the section on American grand strategy.

Marxism

Marxist theories are another example of an inside-out explanation in that they emphasize the economic determinants of American foreign policy. Rather than accentuating the structure of the domestic political system, Marxism underlines the capitalist economy of the United States and the pressures that it exerts on an expansionistic and imperialistic foreign policy. By one account, the foreign policy of the United States simply serves the interests of the capitalist class and the large corporations that they own. Proponents of this theory argue that most of the interventions, covert or otherwise, that the United States has perpetrated in Latin America, the Caribbean, the Middle East, and elsewhere stem from the domestic needs of the American economy for markets and cheap sources of raw materials, for example oil (Kolko 1969). Marxist theories interpret the history of American foreign policy as one of imperialism and empire building, and locate the source of this behaviour in the capitalist economic system of the United States (Chomsky 2004). The American economy, like other capitalist economies, is prone to crises—unemployment, overproduction, downturns—and Marxists argue that elites attempt to solve them by searching for new sources of capital, raw materials, and markets abroad. In order to satisfy the interests of the capitalist class, Marxists argue that American foreign policy promotes their interests by providing a stable international environment for the expansion of capitalism. Marxists argue that the military power of the United States and the wars that it has fought in places like Vietnam, Bosnia, and now Iraq are meant to provide the international stability that capitalists require in

order to invest in foreign lands and accrue greater rates of profit.

The Open Door school of American diplomacy, which was largely inspired by a non-dogmatic Marxism, holds that the mainspring of United States foreign policy has been the search for markets and the desire to integrate the entire world into an open, free trade economic system. The most famous proponent of the open door interpretation of American foreign policy was William Appleman Williams in his classic book *The Tragedy of American Diplomacy* (1972). According to Williams, the United States has attempted to solve its domestic economic problems by expanding abroad in search of overseas markets, cheap raw materials, and investment opportunities. Expansion was deemed to be the answer to America's woes and thus Williams argues that the foreign policy of the United States is determined by domestic factors. For policy makers who embraced the Open Door outlook on the world, America's prosperity at home depended on access to markets abroad. For Williams, the result of the United States pursuing an open door foreign policy is the creation of an American empire. These views became the bedrock of the revisionist interpretation of the Cold War, which held that America's open door economic interests, and not Soviet expansionism, were largely responsible for US intervention in the third world.

Toward a synthesis: neoclassical realism

We would be remiss if we did not mention one attempt to combine systemic and domestic factors into a comprehensive theory of foreign policy. The best example of this undertaking is the theory of neoclassical realism. According to neoclassical realism the only way to understand the foreign policy behaviour of the United States is to consider the manner in which systemic and domestic factors interact with one another. Systemic factors, especially the relative amount of power that a state has, are important for establishing the broad parameters of foreign policy; they help to establish what is and what is not possible.

Yet the distribution of power alone cannot, according to neoclassical realism, explain the particular foreign policy behaviour of the United States. They argue that domestic factors are needed to explain how systemic factors are actually translated into specific foreign policy decisions. Stephen Walt explains that the causal logic of neoclassical realism 'places domestic politics as an intervening variable between the distribution of power and foreign policy behavior' (Walt 2002: 211). Two important intervening variables that neoclassical realism highlights are decision makers' perceptions of the distribution of power and domestic state structure. In other words, for neoclassical realists, both individual decision makers and domestic politics, including the governmental structure, matter in understanding the foreign policy of the United States.

Constructivism

Whereas the previous theories all tended to emphasize material factors to explain American foreign policy, constructivists accentuate the role of ideas and identity that they argue play a major role in foreign policy. Constructivists treat identities and interests as malleable social constructions and are interested in the social processes that lead foreign policy officials to regard America as an 'exceptional' state or a 'virtuous city on the hill'. National identity, according to constructivism, should be the starting point of foreign policy analysis. The identity of the United States is, in part, a function of both its domestic self-image and foreign policy. Constructivist scholars note that identity is never self-referential, but rather is always relational and emerges by differentiating oneself from others. Thus the identity of the United States during the Cold War as the defender of liberal democracy and freedom was, in part, derived by juxtaposing itself to the evil and totalitarian Soviet Union. Constructivists can point to the role of ideas in fostering these identities in documents such as NSC-68 that outlined the United States' Cold War policy of containment and sharply differentiated the national identities of the United States and the Soviet Union.

One of the reasons why constructivist approaches to the study of American foreign policy consider identity to be so important is because they argue it is the basis of interests, which greatly affect the formulation of foreign policy. Contrary to material-based theories such as realism that consider interests to be a function of material capabilities, constructivists argue that they are largely a function of ideas. The ideas that American foreign policy officials hold about the United States form the basis of the American national interest. From a constructivist point of view, one way to understand the United States' global war on terror is in terms of the identity of America as the global guardian of liberty and freedom. And this interest of defending liberty and freedom in order to preserve the identity of America obviously has important implications for the conduct of American foreign policy. Yet American foreign policy is always susceptible to change because

---

KEY POINTS

- ❏ Systemic theories such as defensive and offensive realism argue that the most important influence on America's foreign policy is the international system and specifically the relative amount of power that the United States possesses.
- ❏ Defensive and offensive realism disagree about the manner in which the international system influences the conduct of American foreign policy.
- ❏ Theories that follow the tradition of *Innenpolitik* stress the influence of domestic factors on foreign policy.

- ❏ Liberalism and Marxism are two examples of theories that accentuate internal factors to explain American foreign policy.
- ❏ Neoclassical realism is a theory of American foreign policy that simultaneously seeks to combine systemic and domestic level factors.
- ❏ Constructivism emphasizes the role of ideas and identity in American foreign policy.

identities and interests are malleable. According to constructivists, the interests of the United States are derived endogenously through the process of social interaction. This helps to explain why the United States behaves one way when interacting with other liberal democracies and another way with non-democracies (Nau 2002). By emphasizing ideas, norms, and the social construction of identity, constructivists have a keen interest in explaining the sources of change in American foreign policy.

Origins of the Cold War

The theoretical controversy over whether American foreign policy should be understood as shaped primarily by the external or internal environment has had a far-reaching effect on the debate on the origins of the Cold War. A number of different answers have been given to the question of who was responsible for the Cold War. The Cold War period of American foreign policy (1945–89) has been a subject of intense interest by political scientists and diplomatic historians. The conventional wisdom is that American foreign policy underwent a tremendous transformation between the time the United States entered the Second World War in 1941 following the Japanese attack on Pearl Harbor and the time after the United States and the allies emerged victorious over Germany and Japan. This is often described as a change from isolationism to globalism in which the United States used its preponderant power to assert itself on the world stage. Yet throughout the post-Second World War period American power was challenged by the Soviet Union, which resulted in a tense Cold War that was most dramatically illustrated by the nuclear weapons arms race between the two countries. A key question shaping the historiography of the Cold War is: what led the United States and the Soviet Union to go from allies during the Second World War to bitter rivals locked in a global struggle for power from 1945 to 1989?

External explanations

From a purely systemic, structural realist viewpoint, neither the United States nor the Soviet Union is to blame for the Cold War. The Second World War created a vacuum of power in Europe that was filled by the only two great powers that remained standing: the United States and the Soviet Union. According to this view, the change from a multipolar to a bipolar distribution of power after the Second World War largely explains the behaviour of the United States as structural realists argue that the external environment determines foreign policy behaviour. Thus the ensuing rivalry and competition between the United States and the Soviet Union can be simply explained in terms of the bipolar distribution of power that existed after 1945. One problem with this account is that there is no agency; there are no villains in which to assess blame and responsibility for the origins of the conflict.

Another version of a realist, external explanation of the Cold War holds that in addition to a bipolar distribution of power after 1945, one of the two poles, the Soviet Union, was an expansionist power that was bent on world domination. According to this view, United States foreign policy throughout the Cold War was a successful response to the threatening and expansionist behaviour of the Kremlin. Within diplomatic history, this is referred to as the orthodox account of the origins of the Cold War and, not surprisingly, is popular with many American historians. The orthodox explanation places the blame for the Cold War squarely on the shoulders of the Soviet Union and its leader Joseph Stalin. The United States, in documents such as the famous NSC-68, interpreted Soviet intentions as inherently aggressive and a direct threat to American national security. Given this interpretation of Soviet intentions, the United States, as the only other great power in the international system, had no choice but to respond to this threat and try to check the power of the Soviet Union. This formed the basis of the American policy of containment that is often credited to George Kennan, who was a prominent diplomat stationed in Moscow. On the basis of Kennan's understanding of the Soviets' ideology, he argued, 'it is clear that the main element of any United States policy toward the Soviet Union must be that of a long-term, patient but firm and vigilant containment of Russian expansive tendencies' (Kennan 1984: 119).

Internal explanations

As the Cold War dragged on a new set of historians arose that challenged the notion that American foreign policy was simply a response to the alleged external threat posed by the Soviet Union. Instead of assigning responsibility to the distribution of power in the international system and to the expansionistic ideology of the Soviet Empire for America's behaviour throughout the Cold War, the revisionist school of historians looked inside the United States. And when they closely examined the domestic interests of the United States, the revisionists argued that since at least the late 1800s the overriding goal of American foreign policy was to promote the spread of capitalism so as to ensure a world of free markets that would provide access to American goods and services. This economic thesis was most eloquently put forth by William Appleman Williams (1972) who argued that the promotion of an open door world whereby other states embraced America's liberal ideology and opened their markets to US economic expansion was a constant pattern of behaviour in American foreign policy. Thus for the revisionists, especially those writing during and after the Vietnam War, the United States' expansionistic and even imperialist

behaviour was responsible for the onset of the Cold War. The only threat that the Soviet Union posed after the Second World War was that it openly challenged America's vision of an open, liberal economic world run and managed by the United States. Here Williams went beyond a Marxist analysis as he also underlined the liberal ideological dimension of US foreign policy whereby American policy makers believed that domestic prosperity and tranquillity at home depended on continuous expansion overseas.

Neoclassical explanations

A neoclassical explanation holds that both external and internal factors are necessary to understand the origins of the Cold War. The starting point for a neoclassical explanation is the distribution of power that existed in the international system after the Second World War. Here neoclassical realists such as Chris Layne concur that in 1945 the United States held a significant power advantage over all the other states in the international system. This favourable distribution of power provided the opportunity for the United States to expand its interests around the globe. But for Layne (2006), it is domestic factors, namely Open Door economic and ideological imperatives, which explain why the United States chose to expand its interests and deliberately pursue a Cold War with the Soviet Union from 1945 to 1989. Layne puts forth extra-regional hegemony theory to argue that even if the Soviet Union had not existed after the Second World War, 'America's Open Door aims on the Continent would have led to the establishment of U.S. hegemony in Western Europe' (Layne 2006: 70).

KEY POINTS

- ❏ A number of different answers have been given to the question of who was responsible for the Cold War.
- ❏ External explanations emphasize the bipolar distribution of power that existed after the Second World War and argue that the Soviet Union was inherently expansionistic and the United States attempted to contain the spread of communism.

- ❏ Internal explanations such as those put forth by the revisionist school argue that the United States economic expansionistic and even imperialist behaviour was responsible for the onset of the Cold War.
- ❏ Neoclassical explanations argue that the United States favourable position in the international system coupled with the domestic imperatives of the Open Door explain why it pursued a Cold War with the Soviet Union.

Grand strategy

Since the end of the Cold War there has been a debate over the best grand strategy for the United States to follow. Grand strategy may be defined as the overall vision of a state's national security goals and a determination of the most appropriate means to achieve these goals. Debates about grand strategy are explicitly related to the different theories of American foreign policy discussed in a previous section. Competing grand strategies reflect different views about the character of international politics and the role that the United States must play in order to achieve its core national security interests. Different grand strategies also have competing ideas about the content of America's core interests as well as about the most appropriate means to realize these interests. The aim of this section is to provide an overview of three different grand strategies—neo-isolationism, liberal internationalism, and primacy—and to underline the theory of American foreign policy that informs each of these competing strategies.

Neo-isolationism

Neo-isolationism or what is sometimes called an 'interest-based' foreign policy or a 'strategy of restraint' harks back to an earlier period of American foreign policy when the United States was not as deeply involved in managing the affairs of other states and had not assumed the role of global hegemon. Like its advocates in the past, neo-isolationists are not arguing that the United States should cut itself off from the rest of the world, but rather that America should focus first and foremost on its own national interests. While the exigencies of the Cold War necessitated that the United States played a more activist role in international affairs and violated President Jefferson's warning against entangling alliances, the cessation of the global struggle against communism provides an opportunity for America to come home (Gholz, Press, and Sapolsky 1997). The core argument is that the United States is extraordinarily secure, which is a function of its favourable geographically insular position, weak neighbours to the north and south,

immense military capabilities, and relative standing in the global distribution of power, which allows for a drastic reduction in America's security commitment to Europe, Asia, and much of the rest of the world. Neo-isolationists argue for a restricted conception of the American national interest in terms of the physical protection of the territory and people of the United States as well as its continued economic prosperity.

Neo-isolationism is firmly anchored to the theory of defensive realism. According to neo-isolationists, America has more than enough power for its security, and its overriding national security objective should be to safeguard its position by greatly limiting its involvement in the affairs of, and conflicts between, states in Europe and Asia. Yet, neo-isolationists argue, America is eroding its own power position by continuing to underwrite the security of other states in Europe and Asia. Not only is this no longer necessary, but it is undermining America's own power, which is contrary to the national interest. Moreover, by continuing to spread its military presence around the world and enlarging the tangling alliance that it created in 1949 (NATO), other states are actually attempting to counterbalance against the United States in a more systematic fashion than if the United States simply focused on its own backyard (see Controversies 1.1). Neo-isolationists recommend: the dismantling of NATO, the removal of American troops from states such as Japan and Germany, a reduction of defence spending, and, most importantly, a focus on America's own needs and interests so as to preserve its secure and prosperous position in the world.

Perhaps the biggest criticism of a neo-isolationist grand strategy is that 9/11 demonstrated that America is not nearly as secure as many had assumed. Yet neo-isolationists have a response, namely that there is a direct correlation between America's overseas military presence, particularly in the Middle East, and terrorism directed at the United States. Neo-isolationists argue that the threat of terrorism can be greatly diminished if the United States exercises restraint, reduces its overseas military presence, and refrains from meddling in the affairs of other states.

Liberal internationalism

Proponents of liberal internationalism would argue that neo-isolationists fail to understand that the reason America is so secure and prosperous is exactly because the United States has been exercising global leadership since the end of the Second World War. As a liberal hegemon, America plays a vital role in maintaining international order that has direct benefits to both the United States and much of the rest of the world. Ikenberry (2002) argues that in addition to the realist-based containment order that existed after the Second World War, the United States also established a liberal democratic order that was based on economic openness, international institutions such as the United Nations and the Bretton Woods system, and democracy. This liberal internationalist grand strategy is rooted in the construction of multilateral institutions that are believed to provide cooperative solutions to pressing security and economic issues. While the United States played a key role in the creation of these multilateral institutions, the argument is that they continue to serve American interests by providing legitimacy and a rule-based setting for its foreign policy behaviour. Thus liberals such as Ikenberry argue that other states do not fear US power because of its institutionalized, legalized, and democratic character. So it makes strategic sense for the United States to continue to adhere to the institutions and rules that it helped to propagate after the Second World War.

It should be self-evident that a liberal internationalist grand strategy is firmly anchored to the theory of liberalism. Most fundamentally, the strategy calls on America to actively promote the spread of democracy and liberty around the world. This is viewed as both a moral duty and a strategy that actually improves American security. The United States is better able to pursue its interests and reduce security threats when other states are also democracies. Closely related to the argument about the pacifying effect of democracy is the liberal idea that the promotion of free trade increases the prosperity of more and more people which, in turn, creates the conditions for democratic governance. Free trade is believed to foster greater interdependence among states that diminishes the economic gains that any state could expect to incur by going to war. Thus the greater degree of economic interdependence between the United States and China is believed to lessen the chance of conflict. Finally, the creation of international institutions and norms is viewed as the best mechanism for managing the array of political, economic, and environmental problems that arise in an interdependent world. In this manner the three key ideas of liberal theory—democracy, interdependence, and institutions—are vital elements of a liberal internationalist grand strategy.

Proponents of this strategy argue that it has been immensely successful to realizing American national interests and lament its erosion over the last few years. It is widely acknowledged that President Clinton adhered to a liberal internationalist grand strategy as evidenced by his *National Security Strategy of Engagement and Enlargement* (1995). Clinton embraced democracy promotion, but he attempted to achieve this through multilateral institutions and without the resort to force. And while American power grew under the Clinton administration, its benign character was largely preserved by remaining wedded to the rules and institutions of the existing order. The Bush Doctrine, with its call for unilateral pre-emptive war and disdain for multilateralism as well as for the reigning rules and norms, is seen by many liberals as a bold new grand strategy that is destined to fail (see Major debates and their impact 1.1).

Primacy

A grand strategy of primacy most fundamentally seeks to preserve America's position as the undisputed pre-eminent power in the international system. Peace among the great powers and American security are held to rest on a preponderance of US power. The goal of, but certainly not the quest for, primacy was stymied by the existence of the Soviet

MAJOR DEBATES AND THEIR IMPACT 1.1: Bush Doctrine—realist or liberal?

There has been a great deal of debate and controversy regarding the Bush Doctrine. One debate centres on whether the doctrine is based more on the principles of realism or liberalism. For many, it seems self-evident that the doctrine is based on a muscular version of realism. The call for the preservation of American primacy, the willingness to use force against enemies who challenge US power and interests, and the enthusiasm to pursue a go-it-alone strategy in order to secure American interests in a hostile world seem to fit comfortably in a realist world view. Yet many realists are critical of the Bush Doctrine especially with respect to how it justified the Iraq War. Realists point to a fourth component of the Bush Doctrine: democracy promotion. A key rationale for the invasion of Iraq was that regime change was necessary in order to install a democratic government in Iraq. Liberals who supported the war argued that democracy in Iraq would help to spread freedom and liberty throughout the Middle East, which would be beneficial to the USA since democratic states do not fight democratic states. Thus rather than being based on the principles of realism, some argue that the Bush Doctrine is grounded on liberal Wilsonianism or what John Mearsheimer describes as 'Wilsonianism with teeth'.

Union. In the aftermath of the Cold War, the United States now holds the position of the sole superpower in the international system. Proponents of primacy view this as an extremely advantageous position and argue that America's grand strategy should be one of preventing any future great powers from challenging the power of the United States. Thus the United States should militarily outspend all other states to preserve its military dominance, continue to station troops in, and underwrite the security of, Germany and Japan, and actively work to prevent the rise of states such as China and Russia that could pose a challenge to American primacy.

While advocates of primacy concur with the proponents of liberal hegemony about the benefits of American leadership, they disagree about the recommended means of keeping America number one. While multilateralism has certain advantages, unipolar powers also have the benefit of being able to act unilaterally to advance their own interests regardless of what other states think. Thus when the situation warrants, such as when dealing with rogue states armed with WMD, advocates of primacy do not hesitate recommending that the United States act alone. Institutions are also regarded with a degree of suspicion as they are largely viewed as restraining rather than enabling American power. Finally, proponents of primacy do not believe that the promotion of democracy should trump other vital US interests. Primacy is largely informed by a power-maximizing version of structural realism that does not give much weight to the character of domestic regimes. Thus if the promotion of democracy in a country such as Iraq erodes US power relative to other great powers such as China, proponents of primacy would conclude that this is antithetical to American national interests. Yet other proponents of US primacy, such as neo-conservatives, argue that democracy promotion is a vital component of American grand strategy.[5] All advocates of US primacy, however, agree that keeping America in its pre-eminent position and the rest of the world off balance is the core national interest.

For advocates of primacy, the Bush Doctrine embodies important elements of a strategy of preserving America's dominant position in the international system (see Major debates and their impact 1.1). The Bush Doctrine openly embraces America's commitment to preserving its unipolar position. The 2002 *National Security Strategy* declares that the US military will be 'strong enough to dissuade potential adversaries from pursuing a military build-up in hopes of surpassing, or equaling, the power of the United States'. The Bush Doctrine also declares America's willingness to act unilaterally, which is most evident in its controversial policy of pre-emptive and even preventive war. The Bush administration's unsympathetic view of international institutions was reflected in its decision to invade Iraq without the authorization of the United Nations Security Council. Critics contend that the strategy of primacy is ultimately self-defeating as inevitably the USA will succumb to the imperial temptation of overextending itself and other states will seek to counterbalance American power (see Controversies 1.1). Rather than trying to preserve the impossible, namely unipolarity, many other realists advocate a policy of offshore balancing that attempts to maintain America's relative power and national interests in an emerging multipolar world.

KEY POINTS

❏ Debates about grand strategy are explicitly related to the different theories of American foreign policy.

❏ Neo-isolationism argues that America is secure and should adopt a policy of restraint and limit its interests to the protection of the territory and people of the United States.

❏ Liberal internationalism advocates continued American leadership of the world through multilateral institutions and the promotion of democracy and free trade.

❏ Primacy argues that the overriding goal of US grand strategy should be to preserve indefinitely America's position as the undisputed pre-eminent power in the international system.

Conclusion

This chapter has attempted to demonstrate that the study and practice of American foreign policy is dependent on theory. At the same time, there are a variety of different theories that attempt to explain American foreign policy. Some theories accentuate the impact that external, systemic factors have on American foreign policy while others highlight the influence of internal, domestic factors. And there are also those that attempt to combine systemic and domestic factors. Theories of American foreign policy are important for understanding past debates such as the origins of the Cold War as well as for the contemporary debate over American grand strategy. While complex, theory is unavoidable when it comes to the task of attempting to explain the foreign policy behaviour of the United States.

? Questions

1. Which of the five sources of American foreign policy identified by James Rosenau do you believe is most important for understanding the external behaviour of the United States?

2. How would you explain the United States' decision to invade Iraq in light of each of the five sources of American foreign policy outlined by Rosenau?

3. Do you agree or disagree that it is impossible to construct a theory of American foreign policy?

4. What are the main sources of disagreement between offensive and defensive realists?

5. Compare and contrast 'inside-out' with 'outside-in' explanations of American foreign policy.

6. Whose interpretation of the origins of the Cold War do you believe is most persuasive?

7. Is Chris Layne's explanation of the Cold War able to bridge the divide between internal and external accounts of the Cold War?

8. Which of the three grand strategies do you believe the USA should be following today?

9. Do you agree or disagree that states are attempting to counterbalance the USA?

10. Which theory do you believe the Bush Doctrine is based on?

Further Reading

For a general survey of the main theories in the field

Dunne, T., Kurki, M., and Smith S. (2007), *International Relations Theories: Discipline and Diversity* (Oxford: Oxford University Press).

Snyder, Jack (2004), 'One World, Rival Theories', *Foreign Policy*, 145: 53–62.

On the Cold War

Gaddis, John Lewis (1997), *We Now Know: Rethinking Cold War History* (Oxford: Oxford University Press).

LaFeber, Walter (2002), *America, Russia, and the Cold War, 1945–2000*, 9th edn. (Boston: McGraw-Hill).

On grand strategy

Ikenberry, G. John (2001), *After Victory: Institutions, Strategic Restraint, and the Rebuilding of Order after Major Wars* (Princeton: Princeton University Press).

Mearsheimer, John J. (2001), *The Tragedy of Great Power Politics* (New York: W. W. Norton).

Endnotes

1. See Waltz (1996). Yet other neorealists such as Elman (1996) disagree with Waltz and have sought to illustrate how neorealism can in fact provide a theory of foreign policy.

2. For a discussion of the offence–defence balance, see Jervis (1978) and Lynn-Jones (1995).

3. Snyder (1991) and domestic pathologies.

4. On the theory that democratic states do not fight wars against other democratic states see Russett (1993). For a criticism of this theory see Layne (1994).

5. For an informative discussion of neo-conservativism and American foreign policy see Halper and Clarke (2004).

Visit the Online Resource Centre that accompanies this book for web links to accompany each chapter, and a range of other resources: www.oxfordtextbooks.co.uk/orc/cox_stokes/

2 American exceptionalism

Daniel Deudney and Jeffrey Meiser

Chapter contents

Introduction: American difference and exceptionality

Since its founding almost a quarter of a millennium ago, the United States of America has thought of itself as, and been widely perceived to be, exceptional. The United States is unlike other nation-states in a myriad of ways. Most obviously, the United States is different from other states and nations because it is by far the most successful great power in late modern times. This success is manifest in its current unprecedented status as the world's sole superpower. It is the seat of the world's largest economy. And it is the ideological leader of the most powerful, appealing, and successful form of political, economic, and social organization in modern times: liberal capitalist democracy. Because of its extraordinary success as a great power, the United States has the capabilities to shape the world in a variety of ways that reflect its preference for how the world should be ordered, a preference rooted ideologically in its conception of itself and its special mission. Extraordinary success also has greatly magnified the effect of every aspect of America on the world, from the sublime to the shameful. This success and influence makes an understanding of the United States and its agenda vital to understand major features of contemporary world politics. Understanding how America is different and how it is exceptional is, for better or worse, essential for understanding not just US foreign policy, but major aspects of contemporary world politics.

Success makes the United States different and influential in far-reaching ways, but the core reason the United States is widely viewed as exceptional is because of its intensely liberal character. America is exceptional, both in fact and perception, because more than any other state in history it has embodied and advanced an ideological vision of a way of life centred upon freedom, in politics, in economics, and in society. Prior to the last half of the twentieth century, what were then called republics were very rare in world politics, and the American founding and expansion marked a decisive turning point in the long and largely tragic story of free and democratic government. Convinced they embodied, in the words of President Abraham Lincoln, 'the last best hope of mankind', Americans have been audacious, at times reckless, innovators in turning the abstract and lofty Enlightenment goal of a fully free society into a practical working arrangement. This project has been marred by contradictions, seedy opportunism, and startling blunders. But over nearly twenty-five decades it has relentlessly progressed and come far closer to realization than even the founders dared to imagine. From the outset, this anomalous and experimental polity saw itself not just as liberalism in one country but as the model, the vanguard, and at times vital facilitator, of a universally appealing and universally realizable way of life. This vision of an eventual liberal republican end of history, as the German philosopher Immanuel Kant called it, has been deeply attractive, even intoxicating, to many, while being a frightening threat and a writ for upheaval and imperialism to others.

Given its influence in the world and its highly developed sense of itself as the embodiment of a universal and revolutionary ideology, the claim that the United States is exceptional is highly charged with contentious ideological connotations. In contemporary American and world politics, the expression American exceptionalism means very different things to different people. For some it is a vision, for others a sham, and for others a nightmare. For some Americans, particularly recent neo-conservatives, intoxicated with power and righteousness, American exceptionalism is a green light, a legitimizing rationale and an all-purpose excuse, for ignoring international law and world public opinion, for invading other countries and imposing governments, and for routinely identifying particular and often provincial and pedestrian American interests with the universal pursuit of progress and freedom. For others, American exceptionalism is code for the liberal internationalist aspiration for a world made free and peaceful not through the assertion of unchecked American power and influence, but rather through the erection of a system of international law and organization that protects domestic liberty by moderating international anarchy. This vision sees all states, and particularly large and powerful states, as inherently dangerous and seeks checks, both domestic and international, to restrain the worst impulses of all nations, including the United States. For liberals and internationalists American exceptionalism provides a standard against which much of American history is found wanting in various ways. It is a reminder that much remains to be done and is a perpetual call to action to bring American practices ever closer to American ideals.

Difference, exceptionality, and success

Exceptionality and the hard test of realism

The indispensable baseline for assessing the effects of any domestic factors, such as American liberal republicanism and the exceptionalist ideology associated with it, is the simple realist model of security, power, and interests. In this view, states above all seek security, and they need and seek power to achieve security. They in turn use their power to realize various interests, particularly economic interests, which in turn enhances their power and thus their security. This baseline realist model poses the vital first question: what in actual American behaviour *cannot be explained* by the pursuit of security, power, and interest? Only if this simple model fails to explain do we even need to consider the possible influences of other factors, among them ideology, on American behaviour. However, applying this simple model to any state, particularly a large and powerful state, is rarely a straightforward task. What security requires, what the contours of power look like, and what content interests actually have, are often ambiguous and fraught with misperception and debate, not only by actors in the heat of actual political decision making, but also among scholars making after-the-fact evaluations. Furthermore, as constructivist theorists remind us, identity, ideas, and ideology shape what are understood as threats and interests, and also powerfully shape, in both positive and negative ways, the capacity of states to mobilize power for the pursuit of security, power, and interest.

Applied to the United States, the simple realist model has considerable explanatory power, but also has important blindnesses and limitations. Well articulated through American history in varying degrees of clarity, and richly developed in recent decades by international theorists, the realist view is that the United States is not in any significant way fundamentally different from other states. This conclusion provides the basis for the routine dismissal of the entire discourse of American exceptionality. Realists hold that all the main steps in the trajectory of American foreign policy such as relentless continental expansion against weak adversaries, regional hegemony in the New World often exploited for economic gains, global great power balancing and alliance leadership against predatory revisionist states, and then Western and global hegemony are essentially what any state (seeking security, power, and interest), would have done if it were in the thoroughly enviable position of the United States in the international system.

The realist view of the United States does, however, clearly recognize that the liberal republican character of the United States has two significant distinguishing manifestations: early isolationism and later internationalism. For realists, liberalism has indeed mattered for US foreign policy, but in largely negative ways. For realists, the early American posture of isolationism was made possible by the relative isolation of the United States from the great powers of Europe. But as the industrial revolution unfolding in the twentieth century brought about the end of this isolation, the United States clung for too long to an isolationist foreign policy, with nearly disastrous consequences for the preservation of the balance of power in Europe. Forced to deal with the world, the United States sought to transform the world through the realization of its liberal internationalist programme for democracy promotion within states and international law and organization between them. For realists, this agenda, particularly in its more urgent and crusading forms, entails an unrealistic and utopian hope for human improvement and political change, and is seen as a cloak for raw American power interests. Its pursuit is seen as a chronic source of mischief and disorder, and realists aspire for the United States to abandon its exceptionalist pretences and behave like a normal great power.

Yet the realists' critical and dismissive posture toward the liberal elements that sit at the core of American exceptionalism fails to do full justice to liberalism and its internationalism. The realists correctly see that the American liberal internationalist project has an agenda that is revolutionary to a Westphalian version of world order and to the types of states traditionally associated with this order. But they fail to appreciate the extent to which the extraordinary levels of peace, prosperity, and freedom that prevail within the core of the American system of the Western liberal democratic states are in significant measure the realization of the American liberal internationalist project. Realists also fail to see that this internationalist agenda (which is increasingly best advanced by Europeans rather than Americans) holds the key to whatever hopes there are to address the myriad of real and significant global problems that are being produced by rising levels of global interdependence.

The dark side of American exceptionalism

The landscape of argument about American exceptionalism is further complicated by the fact that the United States is not purely a combination of the very standard realist goals and behaviours and liberal elements, but is also shaped, like all other states, by idiosyncratic factors of national identity rooted in ethnicity, religion, and race. Here are factors that at times powerfully compromise and subvert the liberal democratic vision of the American Creed, and their net effect has been to add streaks of stark eccentricity and blatant hypocrisy to American pretensions to embody the overall liberal project of human freedom (Lieven 2004).

These non-liberal and anti-liberal aspects of American identity and behaviour are distinct from another contemporary view, widely held in Europe, of American exceptionalism as a marker for a cluster of retrograde and dangerous American tendencies. The pro-American liberal narrative of exceptionality emphasizes the historically progressive and internationally indispensable role of the United States as the standard bearer of the liberal cause. But this has been and is being challenged, not just by the Realists, but also by an older line of conservative anti-liberal European thinking and by a contemporary pro-liberal European position. The old European conservative line, echoed today in harsh terms by Islamicists today, is that America's liberalism is a licence for popular anarchy and cultural levelling. For non-Western traditionalists, American liberty is a writ for the libertine, and the United States is the leading purveyor of 'westoxification' (Katzenstein and Keohane 2007).

Perhaps even more telling is the contemporary sceptical view of European liberal democrats, which has grown rapidly more widespread in reaction to the policies of the second Bush administration. At times, for such critics, it seems as if the United States has become something like the world's greatest and most dangerous rogue state. This new European view of exceptional America as liberal laggard emphasizes the ways in which more messianic and crusading aspects of the American liberal agenda, most manifest in contemporary American neo-conservativism, have linked up with some of the more parochial anti-liberal American religious and cultural tendencies, to serve as the ideological façade for the exercise of a blatant and short-sighted pursuit of American power and interest. Given the vastness of American power, particularly military power, claims of American exceptionalism take on a frighteningly imperial character.

American success and its sources

The single most distinguishing feature of the United States has been its extraordinary success. This fact may not be universally liked, but it is universally recognized. Over the roughly two and half centuries since its founding, the United States of America has been by far the most successful state in the international system. This success is the indispensable basis for the vast influence the United States has had on the world and it has nourished the widespread sense among Americans of their special world role.

The United States has been uniquely successful among the great powers over the last century, dubbed by the influential publisher Henry Luce 'the American Century'. The great powers of Europe, most notably Britain, Germany, and France, emerged from the First and Second World Wars either in ruins or ruinously sapped in strength, while the United States emerged largely unscathed. During the second half of the twentieth century, marked by the bipolar Cold War struggle between the Western capitalist democracies, led by the United States, and the socialist-communist coalition led by the Soviet Union, the United States and its allies also emerged victorious after the unexpected (and unexpectedly peaceful) Soviet collapse. Due to this outcome, the United States stands at the turn of the twenty-first century in a position of military ascendancy unprecedented in the modern European and global state systems. As the world's sole superpower, the USA spends more on its military than most of the rest of the world combined and holds something approaching worldwide military supremacy.

Success requires power and power is based, particularly in the industrial era, on wealth. The United States has been the world's largest economy for over a century. Even in the wake of rapid economic growth in large previously underdeveloped countries over the last several decades, the American economy is larger than the next two countries combined. And the United States has sustained its economic leadership across recessions, depressions, and a dizzying succession of technological transformations.

America's economic liberalism—its robust capitalism—has also significantly contributed to American success. The strong commitment to individual achievement and obsession with economic accumulation is supportive of technological innovation and economic growth generally. These ideas are exemplified by the Horatio Alger myth: nobody's class position is fixed by birth, everyone has an equal opportunity for economic success (Hartz 1991: 62–3, 11–3, 219–24). From this perspective, a liberal society can win the allegiance of even the poorest members because of the promise of becoming rich. Regardless of whether the Alger myth is real, Americans believe it, and so do many people around the world. Economic opportunity and prosperity have been self-reinforcing. The lure of economic opportunity was a major factor in the ability of the United States to attract skilled and hard-working immigrants.

In sum, the belief in American exceptionalism is based upon a number of core realities including American military primacy, economic dynamism, and political diversity.

In order to further explore and assess the diverse conceptual landscape of what is at stake in the assertion of American exceptionalism, the remainder of this chapter is divided into four parts. The first part considers the meaning of exceptionalism, the critics of American exceptionalism, and the roots of American success. The second part examines the liberalism which makes the United States exceptional. The third part examines peculiar American identity formations of ethnicity, religion, and 'race' which interact with and often subvert the liberalism of America. Part four examines the role of American exceptionality across the five major epochs of American foreign policy, from the founding to the present.

Liberal exceptionalism

The free world project of American liberal republicanism

The fact that the United States has been so successful makes it different. But the fact that it has been so liberal is what makes it exceptional. A liberal republic, in the language of the Enlightenment which originally conceptualized it, is a distinctly modern type of political regime, composed of a complex matrix of related elements, some of which are in perpetual tension with each other. A liberal republic, a polity liberal in the full and broad sense of the term, is animated and ordered by a set of values, institutions, and practices. The components of a modern liberal republic are individual freedom and institutionalized civil rights, popular sovereignty, limited government specified in a constitution, multiparty electoral democracy, private property and market capitalism, rule of law and independent courts, and religious liberty and separation of church and state. These ideas are codified in the founding documents of the republic: Declaration of Independence, US Constitution, individual state constitutions, and Bill of Rights. It is common to speak of the 'American Creed' as a distillation of liberal democratic values: 'liberty, egalitarianism, individualism, populism, and laissez-faire' (Lipset 1996: 19) or 'liberty, equality, democracy, individualism, human rights, the rule of law, and private property' (Huntington 2004: 46). Each of these elements is complex and Americans, like citizens of other modern liberal democracies, are in perpetual ferment about their secondary features and the tensions among them. So important has liberal republicanism been to the United States and the United States to liberalism that it is impossible to understand the one without the other.

The American project of freedom did not, of course, spring fully formed out of the historically thin (if bracing) air of the New World. It was initially almost entirely an import of English institutions, practices, and values from the revolutions of the seventeenth century, which were then richly nourished by the moderate European Enlightenment in the eighteenth century. But unlike the long-established polities of Europe, where the traditional hierarchies of the crown and church held sway, and only slowly and reluctantly yielded to popular pressures over the last two centuries of reform, revolution, and war, the United States was born far more fully, and uncontestedly, liberal than any modern Europe state.

Anti-statism, state building, and militarism

Anti-statism is deeply rooted in liberal thinking. The United States is different and exceptionally liberal compared to other liberal democracies in the degree to which this anti-statism has been institutionalized and made the object of sustained popular pressure and shaped its foreign policy. Anti-statism and the fear of despotism led the American founders to create a state structure that is fragmented, decentralized, and accountable. Separation of powers allows different branches of government to 'check and balance' one another. The United States exhibits the foreign policy tendencies of both a democracy and a weak state. The open structure of Congress and its frequent elections provides access to individuals and groups that seek to affect foreign policy. Aversion to taxation, another aspect of American anti-statism, has made state building difficult and led to a consistent underfunding of the public sector. Mobilization of the state has been dependent upon outside security threats, or similar systemic shocks.

Anti-statism is integral to liberal republicanism because strong states, governmental apparatuses large in size and amply equipped with violence capabilities and uncontestedly authoritative, are seen as inherent threats to popular security and liberty. American anti-statism sometimes spawns ridiculously paranoid suspicions. For example, as the internationalist project started to bear fruit, popular anti-statism has produced a strong fear and hostility toward international organizations, thought to be seeds of a dark end of history in one-world despotism. In this view, world governance and organization, being big and further away, is less accountable and less checkable, and therefore intrinsically undesirable.

Over time, American anti-statism has been severely compromised by the need to combat foreign threats. The state and war feed on one another, and the single most important factor in overcoming the institutional and attitudinal barriers to American state building has come from war. The Civil War, and then the First World War, produced a great rise in the size and capacities of the federal government, which then quickly declined with the return of peace. But beginning with the mobilization for the Second World War and extending through the long and perilous decades of the Cold War, the United States built a permanent strong state structure, heavily centred on military capability, that went far beyond the vision and constitutional architecture of the founders. The erection of this American National Security State has been largely popular, often wildly so, at the same time as many Americans still voice severe doubts about its longer-term impact on limited government (Johnson 2004).

Over this long war, a peculiarly American style of militarism has arisen. The cumulative weight of a high and enduring mortal foreign threat, a vast military and military industrial complex, and large numbers of politically active veterans has combined to produce increasing militarism in American culture and national life. This has also been fed by the extraordinary 'gun culture' in the United States, marked by widespread firearms ownership, chronic domestic gun violence, as well as the widespread conviction that gun possession is not only necessary as a check on criminals, and possibly even foreign invaders, but also on the US government itself, making gun possession the most basic right of a free society. These features of the American cultural landscape loom large in the increasing scepticism of liberal Europeans and others about the United States. But this militarism

may have much more bark than bite, because it coexists with an extreme reluctance to have Americans killed in battle, and a startling willingness to abandon wars which become more costly in blood than anticipated. Popular theatrical militarism is also tempered by the extreme reluctance of the US military to go to war except in overwhelmingly important and readily winnable conflicts.

American capitalism and prosperity

Among major states, the United States is the most distinctly pro-capitalist, and one of its most distinctive features is high levels of economic growth and widely distributed prosperity. America was capitalist or proto-capitalist from the beginning, a utopia of Lockean liberalism. This pervasive capitalist individualism has figured prominently in the seminal interpretations of the American experience, from Tocqueville in the middle of the nineteenth century to Louis Hartz in the middle of the twentieth. Because the United States was so purely capitalist, American political development has been profoundly different from Europe's, and many of the major features of European life, most notably the feudal stage with its *ancien régime* and working-class socialist movements, are almost completely absent in the United States.

Much of the attractiveness of freedom in the United States has been associated with the freedom to own and accumulate property. The early success of liberal capitalism in the United States was made possible by the availability of large quantities of cheap rich agricultural land.

The social mobility produced by economic advance fostered by abundant land in early America reinforced the belief that individual effort would lead to individual achievement, and helped account for the widespread economic equality which was in stark contrast to the extreme socio-economic stratification virtually everywhere else. This widespread economic opportunity also reinforced American anti-statism, by creating widespread strata of prosperous property owners attached to capitalist ideas, hostility to both a large and intrusive state and socialist redistribution.

America's deep commitment to capitalism and private property has had a significant impact on US foreign policy. American expansion in the nineteenth century was propelled by Americans seeking new and more abundant land for private ownership. Since the late nineteenth century, the United States has intervened abroad to protect American property beyond its borders (Kinzer 2006: 9–108) and has repeatedly sought to 'open' other countries to trade and investment. And much of twentieth-century American foreign policy, from the Spanish American War to the Marshall Plan and the erection of GATT and the WTO, is intimately connected to the interests of American corporations. This deep support for capitalism and private property also contributed to the strong American opposition to third world nationalists. In Guatemala, Iran, and Chile and elsewhere, the US government supported violent coups of right-wing groups to overthrow left-leaning regimes (Kinzer 2006: 111–216), contradicting American support for democracy, and any government, whether elected or not, which favoured the seizure of foreign property ('nationalization') and redistribution. And the Soviet Union seemed so threatening to Americans not just because it was a very powerful great power, but also because it was the central base of a worldwide movement to eliminate private property.

Trade policy is the most consequential domain where American capital has sought to strengthen and use state power, rather than oppose it. American trade policy has changed several times in major ways and from the beginning trade policy has been a central political topic, pitting different interests and regional 'sections' against one another. Initially, under the sway of Jefferson's vision of a decentralized agricultural polity of free proprietor yeomen farmers, and in the interest of the vast majority of Americans who lived and worked on farms, the United States pursued a low-tariff policy, and during this period the United States was part of the colonial 'periphery' in the capitalist world system. Like Brazil, Canada, and Latin America, the United States was mainly an exporter of unfinished raw materials and importer of manufactured goods from Europe.

But the alternative economic vision of protectionism had been articulated from the beginning, most notably by the first Secretary of the Treasury, Alexander Hamilton, in his *Report on Manufacturers* (1790). This protectionist programme was fully implemented during the Civil War when the new Republican Party (in a congressional supermajority with the South absent) established a national currency, a national banking system, and a high tariff to protect American industry. Behind this tariff wall, progressively raised across the decades of Republican Party ascendancy, the United States rapidly industrialized and grew into the world's economic colossus.

Yet another reversal—back to free trade—was triggered by the Great Depression, and the realization that the United States, as the world's largest and lowest-cost industrial producer, could gain from free trade. This shift in economic interest combined with the realization that the spread of capitalism was vital to securing weak democracies against communist domination. With this new power and agenda United States became, from FDR's presidency through to the present, the leader in the worldwide effort to lower tariffs and other trade barriers. This effort not only helped trigger fifty years of global economic growth, but also produced the GATT (now WTO) and ancillary pro-capitalist global organizations and institutions such as the IMF and the World Bank.

The American state has sought to pursue an 'open door' policy of opening up the global economy to American inward investment and has opposed governments that have sought to resist American expansionism.

MAJOR DEBATES AND THEIR IMPACT 2.1: Exceptionalism and ideology

To what extent is American exceptionalism a reality or an ideology that justifies imperial behaviour? Throughout history, many states, both great and small, have claimed some degree of 'specialness' and exceptionalism. In fact, it is exceptional to find a state or a people that does not feel that they are in some ways special. This is especially the case when that historical state has been strong and/or had expansionist tendencies. One only has to think of Ancient Rome, or the Greek city-state of Sparta.

In a sense, then, exceptionalism as an ideology has run throughout history and has often coincided with an imperial foreign policy that serves to justify conquest and overseas expansion. The exceptionalism of the imperial state can be justified in a number of ways that may include a claim to cultural or civilizational greatness (Christianity, democracy, or a civilizing mission) or it may instead rely upon a claim to economic development (capitalism as the end point of history). In some extreme cases, exceptionalism as an ideology may reside in the exceptional state's military preponderance and this can be married to a racial narrative of superiority. Nazi Germany would be a good example of this, and in a lesser sense imperial Britain with its superiority of arms and sense of 'white man's burden'. The central debate then is what comes first, exceptionalism as an ideology or exceptionalism as material fact? As Weber argued, do the cultural enabling conditions and self-belief precede the state of exceptionality or do the economic, political, or strategic conditions have to be in place before the ideology of exceptionalism develops? Ask yourself, would America regard itself as exceptional if it were a middle-ranking power upon the world stage?

Peculiar Americanism

Ethnicity, immigration, and foreigners

The full story of immigration to the United States is very complex, but a broad pattern, identified by the political historian Michael Lind as the 'three American nations', captures much of the pattern. The first American nation, 'Anglo-America', was composed of settlers and their descendants mainly from England and Scotland, and this group and its mores continue to provide the base template of American ethno-national identity. Anglo-America was white Protestant and English-speaking, and these traits, combined with an affiliation for Britain and other British settler colonies, have remained prominent features of the American scene. The second American nation, 'Euro-America', resulted from the immigration of a vast tide of people, from the early 1800s to the early 1900s, from all over Europe, particularly Germany, Ireland, Italy, and eastern Europe. Not speaking English, often Catholic, and poor, these new Americans largely, but not completely, 'assimilated' to the traits of the earlier Anglo nation.

Finally, beginning in the 1960s, with the reform of immigration laws to permit more Asians, Africans, and Latin Americans, combined with sudden influxes of political refugees from revolutions and wars in places like Cuba and Vietnam, there has emerged the third American nation, 'global America'. As earlier, the new wave of immigrants are partly assimilating, but also retain far more active contact, through modern air transport and communications, with extended networks of people in the countries from which they emigrated.

Religion

The desire to practise freely their religious beliefs and realize their religious ideals inspired the founding of several of the early English colonies. American religion has been floridly diverse, benefiting from robust freedom of religion and the 'separation of church and state'. Various strands of Protestant Christianity have been particularly prevalent and influential, in ways both direct and subtle. The overall Christian theme of equality reinforced democracy and the overall Protestantism theme of individualism reinforced liberalism and capitalism. Both the Calvinist and evangelical Baptist tendencies of early American religious sects, such as the Puritan founders of Massachusetts Bay Colony, have also infused American life and foreign policy with a messianic sense that the United States was, in the often-quoted words of the seventeenth-century Puritan preacher John Winthrop, a religiously special place, a 'city upon a hill' that would inspire and help lead mankind from wickedness. Overall, American religious participation helped compensate for the sharper edges of capitalism and provided large numbers of Americans with an intense experience of community otherwise absent in the starkly individualistic society. Periodic religious revivals of fervour and inspiration also motivated major movements of social reform such as the Abolitionist attack on slavery and the Temperance Movement's attack on alcohol consumption, as well as the recent movement for African-American Civil Rights (Morone 2003).

Religiously inspired social reform and messianism in America has also directly spilled into the international arena. Throughout the nineteenth century, when the United States government was small and inward-looking, American missionaries were actively proselytizing around the world, but also providing services such as basic education and medical care and promoting human rights and foreign aid (Mead 2001: 141–7). Yet at the same time, religious leaders provided a rationale for American imperialism as part of an effort to spread Christianity to heathen peoples, and missionaries also served as the vanguard of American imperial military and economic expansion (LaFeber 1963). In recent decades Protestant evangelicals and Catholics have been active and influential in opposing abortion and contraception services, as well as in mobilizing opposition to extreme human rights abuses, such as the genocide now occurring in the Darfur region of Sudan. Various American Christian groups have also become increasingly active and influential in supporting the United States' pro-Israel policy in the Middle East, and their theme of 'crusades' has become another volatile element in the current war on terrorism against violent Islamic fundamentalism.

Race

The inheritance from Europe with which the United States was born was not purely liberal, but also included a radically illiberal system of African slavery, whose presence and eradication profoundly shaped American politics and foreign policy. As part of the colossal global predation and audacious outburst of mercantile, imperial, and colonial activities that brought the global economy and state system into existence in the early modern period, the Europeans coercively moved millions of people, mainly from Africa, across the oceans to labour in the New World's plantations and mines. This brutally coercive economic system was legitimized by, and in turn legitimized, virulently racist attitudes that remained long after slavery was abolished. Tocqueville caught the stark reality when he observed that each of the three 'hostile races' of North America 'follows a separate destiny' and that 'two unlucky races [i.e. Africans and Amerindians] suffer the effects of tyranny, and, though their afflictions are different, they have the same people [i.e. whites] to blame for them' (Tocqueville 1988: 317).

African slavery and white racism stand as the greatest exception to the exceptionally liberal character of the United States. The fact that this brutal system of slavery and racism was so thoroughly capitalist underscores the fact that markets are not inherently free but can be compatible with extreme conditions of unfreedom unless they are embedded in a fuller matrix of political and civil rights. Throughout the nineteenth century, racist ideas of Anglo-Saxon superiority shaped and legitimized 'manifest destiny', providing a convenient justification for the displacement of Indian tribes and Mexicans. The racism of America's dominant white populations, nourished by various 'scientific' Darwinist theories, reached its climax in the oppressive and bloody conquest and rule of the

Philippines in the early years of the twentieth century (Kramer 2006).

The slow and halting but cumulatively largely successful struggle to eradicate first slavery and then institutionalized racism over the history of the American republic has had wide-ranging effects. During the first decades of the American republic conflicts over slavery touched upon everything, and part of the reason the American Constitution created such a weak state was that slave owners, the dominant economic and political group in the southern states, feared that too strong a government could potentially jeopardize their peculiar institution. Catalysed by growing liberal Abolitionist sentiment in the non-slave states in the North, slavery was only abolished by the Union victory in the major bloodbath of the Civil War (1861–5), by far the most destructive war in American history. The second lengthy phase of African-American liberation began after the Union armies left the South in 1876 and the white southerners quickly erected an elaborate system of legalized, or de jure, segregation of so-called 'Jim Crow' laws. Struggles against this domestic regime of racial oppression stretched across decades and it was only in the middle years of the twentieth century when landmark liberal Supreme Court rulings combined with a mass mobilization of African Americans and their white liberal allies in the Civil Rights Movement that formal equality was achieved. Throughout the era of segregation, white southerners, operating as a political bloc and occupying key positions in Congress, not only resisted pressures for domestic change, but also vigilantly opposed US participation in any international human rights regime or organization asserting universal rights, fearing they might weaken the South's system of discrimination. As late as the 1980s, the United States, while serving as the leader of the free world against communist tyranny, was also, embarrassingly, a principal ally of the white apartheid regime in South Africa and this was only reversed by sustained international pressure and the mobilization of a boycott of corporations doing business there.

In the twentieth century, America's growing global role also contributed to the weakening of racial barriers and the delegitimization of racism. As part of the national mobilization for the Civil War and the world wars, African Americans were drawn into military service in large numbers, increasing the ability of African Americans to claim full citizenship. During the Cold War racial segregation was seen as an embarrassment and liability in the battle for 'hearts and minds' in the third world, a major battleground of the struggle. American segregationist policy, in contrast to the official communist hostility toward racism, meant that racism had become a national security liability. The first important step toward desegregation was the integration of the US Army through an executive order from President Truman at the close of the Second World War. The Civil Rights Movement eventually succeeded in ending lawful segregation in the United States and domestic race relations have continued to slowly improve. Racism is now much less powerful a factor than in early periods of American history, a change reflected in the rise in legal emigrants from third world nations.

Race, religion, and immigration have served to make America a 'melting pot' that has been infused with successive cultural waves.

This form of regeneration and vibrancy has added to the sense of American exceptionalism.

KEY POINTS

❏ American liberal exceptionalism has pushed US foreign policy in directions that contradict and transcend the imperatives of power politics. The effect of exceptionalism is visible in American impulses toward the seemingly contradictory positions of isolationism during times of weakness, and internationalism during times of relative strength.

❏ The American founding was a manifestation of the original American internationalism. Following the War of Independence, thirteen sovereign states replaced their ad hoc confederation with a 'states-union' in order to replace international anarchy with binding law and organization.

KEY POINTS (continued)

❏ Throughout most of the nineteenth century, the USA adopted an isolationist posture fostered by national weakness relative to European powers and the republican ideological belief that the United States should serve as a model for the rest of the world and focus on internal progress rather than external interactions.

❏ The twentieth century marked a major departure in American foreign policy: the rise of the USA to world power status under the strategy of liberal internationalism. As changes in technology shrank the globe, the United States sought to remake the world in its own liberal image while at the same time generating sufficient state capacity to prevent the eclipse of the free world by the twin totalitarian threats of Nazi Germany and the Soviet Union.

❏ The end of the Cold War and subsequent collapse of the Soviet Union produced an American-led global liberal hegemony. This 'moment' of liberal triumphalism has seemingly been undermined by the Bush administration, suggesting an uncertain future for liberal internationalism and America's exceptional effect on the international system.

Exceptionality and foreign policy

Liberalism, exceptionalism, and US foreign policy

Various strands of American particularistic national identity, whether ethnic, religious, or racial, have been omnipresent and often influential on American foreign policy. But in the overall trajectory of American foreign policy, they are ultimately less central to the story of American exceptionalism than the truly central axis of the story, which derives both in fact and in perception from the liberal republican core of the American polity. And in turn these liberal influences on US foreign policy have been bounded by the exigencies of great power politics, because the United States, like all states living in international anarchy full of uncertain threats and opportunities, has been by necessity keenly attentive to the requirements, often arduous, of great power balance of power politics. The USA did not emerge so successfully through its long succession of wars by ignoring the demands of power and interest, but by being exceptional in their mastery. But the USA is not simply another great power with a particularly outstanding track record. Its deeply liberal character has powerfully shaped its foreign policy. Sometimes the influence of its liberal democratic polity has worked in ways that contradict the dictates of realpolitik, and even more importantly, in ways that escape and transcend it. What is exceptionally liberal about American foreign policy can be captured in two, at first glance, contradictory patterns: isolationism and internationalism.

At first glance isolationism and internationalism appear to be unrelated, indeed almost opposite approaches to foreign policy. Isolationism is introverted, and seeks as much non-involvement as possible. Internationalism is extroverted and seeks to make the world more like the United States. In reality, of course, American foreign policy has never been purely isolationist or internationalist. At times it has been an odd mixture of both, and has also exhibited other unrelated tendencies.

In the American context, however, isolationism and internationalism are profoundly linked. They can best be viewed as different strategies to achieve the same, essentially liberal ends, but in different circumstances. Isolationism served liberal ends when the United States was relatively isolated (and isolatable) and weak. Internationalism serves liberal ends when the United States is inescapably interdependent with other states and when it is strong enough to influence a larger sphere beyond its borders (Deudney 2007).

In order to examine the actual roles that American exceptionalism, both liberal and illiberal, has played in the overall trajectory of American foreign policy, it is necessary to examine their roles in the different major epochs of American foreign policy, and to see how they have intertwined with the pursuit by the United States of security, power, and interest in the often harshly competitive international system. Five periods, partially overlapping, deserve closer examination: the Founding (1774–87), Hemispheric Isolationism (1787–1917), Great Power Rivalry and World War (1900–91), Liberal Internationalism (1919–2007), and Unipolarity, the War on Terrorism, and Unilateralism (1991–2007).

Original American federal internationalism

Narratives of American foreign policy commonly begin after the founding of the government of the United States by the Constitution of 1787. In reality, however, the founding itself was not solely a 'unit-level' event of 'state formation' but rather had far-reaching 'international' aspects, with deep connections to what would later come to be called liberal internationalism. Although it is commonly held that American internationalism is largely a phenomenon of the twentieth century, and particularly the later post-Second World War part of it, in reality the United States, as a state, had extensive 'international' internal features that were very pronounced at its founding and in the decades that followed. The deep historical roots of internationalism in the American political experience are often overlooked by international theorists, particularly realists, but they provide a template for twentieth-century liberal internationalism.

The founding of the United States took place through a process of confederation and federation among thirteen separate states. The organization of the British colonial activity in the New World was highly decentralized and colonies had a significant measure of local autonomy. After banding together to reach their common goal of independence, the thirteen states then formed a more substantial union with a weak central government. This negotiated union was a 'peace pact' that created the 'Philadelphian System' as an explicit antithesis to the Westphalian system of hierarchies in anarchy that marked European politics (Hendrickson 2003; Deudney 1995). The small professional army, minuscule national bureaucracy, and substantial state militias prevented the resolution of state and sectional conflicts through coercion.

The politics of antebellum America was one of internal sectional rivalry, between the 'free' and slave states. The vexed question of western expansion, potentially upsetting the intersectional balance within the union, was dealt with by diplomatic settlements, the so-called 'Great Compromises' of 1820, 1833, and 1850, that were negotiated between the sections, much like the diplomatic deals of European nation-states with each other. When the issue of slavery could be finessed no longer, the sections fought a war that was largely conducted as an international or interstate war fought between clashing uniformed armies that largely followed the European laws of interstate war, belying its label as the 'Civil War'. The Union victory in the War of Southern Succession saved the Union from dissolution and deepened its liberal character by eradicating slavery. But the Union victory and the assumption of authority and capacity by the central government also marked the evolution of the states-union quasi-international system into something resembling a federal national state. Despite this change, the idea that the United States is, or at least was, as much a liberal 'states-union' as a 'liberal state' continues to serve as an inspiration and model to liberal internationalist aspirations to replace international anarchy with binding international law and organization.

The isolationist liberal republic

During its first century of existence, the United States' foreign policy centred on North America and to a lesser extent the western hemisphere. Americans were largely inward looking, highly focused on issues of internal development. The United States was relatively isolated and therefore had the option of pursuing a policy of isolationism. As the United States was weak, excessive interaction with European states would be on unfavourable terms, and would risk corrupting the American experiment. Instead of taking an active role in international politics, the United States would seek to be an example for the rest of the world to follow by perfecting its own liberal democratic political system and avoiding the corrupting influences of European war and diplomacy. Avoidance of foreign entanglements was a guidepost of American foreign policy. Despite this aspiration, the United States was in an international political and military system that it could neither fully escape nor significantly control. Because it had to fear European predation, the United States necessarily had to pay close attention to European politics and the balance that kept its powerful states in some degree of check. Because of its integration into the world economy centred in Europe, trade and the protection of trade played major roles in US foreign policy, and these economic connections drew the United States into war with European states during both the Quasi-War of the 1790s with France, and the War of 1812 with Britain.

Isolationism also appealed to Americans because of their fear of a large standing army derived from republican ideology and reinforced by recent experience leading up to the War of Independence. It was thought that international engagement would inevitably lead to conflict and war. Furthermore, war would require large-scale extraction of societal resources to fund a large standing army. High taxes and military dictatorship would become necessary to effectively compete within the European state system. Therefore, isolationism had beneficial implications for the American constitutional project.

In 1823, the Monroe Doctrine extended isolationism to the western hemisphere with the declaration that the United States would not allow European powers to involve themselves in the domestic affairs of New World republics. This approach had an imperialistic dimension, in that Central and South American states were assumed to only have partial sovereignty, but the main effect was to assert separation between Europe and the Americas. Within a general framework of isolationism, the United States

pursued an abbreviated policy of imperialism in the Spanish–American War of 1898. This brief, one-sided war also marked a step toward the abandonment of isolationism. While ejecting Spain from the western hemisphere was the unfinished business of the Monroe Doctrine, the war also led to an expansion of American interests deep into the Pacific Ocean and East Asia with the occupation of the Philippines and annexation of Hawaii in 1898. Americans were, however, highly conflicted about the occupation of the Philippines and the counter-insurgency warfare against Philippine nationalists that followed. Many also felt that imperialism was inconsistent with the Constitution.

Great power rivalry and world war

The second century of American foreign policy was very different from the first. Isolationism became increasingly unworkable as America's relative isolation was diminished by the new industrial technologies of communication and transportation. With the 'abolition of distance' as it was referred to in the later nineteenth century, Europe and its great powers and their wars were now no longer buffered and distant from the United States. Beginning between 1890 and 1914, and abruptly ending in 1989–91, the United States was drawn into a series of world wars and struggles that profoundly shaped not only international politics, but the position of the United States in the system. Drawn late into the First World War, the United States, after proposing a largely aborted scheme for an international peacekeeping league, pulled back into a semblance of hemispheric isolation. Initially also uninvolved in the wars in Europe beginning in 1939 and in Asia in 1936, the United States was inexorably drawn into the conflict and was able to serve as the most successful combatant due to the rapid military mobilization of its massive industrial base. With the war having two main victors, the Soviet Union and the United States fell into a struggle for global mastery that lasted over four decades and saw both sides deploy vast nuclear arsenals of global-range strike weapons, whose even partial use would have wiped out much of urban-industrial civilization on the planet. These total stakes seemed raised even further because the two blocs represented the vanguard of radically opposing socio-economic and political systems, which both sides believed were destined to become globally universal.

For America as an 'exceptional' state, these conflicts had two quite contradictory consequences. On the one hand, the specialness of the United States in the project of freedom as Americans understood it became greatly magnified. The United States became the leader and protector of liberal democracies everywhere, and had it not been for American power and purpose between 1940 and 1990, liberal democracy might well have been eliminated from the planet. The United States was no longer simply the leading exemplar of the project of freedom, but the indispensable 'leader of the free world' whose every major action seemed ripe with world historical significance. On the other hand, the rigorous exigencies of these struggles forced the United States to become what it had always claimed to fear becoming, a polity with a vast standing military and state security apparatus, and a vast panoply of allies, clients, and protectorates. Its grand strategy, while still wrapped in the rhetoric of liberal purpose, was in actuality first and foremost about survival and success in the global great power system,

and guided by the precepts of realism. While democracy survived, and in some ways even thrived alongside the National Security State, and while American lack of interest in formal territorial annexation kept its imperial presence from crossing over the line, at least as historically defined, into empire, there was no escaping the fact that the United States had become in important ways quite ordinary as a state, quite like the European national states that the founders had believed to be the antithesis of a republic.

Internationalist liberalism and world order

As impressive as America's success in the great power rivalries of the twentieth century is, what is most exceptional in American foreign policy is not its ascent from a weak regional state to the top of the global great power system, but rather the ways in which it has sought to remake the world according to a liberal vision. This vision is in its logic an extension of the principles of the original American internationalism of the founding. The trigger for the articulation and pursuit of the liberal one-world vision was the same as the move to great power global balancing,

---

 CONTROVERSIES 2.1: Idealism in American foreign policy

One of the exceptional features of US foreign policy is extent to which values affect American foreign policy. A consistent debate in American foreign policy is what role values should play in foreign policy decision making. One perspective is that values should be the driving force in determining the policies that the USA pursues. From this perspective, US foreign policy should be based on a sincere commitment to values such as democracy, human rights, rule of law, and economic opportunity. The rationale for this approach is that American values are attractive to the rest of the world and policies based on these values enhance American legitimacy and increase the soft power of the United States. A second approach is that values should play no role in the decisions made by American leaders. Instead, US foreign policy should

be based on a 'realistic' appraisal of national interests. These interests included pursuing policies that increase American power such as gaining access to foreign markets, and maintaining military and economic superiority. Scholars, policy analysts, and politicians that follow this approach often condemn US foreign policy as being overly moralistic and unrealistic. A third way of conceptualizing the role of ideas is to view them as instrumental. In other words, values are a means of achieving a goal. For example, some international relations theorists argue that the American people will only support an internationalist US foreign policy if they feel it is consistent with American values. Thus, American leaders must frame their preferred policy in terms of how it fosters American values.

namely the realization that as the world shrunk the survival of the United States Constitution required a foreign policy of global scope. As outlined by President Woodrow Wilson and progressive theorists in the early years of the twentieth century, the American liberal internationalist project has two overall aims, to abridge international anarchy through the erection of binding international law and organization, and to change the other units in the system away from hierarchy toward constitutional democracy. Of course this project has never been the sole aim of US foreign policy, which has been, by necessity, focused on the balance of power among the great powers. Many Americans have been ambivalent or hostile to it, and the United States has not always been a consistent adherent to the international arrangements it has played such a major role in creating. Nor has this project been pursued without or against power, but rather as the aim of power.

This basic vision has produced a wide array of efforts, whose real-world impact has ranged from abject failure to stunning success. In the early years of the twentieth century, the United States was the leading force behind the creation of a World Court to arbitrate disputes among states. At the end of the First World War, Wilson's ambitious proposal for a League of Nations was a key, if ultimately unsuccessful, part of the settlement of the Versailles Conference. In the wake of the near disaster of the Great Depression and the Second World War, the United States made a much more serious, sustained, and successful effort to erect a new liberal international order, with measures such as the establishment of the United Nations, the Bretton Woods institutions (IMF and World Bank), the multilateral free trade regime under the auspices of GATT, numerous proposals for bilateral and multilateral nuclear arms control (the Baruch Plan, Atoms for Peace, the Nuclear Non-Proliferation Treaty, and the Strategic Arms Limitation Treaties of the Nixon era), and the emergence of a range of global international regimes, varying greatly in almost every regard. These measures, taken as a whole, provided a greater degree of world public order and governance than ever before in history.

Conclusion: unipolarity, war on terrorism, and unilateralism

The fifth, and still unfolding, period of US foreign policy was inaugurated with the unexpected collapse of the Soviet Union, an event which shifted the overall international system from Soviet–American bipolarity to American unipolarity. The period since the end of the Cold War has been short, is still unfolding, but has been unexpectedly marked by great inconstancy in the direction of US foreign policy.

The first part of this period, stretching from the end of the Cold War to the two Clinton administrations, is in many ways the historical high-water mark of American power and influence, and was accompanied by an array of remarkably progressive developments in world politics. The heady optimism and sense of breakthrough and potential of this period found expressions in notions that the long envisioned liberal 'end of history' was at hand. The collapse of the Soviet Union and the communist project it had spearheaded meant that for the time in history the liberal coalition of states was unmistakably hegemonic globally. The first Bush administration, following in the steps of Reagan's breakthrough diplomacy with Soviet reform leader Mikhail Gorbachev, negotiated a set of far-reaching nuclear arms reduction agreements, the Soviet withdrawal from eastern Europe, and the reunification of Germany as a liberal democracy. Throughout the 1990s, the liberal cause globally relentlessly pushed forward, as dozens of previously authoritarian or totalitarian states moved rapidly to try to become democracies, as the European Union both widened its membership and deepened its institutional capacities, as NATO expanded to encompass many former Soviet satellites in eastern Europe and beyond, as the liberal international trading regime was both strengthened with the establishment of the WTO and widened with the admission of many previously communist or socialist economies. The United Nations also seemed to have new possibilities without the Cold War deadlock, and under its auspices members of the international community made increased efforts to deal with humanitarian crises, failed states, and ethnic cleansing and genocide, and establish a permanent international court for crimes against humanity.

Somewhat unexpectedly, however, the administration of George W. Bush has taken US foreign policy on very different paths, marked by a near reversal of American leadership to strengthen international law, organizations, and regimes. 9/11 and the Bush administration's responses to it have greatly amplified the intensity and impact of this new foreign policy direction. Even before 9/11 the administration had assumed a largely new American role as the leading opponent and critic of most international organizations and regimes, and the leading laggard in dealing with issues arising from global interdependence, perhaps most notably global warming. The administration withdrew from landmark arms control treaties, sought to impede the establishment of the ICC, effectively scuttled the Kyoto Protocol, and simply walked away from an almost completed negotiation to strengthen the Biological Weapons Convention.

Observers of this American turn against the liberal internationalist agenda have emphasized the new tendency for the United States to act unilaterally. Of course all states, particularly large and powerful ones, routinely act unilaterally, and US foreign policy in the nineteenth century was largely unilateral. But against the twentieth-century American role as multilateral alliance leader and institution builder, this turn (or return) marks a sharp departure from the policies of every administration since FDR.

The 9/11 terrorist attacks on the World Trade Center and the Pentagon seemed to draw an even sharper closure to the optimism and progress of the years after the fall of the Berlin Wall. Initially, with world public opinion solidly behind it, the United States executed a quick and bold campaign to overthrow the Taliban regime in Afghanistan that had sponsored and

sheltered the al-Qaeda leaders of the 9/11 attacks. But the Bush administration saw the attacks as harbingers of further far more serious attacks, possibly employing nuclear or biological weapons, and set in motion a far-reaching reconfiguration of American state capacities and foreign policy. On the domestic front, a giant new Department of Homeland Security was created, and the Bush administration began to claim (and act) as if the President, as commander-in-chief of the armed forces, is free to act in wartime outside the limits of international law and constitutional constraints.

Internationally, the initial success in Afghanistan was followed by the remarkable disaster of the United States invasion of Iraq. This invasion seems to have been motivated by several goals: to preclude the emergence of a revisionist and anti-American nuclear power, to sustain American hegemony and alliances in the Middle East oil-producing region vital to the entire world economy, and perhaps even to catalyse the emergence of democratic states in the region. Whatever its purposes, the American occupation of Iraq has turned out to be a disastrous quagmire, bleeding American strength and strengthening the radical Islamic regime in Iran, which had previously been held partially in check by the Saddam Hussein dictatorship in Iraq. As a result of this morass, and the growing backlash against many measures of Bush's open-ended 'Global War on Terrorism', both domestic and international support for the administration and its novel policies has almost completely evaporated.

In one sense the sudden turn of the United States in the Bush years marks a serious diminution of the exceptionalist liberal strand in US foreign policy. While still bellowing its claims to special status as the global palladium of liberty, the United States is now acting with an updated version of the simple realist script, doing what immediate security threats seem to make necessary, with little regard for their cost or international institutional fallout. Whether this new anti-exceptionalist turn has suffered a temporary or permanent setback because of the Iraq and Middle East mess hangs in the balance and with it much of the historical liberal exceptionalism of American foreign policy.

> ❝ **KEY QUOTES 2.1:** The origins of American exceptionalism

The United States, almost from its start, has had an expanding economic system. The nineteenth-century American economy, as compared to European ones, was characterized by more market freedom, more individual landownership, and a higher wage income structure—all sustained by the national classical liberal ideology. From the Revolution on, it was a laissez-faire country par excellence.

(Lipset 1996: 54)

Hence there was a strong family likeness between all the English colonies as they came to birth. All, from the beginning, seemed destined to let freedom grow, not the aristocratic freedom of their motherland, but a middle-class and democratic freedom of which the world's history had not previously provided a complete example.

(Tocqueville 1988: 34)

The English colonies—and that was one of the main reasons for their prosperity—have always enjoyed more internal freedom and political independence than those of other nations; nowhere was this principle of liberty applied more completely than in the states of New England.

(Tocqueville 1988: 39)

I have already said enough to put Anglo-American civilization in its true light. It is the product (and one should continually bear in mind this point of departure) of two perfectly distinct elements which elsewhere have often been at war with one another but which in America it was somehow possible to incorporate in to each other, forming a marvelous combination. I mean the spirit of religion and the spirit of freedom.

(Tocqueville 1988: 47)

There is therefore at the bottom of democratic institutions some hidden tendency which often makes men promote the general prosperity, in spite of their vices and their mistakes, whereas in the aristocratic institutions there is sometimes a secret bias which, in spite of talents and virtues, leads men to contribute to the afflictions of their fellows. In this way it may come about that under aristocratic governments public men do evil without intending it, and in democracies they bring about good results of which they have never thought.

(Tocqueville 1988: 235)

? Questions

1. Is America an exceptional country?
2. To what extent is US foreign policy characterized by either isolationism or internationalism?
3. How do we measure exceptionality and is it an 'objective fact'?
4. Is the belief of exceptionalism an ideological construct?
5. Are exceptionalism and imperialism two sides of the same coin? Explain your answer.
6. What is the basis of American exceptionalism?
7. To what extent was the belief in American exceptionalism rooted in American cultural history?
8. American exceptionalism is a logic outcome of its commitment to free markets and its victory in the Cold War. Critically discuss.
9. Ethnic, religious, and racial difference have given the USA its exceptional nature. Critically discuss.
10. To what extent is the USA a liberal power within world politics and in what ways does this influence the belief in exceptionality?

》   ## Further Reading

Deudney, D. (2007), *Bounding Power: Republican Security Theory from the Polis to the Global Village* (Princeton: Princeton University Press).

Deudney 'brings America back in' to international relations by showing how the construction of the American states-union in 1789 succeeded in preserving democracy in a system populated by predatory monarchical, despotic, and totalitarian nation-states. Only against the backdrop of the long tradition of republican security theory can the importance of the USA fully be realized.

Hartz, L. (1991), *The Liberal Tradition in America: An Interpretation of American Political Thought since the Revolution* (San Diego: Harcourt Brace Jovanovich).

American exceptionalism emerges from a political culture dominated by 'absolute and irrational Lockean liberalism'. This conformist and unique national identity limits the effectiveness of American foreign policy by fostering a sense of intolerance toward different political, cultural, and economic systems.

Lieven, A. (2004), *America Right or Wrong: An Anatomy of American Nationalism* (New York: Oxford University Press).

American identity is a composite of civic nationalism based on universalistic liberal values and chauvinistic nationalism based on religious and ethnic particularities. These two aspects of American exceptionalism foster contradictory impulses in US foreign policy: civil nationalism encourages a moderate internationalism while chauvinistic nationalism fosters isolationism, messianism, and, most ominously, imperialism.

Lipset, S. M. (1996), *American Exceptionalism: A Double-Edged Sword* (New York: W. W. Norton).

As the most prominent contemporary advocate of the idea that America is qualitatively different from other countries, Lipset presents an analysis of how the American Creed—'antistatism, individualism, populism, and egalitarianism'—fosters exceptionalism in American politics, policy, and culture. One important finding is that American exceptionalism is 'double-edged', meaning that the USA is different, but not necessarily better than other countries.

Mead, W. R. (2001), *Special Providence: American Foreign Policy and How it Changed the World* (New York: Routledge).

American foreign policy is an expression of four sometimes complementary and sometimes contradictory traditions: Hamiltonian economic realism, Jeffersonian republican isolationism, Jacksonian populist militarism, and Wilsonian religious moralism. American foreign policy works best when it draws on the strengths of each tradition.

Nau, H. R. (2002), *At Home Abroad: Identity and Power in American Foreign Policy* (Ithaca, NY: Cornell University Press).

The exceptionalist American identity prevents the United States from establishing a stable, moderate, internationalist foreign policy. Only when the USA realizes that American values have in large part come to dominate the international system will it finally feel 'at home abroad'.

Tocqueville, A. de (1988), *Democracy in America*, trans. G. Lawrence (New York: Perennial Library, Harper & Row).

Writing in the 1830s, Tocqueville studied the USA in the context of failed European social revolutions. He saw the USA as an exceptionally successful democracy rooted in mores, laws, political decentralization, and most importantly social equality.

   Visit the Online Resource Centre that accompanies this book for web links to accompany each chapter, and a range of other resources: www.oxfordtextbooks.co.uk/orc/cox_stokes/

Section 1

Historical Contexts

3 The US rise to world power, 1776–1945

Walter LaFeber

Chapter contents

Introduction

Americans like to think of themselves as a powerful nation and a vibrant democracy. At pivotal points in their history, they have also thought of the United States as an *empire*—that is, a collection of various tribes, states, or nations which their central government controlled. That they held this view is somewhat surprising. After all, in 1776 Americans opened a new chapter in world history by successfully rebelling against an empire—the great British Empire.

From the beginnings of United States history, then, empire should have been a bad word. But it was not. Having grown up within the British Empire, George Washington, Thomas Jefferson, and other founders easily thought of their new nation as an empire—although, of course, a decent, democratic, and just empire, quite unlike the British model which they condemned for having corrupt kings and exploited colonies. Once free to conduct their own foreign policies, Americans rapidly grew into a continental power stretching from the Atlantic Ocean to the Pacific. The Civil War of 1861–5 interrupted this era of landed expansion. But the war between North and South also cleared the way for triumphant northern capitalists to create by 1900 the world's number one industrial and agricultural power. Producing far more than they could consume, Americans naturally looked overseas for new markets. The search led them into economic competition with the great imperial powers (Great Britain, France, Germany, Russia, and Japan), and into military competition as well. Not surprisingly, in the late 1890s Americans began to think again of themselves as an empire, only this time as an overseas (not merely a continental) empire.

But, as in 1776, they again also thought of themselves as different from the other imperialists. They saw themselves as representing middle-class order, democracy, and capitalistic success. And, as they demonstrated in the First and Second World Wars, they could build a highly efficient military to ensure their success. In 1945, that military power included the first atomic bombs.

Out of this stunning economic-military combination appeared the US foreign policies which dominated the post-1945 years. By 1991, the United States and its allies had defeated Russian communism to win the four-decades-long Cold War. Before as well as after the 11 September 2001 terrorist attacks on New York City and Washington, DC, many Americans again thought of themselves as living in a nation which headed nothing less than a global empire—an empire now occupying some 700 military bases around the world, and with its economic and cultural power penetrating all corners of the globe (Johnson 2004; Ferguson 2004). This post-1991 version of American empire can only be understood by viewing it as the result of the previous two and a half centuries.

Some widely noted authors thought this post-1991 US empire was good for both Americans and, indeed, the entire globe. Just as Americans had settled and developed a continent before 1945, these authors argued, so they could now bring order and development to crucial parts of a suffering, supposedly less civilized world. Americans in the mid-nineteenth century had followed what they believed to be a 'manifest destiny' (a term first used in New York City and Midwestern newspapers during the 1840s to indicate the right given by God to Americans to populate and develop the continent from the Atlantic to Pacific oceans). After 1917 and especially after 1991, they followed what they believed to be a new manifest destiny to stabilize, democratize, and profit from many parts of the globe.

From colonies to continental empire, 1776 – 1865

From their earliest days of independence, and even during the darkest days of their often-sputtering war against the British, Americans thought of their fortune in imperial terms. As the Revolution ground down to its end in 1783, US soldiers, long unpaid by a bankrupt Congress, threatened to overthrow that Congress and install their commander, George Washington, as a virtual monarch. The General quickly stopped the uprising and possibly saved what was to be an American republic. He passionately condemned anyone 'who wickedly attempts to open the floodgates of civil discord and deluge our rising empire in blood' (Van Alstyne 1960: 1, 29) ...ubt that it

...en states ...one that, ...esidency ...conomic ...oited the ...rderous ...ne. The ...1793–4 ...France ...nd John ...790s to ...s from

...lomacy ...up the ...Euro... ...l, keep ...eize all ...ry and ...c defi... ...ldress' ...ard to ...l rela... ...on as ...erson ...n his ...onest

...with none' (Gardner et al. 1976: i. 56–65). If only Americans could maintain freedom of action, Jefferson concluded, there were few limits to their empire. '[I]t is impossible not to look forward to distant times, when our rapid multiplication will expand itself beyond [present] limits, and cover the whole northern, if not the southern continent,' he wrote a friend in 1801, 'with a people speaking the same language, governed in similar forms, and by similar laws' (Jefferson 1903: x. 296).

Jefferson and his fellow Americans, obviously, did not think small. But the grave dangers inherent in building empires nearly overwhelmed the Virginian

at the beginning of his presidency. In 1801, France's ruler, Napoleon Bonaparte, was pushing Spain out of New Orleans and the vast Spanish holdings west of the Mississippi River. Napoleon intended to create a New World empire for France which would dwarf all others. Jefferson and Secretary of State James Madison immediately saw that by controlling the port of New Orleans, Napoleon could dominate access to the Mississippi River, which drained the port.

Madison quickly identified the grave danger to the American empire. Perhaps the most influential member of the 1787 Constitutional Convention, he had constantly argued that Americans needed ever more territory because they produced so many children. Madison accurately did the arithmetic for his American multiplication table, as it became known (note Jefferson's use of 'multiplication' above). He concluded that the US population was actually doubling every 21–2 years. These families of six to twelve, and more, could not be allowed to overcrowd and corrupt eastern cities. They had to be encouraged to find their own space and income for their families in the west. Once in the west (or, as it is now known, the Midwest), these families would depend on the magnificent river system linked to the Mississippi. If Napoleon held New Orleans and, consequently, controlled the Mississippi, it would be only a matter of time before those thousands of American settlers might have to become citizens of Napoleon's French empire.

Jefferson and Madison exerted intense diplomatic pressure on the French. They even mobilized the small US Army for a possible attack on New Orleans itself. Faced with Jefferson's growing opposition, Napoleon decided his better opportunity lay in reopening war against the British and attempting to conquer much of Europe. He consequently stunned Jefferson by offering in early 1803 to sell for $15 million not only New Orleans, but all of the former Spanish empire which reached from the Mississippi to the Rocky Mountains—and possibly beyond, although few at the time actually knew what lay in the Rockies and beyond. Americans suddenly more than doubled their territory, drove out the French, established complete control over the Mississippi, and gained their first vague claims to lands bordering the Pacific Ocean.

Now Jefferson confronted the central problem which would haunt US leaders from 1787 until the early twenty-first century, and no doubt long thereafter. Having obtained a territory which, he told a friend, would become an 'empire of liberty' for untold generations of Americans, how could the President maintain order and safely govern such a huge, distant holding? (Ferguson 2004: ii. 30–7). New Orleans, for example, held criminals and others who had fled from the United States. They wanted no part of a US-controlled government. In 1776, Jefferson's Declaration of Independence had trumpeted the belief that people held 'inalienable rights'. In late 1803 as he had to deal with Louisiana, however, he ditched that belief. The President set up military control, not a democratic system, over New Orleans and the surrounding territory.

Jefferson believed in democracy, but he did not believe that all people could be trusted to make democracy work properly. Democracy, he knew, was not merely casting a vote. It required, among other things, a fair code of laws, the people's faith that their economic system properly functioned, and the settlers' allegiance to central and state governments which made all this work.

Louisiana was thus made a part of the growing American empire, if not immediately given a democratic system. Then another severe danger loomed. As Britain and France again went to war after 1803, a series of crises between London and Washington on the high seas and along the US–Canadian border finally exploded into war in 1812.

Madison, now the President, planned not only to stop the British mistreatment of American ships and commerce. He also ordered the invasion of Canada in the hope of expanding US landed empire northward. Many Canadians, however, had left the United States in the 1770s because they preferred living under London's rule. They fought back, virtually wiping out the US invaders. In 1814, British forces invaded and burned down Washington, DC. James and Dolly Madison fled in such a hurry that they left plates and utensils set for dinner on the Executive Mansion's dining table. A potential catastrophe was avoided

only by several US naval victories, skilful American diplomacy at the peace negotiations in late 1814, and—especially—British preoccupation in the last months of their victory in Europe over Napoleon.

By 1815, with some twenty years of European wars finally ended, Americans seized the opportunities to expand their growing trade with now-peaceful Europe and also Latin American nations which were declaring their own independence of European colonialism. In 1823, Madison's successor, President James Monroe, declared that henceforth the United States would not tolerate any attempt by Europeans to restore their hold on these New World nations. This Monroe Doctrine was historic not because Americans had the military needed to keep Europeans away from the Americas. Such power would not appear until the 1890s. The Doctrine was a turning point because it announced the US belief that henceforth the Old World should no longer attempt to dominate the New. Three hundred years of European colonialism in the western hemisphere were over.

Or, to look at Monroe's announcement from another perspective (as many Europeans and Latin Americans certainly did), it was a declaration that since the United States was the most powerful of New World nations, its people would hereafter have the dominant voice in defining the western hemisphere's affairs. Monroe and his Secretary of State, John Quincy Adams, had already demonstrated this dominance. Adams is ranked as the greatest Secretary of State in American history, a ranking due in large part to his shrewd negotiations with a declining Spain between 1819 and 1821. Adams talked the Spanish into selling Florida (where many Americans had already settled), and giving the United States Spain's claims on the Pacific coast. Known as the Continental Treaty, Adams's brilliance provided, finally, the formal, internationally recognized claim of Americans to that coast.

Adams barely missed taking Texas from Spain as well. But the American multiplication table took care of that. By the 1830s, Mexico (which then included the present state of Texas) had become independent of Spanish rule. Thousands of Americans moved into the weakly governed Texas region. Mexico had prohibited slavery, but slaveholders from US Southern states easily moved west to establish Texan plantations. When Mexican officials tried to reassert their authority (and anti-slave laws), the new settlers fought back. Despite having 187 settlers wiped out at the battle of the Alamo, the rebels won a series of battles and established an independent country in 1836.

In 1845, newly elected President James K. Polk, a Tennessee slaveholder, worked out a deal in Congress to annex the region. Polk then used a dispute with Mexico over Texas's southern boundary as an excuse to declare war, invade Mexico itself, and demand what he most wanted: the Mexican northern regions, an area now including the states of California, Arizona, New Mexico, Nevada, and Utah. Polk, in other words, launched a war of aggression. The conflict dragged on through 1847 as Mexico refused to surrender. Worst of all, the seemingly never-ending conflict ripped open a debate in Washington. That debate raged around a central question: whether slaveholders should be allowed to take their human property into the newly seized territory.

The seemingly inevitable (even in some minds, apparently blessed-by-God) rise of the United States to world power had become intimately tied to the question of whether this success story required the continual expansion of slavery as well. It was the slaveholders, after all, who exported an ever increasing amount of cotton and tobacco which enriched the US economy. Congressional compromises in 1850 and 1854 tried to quiet the question by allowing the new states to decide on their own whether to be free or slave.

At first glance, these compromises seemed to be the answer. Indeed, giving the people at the grass roots the power to make such fundamental decisions (that is, by exercising their democratic rights) seemed happily American. But in the 1850s an ever larger number of those Americans violently disagreed with such a grass-roots, democratic solution. Living largely in the north-east and Midwest, they believed it was evil to expand slavery, regardless of how it might be justified. Northern, non-slaveholding

farmers especially thought it evil if they lost the chance to buy and exploit good western soil simply because slaveholders were protected by state law as they snapped up the land.

The slaveholders saw it quite differently. Correctly figuring that their multiplication table was not multiplying as rapidly as the North's, southerners believed it was only a matter of time until they would be outnumbered—and thus outvoted in Congress whenever issues involving slavery arose. They also needed new land to replace the soil which cotton and tobacco growing depleted. Southerners thus demanded the annexation of possible slave lands to the south, particularly Cuba (where Spain had installed a vicious slave system for the sugar industry), and Central America.

At this point, Abraham Lincoln entered American history. By 1860 the 51-year-old Illinois politician was a leading figure in the new Republican Party. The Republicans had been founded in 1854–5 to oppose the expansion of slavery. Lincoln was direct in declaring he would not interfere in states where it already existed. Given their dependence on continued expansion into Latin America, however, southerners bitterly condemned his and the Republicans' position of no more slave expansion. When Lincoln won the presidency in 1860, the slaveholding states prepared to leave the Union. A last-minute compromise tried to avert civil war. One part of the deal attempted to pull the southerners back in by guaranteeing federal protection for slavery south of the Kentucky–Missouri boundary lines. Lincoln rightly understood that this provision opened the way for seizing and extending American slavery into areas as far south as Cuba and other Caribbean nations. He rejected the compromise. And so the killing began.

Lincoln became the first President to say no to the continued expansion of Washington's and Jefferson's landed empire. Throughout the 1830s to 1850s, Americans liked to believe this expansion was part of what they termed manifest destiny: an expansion, that is, watched over by a God which blessed the spread of American democracy and capitalism. By 1864–early 1865, however, after three years of terrible war,

Lincoln was questioning why this God, claimed as the President noted by both North and South, would allow the nation to suffer such horrible bloodshed.

After his assassination in April 1865, and as the war finally ended, few of his fellow Americans picked up Lincoln's tortured, fundamental question: if the remarkable US expansionism of both territory and a democratic system was manifest destiny, why did it climax in the Civil War?

KEY POINTS

❑ Driven by their quests for both more territory for their multiplying families and wealth and security for themselves, Americans set out after their War for Independence to establish a continental empire.

❑ Jefferson called this an 'empire for liberty', but he carefully did not give democratic rights to the freshly acquired New Orleans region, and by the early nineteenth century, the United States had become part of an empire containing human slavery.

❑ Lincoln determined to stop the territorial expansion of this slavery and, thus, helped bring about the Civil War.

From old empire to new empire, 1865 – 1913

The North's victors had happier subjects to think about after 1865. When the southerners left Washington in 1861, the northerners who now controlled Congress quickly passed a series of laws which created a foundation for the American industrial and financial complexes which soon dominated world affairs. The legislation included, for example, a much higher tariff to protect northern producers against cheap European goods. Such a tariff had long been opposed by southerners, whose plantation owners wanted access to the cheapest (that is, British) industrial products. Now protected by the ever rising tariff, northern steel makers such as Andrew Carnegie joined the creators of other new industries, such as John D. Rockefeller's Standard Oil Company, to build an industrial complex which became the world's most productive by 1900. A new, overseas economic empire was being developed by Americans.

Landed expansion did continue. In 1867, Alaska was bought for $7.5 million from Russia. By 1875, trade deals were made with Hawaii, deals which led some twenty-three years later to the annexation of those islands. But this post-1865 landed expansion was radically different from the pre-1860 expansionism. The earlier expansion was one of settlement across adjoining territory. When native Indian tribes occupied those lands, or at times tried to fight back against the white settlements, the Indians were killed or forced to live on reservations. The new, post-1865 expansion, however, was not the movement of settlers across the land, but of traders and financers across the oceans. Americans had once viewed these oceans as great walls which helped protect them against foreign invasion. They now viewed them as great highways on which they could ship ever larger amounts of their farm and industrial goods to foreign markets.

Americans continued to follow the advice of Washington and Jefferson not to form any overseas political alliances. The resulting freedom of action allowed the United States to stay out of squabbles in Europe and Asia, while selling goods to all sides. It also led newly wealthy American families to marry their daughters and sons to European, especially British, aristocratic families. The Europeans thus obtained American money, the Americans obtained European class. These links even helped determine which side Americans would favour, and finance, in later wars.

Fuelled by the industrial revolution of the late nineteenth century, which produced the first telephones, automobiles, aeroplanes, and steel complexes as well as the transatlantic marriages, US foreign policy's focus moved from the North American continent to markets of Europe, Latin America, and Asia. This was nothing less than a 'new empire', as one influential observer termed it at the time (Adams 1902). In this new empire, landed expansion aimed primarily not to find new areas for Americans to settle. It instead intended to develop naval bases, an isthmian canal in Central America, and coaling stations to protect and accelerate US overseas trade.

In 1874, the United States also embarked on this new era when, for the first time, it began consistently to sell more goods overseas than it bought. (This favourable balance of trade lasted more than seventy-five years until the expenses of the Cold War created steady deficit trade balances in the 1960s and after.) US international commerce generated such great profits that New York City was becoming a world financial centre. By 1904–5, some of the city's financiers even helped determine the outcome of the Russian–Japanese War by providing vast sums of money to help Japan—and thus to oppose the Russians who were both clashing with US economic interests in Asia and deeply angering many Americans by conducting bloody campaigns against Russian Jews.

The economic foundation for this new empire was thus laid in the 1860 to 1890s era. The new empire's political structure strikingly appeared on this foundation between the 1890s and 1913. In 1895, Cubans rebelled against their Spanish rulers. Some $50 million of US investments in Cuba were endangered in the conflict. In April 1898, President William McKinley, a Republican, decided he had to go to war against Spain. Especially important in his thinking was a fear that the Cuban revolutionaries were winning their rebellion against Spain and, if triumphant, might threaten US property while ignoring American interests.

McKinley thus moved in the War of 1898 to drive Spain out of Cuba and, as well, to ensure that the Cuban revolutionaries would not control their country. As Jefferson had severe doubts about allowing democracy in New Orleans during 1803, so McKinley doubted that democracy was best for American interests in Cuba in 1898. In what Secretary of State John Hay called 'a splendid little war', US forces defeated Spain in less than three months. Cuba and Puerto Rico were taken from Spain, along with the Philippine Islands in the south-west Pacific. The Philippines were a prize McKinley and Hay wanted because control of the Filipino ports for the US fleet would suddenly make the United States a force in Asia and its vast markets. McKinley also annexed the Hawaiian Islands in 1898, thus setting up another link between Americans and Pacific markets. Cuba finally received what was termed independence, but Americans controlled the country and took over a potentially superb naval base at Guantánamo.

In 1899–1900 Hay issued two historic *open door* notes which defined the main principles for the new empire: China (then under attack by European and Japanese colonial powers), must remain whole, united, and under Chinese control, Hay proclaimed, so the entire country would be open to US trade and missionaries. His open door notes opposed colonialism and vigorously supported open foreign markets (in which the new American economic dominance could compete successfully against anyone). These two principles dominated US foreign policy into the twenty-first century.

In 1903, President Theodore Roosevelt helped Panamanians revolt successfully against Colombia, then seized a 10-mile-wide area through Panama. He began building an isthmian canal which opened in 1914. Given its economic power and great battleship fleet (now one of the world's four largest), the United States could even act as a New World policeman. Indeed, Roosevelt actually announced in 1904–5 with his own corollary to the Monroe Doctrine that Americans would be the region's cop on the beat. The irrepressible TR, moreover, won the Nobel Peace Prize for mediating in 1905 a settlement between Russia and Japan after their war. The United States had become a major international power.

Wilson's empire of ideology—and the bitter reaction, 1913–33

In 1917 the United States finally dropped its long-held refusal to become involved in European affairs. It joined the British and French in their war against Germany and Austria-Hungary. By this time, the world was not only gripped by war but by massive class revolution in such vital areas as Russia and China. President Woodrow Wilson tried to set out plans to deal with both the world war and the spreading revolutions. He and his allies won the conflict. But they could not agree on peace terms or stop the revolutions. During the 1920s Americans tried to build the foundations for peace, especially through their economic power. In 1929 that power collapsed in an economic panic which dragged down much of the world and helped create Japanese and German militarism that took the world into another, much greater, world war.

The first great era of *globalization* (that is, the ever closer linking of the world's peoples through economic ties and technology) developed between the 1860s and 1914. Faster, oil-driven ships, then primitive aeroplanes, automobiles, and global telegraph lines, shortened time and distance. By 1910, widely read authors predicted that because peoples were becoming so closely linked, major international wars were impossible.

In the summer of 1914 that conflict nevertheless began. The First World War broke out because of misunderstandings and miscalculations between the Allies (British, French, Russians, and Japanese), and the Central Powers (led by Germany and Austro-Hungary). Both sides had believed that civilized nations, like themselves, would never allow the mass killing now possible with modern arms in a full-scale war, so they felt safe in taking chances. Within months, thousands of lives were being snuffed out in a single day on the blood-drenched fields of France and Russia. Great Britain, France, and Germany, three of the world's wealthiest nations, suddenly had to mobilize such immense forces that, to their surprise, they were going bankrupt.

This brought the United States into the picture. President Woodrow Wilson (1913–21) had demanded at the war's beginning that Americans remain neutral in thought and action. Meanwhile those Americans could profit by selling food and war supplies to both sides. As bankruptcy threatened the belligerents, however, they begged Wilson for help. He initially resisted. The President rightly feared becoming too closely tied economically to either side. But for three centuries Europe had been the most important market for Americans. As that market began to be unable to pay cash for US goods, and as economic depression threatened the United States, Wilson changed his mind. He allowed his nation's bankers to offer both sides dollars and credits so they could continue to purchase American products. The Allies, helped by long-time British ties to New York and Boston banks, borrowed $2.5 billion between 1915 and 1917. This was ten times the amount Germany and Austria-Hungary could obtain.

Wilson's decision to loan vast amounts of money was legal, but it turned out not to be neutral. As ships carrying US goods headed for British and French ports, Germany's submarines sank increasing numbers of those vessels and claimed hundreds of American lives. Wilson recognized the historic right of the British surface fleet, which controlled the oceans, to stop goods headed for the Central Powers. But no firm international law dealt with Germany's new weapon, underwater U-boats, so the President insisted that the submarines' attacks on US ships cease. The Germans complied until late 1916. In January 1917, however, they determined the American shipments to the Allies had to be stopped. The submarines again attacked US ships. In April 1917, the United States declared war on the Central Powers.

Americans now not only found themselves immersed in the bloodiest conflict in human history, but in a world racked by revolution. The twentieth century was to be shaped by these revolutions. Americans grew to hate and oppose them. The first major upheaval had occurred in Mexico after 1911. As that outbreak threatened US lives and interests (especially oil holdings), Wilson several times sent in troops. Instead of taming the revolution, however, the President's military intervention helped make Mexicans both more radical and more anti-United States. At the same time, the great Chinese Revolution erupted. Preoccupied with Mexico, Europe, and the Caribbean, where outbreaks also threatened, Wilson could do relatively little in China.

When, however, the Russian Revolution of February–March 1917 exploded, the world changed for everyone, including Americans. Devastated and impoverished by fighting against Germany, the Russians overthrew their tsarist rulers, then rapidly moved to the left until in November 1917 a communist regime led by Vladimir Lenin seized power. The Soviet leader moved to place private property under state control and to close religious sanctuaries—two acts which shocked the West. Lenin further stunned the Allies by pulling bankrupt Russia out of the fight against Germany. The new leader in Moscow also angered Wilson by threatening to spread communism throughout Europe. It was not an empty threat. The Austro-Hungarian Empire was fragmenting. Peoples in Africa and Asia ruled by British and French colonial officers began to demand independence. The entire globe seemed to be flying apart in 1917–18 and offering communism golden opportunities.

Wilson moved to control the revolutionary outbreak by demanding that the new nations be governed by American-style democracy, not by Leninist-style communism. In doing so, the President set in motion the US challenge to Russian communism—a challenge which characterized American–Russian relations for nearly the whole of the twentieth century. He was determined, as he said, 'to make the world safe for democracy'. Wilson vowed to end, 'once and forever', the centuries-long 'old order' of international affairs which had tried to maintain peace by what 'we used to call the "balance of power"—a thing in which the balance was determined by the sword' (Gardner 1984: 2).

Peaceful voting, the American way, was to replace bloody swords as the method for making changes. Europeans, including the British and French with whom Wilson fought, had little use for his version of democracy. They pointedly noted that in destroying or isolating the Indian tribes and Mexicans who had once populated large parts of North America, US officials had waged war—not conducted elections to see how the Indians and Mexicans might vote. Nor had the North decided the results of the Civil War by holding democratic voting.

The British and French knew, moreover, that elections in Africa and Asia would quickly end their own colonial empires. On this question, Wilson seemed at times to agree with his allies. A Virginia-born racist who as President presided over the segregation of African Americans in Washington, DC, Wilson doubted that many Asians and Africans, or some Latin Americans, could be trusted with democracy.

The President even successfully opposed a Japanese effort to write a clause in the post-war peace agreements which would support racial equality.

Wilson, it became apparent, had never thought through these dangerously complex problems in regard to democracy. He and his associates in London and Paris won the First World War, but they divided and lost the peace. They could not figure out how to deal with (that is, remove) Lenin. In 1918, Wilson had actually joined with the British and French in sending military forces into Russia to try to weaken the communist regime. The intervention backfired as Russians supported Lenin's government against the foreign invasion.

The President's dreams of democracy also turned to nightmares at home. As the leader of the Democratic Party he made pivotal mistakes in 1918 which helped lead to a Republican victory in that year's congressional elections. Republican leaders had grave doubts about Wilson's peace plans, above all his famous proposal to create an international organization, the League of Nations, to maintain the post-war peace. The President, of course, saw the United States, under his leadership, as shaping and leading the new League. For nearly 120 years, however, Americans had steadfastly followed the advice of Washington and Jefferson to stay clear of international alliances. As they prepared to debate the post-war treaty and the League in 1919, Republican leaders in the US Senate decided to oppose Wilson's plans. The President fought back by beginning a gruelling speaking trip across the country. In Colorado, he was stricken by a massive stroke which made it nearly impossible for him to speak. The post-war debate was over. The United States would not join the League of Nations. Wilson's vague, often contradictory, plans for making the world safe for democracy disappeared—at least for a while.

Americans instead set out on their own to help economically reconstruct the war-torn world. In this way they could both make some money and help insure those areas against the seductive promises of communism. Their booming industrial, banking, and farm complexes made impossible any isolation from world markets.

When a military spending race to build battleships threatened to break out after the war, US officials called a conference in Washington for 1921–2. With imagination and bravado, Secretary of State Charles Evans Hughes worked out a Five-Power Treaty with the British, French, Italians, and Japanese (the Russians of course were not invited), which sharply limited naval spending and even forced the signatories to destroy some of their ships. Hughes also seized the opportunity to work out a Nine-Power Treaty. This pact set out a peaceful approach to handling revolutionary China, including an agreed-upon open door approach to the vast Chinese markets. The 1921–2 Washington Conference was the greatest American diplomatic success in the era between the two world wars.

US officials also enjoyed success in helping rebuild Europe. In 1923 the German economy had begun to spin out of control. The war had devastated it, and the Paris Peace Conference in 1919 had then forced Germany to pay billions of dollars in penalties for the war's destruction of property. France tried to grasp the opportunity by seizing territory long disputed between itself and the Germans. A crisis loomed, not least for US bankers and exporters. They long had understood that Germany was the most powerful industrial nation on the continent. If Germans were not economically healthy then all of Europe could sink into depression. The United States consequently quickly convened a conference in 1924 to deal with the crisis. Led by US Vice-President Charles Dawes, a former Chicago banker, the conference worked out a solution. The so-called Dawes Plan proposed massive private loans from US banks to rebuild the German economy. France retreated from its land grab. Europe seemed finally to be at peace and safe from communist infections.

But appearances were deceiving. The economic centre of Europe, Germany, and the most powerful nation in Asia, Japan, heavily depended on US banks for needed capital. By 1928 and early 1929, however, the American economy began to stumble. The immediate cause was the New York Stock Exchange. Its stock prices had ridden the booming economy upward until in 1929 over-speculation and corrupt investment practices set in motion a sharp downward spiral of those prices. Capital began to disappear. Between October 1929 and mid-1931, the New York Exchange's stocks suffered the single greatest loss in history to that time. Some suddenly bankrupt investors chose to commit suicide. As the economy continued to sink in 1932–3, unemployment doubled during those years to an unheard-of number of 25 million. Little help came from most states or the federal government.

The two most important regional powers, Germany in Europe and Japan in Asia, had been supported (as in the 1924 Dawes Plan, noted above) by the dollar. When that currency began to weaken after 1929, so did German and Japanese ties to the United States. The civilian-based governments in Germany and Japan declined along with their economies. A militarily dominated regime emerged in Japan and then, in 1933, Adolf Hitler's Nazi Party seized power in Germany.

The meaning of all this for US foreign policy was immediate—and catastrophic. The United States was unable either to help Tokyo or stop its military plans. The Japanese invaded Manchuria in September 1931. US President Herbert Hoover (1929–33) refused to try to stop Japan. He was frightened of anything that might threaten the long US–Japanese friendship. He also preferred that if someone were going to exploit weakened, revolution-racked China, it would be Japan and not the neighbouring Soviet Union.

Moments occur in US history when events, usually catastrophic events such as the Civil War, the 1929–33 Crash, or the 2001 attacks on New York City and Washington, should force Americans to rethink a world they thought they knew well. Such rethinking is incredibly difficult, especially if the years before the catastrophic events were marked by American successes, and in every instance (before the Civil War, the 1929–33 Crash, or the 2001 attacks), that had indeed been the case. In 1861 Abraham Lincoln provided the rethinking by stopping centuries-long American expansion in order to kill the institution of slavery.

After the 1929 crash, no Lincoln appeared. President Herbert Hoover had considerable international experience, both as a successful engineer in Asian mining ventures and as a close adviser of Woodrow Wilson's between 1917 and 1920. But he was unable to deal with the failures of the nation's economic system. He largely stood immobile as prices collapsed and unemployment soared. Nor could Hoover fundamentally reconsider the foreign policies of the 1920s which had rested on US economic power and cooperation with Japan and Germany. And so, along with the British and French, he did little as Japan invaded Manchuria and China and as Germany slid downwards into Nazism.

KEY POINTS

- The globe was shaken after 1911 not only by the First World War (1914–18), but by revolutions which struck, among others, Mexico, China, and Russia.
- The United States was swept into the First World War by its historic ties to the British and French, and by President Wilson's hope that he could help create a world safe for democracy, not revolution.
- Wilson and other victors failed to create this world at the Paris Peace Conference (1919), and Americans refused to join the League of Nations.

- Americans thus retained their freedom of action, but because of economic and security interests, they had to take the lead with the Washington Conference (1921–2) to limit military spending, and with the Dawes Plan (1924) to rebuild Germany.
- The American economic system, however, sank into depression between 1929 and 1933 to help trigger a global depression which created conditions for the emergence of a militarist regime in Japan and the Nazis in Germany.

The road from economic depression to the Cold War, 1933–45

In 1933, Hoover was replaced in the White House by New York Governor Franklin D. Roosevelt (1933–45). The new President spent his first six years in office trying to end the economic depression at home. Conditions seemed slowly to improve, but for some months in 1938, the nation suddenly suffered one of the steepest economic downturns in its history. Within a year, however, Roosevelt's greatest concern was not the economy but the outbreak of the Second World War in Europe. Indeed, new military spending after 1939 finally lifted the nation out of the depression. In late 1941, the United States entered the conflict. The President spent the next four years not only winning the war, but trying, with much less success, to work out a post-war peace with the other two victors, Great Britain and the Soviet Union.

Roosevelt, much like Hoover, was an internationalist, an Assistant Secretary of the Navy under Woodrow Wilson, and a young vice-presidential nominee for the Democrats in the 1920 election who had strongly favoured joining the League of Nations. In dealing with the 1930s economic crisis, however, FDR moved away from internationalism. His domestic, so-called New Deal, programmes tried to clean up and regulate the stock markets and banking system, while providing direct, immediate federal governmental help to out-of-work Americans. By 1936, the nation's economy had slightly improved, employment rose, and Roosevelt won a second term.

But he had accomplished this improvement at home with little rethinking of American foreign policy. Roosevelt believed he could best raise prices in the United States only through internal manipulation, not difficult international negotiations with trading partners. The President's isolationist (that is, having maximum freedom of action, free of overseas political and also many economic commitments) foreign policies were driven in part by his desire to have an unrestrained hand to revive, quickly, his nation's economy. His policies were also shaped by an isolationist Congress which wanted to concentrate on the domestic crises, not foreign developments. The desire of Americans to stay free of overseas commitments intensified as Hitler's Germany began a series of military aggressions which seized Austria and parts of Czechoslovakia in 1937–8, and as Japanese militarists renewed their invasion of China in 1937.

In 1938, the British and French weakly went along in an international conference at Munich to allow Hitler to seize parts of Czechoslovakia which contained large German populations. Roosevelt agreed with this policy of appeasement (allowing an aggressor—Hitler, in this case—to take territory in the hope it would satisfy the aggressor and bring about long-term peace). Hitler, however, absorbed the slice of territory granted by the British and French, then, to the shock of Americans and the rest of the world, also seized the remainder of defenceless Czechoslovakia. Appeasement and 'Munich' became dirty words in US and international politics, then and after 1945 (Record 2006: 8).

By the summer of 1939, Hitler was prepared to attack other parts of Europe. But he first wanted to neutralize his most important military opponent, the Soviet Union headed by dictator Josef Stalin. Throughout the 1933 to 1935 era, Stalin, deeply frightened of Hitler, had asked Roosevelt, along with British and French leaders, to cooperate in stopping the German aggression. The Westerners were not prepared to do so. They also doubted whether it was possible to work with a communist such as Stalin. In August 1939 the Soviet dictator stunned the West by making a deal with Hitler to stand aside while Germany attacked Poland. The Soviets and Germans then divided Poland between themselves. On the first day of September 1939, the Second World War began with that German invasion. The British and French declared war against Hitler, but the Americans remained neutral in the hope that they could somehow avoid the spreading flames.

By mid-1940 France and most of continental Europe had fallen under Nazi control. President Roosevelt, however, made only measured responses. London and other major British cities were being struck every night by Nazi planes in the so-called Battle of Britain, while a German invasion seemed imminent. The new British leader, Winston Churchill, begged Roosevelt for help. The President responded with large amounts of economic assistance. Equally important, he secretly ordered US warships to track and if necessary sink any German submarines which threatened to interrupt the growing US trade with Great Britain.

But the greatest help for the British came, in a stunning surprise, from the Soviet Union. Hitler was growing tired of dividing up parts of Europe with Stalin and hoped to obtain badly needed petroleum by seizing Soviet oil fields. In June 1941 the Nazi leader launched the largest military operation in history with his invasion of the Soviet Union. His armies soon approached the Russian capital, Moscow, and the Soviet oil fields. Despite encountering considerable opposition, especially in Congress, Roosevelt quickly began sending large amounts of war matériel to Russia. FDR and Churchill agreed that the Soviet dictator was not the person they would most like to work with, but Stalin was certainly to be favoured over Hitler. By autumn 1941, several encounters between American ships and Nazi submarines indicated it was only a matter of time before the United States would go to war, much as it had in 1917.

Instead, war surprisingly struck Americans from the opposite direction. Throughout 1940, Japan had moved into China and South-East Asia in a quest for regional domination and, especially, badly needed oil fields. By mid-1941, as the Japanese seized control of French Indochina, US officials responded by shutting off American petroleum shipments to Japan. In a series of talks, no settlement could be reached between Japan and the United States in regard to the oil or—more importantly—China. Roosevelt refused to recognize Japanese domination of parts of China. Such recognition would have surrendered the historic US open door policy in that country.

Japan's military-dominated government secretly decided to launch a surprise attack on the American naval base in Hawaii, Pearl Harbor. Japanese officials hoped to destroy enough of the US Pacific fleet so Roosevelt, also faced with possible war in Europe, would be willing to meet most of Tokyo's demands in Asia. Japanese planes devastated Pearl Harbor on Sunday 7 December 1941. The attack stunned Americans, but instead of considering a settlement, as the Japanese hoped, Congress, at Roosevelt's request, declared war against Japan. On 11 December, Japan's sometime partner, Hitler, declared war against the United States.

The early months of American involvement in the Second World War were among the darkest in the nation's history. Japan seized a number of US bases in the Pacific, including the strategic Philippines, and threatened to invade Australia. US naval victories, especially in mid-1942 at the Midway Islands, finally began to turn the tide of battle. In Europe, Hitler's offensive continued until mid-1943 when Stalin's armies were able to stop the Nazi advance. Fighting the Second World War, the Soviets paid a horrible price of at least 25 to 30 million dead. Throughout 1942–3, Stalin desperately asked Roosevelt and Stalin to help by opening a second military front in France, and thus force Hitler to shift troops away from Russia.

The US and British leaders refused to open that second front until June 1944. Their refusal came in part from FDR's belief that Anglo-American armies were not prepared for such an invasion of France, and in part from Churchill's determination to fight first in the Mediterranean, where the British Empire had major interests. Thus US and British forces invaded not France, but German-controlled North Africa in 1942 and then Italy. Stalin grew suspicious that his allies were hoping his armies would exhaust themselves fighting Hitler and thus not be in a position to threaten US and British plans after the war.

The United States was beyond question becoming the world's greatest power. British, Russian, Japanese, and western European industries and cities were largely reduced to smoking ashes between 1941 and 1945. But untouched US industrial production shot up by 90 per cent. Americans came to understand what this meant: they no longer needed to fear becoming politically involved with the world because now, they believed, they finally held the raw power to control and run that world. For example, in 1942, when Roosevelt announced a new United Nations organization which was to replace the failed League of Nations, most Americans immediately accepted the UN because they believed they (unlike Wilson with the League in 1919) would be able to control it. (And they did—until the 1960s and 1970s when membership in the UN of many new African and Asian nations threatened US control. Then Americans cooled considerably toward the UN.)

A consensus emerged among US leaders during the conflict that they would hold post-war power. But for what purpose? What kind of world should Americans try to construct? Here Roosevelt and Truman encountered the haunting problem which, finally, doomed Americans' post-war hopes and swept the nation into a forty-five-year Cold War—and beyond.

On the one hand, they were determined to construct an open, integrated post-war world in which trade could move freely. War-torn nations were to be rebuilt rapidly. There was to be no more high-tariff and other forms of economic warfare which had destroyed international relations in the 1930s and climaxed in the Second World War. Roosevelt first moved against his own ally, Great Britain. The British had tried to preserve their empire by setting up trade walls around it during the 1930s. In return for providing all-important US military help in 1941, Roosevelt asked Churchill to promise that after the war the British would remove those walls (and allow Americans, for example, to trade freely with such parts of the British Empire as India, Canada, and South Africa). The British leader complained bitterly, and tried to add reservations, but he had no choice except to give in to the Americans if he expected US help.

Washington officials followed this up in 1944 by establishing the economic side of the new United Nations: the World Bank and International Monetary Fund (IMF). The World Bank was to provide international cooperation in investment to rebuild the post-war world. The IMF was to create international financial cooperation so the deadly economic wars between nations which had marked the 1930s could not be repeated. Because Americans controlled half the world's wealth in 1945, there was no doubt who would provide the financial resources for these two institutions—and thus control the institutions themselves.

Ominously, the Soviet Union refused to join the World Bank or the IMF in 1945–6. Stalin refused to allow any international organization controlled by the United States to examine Soviet records or try to shape the Russian economy. The dictator's refusal to cooperate with the US policy of an open economic world was also linked to the failure of the Russians and Americans to agree on how the post-war world should be rebuilt politically. Through three war-time summit conferences (at Tehran, Iran, in 1943, the Soviet city of Yalta in February 1945, then Potsdam, Germany, in July 1945), the US, British, and Soviet leaders failed to reach agreement on the crucial European question: how to rebuild a defeated Germany. Roosevelt at first was willing to make the Germans pay by stripping them of all industry (a position Stalin happily agreed with). But FDR then changed his mind when he realized Europe could never be quickly rebuilt and kept open unless its long-time economic power centre, Germany, was rebuilt first. Stalin's armies finally took the decision out of Roosevelt's hands by reaching the German capital of Berlin ahead of US and British forces, and then holding on to eastern Germany. While the leaders debated, the Soviets stripped eastern Germany of all the resources they could ship back to Russia. Germany would remain divided for the next forty-five years.

The German and other central post-war issues had not yet been fully decided on 12 April 1945, when Roosevelt suddenly died of a massive stroke. FDR, however, had worked hard to stay on good terms with Stalin (recall his sending of massive US aid to the Soviets in mid-1941 even before the Americans entered the war), although the relationship was in decline during the months before Roosevelt's death. His successor, Vice-President Harry S. Truman, was a parochial Missouri politician who knew little about foreign policy, nor did FDR ever try to help him understand the deteriorating relationship with the Russians in early 1945.

Understandably highly insecure personally, as well as unprepared, Truman quickly tried to show he was tough by demanding that the Soviets back down from their control of Poland and hold open elections in that country. The new President privately bragged that he had given the Russians 'the straight one-two to the jaw' (Sherwin 1975: 72; Stimson and Bundy 1949: 609). Stalin responded with a one-two of his own which turned out to be more effective. He pointed out that he did not protest US and British policies in countries close to those two nations' interests (such as Italy, Belgium, France, and Mexico)—so Americans should understand that the Soviets had comparable interests in eastern Europe, through which, after all, the Germans had twice invaded Russia in just twenty-seven years. Stalin determined there would not be a third invasion.

Truman attended his first summit with Churchill and Stalin at Potsdam in July 1945. The President believed he had a secret weapon which would help him pressure Stalin to cooperate on American terms. That weapon, the atomic bomb, was first tested while Truman was in Potsdam. He told Stalin about the successful test. The Soviet leader seemed unimpressed.

(He had learned a good deal about the bomb's development from Russian spies.) Despite the President's pressure, the Soviets refused to back down on Germany or eastern Europe.

Stalin did renew his earlier pledge to Roosevelt that the Russians would enter the war against Japan about 8 August. Truman, however, was by now little interested in having the Soviets involved in Japan. The United States dropped the first atomic bomb on Hiroshima on 6 August 1945, instantly killing more than 80,000 Japanese. On 8 August, the Soviets declared war on Japan. The next day the President dropped the second bomb on Nagasaki which quickly killed more than 65,000 people. Within a week, Japan surrendered. Truman believed he had avoided the terrible bloodshed which would have resulted from an invasion of the Japanese home islands. The President rushed occupation teams into Japan so he would not have to share final control of the occupation with either the British or Soviets.

The struggle against Hitler and the Japanese militarists had ended in triumph. But a new war had erupted between the United States and Great Britain, on the one hand, and the Soviets on the other. The conflict was over the question of whether the world was to be open to trade, investment, and cultural influences (which the virtually untouched American society, enriched by the war, could command), or whether strategic areas of the globe, particularly central and eastern Europe which had recently given birth to two world wars, were to be controlled and closed off by victorious Soviet armies. The Cold War had begun.

KEY POINTS

❑ During the 1930s the United States could neither solve its own economic depression nor cooperate with those nations concerned about the rise of Hitler in Germany or militarism in Japan.

❑ When the United States entered the war after being attacked by Japan in 1941, US officials began extensive planning for an open post-war world free of both British colonialism and Soviet occupation.

❑ Neither Roosevelt nor Truman, however, could find the means to force Stalin to retreat from eastern Germany and eastern Europe—two areas the Soviets believed were fundamental for assuring their own security.

Conclusion

In the early 1830s (that is, as Americans were convinced they were manifestly destined to build a North American continental empire), a shrewd French visitor, Alexis de Tocqueville, wrote a two-volume work, *Democracy in America*. It is perhaps the best analysis ever made of the nation's society—and its destiny. Tocqueville predicted that although both peoples were only beginning to be players on the international stage, Americans and Russians were each 'marked out by the will of heaven to sway the destinies of half the globe' (Tocqueville 1948: i. 434). In the 1940s, Tocqueville's prediction of 110 years before seemed to be coming true.

Americans had seldom doubted their own destiny. They began with thirteen colonies on the western rim of the Atlantic Ocean, then, within less than eighty years after achieving independence, spread their system, which their leaders called an 'empire', from the Atlantic to the Pacific. The landed expansion was in part based on, and profited from, the institution of human slavery. In 1861, Lincoln stopped any further landed expansion which might benefit those who owned slaves. The result was the war which took more American lives than any other in the nation's history.

When the Civil War ended with the North's victory, a forcefully reunited nation proved so effective in exploiting and developing the continent that a new empire had to be developed after 1865. It was an empire of global markets, protected by naval bases in such places as Panama and the Philippine Islands, which could absorb the extraordinary production spewing out of American farms and factories. By 1900, the United States had become by many measurements the world's number one producer. Its interests swept it into two world wars. Faced in 1917–20 with a dangerously revolutionary world, Woodrow Wilson tried to organize that world by replacing radical revolution with his determination to 'make the world safe for democracy'. He failed,

as did later American leaders who falsely assumed that political institutions arising out of centuries of American and British history could easily be translated into similar institutions in, say, Asia, the Middle East, and Africa, whose history and traditions were vastly different.

Indeed, the American system itself broke down in 1928–9 and helped trigger a global depression which in turn gave birth to military regimes in Japan and Germany. By 1941, Franklin D. Roosevelt was concerned not with expanding democracy but stopping Japanese and German expansion. The United States finally won the Second World War, but only with the help of the British and, especially, Soviets. Of the 13 million Germans who perished in the war, Stalin's armies killed more than 10 million, although at the cost of probably three times that number of Russian lives. The Soviet dictator determined to hold eastern Europe and part of Germany as a security area for the Soviet Union.

US officials could not accept such results of the war. They believed the world had to be open and developed economically along capitalist lines (thus the creation of the World Bank and International Monetary Fund in 1944–5), while the globe was also being opened, decolonized, and slowly integrated politically (thus the creation of the United Nations between 1942 and 1945). When he issued his prophecy in the 1830s, Tocqueville had noted that although they were each destined to create an empire dominating half the globe, nevertheless the Russian and American 'starting point is different and their courses not the same' (Tocqueville 1948: i. 433–4). The Frenchman was correct. The Americans' view of why they had become the world's greatest power in 1945, and why they now had to fight that Cold War, can only be understood by understanding how they developed their continental empire and then their new empire over the previous 170 years. They were, and continue to be, the products of their own, long history.

? Questions

1. What were the major characteristics of the first American 'empire'?

2. When and why did the first American 'empire' transform into a 'new empire'?

3. Jefferson is famous as a father of American democracy, so why did he deny democracy to the New Orleans region after he bought Louisiana in 1803?

4. Why did American expansion across the continent, which was supposedly blessed by 'manifest destiny', lead to the outbreak of the Civil War?

5. Why do the War of 1898 and its immediate results exemplify a new era, a 'new empire', in American history?

6. In 1918, much of the world (outside the Soviet Union) saw Woodrow Wilson as its greatest hope. Why, then, did Wilson fail to 'make the world safe for democracy' between 1918 and 1920?

7. Why was the US stock market crash of 1929 such a blow to the American foreign policies which had been forged, with considerable success, between 1921 and 1929?

8. With the world facing increased danger during the 1930s from Japanese and German military aggression, why did President Franklin D. Roosevelt follow isolationist foreign policies which offered little resistance to that aggression?

9. What were the major differences between the Soviet Union and the United States which developed when they were allies between 1941 and 1945 and led them into the post-1945 Cold War?

10. Why did the United States follow an 'open door' policy throughout much of its post-1890s foreign relations and, notably, in its planning during the Second World War for the post-war peace?

11. Given their history to 1945 of trying to expand democracy, should Americans make the expansion of democratic institutions throughout the world a central principle of their diplomacy?

» Further Reading

Cohen, W. I. (2000), *The American Response to China*, 4th edn. (New York: Columbia University Press).

This excellent survey of the entire US–China relationship includes most useful reading guides.

Cole, W. (1983), *Roosevelt and the Isolationists, 1932–1945* (Lincoln, Nebr.: University of Nebraska Press).

Cole's volume is the best overall analysis of isolationism in the period and Franklin D. Roosevelt's relationship to it.

Gardner, L. C. (1984), *Safe for Democracy: The Anglo-American Response to Revolution, 1913–1923* (New York: Oxford University Press).

A superb, detailed analysis of Woodrow Wilson's response to the revolutions, this volume also provides important perspective by comparing Wilson's with the British response before, during, and after the First World War.

Hunt, M. H. (1987), *Ideology and American Foreign Policy* (New Haven: Yale University Press).

In a splendid post-1780s overview, Hunt emphasizes the role of race and anti-revolutionary sentiment in the formulation of US foreign policies.

Iriye, A. (1993), *The Globalization of America, 1913–1945* (New York: Cambridge University Press).

A provocative overview, this volume includes most helpful bibliographical references.

LaFeber, W. (1993), *The American Search for Opportunity, 1865–1913* (New York: Cambridge University Press).

An overview emphasizing the American role in stimulating revolution, as well as opposing it, the book also has extensive lists for further reading.

Langley, L. (1990), *America and the Americas: The United States in the Western Hemisphere* (Athens, Ga.: University of Georgia Press).
A valuable survey, with most helpful guides for further reading, this book notes the Latin American developments as well as US policies toward the southern hemisphere.

Perkins, B. (1993), *From Sea to Sea, 1776–1865* (New York: Cambridge University Press).
Written by a leading scholar of the era, this detailed overview has important interpretations as well as select lists of books and articles for further research.

Weinberg, A. K. (1935), *Manifest Destiny* (Baltimore: Johns Hopkins University Press).
A classic work of writing, scholarship, and interpretation, Weinberg's analysis is notably important for its questioning and, at times, its sarcasm.

Wilkins, M. (1970), *The Emergence of Multinational Enterprise: American Business Abroad from the Colonial Era to 1914* (Cambridge, Mass.: Harvard University Press).
This is the pioneering work on US financial expansion overseas and, although it is not identified as such, on the first great age of globalization between 1860 and 1914.

 Visit the Online Resource Centre that accompanies this book for web links to accompany each chapter, and a range of other resources: www.oxfordtextbooks.co.uk/orc/cox_stokes/

4 American foreign policy during the Cold War

Richard Saull

Chapter contents

Introduction

This chapter seeks to provide a theoretically informed overview of American foreign policy during the Cold War covering the main historical developments in US policy from the breakdown of the wartime alliance with the USSR and the emergence of US–Soviet diplomatic hostility and geopolitical confrontation, through to the spread of the Cold War beyond Europe and US military interventions in the third world, and the US role in the ending of the Cold War. The chapter will discuss these historical developments through drawing on different theoretical explanations of US foreign policy; those that focus on the role of geopolitical, ideational, and/or socio-economic factors. It aims to highlight the twin pillars of US foreign policy—one based on the geopolitical threat from the USSR and the other based on the US role in the international capitalist economy and the evolving and sometimes contradictory relationship between these two concerns and how they were resolved by US policy makers.

The discussion of American foreign policy during the Cold War has been dominated by three analytical questions: (1) the role of the USA in the emergence of the Cold War; (2) what factors best account for US foreign policy during the Cold War; and (3) the role of US policy in the collapse of Soviet communism and the end of the Cold War. Within the scholarly literature on US foreign policy two theoretical responses have tended to dominate the discussion of these questions. The first has emphasized the role of material or geopolitical factors in accounting for American foreign policy. Simply put, US policy was concerned with addressing the geopolitical and military threat to its security from the Soviet Union. The second response, whilst recognizing the significance of the geopolitical challenge to American security and international interests, has focused much more on the ideological characteristics of US foreign policy; meaning that it was the communist ideological character of the USSR that was as much of a concern to US policy makers as

the geopolitical threat, and, further, the fact that the domestic liberal-democratic characteristics of the USA also informed the ends and implementation of foreign policy.

This 'mainstream' debate on American foreign policy during the Cold War has done much to illuminate our understanding of both the Cold War and the nature of American foreign policy. However, it rests on a contestable assumption as to what the Cold War was about, namely the post-war bipolar US–Soviet relationship. This—what could be considered as the—conventional account of the Cold War and US foreign policy within it has tended to overlook the socio-economic dimensions of US foreign relations. This refers to the place of economic actors and processes in American foreign policy, as well as the wider concerns—extending beyond the Soviet threat—to include other (communist) states and radical and revolutionary movements that confronted the USA after 1945, and which came to inform the decisions and policies of the US foreign policy bureaucracy during the Cold War. Further, the conventional account has not sufficiently addressed the relationship between the USA and its Cold War allies—in western Europe in particular—and how these relations contributed to the overall dynamic of the Cold War.

What I intend to do in this chapter is to provide a theoretically engaged discussion of American foreign policy during the Cold War addressing the main historical developments within the evolution of the Cold War. As well as addressing the arguments within the mainstream debate on US foreign policy in the Cold War, I will also engage with a wider academic literature, particularly those scholars who draw on an analytical framework informed by a Marxist understanding of international relations, to provide a historically richer and more theoretically informed survey of American foreign policy during the Cold War.

The rest of the chapter is organized in the following way: first, I will provide a brief overview of the main theoretical frameworks accounting for American foreign policy during the Cold War; secondly, I will then move on to a survey of the history of US foreign policy in the Cold War weighing up the explanations offered by each theoretical perspective.

The Cold War and theorizing American foreign policy

Realism

There are two strands to realist explanations of American foreign policy during the Cold War. On the one hand there are those 'Cold War realists' (Kennan 1984; Kissinger 1961, 1994; Lippman 1947; Morgenthau 1951) who sought to account for the emergence of the Cold War and, later, became public critics of US foreign policy during the Cold War, and, on the other hand, there are international relations theorists (Mearsheimer 2001; Waltz 1979) who have addressed the bipolar relationship and the US role within it. What links these two sets of scholars is their common concern with what they regard as the shifting geopolitical contest between the USA and the USSR for ascendancy over post-war Europe and other strategically important areas (the Middle East and East Asia) after the war, and the way in which concerns centred on geopolitical and military power—security—guided US foreign policy. These scholars, then, have—in different ways—questioned the ideological motivations (of anti-communism and/or the upholding and expansion of liberal-democratic values) of US policy.

Where they differ is in their respective emphasis on US policy in the Cold War. Thus, Mearsheimer and Waltz emphasize the stability of the Cold War encapsulated in Gaddis's (1987) term the 'long peace', highlighting how US power countered or balanced Soviet power after 1945 and through the mutual deterrence of nuclear weapons reduced the likelihood of geopolitical competition triggering war. In this sense the Cold War was relatively stable because US policy was driven by geopolitical concerns.

This contrasts with the public criticisms of US foreign policy voiced by Cold War realists who regarded US foreign policy as too dependent on a militarized form of containment (Kennan 1984) and too influenced by an ideological commitment to spreading liberal-democratic (Wilsonian) values in its foreign policy (Morgenthau 1951). The upshot of these failings according to these critics—of not being realist enough—was that the USA became involved in areas of the world, such as Vietnam, where it had few if any strategic interests, getting embroiled in costly wars that did not best serve the national security interests of the USA. Consequently, whilst the Cold War realists agreed with the orthodox view on the origins of the Cold War—that the USA had no choice but to react to aggressive moves by the USSR in east-central Europe after 1945 with the doctrine of containment—they disagreed with the orthodox claim that Soviet policy was driven by communist-ideological expansion (Feis 1970) rather than traditional Russian great power manoeuvring. The Soviet threat and the key concern of US policy, then, was the Red Army's military presence in east-central Europe (and the wider expansion of Soviet geopolitical power throughout the Cold War) rather than the declared revolutionary aims of Moscow as the centre of the international communist movement.

Ideational approaches

In opposition to realist arguments ideational explanations of American foreign policy during the Cold War (Crockatt 1995; Lebow 1994; Schlesinger 1967) dwell on the way in which US foreign policy decision making was to a significant extent conditioned by the prevailing political values and ideological frameworks located within American domestic politics. According to these scholars, the liberal-democratic characteristics of the American polity and the way in which American policy makers viewed themselves—what it meant to be an American and what American values were—influenced not only the foreign policy objectives of the United States, but also how those objectives were realized.

Such accounts emphasize the dismay and revulsion of American leaders towards Soviet political practices in east-central Europe after the war and the way in which an ideological commitment to liberal-democratic political and economic values conditioned US policies towards western Europe after the war. Some scholars, such as David Campbell (1998), go as far as to stress how US foreign policy in the Cold War and the representation (and manipulation) of a Soviet threat was a key factor in the construction of a post-war American national identity based on the idea of 'freedom' as a uniquely American characteristic in contrast to the 'foreign' and 'hostile' ideas and values of socialism, equality, and collectivism.

In contrast to realism's emphasis on supposedly impersonal and objective geopolitical interests as the guiding principle informing foreign policy, scholars within the ideational-constructivist school give greater analytical purchase to the way in which a clash of ideological mindsets and world views between Soviet communism and American liberalism after the war was played out. This was reflected in the manner in which each superpower related to each of the two halves of divided Europe and the nature of the political institutions each sought to establish. Thus, these scholars argue that whereas the Marshall Plan and NATO reflected and institutionalized liberal-democratic values, the institutions created by the USSR in east-central Europe bore the hallmark of communist dictatorship.

With regards to the origins and evolution of US foreign policy during the Cold War, ideational approaches have also tended to reflect on the language and principles guiding US actions towards the USSR. In a word, although the USA was obviously concerned with the Soviet geopolitical presence in Europe, this became a Cold War because of the way in which that presence was combined with the articulation and institutionalization—through the imposition of communist rule—of a conflicting ideological vision of the post-war world (Schlesinger 1967) in opposition to liberal-democratic principles.

Further, as Mervyn Leffler (1994) has argued, US policy towards the USSR after 1945 was strongly influenced by a deep-rooted institutional and wider societal mentality of suspicion and hostility towards the ideology of communism dating from the 1917 Bolshevik Revolution and the way in which this—in some respects—virulent anti-communism made recognition of what some scholars regarded as 'legitimate' Soviet defensive security interests in east-central Europe after the war difficult. This approach also suggests that US policy makers were unable—as the Cold War progressed—to recognize that communism was not as centrally dominated by Moscow as the prevailing ideological mindset of the US national security bureaucracy believed (LaFeber 1989; Barnet 1972). The failure to compromise or engage the USSR at certain moments in the Cold War, then, is regarded as reflecting the way in which ideational assumptions about communism informed US foreign policy. Such assumptions continued into the closing stages of the Cold War as a number of senior figures in the Reagan and Bush administrations continued to harbour ideologically determined reservations and suspicions (Risse-Kappen 1991–2) about Gorbachev's policies and commitment to fundamentally reforming Moscow's relations with Washington.

Socio-economic approaches

Those scholars that focus on the way in which socio-economic structures and processes are central to explaining American foreign policy making during the Cold War (Cox 1984; Halliday 1986; Horowitz 1967; Kolko 1969; Saull 2001, 2007) have been concerned with the specifically capitalist properties of American foreign policy. These writers highlight two dimensions to the capitalist character of American foreign policy. First, is that both American (economic) actors (businesses, corporations, and individuals—and trade unions) and processes (production, investment, trade, distribution, and consumption, as well as conflicts between capitalists and workers) located within the sphere of the market economy played an important role in the international relations of the United States during the Cold War. In particular, these actors and processes conditioned the implementation and impact of American foreign policy, notably towards other capitalist states with respect to the way in which such processes helped promote stability, cooperation, and economic development within and amongst these states, as well as furthering American national security interests.

As much as American foreign relations during the Cold War, then, were concerned with physical security encapsulated in military power and strategic alliances, so they were also concerned with issues of economic security and prosperity, particularly with respect to the way in which international economic processes influenced the health and prosperity of the domestic political economy of the United States. Thus, the upholding of a liberal, open, and capitalist American economy was, in part, conditional on the existence of a wider international capitalist system that was also characterized by liberal principles of openness.

The second capitalist dimension of American foreign policy is that the American state is capitalist: meaning that its institutional structure, jurisdiction, and policies not only rest on the separation of the sphere of the state (politics) from economic activities of production, exchange, investment, and consumption located in the market, but that the policies of the American state seek to uphold this particular organization of society. According to these scholars, then, when we refer to American foreign relations we are in fact referring not only to formal diplomatic relations between states, but also to other (socio-economic) actors and processes committed to preserving and expanding capitalist relations of production and exchange.

This approach to American foreign policy is as much concerned to account for US relations with other capitalist states as it is the bipolar relationship after the war and the way in which capitalist *social* or class interests pervaded US national security policy. Consequently, for these scholars the Soviet threat was not primarily because of its geopolitical presence within east-central Europe but rather that this geopolitical presence was based upon a different and antagonistic set of socio-economic arrangements encapsulated in the communist organization of society and politics.

It was not then—as suggested by ideational scholars—mainly a concern with the different ideological values of the Soviet leadership and the way in which this challenged US post-war goals, but rather the fact that the socio-economic organization and reproduction of the Soviet type of society (and its expansion into east-central Europe and beyond) removed a geo-economic space from involvement in capitalism, cutting off potential markets for US and international capital, as well as claiming to be a societal alternative to American-led capitalism. Further, it was not only the case that the USSR threatened the international (and domestic American) social reproduction of a capitalist kind of society, but other revolutionary states—which emerged throughout the history of the Cold War—extended this threat, as well as those revolutionary and communist social and political movements active throughout the Cold War which were committed to overthrowing capitalist social arrangements (Halliday 1986; Saull 2001, 2007).

Now that I have provided an overview of the main theoretical perspectives on explaining American foreign policy during the Cold War giving a flavour of their main arguments, I will spend the rest of the chapter examining the key historical developments in American foreign policy during the Cold War, interspersing the historical narrative with reflections on the varying analytical strengths of each of the three approaches outlined above.

KEY POINTS

❏ Three main theoretical approaches to American foreign policy during the Cold War: realists, ideational, and socio-economic approaches.

❏ Two aspects to realist approaches to US foreign policy in the Cold War: (1) Cold War realists who accounted for the origins of the Cold War and later became critics of US policy; and (2) IR theorists concerned with the US role in the post-war bipolar relationship.

❏ Both concerned with the role of geopolitical factors in US foreign policy towards the USSR and have tended to downplay the ideological motivations in determining US policy.

(continued)

The origins of the Cold War and containment

The debate on the origins of the Cold War

The analysis of American foreign policy in the early period after the Second World War has been dominated by the debate over the US role in causing the breakdown of the wartime alliance and in triggering diplomatic hostility and geopolitical confrontation between Washington and Moscow. This has been framed in the so-called 'orthodox-revisionist debate on the origins of the Cold War'. Whilst the 'orthodox interpretation' of the origins of the Cold War sees US diplomacy as rather passive and reactive in the face of acts of Soviet aggression in east-central Europe (Kennan 1947; Feis 1967; Schlesinger 1967) highlighted by the creeping Sovietization of the region between 1945 and 1948, the alternative, revisionist view, stresses the conservative (rather than revolutionary) and defensive character of Soviet policy and the more proactive and expansionist policies of Washington.

In this account revisionist scholars (Horowitz 1967; Kolko and Kolko 1972) argue that the US used its post-war economic power and dominance to not only try to undermine Soviet influence in east-central Europe through drawing these states into a US-led international economic system decoupling them from economic links with the USSR, but also used this power to pressure other capitalist states (in western Europe and Britain in particular) to agree to and adopt the policies that would realize a distinctly American vision of how the post-war international economy should be organized—a vision that would have forced these states to not only open up their economies to US investment, but to dismantle their imperial trading blocs that had closed off access to American capital.

This debate has generated a huge scholarly literature (Ambrose and Brinkley 1997; Gaddis 1987, 1997; Leffler and Painter 1994; Paterson 1988) that has benefited from and expanded with the post-Cold War opening of Soviet diplomatic archives. I do not have the space to address many of the issues discussed in this literature or provide a historical narrative of the key events in the move from alliance to confrontation. Instead, I will make reference to some of the key historical developments that each of the three different theoretical approaches highlight to assess their relative merits in explaining US foreign policy in the early Cold War and, in doing so, highlight the relative strengths and

CONTROVERSIES 4.1: The orthodox – revisionist debate on the Cold War

The orthodox argument:

- The origins of the Cold War are found in Marxism-Leninism and its doctrine of class struggle leading to world revolution.
- The USSR was hostile to capitalist states and pursued policies to undermine the authority of these states.
- After the war the USSR was committed to extending Soviet power over Germany as much as east-central Europe.
- Roosevelt and Truman misjudged the expansionist nature of Soviet policy, naively harbouring vain hopes about integrating the USSR into a post-war liberal-democratic world order.
- US leaders did not have a clear vision of the post-war world and they were prepared to make political concessions (over east-central Europe) to Moscow for short-term military gains.
- Despite evidence of increasing Sovietization of east-central Europe the Truman administration continued to make concessions to Moscow (e.g. proposing, in the Baruch Plan, joint US – USSR control over the production of nuclear weapons, and inviting the USSR and east-central European states to participate in the Marshall Plan in 1947).
- Soviet hostility and aggression forced the USA to change policy by coming to the aid of western Europe and accepting the division of Germany.
- The Soviet response was further aggression in east-central Europe highlighted by the Czech coup of February 1948.
- With the Berlin blockade the US finally realized that it had to make a military commitment to the defence of western Europe with the creation of NATO.

The revisionist argument:

- Rejects the orthodox account as misreading Soviet actions and objectives and overlooking the expansionist character of US policy.
- The USSR cannot be held responsible for the Cold War by highlighting the impact of the war on the USSR and the military (monopoly on nuclear weapons) and economic advantages (massive increase in economic power of the USA through the war) of the USA after the war.
- Soviet policy after the war was concerned with domestic economic reconstruction (after the devastation caused by the war) and ensuring that Germany would never again pose a military threat.
- The Cold War emerged out of the needs of the American capitalist system to expand into new markets as a way of overcoming the problem of overproduction within its domestic economy.
- The expansion of American economic influence resulted in the spread of American political power.
- Because the USA was the leading economy after the war, inevitably it would benefit most, and policies of 'free trade' and 'equal opportunity' in all foreign markets would lead to US domination.
- The decisive reason for US involvement in the war was the aim to maintain and expand its influence in the world economy over other capitalist states.
- During the war and in negotiations afterwards, the USA was primarily concerned with breaking up the British Empire and ending the policy of imperial preferences that discriminated against American producers.
- When the 'open door' of American economic expansion was applied to east-central Europe, the USSR saw a threat to its legitimate security interests and was forced to act to prevent the spread of US economic and political influence.
- The Truman administration applied economic pressure on the USSR (ignoring Soviet requests for economic aid after the war, abruptly ending lend-lease deliveries at the end of the war, refusing to grant German reparations to Moscow at the Potsdam Conference) to try to extract concessions from Moscow over the future of east-central Europe and Germany.
- The Marshall Plan was an attempt to impose liberal-capitalism on east-central Europe, thus expelling Soviet influence.
- It was US policy that caused the division of Europe. When it became clear that the USA could not force changes in Soviet policy, by 1946 it pursued a policy of containment and division, which forced Moscow to act.

weaknesses of the orthodox and revisionist accounts of the early Cold War, respectively.

As suggested above, in my survey of the different theoretical perspectives on US foreign policy each approach emphasizes one or other set of factors to account for American behaviour: geopolitical, ideational, and/or socio-economic. To what extent, then, can we explain the shift in US foreign policy towards Cold War through a focus on each of these factors? The end of the war saw Europe and—though to a lesser extent—the world beyond continental Europe structured around the geopolitical dominance of the United States and the Soviet Union—the superpowers. This geopolitical outcome was coloured by the differing political and ideological values associated and institutionalized within each superpower; on the one hand liberal democracy and on the other communist dictatorship. Further, these differences in ideology and political values were matched by the very different forms of societal organization and socio-economic structure that characterized the USA and the USSR respectively.

The emergence of containment

What is clear is that the post-war geopolitical arrangement did not immediately settle into the fixed and frozen division and strategic competition that was to characterize the Cold War. Initially, at least, the USA did not automatically see this military outcome of the war as a necessary cause for geopolitical hostility to develop with Moscow. It was to be the combination of Soviet actions in east-central Europe and the American response to them that would trigger confrontation. In this sense both orthodox and revisionist arguments contain elements of truth, as Soviet policy was perceived as aggressive and against the spirit, if not the letter, of the Yalta and Potsdam agreements over the future of post-war Europe by the USA, and US policies, particularly towards Western-occupied Germany, were seen as hostile to Soviet security interests. The key analytical issue here is that issues of perception, interpretation, and,

crucially, domestic politics within the United States were to play an important role in determining the response to Soviet actions in east-central Europe, something which both orthodox and revisionist approaches do not sufficiently recognize.

The 'Sovietization' of east-central Europe and the particular way that this was carried out—through the gradual elimination of non-communist political forces and the coercive economic integration of east-central Europe into the Soviet economic system between 1945 and 1948—was crucial to shifting US perspectives on how the post-war international system would be organized. These developments and their militarized character not only entrenched the geopolitical consequences of the war but they also appeared to threaten the political security of western Europe and other areas (Iran and Turkey) that bordered the Soviet Union. The illiberal and undemocratic character of Soviet policies were, then, important in colouring the geopolitical outcome of the war. In other words, for US leaders, Soviet actions communicated that Moscow could no longer be seen as a partner or ally, but rather a competitor and foe committed to establishing a very different if not antagonistic set of post-war arrangements over east-central Europe.

However, this change in the geopolitical outlook of the post-war world recognized by Truman and his advisers in the early months after the end of the war needed to be conveyed to the American public and Congress who had to be persuaded to support a shift in US policy to a more forthright opposition to Soviet actions. In this regard Soviet policies, notably the rigged elections in Hungary and Poland in 1947, the coup in Czechoslovakia in February 1948, and the Berlin blockade later that year, provided helpful ammunition for the struggle to persuade the American public, but it took a campaign of speeches, publicity, and, to some extent, manipulation, exaggeration, and propaganda waged by US government agencies and sympathetic newspapers and other opinion formers to mobilize public and congressional support behind a policy of containment and confrontation.

> **KEY QUOTES 4.1:** Kennan and the origins of containment

Excerpts from 'The Long Telegram', 22 February 1946

At the bottom of the Kremlin's neurotic view of world affairs is traditional and instinctive Russian sense of insecurity. . . .

After establishment of Bolshevist regime, Marxist dogma, rendered even more truculent and intolerant by Lenin's interpretation, became a perfect vehicle for sense of insecurity with which Bolsheviks, even more than previous Russian rulers, were afflicted. In this dogma . . . they found justification for their instinctive fear of outside world, for the dictatorship without which they did not know how to rule, for cruelties they did not dare not to inflict, for sacrifices they felt bound to demand. In the name of Marxism they sacrificed every single ethical value in their methods and tactics. Today they cannot dispense with it. It is fig leaf of their moral and intellectual respectability. Without it they would stand before history, as best, as only the last of that long succession of cruel and wasteful Russian rulers who have relentlessly forced their country on to ever new heights of military power in order to guarantee external security for their internally weak regimes. This is why Soviet purposes must always be solemnly clothed in trappings of Marxism, and why no one should underrate the importance of dogma in Soviet affairs. . . . Wherever it is considered timely and promising, efforts will be made to advance official limits of Soviet power. For the moment, these efforts are restricted to certain neighbouring points conceived of here as being of immediate strategic necessity, such as northern Iran, Turkey, possibly Bornholm. However, other points may at any time come into question, if and as concealed Soviet political power is extended to new areas . . . Russians will participate officially in international organizations where they see opportunity of extending Soviet power or of inhibiting or diluting power of others. In summary, we have here a political force committed fanatically to the belief that with US there can be no permanent *modus vivendi*, that it is desirable and necessary that the internal harmony of our society be disrupted, our traditional way of life be destroyed, the international authority of our state be broken, if Soviet power is to be secure. This political force has complete power of disposition over energies of one of the world's greatest peoples and resources of the world's richest national territory, and is borne along by deep and powerful currents of Russian nationalism.

(Kennan 1967: 547–59)

'X': the sources of Soviet conduct

[W]e are going to continue for a long time to find the Russians difficult to deal with. It does not mean that they should be considered as embarked upon a do-or-die program to overthrow our society by a given date . . .

In these circumstances it is clear that the main element of any United States policy toward the Soviet Union must be that of a long-term, patient but firm and vigilant containment of Russian expansive tendencies. It is important to note, however, that such a policy has nothing to do with outward histrionics: with threats or blustering or superfluous gestures of outward 'toughness.' While the Kremlin is basically flexible in its reaction to political realities, it is by no means unnameable to considerations of prestige. Like almost any other government, it can be placed by tactless and threatening gestures in a position where it cannot afford to yield even though this might be dictated by its sense of realism. The Russian leaders are keen judges of human psychology, and as such they are highly conscious that loss of temper and of self-control is never a source of strength in political affairs. They are quick to exploit such evidences of weakness. For these reasons, it is a sine qua non of successful dealing with Russia that the foreign government in question should remain at all times cool and collected and that its demands on Russian policy should be put forward in such a manner as to leave the way open for a compliance not too detrimental to Russian prestige. . . .

In the light of the above, it will be clearly seen that the Soviet pressure against the free institutions of the Western world is something that can be contained by the adroit and vigilant application of counterforce at a series of constantly shifting geographical and political points, corresponding to the shifts and manoeuvres of Soviet policy, but which cannot be charmed or talked out of existence. The Russians look forward to a duel of infinite duration, and they see that already they have scored great successes.

(*Foreign Affairs*, July 1947)

The Truman doctrine

What is also significant in the move towards the containment of the USSR is that two crucial developments, which triggered policy responses that became landmarks in the onset of the Cold War, did not directly involve or concern the USSR. Thus, although US policy was directed towards the USSR, in some cases US policy was in *response* to actions carried out by other communist or revolutionary states or movements. In this sense, US foreign policy in the beginning of the Cold War—as it was to be throughout the Cold War—was as much concerned with responding to the actions of non-Soviet forms of communist power, as it was to Soviet actions.

The first development concerned the situation in Greece where communists were fighting a civil war against a right-wing pro-Western government supported by British troops. It was the decision by the British government to end its support of the Greek government in February 1947—due to economic exigencies—that raised the spectre of communist victory. Such a development was seen as posing a threat not only to the security of Turkey, but also the wider Middle East, and it was this that led Truman to deliver a speech—what became known as the 'Truman Doctrine'—in early March to both houses of Congress, and to the wider audience of the American public, calling on the American people to shoulder the burden of 'support[ing] free peoples who are resisting attempted subjugation by armed minorities or by outside pressures'.

Although Congress took further convincing to grant Truman's demands for aid to Greece, this was to become the first step in America's political and military commitment to the security of western Europe and, later, a global commitment to containing communist expansion. The significance of this for our understanding of American foreign policy was that US policy was in response to how the prospect of a local communist revolution could have geopolitical consequences—by extending communist power allied to the USSR—and, further, the crucial role played by politics and perception and, to a not insignificant degree, personality in determining what the USA did.

The Marshall plan

The other key development concerned the economic future of post-war Europe and how this related to US concerns to organize the post-war international economy in a way that would not only prevent the likelihood of another global economic crisis—as occurred in the 1930s, which provided an important context for the origins of the Second World War —but would also allow the USA to best realize its economic interests. The framework for organizing the post-war international economy was decided—under the guidance of the US Treasury—at the Bretton Woods conference in New Hampshire in 1944. The agreement laid out a framework for a liberal and open international trading system; that is, a framework that not only tended to reflect US political and ideological interests and values, but also a framework that would ensure significant economic benefits would flow towards the USA as western European economies (and their imperial possessions) would be opened up to take American goods. The Bretton Woods agreement, then, seemed to bear out revisionist claims and, more broadly, socio-economic approaches to a significant degree, with respect to explaining the importance of socio-economic interests—that of American exporters and the American economy as a whole—on US foreign policy.

However, the original Bretton Woods blueprint was to be short-lived, as a combination of developing geopolitical tensions with Moscow and mounting economic difficulties within western Europe during 1946–7 caused a US rethink. The growing economic crisis in western Europe raised two prospects of concern for the USA. First, that an economic crisis in western Europe would force these economies to move towards protectionist economic policies thus closing off their economies from meaningful international economic exchange and scuppering the hopes and plans of the USA. This would not only have had negative consequences on the US economy—depriving US exporters of foreign markets—but would have also removed a source of leverage over the post-war political future of western Europe

> **KEY QUOTES 4.2:** The Truman Doctrine

President Truman's address before a joint session of Congress, 12 March 1947

The peoples of a number of countries of the world have recently had totalitarian regimes forced upon them against their will. The Government of the United States has made frequent protests against coercion and intimidation, in violation of the Yalta Agreement, in Poland, Rumania, and Bulgaria. I must also state that in a number of other countries there have been similar developments.

At the present moment in world history nearly every nation must choose between alternative ways of life. The choice is too often not a free one.

One way of life is based upon the will of the majority, and is distinguished by free institutions, representative government, free elections, guarantees of individual liberty, freedom of speech and religion, and freedom from political oppression.

The second way of life is based upon the will of a minority forcibly imposed upon the majority. It relies upon terror and oppression, a controlled press and radio; fixed elections, and the suppression of personal freedoms.

I believe that it must be the policy of the United States to support free peoples who are resisting attempted subjugation by armed minorities or by outside pressures.

I believe that we must assist free peoples to work out their own destinies in their own way.

It is necessary only to glance at a map to realize that the survival and integrity of the Greek nation are of grave importance in a much wider situation. If Greece should fall under the control of an armed minority, the effect upon its neighbor, Turkey, would be immediate and serious. Confusion and disorder might well spread throughout the entire Middle East.

Moreover, the disappearance of Greece as an independent state would have a profound effect upon those countries in Europe whose peoples are struggling against great difficulties to maintain their freedoms and their independence while they repair the damages of war.

It would be an unspeakable tragedy if these countries, which have struggled so long against overwhelming odds, should lose that victory for which they sacrificed so much. Collapse of free institutions and loss of independence would be disastrous not only for them but for the world. Discouragement and possibly failure would quickly be the lot of neighboring peoples striving to maintain their freedom and independence.

(*Public Papers of the Presidents* 1963: 176)

and the wider international economy, as these economies would have removed themselves from American influence.

The second concern was that communist and other pro-Soviet forces in western Europe would take advantage of any crisis to seize power and push western Europe in a pro-Soviet direction. In this case the USA was concerned less with Soviet policies and more with how potentially revolutionary domestic political developments within western European states could have geopolitical consequences favourable to the USSR. The US response to the growing economic difficulties in western Europe and the possibility of one or other of the two possible future scenarios emerging was the Marshall Plan, announced by the US Secretary of State, George Marshall, in a speech at Harvard University in June 1947.

The Marshall Plan was aimed at aiding European economic recovery, thus thwarting economic crisis, but also drawing those states in receipt of Marshall Aid into closer economic links with the USA and implementing policies—revised from Bretton Woods—that the USA found acceptable. Further, the diplomatic and institutional framework that the USA developed to deliver Marshall Aid—through the Organization of European Economic Cooperation (OEEC)—would provide a vehicle for developing links with east-central European countries. On this point, revisionist arguments have some substance. Any moves by east-central European states to join the Marshall Plan framework would have not only integrated them into a pro-US liberal institutional and political framework, it would have also fundamentally challenged Soviet economic and security interests in the region by weakening the ability of the USSR to determine internal political and economic developments within these states. Consequently, Moscow compelled east-central European states to reject such overtures.

The Marshall Plan is significant for understanding US foreign policy in the early Cold War for a number of reasons. It highlights how US foreign policy was concerned with developments within the domestic politics of other capitalist states, particularly in western Europe. Thus, contrary to orthodox (and realist) approaches, it was not only the case that the USA did meddle in the domestic affairs of western European states in the early Cold War—and after—as a way of influencing political developments in a way compatible with US interests, but this was also a crucial area of concern for US foreign policy.

This suggests that the Cold War was not, then, just about international diplomatic and geopolitical relations between the superpowers, but also concerned political and economic developments within the domestic politics of other capitalist states. In this respect, whilst the USSR was a geopolitical threat, the flow of political developments, conflict, and economic instability and crisis within other capitalist states was—throughout the history of the Cold War—a socio-economic challenge to the USA, as the possibility remained that a government could come to power and not only oppose US economic interests, but also alter the geopolitical relationship with the USA by opting for neutrality or withdrawal from alliance with the USA (Colás and Saull 2005: 12–17). The fact that this never occurred does not mean that it was not a constant concern for the USA or that the USA did not implement policies to ensure that it did not happen.

Whilst Marshall Aid provided an economic means for the USA to realize its foreign policy objectives of preventing economic crisis as well as tying west European states into closer diplomatic relations with the USA, this concern with domestic political developments saw the USA—or, more precisely, the newly created CIA—play an important role in thwarting the constitutional political ambitions of the Communist Party in Italy in the 1948 elections. The Marshall Plan also alerts us to the *form* of US foreign policy. Whilst the formal machinery of diplomacy was utilized to introduce the Marshall Plan, as a number of scholars have highlighted (Carew 1987; Rupert 1995; Saull 2007) Marshall Aid was organized through a broader coalition of private, non-governmental agencies. US companies and trade unions (the American Federation of Labor-Conference of Industrial Organizations) played a key role in 'selling' Marshall Aid to European trade unionists and workers and encouraging the establishment of anti-communist trade unions.

The analytical significance of this goes beyond how we think about the nature and delivery of the Marshall Plan; it also highlights the socio-economic or class dimensions of Marshall Aid and American foreign policy more generally. The foreign policy of the USA (or any other state for that matter), then, is likely to have uneven socio-economic consequences, not only for the society at which a policy is directed, but also for the 'home' society where the policy is made. Thus, whilst the USA did have to make revisions to its original blueprint regarding the character of the post-war international economy, it was a price worth paying in that private property rights were protected and the interests of capital tended to take preference over those of workers (Cox 1987; Rupert 1995: 43–9). In sum, then, the Marshall Plan could be seen as reflecting an attempt to promote a particular form of societal organization within western European states that maintained a balance of promoting economic stability, thus social peace and political alliance with Washington.

The twin pillars of US Cold War foreign policy

By early 1948, then, the USA had established the key pillars of its Cold War foreign policy. On the one hand was the military-geopolitical dimension of containment highlighted in its commitment through the Truman Doctrine to the defence of 'free peoples' facing 'communist subversion and aggression'. Once this threshold had been crossed, it became much easier for Truman and future presidents to persuade Congress and the American public to shoulder further and heavier burdens in the struggle against Soviet and communist expansion. Thus, in April 1949 the implicit commitment to the military defence of its

> **KEY QUOTES 4.3:** The Marshall Plan

Speech given by Secretary of State George C. Marshall on 5 June 1947 at Harvard University, in which he outlined a programme of economic assistance to post-war Europe.

The truth of the matter is that Europe's requirements for the next three or four years of foreign food and other essential products—principally from America—are so much greater than her present ability to pay that she must have substantial additional help or face economic, social, and political deterioration of a very grave character . . .

Aside from the demoralizing effect on the world at large and the possibilities of disturbances arising as a result of the desperation of the people concerned, the consequences to the economy of the United States should be apparent to all. It is logical that the United States should do whatever it is able to do to assist in the return of normal economic health in the world, without which there can be no political stability and no assured peace . . .

Its purpose should be the revival of a working economy in the world so as to permit the emergence of political and social conditions in which free institutions can exist . . .

Any government that is willing to assist in the task of recovery will find full cooperation; I am sure, on the part of the United States Government. Any government which manoeuvres to block the recovery of other countries cannot expect help from us. Furthermore, governments, political parties, or groups which seek to perpetuate human misery in order to profit therefrom politically or otherwise will encounter the opposition of the United States.

It is already evident that, before the United States Government can proceed much further in its efforts to alleviate the situation and help start the European world on its way to recovery, there must be some agreement among the countries of Europe as to the requirements of the situation and the part those countries themselves will take in order to give proper effect to whatever action might be undertaken by this Government . . .

It would be neither fitting nor efficacious for this Government to undertake to draw up unilaterally a program designed to place Europe on its feet economically . . .

The initiative, I think, must come from Europe. The role of this country should consist of friendly aid in the drafting of a European program and of later support of such a program so far as it may be practical for us to do so. The program should be a joint one, agreed to by a number, if not all, European nations.

(http://marshallfoundation.org/documents/Marshall_
Plan_Origins.pdf)

west European allies of the Truman Doctrine was formalized with the establishment of NATO.

However, in recognizing this we also need to acknowledge the dynamic within the relationship of not only Soviet policy, but also—as will become clearer below—of other communist movements and states, and the way in which the US leadership was unable—for much of the history of the Cold War—to differentiate the diplomacy of Moscow from the policies of other communist states and the actions of communist movements. This highlights the strengths of ideational approaches to understanding US foreign policy: that is, how political developments in other states were *interpreted* as having negative international consequences for the United States.

Further, we also need to recognize the way in which US foreign policy decisions—in the early period of the Cold War (and throughout)—were influenced by the behaviour of its key allies. In this regard the US decision to make a political and military commitment to the defence of western Europe was conditional on the policy decisions of these states. Geir Lundestad's (1998) phrase 'empire by invitation' nicely captures the character and dynamic within the relationship between the USA and its western European allies after 1947. Western European states, spurred on by Churchill's 'iron curtain speech' of March 1946, which called for a Western Alliance against what he regarded as a growing Soviet threat, effectively requested and welcomed US diplomatic and military support and protection.

Thus, whilst recognizing the hierarchy and distribution of political and military power within the Atlantic Alliance during the Cold War we also need to recognize the way in which the USA made efforts to accommodate the interests and concerns of its allies. This has already been mentioned with regard to the Marshall Plan and the way it was organized and delivered through the multilateral OEEC, but it goes beyond this in that the ruling elites within western Europe tended to share the concerns of US policy makers to a significant degree, thus assisting the implementation of US policy and facilitating the legitimacy of institutions such as NATO and the basing of tens of thousands of US troops in western Europe.

The second pillar concerned the economic framework governing the international capitalist economy and US relations with the other advanced capitalist states. Here, the USA was forced to make concessions to the economic and social needs of other capitalist states, even if that meant—in the short term—tolerating

economic policies it found a little problematic. Further, and in contrast to the revisionist argument over the aim of US foreign relations, US policy contributed to the economic growth of the other capitalist states, to such a degree that by the late 1960s these states—Germany, Japan, and France in particular—were beginning to eat away at US post-war economic ascendancy in the production of manufactured goods. However, whilst recognizing the economically benign consequences of US policies we also have to acknowledge the way in which these arrangements also rested on a rather uneven distribution of social or class power within these states, reflected in the disproportionate flow of benefits to owners and managers of capital.

KEY POINTS

❑ Discussion of role of the USA in the origins of the Cold War is dominated by the 'orthodox – revisionist' debate. The orthodox approach argues that the USA was naive about the nature of Soviet power and responded to Soviet aggression in east-central Europe whilst the revisionists argue that the USA tried to impose its economic system on east-central Europe causing the division of Europe and provoking Soviet hostility.

❑ Containment emerged out of the dynamic within the differing policies of Moscow and Washington towards Europe immediately after the war and, in particular, the way the USA interpreted Soviet policies as being hostile.

❑ The Truman Doctrine was announced in a context of what were seen as aggressive actions by the USSR in east-central Europe and the inability of Britain to continue to aid anti-communist forces in the Greek civil war. It was this context that allowed the Truman administration to persuade the American public that

it needed to shoulder the responsibility of containing communism.

❑ The US security commitment to western Europe was also influenced by the policies of west European governments, who 'invited' the USA to be responsible for their defence from the Soviet threat.

❑ The Marshall Plan was concerned with addressing the post-war economic crisis within Europe and, thus, ensuring that west European states did not pursue economic policies that challenged American economic interests.

❑ The Marshall Plan saw the US compromise on its original (Bretton Woods) plan for how the post-war international economy would be organized by accepting some of the economic needs of west European states.

❑ Marshall Aid saw the involvement of US non-state actors (businesses and trade unions) in the implementation of the Marshall Plan. It also helped promote economic growth in western Europe which promoted political stability, whilst preserving capitalism.

Korea, NSC-68, and the militarization of US foreign policy

Thus far I have focused on US policy towards Europe in the early period after the war. The relations with both its allies and its Soviet foe were to remain

relatively stable after 1949. With the seeing off of the attempt by the Soviets—through the almost year-long (June 1948–May 1949) blockade of Berlin—to thwart western policy towards divided Germany, the division of Germany and Europe into two opposing zones was sealed. This division was soon to become highly militarized with the stationing of massed divisions of tanks and troops on either side of the divide, which effectively froze the European Cold War, ushering in a period of military-enforced stability until the late 1980s. However, the momentum of events in Europe and the direction of US policy were to be influenced by events elsewhere—in Asia—which would result in a much greater militarization of US foreign policy and containment.

Two events would propel the USA towards a much bolder and ambitious containment policy, thus assisting those tendencies within the US polity that favoured such a posture and making it easier to convince Congress and the American public of the need to militarize containment. The two events were the communist revolution in China in 1949 and the outbreak of the Korean War in June 1950 with the invasion of the pro-western South by the communist North. The significance of these developments was to be profound. They were to inaugurate US military interventions in the former colonial or third world, which would culminate in the debacle in Vietnam between 1965 and 1973. As the dynamic of Soviet policy in Europe conditioned and triggered US responses there, rather than the USA having a grand design (as suggested by revisionists) regardless of Soviet actions, so developments involving other communist movements and states would provide the key factors in the shaping of containment, leading to the involvement of the USA in a number of 'hot wars' in the third world.

The failure of US policy towards China, what critics of the Truman administration called 'the loss of China', was a major strategic setback (Paterson 1988: 54–75) as US post-war planning had always assumed that China would be a source of post-war stability and alliance in Asia. It also had consequences for US policy towards Japan, as Japan now became much more central to US security in the Pacific and, with China going communist, more at risk from communist expansion.

Following its policy in Europe, and the rapid demobilization of its military forces at the end of the war in the Pacific, US policy was filtered through local agents, specifically the anti-communist Kuomintang government. Here, US policy was characterized by ineffectiveness and frustration despite providing significant financial and military aid to the Kuomintang in its struggle with the Chinese communists. Unable to intervene themselves—the scale of any intervention in a country the size of China would have required tens of thousands of troops, as well as contradicting Washington's commitment to decolonization and national self-determination—the USA was reliant on the incompetent, corrupt, and feckless Kuomintang.

The Korean War

However, despite the shock of the communist victory in China it was to be the North Korean invasion of South Korea—what the USA interpreted as an act of aggression across a recognized international boundary—that would be the defining event in shifting containment from a policy of diplomatic threats to the construction of a major military alliance in NATO and Japan (with the 1951 Mutual Defence Treaty) and active military interventions in the third world beginning with the dispatch of US combat forces to the Korean peninsula soon after the invasion. Whilst the 'loss of China' was a much greater strategic setback, this came through the result of an internal civil war. This contrasted with Korea where—despite the fact that the boundary dividing the north and south of the peninsula had no legal basis—the communist invasion appeared to signal a new brazenness and aggression in communist policy. The invasion appeared to bear out the arguments of anti-communist hardliners in the US government who interpreted events in Korea as part of a coordinated pattern of communist expansion directed by Moscow, rather than as a local civil war only cautiously supported by the Soviets and Chinese (Cumings 1981/1990).

NSC-68

Other than the decision to send troops to repel North Korean forces, the defining decision relating to the war was Truman's approval of the proposals outlined in National Security Council Report number 68 (NSC-68) in September 1950. Truman's decision moved the US towards containment of Soviet and communist advances by military means, primarily because the Truman administration—and later US administrations—regarded Soviet/communist advances as occurring through military aggression, across territorial boundaries, rather than, as in the case of Korea (and other, later cases), the result of internal political, socio-economic, and military dynamics. With US troops engaged on the ground against Soviet- and Chinese-backed communist invaders (and after the Soviets had detonated an atomic device in August 1949 earlier than the USA had anticipated) the perception of a much more threatening global context led to momentous changes in US foreign policy.

In the following months and years the USA moved towards implementing the recommendations of NSC-68—something much less likely without the events of June 1950. US troop strengths in Europe were strengthened and NATO was to be given much greater military bite with the decision—supported by the USA—for the rearmament of West Germany in May 1955. By 1953 US military production was seven times that of 1950, the army grew by 50 per cent, and the USA also doubled the number of air groups to ninety-five (Ambrose and Brinkley 1997: 122; Leffler and Painter 1994: 118). Another key consequence of the Korean War was the stepping-up of US military aid to French forces in Indochina fighting communist-led anti-colonial forces. This was to be the first step in what would eventually become the Vietnam War.

KEY POINTS

- Significance of the spread of the Cold War to Asia on US policy towards western Europe and the increasing militarization of containment after 1950.
- 1949 communist revolution in China seen as a failure of US policy by critics of the Truman administration. US failure due to its dependence on the corrupt and incompetent Kuomintang government.
- The communist victory in China undermined US plans for the post-war future of east Asia, increasing the importance of Japan to US interests, as well as making Japan more vulnerable to communist influence.
- Despite the shock of the Chinese Revolution the key turning point for US policy came with North Korea's invasion of South Korea in June 1950. This was perceived as an act of aggression across a territorial border, triggering US military intervention in defence of the South and ushering in a policy of US military interventions in third world conflicts.
- As well as dispatching troops to the Korean peninsula, the US initiated a massive programme of rearmament—as proposed in NSC-68—instigating the militarization of containment.
- The Korean War also saw a major increase in US aid for French forces fighting communist forces in Indochina and the USA agreeing to the rearmament of West Germany within NATO.

Cold War in the third world

As indicated in the previous section, the US military intervention in the Korean civil war from 1950 initiated what would become a dominant and increasingly controversial aspect of US foreign policy in the Cold War—military interventions in support of allied governments and/or against revolutionary states.[1] The outstanding case in this regard was the US military intervention in Vietnam between 1965 and 1973. The scale and length of the US intervention in Vietnam (which actually began in 1950 through its support for the French and then, after, through its support of the attempts to create a post-colonial independent anti-communist state in the south of Vietnam from 1954) contrasted with numerous other interventions

> **KEY QUOTES 4.4:** NSC-68

VII. Present risks

A. GENERAL

[T]he integrity and vitality of our system is in greater jeopardy than ever before in our history. Even if there were no Soviet Union we would face the great problem of the free society, accentuated many fold in this industrial age, of reconciling order, security, the need for participation, with the requirement of freedom. We would face the fact that in a shrinking world the absence of order among nations is becoming less and less tolerable. The Kremlin design seeks to impose order among nations by means which would destroy our free and democratic system. The Kremlin's possession of atomic weapons puts new power behind its design, and increases the jeopardy to our system. It adds new strains to the uneasy equilibrium-without-order which exists in the world and raises new doubts in men's minds whether the world will long tolerate this tension without moving toward some kind of order, on somebody's terms . . .

The risks we face are of a new order of magnitude, commensurate with the total struggle in which we are engaged. For a free society there is never total victory, since freedom and democracy are never wholly attained, are always in the process of being attained. But defeat at the hands of the totalitarian is total defeat. These risks crowd in on us, in a shrinking world of polarized power, so as to give us no choice, ultimately, between meeting them effectively or being overcome by them . . .

B. SPECIFIC

It is quite clear from Soviet theory and practice that the Kremlin seeks to bring the free world under its dominion by the methods of the cold war. The preferred technique is to subvert by infiltration and intimidation. Every institution of our society is an instrument which it is sought to stultify and turn against our purposes. Those that touch most closely our material and moral strength are obviously the prime targets, labor unions, civic enterprises, schools, churches, and all media for influencing opinion. The effort is not so much to make them serve obvious Soviet ends as to prevent them from serving our ends, and thus to make them sources of confusion in our economy, our culture, and our body politic. The doubts and diversities that in terms of our values are part of the merit of a free system, the weaknesses and the problems that are peculiar to it, the rights and privileges that free men enjoy, and the disorganization and destruction left in the wake of the last attack on our freedoms, all are but opportunities for the Kremlin to do its evil work . . .

Since everything that gives us or others respect for our institutions is a suitable object for attack, it also fits the Kremlin's design that where, with impunity, we can be insulted and made to suffer indignity the opportunity shall not be missed, particularly in any context which can be used to cast dishonor on our country, our system, our motives, or our methods. Thus the means by which we sought to restore our own economic health in the '30's, and now seek to restore that of the free world, come equally under attack. The military aid by which we sought to help the free world was frantically denounced by the Communists in the early days of the last war, and of course our present efforts to develop adequate military strength for ourselves and our allies are equally denounced . . .

At the same time the Soviet Union is seeking to create overwhelming military force, in order to back up infiltration with intimidation. In the only terms in which it understands strength, it is seeking to demonstrate to the free world that force and the will to use it are on the side of the Kremlin, that those who lack it are decadent and doomed. In local incidents it threatens and encroaches both for the sake of local gains and to increase anxiety and defeatism in all the free world . . .

The risk that we may thereby be prevented or too long delayed in taking all needful measures to maintain the integrity and vitality of our system is great. The risk that our allies will lose their determination is greater. And the risk that in this manner a descending spiral of too little and too late, of doubt and recrimination, may present us with ever narrower and more desperate alternatives, is the greatest risk of all. For example, it is clear that our present weakness would prevent us from offering effective resistance at any of several vital pressure points. The only deterrent we can present to the Kremlin is the evidence we give that we may make any of the critical points which we cannot hold the occasion for a global war of annihilation.

(*Foreign Relations of the United States* 1950)

in Latin America, the Caribbean, sub-Saharan Africa, the Middle East, and other parts of Asia through smaller-scale military and covert interventions involving the CIA and/or the funding, training, arming, and directing of local anti-communist forces waging forms of armed struggle against revolutionary states.[2]

Space does not allow me to detail these many interventions and the specific reasons for US decisions to mount them. Instead, I will focus on the Vietnam War as reflective of a broader US concern about the spread of communism in the third world and, with it, the political and geopolitical expansion of Soviet global power.

Vietnam

In Vietnam, as in many other parts of the third world—with the exception of Cuba after the 1959 revolution and Chile between 1970 and 1973—US economic interests were rather marginal as a direct cause of US intervention, since in most cases revolutionary seizures of power did not tend to result in major setbacks for the direct national economic interests of the United States. Further, and as highlighted by the Cold War realists mentioned earlier, many of the countries and regions were not regarded—at least by some high-profile realist thinkers (Morgenthau 1969)—as being of strategic interest to the United States.

Thus, whilst the Korean War could be seen as reflecting a geopolitical challenge to the United States, for some realists, at least, this was less the case with Vietnam and the many other US interventions in the third world. How, then, do we explain the US intervention in Vietnam and what does this tell us about American foreign policy towards the third world (and revolutionary political change) more generally throughout the Cold War? To address this question we have to look at the actual steps leading up to the intervention—a basic narrative of events—and then assess the reasons for the intervention and the role of different factors and explanations.

In the case of Vietnam, US intervention proceeded in a step-by-step fashion conditioned by developments on the ground in Vietnam, the wider regional and global context of the Cold War, and, finally, the complexion of political opinion within the United States. As I have already mentioned, the initial US intervention—in support of the French between 1950 and 1954—was largely determined by the wider regional context of war and communist expansion across geographical borders. It was this that gave rise to the idea of the 'domino theory' whereby those countries neighbouring a newly created revolutionary or communist state would become 'infected' with the 'communist contagion' and would fall over like dominoes—becoming communist. Hence, the importance of those countries—like (South)Vietnam and South Korea—in the front line in the struggle to contain the spread of communism.

With the departure of the French and the division of Vietnam into a communist North and anti-communist South in 1954, the USA picked up where the French had left off in providing the financial and military support for the construction of an independent South Vietnamese state. In this sense the USA was following the pattern established in Korea—a divided peninsula after the 1953 armistice—with the USA committed to supporting the construction of a strong pro-Western and capitalist regime in the South. From this point on, having made a political commitment to the future of South Vietnam, the flow, implementation, and success of US policy became dependent on its relationship with its local ally and the social and political forces associated with the South Vietnamese ruling elite.

In a similar fashion to its relationship with the Chinese Kuomintang (1945–9), between 1954 and 1973 US policy was concerned not only with addressing the escalating communist political and military threat—especially after 1960 when the communist-led National Liberation Front (NLF) launched its struggle in the South—but also with getting its local ally to pursue policies that the USA favoured and regarded as the best way of constructing a stable and credible non-communist state in the South.

With the launching of the NLF offensive in 1960 (after the Saigon regime had arrested, tortured, and assassinated thousands of communists and suspected communists in the South in the preceding months) the US commitment to Vietnam became increasingly militarized, resulting in a steady increase in the number of US troops and advisers dispatched to Vietnam.[3] The key point here is that it was the actions of the Saigon government that triggered the upsurge in guerrilla activity in the South and it was to be this dynamic—the policies and failures of the South Vietnamese—that would effectively drive US policy on the ground. This was particularly so as the Saigon regime's military ineptitude and political and economic incompetence and corruption quickly showed it to be unable to effectively deal with the NLF offensive, and its economic and agrarian policies—in spite of US advice and pressure for reform—actually aggravated the political and security situation in the countryside.

Faced with this situation as 1965 approached, and as US troop numbers and involvement increased (along with casualty figures), the USA had two options. First, it could withdraw and leave Saigon to deal with the communist threat with the likelihood that it would fail and the South would go communist. Such an outcome would have had dramatic consequences for US standing in the world, questioning the will of the USA to meet communist threats, potentially undermining the regional security of other US allies in the region, and questioning the effectiveness of US policy. Such a dilemma confronts the US leadership today with regard to Iraq with similar consequences for what could be seen as a precipitous withdrawal. Second, the USA could become much more involved, effectively taking over responsibility for directing the war in the countryside against the NLF.[4]

The USA chose the latter and, as in the case of those other key moments in modern US history where the USA has decided to take on a much bigger military commitment likely to have a significant impact on US domestic politics (Pearl Harbor, Korea, 9/11), a *casus belli*—an 'unprovoked' act of aggression on the USA or its forces—was required that would be used to convince the American public of the need to take on a military burden involving the dispatch of large numbers of troops overseas to fight.

This was 'provided' with the 'Gulf of Tonkin incident' where US ships were supposedly[5] attacked by North Vietnamese forces. This apparent 'act of aggression' highlighting the involvement of the North in the war in the South provided the basis for the infamous 'blank cheque' granted by Congress—the Gulf of Tonkin Resolution—to the Johnson administration to intensify the war through increasing the numbers of US troops in South Vietnam (reaching a peak of just under half a million in 1968) and through launching bombing raids—Operation Rolling Thunder—on the North.

After 1965, then, the USA became involved in a drawn-out and bloody war in the jungles of South-East Asia, propping up a rotten and corrupt state and—in spite of the huge and horrific levels of bombs (and chemical weapons) dropped on the peoples of Vietnam, South and North—and along with killing far more Vietnamese than the combined communist forces were able to kill US troops, failed to deliver the knock-out blow to win the war. Instead, as the war prolonged and, particularly after the political debacle and humiliation of the 1968 NLF Tet Offensive—when NLF guerrillas seized control of the US embassy in Saigon—American domestic politics began to play a much more important role on US policy as the campaign for withdrawal gathered pace in the USA.

Although the anti-war movement did not force the USA to withdraw it played a key role in ending the policy established under Johnson after 1965 highlighting, again, the importance of domestic political opinion on US foreign policy. With the election of Richard Nixon in late 1968 US policy changed as it sought an exit from Vietnam.

Although the US commitment to Vietnam was singular, what does the US experience in and with Vietnam suggest about American foreign policy towards the third world? As recognized by the Cold War realists, US involvement was not—primarily—driven by geopolitical concerns. However, although Vietnam and the many other sites of US intervention were not—in themselves—of geopolitical significance, whether or not communist expansion took place within them was.

Although not in all cases (but in enough), revolutionaries (not just communists) coming to power did tend to open up avenues for the expansion of Soviet influence and power, and the expansion of communist and Soviet influence did tend to have an impact on wider regional international relations and the security of neighbouring states. This is not to suggest that the 'domino theory' was to be borne out in South-East Asia after the 1975 communist victory in Vietnam, but it does suggest that revolutions had international repercussions that had an impact on the international and domestic politics of neighbouring states even if they did not succumb to revolution.[6]

The international and geopolitical consequences of revolutionary change were most evident in developments in Cuba after the 1959 revolution, which led into the 1962 Missile Crisis through the attempt by Moscow to alter the strategic balance of power by deploying nuclear missiles on Cuba. Whilst we might argue that openings only emerged for Moscow because of US hostility to revolutionary change (highlighted in its sponsorship of the ill-fated 'Bay of Pigs' invasion by counter-revolutionaries in April 1961), we still have to recognize the very different and antagonistic domestic and foreign policy priorities of most, if not all, revolutionary states during the Cold War with respect to US priorities and interests.

The threat of revolution, then, could be seen in geopolitical terms. However, US responses to revolutionary change were also a product of the prevailing anti-communist ideational mindset within the US national security bureaucracy which also pervaded wider US society. Consequently, most if not all revolutionary changes tended to be seen as communist inspired or—in one way or another—involving Moscow. This was obviously not always the case, as revolutionary change carried out by nationalist movements—mainly against European colonial powers—in the third world was a product of very local political and economic developments with little or nothing to do with Moscow. Consequently, on one level, then, we could see the struggles of nationalist movements for political and economic independence in the third world as being separate from the Cold War. This highlights a further layer of complexity in surveying American foreign policy as US policy was concerned not only with the USSR and other communist states, but also with thwarting the domestic and international ambitions of a number of third world states. And, not because they were communist, but because they refused to accept or involve themselves in American-constructed international security and economic frameworks.

KEY POINTS

- Initial US intervention in Vietnam (Indochina) between 1950 and 1954 was conditioned by wider regional (the Chinese Revolution and Korean War) and international (formation of NATO) developments.
- Role of the 'domino theory'—that states surrounding a newly created communist state would become 'infected' with communism and at risk of communist subversion—in US policy towards Vietnam.
- After 1954 the USA committed itself to building a stable anti-communist state in South Vietnam, the success of which was dependent on its relations with local political forces in South Vietnam.
- Increasing US (military) involvement in South Vietnam after 1960 due to the failings of the South Vietnamese government. By the mid-1960s faced a dilemma: to pull out of Vietnam and see a likely communist victory or become more involved, effectively running the war.

- The significance of the 'Gulf of Tonkin incident' in 1965 in justifying the escalation of US military involvement in Vietnam.
- The prolonging of the war and the humiliation caused by the NLF's 1968 'Tet Offensive' meant that American domestic politics became much more influential on American policy leading to the eventual withdrawal of US troops by 1973.
- The significance of revolutionary change in the third world is that it opened up avenues for the expansion of Soviet geopolitical power, as well as the way new revolutionary regimes threatened to undermine the political stability of neighbouring states.
- The geopolitical consequences of revolutionary change were most evident in how the 1962 Cuban Missile Crisis developed out of the 1959 Cuban Revolution.

> **KEY QUOTES 4.5:** The Gulf of Tonkin incident and resolution

President Johnson's Message to Congress, 5 August 1964

Last night I announced to the American people that the North Vietnamese regime had conducted further deliberate attacks against U.S. naval vessels operating in international waters, and I had therefore directed air action against gunboats and supporting facilities used in these hostile operations. This air action has now been carried out with substantial damage to the boats and facilities. Two U.S. aircraft were lost in the action.

After consultation with the leaders of both parties in the Congress, I further announced a decision to ask the Congress for a resolution expressing the unity and determination of the United States in supporting freedom and in protecting peace in southeast Asia.

These latest actions of the North Vietnamese regime has given a new and grave turn to the already serious situation in southeast Asia . . .

The threat to the free nations of southeast Asia has long been clear. The North Vietnamese regime has constantly sought to take over South Vietnam and Laos. This Communist regime has violated the Geneva accords for Vietnam. It has systematically conducted a campaign of subversion, which includes the direction, training, and supply of personnel and arms for the conduct of guerrilla warfare in South Vietnamese territory. In Laos, the North Vietnamese regime has maintained military forces, used Laotian territory for infiltration into South Vietnam, and most recently carried out combat operations—all in direct violation of the Geneva Agreements of 1962.

In recent months, the actions of the North Vietnamese regime have become steadily more threatening . . .

As President of the United States I have concluded that I should now ask the Congress, on its part, to join in affirming the national determination that all such attacks will be met, and that the United States will continue in its basic policy of assisting the free nations of the area to defend their freedom.

As I have repeatedly made clear, the United States intends no rashness, and seeks no wider war. We must make it clear to all that the United States is united in its determination to bring about the end of Communist subversion and aggression in the area . . .

Joint Resolution of Congress RES 1145, 7 August 1964

Resolved by the Senate and House of Representatives of the United States of America in Congress assembled,

That the Congress approves and supports the determination of the President, as Commander in Chief, to take all necessary measures to repel any armed attack against the forces of the United States and to prevent further aggression.

Section 2. The United States regards as vital to its national interest and to world peace the maintenance of international peace and security in southeast Asia. Consonant with the Constitution of the United States and the Charter of the United Nations and in accordance with its obligations under the Southeast Asia Collective Defense Treaty, the United States is, therefore, prepared, as the President determines, to take all necessary steps, including the use of armed force, to assist any member or protocol state of the Southeast Asia Collective Defense Treaty requesting assistance in defense of its freedom.

Section 3. This resolution shall expire when the President shall determine that the peace and security of the area is reasonably assured by international conditions created by action of the United Nations or otherwise, except that it may be terminated earlier by concurrent resolution of the Congress.

(*Department of State Bulletin*, 24 Aug. 1964)

Ending the Cold War

The discussion of the role of American foreign policy in the ending of the Cold War has focused on the policies of the Reagan administration and, in particular, the claims by some scholars and former members (Weinberger 1990) of the Reagan administration that 'Reagan won the Cold War'. The claim, then, is that Reagan's arms build-up and policy of confronting the USSR and its allies in the third world (after a spate of revolutions during the 1970s that saw an expansion of Soviet power) through supporting anti-communist guerrilla movements forced the USSR into making strategic and political concessions that effectively ended the Cold War between 1987 and 1989. So, did Reagan's policies of confrontation force Soviet concessions, effectively ending the Cold War?

In assessing the impact of Reagan's policies most scholars tend to highlight the differences between the first and second terms. Whilst the first term was characterized by a more aggressive and confrontational stance towards the USSR, the second term—in part reflected in the turnover in key personnel and a more assertive Congress—saw a gradual shift away from confrontation and, with Gorbachev's accession to the Soviet leadership in 1985, an opening to negotiations with Moscow.

In terms of timing, then, Reagan's policies did *not* force Soviet concessions, as the developments

CONTROVERSIES 4.2: US policy and the end of the Cold War

A number of scholars and former members of the Reagan administration argued that the Cold War ended because the USSR was forced to make strategic concessions due to the pressure imposed on the USSR by Reagan's arms build-up and the policy of confronting and intervening against Soviet allies in the third world. Other scholars argued that Reagan's policy had either little impact on Soviet policy—which was driven by domestic factors—or actually made Soviet reform less likely because of the hostile international environment created by Reagan's policies. This debate about the role of US military power and reform ideas within the USSR dominated the pages of a number of leading international relations journals (*International Security and International Organization*) during the early 1990s.

> **KEY QUOTES 4.6:** Reagan's 'evil empire' speech

President Reagan's 'evil empire' speech to the House of Commons, 8 June 1982

From Stettin on the Baltic to Varna on the Black Sea, the regimes planted by totalitarianism have had more than thirty years to establish their legitimacy. But none—not one regime—has yet been able to risk free elections. Regimes planted by bayonets do not take root . . .

If history teaches anything, it teaches self-delusion in the face of unpleasant facts is folly. We see around us today the marks of our terrible dilemma—predictions of doomsday, antinuclear demonstrations, an arms race in which the West must, for its own protection, be an unwilling participant. At the same time we see totalitarian forces in the world who seek subversion and conflict around the globe to further their barbarous assault on the human spirit. What, then, is our course? Must civilization perish in a hail of fiery atoms? Must freedom wither in a quiet, deadening accommodation with totalitarian evil? . . .

The decay of the Soviet experiment should come as no surprise to us. Wherever the comparisons have been made between free and closed societies—West Germany and East Germany, Austria and Czechoslovakia, Malaysia and Vietnam—it is the democratic countries that are prosperous and responsive to the needs of their people. And one of the simple but overwhelming facts of our

time is this: of all the millions of refugees we've seen in the modern world, their flight is always away from, not toward the Communist world. Today on the NATO line, our military forces face east to prevent a possible invasion. On the other side of the line, the Soviet forces also face east to prevent their people from leaving . . .

The objective I propose is quite simple to state: to foster the infrastructure of democracy, the system of a free press, unions, political parties, universities, which allows a people to choose their own way to develop their own culture, to reconcile their own differences through peaceful means . . .

What I am describing now is a plan and a hope for the long term—the march of freedom and democracy which will leave Marxism-Leninism on the ash heap of history as it has left other tyrannies which stifle the freedom and muzzle the self-expression of the people. And that's why we must continue our efforts to strengthen NATO even as we move forward with our zero-option initiative in the negotiations on intermediate-range forces and our proposal for a one-third reduction in strategic ballistic missile warheads . . .

(*Public Papers of Ronald Reagan*, 1982, available at www.reagan.utexas.edu/archives/speeches/ 1982/60882a.htm) that realized the end of the Cold War confrontation emerged out of a rather different political and geopolitical context. Further, for as long as the USA kept the pressure on, Moscow continued to—in the main—meet its international commitments and, further, did not move towards making concessions to the USA (Halliday 1994; Saull 2007: 165–79). This was the case even in the early stages of the Gorbachev leadership during 1985–6.

We do not know what might have happened had the second-term Reagan administration continued with the hard-line policies of the first term, but the reduction of international tensions certainly made it easier for Gorbachev to usher in the changes that he made in Soviet foreign and domestic policies that broke the geopolitical and ideological framework that had dominated US–Soviet relations since 1945. Further, it was only in this altered—more benign—geopolitical context that the Soviet leadership could tolerate the developments in east-central Europe in 1989, which saw the collapse of communist power within these states and the dissolution of the Warsaw Pact.

However, in recognizing the paradoxical role played by Reagan's policies in ending the Cold War, we also need to take stock of the longer-term consequences of US geopolitical hostility towards the USSR and the economic burdens that this posed on the USSR. Thus, whilst the Reagan doctrine may not have forced the USSR to end the Cold War, the longer-term impact of US policy towards the USSR and international revolution, more generally, posed huge burdens that could only undermine the domestic political and economic legitimacy of the USSR and its allied regimes—thus bearing out Kennan's prognosis in the 'The Sources of Soviet Conduct' that the USA should contain Soviet power until the domestic problems within the USSR forced political change—particularly through the way in which economic resources were channelled towards maintaining the military-geopolitical balance with the USA. In this regard, the wider international capitalist socio-economic dimensions of US power and the way in which the USA took advantage of economic resources beyond the national economic space of the United States proved to be a defining factor in the long-term struggle with the USSR.

KEY POINTS

❑ The role of American foreign policy in the ending of the Cold War has focused on the claims by some scholars and former members of the Reagan administration that Reagan's hard-line policies forced the USSR into making concessions that ended the Cold War.

❑ Most scholars highlight the differences between the first and second terms of the Reagan presidency. Whilst the first term was dominated by confronting the USSR in the third world and imposing an economic burden on Moscow through a massive arms build-up, the second term saw Reagan move towards negotiations with Moscow.

❑ Historical evidence suggests that Reagan's hard-line policies had little impact on changing Soviet behaviour during his first term.

❑ It was the changed circumstances (and policies) of Reagan's second term that made Gorbachev more willing and able to implement his reform programme that ended with the collapse of communist power and dissolution of the Warsaw Pact.

❑ Whilst Reagan's hard-line policies may not have 'won' the Cold War, the long-term costs imposed on the USSR by containment played a very important role—as suggested by Kennan—in undermining the political and economic legitimacy of communist rule in the USSR and east-central Europe.

Conclusion

This chapter has provided a historical survey of American foreign policy during the Cold War covering a number of major developments and changes in US policy. It has sought to account for US policy by drawing on and evaluating contrasting theoretical arguments that stress the role of geopolitical, ideational, and/or socio-economic factors in US foreign policy. The chapter has demonstrated the explanatory uses and limitations of each approach. Its main conclusions are that the making of US foreign policy during the Cold War was centred on how external developments involving the USSR and other revolutionary states and changes in the international capitalist economy were mediated through the institutions of the US state and domestic political debates involving the American people and their political representatives.

In this sense the realm of domestic politics and the prevailing ideational and ideological currents within state institutions and wider society were crucial in determining the US response to geopolitical changes and challenges and in responding to changes in the international capitalist economy. Further, the chapter has tried to expand our intellectual gaze beyond the traditional focus on US diplomatic and interstate relations through highlighting the connections between geopolitics and international economic relations.

US foreign policy then and now has been preoccupied with these two concerns—geopolitical and socio-economic—and in this regard the reordering of the international economy after the war based on US leadership and a US model of political economy could be seen as *the* transformation in world politics after the war now that the Cold War has ended. The interesting point for the future of US global power is that the Cold War was integral to those post-war international economic arrangements.

? Questions

1. In what ways did domestic political developments influence American foreign policy during the Cold War?
2. Critically assess orthodox–revisionist debate on the origins of the Cold War. Which account do you find more convincing and why?
3. Throughout the history of the Cold War the United States used and manipulated the Soviet threat to secure its leadership over the Western world. Discuss.
4. How useful is the concept of imperialism in explaining American foreign relations during the Cold War?
5. Why did the United States intervene in Vietnam? Why was it unable to overcome communist forces?
6. American policy toward third world revolutions was as much about misperception as it was about confronting communist expansion. Discuss.
7. To what extent was the US policy a case of 'containment by other means'?
8. Did the USA cause the 'new' Cold War?
9. Did Reagan 'win' the Cold War?
10. What impact did the end of the Cold War have on American foreign policy?

» Further Reading

Chomsky, N. (1991), *Deterring Democracy* (London: Verso).
   Survey of American foreign policy from one of its leading radical critics.

Gaddis, J. L. (1997), *We Now Know: Rethinking Cold War History* (Oxford: Clarendon Press).

An important study of the Cold War drawing on the interpretation of declassified Soviet documents.

Garthoff, R. (2006), *A Journey through the Cold War: A Memoir of Containment and Coexistence* (Washington, DC: Brookings Institution Press).

A personal survey of Cold War history from a leading diplomatic historian of the Cold War.

Kolko, G. (1988), *Confronting the Third World: United States Foreign Policy, 1945–1980* (New York: Pantheon Books).

Survey of American foreign policy towards the third world from a leading Cold War revisionist.

Lebow, R., and Risse-Kappen, T. (eds.) (1995), *International Relations Theory and the End of the Cold War* (New York: Columbia University Press).

Collection of articles drawing on different theoretical perspectives debating the end of the Cold War.

Pollard, R. (1985), *Economic Security and the Origins of the Cold War: The Strategic Ends of US Foreign Policy, 1945–1950* (New York: Columbia University Press).

Excellent analysis of the role of economic considerations in US foreign policy after the war.

Young, M. (1991), *The Vietnam Wars, 1945–1990* (New York: Harper Collins).

Excellent survey of the US military intervention in Vietnam.

 Endnotes

1. Prior to this the USA had shown itself committed to using force—through numerous interventions—against revolutionary movements and states in the western hemisphere in the early decades of the twentieth century. See Horowitz (1969).

2. Many of which formed the basis of presidential national security doctrines throughout the Cold War.

3. Between 1961 and 1962 the number of US military personnel in South Vietnam more than tripled from 3,000 to 11,000, increasing to over 16,000 in 1963 and more than 23,000 before the formal introduction of combat troops in March 1965. By the end of 1965 there were 184,000 US military personnel in South Vietnam. See Young (1991: 332–3).

4. See Saull (2001: 189–99; 2007: 109–12, 120–7) for a detailed analysis of US policy in Vietnam.

5. An alternative view is provided by in the 'Pentagon Papers' which state that the USA deliberately provoked the North Vietnamese attack on the two US vessels—the *Maddox* and *Turner Joy*. See Sheehan (1971) and Prados (2004).

6. This was evident in Indonesia in the mid-1960s with the growing power of the Indonesian Communist Party. The result was a pre-emptive counter-revolutionary *coup d'état* by right-wing and pro-American elements within the armed forces—led by General Suharto—that overthrew the radical nationalist government in 1966 ushering in the massacre of tens of thousands of communists and other leftists by the military regime over the following months.

 Visit the Online Resource Centre that accompanies this book for web links to accompany each chapter, and a range of other resources: www.oxfordtextbooks.co.uk/orc/cox_stokes/

5 America in the 1990s: searching for purpose

John Dumbrell

Chapter contents

Introduction: post-Cold War American internationalism

Between the late 1940s and 1989, the guiding principle of American foreign policy was straightforward: the containment of Soviet international power. With the collapse first of the Berlin Wall, and subsequently of Soviet communism itself, the United States stood in need of a new way of grounding its internationalist engagement. A lengthy debate ensued as to the proper scope and purpose of this new foreign policy. Post-Cold War foreign policy was developed under the contrasting leadership of President George Herbert Walker Bush and Bill Clinton. This chapter surveys and evaluates US foreign policy debates and policy management during the last decade of the twentieth century.

The history of US foreign policy, since the early years of the twentieth century, has been punctuated by a series of key, catalysing, events, shaping and reshaping the course of American internationalism. Some of these events, notably the rejection by the US Senate of the Treaty of Versailles in 1919, derived primarily from internal American political debates. Others, notably the Pearl Harbor attack of 1941 and the terror assaults of 11 September 2001, were external shocks. The 'long' 1990s constituted a distinct phase in the history of American internationalism, the era between two recent external shocks. The first was the benevolent shock of 1989, the fall of the Berlin Wall and the subsequent ending of the Cold War. The second, this time malevolent, shock, of course, was 9/11.

The present chapter concerns itself with the American policies, politics, and policy debates associated with the era which closed on 11 September 2001 with an event just as extraordinary and transformative as the one which stood at its opening. The post-Cold War era, now clearly discernible as a distinct chapter in the story of American foreign policy, had its own defining characteristics. The USA continued to hold Russia (after 1991, post-Soviet Russia) at, or at least near, its centre of attention. Washington also, however, became aware of the *limits* of the Cold War

victory. The world's most populous country, China, of course, was still communist. Visions of international disorder also attended the demise of the Cold War system.

Despite such worries, the apparent triumph of liberalism—the putative 'end of history' (Fukuyama 1989)—seemed to point away from the kind of global geopolitical/ideological intermixture which had defined the Cold War. Norman Ornstein (1994: 114) wrote in 1994: 'geoeconomics increasingly drives geopolitics, compared to a Cold War agenda where geopolitics drove geoeconomics.' In the 1990s, economic foreign policy constituted a kind of operational cutting edge, providing purpose and coherence to wider strategies of US international engagement. The 1990s also witnessed the emergence of new agendas, often 'old' issues transformed by circumstance and perception. New agendas centred on what the Clinton administration came to call 'borderless threats': environmental problems; the rise and transmogrification of international terrorism; and, most obviously, international disintegration, manifested very swiftly and conspicuously in the Balkans. American foreign policy in the 1990s operated in an environment of dislocation and of possibility. Elation at the Cold War victory clashed with worries about global disorder and about America's ability to cope with disorder. These were years of intense democratic possibility, yet also—from Rwanda to Bosnia—of atavistic negativity and irrationality. How should the USA respond to a world which was apparently both rapidly integrating and rapidly disintegrating?

Perhaps, above all, at least from the point of view of our concern here with the course of US foreign policy, the post-Cold War era saw a conscious and complex debate, conducted at both elite and public levels, about the very point and purpose of American internationalism. Should America continue to lead? Was leadership, or even sustained global engagement, good for America?

BOX 5.1:   Chronology of key events, 1989 – 2001

1989	January: inauguration of President George H. W. Bush June: Tiananmen Square massacre in Beijing November: fall of Berlin Wall December: Bush – Gorbachev Malta summit US invasion of Panama
1990	May – June: Bush – Gorbachev summit in Washington and Camp David superpower agreement on reunification of Germany August: Iraq invades Kuwait Operation Desert Shield launched September: Bush's New World Order speech November: European conventional force levels treaty signed
1991	January: Congressional Gulf War debate January – February: Operation Desert Storm: liberation of Kuwait July: First START (superpower strategic arms treaty) signed August: failed coup in Moscow Soviet parliament bans the Communist Party December: USSR replaced by 'Commonwealth of Independent States'
1992	June: Washington summit: Russia recognized as the 'successor state' to the USSR December: Operation Restore Hope begins in Somalia
1993	January: inauguration of President Bill Clinton June: air assault on Iraq September: Oslo Declaration of Principles on Middle East peace

	October: 18 US military personnel killed in Somalia November: NAFTA (North American Free Trade Agreement) approved by the US Congress
1994	April: US forces leave Somalia September: US invasion of Haiti October: North Korean nuclear agreement
1995	January: Republicans assume leadership of both houses of the US Congress US rescue operation for the Mexican *peso* July – August: Congress votes to lift the arms embargo on the Bosnian government August: US diplomatic initiative in Bosnia November: Dayton Peace Accords agreed
1996	February: Presidential Directive 25 issued November: Clinton re-elected
1997	May: NATO-Russia Founding Act signed
1998	April: Good Friday (Belfast) Peace Agreement August: missile attacks on Sudan and Afghanistan December: US – UK air strikes on Iraq
1999	March: NATO air strikes on Serbia begin April: NATO 50th anniversary summit: formal admission of Poland, Hungary, and the Czech Republic October: US Senate fails to ratify the Comprehensive Nuclear Test Ban Treaty
2000	July: Israel – Palestine peace talks begin at Camp David November: George W. Bush wins the presidential election

Searching for purpose: the 'Kennan sweepstakes'

Post-Cold War options

Beginning in the late 1980s, the American foreign policy community was exposed to a sometimes bewildering and prolonged national public meditation on possible options for an America without a Soviet threat. During the first year of Clinton's presidency, the debate became known in administration circles as the 'Kennan sweepstakes': a conscious effort to find a post-Soviet statement of purpose to rival George

Kennan's early Cold War concept of 'containment' of communism (Brinkley 1997). The debate was at first deeply influenced by the notion of American decline (Kennedy 1998). Since the mid-1980s, the USA had been a net debtor nation; by the end of the presidency of Ronald Reagan (1981–9), America was the world's biggest debtor. Perceptions of relative decline were, however, even in the early 1990s, undercut by the contemporary advances for liberal democracy, not only in former communist countries, but also in Latin America and South Africa. Commentators began to develop the notion of the 'democratic peace', an idea derived from Enlightenment philosopher Immanuel Kant which was profoundly to influence the foreign policy thinking of the Clinton administration (Russett 1993; Doyle 1995). Moreover, as the Soviet Union imploded, American military eminence became obvious. Even before the formal break-up of the USSR, neo-conservative commentator Charles Krauthammer (1991) was discussing the 'unipolar moment'. From a liberal perspective, Joseph Nye developed the idea of 'soft power', involving the ability to co-opt rather than coerce, to set the assumptions, even the organizational framework, for international behaviour. Nye (1991: 259–60) concluded: 'America is rich but acts poor.' For Nye, who worked in the Departments of State and Defense under President Clinton, the prevailing view was that 'we can't afford' international leadership 'despite the fact that US taxes are a smaller per cent of GNP [gross national product] than in most other' developed countries.

Perceptions of American decline derived not only from the huge federal deficits, trade and budget, inherited from the Reagan years. They were associated also with the continuing backwash from the defeat in Vietnam, as well as with other humiliations in the developing world (notably the 1979–80 Iranian hostage crisis), and with perceived problems of US economic competitiveness. Though the case for decline weakened rapidly with the burgeoning success of the 1990s and the elimination of the Reagan budget deficit, declinism did affect the debate over post-Cold War options. Despite this, the options debate exuded a sense of liberation. America, whatever its economic problems, seemed to have a real choice. There was no single focus of 'threat' which now determined the choice of foreign policy future.

The range of options on offer in the early 1990s was conveniently arranged along a spectrum leading from strong internationalist assertion (to the point of actual imperialism) at one end, to contractionism (to the point of isolationism) at the other (Crabb, Sarieddine, and Antizzo 2001). The major fear in elite discourse was that of a new isolationism. With the Soviet threat extinguished at last, perhaps America really was homeward bound? Robert E. Hunter (1992: 3, 18) warned that the USA must not react to its Cold War victory by folding its tent and quietly stealing away. Elites must win the battle for internationalism. Ronald Steel (1995: 85) discerned 'a chasm between a foreign policy establishment mesmerized by notions of American leadership and "global responsibilities" and an American public concerned by drug trafficking and addiction, jobs, illegal aliens' and other domestic issues. By 1998, Samuel Berger, Clinton's second National Security Adviser, was arguing that the real danger came from 'those who would "talk the talk" of internationalism, but "walk the walk" of isolationism' (Berger 1998: 188). Successful internationalism required the nerve to spend money and to take risks even when America was not directly threatened. In these debates, 'isolationism' was generally a term of abuse, though some commentators—notably Eric Nordlinger (1995)—were prepared to employ it in a positive, approving sense.

KEY POINTS

❑ Both the George H. W. Bush and the Clinton administrations wrestled with the problem of deciding on a clear, publicly defensible, strategy for US foreign policy in the new era.

❑ Debates prior to 1995 were affected by perceptions of American decline.

❑ Post-Cold War options ran a gamut from expansionist/imperialist to contractionist/isolationist.

MAJOR DEBATES AND THEIR IMPACT 5.1: The 'end of history' and the 'democratic peace'

'End of history'

What we may be witnessing is not just the end of the Cold War, or the passing of a particular period of post-war history, but the end of history as such: that is, the end point of mankind's ideological evolution and the universalization of Western liberal democracy as the final form of human government. . . .

The end of history will be a very sad time. the struggle for recognition, the willingness to risk one's life for a purely abstract goal, the worldwide ideological struggle that called forth daring, courage, imagination, and idealism, will be replaced by economic calculation, the endless solving of technical problems, environmental concerns, and the satisfaction of sophisticated consumer demands.

(Fukuyama 1989)

Against Fukuyama, I will argue that what he calls 'democratic capitalism' has no prospect of becoming universal. A world consisting only of liberal democratic regimes is not an inevitability: it is a utopia, a state of affairs made unrealizable by some of the most powerful forces of the age.

(Gray 1998)

Fukuyama predicted the end of ideological conflicts, not history itself, and the triumph of political and economic liberalism. That point is correct in a narrow sense: the secular religions that fought each other so bloodily in the last century are now dead. But Fukuyama failed to note that nationalism remains very much alive. Moreover, he ignored the explosive potential of religious wars that has extended to a large part of the Islamic world.

(Hoffman 2002)

The 'democratic peace'

The end of ideological hostility matters doubly because it represents a surrender to the force of Western values of economic and especially political freedom. To the degree that countries once ruled by autocratic systems become democratic, a striking fact about the world comes to bear on any discussion of the future of international relations: in the modern international system, democracies have almost never fought each other.

(Russett 1993)

President Bush Senior and 'the vision thing'

President Bush was actually an unlikely post-Cold War visionary. Rather, he brought to the White House the pragmatic conservatism of an 'American tory' (Polsby 1990). Bush famously denied any skill with 'the vision thing'. In the frenetic immediate post-Cold War climate, he was not short of advice. Former Defense Secretary Robert McNamara (1989) urged him to cut defence spending by 50 per cent. At the other extreme, the 1992 Defense Planning Guidance, written in his Department of Defense and leaked to the press in April 1992, envisaged an America which would enjoy permanent military primacy, retaining 'the pre-eminent responsibility for addressing selectively those wrongs which threaten not only our interests, but those of our allies and friends, or which

could seriously unsettle international relations' (Petras and Morley 1995: 13–24).

Bush's natural caution was tempered by the demands of occupying the White House as the Cold War order expired. His advice to aides included the injunction to 'think big', as well as to 'work as a team' under close presidential direction (Kolb 1994: 6). An August 1990 speech in Colorado represented an early effort to map out a post-Cold War foreign policy. The USA needed to meet new, unspecified threats, 'wholly unrelated to the earlier patterns of the US–Soviet relationship'. Only 'a strong and engaged America' could respond adequately to threats which might emerge in any corner of the globe (Melanson 1996: 219).

The elder Bush's main contribution to post-Cold War role setting was the concept of a New World Order, outlined to Congress following the 1990

> **KEY QUOTES 5.1:** The New World Order

Out of these troubled times . . . a new world order can emerge . . . Today, that new world order is struggling to be born, a world quite different from the one we have known, a world where the rule of law supplants the rule of the jungle, a world in which nations recognize the shared responsibility for freedom and justice, a world where the strong respect the weak.

(President George H. W. Bush, 11 Sept. 1990)

'World Orders, Old and New': the rule of the 'rich men of the rich societies . . . assisted by the rich men of the hungry nations who do their bidding'.

(Chomsky 1994)

Using force makes sense as a policy where the stakes warrant, where and when force can be effective, where no other policies are likely to prove effective, where its application can be limited in scope and time, and where the potential benefits justify the potential costs and sacrifice.

(President George H. W. Bush, 5 Jan. 1993)

invasion of Kuwait by Saddam Hussein's Iraqi army. Though it contained a general commitment to democratic idealism, the New World Order was far from an American-led campaign for global democracy. It represented rather a brand of 1990s internationalism which was closely attuned to a keen awareness of the limits of American power. Following the 1991 victory in the Gulf against Iraq, Bush famously, and rather prematurely, boasted of having buried the 'specter of Vietnam' in 'the desert sands of the Arabian peninsula' (Tucker and Hendrickson 1992: 72). Yet, just as the New World Order was no unabashed call to arms, Bush's farewell speeches at the close of his presidency emphasized constraints as well as opportunities. At West Point military academy in January 1993, Bush rhetorically reserved the use of force for occasions 'where its application can

be limited in space and time, and where the potential benefits justify the potential costs and sacrifice' (*Public Papers* 1993: 2229).

Bill Clinton

Clinton's 1992 presidential campaign was dominated by domestic issues; indeed a major Clinton criticism of Bush was that the latter had become excessively oriented towards foreign policy. By the time Clinton entered the White House, however, it was clear not only that an entry had to be found for the 'Kennan sweepstakes', but that Bush's New World Order—terminology and concept—had to be recast. Clinton was now looking for a vision that combined a commitment to geo-economics, and an awareness of limits, with moral purpose. The key task was to delineate the conditions for engagement, military or diplomatic. Various administration spokesmen advanced notions of 'assertive humanitarianism'. Undersecretary of State Peter Tarnoff promoted a highly restrained version of 'assertive mulilateralism', based on a 'case by case decision to limit the amount of American engagement' . Secretary of State Warren Christopher responded, slightly unconvincingly, that 'our need to lead, our determination to lead, is not constrained by

KEY POINTS

- ❏ The New World Order was President Bush Sr.'s main contribution to thinking beyond the Cold War.
- ❏ Bush's concept combined awareness of constraints on American power, as well as opportunities for exercising it.

our resources' (Brown 1994: 609). As they developed in the early phase of Clinton's presidency, the 'tests' or conditions for engagement seemed to centre on the domestic overspill from regional conflict, alliance obligations, and demonstrable US economic interest.

The administration's prize entry in the 'Kennan sweepstakes' was 'democratic enlargement', defended and defined by National Security Adviser Tony Lake in September 1993. Lake made it clear that 'democratic enlargement' had economics at its heart. The replacement for anti-communist containment would be 'a strategy of enlargement . . . of the world's free community of market democracies' (Brinkley 1997: 116). 'Democratic enlargement' never gained wide currency as a slogan; for one thing, it became hopelessly confused in the public mind with enlargement of the North Atlantic Treaty Organization (NATO). It was superseded in later declarations of purpose by the formula 'engagement and enlargement'. Yet, 'democratic enlargement' did capture what was to become the central, integrating purpose of the Clinton foreign policy: to position the USA at the head of economic globalization.

As it developed in the mid- and late 1990s, Clinton administration 'big thinking' on post-Cold War foreign policy reflected both a new confidence and a new caution. Confidence derived from the retreat of declinism. By mid-decade, the computer revolution, growth in global free trade, and the US consumer spending boom had transformed the recessionary economic climate which had affected the election of 1992. The reversals in Somalia, however, raised doubts about the future of 'assertive humanitarianism'. From January 1995, Clinton had to share power with a Republican congressional majority which was contemptuous of anything resembling naive altruism in foreign policy. One expression of the post-Somalia mood was Presidential Decision Directive (PDD) 25, drafted in May 1994. The document laid out conditions for US participation in UN peacekeeping operations. It was actually a little less cautious than similar directives from Bush. Under PDD 25, the USA would contribute across its full range of capabilities, not just its 'unique' ones. However, US troops would support UN operations only if risks were 'acceptable' and objectives clear (Daalder 1996).

Administration thinking in the second Clinton term focused on the desired globalization of market democracy, a concept encapsulated in the phrase 'family of nations'. Excluded from the family were 'rogue' or 'backlash' states, later dubbed 'states of concern'. Such states included familiar international 'bad boys': Iraq, Iran, Cuba, North Korea, Libya. The post-Cold War 'democratic peace' was to be extended and protected by exposing and marginalizing the rogues (Lake 1994; Dumbrell 2002). Against Republican arguments that 'Americanism' and narrowly defined national interest should guide foreign policy, second-term Clintonites—notably Madeleine Albright, Secretary of State 1997–2001—argued for the US role as 'indispensable nation'. For Albright (2003: 420), the final decade of the twentieth century was 'the global era, a time characterised by heightened interdependence, overlapping national interests, and borders permeable to everything from terrorists and technology to disease and democratic ideals'. The USA would not and could not do everything; yet it could guide and shepherd the global progress towards market democracy. Democratic idealism was still part of the administration's conceptual apparatus in the second term. However, it was an idealism which had by this time been severely tested against the stubborn refusal of traditional security concerns to disappear, even in the era of post-communism. The 'security agenda', especially in relation to the Korean peninsula, Russia, and China, appeared to subsume 'global freedom' in a major foreign policy address in San Francisco in February 1999 (McCormick 2005: 192).

KEY POINTS

- ❏ Clinton's post-Cold War vision shifted from 'democratic enlargement' to 'engagement and enlargement'.
- ❏ Clinton increasingly looked towards extending the sway of market democracy and to marginalizing 'rogue states'.

KEY QUOTES 5.2: The Clinton administration: globalization, democracy promotion, and rogue states

With NAFTA, we'll be creating the biggest trading block in the world right at our doorstep, and led by the United States.

(President Bill Clinton, radio address, 18 Oct. 1993)

. . . our policy must face the reality of recalcitrant and outlaw states that not only choose to remain outside the family but also assault its basic values. There are few 'backlash states': Cuba, North Korea, Iran, Iraq, and Libya. For now they lack the resources of a superpower, which would enable them to seriously threaten the democratic order being created around them. Nevertheless, their behaviour is often aggressive and defiant. The ties between them are growing as they seek to thwart or quarantine themselves from a global trend to which they seem incapable of adapting.

(Lake 1994; Anthony Lake was a US National Security Adviser)

The world is no longer divided into two hostile camps. Instead, we are building bonds with nations that once were our adversaries. Growing connections of commerce and culture give us a chance to lift the fortunes and spirits of people the world over. And for the very first time in all of history, more people on this planet live under democracy than dictatorship.

(President Bill Clinton, second inaugural address, 20 Jan. 1997)

Today, as President Clinton leaves office, America is by any measure the world's unchallenged military, economic and political power. The world counts on us to be a catalyst of coalitions, a broker of peace, a guarantor of global financial stability. We are widely seen as the country best placed to benefit from globalization.

(Sandy Berger (National Security Adviser), 'A Foreign Policy for the Global Age', 17 Jan. 2001)

BOX 5.2: The USA and Somalia, 1992 – 4

Clinton and Somalia

The Bush intervention, 1992

In December 1992, shortly after his defeat in the presidential election, President George H. W. Bush announced, during a congressional recess, the start of Operation Restore Hope, involving some 28,000 US troops in a humanitarian aid intervention in Somalia, a country torn apart by civil conflict. The original intention was to have US troops withdrawn before Clinton's inauguration. A United Nations authorization in December recognized that the force would be commanded by the United States. Divisions quickly opened between the USA and the UN, while domestic opinion focused on the possibility of 'another Vietnam'. The troop commitment took place with a minimum of reference to the 1973 War Powers Resolution. When the first US Navy SEAL commandos landed in Somalia on 8 December, they were greeted by television lights and cameras of the international media.

Clinton and Somalia

Following some initial apparent success, the intervention developed into a messy crash landing for Clinton.

The new President made references to his need to inform Congress under the War Powers Resolution, but held that continued deployment of US forces was a function of his 'inherent powers' as commander-in-chief of the armed forces. The situation deteriorated sharply after the UN Security Council, prodded by US Ambassador Madeleine Albright, adopted a 'nation-building' brief for the mission. US forces were tasked with arresting Mohamed Farah Aideed, the Somalian warlord blamed for the murder of twenty-three Pakistani peacekeepers in June 1993. Eighteen US military personnel were killed in a Mogadishu firefight in October. By this time, the intervention was unpopular and beginning to stimulate congressional calls for withdrawal. The Democratic leadership in Congress, however, effectively protected the new Democratic President from any radical assault on his authority. Clinton announced, following the Mogadishu killings, that all US troops would be withdrawn by April 1994. Congress raised the prospect of a funding cut-off thereafter, though it allowed limited troop deployment until early 1995.

(continued)

BOX 5.2: (continued)

Rationale and significance

Bush's decision to commit troops to a region without significant immediate security interest for the United States was, in effect, the New World Order in action. Here was the USA acting as chairman of the international board of post-Cold War peace and order imposition. Moreover, this was an intended demonstration that Vietnam-era constraints on US military action had now evaporated. Bush's decision was rooted in a genuine concern to advance humanitarian interventionism in the new order, as well as to compensate for his administration's perceived inability to affect the worsening security and humanitarian situation in the former Yugoslavia. The deployment reflected the 'CNN effect': the putative ability of media coverage of post-Cold War humanitarian disasters to shape Washington's agenda. Clinton was bequeathed something of a poison pill. The shift in purpose, from humanitarian relief to nation building, indicated the dangers of 'mission creep' in the new international environment. The Somalian failure illustrated the shallowness of the US public and legislative commitment to the kind of expansive internationalism envisaged by Bush's New World Order.

Foreign policy making in the new order

Policy making under Bush and Clinton: executive organization and legislative prerogatives

In the early 1990s, there was a wide consensus to the effect that the form as well as the content of US foreign policy would change in the new world. At one level, so it was argued, the USA needed to develop and embed policy processes which reflected the requirements of a globalizing world economy, increasingly shaped by the dynamics of free trade. Robert Paarlberg (1995: p. xx) wrote that 'cross-border economic integration' would require political leaders to 'challenge the assumptions of national political sovereignty'. America's domestic political process appeared likely to become increasingly decentralized, less hierarchical, and more open to legislative and domestic interest group pressure. With the integrating force of immediate threat removed, the line between foreign and domestic policy seemed about to become even more blurred than previously. Presidents would no longer be able to assert authority under the cover of perpetual international crisis. Even state and local governments appeared to be getting in on the act, as they developed quasi-independent trade strategies (McHenry 1994).

Despite all this, the foreign policy process under President George H. W. Bush retained more of a Cold War than a 'New World Order' aspect. The practical efficiency of the Bush foreign policy team was impressive. It coped well with much of the 'high politics' management, notably the reunification of Germany, which accompanied the end of the Cold War. Inside the White House, Bush operated a closely structured National Security Council (NSC) committee system, deferring always to the President. Many key decisions were made by ad hoc groups chaired by Bush himself. The President and his foreign policy elite were unenthused by the possibility of post-Cold War legislative resurgence, a development they managed to keep at bay. The congressional debate which preceded the 1991 Gulf War was a set-piece for the articulation of legislative war-making prerogative; narrow victories were achieved for the presidential line in both houses. As with the Panamanian invasion of 1989, the 1991 Gulf conflict nevertheless proceeded with a minimum of legislative involvement. When asked in 1992 about his failure to achieve domestic success to match his victory in the Gulf, Bush replied: 'I don't have to get permission from some old goat in Congress to kick Saddam Hussein out of Kuwait. That's the reason' (Fisher 1995: 151).

Policy making in the Clinton years did provide evidence of a decentralized post-Cold War process. East European ethnic lobbies in the USA, for example, played an important role in energizing the presidential commitment to NATO's eastward expansion (Kirschten 1995; Asmus 2002: 80). In post-Soviet conditions, policy towards Cuba lost its high-security profile and became influenced by congressionally oriented expatriate anti-Castro lobbies in Florida, notably the Cuban-American National Foundation (Kiger 1997; Haney and Vander-bush 1999). Clinton made important bureaucratic changes, designed to recognize the newly central international economic agenda. The National Economic Council (NEC)—originally headed by Robert Rubin and later by Laura Tyson—was established in order to raise economic foreign policy to the same status as foreign diplomatic policy. Clinton (2005: 636) boasted that the NEC became the 'most important innovation in White House decision making in decades'.

The early Clinton foreign policy operation was hampered by the President's own preoccupation with domestic policy. The post-1992 foreign policy team was not as effective as that associated with Clinton's predecessor. At times, especially in relation to Balkans policy before 1995, the process was in frank disarray (Bert 1997). By 1995, Clinton was concentrating more clearly and effectively on foreign policy, and continued to do so during the second term. Republican challenges on domestic issues, effectively ending the prospects for a successful presidential reform agenda, made a contribution here. Despite all the difficulties, the key Clinton players—Warren Christopher and Tony Lake in the first term; Madeleine Albright, Sandy Berger, and (Republican) Secretary of Defense William Cohen in the second—worked reasonably well as a team, avoiding the conspicuous public disagreements that had damaged previous administrations.

The post-1994 Republican Congress quickly asserted itself in regard to policy in Bosnia. During the second term, Clinton suffered defeats when the Senate refused to confirm the Comprehensive Nuclear Test Ban Treaty in 1998, and when Congress subsequently removed the presidential 'fast track' trade-negotiating authority. Battles were fought over foreign aid, economic aid to Mexico, and reorganization of the State Department. Yet policy initiation remained firmly in the White House. Clinton achieved Senate ratification in 1997 of NATO expansion. When the USA began its air bombardment of Yugoslavia in 1999, Congress was 'consulted' rather than substantively included in decision making. Sandy Berger opined that Clinton had 'ample constitutional power' to act militarily without specific legislative authorization (Hendrickson 2002: 122).

Public opinion

Bush's New World Order was, among other things, an effort to sell a reordered American globalism to a sceptical American public. The notion of a post-Cold War 'homeward bound' public, even of a neo-isolationist 'new populism', profoundly influenced the foreign policy debates of the 1990s. 'New populist' candidate Pat Buchanan made waves in the 1992 and 1996 Republican primary elections, arguing for a foreign policy based on narrow nationalist principles. Following the 1994 elections, Senator Jesse Helms of North Carolina, inveterate opponent of foreign aid and of the United Nations, headed the Senate Foreign Relations Committee. The 'new populism' had to be taken seriously.

There was little public encouragement in the 1990s for the USA to become actively engaged in apparently remote regional conflicts. Foreign aid and 'global altruism' slipped down all polled lists of public priorities (Rosner 1995–6; Bacevich 1996). The gap, identified by Ronald Steel and referred to above, between elite and public perspectives—global leadership versus domestic concerns—was evident, for example, in Chicago Council on Foreign Relations polling in the mid-1990s (Rielly 1995).

Yet truth was more complex. The 'new populism' was itself as much an expression of electoral opportunism as of mass preference. Would-be 'new populist' leaders of right (Pat Buchanan) and left (Democrat Jerry Brown) attacked globalization and elite free trade policies in the name of the ordinary American. The post-1994 congressional Republicans certainly had a 'new populist' tinge; they showed considerable distaste for 'entangling alliances' and tended to favour unilateralism in foreign policy. However, post-Cold War public opinion *per se* was complex. It retained from the earlier post-Vietnam War era a prudent attitude towards military intervention, especially if goals were vague and American interests indistinct (Jentleson 1992). Post-Cold War public introversion had its limits. The saliency of foreign policy to the US public certainly decreased in the 1990s; yet there was little public enthusiasm for quitting international bodies such as the United Nations

and NATO (Kull 1995–6). Both Bush and Clinton were able to lead America along the internationalist path, with the latter conspicuously succeeding in eliciting public approval for troop commitments to Bosnia in 1995–6.

KEY POINTS

❑ The 1990s saw a widespread expectation that foreign policy making would become more decentralized and less dominated by presidents.

❑ The post-Cold War presidents were, to varying degrees, able to resist the decentralizing dynamic and, in particular, showed scant regard for congressional war powers.

❑ 'Homeward bound' public opinion was a major potential constraint on executive policy making in the new era.

US foreign policy in the post-Cold War era

President Bush Senior, 1989 – 93

Despite the centrality of 'big thinking' in the 1990s, much foreign policy leadership remained as it had always been: the management of complex international interactions, especially in the context of more or less unexpected crises and emergencies. George H. W. Bush's main concern in 1989–90 was how to manage the extraordinary, and largely unexpected, transformations that were taking place in Russia and eastern Europe. The hallmarks of the Bush approach were procedural deftness, restraint, and caution (Zelikow and Rice 1995; Hurst 1999; Bush and Scowcroft 1998). At times, strategic caution resembled stasis. Bush offered a process of 'testing' both Soviet premier Mikhail Gorbachev's good faith and his security in office. Washington sought also to integrate a reforming USSR into Western capitalist economic and political networks. The collapse of communism in eastern Europe was greeted in official Washington with diplomatic equanimity; Bush famously declined 'to dance on the Berlin Wall'.

The Bush policy, as it evolved between November 1989 and the extinction of the Soviet Union just over two years later, was one of attempting to bolster Gorbachev's domestic position where possible, but also of stopping well short of complete commitment to the Soviet reformer. There was to be no 'grand bargain', wherein Soviet reform might be underpinned by massive American aid. At the Malta summit in late 1989, Bush effectively promised that Washington would not 'create big problems' if Moscow intervened to pacify the Baltic republics (Beschloss and Talbott 1993: ch. 7). The unpredictability of Soviet politics was underlined by the failed anti-Gorbachev coup of August 1991. The coup attempt followed an uncharacteristically incautious Bush speech, delivered in Ukraine on 1 August. A denunciation of nationalist fragmentation delivered against Gorbachev's wishes, the 'chicken Kiev' speech may have encouraged the August plotters. Bush supported Boris Yeltsin, the leader of the newly independent Russia, throughout 1992, though again with relatively little in the way of concrete aid. Though criticized for its hesitancy,

Bush's Soviet/Russian policy had much to commend it. Two superpower strategic arms (START) treaties were signed by early 1993. Above all, the huge shift in the geopolitical landscape had been managed, at least beyond the immediate disorder in the former Yugoslavia, in a way broadly congruent with the White House's desire to avoid violent disintegration of the Soviet state system. Bush's pragmatic conservatism applied also to relations with China, with only muted criticism being offered following the 1989 massacre of student activists in Tiananmen Square, Beijing.

Bush's policy elsewhere was notably more incautious. In December 1989, the USA invaded Panama. The invasion followed the 'voiding' of elections by Panamanian dictator Manuel Noriega. The White House offered a range of justifications for the action: 'to safeguard the lives of Americans, to defend democracy in Panama, to combat drug trafficking, and to protect the integrity of the Panama Canal' (Maechling 1990: 123). It was rather remarkable that this invasion, the first such use of military force in what were (just) post-Cold War conditions, had very little basis in international law (Fisher 1995: 145–8). Noriega, one-time US intelligence 'asset', had become a severe embarrassment to Washington. The invasion served as an indication of Washington's resolve to act decisively in the new international era, especially in its own hemisphere.

In contrast to Panama, the US response to Iraq's illegal August 1990 invasion of Kuwait was strongly backed by the United Nations. Saddam Hussein, like Noriega, was a former recipient of American aid who was now seen by Washington as an international menace. The US diplomatic and military response to the Kuwaiti invasion, Operations Desert Shield and Desert Storm, however, was multilateral and measured. As Freedman and Karsh (1994: 441) argued, the 1991 ouster of Iraq from Kuwait 'saw the return of the United States to a self-confident and an effective role at the heart of international affairs'. Bush's justification for action, centring on international law and on the threat the Iraqi action mounted to oil supplies, was internationally persuasive. Controversy extended to the way in which mission goals—defending Saudi Arabia from attack, expelling the illegal invader, at times even destroying the Iraqi regime—shifted. The US commitment noticeably expanded following the 1990 mid-term elections. The US attacks on virtually defenceless retreating Iraqi troops at the war's end were also highly controversial. Bush's reasons for allowing Saddam to remain in power—primarily concern for the integrity of the allied Gulf coalition and for the limited UN mandate, as well as the desire to avoid involvement in prolonged and unpredictable Iraqi nation building—were coherent. The raising and subsequent disappointing of the hopes of the Shi'a population of southern Iraq, that the USA would intervene further in Iraq itself, profoundly damaged the prospects of a successful invasion by American troops in 2003.

KEY POINTS

❑ Bush's management of the geopolitical convulsions which accompanied the end of the Cold War was generally sure-footed, if rather uninspired.

❑ The 1989 Panamanian invasion and the 1991 Gulf conflict were transformative assertions of post-Cold War US military force.

President Clinton, first term, 1993–6

Much of the early Clinton foreign policy agenda consisted in confronting issues inherited from the momentous Bush years: ratification of the North American Free Trade Agreement (NAFTA) between the USA, Canada, and Mexico; attempting to achieve a post-Cold War settlement with Russia; continuing Bush's moves towards a military posture appropriate for the new era; and developing a credible policy for the disintegrating Yugoslavia.

The November 1993 congressional endorsement of NAFTA (234–200 in the House; 61–38 in the Senate) was a major victory for the President and for the principle of regional free trade. It was a defeat for protectionist and 'new populist' forces, including those represented by Ross Perot, whose 19 per cent national support in the 1992 presidential election had done so much to usher Clinton into the White House. The NAFTA vote set the foundation of a presidential record that was to be distinguished by its commitment to both bilateral and multilateral free trade policies. The administration set its sights on 'big emerging markets', including China, India, Brazil, and South Africa. The interpenetration of global security and economics was exemplified in the administration's policy of free trade with China, more or less without regard for Beijing's human rights record.

Policy towards Russia combined various elements, some of them mutually irreconcilable: a recognition of Boris Yeltsin as the only credible leader of the former superpower—the 'Yeltsin drunk or Yeltsin sober' policy, as it came to be known in Washington; a generalized commitment to Russian and east European democratization; the real need to control and decommission nuclear weapons in various parts of the old USSR; a concern to marginalize Russia as a future international security player; and the playing of a central role in the over-rapid marketization of the Russian economy (Clark 2001: 103–7; Talbott 2003; Marsden 2005; Maclean 2006). Policy towards Russia was also complicated by what was to become a major achievement of the Clinton administration: the expansion of NATO into eastern Europe. The result of these competing policy concerns was a stance towards Russia which continually risked either provoking a nationalist counter-reaction or a capitulation to the 'new oligarchs' who came to dominate the Russian economy. Regarding the post-Cold War military, Clinton continued the Bush dynamic of resetting capabilities. In 1993, it was announced that, by 1998, defence spending as a percentage of GNP would be less than half what it had been in the era of the Vietnam War. The US defence posture would be organized around the ability to fight two near-simultaneous major regional conflicts.

Clinton's early Bosnian policy continued the Bush administration's unwillingness to accept the need for direct US involvement in what Warren Christopher called in 1993 a 'European situation' (Hendrickson 2002: 73). Tony Lake subsequently recalled the frustration of this period: 'We kept looking for something—reading and rereading everything there was about the area' (Halberstam 2003: 199). Deadlock was broken only in 1995, with the threat of a Republican takeover of Bosnian policy, and with the massacre at Srebrenica. Richard Holbrooke, Assistant Secretary of State for European Affairs, began a diplomatic offensive which led within a few months to the Dayton Accords.

The Somalian disaster cast a long shadow. The Rwandan genocide of 1994 proceeded with a minimum of attention from either the UN or the USA. Clinton was later to describe relative non-involvement in Rwanda as the greatest shame of his administration. Military action did occur in Iraq, initially as part of the policy of 'keeping Saddam in his box' and of the commitment to 'dual containment' (of Iraq and Iran). Clinton emerged as an enthusiastic and frequent user of small-scale military force. Iraq was attacked from the air in 1993, 1994, 1996, 1997, 1998, and 1999. In 1994, the USA launched what was to be a virtually bloodless invasion of Haiti. Designed to restore the rule of elected leader Jean-Bertrand Aristide, the invasion followed domestic pressure, associated particularly with the large refugee influx from Haiti. The Clinton peace agenda was also followed in the first term by the initiation of intense engagement in the affairs of Northern Ireland, an agreement over North Korean nuclear development, and a degree of progress in the Israel–Palestine dispute. An agreement, brokered by Norway, in 1993 recognized the principle of Palestinian self-determination.

Reviewing the first Clinton term, Warren Christopher (1995: 8) asked: 'What would the world be like without American leadership just in the last two years? We might have four nuclear states with the breakup of the Soviet Union instead of one; a North Korea building nuclear bombs; a rising protectionist tide rather than rising trade flows . . . brutal dictators still terrorizing Haiti and forcing its people to flee; and Iraqi troops very likely back in Kuwait, threatening the world's oil supplies.' Christopher's summary was a reasonable one, despite the conspicuous omission of Bosnia, Somalia, and Rwanda from his survey.

President Clinton, second term, 1996–2001

As is the case with most presidencies, Clinton's second term witnessed a noticeable shifting of gear. The shift proceeded partly from the 1995 transformation in policy towards Bosnia. With declinism now a philosophy of the past, the post-1995 White House exuded greater confidence in America's ability to exercise global leadership. Above all, the Republican Congress began to make its presence felt, pressing the executive towards unilateralist foreign policy options, and towards a new commitment to military spending. The second term witnessed important presidential reverses at the hands of the Congress, as well as international failures such as the failure to prevent India and Pakistan becoming viable nuclear powers.

The later security agenda extended also to Taiwan, where in 1996 Clinton moved to deter the threat of a Chinese invasion; to Iraq; to international terrorism; and to the Balkans. Regarding Iraq, the containment of the Baghdad regime gave way to a willingness to countenance the possibility of 'regime change' (Ritter 2005). The international terrorist threat climbed swiftly up the bureaucratic tree. In August 1996,

---

BOX 5.3: Clinton and Northern Ireland

The policy

The Clinton administration followed a newly activist strategy towards the settlement of the conflict in Northern Ireland. In February 1994, a visa was issued to enable Gerry Adams, leader of Sinn Fein, to visit the United States. The visa was widely interpreted as an effort to bring the political wing of the Provisional Irish Republican Army 'in from the cold'. It was part of a strategy designed to put American diplomatic weight behind those forces within violent republicanism that were looking to achieve an end to the conflict. The first IRA ceasefire (August 1994) was widely linked to American encouragement. In December 1994, Clinton appointed former Senator George Mitchell as 'peace envoy' to Northern Ireland. The White House extended its diplomatic net to include Official Unionists. Clinton visited Belfast in November 1995 and in September 1998. Mitchell was appointed in February 1996 to head an international commission on arms decommissioning. The breaking of the IRA ceasefire in early 1996 was a major setback for Clinton's strategy. However, the USA remained intimately involved in the diplomacy which resulted in the 1998 Good Friday (Belfast) Agreement.

Rationale, drawbacks, and achievements

American activism towards Ireland is often interpreted as an effort to secure 'the Irish vote' in the USA. In fact, there is no such thing as a cohesive 'Irish vote'. Clinton was influenced by new groupings within Irish America and within the Democratic Party. However, Clinton was attracted to Irish activism by the possibility of achieving diplomatic success in a regional conflict which did not involve the possibility of US troop commitment. He intervened in complex bureaucratic rivalries in order to secure the visa for Adams in 1993. The policy not only ran the risk of upsetting some elements of the US foreign policy bureaucracy, notably the State Department; it caused huge resentment in London, at least during the pre-1997 period. The USA, especially in the new post-Cold War environment, was not especially concerned about London's sensibilities. Tony Blair (Prime Minister from 1997) welcomed the Clinton interventions. The policy contributed to the polarization of Northern Irish politics, since it strengthened both Sinn Fein and the rejectionist Democratic Unionists, at the expense of centrist nationalist and loyalist parties. Nevertheless, Clinton's activism was a vital part of the dynamic which led to the 1998 Agreement.

Clinton described international terrorism as 'an equal-opportunity destroyer, with no respect for borders' (Clinton 2005: 719). Attacks on US embassies in East Africa and the 2000 assault on the USS *Cole* kept these issues firmly on the agenda. George Tenet (2007) later accused the Clinton team of inactivity towards terrorism. The judgement of the 9/11 Commission (2004: 340) is probably correct. According to the Commission, the Clinton people 'took the threat seriously, but not in the sense of mustering anything like the kind of effort that would be gathered to confront an enemy of the first, second, or even third rank'. The missile attacks on putative terrorist targets in Sudan and Afghanistan were ineffectual and probably counter-productive.

In March 1999, NATO forces, led by the USA, instituted a seventy-eight-day bombing campaign against Serbia. The action, which Clinton dubbed 'the first ever humanitarian war' (DiPrizio 2002: 130), was taken following Serbian leader Slobodan Milosevic's refusal to sign the Rambouillet Agreement, setting terms for a cessation of violence against the Albanian minority in the Serbian region of Kosovo. The action—extremely controversial, and at least arguably taken after impossibly humiliating demands had been placed on Serbia—led to Serb government capitulation and the entry of NATO forces into Kosovo. The bombing was hailed by sympathetic observers as not just the first humanitarian war, but also the first war ever to be won by air power alone, albeit with a (more or less) credible threat of ground invasion. The war was waged outside any UN remit; Russia would almost certainly have vetoed the action in the Security Council. The willingness of the administration to follow unilateralist or quasi-unilateralist paths was evidenced further in its opposition to American involvement in the International Criminal Court, a position which Clinton reversed in his very final days in office. Republican pressure, along with administration re-evaluation of US military preparedness, led also to defence spending increases. Particularly conspicuous here was the revival of anti-missile defence, a cherished Republican cause harking back to President Reagan's Strategic Missile Defence programme.

Clinton's final year in office was dominated by the effort to achieve a Middle East peace settlement, building on the 1998 Wye River Accords between Israel and the Palestinians. Important concessions were made by both sides. Palestinian negotiators accepted that some Israeli settlements, with Israel providing security, could continue in the West Bank; and that Jewish areas of east Jerusalem could be part of Israel. Israelis accepted various logistic positions on the viability of a new Palestinian state (Ross 2004). Major issues, however, notably the Palestinian refugee question, remained unresolved. The process failed, ultimately, to overcome decades of distrust and also the unwillingness or inability of Palestinian leader Yasser Arafat to move beyond long-held positions. A conscientious effort to secure a historic peace, the Clinton peace process eventually confirmed in the minds of the incoming Republican administration that conditions for peace in the region simply did not exist.

During the election campaign of 1992, candidate Bill Clinton announced that 'the cynical calculus of power politics is ill-suited to a new era'. In a turn-of-the-century survey of Clinton's foreign policy, Stephen Walt concluded that hopes of transcending 'power politics' in the post-Cold War era had not been achieved. Clinton continued, indeed confirmed, the willingness of the USA to use military force, justified by a mixture of ideals and interests, in ways that would have familiar to many pre-Cold War presidents. In his last year in office, for example, the USA greatly extended its commitment to intervention against guerrilla movements in Colombia. Clinton's main concern was to find a foreign policy that reconciled expansive internationalism with the contractionist climate of the 1990s. As Walt put it, Clinton sought 'hegemony on the cheap' (Walt 2000: 78–9).

KEY POINTS

❑ Clinton's second term involved a noticeable turn towards unilateralism and remilitarization.

❑ The 1999 Kosovo campaign involved a denial of traditional notions of national sovereignty.

CONTROVERSIES 5.1: Evaluating the presidents

Evaluating presidents and their foreign policy leadership

Evaluation of presidential performance is plagued by problems of subjectivism. Regarding presidential performance as a whole, congressional success scores and the achievement of 'landmark' legislation are often regarded as key indicators of presidential success. In foreign policy, where legislation is less central than in the domestic arena, 'objective' congressional voting success scores are less helpful. Successful foreign policy leadership seems to reside in the following:

- Clarity of purpose and 'vision': this was especially important if policy was not merely to drift following the end of the Cold War.

- Effective procedures and skilled foreign policy management.

- Maintenance of a domestic foreign policy consensus.

- Protecting US security and international economic interests.

- Observing the requirements of domestic and international law.

- Avoiding manifest foreign policy disasters.

Evaluating G. H. W. Bush and Clinton

Both presidents struggled with the development and articulation of a post-Cold War foreign policy 'vision' for the United States. Bush's procedural management was generally sure and effective. Clinton's management was less sure-footed, but bears comparison with that of most presidents. Despite setbacks, both presidents managed to maintain a general domestic consensus behind at least a moderately expansive American internationalism. American global power—military, economic, and cultural—skyrocketed throughout the 1990s. Both presidents were committed to multilateralism in pursuit of American international interests, though Clinton's later foreign policy was marked by a move towards unilateralism. Both Bush and Clinton followed a 'presidentialist' foreign policy, with relatively little concern for the rights and prerogatives of Congress. Foreign policy 'disasters' on the model of the Vietnam War did not occur in the 1990s, despite missed opportunities (for example, in the Balkans before 1995), outright failures (as in Somalia), and misjudgements (such as the assault on Sudan in 1998).

Conclusion

Despite important temperamental and philosophical differences between the two post-Cold War presidents, foreign policy leadership during the 'long' 1990s showed considerable unity of purpose. Both Bush and Clinton devoted time to conceptualizing new threats to America's security. However, compared to the Cold War and the post-9/11 eras, the 1990s were the years without threat. Bush's New World Order and Clinton's various formulations—'assertive humanitarianism', 'selective engagement', 'democratic enlargement', 'assertive multilateralism', 'engagement and enlargement'—were all attempts to keep expansive US internationalism alive in this new environment. They were also efforts to articulate a foreign policy which looked beyond narrowly conceived national interest. The 1990s were years in which US leaders bolstered their internationalism with an optimistic commitment to democratizing purpose.

In general, while they recognized limits to US global ambition, the post-Cold War presidents managed to restrain the more extreme variants of neo-isolationism and 'new populism', sometimes by deliberately exaggerating the strength of those forces. US foreign policy leaders in the 1990s sought to manage transition, to infuse short-term crisis management with longer-term vision, to reset the diplomatic compass. Between them, Bush and Clinton, for good or ill, preserved American global hegemony—albeit an overextended 'hegemony on the cheap'—and protected executive domination of the foreign policy process.

? Questions

1. To what extent were the 'long' 1990s (1989–2001) a distinct phase in the history of US foreign policy?
2. What foreign policy options were available to post-Cold War foreign policy leaders?
3. How coherent was President Bush Sr.'s vision for post-Cold War US foreign policy?
4. How coherent was President Clinton's vision for post-Cold War US foreign policy?
5. To what extent did the 1990s see a reassertion of congressional influence over US foreign policy?
6. How influential was the 'new populism' in the making of 1990s US foreign policy?
7. What were America's objectives in the 1991 Gulf War and how comprehensively were they achieved?
8. How successful was President Bush Sr.'s foreign policy management?
9. How successful was President Clinton's foreign policy management?
10. In what senses did US foreign policy in the 1990s exemplify Francis Fukuyama's 'end of history' thesis?

» Further Reading

Bush, George, and Scowcroft, Brent (1998), *A World Transformed* (New York: Alfred A. Knopf).

   Memoir of the Bush management of the geopolitical changes of the 1990s.

Clinton, Bill (2005), *My Life* (London: Arrow Books).

   Uneven, sometimes pedestrian, but indispensable presidential memoir.

Cox, Michael, Ikenberry, G. John, and Inoguchi, Takashi (eds.) (2000), *American Democracy-Promotion: Impulses, Strategies and Impacts* (Oxford: Oxford University Press).

   Essays covering vital themes in post-Cold War US foreign policy.

DiPrizio, Robert C. (2002), *Armed Humanitarians: US Interventions from Northern Iraq to Kosovo* (Baltimore: Johns Hopkins University Press).

   Survey of 'assertive humanitarianism' under Bush and Clinton.

Fukuyama, Francis (1992), *The End of History and the Last Man* (London: Hamish Hamilton).

   Redolent of American hopes and fears in the 1990s.

Hendrickson, Ryan C. (2002), *The Clinton Wars: The Constitution, Congress, and War Powers* (Nashville: Vanderbilt University Press).

   War powers debates from Somalia to Kosovo and Iraq.

Ross, Dennis (2004), *The Missing Peace: The Inside Story of the Fight for Middle East Peace* (New York: Farrar, Straus and Giroux).

   Detailed, compelling memoir from a leading US peace negotiator.

 Visit the Online Resource Centre that accompanies this book for web links to accompany each chapter, and a range of other resources: www.oxfordtextbooks.co.uk/orc/cox_stokes/

Section 2

Institutions and Processes

6 The foreign policy process: executive, Congress, intelligence

Michael Foley

Chapter contents

Introduction

The United States system of government was originally conceived to be a complex model of power sharing and reciprocal restraint. In many respects, the foreign policy process reflects that initial design but it also reveals the effects of political, institutional, and constitutional evolution in which the distribution of decision making has changed in favour of a more centralized and functional matrix. The emphasis upon rationality, specialization, and management has increased along with the expansion of the United States as a global superpower with a profusion of international interests requiring supervision. The presidential office has been at the centre of this transformation but it has also acted as a catalyst for periodic revivals of constitutional fundamentalism in which systemic indictments lead to demands for greater democratic participation in the service of republican values.

Challenge of foreign policy to state formation

It is customary to regard the area of US foreign policy making as having been the subject of a transformative process which has mirrored the American republic's rise from an isolated small power to that of a global hegemon. The prevailing conception of policy formulation in the area of international affairs has been one of a disjuncture between (1) on the one hand the notion of an original condition in which a rural and rules-based polity was predominantly concerned with internal expansion, and (2) on the other hand the concept of a great international power centre with a more modern and utilitarian approach to the complexity and imprecision of engaging with world politics. The conventional narrative of the foreign policy process in the United States, therefore, is one in which an interest in, and a capacity to deal with, the international sphere has had to emerge from a prior set of institutions, processes, and outlooks oriented towards the demands of domestic governance. In fact, in many instances the contemporary infrastructure of what has been termed the 'national security state' or the 'foreign policy establishment' is seen as a living testament to the way that an earlier preoccupation with internal issues and legal formalities has been displaced by a de facto system of open-ended adaptation in response to international circumstances.

Attractive though this depiction may be, it offers an oversimplified perspective of governmental evolution. Moreover, it is a view that not only distorts the position of foreign policy as an issue in the formative processes of the republic, but also misrepresents the nature and depth of the political transformation commonly ascribed to the driving imperatives of foreign policy in American government. Under closer scrutiny, a more intricate picture emerges in which the relationship between sovereign states becomes central both to the formulation of the American Constitution and to the subsequent processes of foreign policy making in the United States.

Interstate relations and the US Constitution

Various elites became so perturbed by this course of events that in 1787 they advocated the wholesale revision of the Articles of Confederation that had provided a modicum of central governance since 1781. The Founding Fathers, who devised what was to become the US Constitution, were confronted by the need to reverse the centrifugal forces of states' rights and assembly-driven government. The Founders' concerns over the condition of the states were threefold. First, the states were accused of civic immaturity in not being able to maintain internal order or to ensure the rights and freedoms of their own citizens. Second, their sovereignty and their behaviour were seen as impeding the development of commerce through import and export levies, separate currencies, and a host of other restrictive practices designed to protect their own economic activities. In doing so, they were preventing the emergence of a huge free trade area that would maximize the collective economic potential of the republics.

Third, and probably most significantly, the Framers saw the states as a danger to themselves in the realm of international power politics. By acting as independent sovereign communities with their own international interests and foreign policies, the newly emancipated republics were considered as having placed their own collective security in jeopardy. There were serious concerns that these new states—either individually or in groups—could be turned into de facto client states or even into quasi-colonies by European empires which were still highly active in the western hemisphere. The situation was further exacerbated by the regional variations in economic structures and international trading partnerships. New England, for example, had strong shipping and commercial interests, while the South's slave economy was dependent upon cash crops, slave supplies, and unrestricted access to foreign markets.

Many of the debates in the constitutional convention of 1787 centred upon the relationships between states in North America, and between them and the geopolitics of their position in relation to other powers. Designing a constitution that would reduce the various tensions sufficiently to achieve consent was a difficult undertaking that required a complex system of contiguous powers, reciprocal restraints, and negotiated settlements. Two elements are particularly noteworthy in the context of a foreign policy-making capacity. First was the existence of rivalries between different states and regions. These led to a distribution of power within the federal government which was intended to create a balance of power between the North and the South. The North had wanted navigation laws to be passed by simple majority votes in Congress. Southerners feared that the northern shippers would be able to charge what they liked for carrying southern goods and therefore pressed for such laws to be made subject to the requirement of two-thirds majorities. In the end, the South agreed

to drop its objections to simple majorities in return for a raft of concessions aimed at protecting the South's slave economy and slave culture. One of the most significant elements of the accommodation was the agreement whereby treaties with other nations would have to receive the assent of two-thirds of the Senate in order to become law. The South may have been able to trust the North with domestic navigation laws through simple majority rule, but that trust did not extend to the area of treaties—especially as they might well have affected its relationship with their trading partners (Rakove 1982).

The Senate 'switch'

The second noteworthy aspect was that after having enumerated the new government's jurisdiction in the key areas of revenue, commerce, and the organization of the western territories, the Framers turned their attention to the institutions of government and their respective powers in relation to one another. Many delegates had been disappointed over the limited range of federal powers and over the creation of a second chamber in the form of a Senate that would give physical expression to the separate sovereignties of the states. Initially it was thought in some quarters that a Senate of twenty-six members would provide an aristocratic element to the new government. The possibility of it acting as a Council of State was reflected in the original assignment of foreign policy powers to the chamber. The power to appoint ambassadors and make treaties was originally earmarked for the Senate, but following what was considered to be a number of strategic defeats inflicted on those who proposed a more centralized government, these foreign policy powers were switched at a late stage to the executive branch of the presidency. This was both to boost the status and independence of the presidency, and to give some additional weight to the federal government's singular claim of representing the national interest (McDonald 1985: 230–7, 250–62; Rakove 1997: 244–87).

The interstate and international background to a constitution devised in the midst of an era of imperial power politics gave the federal government a foundational prospectus of creating a framework for national cohesion. Whether by political circumstance or conscious design, the embryonic executive branch was afforded a potential for integrated governance that was to become closely related not only to the federal government's own formative processes but also to the generative forces of international affairs in the expansion of federal authority and in the construction of the modern structure of foreign policy making.

KEY POINTS

❑ Interstate relations and security concerns were central issues in the formation of the United States.

❑ Regional politics shaped the Constitution's outlook on foreign policy governance.

❑ The Senate was originally assigned the major role in foreign policy making until a late 'switch' to the presidency.

Foreign policy as a primary agency of governmental adaptation

As has been noted, the Constitution's architects did not have a clear sense of foreign policy responsibilities lying necessarily within the executive sphere of action. Their main concern was in establishing a federal level of governance in the conduct of international affairs. And yet, the predominant pattern to have emerged over American history has been the rise of the presidential office in the formulation of foreign policy and in the responsibility for American lives and interests abroad. This has been, and remains, a controversial development in a system of government specifically designed to be one of limited powers and reciprocal restraints. But over the course of the republic, the presidency has been able to claim the existence of a synergy of development between the executive office and the policy sector of foreign policy. Together they have provided the main engine room not only for constitutional change but for altering the fabric of American society and ultimately the nature of the world order. Foreign policy issues have been instrumental in the evolutionary transformation of American government into an extensive and centralized system of administration relating to the resources and actions of a world power. In like manner, the development of the presidency has been closely tied to the numerous and urgent demands of the international sphere and to the need of the United States to have the capacity to attend to them with the appropriate levels of decisiveness and judgement (Hargrove 1974: 98–174; Corwin 1957: 170–262).

In one sense, it is a measure of the influence assigned to the federal government's responsibilities in foreign policy that this sector has been able to generate such substantial changes to the scale of the federal government and to the internal distribution of power within it. In another sense, the integrity of the Constitution and its derivative processes has always been a subject of great sensitivity in a polity whose identity is closely bound up with the tradition and legitimacy of its governmental processes—and in particular its ability to address the litmus test issue of restraining executive power. The net effect has been a largely continuing tension between need and law; between security and due process; and between unified executive direction and the claims to a rightful and productive pluralism.

Very often the executive has prevailed and it can be claimed that these instances and even periods of executive dominance have led to a definite and irreversible historical drift towards an executive-centred policy process. But such a conclusion not only overlooks the developmental contingencies of constitutional change, but also diminishes its contested nature. What appear to be historically settled patterns of foreign policy making can on occasion experience seismic shifts of complaint based not just on the substance of the policy output but, more significantly, on the structure and authority of the policy process (Schlesinger 1974: 208–419). It is on these occasions that the constitutional and political basis of United States foreign policy can be seen as being far from settled in favour of presidential government. It is against such a background, and with this caveat in mind, that we must attempt to account for the rise to prominence of the presidency in this field—and for the conditioning factors in such a position of conspicuous responsibility.

The executive as the lead agency of systemic evolution

The primary focus of America's foreign policy-making systems lies with an executive infrastructure of departments and agencies whose roots and authority are drawn from the initial grant of constitutional power to the presidential office. Of all the Framers' creations, the presidency is the one structural feature of the Constitution that can only be fully comprehended, and satisfactorily accounted for, by reference to a process of development. And this emphasis upon precedent, continuity, and jurisdictional sensitivity remains central to a branch of government whose resources have had to be claimed and rationalized

through time, rather than through definitive and final grants of power. It is true that the Constitution did assign to the presidency a number of specific roles in relation to foreign affairs. But in time, it became increasingly evident that presidents were being placed in positions where they had to supplement their enumerated functions with additional roles that were occasioned by changing conditions, issues, and requirements that were not clearly reducible to the minimalist features of the Constitution. Whether this was seen as filling in the gaps, or taking up the slack of a short and tersely composed constitution, the net effect was that presidents quickly assumed the central position in a dynamic that conjoined the presidency with issues of peace and security in the furtherance of constitutional evolution (Pious 1979: 332–415; Fisher 2007).

This is not to say that the presidency's rise to prominence has been uncontested or that the office has been immune to the American system of checks and balances. Nevertheless, presidents have been able to exploit their associations with concepts like the national interest and the popular will, along with the themes of public safety and social stability, to make persuasive cases in support of an expansive role. Apart from the instrumental argument of executive responsiveness to palpable need, presidents have been effective in advocating the property of executive virtue that gathers power in support of causes considered to be just.

Through an accumulation of precedents, the presidential office has in many respects introduced a common law ethos into the 'black letter' formalism

---

BOX 6.1: Defence and foreign policy-related powers granted to the president in the US Constitution

The President shall be Commander-in-chief of the Army and Navy of the United States, and of the Militia of the several States, when called into the actual Service of the United States; he may require the Opinion, in writing, of the principal Officer in each of the executive Departments, upon any subject relating to the Duties of their respective Offices, and he shall have Power to Grant Reprieves and Pardons for Offenses against the United States, except in Cases of impeachment. He shall have Power, by and with the Advice and Consent of the Senate, to make Treaties, provided two thirds of the Senators present concur and he shall nominate, and by and with the Advice and Consent of the Senate, shall appoint Ambassadors, other public Ministers and Consuls.

(United States Constitution, Article II: Section 2)

> **BOX 6.2: Expansive presidents up to and including the inception of the modern presidency**
>
> | | | |
> |---|---|---|
> | Presidents who played an active role in expanding the scope of the office in national security and foreign affairs, and who have had lasting effects on the development of the presidency in these areas of policy making. | Andrew Jackson | (1829–1837) |
> | | James Polk | (1845–1849) |
> | | Abraham Lincoln | (1861–1865) |
> | | Theodore Roosevelt | (1901–1909) |
> | Thomas Jefferson   (1801–1809) | Woodrow Wilson | (1913–1921) |
> | James Monroe   (1817–1825) | Franklin D. Roosevelt | (1933–1945) |

of the Constitution. In doing so, the presidency has not only pushed the specified powers of Article II into new meanings through the aggregation of usage, but also pursued the logic of an executive office in a system of government otherwise burdened with a complex of countervailing dynamics. As a consequence, presidents have injected an instrumental realism, and often a utilitarian spirit, into the framework of government. Presidents, and especially those designated as 'great' or expansive presidents, have used the issue of national security and international relations to widen the parameters of the executive branch and the federal government as a whole.

Expansionist presidents have coincided with various expansionary features of the United States not just in terms of state formation and social integration, but also in respect to its status as an international power. The presidential office has provided a means by which the federal government has been able to provide a centre of responsive and timely decision making. It has done so by exploring the opportunities for power accumulation within the system and by developing a linkage between external challenges to the system as a whole and the need for some agency of systemic adjustment. In no field has this inventiveness been more evident than in the area of war. The prospect, or actual condition, of a supreme emergency has been particularly significant in disclosing the full rationale of the presidential position in the constitutional framework of the US government. It is not simply that war tends to transform political and social institutions into a different configuration. It is that issues of war and peace open up the interior properties and implicit premises of the executive function in a much more explicit manner than is usually the case in other less urgent areas of public life.

Executive prerogative

Even though the United States is renowned for its reliance upon a sovereign constitution whose logic ensures that all its components are reducible to its central provisions, the issue of security has always been particularly problematic. In the main, this is because a society's need to maintain itself against threats generates demands for an exceptional sphere of authority that will not necessarily be wholly derived from the explicit framework of the Constitution. The authority in question is the mercurial theme of executive prerogative. In the British constitution, the crown prerogative allows for the remaining elements of the monarchy's original authority to be exercised by ministers. Given the self-professed republicanism of the Founders, the US Constitution allows for no express provision for any notion of prerogative powers.

Nonetheless, the Framers would have been aware of the difficulty of confining all state activities and responsibilities to the forms of due process and representational consent. Even John Locke (1632–1704), whom many of the Founders regarded as their philosophical mentor, found it difficult to liberalize the state to the point where it would no longer be necessary to have any recourse to an executive prerogative operating in the absence of law or even contrary to its enactments. At one level, it would appear that the US Constitution is purposefully devoid of such discretionary powers. But constitutions invite interpretations of their defining logic and operating principles. They also depend upon usage and precedent to accumulate meanings. In the case of the United States Constitution, it is clear that presidents have sought to make explicit what in their view was implicit in the very creation of an executive branch of government: namely a responsibility to act in the nation's self-interest.

The possession of the physical means of coercion, as well as its functional capacity of initiative and decisiveness, has permitted the creation of a set of powers that are interpreted as being implied by the Constitution's original construction of an executive. Just as presidents have often been in a position to claim such powers, so other centres of power have often been prepared to acquiesce in the emergency nature of such presumptions (Pious 1979: 47–84; 2007). Aware of the possible weaknesses of democratic government described by Alexis de Tocqueville (1805–59), other branches have not always disputed the rights and judgements of presidential leadership in an area of governance rich in the potential for prerogative privilege. On the contrary, they have had a pronounced tendency to defer to the asserted realism and pragmatism of executive-led decisions over military action.

Judicial recognition of inherent executive power

This outlook of pragmatic acquiescence has been evident in the limited number of Supreme Court cases relating to the president's responsibilities in foreign policy. The general absence of cases in this area is itself significant. It not only demonstrates a disinclination on the part of the judiciary to involve itself in this field of policy, but reveals the ambiguous relationship between the principles of constitutionalism

---

BOX 6.3: Observations made by Alexis de Tocqueville on the weaknesses of democratic government in the area of international relations

Foreign politics demand scarcely any of those qualities which are peculiar to a democracy; they require, on the contrary, the perfect use of almost all those in which it is deficient. Democracy is favorable to the increase of the internal resources of a state, it diffuses wealth and comfort, promotes public spirit, and fortifies the respect for law in all classes of society: all these are advantages which have only an indirect influence over the relations which one people bears to another. But a democracy can only with great difficulty regulate the details of an important undertaking, persevere in a fixed design, and work out its execution in spite of serious obstacles. It cannot combine its measures with secrecy or await their consequences with patience. These are qualities which more especially belong to an individual or an aristocracy; and they are precisely the qualities by which a nation, like an individual, attains a dominant position.

If, on the contrary, we observe the natural defects of aristocracy, we shall find that, comparatively speaking, they do not injure the direction of the external affairs of the state. The capital fault of which aristocracies may be accused is that they work for themselves and not for the people. In foreign politics it is rare for the interest of the aristocracy to be distinct from that of the people. . . .

Almost all the nations that have exercised a powerful influence upon the destinies of the world, by conceiving, following out, and executing vast designs, from the Romans to the English, have been governed by aristocratic institutions. Nor will this be a subject of wonder when we recollect that nothing in the world is so conservative in its views as an aristocracy. The mass of the people may be led astray by ignorance or passion; the mind of a king may be biased and made to vacillate in his designs, and, besides, a king is not immortal. But an aristocratic body is too numerous to be led astray by intrigue, and yet not numerous enough to yield readily to the intoxication of unreflecting passion. An aristocracy is a firm and enlightened body that never dies.

(Tocqueville 1948: i, ch. 13 'Government of the Democracy in America', http://xroads.virginia.edu/~HYPER/DETOC/ toc_indx.html)

and the realism of executive prerogative. For example, in *The Prize Cases* (1863), the Court was asked to consider whether President Lincoln had any authority to blockade southern ports at the outset of the Civil War (1861–5). According to the Constitution, a state of war could only exist if Congress had formally declared war, but in this instance the President had acted without such express authorization. Although the Supreme Court is tasked to protect the integrity of the Constitution, on this occasion it saw fit to affirm the president's judgement in superseding the precise demands of due process. The very nature of the emergency created its own momentum for executive action and prompted a recognition that under certain conditions executive prerogative possessed a legitimacy that was not reducible to the Constitution:

❝[T]he President is . . . bound to resist force with force. He does not initiate the war, but is bound to accept the challenge without waiting for any special legislative authority. And whether the hostile party be a foreign invader, or states organized in rebellion, it is none the less a war . . . [In] this greatest of civil wars . . . [t]he President was bound to meet it in the shape that it presented itself, without waiting for Congress to baptize it with a name. (Prize Cases: 669) ❞

Another keynote decision was prompted by the growing instability of the international order during the 1930s. The rise of international tensions and the threat of war led the Supreme Court to make a concerted case in favour of presidential authority and, in doing so, to incorporate the theme of executive prerogative firmly within the Constitution. In the case of *United States* v. *Curtiss-Wright Export Corporation* (1936), the Court went to great lengths in underwriting the need for executive authority in the conduct of foreign relations. The decision was based not merely upon the powers implied in the Constitution but also on the authority vested in the executive by virtue of the fact that it was an executive office. The president's powers therefore were not strictly limited to the Constitution's provisions, or to statutory grants from Congress. They were supplemented

---

BOX 6.4: *United States* v. *Curtiss-Wright Export Corporation* (1936) 299 US 304, 318–20

It results that the investment of the federal government with the powers of external sovereignty did not depend upon the affirmative grants of the Constitution. The powers to declare and wage war, to conclude peace, to make treaties, to maintain diplomatic relations with other sovereignties, if they had never been mentioned in the Constitution, would have vested in the federal government as necessary concomitants of nationality. . . .

Not only, as we have shown, is the federal power over external affairs in origin and essential character different from that over internal affairs, but participation in the exercise of the power is significantly limited. In this vast external realm, with its important, complicated, delicate and manifold problems, the President alone has the power to speak or listen as a representative of the nation. He makes treaties with the advice and consent of the Senate; but he alone negotiates. Into the field of negotiation the Senate cannot intrude; and Congress itself is powerless to invade it. . . .

It is important to bear in mind that we are here dealing not alone with an authority vested in the President by an exertion of legislative power, but with such an authority plus the very delicate, plenary and exclusive power of the President as the sole organ of the federal government in the field of international relations—a power which does not require as a basis for its exercise an act of Congress, but which, of course, like every other governmental power, must be exercised in subordination to the applicable provisions of the Constitution. It is quite apparent that if, in the maintenance of our international relations, embarrassment—perhaps serious embarrassment—is to be avoided and success for our aims achieved, congressional legislation which is to be made effective through negotiation and inquiry within the international field must often accord to the President a degree of discretion and freedom from statutory restriction which would not be admissible were domestic affairs alone involved. Moreover, he, not Congress, has the better opportunity of knowing the conditions which prevail in foreign countries, and especially is this true in time of war. He has his confidential sources of information. He has his agents in the form of diplomatic, consular and other officials. Secrecy in respect of information gathered by them may be highly necessary, and the premature disclosure of it productive of harmful results.

by a range of supports that arguably were not strictly constitutional in nature (e.g. historical tradition, force of circumstances, threat levels, executive skills, and the nature of international negotiations). The judgement in this landmark case represented an extraordinary piece of constitutional metamorphosis. It could be claimed that this set of extravagant—and arguably extra-constitutional—propositions represented a departure from constitutional government. The principle of shared and concurrent powers, which lies at the heart of American constitutionalism, had been largely replaced in the area of foreign policy by one of condoned presidential primacy under the pressure of external developments.

The *Curtiss-Wright* judgment became the linchpin of presidential claims to extraordinary legitimacy and to a widening remit of executive prerogative. Its implications quickly became evident during the Second World War which witnessed the establishment of an entire defence infrastructure in American society. The logic of a sustained emergency continued with the Cold War when global conditions and the advent

of nuclear arsenals ensured that even greater power flowed to the centres of executive direction. The need for sophisticated structures of decision making, intelligence assessment, and crisis management led to the 'national security state', to the further enhancement of the president's own Executive Office (e.g. National Security Council), and to the formal establishment of a range of intelligence resources (e.g. Central Intelligence Agency) (Nathan and Oliver 1987: 21–105; Hart 1995; Andrew 1996; Inderfurth and Johnson 2004). References to an emergent and necessary form of 'presidential government' seemed prosaic as the executive prerogatives of foreign policy had become as self-evident as the international threat to American security (Burns 1973; Koh 1988). Even after the Cold War, the scale of the executive establishment in this area continued to grow so that by 2006 the USA accounted for 48 per cent of the world's military expenditures with the president as commander-in-chief of the world's most lethal form of force projection.

KEY POINTS

❑ Foreign policy became increasingly recognized as an exceptional issue area in the governing responsibilities of the USA.

❑ The requirements of foreign policy were a powerful motive force in the adaptive capacity of the federal government.

❑ The presidency has acted as the chief agency and main beneficiary of governmental evolution in response to foreign policy needs.

❑ Executive prerogative and inherent powers—especially in relation to war—have marked the emergence of presidential power and the rise of the USA as a world power.

Congress and the challenge of co-equality

In the field of foreign policy, the United States system of government is distinguished by an extraordinary mixture of movement and stasis; of evolutionary modernity and fixed tradition. Nothing better illustrates this dualism than the continued presence of Congress as a co-equal constitutional partner in the sphere of public policy. In most respects, Congress

represents a traditional order of governance that is rooted in a strict formal sequence of government process, whereby laws are first enacted by legislative assent and subsequently implemented by the executive. It has already been noted that the requirements of foreign policy do not fit easily into such a formulaic process and that the presidency has had to lead the way in recalibrating the process of government in line with the exigencies of the international sphere. As a result, Congress has often had to resort to a rearguard strategy of adaptation and repositioning in order to maintain a meaningful role in the area of foreign policy. In this it has been able to call on the support of the Constitution and the principle of the rule of law as well as different sectors of the public and various elements of the executive. The net effect has been one of ambiguity and dispute which have generated a host of repercussions throughout government and the policy process.

Congress as a model of compliance

It is possible to view the role of Congress in foreign policy as something of an anomaly in that it is suggestive of an *ancien régime* of a simpler age when governments were altogether smaller in size and scope, and when the United States had the option of keeping the world at bay through geographical and political isolation. The heyday of congressional activism in foreign policy is often cited as the 1930s when the legislature sought to prevent President Roosevelt from implicating the United States in international disputes by a series of enactments intended to secure American neutrality in the face of rising European fascism and growing Japanese expansionism. The congressional position of isolationism may have been a politically responsive position, but in retrospect it was seen as thoroughly misguided, short-sighted, and dangerous. Congress's efforts to maintain security through appeasement became so discredited that they ushered in the rise of presidential initiative, executive judgement, and specialist foresight in the formulation of American foreign policy. The mindset of the Cold War merely intensified the transition of Congress into something of a support agency for executive action against communism as well as an institutional embodiment of America's social consensus against the communist threat (Spanier 1981; Sundquist 1981: 91–126).

According to this perspective, Congress was an institution that was simply too big, too decentralized, and too disorderly to be a responsible partner in the conduct of foreign policy. To much of its membership, Congress could neither compete with the executive's sources of information, nor challenge its expertise in the way it was appraised and acted upon. Just as the executive accepted the responsibility of setting the agenda, so Congress in many ways believed that the virtues of institutional responsiveness and political responsibility were based upon the merits of public affirmation and strategic compliance. Policy initiatives and constitutional powers

---

BOX 6.5: Gulf of Tonkin Resolution (1964)

Joint Resolution of US Congress (HJ RES 1145; Public Law 88 – 408), 7 August 1964, approved on 10 August 1964.

The Joint Resolution was passed by the House of Representatives (414 – 0) and by the Senate (88 – 2).

Resolved by the Senate and House of Representatives of the United States of America in Congress assembled,

That the Congress approves and supports the determination of the President, as Commander-in-chief, to take all necessary measures to repel any armed attack against the forces of the United States and to prevent further aggression.

Section 2. The United States regards as vital to its national interest and to world peace the maintenance of international peace and security in southeast Asia. Consonant with the Constitution of the United States and the Charter of the United Nations and in accordance with its obligations under the Southeast Asia Collective Defense Treaty, the United States is, therefore, prepared, as the President determines, to take all necessary steps, including the use of armed force, to assist any member or protocol state of the Southeast Asia Collective Defense Treaty requesting assistance in defense of its freedom.

Section 3. This resolution shall expire when the President shall determine that the peace and security of the area is reasonably assured by international conditions created by action of the United Nations or otherwise, except that it may be terminated earlier by concurrent resolution of the Congress.

were delegated to the executive (Schlesinger 1974: 127–207). Presidential pre-eminence afforded executive discretion to expand the usage of 'executive agreements' between states in place of the legal formalities of the treaty process. Furthermore, the sharing of war powers was gradually superseded through the commander-in-chief's capacity to deploy the armed forces in the absence of any formal declarations of war. When Congress was asked for its support, it was customary to give it in extravagant terms such as the Gulf of Tonkin Resolution of 1964. Anything less may have been construed as questioning the executive's action in a crisis, which in turn could be interpreted as signifying a lack of national resolve in confronting an adversary.

Congress as a model of assertion

This picture of model compliance and institutional subordination has become a well-established impression of Congress in the sphere of foreign policy. And yet, whilst acknowledging the inherent structural deficiencies of such a body, it is possible to arrive at quite a different estimation of Congress's contribution to this area of policy making. An alternative view can be drawn from three main sources.

First, the characterization of Congress as a collectively supine branch always amounted to something of an overstatement. Even during the Cold War, representatives remained attentive to, and active within, a number of international areas (e.g. trade, transport, communications, immigration, foreign aid) and were often prepared to assert their positions in the form of legislative enactments. In addition to its influence upon the structural configuration of the military's distribution of resources, therefore, Congress was, and has remained, far from passive in a range of issue areas relating to foreign policy.

Second, as the intensive nature of the Cold War subsided in the 1970s and 1980s, the basic imperatives of executive-centred foreign policy diminished in scale. When this relaxation in Cold War disciplines was combined with the onset of greater congressional decentralization and with increased budgetary

pressures upon federal expenditures, the effect was to bring many aspects of foreign policy under closer scrutiny. It was during this period that the differentiation between foreign policy and domestic policy began to erode as international dimensions intruded increasingly upon domestic issues and as constituency concerns began to be extended to America's policies abroad. The net effect was that more members of Congress found that they had more discretion in challenging the executive in its positions and judgements (Lindsay 1994). Congress also became better positioned to involve itself more deeply in the bureaucratic politics of the executive branch, particularly as its specialized subcommittees were increasingly embedded in the policy communities, or sub-governmental networks, that incorporated private sector interests, legislative connections, and agency agendas.

Third, the mystique that had conjoined foreign policy with executive sophistication in the Cold War was seriously compromised in the circumstances surrounding the Vietnam War. The level of misrepresentation, concealment, and deception in the highest reaches of government, the ambiguous nature of the commitment undertaken by the United States, and the volume of casualties and costs incurred by a war that America found it could not win were all factors in the public's disenchantment with the conflict. But more significantly for the processes of governance, the Vietnam War aroused a deep-set American reaction over the conduct of its politics in having allowed US forces to become so embroiled in an Asian land war. In essence, the war stimulated a fundamentalist response that proceeded on the basis that Vietnam was not simply the consequence of mistaken intelligence or poor decisions by a particular administration but instead indicated a dysfunctional imbalance within the structure of government (Schlesinger 1974: pp. vii–x, 208–419).

The notion of systemic defect that had permitted what was widely interpreted to be an abuse and even a usurpation of power prompted Congress into a series of direct countermeasures to correct the perceived imbalance. In an atmosphere of heightened republican fervour and Constitutional revival, Congress engaged in a quantum leap of foreign policy activism. Its challenge ranged from 'end the war' amendments and war budget cuts to critical appraisals of weapon system projects and military performance indicators; from investigations into the conduct and legitimacy of intelligence agencies to interventions into areas of high strategic and diplomatic value (e.g. nuclear non-proliferation, human rights, regional security); and from the establishment of procedures enabling Congress to acquire information and to underpin its rights of consultation and participation in the formulation of foreign policy (e.g. arms sales, military assistance, executive agreements) to measures challenging the presidency's acquired prerogatives in the field of war powers.

Collectively, this release of political energies represented a radical shift both in attitudes and in the ecology of institutional relationships. The forcible intrusion of Congress into international affairs appeared to run counter to a pattern of precedents that had come to be seen as entrenched and geared to the logic of an ineluctable executive hegemony. Although Congress was more structurally fragmented and atomized in outlook than ever, its indiscipline allowed it to offer the prospect of critical oversight and to create an impression that foreign policy was now as amenable to legislative politics as it had been to bureaucratic politics.

The resurgence of Congress into the foreign policy field has sometimes been referred to as such an emphatic reversal of power away from the executive that it constituted a 'revolution' in Washington politics (Franck and Weisband 1979; Sundquist 1981: 238–314; Ripley, Lindsay, and Farrell 1993). But in the same way that it is important not to exaggerate the diminished status of Congress during the Cold War, so it is equally important that Congress's contemporary role is not overstated (Hinckley 1994). The general position lies in the intermediate area between the two extremes of an 'imperial presidency' and an 'imperial Congress'.

Congress as a mixed model

Throughout the 1980s and 1990s, Congress continued to depend upon the executive for the day-to-day responsibilities of foreign policy, but at the same time it retained its right to intervene on a selective basis, in order to draw attention to an issue, or to reorder a set of priorities, or to challenge a policy direction. President Reagan, for example, expended considerable political capital in long-running disputes with Congress over the issue of economic sanctions on South Africa, and over American military assistance to the contra rebel forces in Nicaragua. President Clinton also struggled with Congress over foreign policy issues (e.g. NATO enlargement and the commitment of US troops to peacekeeping in former Yugoslavia).

Congress has devised new ways to ensure greater consultation and transparency in the conduct of foreign policy (e.g. conditional authorizations, reporting requirements). Further developments in congressional organization mean that legislative initiatives in foreign policy have the effect of often circumventing the traditional channels of influence away from the previous centres of dominance towards new bases of influence. The Senate, for example, with its constitutional powers over treaties and appointments, together with the prestige of its Foreign Relations Committee, has traditionally been central to the legislature's capabilities in foreign policy. Now, in many ways, the emphasis has shifted to the usage of budgetary devices in influencing foreign policy which gives the House of Representatives greater leverage than the Senate in the international politics surrounding the US government's appropriations process.

Congress has continued to benefit from an expanded licence to contest foreign policy with executive departments. Its oversight role has also been enhanced by the contemporary proliferation of interest groups in the area of foreign policy. They may be economic or ethnic in foundation; they may be values-based advocacy organizations; or they may be lobbying consultants operating openly on behalf of foreign governments. Whatever their source, the trend has been that of a deepening synergy between organized interest group activity and Congress's representational role. James Lindsay has observed the dynamic leading to the surge in legislative activism: 'With more groups active on more foreign policy issues, members find themselves under greater pressure to address foreign policy.

At the same time, the rise of interest group activity means that suddenly members stand a good chance of benefiting politically by undertaking detailed legislative work on foreign policy' (Lindsay 1994: 29).

While it is true that congressional involvement in foreign policy issues has increased, it remains the case that its participation is variable across different subfields of foreign policy and that it is the presidency that retains the mainline obligation of coordinating and overseeing America's position in the international sphere. The office possesses enormous reserves of influence in foreign policy not just because of the prodigious resources that are available in the federal bureaucracy but also because of the executive privileges of secrecy, initiative, and rapid response. On this basis, the president can offer to provide a leadership role in a system that arguably requires its force, and denies its legitimacy, in equal measure. Even in a post-Cold War setting, Congress still suffers from chronic problems in matching the presidency as a co-equal partner in foreign policy. It is not simply that congressional attempts to restrict the presidency by legislative means have often led to the White House reinterpreting them as sources of authorization. It

---

 CONTROVERSIES 6.1: Presidential leadership

The emphasis given to presidential leadership in foreign policy is not to deny, or even to diminish, the significance of other actors, agencies, or influences upon the policy process. The literature on the formulation of America's position in international affairs correctly refers to the importance of such generic elements as international, societal, governmental, and bureaucratic factors—as well as to the more specific factors such as particular regional histories and individual crises. Nevertheless, the presidency does retain a close association with foreign policy. It is largely a matter of supply and demand. In many of the most important and conspicuous areas of foreign policy, American society requires a focal point of national unity to give material form to the idea of solidarity and patriotism in the face of possible adversity. For their part, presidents naturally gravitate towards the illustrious roles and political theatre of international affairs where the office's constitutional status as head of state and its capacity for political symbolism receive their maximum expression.

For example, it is presidents who are the chief instigators, and the primary embodiments, of the 'rally-round-the-flag' effect (Mueller 1973; Hetherington and Nelson 2003; Mueller 2005). This refers to those occasions when the American public is mobilized in response to an international crisis involving the United States. It is the president who benefits from these public reactions not just because of being personally involved in an international event but because of the presidency's representational significance as the only nationally elected office in American democracy.

The president's leadership role is discernible in a wide variety of contexts from imposing a particular imprint upon the management of the national security structure to shaping the posture and future planning of America's relationship with the rest of the world; and from giving public expression to the purposes and values of American foreign policy to the issue of whether and when to commit US forces abroad. Just as US strategic positions become defined as presidential 'doctrines' (e.g. Truman Doctrine, Nixon Doctrine, Bush Doctrine), so American military interventions tend to become known as presidential wars. The intimate connection of significant foreign policy issues with the presidency has become part of a high exposure form of governance in which presidents continually seek to enhance their national credentials but also to cultivate a direct relationship with the public in a process that has been likened to a permanent election campaign (Ornstein and Mann 2000).

The shift toward a 'public presidency' (Kernell 2007) of maximum engagement and outreach can relate well to the more traditional role of national leadership. But at the same time, the drive to widen the support base can also lead to an erosion of more institutional foundations to presidential power. This can in turn result in presidents becoming increasingly exposed in terms of personalized blame and accountability. Just as 'rally-round-the-flag' incidents tend only to lead to short-term gains in presidential support, so the decline and fall of many presidential leaderships have been marked by public reactions to what are perceived to be foreign policy failures. In this way, foreign policy can become the access point for presidential critique and the means by which a president's reputation for leadership and even for competence can be undermined.

is that Congress's own determination in following through on its own conditions and pre-requirements has often been less than robust.

The relationship between the Congress and presidency continues to be a changeable mix of conflict and cooperation—of legislative enquiry and assertion coexisting with executive discretion and residual responsibility. Congress cannot be an exact equivalent of the presidency in such a field but what it can do is to reveal the contested nature of foreign policy and to ensure that foreign policy issues are forced onto the political agenda. Arguably, its role has a much wider significance. Congressional oversight can serve to underline the importance not merely of what policy decisions are made and how they are arrived at, but also the values that have informed both the process and outcomes of policy production.

KEY POINTS

❑ Congress represents not only its electorates but also traditional precepts of democracy, the rule of law, due process, and constitutional government.

❑ Although a formal co-equal in status, the legislature faces considerable political and technical difficulties in matching the executive in foreign policy.

❑ Fluctuations occur in the relationships between the two institutions in this litmus test area of governmental responsibilities and political legitimacy.

❑ While global integration has increased congressional interest in more foreign policy sectors, it still suffers from serious disadvantages in the more strategic areas associated intelligence information, executive agreements, and military deployments.

Democratic dilemmas

The practice of making foreign policy generates a profusion of issues relating to the principles and practices of good government. In the United States, the disputes concerning this area of policy formulation are almost invariably reduced to questions of 'democracy'. Just as the process of government decision making is tested to its fullest extent by the exigencies of international demands, so the society's understanding of, and attachment to, the terms and conditions of democracy tend to be measured by its government's conduct in an area that is often deemed to be inherently ambivalent over the requirements of democracy. Given the degree to which the identity and discourse of American politics is permeated by its cultural associations with democratic principles, foreign policy issues often become the source of political disputes that occasionally deteriorate into intensive and highly divisive controversies over the criteria of democratic authenticity. By one means or another, such issues are generally sharpened into critical focus by the way that they can be translated into the normative constituents of legislative–executive relations. The contested claims of the Congress and the presidency can bring many of the 'democratic dilemmas' occasioned by foreign policy to the surface of political exchange. Four of the most contentious dilemmas are examined below.

Democratic diversity/ governmental unity

The *first* source of tension relates to the strain between the open-textured characteristics of democratic diversity and civic equality on the one hand, and the way that foreign policy making seems to gravitate towards a small and enclosed group of individuals with claims to specialist knowledge. Instead of a broad range of opinions from a wide distribution of sources in an extended process of consensus building, many of the most important foreign policy decisions are presented as the outcome of highly advanced decision-making processes. These are operated by a narrow band of sophisticated and highly knowledgeable elites working on the premiss of a basic pre-existing consensus. The presumption of social unity is matched by the presumption on the part of foreign policy specialists that they are able to reveal or to construct foreign policy decisions best suited to the interests of the society.

Because international affairs are thought to be complex in nature, then it can be argued that the subject area requires high levels of in-depth understanding and even inside track knowledge of the pertinent factors. Detachment in such a context is generally depicted as a virtue rather than a vice. Moreover, the conduct of foreign policy is in many respects centred upon the calculation of risks and the need to have an accurate grasp of the dynamics of negotiation which will often be dependent upon the trust existing between limited numbers of principal parties. If international relations can be characterized as an intricate game, then it can be regarded as one which is necessarily confined to a largely exclusive set of players that understand the nuances of its methods and rules. The higher the stakes, or the closer the connection an issue has to the high politics of national security, then the consequence is likely to be one of a proportionately smaller set of elites making their judgements on behalf of the people.

Open government/ operational secrecy

This drive to confine the domestic parameters of decision making in order to enhance the ability to engage effectively with the diverse centres of power in the outside world leads to a *second* problematic area between democracy and foreign policy. The multidimensional and interdependent properties of the latter will often increase the attraction of concealment as a regular *modus operandi* in foreign affairs. While democracy has close associations with open government, transparency, and the attribution of accountability, foreign policy governance is distinguished by a tendency to value the element of discretion to the point of endorsing secrecy not only as a medium of policy making but also as an instrument of policy itself.

The establishment of a range of intelligence agencies has created prodigious problems of democratic oversight in the American system not least because of the conundrum of trying to reconcile open enquiry with a rationale of confidentiality and operational integrity. The resort to secrecy has many dimensions in its own right. Concealment, for example, can be used as an instrumental device against an international adversary, but at the same time it can be deployed to evade scrutiny by elected compatriots representing the public and advancing claims of a 'right to know'. Likewise, covert action undertaken by the United States needs by its very nature to remain undetectable. And yet, its secrecy raises profound questions over the viability, timing, and scope of any form of prior approval by Congress—or rather by a very small and carefully vetted elite of trusted representatives whose discretion can be relied upon (Johnson 1991; Jeffreys-Jones 1998; Johnson 2004).

Rule of law/realpolitik

A *third* dilemma is posed by the unequal relationship between the traditionally law-centred ethos of democracy, and the international realm in which the rule of law has at best a secondary significance. The main formats and principles of democracy are strongly suggestive of a process of law. On behalf of the public, elected representatives make laws that are expected to be explicit and ascertainable in content and for which legislators are accountable to the electorate. In contrast to this kind of formal-legal regime, foreign policy making is often distinguished by its implicit exemptions from the standard operating procedures of domestic governance. Not only does foreign policy have the reputation of being externally driven and, therefore, necessarily susceptible to the considerations of contingency, but it is seen as having to be adaptive to changing conditions and free from any strict attachment to a particular sequence of validation. As a consequence, the linkages of democratic authority, consent, and accountability that inform the domestic policy process are more difficult to trace in the more amorphous yet functionally grounded realm of foreign policy.

Rationality/responsibility

A *fourth* type of friction centres upon the disruptive effect that foreign policy can have upon the collective integrity of what are deemed to be separate constituents of democratic government. Categories that can seem to be more easily inclusive in other fields of public policy can be interpreted quite differently in the foreign policy sector. Democratic themes can become dissociated from what are taken in some quarters to be mainline obligations on the part of government.

One commonly cited disjunction pits rationality against responsibility. Robert Dahl used President Franklin D. Roosevelt's surreptitious methods of implicating the United States in the Allied cause before Pearl Harbor, in order to demonstrate how a president initiated a foreign policy that would not have received majority support in Congress or amongst the public. Key decisions were made not only without prior or subsequent congressional approval, but were designed to evade Congress's express commitment to neutrality. This was because the legislature was not considered to be sufficiently competent to reach an accurate assessment of the severity of the impending international crisis. To Dahl, the issue represented a profound conflict between 'rationality, understood by the President and State Department, and responsibility as seen by Congress' (1964: 180). The former thought that they had superior information and experience that allowed them to grasp the significance of unfolding developments in a way that Congress and the public could not, or would not. As a consequence, the foreign policy experts 'chose to

avoid Congressional control over aspects of foreign policy' (1964: 180). Dahl continues:

> **"**Those who regard political responsibility as the highest obligation of democratic leadership will argue that the President should have based his foreign policies on Congressional and popular consent, even if this had meant the self-destruction of the nation. . . . Those who place the highest value on rationality may argue that the President has a *'higher'* responsibility . . . to pursue foreign policies even if these could not be based on popular consent. (1964: 180–1)**"**

While Dahl looks for ways by which these two approaches can be reconciled and conjoined in a functioning democracy, he along with a great many other observers recognizes that where security is under threat the dominant political disposition has been to privilege 'presidential government' over the reservations of 'congressional democracy'.

Competing interpretations

The problematic issues emanating from the relationship between foreign policy and democracy have led to numerous constructions in the form of solutions to, or rationalizations of, the interaction in terms that are acceptable to a society with self-image as a model democracy. In some accounts, legislative–executive relations can be configured as a process of mutual dependency and joint assistance in which both branches can collaborate in the management of politically contentious aspects of foreign policy. More typically the relationship between the institutions—and through them the relationship conceived between foreign policy and democracy—is characterized as being competitive in nature but at the same time contributing to a positive equilibrium from the negative properties of the exchange. Another perspective views the democratic issue as one that can be addressed through a variation of the notion of a virtuous circle. If the requirements of democracy can be more or less satisfied by the institutional and political inputs into foreign policy, then it can be deemed democratic by reference to its origins. If, on the other hand, the policy outcomes are judged to be democratic in effect, then the methods can be supported on the grounds of the democratic ends that are served by such a process.

For others of a less sanguine outlook, the implied symmetries surrounding political and moral equivalence of inputs and outcomes possess a coherence that is misleading. The constitutional historian Edward S. Corwin famously summarized the purpose and effect of the Constitution's respective grants of power to the Congress and the presidency as amounting to an 'invitation to struggle for the privilege of directing American foreign policy' (1957: 171). In effect, Corwin attempted to apply the self-regulating doctrines of pluralism to governing institutions. Nevertheless, what in many respects is a rationalization of constitutional indeterminacy—as well as an explanation of the subsequent contestation between institutions—leaves a great many questions unanswered concerning the proper or feasible relationship between the two bodies and what they represent.

The imprecision concerning the parameters of each branch in the field of foreign policy can suggest an exchange of comparable clusters of roles and responsibilities. On the other hand, the 'struggle' might pertain to the forced conjunction of unresolved opposites within a single constitutional structure. It is equally plausible to construe that the struggle in reality represents two different approaches to the process of policy making, or even that it constitutes two entirely different policy processes. In similar vein, it can be difficult to determine whether the imperatives of foreign policy reveal dimensions to the Constitution that under normal conditions remain largely concealed; or whether foreign policy operates under what is in essence a different constitution from that at work in domestic affairs; or whether during periods of strain the Constitution is itself held in a state of suspension for the greater good of society and to ensure the long-term future of constitutional democracy.

While these interpretative disputes continue, one factor remains constant: namely the way that foreign policy issues can be the catalyst for intense spasms of political introspection by a society that retains the normative sensitivities and the civic capacity to subject established patterns of convention to rigorous and often disruptive inspection.

KEY POINTS

❑ Foreign policy has highlighted several points of tension which can be seen as democratic dilemmas. These include:
- the influence of specialist elites in the international affairs;
- the issue of secrecy and open government;
- foreign policy exemptions from the rule of law and due process;

- the extent to which notions of urgency and necessity should have priority over popular consent.

❑ Attempts to resolve these dilemmas have led to varied rationales concerning the distribution of power and responsibilities between the Congress and the presidency.

9/11, the war on terror, and new tensions

Notwithstanding the unprecedented nature of the terrorist attacks on the United States in 2001, the overall configuration of the policy processes and disputes surrounding America's reaction revealed a marked resemblance to previous foreign policy crises. In the aftershock of the attacks, American society looked to the White House for a focal point of national consciousness and collective solidarity. President

Bush was adept at using the 'rally around the flag' effect for the purposes of framing the issue of international terrorism and shaping political support for the selected reactions. Governments have long been able to use fear and insecurity to mobilize resources and to accumulate powers on a scale that would be inconceivable without the stimulus of aroused public anxiety. The Bush administration was no exception in making full use of the transformative energies of a crisis. The president was able to secure the accelerated passage through a compliant Congress of the Patriot Act which not only radically reshaped the federal government's structure of internal security, but dramatically increased its powers of surveillance and detention. In effect, the Cold War apparatus of the national security state was deepened and combined with a homeland security society that reached into areas previously protected civil liberties and constitutional limitations (Brzezinski 2005; Arnold 2006; Amnesty International 2007).

Although the initial reaction of the Bush administration had been cautious in respect to overseas retaliation, the White House used the issue of international terrorism to reaffirm its prior scepticism of international institutions and multilateral processes. This set the stage for a new form of international coalition building that would bypass established processes in favour of an ad hoc task force dedicated to a 'war on terror'. Bush's populist disregard for traditional diplomacy and institutional formalities was prompted by the nature of the threats against the United States, by the mercurial character of terrorist organizations like al-Qaeda, and by the calculation that urgent action was required to pre-empt the danger of the USA being attacked through groups covertly acquiring and deploying weapons of mass destruction. To the administration, the special character of the danger required a different kind of warfare and a different set of executive prerogatives to go with it.

The initial military response by America was seen as reasonable by the international community. The intervention in Afghanistan (2001) was widely supported. Because the Taliban regime had given sanctuary within its borders to al-Qaeda groupings, the

United States was easily able to organize a broad-based coalition that included NATO forces. But when President Bush extended his anti-terrorism agenda to include Iraq as part of the 'axis of evil', the level of international support suddenly diminished, leaving an increasingly unilateralist White House reliant upon its option of a 'coalition of the willing' (Bush 2002). The objections lodged by the traditional channels of international governance found very little resonance inside the United States. On the contrary, supported by high public approval ratings, by solid congressional support, and by a generalized fear of further attacks, President Bush was able to establish a public perception that Iraq was not only implicated in the attacks on 9/11 but possessed WMD which would be passed on to Islamic extremists. In a move that was strongly suggestive of the need to compensate for the intelligence failures surrounding 9/11, the White House projected intelligence information and its assessment to the forefront of its adopted causes of war against Iraq. The intelligence-led linkage between Iraq, 9/11, WMD, and terrorism was clearly evident in the congressional resolution authorizing the threat posed by the regime of Saddam Hussein.

After the initial success of the invasion and the removal of Saddam Hussein, United States-led coalition forces became increasingly involved in a costly campaign of establishing security against a backdrop of sectarian violence and social disintegration. As the temporary intervention turned into a long-term occupation and a war of attrition against insurgents, the Bush presidency came under severe pressure. The issue of terrorism, national security, and regional stability, which had boosted his political influence in 2001–3, was transmuted into an instrument of indictment during his second term of office. The claims and assumptions made by the Bush White House in support of both the war and the president's own rights to determine policy were increasingly subjected to critical review in light of what was being interpreted as a policy failure. In the forefront of the critiques was the charge that the Bush administration had politically manipulated the intelligence on Iraq for the purposes of mobilizing public support for the

BOX 6.6: Authorization for use of military force against Iraq Resolution of 2002
(Public Law 107–243, 116 Stat. 1497–1502)

The Joint Resolution, authorizing the use of United States armed forces against Iraq, was passed by the House of Representatives (296–133) on 11 October 2002, and by the Senate (77–23) on 12 October 2002.

- Whereas the attacks on the United States of September 11, 2001, underscored the gravity of the threat posed by the acquisition of weapons of mass destruction by international terrorist organizations;

- Whereas Iraq's demonstrated capability and willingness to use weapons of mass destruction, the risk that the current Iraqi regime will either employ those weapons to launch a surprise attack against the United States or its Armed Forces or provide them to international terrorists who would do so, and the extreme magnitude of harm that would result to the United States and its citizens from such an attack, combine to justify action by the United States to defend itself; . . .

- Whereas the President and Congress are determined to continue to take all appropriate actions against international terrorists and terrorist organizations, including those nations, organizations, or persons who planned, authorized, committed, or aided the terrorist attacks that occurred on September 11, 2001, or harbored such persons or organizations;

- Whereas the President has authority under the Constitution to take action in order to deter and prevent acts of international terrorism against the United States, as Congress recognized in the joint

resolution on Authorization for Use of Military Force (Public Law 107–40); and

- Whereas it is in the national security interests of the United States to restore international peace and security to the Persian Gulf region: Now, therefore, be it *Resolved by the Senate and House of Representatives of the United States of America in Congress assembled,* . . .

Sec. 2. Support for United States diplomatic efforts.

The Congress of the United States supports the efforts by the President to (1) strictly enforce through the United Nations Security Council all relevant Security Council resolutions regarding Iraq and encourages him in those efforts; and (2) obtain prompt and decisive action by the Security Council to ensure that Iraq abandons its strategy of delay, evasion and noncompliance and promptly and strictly complies with all relevant Security Council resolutions regarding Iraq.

Sec. 3. Authorization for use of United States armed forces.

(a) AUTHORIZATION
—The President is authorized to use the Armed Forces of the United States as he determines to be necessary and appropriate in order to (1) defend the national security of the United States against the continuing threat posed by Iraq; and (2) enforce all relevant United Nations Security Council resolutions regarding Iraq.

war. In misrepresenting intelligence materials over WMD, the president was accused not only of misrepresenting the causes of war but of misappropriating the legal processes relating to decisions over entering into a state of war.

The White House had previously aroused anxieties over the magnitude of its constitutional assertions. For example, it claimed a unilateral power to initiate wars without any congressional approval, and it assumed it could interpret, terminate, or suspend international treaties at its discretion (Yoo 2005). The

protracted nature of the Iraq War allowed these concerns to resurface as part of a more general reaction against the style of the Bush presidency. Under Bush's leadership, the administration had authorized the detention of prisoners without trial at Guantánamo; placed 'illegal combatants' beyond the scope of the Geneva Conventions; claimed that Congress could not restrict the president's authority in instituting harsher methods of interrogation; and insisted that the inherent powers of the presidency permitted the National Security Agency to breach the provisions of the Foreign Intelligence Surveillance Act (1978) and to monitor the phone call records of millions of Americans. All these positions came under critical review not least by the Supreme Court, which broke its customary reticence over considering foreign policy issues in *Hamdan* v. *Rumsfeld* (2006). In the case, the Court declared that the administration's plan to try terrorist suspects at Guantánamo by military commissions denied them not only the protections of the Geneva Conventions but the rights of due process that would be afforded by a court martial or a civilian tribunal.

Prior to the Iraq action, Congress had been complicit in what was retrospectively seen as a rush to war. Louis Fisher concluded that in authorizing military action by a measure comparable to the notorious Gulf of Tonkin Resolution, the legislature had failed in its constitutional duty: 'instead of acting as the people's representatives and preserving the republican form of government, they gave the president unchecked power' (Fisher 2003: 405). But following the 2006 mid-term elections when the Democrats regained control

of the House and Senate, Congress became much more vocal in its assaults upon the presidency in the key area of war powers. As institutional and political interest in the venerable dogmas of the separation of powers revived, so public scepticism of the war and the Bush presidency intensified. Personal culpability for individual judgements and choices was directed to the White House but, in line with American traditions of political accountability, responsibility was not confined to President Bush. The issue of causality was characteristically widened into that of a systemic failure of the decision-making structure—stretching from bureaucratic disarray and confused agendas to intelligence mismanagement and the abandonment of checks by alternative centres of political and media opinion (Ricks 2006; Gordon 2007). These in turn led to calls not for new frameworks of governance but for a return to the fundamentals of a balanced constitution. However, as we have seen, the comforting prospect of constitutional certainty is a chimera, for the only precision afforded by its provisions remains that of strategic ambiguity.

KEY POINTS

- ❏ Terrorist attacks, and further threats of international terrorism, prompt President Bush into new kinds of warfare and new claims of inherent executive powers.
- ❏ Sweeping powers of surveillance, arrest, detention, and interrogation raise issues over the relationship of security to civil liberties.

- ❏ The use or misuse of intelligence in mobilizing support for the war on terror, combined with the outcome of the 2006 mid-term elections, revive interest in the constitutional balance between the presidency and the Congress.

Conclusion

This chapter has examined the various tensions that exist between a system founded upon a rules-based conception of limited powers, and the requirements of a policy sector that is externally driven, highly reactive, and expansionary in its effect upon power accumulation. While the foreign policy process can often be presented as the height of organizational modernity with its emphasis upon sophisticated

information-processing and decision-making systems, it also retains a capacity for reverting into heated debates over the demarcation and distribution of authority within the government (Henkin 1990). Such principles as representation, consent, accountability, transparency, legal propriety, and the 'right to know' amount to criteria of governance that generally have to be at least implicitly acknowledged by decision makers. But occasionally, they assume a far greater significance and even exert a controlling influence upon the policy process. In this way foreign policy outputs can point up the tensions between notions of functional responsiveness and institutional realism on the one hand, and the continued importance of civic norms and due process on the other. A foreign policy failure in the United States, therefore, is still largely conceived as a systemic failure on the part of the participants to adhere to traditional principles of governance. According to the old maxim, the Constitution is an invitation for the president and the Congress to struggle for the control of foreign policy. As this section has attempted to show, that struggle is as much about the dispute over what role a foreign policy has in American government.

? Questions

1. What role did interstate relations play in the origins and scope of the US Constitution?
2. What is the significance of the landmark case of *United States* v. *Curtiss-Wright Export Corporation*?
3. How can Congress influence the formulation of foreign policy?
4. Describe and evaluate the significance of presidential leadership in the area of foreign policy.
5. What is meant by the term 'rallying round the flag' and how important is it to presidential leadership in times of crisis?
6. Examine the challenges to democratic principles posed by the requirements of foreign policy.
7. What conclusions do you draw from the wording of the Gulf of Tonkin Resolution (1964) and the Authorization for Use of Military Force against Iraq Resolution (2002)?
8. Is secrecy a necessary and indispensable element of effective policy making? What problems does it pose for the processes of accountability?
9. Is it accurate to describe the foreign policy process in the United States as a struggle between Congress and the presidency?
10. Examine the political and constitutional difficulties of ending a war.

» Further Reading

Wittkopf, E. R., Kegley, C. W., and Scott, J. M. (2002), *American Foreign Policy*, 6th edn. (Belmont, Calif.: Wadsworth).

An established text divided into analytical sections that examine the external, societal, and governmental sources of American foreign policy. Its usage of historical and contemporary sources, combined with its recognition of the importance of American principles, values, and interests, provides a highly accessible overview of the policy-making process.

Fisher, L. (2004), *Presidential War Power*, 2nd edn. (Lawrence, Kan.: University Press of Kansas).

A leading congressional scholar navigates his readers through the complex and contentious debates over the allocation of war powers. By locating the disputes in their historical, political, and constitutional contexts, Fisher is able to reach a critical appreciation of the trend lines in presidential war making and the need for an institutional balance to be restored.

Inderfurth, K. F., and Johnson, L. (eds.) (2004), *Fateful Decisions: Inside the National Security Council* (New York: Oxford University Press).

Karl Inderfurth and Loch Johnson guide the reader through the structures and processes of the National Security Council. Their team give an array of valuable insights into the origins, workings, strengths, and weaknesses of the NSC. The book not only assesses the contribution of the NSC over the period 1947 to 2003, but offers reform proposals to improve the Council's performance.

Mann, T. E., and Ornstein, N. J. (2006), *The Broken Branch: How Congress is Failing America and How to Get it Back on Track* (New York: Oxford University Press).

A study that is illustrative of the critiques levelled at Congress and of the need for reform. It argues that the recent developments of high partisanship and procedural arbitrariness have led it to become increasingly dysfunctional.

Cronin, T. E., and Genovese, M. A. (2003), *The Paradoxes of the American Presidency*, 2nd edn. (New York: Oxford University Press).

By exploring the presidency through the analytical device of paradoxes, Cronin and Genovese are able convey the way that the office attracts increased expectations at the same time as the system restricts the resources and power that would enable the presidency to fulfil the promises of effective governance.

 Visit the Online Resource Centre that accompanies this book for web links to accompany each chapter, and a range of other resources: www.oxfordtextbooks.co.uk/orc/cox_stokes/

7 Military power and US foreign policy

Beth A. Fischer

Chapter contents

Introduction

This chapter considers the role that military power has played in the conduct of US foreign policy since the end of the Second World War. It discusses key strategies governing the use of military power, such as containment, deterrence, the Powell Doctrine, and pre-emption. It also considers the various ways in which military power has been used, and its effectiveness in attaining political objectives.

How has military power been reconceptualized over time in the United States? For what purposes has the United States deployed its military? How effective is military power in achieving political objectives? This chapter will consider the rise and use of American military power since 1945. It will also consider important debates regarding containment, deterrence, pre-emption, and the limits of military power.

Rise of American military power, 1945 – 91: containment and deterrence

The United States emerged from the Second World War as a military great power. It had the largest navy in the world, and, more importantly, it was the only state to have the atomic bomb. This military capability grew throughout the Cold War. By the time the Soviet Union collapsed in 1991 the United States' military power was unrivalled. Two concepts governed US military power and strategy throughout the Cold War: containment and deterrence.

The military implications of containment

Containment was the foundation of American foreign policy throughout the Cold War. Each administration had its own version of containment, but the ultimate goal remained the same: to contain the spread of Soviet communism. Containment sought to prevent Soviet expansionism.

During the 1950s the United States sought global containment. That is, it sought to aid all those resisting communism throughout the world. All countries were considered vital to American interests in the belief that if one country fell to communism, its neighbours would be destabilized and fall to communism as well. This analogy is known as the 'domino theory'.

These perspectives led to American military involvement in Korea between 1950 and 1953. In this case the United States went to war so as to prevent communist North Korea from controlling democratic South Korea. American policy makers feared that if North Korea could gain control of the South, it would lead to further communist expansion throughout Asia. Although the Korean War ended in 1953, US troops remain posted along the border between North and South.

The desire to contain the spread of communism in Asia led to another war, this time in Vietnam. Although the political objective was the same, the Vietnam War was a far different type of conflict. The Korean War had been a traditional war fought between massive, organized armies with relatively clear front lines. The Vietnam War was less traditional: the front lines were often unclear, battles often took place in muddy jungles, and most importantly, Vietnamese civilians engaged in guerrilla-style attacks on US forces. The US military was ill prepared to counter this kind of insurgency. It was structured, trained, and equipped to fight a large-scale conventional war. The United States originally sought to fight a 'limited war'. However, throughout the late 1960s the White House incrementally increased the amount of US troops in Vietnam. By late 1968 there were over half a million US troops in the region and Washington was spending $35 billion per year on the conflict.

Nonetheless, the United States was unable to win the war. By the time a ceasefire was signed in January 1973 58,000 US soldiers had been killed, along with countless Vietnamese. American involvement truly ended in April 1975 when Saigon fell to the North Vietnamese and all remaining Americans were evacuated. Despite the fact that the United States was a military superpower, it had suffered a humiliating defeat.

The Vietnam War was both unpopular and devastating for Americans. It led to an era in which Americans lost faith in their political and military leaders. The Vietnam War had several important implications for the way in which military power was conceptualized in the United States.

For one thing, the loss in Vietnam led Americans to reject containment on a global scale. Many believed that the United States had overextended itself: the United States did not have the resources to protect all peoples fighting communism. President Nixon reflected these views in 1970 when he declared that the United States would continue to provide military and economic assistance to friends, but those nations must be responsible for their own security. Nixon implicitly acknowledged that there were limits to American military power and what it could achieve. This decision to 'scale back' containment became known as the Nixon Doctrine.

Secondly, the defeat in Vietnam has led to what some call a 'Vietnam Syndrome'. In this view Americans have been so haunted by the loss that they have sought to avoid involvement in other wars at almost all costs. Thus, although American military power has been growing for the past thirty years, there has also been a strong reluctance to actually use this power. The Vietnam Syndrome is wrapped in both fact and myth. While Americans continue to be scarred from Vietnam, the USA has, in fact, repeatedly deployed its military power since 1975, as will be discussed.

The experience in Vietnam has also led US military leaders to revamp military strategies. Some contend that the attempt to fight a 'limited war' in Vietnam contributed significantly to the United States' defeat. In this view the gradual increase in troop deployments did not allow the United States to make maximum use of its military capabilities. Consequently, in future wars the United States must deliver massive force right from the outset. This perspective is often called the Powell Doctrine, after General Colin Powell, who served as chairman of the Joint Chiefs of Staff for

the first President Bush, and as Secretary of State for the second President Bush. General Powell had spent a career in the military, including two tours of duty in Vietnam. In his view, in order to address the mistakes of Vietnam future military deployments must meet three criteria: the aim of the mission and the rules of engagement must be clear, the United States must send overwhelming force right from the outset, and there must be a clear exit strategy so as to avoid mission creep. Powell also emphasized the need for strong public support for such operations (Powell 1992–3).

The military implications of deterrence

At the conclusion of the Second World War the United States was the only state with an atomic weapon. Although the Soviet Union had a larger conventional army, American leaders believed the US monopoly on nuclear weapons was the 'great equalizer'. That is, the destructive capacity of nuclear weapons made up for the relative weakness in conventional (non-nuclear) military power.

In August 1949 the Soviet Union tested an atomic weapon of its own. This event profoundly changed the nature of the Cold War. The USA responded to the Soviet test with a policy review, called NSC-68. This document claimed the United States was now in a dangerously inferior position. Consequently, it needed to build up its own military strength so that it surpassed that of the Soviet Union. The United States needed to achieve and maintain a position of military superiority. NSC-68 led to a dramatic increase in US defence spending, as well as to a global network of US military bases and alliances. The Cold War was no longer simply an ideological and political contest—it now entailed an arms race of epic proportions.

The United States also adopted a strategy of deterrence. Deterrence entails dissuading an enemy from attacking by convincing him that the costs of an attack would far outweigh any benefits. During the Cold War the United States deterred the Soviets from launching a nuclear attack by threatening to respond in kind. That is, if the Soviet Union were to launch a nuclear strike against the USA or its allies, the United

States would respond with a retaliatory nuclear attack on the Soviet Union. Such retaliation would bring unacceptable damage to the USSR. In effect, a nuclear attack on the USA would have been suicidal for the Soviets. This strategic doctrine was called mutual assured destruction, or MAD.

MAD generated a *nuclear* arms race. In order to effectively deter the Soviet Union from launching a nuclear attack, the USA needed to be able to maintain a nuclear arsenal that was large enough to withstand the initial attack, with enough weapons left over for a devastating retaliatory strike. But how many nuclear weapons were enough? How many weapons could a Soviet attack be expected to destroy? Because the destructive effects of a nuclear attack could only be speculated, each side could never be certain that it had enough weapons for a retaliatory strike. The logic of MAD created an impetus to continually increase the size and destructive capability of each arsenal. Thus, the Soviet and American arsenals grew into the tens of thousands not because strategic planners believed this many weapons were necessary in order to subdue the enemy, but rather, because they assumed a significant portion of the arsenal would be destroyed during a first strike. The goal was to have enough nuclear weapons standing after the first strike so as to be able to launch a devastating retaliatory strike (see Figure 7.1).

Neither the Soviet Union nor the United States has ever had a comprehensive defensive system to protect itself against a nuclear attack, although the Soviet Union has a limited defensive system around Moscow.

Throughout the Cold War, the logic of MAD dictated that defensive systems were destabilizing and, therefore, to be avoided. For example, imagine that the USSR built a defensive system that protected Soviet territory against a nuclear attack. Moscow would then be able to launch a first strike against the USA without fear of a reprisal. According to the logic of MAD, there would be nothing to deter the Soviets from initiating a nuclear war. Consequently, in 1972 both the United States and the Soviet Union signed the Anti-Ballistic Missile (ABM) Treaty which outlawed the construction of new systems designed to defend against nuclear attack. In essence, the superpowers agreed that mutual vulnerability would lead to mutual security.

Owing to this nuclear stand-off, superpower conflicts were fought primarily through proxies in the third world. Throughout the Cold War the superpowers supported and assisted adversaries throughout Asia, Africa, Latin America, and the Middle East. Indeed, the most blood was spilled not in Europe or North America, but in Latin America.

Questioning deterrence and ending the arms race

For much of the Cold War many experts believed that mutual assured destruction had prevented the superpowers from engaging in direct conflict with one another. However, during the 1980s there was a significant change in both American and Soviet

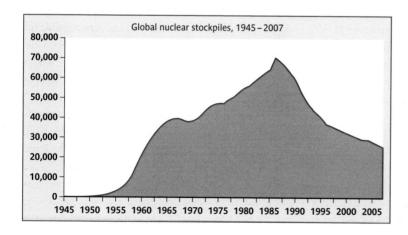

Fig. 7.1 Global nuclear stockpiles, 1945–2007

Source: www.nukestrat.com/graphics/worldnukeshist.jpg

thinking. President Ronald Reagan and Soviet leader Mikhail Gorbachev both abhorred MAD. Each leader believed that the reliance on mutual destruction was not only nonsensical, but irresponsible. Moreover, Reagan and Gorbachev were both concerned about the possibility of a nuclear accident. Both leaders sought to shift away from nuclear deterrence, and to eliminate nuclear weapons.

In 1987 Reagan and Gorbachev signed the landmark Intermediate Nuclear Forces (INF) Treaty. This treaty stipulated that the superpowers would eliminate intermediate-range nuclear missiles from Europe. The treaty was significant because it was the first time the superpowers agreed to actually eliminate nuclear weapons. All previous arms agreements had simply limited the rate at which nuclear arsenals could grow.

By 1990 the superpowers were making substantial progress in dismantling the arms race that had been a cornerstone of the Cold War. In June 1990 Washington and Moscow pledged to destroy a significant percentage of their chemical arsenals by 2002, as well as to accelerate discussions on reductions in strategic nuclear weapons and conventional weapons. In November the USA and its NATO allies and the USSR and its Warsaw Pact allies concluded the Conventional Armed Forces in Europe (CFE) Treaty, which substantially reduced the amount of conventional forces in Europe. In the summer of 1991 the USA and the USSR also signed the Strategic Arms Reduction Treaty, or START. This treaty was the first to reduce the superpowers' long-range nuclear arsenals. In short, by the time the Soviet Union collapsed in December 1991 the superpower arms race had already become defunct.

> ### KEY POINTS
>
> - During the 1950s the United States sought to stop the spread of communism throughout the world. This led to wars in Korea and Vietnam.
> - The loss in Vietnam led the USA to question its military commitments abroad and revamp military strategy.
> - Mutual assured destruction (MAD) generated a nuclear arms race, and led the superpowers to forgo defensive systems.
> - During the late 1980s the USA and the USSR shifted away from deterrence and began to dismantle the arms race.

The post-Cold War era: confronting fundamental questions

During the Cold War the United States had a clearly defined enemy and established alliance systems. When the USSR collapsed in December 1991 US foreign policy lost its focal point. Washington had to confront fundamental questions about its role in the world and its military power.

For what purpose should the US military be deployed?

For what purpose should US military forces be sent abroad, and under what conditions? Throughout the Cold War the United States had focused almost exclusively on the threat of Soviet expansionism. After the USSR collapsed, American leaders sought to envision the threats, challenges, and responsibilities of the post-Cold War world. Establishing priorities was difficult, particularly for a generation of military and political leaders who had gained their expertise during the Cold War.

As indicated in Box 7.1, the US deployed its military repeatedly during the post-Cold War era, for a variety of purposes. Between 1990 and 2001 the United States deployed military forces abroad twenty-one times. These deployments entailed anywhere from a few military advisers to over a half million troops. Nine of these twenty-one deployments entailed

BOX 7.1: US military deployments, 1990–2001

Date	Location	Objective
1990	Liberia	Assist evacuation of US embassy in Monrovia
1990–1	Saudi Arabia/Iraq	Operation Desert Storm: Eject Iraqi forces from Kuwait. Limited US forces deployed to northern Iraq in May 1991 to provide emergency humanitarian relief to Iraqi Kurds.
1992	Kuwait/Iraq	US forces monitor Iraq–Kuwait border and no-fly zones in southern Iraq. US and British air forces engage in sporadic, limited battles in the no-fly zones through 2003.
1992–4	Somalia	Operation Restore Hope, which began as a US-led UN humanitarian mission. After May 1993 US forces continued to participate in the successor UN operation, UNOSOM, which sought political reconciliation in that country. This mission entailed limited military action to quell local violence.
1993–2001	Bosnia	US participation in NATO air actions to enforce UN efforts to stop Bosnian Serb violence against Muslims in the region. By the end of 1995 US troop deployments were increased as part of a NATO mission to enforce the Dayton Peace Accords. US participation gradually reduced.
1994	Rwanda/Burundi	Evacuate US citizens and other third parties. Assist in humanitarian aid.
1994	Haiti	Restore democratically elected leader to power. Began as naval embargo, but evolved to entail troop deployments so as to restore and maintain stability.
1996	Liberia	Evacuate US citizens and other foreign personnel.
1996	Central African Rep.	Evacuate US citizens.
1997, 1998	Albania	Evacuate US citizens and enhance security at US embassy.
1997	Congo & Gabon	Evacuate US citizens.
1997, 2000	Sierra Leone	Evacuate US citizens.
1997	Cambodia	Possible evacuation of US citizens.
1998	Guinea-Bissau	Evacuate US citizens and other foreigners.
1998	Kenya & Tanzania	Disaster assistance and security personnel deployed to US embassies bombed by al-Qaeda.
1998	Afghanistan and Sudan	Airstrikes against suspected al-Qaeda sites in response to bombings of US embassies in Kenya and Tanzania.
1998	Iraq	Operation Desert Fox. Bombing campaign (with the UK) against military targets and industrial facilities suspected of producing WMD. No-fly zones enforced more strictly.
1999	Yugoslavia/Albania/ Kosovo	NATO air campaign to stop ethnic cleansing of Albanian Muslims.

(continued)

BOX 7.1: *(continued)*

Date	Location	Objective
1999	East Timor	Limited support for UN stability force.
2000	Yemen	Disaster response assistance after terrorist.
2001	Various regions	In response to 11 September terrorist attacks forces deployed to a number of nations in the Central and Pacific Command areas of operations.

evacuating American citizens from unstable countries. Five more—Somalia, Haiti, Bosnia, East Timor, and the latter part of the Kosovo mission—entailed operations intended to foster political stability. (However, the Somalia operation began as a humanitarian mission.) In only one instance during this period did the United States engage in a major conventional war—the Persian Gulf War.

The Persian Gulf War, 1990–1, and its aftermath

In August 1990 Iraq invaded Kuwait. The Iraqi leader, Saddam Hussein, calculated that the United States would condemn the invasion, but that Washington would take no action. He reasoned that the Vietnam Syndrome still prevailed in the USA. That is, he believed that after the United States' humiliating loss in Vietnam, Americans would not have the stomach to become involved in another foreign war.

Saddam Hussein calculated wrongly. President George H. W. Bush did not interpret the invasion in terms of the Vietnam War. Rather, he and British Prime Minister Margaret Thatcher considered the invasion to be akin to Hitler's invasion of Poland at the outset of the Second World War. While the lesson of Vietnam may have been to avoid foreign military involvement, the lesson from the Second World War was that aggression must be stopped at the outset. Consequently, President Bush and Prime Minister Thatcher were determined to eject Iraq from Kuwait. Bush's resolve grew when it appeared that Saddam Hussein intended to invade Saudi Arabia as

well. If allowed to gain control of Saudi Arabia's oil fields, Saddam would control nearly 40 per cent of the world's oil supplies, thus allowing him to dictate world oil prices.

President Bush considered Saddam's actions the first test of the 'New World Order', and advocated a multilateral solution that centred on the United Nations. First, the White House worked through the UN to pass a series of resolutions calling on Iraq to withdraw from Kuwait, and placing economic sanctions on Baghdad until it did so. The administration also built an alliance of over thirty states to place further pressure on Iraq. Finally, President Bush deployed military forces to Saudi Arabia so as to deter Saddam from invading that country.

When Saddam Hussein failed to withdraw his forces from Kuwait by the UN deadline of January 1991, the United States and its allies launched Operation Desert Storm. This operation was conducted in accordance with the principles of the Powell Doctrine. First, there was a clear military objective: the coalition was to eject Iraqi forces from Kuwait. Second, the United States employed overwhelming force. The USA sent half a million troops to the region—approximately the same amount of troops that had been deployed at the peak of the Vietnam War. Finally, there was a clear exit strategy: US and coalition forces would withdraw once Iraqi forces had left Kuwait.

The Persian Gulf War lasted forty-two days and was a clear military victory for the USA and its allies. It began with a high-tech bombing campaign, and ended 100 hours into a ground war. It was a large-scale conventional war for which the United States military was well structured, equipped, and trained. However, over

MAJOR DEBATES AND THEIR IMPACT 7.1: What role for nuclear weapons?

It is time—well past time, in my view—for the United States to cease its Cold War-style reliance on nuclear weapons as a foreign policy tool. . . . I would characterize current US nuclear weapons policy as immoral, illegal, militarily unnecessary, and dreadfully dangerous. The risk of an accidental or inadvertent nuclear launch is unacceptably high. . . . How destructive are these weapons? The average US warhead has a destructive power 20 times that of the Hiroshima bomb. Of the 8,000 active or operational US warheads, 2,000 are on hair-trigger alert, ready to be launched on 15 minutes' warning. . . . What is shocking is that today, more than a decade after the end of the Cold War, the basic US nuclear policy is unchanged. It has not adapted to the collapse of the Soviet Union. . . . At minimum, we should remove all strategic nuclear weapons from 'hair trigger' alert. . . . That simple change would greatly reduce the risk of an accidental nuclear launch. It would also signal to other states that the United States is taking steps to end its reliance on nuclear weapons. . . . I have worked on issues relating to US and NATO nuclear strategy and war plans for more than 40 years. During that time I have never seen a piece of paper that outlined a plan for the United States or NATO to initiate the use of nuclear weapons with any benefit for the United States or NATO. . . . To launch weapons against a nuclear-equipped opponent would be suicidal. To do so against a nonnuclear enemy would be militarily unnecessary, morally repugnant, and politically indefensible.

(McNamara 2005; Robert S. McNamara was US Secretary of Defense 1961–8 and president of the World Bank 1968–81)

[O]ver the last decade the nature of the nuclear threat has fundamentally changed, from large-scale attack to the use of one or a few nuclear devices by a rogue nation or subnational group against the United States or one of its allies. Countering the proliferation of nuclear weapons . . . has thus become as high a priority as deterring major nuclear attacks. . . . [W]ith its overwhelming conventional military advantage, the United States does not need nuclear weapons for either war fighting or for deterring conventional war. It should therefore scale back its nuclear activity significantly. . . . The United States should not, however, abandon effective nuclear forces, and it should even leave open the possibility of certain limited kinds of nuclear tests. . . . [N]uclear weapons continue to play a key role in US security. After all, there is no guarantee that geopolitical circumstances will not change dramatically, and the emergence of a more militant China or Russia's return to totalitarianism might compel the United States to place greater reliance on its nuclear forces. Moreover, Washington's commanding nuclear posture still works to limit the nuclear ambitions of other countries. US allies, most notably Germany and Japan, have forsworn establishing their own nuclear programs in exchange for protection under the US security umbrella. . . . Ultimately, Washington must strike a balance between conflicting goals: maintaining a modern nuclear weapons posture, on the one hand, and curbing the spread of nuclear weapons, on the other.

(Deutch 2005; John Deutch was Deputy Secretary of Defense, chairman of the Nuclear Weapons Council, and director of Central Intelligence during the Clinton administration. He was also an Undersecretary of Energy during the Carter administration)

time Americans increasingly questioned whether the Persian Gulf War was a political victory. Although the coalition forces had succeeded in ejecting Iraqi forces from Kuwait, Saddam Hussein remained in power after the ceasefire. Indeed, he remained in power far longer than did President Bush or Prime Minister Thatcher. Bush administration officials repeatedly pointed out that the UN resolutions only called for Iraqi forces to be ejected from Kuwait. They argued that if the United States had sought to remove Saddam Hussein from power, such actions would have violated the UN resolutions and international law, and would have caused the USA to lose the support of most of its coalition partners. However, the president's characterization of Saddam Hussein as an evil dictator had raised expectations that he would be removed from power.

After the war concluded the United States adopted a policy of containment toward Iraq. Small contingents of US forces remained stationed in the region so as to deter the Iraqi leader from further invasions. Two 'no-fly' zones were also established in the northern and southern sections of the country so as to prohibit Iraqi forces from aerial attacks on the Kurds and Shi'ites living in these regions. American and British air forces monitored these no-fly zones, which covered 40 per cent of the country. The United Nations and member states placed sanctions on Iraq, and UN inspectors were deployed in an attempt to prohibit Iraq from developing weapons of mass destruction. However, in October 1998 Saddam Hussein ejected these inspectors. This prompted the USA and Britain to launch Operation Desert Fox. This four-day mission consisted of 650 sorties against security targets in Iraq, which significantly undermined Iraqi military capability. Afterward, US and British forces began to enforce the no-fly zones more strictly, which led to sporadic skirmishes. In addition, the Clinton administration sought to modify the sanctions regime so as to place more pressure on Saddam, yet limit the negative effects on the Iraqi people. Moreover, Congress passed, and President Clinton signed, a bill calling for regime change in Iraq.

What role for nuclear weapons?

In the post-Cold War world are nuclear weapons still useful?

In the 1990s some American military leaders and others began publicly calling for the elimination of nuclear weapons. These so-called nuclear abolitionists contend that the USA should eliminate its nuclear arsenal for numerous reasons. For one thing, the United States has such overwhelming conventional military power that the introduction of nuclear weapons into any conflict is not militarily necessary. Moreover, the implicit threat that the United States could introduce nuclear weapons during a conventional conflict is simply not credible. The use of nuclear weapons would be morally repugnant, thereby eliminating them as a serious policy option. Third, maintaining such a large nuclear arsenal raises the probability of a catastrophic nuclear accident. Furthermore, nuclear weapons are expensive to develop, maintain, and store safely. Since they have little military utility in the first place, it makes little sense to continue to fund them, abolitionists argue.

Others disagree, however, and believe that the United States must continue to retain a nuclear weapons capability. Few have called for a *build-up* of American nuclear arsenals since the ending of the Cold War, but many contend that it is necessary to retain at least a more limited arsenal. For one thing, they argue, nuclear weapons continue to be necessary in order to deter attacks against the United States. In addition, the knowledge of how to make nuclear weapons cannot be destroyed. Thus, it is likely that there will be more nuclear states—and possibly, nuclear enemies—in the future. The United States would be dangerously vulnerable should it completely destroy its arsenal.

The administration of President George W. Bush has agreed with this latter perspective. In the administration's view, it is essential for the USA to retain a nuclear capability, although a significantly smaller capability is sufficient. Towards this end Bush and Russian President Vladimir Putin signed a treaty in May 2002 to reduce nuclear weapons down to a level of 1,700–2,200 warheads each by December 2012. This agreement, known as the Moscow Treaty, or the Treaty on Strategic Offensive Reductions (SORT), will reduce stockpiles to their lowest total since the 1950s.

KEY POINTS

❑ During the post-Cold War era the USA deployed its military abroad repeatedly, and for a variety of purposes.

❑ The Persian Gulf War was a conventional war conducted according to the principles of the Powell Doctrine. It was a clear military victory, although some have questioned whether it was a political victory.

❑ Some believe nuclear weapons continue to be a useful deterrent, while others maintain they should be abolished.

The administration of George W. Bush: terrorism and pre-emption

President George W. Bush came to office during the post-Cold War era, when the United States was still trying to figure out its national security policy for the new international system. During the 2000 presidential campaign Bush's foreign affairs adviser, Condoleezza Rice, outlined the candidate's approach to national

> **KEY QUOTES 7.1:** Condoleezza Rice

The United States has found it exceedingly difficult to define its 'national interest' in the absence of Soviet power. . . . In a democracy as pluralistic as ours, the absence of an articulated 'national interest' either produces fertile ground for those wishing to withdraw from the world or creates a vacuum to be filled by parochial groups and transitory pressures. . . .

Power matters, both the exercise of power by the United States and the ability of others to exercise it. Yet many in the United States are (and always have been) uncomfortable with the notions of power politics, great powers, and power balances. . . . The reality is that a few big powers can radically affect international peace, stability, and prosperity. . . . America's military power must be secure because the United States is the only guarantor of global peace and stability. . . .

[T]he next president will be confronted with a prolonged job of repair[ing US military power.] Military readiness will have to take center stage. . . . [T]he next president should refocus the Pentagon's priorities on building the military of the 21st century

rather than continuing to build on the structure of the Cold War. US technological advantages should be leveraged to build forces that are lighter and more lethal, more mobile and agile, and capable of firing accurately from long distances. In order to do this, Washington must reallocate resources, perhaps in some cases skipping a generation of technology to make leaps rather than incremental improvements in its forces.

The president must remember that the military is a special instrument. It is lethal, and it is meant to be. It is not a civilian police force. It is not a political referee. And it is most certainly not designed to build a civilian society.

(Rice 2000; these extracts outlined what Bush's foreign policy would be should he win the 2000 presidential election. Condoleezza Rice was the National Security Adviser during President George W. Bush's first term in office, and the Secretary of State during his second term)

security in an article in *Foreign Affairs* (see Key quotes 7.1). Rice called for the United States to place greater emphasis on its national interest, and emphasized the need for overwhelming military strength.

Once in office, the Bush administration's national security policy focused primarily on transforming the military and national missile defence.

Transforming the military

President Bush's Secretary of Defense, Donald Rumsfeld, believed the US military had not adequately adapted to the post-Cold War world, and wanted to transform the military into a more nimble, accurate, high-tech force. This so-called revolution in military affairs (RMA) certainly did not begin with the Bush administration.[1] Since the Persian Gulf War, the US military had been deploying weapons systems that made increasing use of robotics, electronics, and information technologies. However, Rumsfeld believed transformation should be a priority. Under

his guidance, military planning shifted from a focus on conventional threats to the need to address 'asymmetrical threats' such as terrorism, cyberattacks, and biological and chemical attacks. The goal was to develop new technologies so as to be able to counter these threats with agility.

National Missile Defence (NMD)

The Bush administration came to office in 2001 committed to developing and deploying a national missile defence system. It maintained that the strategic environment had so changed since the Cold War that defences were now imperative. The primary threat to American security was no longer a large-scale nuclear attack from the USSR, but a more limited attack from a terrorist group or 'rogue state'. Such an attack might be accidental or unauthorized, and would entail tens of warheads rather than thousands.

The Bush administration's NMD system entails radar stations and approximately 100 interceptor missiles based primarily in Alaska and California. (It also uses radar stations in England and Greenland.) Simply put, once radar stations detected an incoming missile, the USA would launch a ground-based interceptor that would home in on the warhead and ram into it at 20,000 miles per hour. The system is intended to intercept dozens of warheads.

The Bush administration has consulted with Poland, the Czech Republic, and Britain regarding the possibility of setting up a European base for the system similar to the one in Alaska (Cowell 2007: A4). Theoretically, a European site would intercept missiles launched from North Africa or the Middle East. Future plans call for more radar stations and interceptors both within the USA and abroad so as to be able to deploy countermeasures that could intercept not only more missiles, but a more sophisticated attack.

The Bush administration's NMD programme has been very controversial, both within the USA and abroad. For one thing, the Bush administration unilaterally withdrew from the ABM Treaty in order to build the system. Critics charge this was a dangerous display of hubris and needlessly antagonized Russia. Supporters counter that the administration's first choice was to modify the treaty, and that it only withdrew once Russian leader Vladimir Putin refused such modifications.

Critics also charge that the Bush administration's NMD system seeks to address threats that are not credible. The White House claims to be defending against rogue states with limited arsenals, such as North Korea, but critics charge that such states do not have the capability, or the will, to launch an attack on the USA.

Third, critics argue that the technology behind NMD is unproven. Many of the early tests of the technology failed, and those tests that were successful were so controlled that they failed to replicate

Table 7.1 Military spending, 2006[1] (figures in 2005 US dollars and exchange rates)

Country	Spending ($ billion)	Spending per capita	World share (%)
United States	528.7	1,756	46
United Kingdom	59.2	990	5
France	53.1	875	5
China[a]	49.5	37	4
Japan	43.7	341	4
Germany	37.0	447	3
Russia[a]	34.7	244	3
Italy	29.9	514	3
Saudi Arabia[b]	29.0	1,152	3
India	23.9	21	2
Australia	13.8	676	1
Canada	13.5	414	1
Spain	12.3	284	1

a Estimated figures.
b The figure for Saudi Arabia includes expenditure for public order and safety, and therefore might be an overestimate.

Source: Adapted from SIPRI, www.sipri.org.

real-world conditions. The administration's defenders counter that test failures are an anticipated part of the development process and allow scientists and engineers to learn about needed modifications.

Critics also argue that NMD is too costly. The Bush administration requested $8.9 billion for the Missile Defense Agency in fiscal year 2008. Missile defence receives more funding than any other weapons programme. Given the lack of a credible threat and the questionable technology, it is foolhardy for the United States to fund such an exorbitant project. The system's defenders argue that the potential devastation of a ballistic missile attack warrants large expenditures.

Finally, detractors argue that the NMD system will be destabilizing, and could provoke arms races. Other states might be tempted to increase their arsenals so as to be able to overwhelm the system, and this could trigger regional arms races.

11 September and the war on terror

The Bush administration remained committed to transforming the military and NMD after the terrorist attacks of 11 September 2001. However, other aspects of its national security policy changed significantly.

Prior to 11 September the United States viewed terrorism primarily as a crime. Crimes are dealt with through a legal process: suspects are captured, put on trial, and, if found guilty, imprisoned. The Bush administration took a different approach. It declared the terrorist attacks of 11 September to be an act of war. It stressed that Osama bin Laden had specifically called for a war against the United States and American citizens, and had engaged in large-scale violence toward this end. President Bush then invoked the United States' right to self-defence under Article 51 of the United Nations Charter. In this understanding, states have the right to defend themselves against an attack through retaliatory military action. Consistent with this view, for the first time in its history NATO came to the defence of one of its members. Within twenty-four hours of the attacks NATO deployed aircraft and ships in support of the United States.[2]

The Bush administration's post-9/11 foreign policy was outlined in the 2002 National Security Strategy (NSS), and reiterated in the 2006 NSS. Two principles outlined in the 2002 NSS have implications for military strategy. First, the NSS declared that the United States would 'make no distinction between terrorists and those who knowingly harbor or provide aid to them'. Thus, the scope of the war on terror is very broad. Second, the NSS also introduced the policy of pre-emption. 'We will cooperate with other nations to deny, contain, and curtail our enemies' efforts to acquire dangerous technologies [and WMD],' the document states. 'And, as a matter of common sense and self-defense, America will act against such emerging threats before they are fully formed.' The NSS goes on to state that the USA 'must be prepared to stop rogue states and their terrorist clients before they are able to threaten or use WMD against the US, our allies and friends'. In short, the Bush administration seeks to prevent adversaries (or potential adversaries) from developing WMD. Although it uses the term 'pre-emption', the policy is more accurately termed 'prevention'.

Thus, the Bush administration rejected the idea of containment, which had been the foundation of US national security policy for decades. In the post-9/11 era containing threats was no longer possible, it reasoned. Instead, the United States would seek to prevent threats from developing in the first place.

It has long been accepted that each state has the right to act pre-emptively in the face of an *imminent* threat. That is, if faced with an imminent attack, a state has the right to use military action so as to forestall that attack. However, the Bush administration's version of 'pre-emption' is not focused on such imminent threats. It seeks to prevent potential adversaries from *developing the capability* to launch an attack on the USA. It seeks to forestall *long-term* threats to its security, rather than imminent attacks.

This doctrinal shift is most striking when compared to US policy during the Cold War. Throughout the Cold War Washington feared and loathed Soviet nuclear weapons, but it implicitly accepted Moscow's right to develop them. The White House sought to contain the Soviet threat; it never asserted a right to prevent the USSR from building WMD in the first place.

Three days after the 9/11 attacks Congress passed a joint resolution authorizing the President to use armed force against those responsible. The resolution gave the President authority 'to use all necessary and appropriate force against those nations, organizations, or persons, he determined planned, authorized, committed or aided the terrorist attacks ... [or who] harbored such organizations or persons'. Within a month US forces were deployed to Afghanistan.

The war in Afghanistan, 2001

On 7 October 2001 the United States launched Operation Enduring Freedom in Afghanistan. This war had several aims. First and foremost, it sought to close down al-Qaeda training camps in that country, and to capture al-Qaeda operatives. The operation also sought to disrupt and end support for terrorism. Additionally, the United States sought to topple the Taliban regime, which had been providing a safe haven for al-Qaeda.

The US invasion of Afghanistan met with little international criticism. For one thing, the Taliban regime was broadly perceived to be illegitimate. Only three countries recognized the Taliban as the official government of Afghanistan, and it had been denied the right to take Afghanistan's seat at the United Nations. Second, the Taliban had one of the worst human rights records in the world, and was particularly harsh toward females. Moreover, diplomatic attempts to resolve the problem had proven fruitless. During the 1990s Washington and the international community had been in talks with the Taliban trying to get them to turn over Osama bin Laden, and to close down the terrorist training camps. The Taliban repeatedly refused. Sanctions had proven futile as well. Finally, many agreed with the Bush administration's assertion that the 9/11 attacks had been an act of war.

The war in Afghanistan was the most high-tech war the United States had ever conducted. Sixty per cent of the bombs dropped during the campaign were guided by lasers or satellites, and early estimates indicated that 75 per cent of the bombs dropped were accurate.[3] Other technological innovations were also on display, such as unmanned aerial vehicles (UAVs), or drones, called Predators, which proved extremely effective in tracking and destroying targets.

Despite these new technologies, the US military found that some of its most effective forces were distinctly low-tech. Special operations forces, which consisted of a dozen or so elite troops or CIA operatives, proved especially useful. Often travelling by horseback, these units blended into local environments, and gathered important intelligence information about enemy movements and targets.

In November 2001 the US war in Afghanistan ended with a clear military victory. Al-Qaeda training camps were largely destroyed, the network was severely disrupted, and the Taliban regime was replaced with a new, more humane government. However, subsequent political developments have been troublesome. For example, during the war the United States captured approximately 5,000 persons suspected of abetting terrorism. While most of these individuals were released, many remain in detention centres under questionable conditions. These detentions have raised questions about the ethics of US foreign policy. Moreover, opium production in Afghanistan has soared, running the risk that it will devolve into a 'narco-state'. Profits from the opium trade are also fuelling a growing insurgency in the southern sections of the country. By 2006 both the Taliban and al-Qaeda appeared to be regrouping under new leadership along the Afghan–Pakistan border. In short, the region remains a threat to international security.

The war in Iraq, 2003

The war in Iraq, which began in March 2003, was the second phase of the Bush administration's war on terror. Whereas there had been international support for the war in Afghanistan, the US war in Iraq was broadly condemned.

Why did the United States invade Iraq? The Bush administration provided several reasons. First, it argued that Saddam Hussein had repeatedly violated UN resolutions which required Iraq to open its military facilities to international inspections. This assertion was undeniable. Saddam had ejected

UN weapons inspectors from Iraq in 1998. Second, it contended that Saddam Hussein was seeking to develop WMD. This assertion seemed plausible at the time, since the Iraqi dictator had previously tried to develop such capabilities. Third, and most controversial, the administration charged that Iraq harboured terrorism. It repeatedly implied that Saddam Hussein had links to al-Qaeda. President Bush suggested that Saddam Hussein had to be overthrown so as to prevent him from transferring WMD to terrorists.

The war in Iraq was the first test of the Bush administration's pre-emption policy. That is, the aim was to prevent Iraq from developing a WMD capability and to prevent it from transferring that capability to terrorist groups. (The Afghanistan war was not an example of pre-emption, as the military operation was launched *after* al-Qaeda had attacked.)

The war in Iraq was divisive for many reasons, not the least of which was military strategy. Within the Bush administration there were several important debates. One centred on whether the USA should go to war with Iraq at all. Secretary of State Colin Powell and others argued that the USA should remain focused on fighting al-Qaeda in Afghanistan. In this view, a war in Iraq would be a potentially dangerous diversion from the war on terror. Others disagreed. Secretary of Defense Rumsfeld, Vice-President Cheney, and others insisted that the Iraqi dictator had to be removed from power.

Once it became clear that the President was heading toward war another debate developed. Powell argued that the United States should try to cobble together a multilateral coalition, similar to the way in which the first President Bush conducted the 1991 Persian Gulf War. In Powell's view, the United States could topple Saddam's regime alone, but it could not single-handedly build a new Iraq. It would need allies to do so. Others disagreed. They preferred a unilateral approach, claiming that multilateralism would slow the process down and perhaps derail it altogether.

A third debate centred on the amount of force the United States would deploy to Iraq. Some believed the war should be conducted in accordance with the Powell Doctrine. That is, the USA should deploy overwhelming force right from the outset. According to some estimates, this would entail 400,000 or so troops. Powell and others maintained that high troop levels would be needed to maintain order after the regime fell and during the period of reconstruction.

Secretary Rumsfeld disagreed. Rumsfeld believed the US goal should be to invade, depose Saddam Hussein, and withdraw as quickly as possible. A large US force would not only appear to be an imperialist occupier, he reasoned, it would take longer to exit Iraq. The longer US forces remained in Iraq, the more anti-American resentment would arise. Consequently, Rumsfeld favoured sending just enough troops to depose Saddam and exit quickly.

In short, whereas one group envisioned a long-term state-building project, the other envisioned a lightning war in which the USA would decapitate the existing regime and rapidly depart so as to allow the Iraqis to rebuild themselves.

Ultimately, the Secretary of Defense's vision prevailed. The United States launched Operation Iraqi Freedom in March 2003, deploying approximately 140,000 troops in the process. Once again, American technology allowed the United States to topple the existing regime quickly. The Defense Department made even more extensive use of Special Operations Forces, and refined much of the technology it had used in Afghanistan, thus making it even more effective.[4]

This initial military success became tempered, however. Although the United States has overwhelming military power and the most technologically sophisticated military, it has found itself bogged down fighting a low-tech, urban insurgency in Iraq. While the US army is adept at fighting large-scale conventional wars, guerrilla-style combat is proving far more challenging.

Political success has been even more elusive. Efforts to build a stable democracy in Iraq have been halting, at best, creating growing instability. Terrorism has flourished. Moreover, the war calls into question the whole concept of pre-emption. The Bush administration launched the war so as to prevent Saddam Hussein from transferring WMD to terrorists. It now appears that Saddam did not have WMD, nor did he have substantive links to al-Qaeda. In order for pre-emption to be a viable policy, a government must have accurate intelligence information on both the capabilities and the intentions of potential adversaries. In this case, US intelligence was mistaken on both counts.

KEY POINTS

❑ Transforming the military and national missile defence have been central components of the Bush administration's national security policy.

❑ The Bush administration considered the 11 September attacks to be an act of war.

❑ The policy of pre-emption entails denying an adversary the ability to develop weapons of mass destruction. This policy was first tested in the war in Iraq.

❑ The wars in Afghanistan and Iraq were quick military victories. However, political victory is proving elusive.

Conclusion

US military power has grown since the end of the Second World War. Today, US military power is unequalled throughout the world. The United States has used its military power in a variety of ways—to counter the spread of communism, to deter attacks, to promote peacekeeping, to assist in humanitarian disasters, to counter terrorism, to promote democracy, and to counter the spread of weapons of mass destruction, among other aims.

This chapter highlights a central paradox: although the USA has the most powerful military in the world, there are limits to what military power can achieve. The war in Vietnam was neither a military victory nor a political victory. US military strategists learned from this defeat and adapted. Consequently, the Persian Gulf War, the war in Afghanistan, and the war in Iraq were all military victories. In all three instances enemy forces were quickly defeated.

However, it is questionable whether these wars were political victories for the United States. Saddam Hussein remained in power far longer than did the first President Bush, and continued to threaten his people and the region throughout the 1990s. In Afghanistan, the Taliban was quickly ousted, but the country remains unstable. Political victory has proven the most elusive in Iraq. Although Saddam Hussein was overthrown with relative ease, the United States has been unable to build a democratic state that can maintain order. This political failure has been destabilizing, both for the country and the region.

The ongoing conflicts in Afghanistan and Iraq highlight another conundrum: although the USA has the largest military force in the world, this force is not well suited to fighting insurgencies and terrorism—the central threats to American security today.

? Questions

1. Why did the United States become involved in the Korean War and the Vietnam War?
2. What is the Powell Doctrine, and how has it influenced military operations?
3. What is Mutual Assured Destruction (MAD)?
4. For what purposes has the United States deployed its military? To what effect?
5. What are the military implications of containment, and how have they changed over time?

6. Do nuclear weapons have a role to play in US security?

7. Why is national missile defence controversial?

8. How can a large conventional army effectively counter terrorism and insurgencies?

9. What are the implications of the Bush administration's policy of pre-emption?

10. Can military power be used to achieve political victories in Iraq and Afghanistan?

» Further Reading

Blackwill, R. D., and Carnesale, Albert (eds.) (1993), *New Nuclear Nations: Consequences for US Policy* (New York: Council on Foreign Relations).

This volume systematically analyses a multitude of diplomatic and military means for coping with nuclear proliferation.

Clark, Wesley K. (2001), *Waging Modern War: Bosnia, Kosovo and the Future of Combat* (New York: Public Affairs Books).

Clark, a US general and former NATO Supreme Allied Commander, draws upon his experiences in the Kosovo war to offer lessons about fighting terrorism and asymmetrical warfare.

FitzGerald, F. (2000), *Way Out There in the Blue: Reagan, Star Wars and the End of the Cold War* (New York: Simon & Schuster).

A detailed, yet engaging book on the Strategic Defense Initiative and national missile defence.

Gordon, Michael R., and Trainor, Bernard E. (2007), *Cobra II: The Inside Story of the Invasion and Occupation of Iraq* (New York: Vintage).

An account of the invasion plans and the manner in which they led to the insurgency.

Kaplan, Robert D. (2006), *Imperial Grunts* (New York: Vintage).

An on-the-ground account of numerous military missions throughout the globe.

Larson, Jeffrey A., and Wirtz, James J. (eds.) (2001), *The Rocket's Red Glare: Missile Defense and the Future of World Politics* (Boulder, Colo.: Westview Press).

This volume provides a reasonably balanced view of many of the key debates surrounding national missile defence.

Woodward, Bob (2004), *Plan of Attack: The Definitive Account of the Decision to Invade Iraq* (New York: Simon & Schuster).

An in-depth account of the Bush administration's decision to go to war in Iraq and the development of its plans for invasion.

Endnotes

1. See the RMA Debate, www.comw.org/rma/index.html.

2. www.nato.int/issues/terrorism/index.html, accessed 1 Mar. 2007.

3. BBC (2002). This figure will probably be revised downward over time.

4. See Woodward (2004, 2006), Gordon and Trainor (2007), and Risen (2006).

 Visit the Online Resource Centre that accompanies this book for web links to accompany each chapter, and a range of other resources: www.oxfordtextbooks.co.uk/orc/cox_stokes/

8 Regional shifts and US foreign policy

Peter Trubowitz

Chapter contents

Introduction

Whatever else future historians say about American foreign policy in the post-11 September era, they will not say that it was a time of consensus. To a degree that no one anticipated in the aftermath of the attacks on the World Trade Center and the Pentagon, the country is mired in a polarizing and bruising debate over foreign policy. The troubled Iraq War is the central issue in this debate, but as public opinion polls indicate, the controversy over the war reflects profound differences over the purposes of American power and the authority to exercise it. As one highly regarded observer of the American political scene puts it, 'a chasm the size of the Grand Canyon' now divides the country over foreign policy (Cook 2007).

This is not the first time that America has been deeply divided over foreign policy. Deep fault lines surfaced in the 1890s and 1930s and debates over foreign policy took on strongly emotional and moral overtones, just as they do today. In each period, the conventional wisdom that politics in the United States 'stops at the water's edge' was betrayed by protracted and divisive conflicts over how the country should respond to the breakdown of the old international order, and to the emergence of new strategic realities and economic challenges. Questions of foreign policy became enmeshed in the nation's electoral politics. In each period, America's leaders experienced great difficulty in articulating a vision of the national interest that commanded broad domestic support.

Why do America's leaders find it so difficult to mobilize broad-based support for their foreign policies? Why is the nation's foreign policy so conflict prone? Some scholars locate the source of conflict in America's political culture. They argue that Americans hold divergent images of what their nation is, or what it should be, and that these differences invariably give rise to profound disagreements over how and when America should use its power. Other scholars argue that America's divided constitutional order is the source of conflict over foreign policy. The 'weakness' of the American state, manifest in the sharing of foreign policy-making powers between the White House and Congress, is considered to be, in Edwin Corwin's famous phrase, 'an invitation to struggle' for control over the authority to make foreign policy.

Despite their many and important differences, both approaches assume that the appropriate level of analysis is national: the focus is on *national* political traits or structures. They ignore what for many scholars of American politics is fundamental: regional difference. All politics may not be local, but as V. O. Key pointed out long ago, in the United States regions are the 'building blocs' of national politics (Key 1964: 229). Like E. E. Schattschneider before him, and Walter Dean Burnham after him, Key underscored the sectional dimension of national politics in the United States (Schattschneider 1960; Burnham 1970). These scholars showed that many of the great struggles in American history over domestic policy were also conflicts between *subnational* coalitions advancing conflicting regional agendas.

This chapter builds on this insight by showing how regionalism also impacts foreign policy. In contrast to accounts that grant primacy to ideas or institutions, it identifies America's *regional* diversity as the most important source of tension and conflict over foreign policy. I show that conflicts over the purposes of American power, as well as the constitutional authority to exercise it, are fundamentally conflicts over the distribution of wealth and power in American society among coalitions with divergent interests and claims on the federal government's resources. They are regional in nature, and they grow out of the uneven nature of the nation's economic development and integration into the world economy.

This argument is developed by analysing debates over American foreign policy in three different periods: the 1890s, 1930s, and in the current era. During the 1890s, the 'Great Debate' over imperial expansion in Latin America and the Pacific Basin pitted the industrial North-East against the agrarian South, with the West playing a decisive 'swing' role. A quarter of a century later, the urban North-East and the South found common ground in an 'internationalist' foreign policy agenda and waged a fierce battle against their 'nationalist' rivals in the rural West. At issue was whether the United States should assume a more assertive role in checking the spread of fascism in Europe and in promoting global economic recovery.

Today, sectional conflicts divide the nation again. What many define as a fight between 'liberals' and 'conservatives' over how to respond to the challenges posed by globalization and terrorism is more usefully understood as a conflict between two broad coalitions of interest: one based in the South and Mountain West; the other grounded in the North-East and Pacific Coast. This pattern of regional polarization, which developed long before 11 September, reflects a deepening division of the electoral map into so-called 'red' states that benefit from military spending, export promotion, and import liberalization, and 'blue' states that do not. Those differences go a long way toward explaining why six years after America was attacked, the country is still debating how it should define and pursue its interests in the world.

Regional interests and foreign policy

Regionally based political competition and conflict is one of the most distinctive features of American politics. Frederick Jackson Turner first identified the significance of regionalism in the United States, and since then a large literature has developed on its sources and impact on national policy. A common theme in this literature is that regionalism in American politics is rooted in the geographically uneven nature of economic growth and development.[1] In other industrialized nations regional economic differentiation is often coterminous with ethnic or religious difference. While ethnic and religious difference is also an important feature of American politics, at the regional level political conflicts are grounded in conflicts of economic interest.

Scholars identify a number of factors to explain these regional differences. Some emphasize geographic disparities in resources, markets, and the costs of factors of production. Others focus on the role that the federal government plays in shaping patterns of uneven regional growth and development. There is also an important literature on how the spatially decentralized structure of political representation in the United States reinforces regional differences that arise from uneven growth. Historically, when the nation's political parties have been rooted in sections of the country with significantly different economic interests, domestic competition over public policy at the national level has intensified. Popular images like 'Red America' and 'Blue America' capture this interplay of party and region.

In the past, much of this literature focused on domestic policy. However, in recent years the effects of regionalism on foreign policy making have received increased attention. A central finding in this work is that regions that stand to benefit, politically as well as economically, from the projection of American power are likely to support more ambitious, expansionist foreign policies.[2] Politicians from these regions are the ones most apt to favour a strong American presence abroad and a powerful chief executive at home. Conversely, regions whose income, profits, or political standing at the national level depend on the home market, or are threatened by international competition, are less

---

BOX 8.1: American exceptionalism? Sectionalism American style

In many countries, regionalism is associated with ethnic or religious difference. These political systems are typically studied within a centre–periphery perspective, where regionalism manifests itself in the form of protest by culturally distinctive peripheries against political and economic exploitation by the centre. While ethnic and religious diversity is also an important feature of American politics, it is most conspicuous and salient at the 'microregional' (neighbourhood and city) level. At the 'macroregional' level, the absence of the kinds of cultural cleavages present in other nations has meant that in the United States sectionalism is usually grounded in conflicts of economic interest.

likely to support the 'overhead charges' of maintaining international openness: a powerful military, easy credit for foreigners, an open domestic market, and so on. Elected officials from these regions are the ones who are most likely to make the case for a more retrained and cost-conscious foreign policy and stress domestic priorities and needs.

Explaining deep and persistent conflict over US foreign policy requires some mapping of the nation's economic geography.[3] Functional position alone, however, is too blunt an instrument to explain fully how regional competition over foreign policy is played out in the national political arena. As mentioned, party politics also plays a role. Party leaders have a long if inglorious record of playing politics with the national interest. Within the structures of a two-party system, they have often used foreign policies to mobilize electoral support and marginalize political opponents. As I show in the cases below, explaining how regional foreign policy coalitions form also requires some attention to electoral geography and party politics.

KEY POINTS

❏ Regionalism is one of the oldest and most distinctive features of American political life.

❏ Regions that benefit, politically as well as economically, from the projection of American power are likely to support more ambitious, expansionist foreign policies.

❏ Historically, when the national parties have been rooted in regions with significantly different stakes in international openness, partisanship has intensified.

The great debate over expansionism

Few periods in American history had a more profound impact on the nation's foreign policy, or have enjoyed more attention by American diplomatic historians, than the 1890s. Having created a continental empire in the nineteenth century, Americans set their sights on more distant frontiers. As every textbook on American diplomatic history states, in the 1890s the United States became a great power, shedding its isolationist past and embracing a more assertive, outward-looking foreign policy geared to opening new markets in Latin America and Asia. America built a modern battleship navy, transformed its protective tariff into a bargaining tool to open foreign markets, and extended its strategic reach through the acquisition of foreign lands.

America's turn toward empire

This shift in American foreign policy is often viewed as the inevitable result of the nation's rise as a world power. Such interpretations begin with the obvious: the country was growing at a spectacular rate. Between the end of the Civil War in 1865 and the beginning of the Spanish–American War in 1898, the population of the United States more than doubled, and the gross national product nearly trebled. Long a world leader in agricultural output, the United States by the turn of the century had surpassed Germany, France, and even Great Britain in steel and coal production, as well as total manufacturing output. A decade later, America alone accounted for fully one-third of the world's industrial production.

As the national economy expanded, so did Americans' financial and commercial interests overseas. Once highly dependent on foreign capital, America's leading banks and corporations now aggressively looked overseas for investment opportunities. Even more impressive was growth in America's commercial trade. Between 1865 and 1898, exports expanded from $281 million to roughly $1,231 million, making America the third greatest exporter in the world behind Britain and Germany. While much of this increase came from agriculture, by the 1890s manufactures were rapidly closing the gap. The bulk of the industrial export trade went to less developed nations in Latin American and Asia. Industrial exports to Europe also increased but not nearly as much; agricultural goods, especially cotton and wheat, made up the single largest class of exports to the Old World.

Fears of overproduction and colonial encirclement fuelled Americans' interest in overseas expansion. Severe depressions in the 1870s and 1890s, and a somewhat milder contraction in the 1880s, contributed to the perception that foreign markets were essential to American well-being. Overproduction was seen as the cause of these crises, and each one sent more and more farmers and manufacturers in search of new markets to sell their surplus goods. The discontent and turmoil engendered by these economic downturns led many to view foreign markets the way an earlier generation had looked to the national frontier: as a 'safety valve' for economic and social problems. There was a growing conviction in the 1890s that continental expansion had reached an end, and this only underscored the sense of urgency that many felt about the 'export solution'.

Great power rivalry was also a source of great concern to many Americans. For most of the nineteenth century, the world economy had revolved around Great Britain. The world's banker, workshop, and policeman, England used its power to establish an international economic order which, at its peak, emphasized free and open trade. Beginning in the 1870s, this system started to fall apart. Economic crises in Europe and Asia led Germany, France, and Japan to contest British hegemony and turn to mercantilism and imperialism to revive their slumping economies and pacify domestic discontent. While great power rivalry, and the 'scramble for empire' it kicked off, did not pose an immediate threat to American security, it did raise questions about the country's ability to guarantee access to its budding export trade to South America and Asia in the near and long term.

These were fundamentally questions about means. If most Americans by the 1890s favoured the goal of commercial expansionism, they disagreed sharply about the appropriate methods: would the acquisition of foreign lands (e.g. Hawaii, Cuba, the Philippines) and a larger navy be needed to promote expanded trade or could America's foreign trade expand without political and military burdens? Should new economic opportunities be sought in underdeveloped or advanced regions, in South America and Asia, or Europe? On these questions of means, consensus gave way to intense domestic conflict and political rivalry. The critical fault line ran along sectional lines. On one side stood the industrial North-East, and on the other, the agrarian South. In between, lay the West.

Sectional bases of the conflict

Many factors explain why expansionism divided the country so sharply along sectional lines, but one was central: the economy. The northern and southern economies differed enormously. Despite the development of a *national* economy after the Civil War, the United States in the 1890s remained in many ways a single nation-state with two distinct *regional* economies: one specializing in manufacturing, the other in agriculture. This meant that these regions had very different things to sell on the world market. It also meant that their elected representatives in Washington had quite different ideas about *where* America should cultivate commercial ties. Seeking outlets for its surplus manufactures, the industrial North-East looked primarily to non-industrialized areas of the globe, particularly South America and Asia. By contrast, the agrarian South was highly dependent on industrial markets for selling its raw materials. It looked to Europe for expanded trade.

Where to expand was one thing; *how* to expand was yet another. For the Republicans who dominated the North-East, a neo-mercantile strategy that put a premium on overseas bases and naval power had distinct advantages. For starters, the Republican North-East was home to the country's most powerful industrial, financial, commercial interests—the very interests that had the biggest stake in securing greater access to, and control over, markets in Latin America and Asia. They viewed territorial expansion and naval power as two sides of the same coin. Naval power, Republicans argued, was needed to promote the spread of American commerce overseas; establishing a strategic presence in places like Hawaii, Cuba, and the Philippines was needed to enhance the Navy's ability to project power. The Republican case for imperial expansion was thus both economic and strategic.

It was also a way for northern Republicans to advance partisan interests. Empire building was a way of addressing the needs of hard-pressed workers. The modernization of the Navy meant jobs for northern workers, which in turn meant votes for northern politicians. A strategy of territorial expansion also helped Republican leaders to shore up and consolidate political support among industrialists, bankers, and merchants who were interested in expanded trade and investment. Additionally, northern Republican leaders found the issue of expansionism helpful at the ballot box, using jingo nationalism to mobilize their partisans at election time and silence discontents. It certainly was not the first time in American history that elected leaders played politics with the national interest.

Expanding the capacity of the federal government to project power abroad also helped to expand the Republican Party's electoral base at home. Republicans used the lure of naval expenditures to win support along the Pacific Coast. In the rural West, efforts to open markets in Latin America through tariff reform served to enhance the Republicans' appeal among hard-pressed western farmers who viewed Latin America as an outlet for their surplus foodstuffs. Expansionism had a hard edge as well.

BOX 8.2: Quo bono? The great debate over American imperalism

Debates over foreign policy are not just about the world 'out there'. They are also about the balance of political power inside the United States. In the 1890s, as during other periods of the nation's history, politicians viewed foreign policy issues against a larger political canvas. The issues of naval spending, territorial expansion, and tariff reform were debated in terms of their impact on each region's overseas commercial interests and on post-bellum political arrangements that continued to make the agrarian South a 'colony' of the industrial North-East. Who stood to gain politically and economically from an expansionist foreign policy, and who stood to lose, was the central question.

Republicans used it to split the western and southern branches of the radical agrarian movement known as the Populists—the most serious political threat to Republican rule in the 1890s.

All of this helps explain why the South so vigorously opposed the North-East's foreign policy agenda. While the North-East and parts of the West could hope to realize gains from a strategy of imperial expansion, the agrarian South could not and, in fact, did not. The South was more dependent on international markets than any other region in the country. Not surprisingly, southern politicians were among the most vocal proponents of expanded trade. For the South, however, there was a key difference: the Democratic South required industrial markets for their goods and thus had powerful reasons for avoiding policies that might provoke or exacerbate great power tensions and, thereby, threaten American access to the great industrial markets of Europe among industrial nations there. Policies that challenged British commercial dominance in the southern half of the western hemisphere raised potential risks for the South.

For the North and South, the decline of British hegemony and the rise of imperial rivalry meant very different things: for the former, it opened possibilities for commercial expansion; for the latter it threatened an already-weakened liberal trading order on which the South was vitally dependent. This is why southern lawmakers in Washington advocated free trade and also helps explain why they opposed building a powerful navy. A more powerful military posed other risks for the South as well. Twenty-five years after the end of the Civil War, the South was still very much a 'colonial appendage' of the North. Many of the region's leaders viewed military expansionism as a way to keep the South in tow. The naval build-up, for example, offered the South little by way of economic or political compensation. Given the paucity of shipbuilders and steel producers in the agrarian South, and the absence of many southerners on the key committees in Congress, there was little hope of winning contracts, jobs, or patronage for the region.

Imperial expansionism also posed a threat to the 'Southern way of life'—or so the South's leaders argued. For every northern Republican who remind-ed Populists that foreign markets were the answer to their woes, there was a southern Democrat claiming that the seizure of 'tropical lands' like Hawaii would mean an influx of 'cheap coolie labour' that would threaten their livelihoods. Preaching the doctrine of 'white supremacy' was one way to deflect the Popu-lists' appeal to southern farmers. Playing on long-standing fears of Republican militarism and political domination was another. What assurances, southern leaders argued, that the large military establishment that would be needed to suppress political resist-ance in foreign colonies would not someday be used to coerce underdeveloped areas within the nation's borders? As in everything else in American politics, the Civil War cast its long shadow on the debate over imperial expansion.

Expansionism abroad; hegemony at home

America's emergence as a great power was forged in the crucible of domestic political struggle. Often depicted as a contest between competing visions of America's purpose in the world, the conflicts over expansionism in the 1890s were bred on conflicts of interests. The stakes were high. Those in the North-East who stood to gain the most faced the challenge of mobilizing a domestic political coalition broad and stable enough to overcome the South's resistance. The key to success lay in the West and this was not lost on Republican leaders. Indeed, the Republicans' foreign policy agenda is best seen as part of a larger electoral strategy in the 1890s that designed to exploit sectional differences in the agrarian periphery and to prevent an alliance against the North-East.

Southern Democrats, well practised in the art of sectional politics, were wise to the game. Being able to do something about it was another matter. In politics, as in war, there are objective realities, and in the late 1890s, the possibilities for a southern–western alliance over foreign policy were remote. The West was not as dependent on foreign markets as the South; its principal market was at home not abroad. Policies that challenged British dominance were thus less risky for the West than the South. Moreover, because it was not as dependent on for-eign markets as the South, western lawmakers could us their votes in Congress on issues of importance to the North-East—naval spending, foreign bases, tar-iff reform—to win concessions on domestic policy matters such as currency reform, railway regulation, and monopoly control that were of great importance in the trans-Mississippi West.

So it was that the West threw its weight behind the Republican North-East's foreign policy agenda. The story of America's rise as a great power is thus also a story about how the Republicans established hegemo-ny at home. With the exception of Woodrow Wilson's presidency, Republicans would control the machin-ery of national government for the next thirty years. Indeed, it took the full force of the Great Depression to destroy the regional alliance between the North-East and the West that formed the backbone of Republican political power. The depth and breadth of Franklin Delano Roosevelt's stunning victory in the 1932 presidential contest created new possibilities for a sectional alliance spanning the Mason–Dixon line and, in so doing, offered a new opportunity to rede-fine the purposes of American power.

KEY POINTS

❏ The 'great debate' over expansionism in the 1890s pitted the Republican North-East against the Dem-ocratic South. In between lay the West, the 'swing region' in late nineteenth-century American politics.

❏ The critical issues of naval spending, territorial expansion, and tariff reform were debated in terms of their impact on each region's overseas commer-cial interests and on post-Civil War political arrange-ments that continued to make the South a 'colony' of the North-East.

❏ In the battle between the North and the South, the key to success lay in political alliance with the West. Recognizing this, northern Republicans, who con-trolled the machinery of the national government, fashioned a foreign policy platform that enabled them to capture western support for their expan-sionist cause.

The struggle over internationalism

The 1930s were years of upheaval and change in America's foreign relations. During this tumultuous decade of depression and war, the United States went from a country that defined its interests in largely hemispheric terms to a nation that saw itself as a global power, with far-flung interests and international responsibilities. The raw, assertive nationalism that had so often characterized America's foreign policy during the preceding quarter-century was abandoned in favour of a new role for the United States, where Washington took the lead internationally in liberalizing the world economy and guarding against the kind of international breakdown that had led to one of history's longest depressions and one of its worst wars.

America's internationalist turn

No figure looms larger in this transition to internationalism than Franklin Roosevelt. Often remembered as a great innovator on the domestic front, Roosevelt was also an extraordinary statesman. Certainly, few in the 1930s had a better appreciation of the perilous international situation confronting the United States. As early as 1933, Roosevelt began urging that he should be given the authority to impose economic sanctions to deter German and Japanese military intimidation and expansionism. The new president also lost little time experimenting with ways to revive the world economy and promote foreign trade. As the political crisis in Europe and Asia deepened in the 1930s, again it was Roosevelt who made the case for giving Britain and others the military means to defend themselves against the Axis powers and rearming the United States itself.

In all cases Roosevelt would have his way with Congress, but not before the country endured one of the most bitter fights over foreign policy in its history. From Japan's seizure of Manchuria in 1931 to Mussolini's invasion of Ethiopia in 1935 to the Nazi occupation of France in 1940, America's leaders fiercely debated *how* the United States should respond. Policy

differences in Washington became less tractable and debates over how the nation should respond to international events became hopelessly embroiled in fights over *means*. Were the new governmental mechanisms Roosevelt was proposing needed to restore the world economy and safeguard against another breakdown? Should the United States assume a more assertive role in deterring expansionism and checking aggression? These were the questions that divided America in the 1930s.

As in the 1890s, fights over foreign policy in the 1930s were inextricably linked to domestic conflicts of interest. So were debates over 'entangling' America in foreign rivalries. Once again, arguments for and against an assertive foreign policy had direct implications for the domestic distribution of wealth and power. What changed, and dramatically so, was *who* lined up on each side of the battle line. This time, it was the West, not the South, that led the fight against the projection of American power—a battle that it, like the South in the 1890s, would lose. In the 1930s, the South favoured a vigorous assertion

---

BOX 8.3: Franklin Roosevelt and the great transformation

When Franklin Roosevelt was inaugurated in March 1933, twelve years of Republican-dominated foreign policy came to an end. During the 1920s, laissez-fairism was America's credo in foreign as well as domestic policy. Instead of looking for ways to capitalize on America's tremendous power after the First World War, Republican presidents throughout the decade looked for ways to minimize American involvement in the affairs of other countries, especially in continental Europe. Although Washington would continue to promote commercial expansion abroad, as it had since the 1890s, the Republican administrations of Warren Harding, Calvin Coolidge, and Herbert Hoover maintained a low political-military profile overseas and for the most part eschewed the kind of multilateralism that Franklin Roosevelt and the Democrats would champion in the 1940s.

of US leadership in world affairs, a position it ironically now shared with the North-East.

Depression, militarism, and the North – South alliance

Once deeply divided over foreign policy, North and South found common cause in the 1930s fight against economic nationalism, military intimidation, and imperial expansion. However much northerners and southerners might disagree on the rights of Negroes and organized labour, sectional rivalry stopped at the water's edge. What explains the rise of a new foreign policy coalition that crossed the once impenetrable Mason–Dixon line? Why did the once-powerful alliance between the North-East and West break down? Though many factors contributed to this domestic realignment over foreign policy, much is explained by a single development: by the late 1920s, the North-East was far more deeply integrated in, and deeply dependent on, the world economy, than it had been in the 1890s.

America's dramatic rise as a mature industrial and financial power in the first quarter of the twentieth century is largely a story of the North-East. The First World War had transformed the world economy and America's place in it. As a result of the war-inflated economic boom, the national trade surplus climbed to over $3.5 billion in 1917, with manufactured goods accounting for over 60 per cent of total exports. Foreign direct investment also grew rapidly. American corporations took advantage of the war to expand into areas long dominated by Europeans, most notably Latin America. The flow of American capital overseas was so great that by the beginning of the Roaring Twenties, the United States was not only the most productive nation in the world, but also its leading source of capital.

This trend in American investment accelerated through the 1920s. The nations of Europe needed foreign capital to fund their recovery from the ravages of the First World War; American investors needed foreign outlets to dispose of surplus capital. America's largest corporations kept pace with the nation's big

Wall Street banks. Once relatively insignificant in the American economy, the nation's overseas assets had become equal to over one-fifth of the gross national product by the time of the 1929 Wall Street crash. Though less dramatic, the growth of America's overseas trade was also important. Exports increased from $1.4 billion in 1900 to over $5.1 billion in 1929. More significant, the composition of this trade changed radically. In the past, the United States had been chiefly an exporter of primary goods to Europe. While cotton remained the leading export commodity, by the 1920s industrial sectors such as automobiles, machinery, and iron and steel had a considerable stake in foreign markets.

As the country's position in the world economy changed, America's leaders reassessed the nation's role in world affairs. Incentives to do so were especially strong in the North-East, where most of the wealth and prosperity generated by the rapid economic growth in the country's overseas trade, investment, and lending was concentrated. With roughly half of the national population, the region stretching from southern New England to the Potomac and west to the Mississippi produced over two-thirds of all manufacturing jobs in the country. More impressive still was the region's productivity. Seventy-five per cent of the total value added in manufacturing came from the manufacturing belt, and most of that was concentrated in the region's powerful industrial and financial centres: Baltimore, Boston, Chicago, Cleveland, Detroit, Philadelphia, Pittsburgh, and New York.

Once a part of the country that depended on economic protection from foreign imports, America's 'manufacturing belt' was now the core region of the world economy, eclipsing the great 'iron triangle' in Europe that ran from Stuttgart to Antwerp to Paris. Hitler's barter system in *Mitteleuropa* and Japan's drive for a Greater East Asia Co-Prosperity Sphere promised nothing good for a region whose representatives now favoured freer trade, open access, and capital mobility. It is thus not surprising that the urban North-East was at the vanguard of support for reviving and liberalizing the world economy, or that its elected officials in Congress now looked to their colleagues from the Deep South rather than the trans-Mississippi West to build a domestic coalition strong enough to sustain a change in international direction.

By any measure, the South was more committed to a vigorous assertion of American power overseas than any other part of the country. Opinion polls consistently showed southerners to be more internationalist and interventionist than non-southerners. The vast majority of the region's newspapers endorsed Roosevelt's foreign policy, even though many took exception to his domestic policies. Southerners even led the country in volunteer enlistment in the armed services. These sentiments were widely shared by the region's representatives in Washington. All but a small minority supported Roosevelt's international economic policies and diplomatic and military efforts to contain the gathering geopolitical threat. No region of the country more avidly supported a 'get tough' strategy toward the Nazis than the South.

Southern support for a more ambitious and decisive foreign policy sprang from multiple sources. Party politics tell part of the story. Roosevelt was remarkably popular among southern voters, and he swept the South by huge margins in each of his runs for the presidency. Yet, party loyalty and Roosevelt's personal charm alone cannot explain southern policy choices. In the final analysis, the South's interests were determined by its near complete dependence on the world economy. Indeed, the South was more vulnerable to the loss of overseas markets than any other sections of the country. On the eve of the Great Depression, southern exports made up 30 per cent of all American exports and accounted for roughly 20 to 25 per cent of the South's total economic production. Cotton and tobacco made up the bulk of southern exports, most of which continued to flow to Europe.

The South was a region that depended heavily on exporting commodities to world markets, and in this regard little had changed since the 1890s. And this explains why most southerners viewed the spread of economic nationalism in the 1920s and 1930s with alarm. For them, the collapse of the liberal European-oriented world system presented a fundamental threat. 'However else the crisis of that world might have been viewed by others,' writes one scholar, 'the articulate South saw Nazi aggression as a dagger thrust at the heart of this system.'[4] If Germany defeated Britain, Hitler and his Axis partners would establish economic hegemony over the European continent and divide the world into exclusive spheres of influence. If Hitler were not stopped, he would close the doors of Europe to American exports and move against US commercial interests elsewhere.

The threat to the South though was not only economic; it was political as well. Closure of the international trading system would not only close off their vital markets, but also would inevitably force the American government into ever-intensifying regulation and control of the domestic economy. While the country and small-town elites who dominated the region's politics desired federal assistance to cope with pain and suffering that the Great Depression had wreaked on the South, they feared and resented federal intervention. Southern leaders thus faced a choice: either actively support efforts by Washington to reverse the partitioning of the world economy, even at the risk of war, or accept the loss of economic and political autonomy that heavy federal intervention in the region would mean. To most southern leaders the choice was clear. If protecting their power and privilege required delegating vast amounts of foreign policy-making power to the executive branch, then so be it.

If internationalism was the credo of the agrarian South, isolationism was the ideology of the West. The same polls that ranked southerners as Roosevelt's strongest supporters on foreign affairs showed westerners to be his toughest critics. Westerners were generally more sceptical than other Americans about the virtues of foreign trade, military preparedness, and aid to Britain and they were less willing to spend American blood and treasure to check Germany's or Japan's drive for hegemony in Europe and Asia. Isolationism reigned supreme in the 1930s in the Great Plains and Mountain West. Western isolationists, steeped in the region's agrarian traditions, looked above the Mason–Dixon line and found allies in other parts of rural America.

Western views were well represented on Capitol Hill. No elected officials defended isolationism more passionately than those from the rural West. Often attributed to ignorance, backwardness, and parochialism, westerners opposed internationalism for very concrete reasons. Unlike the agrarian South, the rural West looked primarily to the domestic market for its prosperity. Wheat growers, who produced the region's leading farm export, sold less than 20 per cent of their crop abroad each year. Producers of other leading crops in the West were even less dependent on overseas markets. Having less at stake in Europe than the South or the urban North-East, it is thus not surprising that the rural West also felt comparatively less urgency in aiding the Allies or expanding the nation's capacity to project military power overseas. If anything, the looming 'threat' of foreign imports of grains, livestock, and minerals caused more apprehension in the rural West than the possibility of 'losing' markets in Europe or Latin America.

When western lawmakers made the case for 'self-sufficiency' and 'self-reliance' on Capitol Hill, they had good reason to believe that internationalism was not in the best interests of the local economies they represented. This did not mean that they envisioned an America cut off, ostrich-like, from the rest of the world. Most westerners did not want to sever trade and credit relations with other nations. Nor were they pro-Nazi, pro-fascist, or pro-Axis. In this sense, the term 'isolationist' can be misleading. What western congressmen favoured was a more narrowly prescribed definition of the nation's interests. For them, the issue was not so much whether and how vulnerable these interests were, and on this critical point, most western leaders did not believe that German control of the European continent, or for that matter Japanese dominance in Asia, would change the underlying realities of the global market.

Politics reinforced western scepticism toward internationalism. No part of the country was more susceptible to claims that American and British bankers had dragged the United States into the First World War. The vast majority of the region's farmers held Wall Street in low repute, and London's standing in the region was not much higher. Few westerners attached much credence to the notion that American and European security interests were interdependent, or to the idea that Britain was America's 'first line of defence'. In western eyes, such talk was nothing more than self-serving British propaganda and Ivy League sophistry. Calls for military mobilization were greeted with the same suspicion. Many farmers blamed US participation in the last European war for the farm crisis that devastated the region in the 1920s and the resulting shift in power from the farm to the city. Why should they support free trade schemes that subsidized Wall Street at their expense?

One consequence is that Republican Party's hold on the region weakened during the 1920s. The national parties were always held in low repute by large numbers of western voters, many of whom viewed the parties as instruments of powerful eastern interests. The Republican Party had carried the region in most presidential contests since the 1890s, but the West's support was always fragile and variable. As the Republican-dominated North-East moved in the direction of internationalism in the 1920s, it became increasingly difficult for the party's leaders to broker intra-party compromises over foreign policy. In fact, Herbert Hoover's efforts to do by pursuing 'semi-internationalism' only exacerbated tensions within the party. By the time Franklin Roosevelt took office in March 1933, the Republican Party was in tatters: deeply divided along regional lines and incapable of offering a programmatic response to the economic and political dislocations caused by the Great Depression.

Internationalism as party building

Republican losses were Democratic gains. Just as the internationalization of the urban North-East weakened the sectional bases of the Republican coalition, it created new possibilities for political alliance that Roosevelt and the Democrats were quick to exploit. In the past, Democratic politicians faced an uphill battle in the staunchly protectionist and Republican North-East. By the 1930s, however, international-ist principles like free trade and collective security were no longer anathema in the region's big urban metropolises. On the contrary, as Roosevelt came to realize, internationalism could be used to broaden the Democratic base in the North-East and to weak-en the Republican Party by exacerbating sectional rivalry within it. Economic nationalism, once the Republican elixir, now divided the party. Still heav-ily Republican, the eastern Establishment advocated liberal internationalism. Western Republicans were nationalism's staunchest supporters.

For Roosevelt there were thus huge political advan-tages in moving decisively toward internationalism. The Democrats were now well positioned to reap the rewards of the urban North-East's internationaliza-tion and the internecine struggles within the Repub-lican Party it touched off over international trade. Because core elements of the Democratic and Repub-lican parties now stood to benefit politically as well as economically from a commitment to maintain order, stability, and openness on the Eurasian landmass, their elected representatives had a strong incentive to support Roosevelt's efforts to stabilize the world economy and prevent the spread of nationalism and militarism overseas. In sum, America's international-ist turn rested on political facts *inside* as well as *out-side* the United States.

American efforts to stabilize the international environment began in the 1930s. An even greater effort occurred after the Second World War. From the late 1940s onward, American policy makers sought to rebuild the world economy along lib-eral lines. They also worked to ameliorate Europe's chronic geopolitical troubles by encouraging eco-nomic integration, interdependence, and growth. The Marshall Plan, the General Agreement on Tar-iffs and Trade (GATT), and the North Atlantic Trea-ty Organization (NATO) were all part of this larger effort to aimed at liberalizing the world economy and preventing the kind of international breakdown

experienced in the 1930s. Under US leadership, new governmental mechanisms were created to regulate the world economy; new institutions and agencies were established to disperse American economic relief; and new military means were developed to strengthen the nation's presence overseas and to deter other nations, most conspicuously the Soviet Union and China, from taking advantage of politi-cal instability on the Eurasian landmass.

The domestic political viability of America's lib-eral internationalism depended on the alliance between the North-East and the South that Roosevelt forged in the 1930s. From the Second World War to the Korean and Vietnam wars this alliance afforded America's presidents, Republican and Democratic alike, considerable latitude in managing the nation's foreign policy. Then, around the 1970s, the first cracks in the domestic foundations of liberal inter-nationalism appeared. While it would not be until later that the regional and party battle lines would be redrawn, the international and domestic process-es that fractured the North–South alliance made it increasingly difficult to manufacture consensus over foreign policy.

KEY POINTS

- ❑ During the Great Depression, the key question was whether or not America should assume an active role in rebuilding the world economy and checking the spread of fascism in Europe and Asia.
- ❑ Internationalists from the urban North-East and the agrarian South favoured active American interna-tional leadership. Because this coalition spanned the Mason–Dixon line and included Republicans as well as Democrats, it overwhelmed nationalist opposition in the West and formed the foundation of the Cold War consensus to come.
- ❑ In the 1930s as in other periods of American for-eign policy, politicians from different parts of the country sought to equate regional interests with the national interests. Foreign policy issues were debated in terms of their immediate impact on regional prosperity and their longer-range regional political and economic consequences.

American primacy and the 'new sectionalism'

With the end of the Cold War, that domestic challenge only became more difficult. While the United States enjoyed unrivalled power internationally, its political ability to convert its power into influence rapidly diminished. Political fissures over foreign policy that opened up two decades earlier became more acutely partisan after the collapse of the Soviet empire. Republicans from the 'red' states of the South and Mountain West espoused fundamentally different views about the purposes of American power from elected officials from 'blue' states in the North-East and along the Pacific Coast. Contrary to all expectations, those foreign policy differences have only hardened since 11 September. Indeed, today Republicans and Democrats are more divided over foreign policy matters than at any time since the Second World War.

End of consensus

For nearly three decades after the Second World War, the nation's foreign policy was based on an alliance between the North-East and the South. These regions were the earliest and largest beneficiaries of the policies of foreign aid, forward defence, and liberal trade that were aimed at promoting an open, interdependent world economy, and at the Cold War isolation or 'containment' of nations that threatened it. Because this coalition was rooted in the regional power base of the Democratic Party and the powerful eastern wing of the Republican Party, it provided an institutional framework for a bipartisan foreign policy. Party politics did not stop at the water's edge during the Cold War years; rather, shared interests kept partisanship in check.

That bipartisan coalition lasted until the 1970s when it began to fall apart under the combined weight of three developments: mounting social tensions triggered by the Civil Rights Movement and the Vietnam War; the economic decline of the industrial North-East and the rise of the so-called 'sunbelt' states of the South and West; and the shift in the Republican Party's centre of gravity from the North-East to the Mountain West. The first two drove North and South apart. The third created opportunities for coalition building between West and South. As the Republican Party aligned itself with the rapidly growing states of the Mountain West, it searched for allies in the country's other late developer, the South.

During the 1970s economic activity began to shift from the North-East to the South and West. Many factors contributed to this process: the diffusion of large-scale, high-technology production, lower transportation costs, regional disparities in labour costs, energy prices, and local tax rates. No less important were the uneven consequences of the erosion of American commercial power in the international economy. The North-East suffered disproportionately from the rise of Europe and Japan in the 1970s as economic competitors. Spatial disparities in federal spending and federal tax policies also played a role in accelerating, if not encouraging, this regional shift in

---

BOX 8.4: The Cold War consensus

American leaders were able to mobilize broad domestic support for their foreign policies during the quarter century that followed the Second World War. Presidents enjoyed considerable latitude, if not deference, on matters of foreign policy—certainly more than they did on domestic policy issues. The absence of foreign policy conflict during this period did not mean that politics stopped at the water's edge. Rather the Cold War consensus rested on a bipartisan alliance that spanned one of America's great political fault lines: the Mason–Dixon line. Northern and southern lawmakers found common cause in Cold War policies aimed at containing the Soviet Union and promoting international economic openness. As that political alliance began to come apart in the 1970s, America's leaders, Republican and Democratic alike, found it increasingly difficult to mobilize and sustain bipartisan support for their foreign policies.

power. Federal expenditures and tax policies spurred the growth of sunbelt cities such as Atlanta, Miami, Houston, and Phoenix while exacerbating economic difficulties in the older north-eastern centres of Boston, Chicago, Detroit, and New York.

The migration of industries, jobs, and people from the manufacturing belt to the sunbelt created 'structural conditions' conducive to political alliance between West and South. Republican stratagems made it a reality. Beginning in the late 1970s western Republicans like Ronald Reagan aggressively pushed domestic and foreign policies that were now antithetical to the interests of the declining North-East. In foreign policy, the Republicans' long-standing commitment to anti-communism was grafted onto a 'new' foreign policy agenda that favoured less international regulation, a strong national defence, and 'bolder, more assertive' leadership. By playing on these and other issues (such as race), Republicans wrought havoc in the Democratic Party. Southerners left the party in droves.

In the 1980s the Democrats' electoral stronghold narrowed to the ageing North-East. No longer restrained by the demands of coalition building, the Democratic leadership adopted a foreign policy strategy that played well in the northern 'rustbelt' and along the Pacific Coast: retrenchment. While most Democratic leaders continued to favour American participation in international institutions, they urged greater restraint in the use of military force, a smaller defence establishment, and a larger role for Congress in the foreign policy-making process. On foreign economic policy, Democrats edged away from their long-standing commitment to free trade, capital mobility, and equal access. Demands for 'fairer trade', job retraining, and industrial policy became as obligatory in Democratic politics as demands for freer trade, 'fast track procedures', and 'FTAs' (free trade agreements) were in Republican circles.

Red America versus Blue America

By the time the Berlin Wall fell in 1989, the domestic underpinnings of liberal internationalism had given way. In its place arose two new coalitions: one, centred in the South and Mountain West, that was dedicated to the projection of American power and the primacy of national security; the other, based in the North-East and Pacific Coast, committed to reducing America's geopolitical footprint and investing greater resources on the domestic side of the ledger. Much of the struggle over foreign policy since the end of the Cold War originates here, in the deepening divide between what political pundits dubbed 'Red America' and 'Blue America'. In contrast to what happened in the 1890s and 1930s, when new hegemonic blocs arose out of the struggles set in motion by uneven growth, the regional and partisan divisions that emerged before the end of the Cold War only intensified afterwards.

Economic trends in the 1990s generally reinforced this 'new sectionalism'. Higher tax rates, labour costs, and energy prices in the North-East made it harder for elected officials from 'blue' states to find common ground on foreign and domestic policy with 'red' state officials who had competing economic concerns. So did the uneven effects of globalization. The outsourcing of American jobs hit the ageing industrial centres of the North-East especially hard. Well-paying, unionized jobs in manufacturing were the first to be lost as production lines were moved abroad and cheap imports arrived from low-wage economies. The North-East moved to the forefront of efforts to rein in America's commitment to free trade. Free trade's most reliable advocates came from the South and, especially, the Mountain West: ironically, the one part of the country that consistently opposed Roosevelt's efforts to liberalize trade in the 1930s.

The South and the West also provided the surest support for foreign policies that put a premium on military power. Some analysts attribute these regional differences to strategic subcultures: southerners are said to be more nationalistic and less willing to accept the constraints on national autonomy that accompany institutionalized multilateralism. Whatever the merits of such claims, changes in the economic and political geography of military spending and production made it harder for politicians from different parts of the country to find common ground on national security policy. Since the 1970s, Pentagon spending on military procurement and research and development benefited the South and West at the expense of the North-East, contributing to the decline of the manufacturing sector in the North. In addition, southern and western states that make up the so-called 'gunbelt' have consistently received a larger share of the resources spent on military bases and personnel.

Seen in this light, the fights between Republicans and Democrats about how America should respond to 'rogue states' like Saddam Hussein's Iraq, or China's rise to great powerdom, or the outsourcing of American jobs to India, take on new meaning. They are battles in a larger, political war for control of the national political economy. This is why Republicans took exception to Bill Clinton's efforts to slow the growth of defence spending and why Democrats opposed the unilateral turn foreign policy took during George W. Bush's presidency. Foreign policies that put a premium on military power and free trade resonate in the southern and western areas Republicans represent. Conversely, foreign policies that shift some of the burden of 'leadership' to other nations and international institutions help Democrats politically in the North-East and Pacific Coast.

To be sure, this gap between Republicans and Democrats is not solely explained by uneven growth or electoral geography. American primacy has also had an effect. For all of its pathologies and shortcomings, the Cold War had a disciplining effect on America's politics. Public anxieties about Moscow's geopolitical ambitions and 'the bomb' also made consensus building easier by forcing politicians to the centre. With the collapse of the Soviet empire Republicans *and* Democrats have found it easier (i.e. politically safer) to use foreign policy to pursue narrower political ends. This is especially true of those elected officials who hail from the 'red' and 'blue' districts and states whose voters are overwhelmingly Republican and Democratic.

The widening gyre

For all it changed, 11 September did not reverse this trend. The initial surge in bipartisan unity in Washington and beyond that followed the attacks on the World Trade Center and the Pentagon quickly subsided.[5] And as the partisan debate over the war in Iraq demonstrates, Republicans and Democrats today are in strong disagreement about the proper mix of power and diplomacy in foreign affairs. Meanwhile, the war on terrorism has done little to quell partisan strategizing and electioneering on Capitol Hill over trade policy, foreign aid, and even homeland security. According to one widely used index, Congress is today more politically fractious and polarized than at any time in the last one hundred years.[6]

George Bush's governing style clearly contributed to this state of affairs. Bush had promised to govern as 'a uniter, not a divider', but his political advisers concluded otherwise (Bush 2000: 4, A20). Even before Bush took office, they had concluded that the once vaunted 'vital center' of American electoral politics had collapsed and political strategies aimed at capturing it would backfire.[7] The most effective policies would be polarizing ones— those designed to mobilize the party's core constituencies. In a divided nation, intense partisanship would be needed to win at the ballot box and on

---

BOX 8.5: Regionalism redux: Red America versus Blue America

America is today experiencing the return of important regional divides; partisan differences are again running along regional lines, making it more difficult for the country's leaders to mobilize broad and consistent support for their foreign policies. One regional coalition, centred in the South and Mountain West, is dedicated to the projection of American power and the primacy of national security; the other, based in the North-East and Pacific Coast, is committed to reducing America's geopolitical footprint and investing greater resources in domestic programmes. In contrast to the 1890s and 1930s, when new hegemonic blocs arose out of the regional struggles set in motion by uneven growth, the contest between what pundits call Red America and Blue America has intensified during the presidency of George W. Bush and shows little sign of abating after he leaves office in January 2009.

the House and Senate floors. Consensus building was subordinated to wedge politics.

Foreign policy became a tool of partisan warfare, especially at election time. In the 2002 campaign, the White House used national security to drive up Republican turnout in key districts and states and deflect public anxiety about a weak economy.[8] In the 2004 presidential election, Bush focused his campaign on the threat of terrorism, charging that the country would 'invite disaster' if the Democrats were to win (Alberts 2004). Vice-President Richard Cheney pursued the same critique of the opposition, warning, 'If we make the wrong choice [of candidates], then the danger is that we'll get hit again' (Silva 2006). The rhetoric continued in the 2006 mid-term elections, with Bush insinuating that a Democratic victory means 'The terrorists win and America loses' (Abramowitz 2006).

> ### KEY POINTS
>
> ❑ Today, Republicans and Democrats are more divided over foreign policy matters than at any time since the Second World War. Partisan differences are again running along regional lines, with the so-called 'red' states of the South and Mountain West on one side and the 'blue' states of the North-East and Pacific Coast on the other side.
>
> ❑ Politicians from Red America champion foreign policies that put a premium on American power. Those who hail from Blue America favour greater reliance on international institutions and multilateral diplomacy.
>
> ❑ These divisions hardened during George W. Bush's presidency but the process of regional restructuring that gave rise to them began before the Bush administration took office in 2001.

Conclusion

Most accounts of American foreign policy making focus on national ideologies and institutions. This reflects the widely held belief among foreign policy analysts that politics in the United States has become increasingly 'nationalized' and divorced from place-specific interests. The regional nature of struggles in America's early years that shaped the political debates over 'non-entanglement' in European affairs and continental expansion is assumed to have withered away in the twentieth century, with the closing of the 'national frontier', the rise of American power, and the nation's steady integration into the world economy. Sectionalism is viewed as a relic of America's past, a primitive impulse that has been displaced by the march of time.

The view of American development confuses a process with an outcome. Despite decades of economic convergence, the American economy is marked by high degrees of regional specialization and differentiation. Moreover, the nation's spatially decentralized system of political representation offers ample opportunity for regional differences to find political expression at the national level, and sometimes as party conflicts, as in the 1890s and again today. Once

again, Republicans and Democrats are advancing fundamentally visions of American power that are shaped in significant ways by the regional interests these parties represent. Republicans who hail from Red America contend that American power depends primarily on the possession and use of military might. By contrast, Democrats who represent Blue America maintain that the nation's power depends more on persuasion than coercion, and on domestic investments in infrastructure and education.

Which vision will dominate American foreign policy in the years ahead? Making predictions is always hazardous, but short of a major political shake-up in 2008 that gives the Democrats *or* Republicans effective control over the national political economy, the most likely outcome is continued conflict and polarization. America's two parties are so deeply entrenched regionally, and so evenly divided nationally, that bipartisan coalition building is likely to continue to be ad hoc, fragile, and short-lived (Kupchan and Trubowitz 2006). America may enjoy unrivalled power internationally, but today it lacks the domestic political will needed to convert that power into programmatic policy.

? Questions

1. Why is the foreign policy-making process in the United States so conflict ridden?
2. Why are some regions of the United States more prone to expansionist foreign policies than others?
3. When are sectional differences over foreign policy most likely to find expression as partisan conflicts? Use historical examples to support your answer.
4. Why did the industrial North-East favour a policy of imperial expansion in the 1890s? Why did the agrarian South oppose expansionism?
5. Why did the North-East and the South find common cause in internationalism in the 1930s?
6. Why were politicians from western states more prone to nationalism and isolationism before the Second World War?
7. Why is the foreign policy-making process in the United States so much more partisan today than it was at the height of the Cold War?
8. How have the North-East's views of free trade changed over time? What explains the shifts in the region's attitudes toward trade?
9. In the 1890s, southern leaders opposed a large peacetime military establishment. Today, southerners are the Pentagon's biggest backers in Congress. What factors contributed to this change in the South's attitude toward military power?
10. Why is bipartisanship unlikely to return to American foreign policy after George W. Bush leaves office in 2009?

» Further Reading

Brzezinski, Zbigniew (2007), *Second Chance: Three Presidents and the Crisis of American Superpower* (New York: Basic Books).

    A critical examination of American statecraft since the fall of the Berlin Wall.

Johnson, Robert David (2006), *Congress and the Cold War* (New York: Cambridge University Press).

    A valuable treatment of Congress's role in the making of foreign policy during the Cold War.

LaFeber, Walter (1993), *The American Search for Opportunity, 1865–1913* (New York: Cambridge University Press).

    A stimulating account of America's rise as a great power and its international consequences.

Reynolds, David (2001), *From Munich to Pearl Harbor: Roosevelt's America and the Origins of the Second World War* (Chicago: Ivan R. Dee).

    An insightful study of America's turn toward liberal internationalism.

Trubowitz, Peter (1998), *Defining the National Interest: Conflict and Change in American Foreign Policy* (Chicago: University of Chicago Press).

    A systematic analysis of how politics, economics, and geography shape US foreign policy.

Endnotes

1. See e.g. Agnew (1987); Bensel (1984); Markusen (1987).
2. See Trubowitz (1998); Silverstone (2004); Narizny (2007).
3. In the discussion below, I utilize the classic tripolar grouping that divides America's states into three 'great regions', divided roughly along the courses of the Mississippi and Ohio rivers: the North-East, South, and West. The North-East refers to states in New England, the Middle Atlantic, and the Great Lakes areas: Connecticut, Delaware, Illinois, Indiana, Maine, Maryland, Massachusetts, Michigan, New Hampshire, New Jersey, New York, Ohio, Pennsylvania, Rhode Island, Vermont, and Wisconsin. The South includes states from the South-East and South-West: Alabama, Arkansas, Florida, Georgia, Kentucky, Louisiana, Mississippi, North Carolina, Oklahoma, South

Carolina, Tennessee, Texas, Virginia, West Virginia. The West refers to states from the Great Plains, Mountain West, and Far West: Alaska, Arizona, California, Colorado, Hawaii, Idaho, Iowa, Kansas, Minnesota, Missouri, Montana, Oregon, Nebraska, Nevada, New Mexico, North Dakota, South Dakota, Utah, Washington, and Wyoming.

4. Paul Seabury (1957), *The Waning of Southern 'Internationalism'* (Princeton: Center of International Studies), 15.

5. See Trubowitz and Mellow (2005).

6. http://voteview.com/.

7. See Edsall (2006: esp. 51–77).

8. On the electoral impact of national security in 2002 see Jacobson (2007: 87–91).

 Visit the Online Resource Centre that accompanies this book for web links to accompany each chapter, and a range of other resources: www.oxfordtextbooks.co.uk/orc/cox_stokes/

9 Media and US foreign policy

Piers Robinson

Chapter contents

Introduction

The attacks of 11 September 2001 transformed the foreign policy agenda of the United States and ushered in a global 'war on terror'. The events themselves were communicated by the world's media almost instantaneously and had a profound impact upon both US and global public opinion. Within weeks, and with overwhelming support from both US media and public, the Bush administration invaded Afghanistan. Then, in a short period of time, the US government mobilized the support of both the US media and public to back the invasion of Iraq. Since then, US strategy in both Afghanistan and Iraq has become increasingly controversial both internationally and within the United States. The increase in US casualties across both war zones, scandal over the treatment of Iraqi prisoners at Abu Ghraib, and a growing perception that US policy is 'failing' have generated significant levels of media criticism and public dissent in the USA. At the time of writing, the Bush administration's war on terror is subject to significant political challenge within the USA. In short, US foreign policy since 9/11 has been conducted under the glare of media and public attention from both within the United States and globally. But what roles have public opinion and media played during these events? To what extent has US media and public been manipulated by the US government, and to what extent, conversely, have public opinion and media shaped US foreign policy during these tumultuous times? Moreover, what are the consequences of public opinion and media for US power in the twenty-first century? Such questions are the subject matter of this chapter.

This chapter introduces students to the range of debates that have dominated research into the relationship between US public opinion, media, and foreign policy. Before grappling with these academic debates, we will discuss the nature of US media and public opinion, including a consideration of democratic expectations of mass media and public opinion. This initial section sets the grounds for a discussion of pluralist and elite models of the public opinion/media/foreign policy nexus. The pluralist model emphasizes both the independence and power of US media and public opinion and their ability to influence US foreign policy. The elite model, discussed next, adopts a different understanding of this nexus and highlights the ability of US political elites to shape both media and public perceptions. The chapter then moves to a discussion of public and media diplomacy aimed at projecting US power abroad. Throughout, attention is paid to the ways in which public opinion and media can be understood as a source of power for, and as a constraint upon, US foreign policy. In conclusion, the chapter discusses contemporary debate concerning the impact of technological developments, including the internet and the rise of global media such as Al-Jazeera, upon US power and influence. First, however, we need to introduce basic concepts regarding media and public opinion.

Concepts

KEY POINTS

❑ Political communication research focuses upon the analysis of mainstream media outlets such as television news and newspapers.

❑ As a whole, US mainstream media are expected to provide US citizens with a full range of relevant viewpoints and opinions.

❑ The US citizens are often categorized as either *isolationist* or *internationalist*.

When discussing *media*, academics are, more often than not, referring to mainstream media outlets such as TV news channels, newspapers, and cable networks such as CNN and Fox News. Whilst other components of US media, such as the film and light entertainment industry, are important with regard to political information (Baum 2003), it is these traditional mainstream news media sources that are understood to be the crucial sites upon which political information is mediated and communicated to the American public. For the sake of brevity, in this chapter the term media is used to mean news media. Key US network television media outlets include CBS, NBC, and ABC and significant cable channels are CNN and Fox News. All these outlets communicate news to a national audience. US newspaper coverage of international affairs is largely led by the *New York Times* and the *Washington Post* (and to a lesser extent the *Los Angeles Times*). As with other US newspapers, these are regionally based, albeit with a minority nationally based readership, but they do have a significant influence upon the remainder of the US regional press.

In terms of journalistic norms, mainstream US media claim to be objective in their approach to covering the news. Even in relation to international affairs coverage, mainstream media disavow suggestions of their news coverage being distorted by patriotism and national bias (Aday, Livingston, and Herbert 2005). Whilst acknowledging a focus on US interests, these media maintain a commitment to telling US citizens the truth about international events. As such, mainstream media in the USA are supposed to function as the central component of the US public sphere within which informed, open, and free-ranging debate can occur. Media are also expected to perform a watchdog role whereby both government and powerful interests are held to account by media. Examples such as the Watergate scandal in the 1970s, when journalists Bob Woodward and Carl Bernstein uncovered political corruption surrounding the Nixon administration, are often cited as seminal examples of watchdog journalism. More recently Seymour Hersh's watchdog journalism highlighted issues surrounding the treatment of Iraqi prisoners at Abu Ghraib in Iraq. The independence of the media from political power is in theory guaranteed through US media operating according to the free market model; that is to say media outlets are privately owned and run as a business in order to make profit. As a consequence, US media are not controlled by government and are, in theory, protected from undue influence and pressure. Public service broadcasting, whereby media is funded through public

money and regulated by the state, does exist in the USA (e.g. PBS, the Public Broadcasting Service) but has a small viewership and minimal influence. As such, the dominance of commercial media in the USA is exceptional, as most Western democracies have developed mixed media systems that contain a greater proportion of public service broadcasting. Overall, the key point here is that the assumption underlying the free market model is that power is sufficiently devolved so as to enable a free and independent media. As such, US media are expected to conform to the pluralist model whereby all groups in US society, from government through business to the public, have access to, and are represented in, the US public sphere.

With respect to public opinion and international affairs, research has traditionally identified two distinct orientations amongst US citizens. The first is the *isolationist* sentiment, the second the internationalist sentiment. Isolationists are opposed to the USA taking an active role in world affairs. Beyond guaranteeing the security of the USA, isolationists believe that the USA should avoid both involvement in international organizations such as the United Nations and attempts to influence the affairs of other states. For example, prior to the attack by Japan on Pearl Harbor in 1941, majority US public opinion was isolationist and, therefore, opposed to becoming directly involved in opposing Nazi Germany's expansionist war. *Internationalists*, conversely, support a more active role for the USA in global affairs including US involvement in international organizations such as the United Nations. Internationalists support the deployment of US forces around the world and attempts to promote values such as democracy and free market economics. For example, since the 9/11 attacks, it is likely there has been an increase in internationalist sentiment with the US public supporting an interventionist foreign policy in order to combat threats and secure US interests. Whilst more recent studies have sought to develop more nuanced descriptions of US public beliefs regarding foreign policy (e.g. Wittkopf 1990), the isolationist/internationalist distinction remains a central analytical tool.

The pluralist model

The pluralist model makes a number of important assumptions. The first is that power is sufficiently dispersed throughout society (including across government, media, and public) so that no one set of interests is able to prevail. Rather, the political process, including media debate and public opinion formation, is the outcome of a range of competing positions negotiated through an open political system, a free media and underpinned by a public that has access to sufficient information in order to develop an independent opinion. More specifically, the pluralist model assumes, first, that the US public are capable of rationally processing news information in order to form their own, independent, opinion. Second, the pluralist model maintains that mainstream media are sufficiently independent from political power to allow them to present a diverse range of political perspectives. Third, the pluralist model assumes the US political system is sensitive to, and therefore influenced by, public opinion and media.

Having clarified what is meant by *pluralism*, we now turn to consider of pluralist accounts of the public opinion/media/foreign policy nexus. I will first examine pluralist accounts of the relationship between public opinion and foreign policy, and then pluralist accounts about the relationship between media and foreign policy.

Public opinion and foreign policy

Historically, tension exists between *realist* and *liberal-democratic* perspectives on the role of public opinion in US foreign policy formulation. Realists traditionally oppose public input to the complex task of foreign affairs. Conversely, liberal approaches advocate greater levels of public involvement in the process of foreign policy making (see Major debates and their impact 9.1). But, what influence does the US public actually wield on foreign policy formulation?

For some academics and many politicians, public opinion is a force to be reckoned with. Perhaps the clearest articulation of this claim can be found in the 'Vietnam Syndrome'. During the United States war in South-East Asia, aimed at preventing the defeat of the South Vietnamese government to communist forces, the US government suffered a significant, albeit gradual, decline in public support for the war. With the eventual defeat of US forces, a perception emerged within some quarters of the US foreign policy establishment that negative public reaction to US casualties was fundamental in draining the commitment of the US government to fight in Vietnam. Belief in the Vietnam Syndrome is so prevalent within military and political circles that it is regularly invoked during debates over US military operations; for example in Somalia 1992–3, Kosovo 1999, and current US operations in Iraq. Unless military victory can be achieved with minimal loss of life, erosion of public support will ultimately contribute to military defeat. According to the Vietnam Syndrome, public opinion acts as a *constraint upon US power* by limiting the ability of the USA to engage in military action.

Whether or not the Vietnam Syndrome exists as a reality, as opposed to a belief, is subject to substantial debate. In fact, evidence exists supporting an inverse relationship between US casualties and public support for war. For example, in *War, Presidents and Public Opinion*, John Mueller (1973) examined opinion polls and casualty counts during the Korean and Vietnam wars, and found that during both a tenfold increase in the number of US military casualties correlated with a 16-percentage-point drop in public support. However, whilst casualties might decrease public support for war, the extent to which this then influences politics is less clear-cut. For example, there exists some evidence that foreign policy issues do have a major impact upon how the US public votes (e.g. Aldrich, Sullivan, and Borgida 1989). However, even if foreign policy issues influence voting and, in turn, impact on a US president in electoral terms, this does

MAJOR DEBATES AND THEIR IMPACT 9.1: Realist and liberal-democratic views on public opinion and foreign policy

The liberal-democratic perspective

The idea that public opinion should influence foreign policy formulation has a long history. In the early twentieth century, President Woodrow Wilson articulated the importance of public scrutiny of foreign affairs in his famous 'Fourteen Points'. Here he called for 'Open covenants of peace, openly arrived at, after which there shall be no private international understandings of any kind but diplomacy shall proceed always frankly and in the public view'. More specifically, a key component of liberal theory is the *democratic peace thesis*. This thesis maintains that liberal democracies are war-averse because, at least in part, the consent of the public is required. As people generally prefer peace to war, public opinion can act as a powerful constraint upon elected leaders and, therefore, the external behaviour of a state. In order for this to occur, public opinion should be able to influence foreign policy. Overall, the liberal-democratic perspective maintains that public opinion can contribute to sound foreign policy; as well as acting as a check against corrupt political elites, incorporating public concerns increases the range of opinions and arguments available to policy makers. As a result, more rational and well-thought-out policies can be devised.

The realist perspective

The realist perspective that foreign policy should be immune from public influence also has a long history. Writing in reference to US public opinion during the early part of the Cold War era, Walter Lippman claimed that '[t]he Unhappy truth is that the prevailing public opinion has been destructively wrong at the critical junctures' (Lippman 1955: 20) (see also Key quotes 9.3). In part, the claim underpinning the realist perspective is that foreign policy elites are best placed to decide what should be done in order to further US national interests; and, at the same time, that the US public are largely ignorant and/or ill informed about international affairs and, therefore, ill equipped to think about the complexities of foreign policy. But the realist claim is also now underpinned by the *neorealist* position that policy makers react to events in the international system, such as emerging threats and shifts in the balance of power, and not to internal factors such as the desires and wishes of the US public. Overall, realism argues that policy makers should remain detached from the pressures of public opinion, formulating foreign policy in response to external events in the international system, and not in response to internal domestic politics including public opinion.

To a large extent, these two competing normative positions on the role of public opinion and media are reflected throughout both policy debate and academic research. For example, some policy makers from a realist perspective have complained that public opinion and media wield too much power vis-à-vis foreign policy formulation, and that this prevents rational policy making. In the case of Vietnam, the apparent impact of public opinion and media suggested to realists that these had prevented the USA from winning that war. For academics, these normative positions are often spoken to in the research questions that they pursue. For example, some research into the CNN effect analyses this phenomenon in order to assess whether policy elites have 'lost control' over the policy process. As such, this research is of direct relevance to policy makers who seek to minimize media impact on policy.

not necessarily mean that actual policy is then influenced. For example, the Republican Party suffered significant losses in the 2006 congressional elections which many analysts put down to the Iraq War. However, the resulting impact of those losses on the Bush administration and its policy towards Iraq has not, apparently, led to a decision to withdraw from Iraq.

Indeed, research documenting the impact of public opinion on actual foreign policy decisions is scarce (see Holsti 1992 for an overview). Part of the problem lies in gathering evidence from meetings that are held in secret. And, even when documentary evidence exists from such meetings, the researcher is still confronted with the task of inferring from this data what was actually going on in the minds of policy makers. A more complicated issue confounding attempts to *measure influence* is the difficulty of disentangling one factor influencing policy making, public opinion, from the multitude of factors that may be relevant.

Overall however, a perception persists that US public opinion does influence US foreign policy. The actual empirical evidence to support this perception is less certain. Whilst evidence points toward the importance of foreign affairs vis-à-vis voting, there is less to support the claim that foreign policy decisions are then influenced as a result. At most, public opinion is one factor amongst many shaping policy decisions. Perhaps of greater importance, however, is the tendency of the public opinion–foreign policy literature to ignore a crucial intervening variable—that of media. In the broadest sense, whilst public opinion might be formed along isolationist/internationalist lines, the details of particular foreign policy issues have to be communicated via mainstream media. In turn, the question of how public opinion is shaped regarding specific issues is linked to the way in which US media present those issues. At the same time, officials use media both as a source of information and as a guide to 'perceived public opinion' whereby policy makers use the agenda and tone of media reports as a guide to public opinion (Entman 2000: 79). In terms of understanding influences upon US foreign policy, it is equally important to examine the way media reports on international affairs. And it is to pluralist accounts of the relationship between media and foreign policy that we now turn.

Media and foreign policy: the CNN effect debate

It was the Vietnam War, again, that elevated interest in the power of media to mould both public opinion and foreign policy. Whilst arguments surrounding the Vietnam Syndrome focused upon the impact of US casualties on public opinion, a parallel argument emerged concerning the role of US media in particular during 1968 Tet Offensive. This offensive involved an uprising throughout South Vietnam organized by communist forces. During this crisis, widespread

fighting occurred across major cities in South Vietnam and in full view of US journalists. A war that had been presented by the US military as one that was being won, suddenly appeared out of control. For some, relentlessly adversarial and critical journalism revealed the horrors of the Vietnam War, both fuelling anti-war sentiment and forcing the hand of policy makers. As with public opinion and the Vietnam Syndrome discussed earlier, the perception was created that media had acted as a powerful constraint, effectively limiting the use of US military power (see Key quotes 9.1). Since that time, the quantity of studies asserting the influence of media on foreign policy has steadily increased. Two developments, in particular, underpinned the thesis that the US media was beginning to wield greater power. The first concerned the arrival of 24-hour news broadcasting epitomized by Cable News Network (CNN). As a news channel attempting to compete with traditional media, CNN promised an orientation toward international news and took advantage of developments in communication technology to provide dramatic real-time reporting from around the world. Largely due to CNN, events such as the collapse of communism, symbolized by the fall of the Berlin Wall, and the 1991 Gulf War, were experienced in real time by many US citizens. The effect of this development, according to some commentators (e.g. Hoge 1994), was to increase the exposure of both the US public and foreign policy establishment as major crises around the world were reported instantaneously. Some spoke of foreign policy being driven by CNN, the so-called 'CNN effect'. The second development understood to have increased media influence was the end of the Cold War. During this period world events had been dominated by the ideological clash between communism and capitalism that had created an ideological bond between US journalists and policy makers. In short, US journalists and US policy makers viewed global events through the same Cold War prism of anti-communism and journalists were disinclined to question their government when under threat from the 'red menace'. Released from the ideological 'prism of the Cold War', US journalists had, it was argued, become freer to cover the stories they wanted to and criticize

> **KEY QUOTES 9.1:** Richard Nixon on media and the Vietnam War

The Vietnam War was complicated by factors that never before occurred in America's conduct of a war . . . More than ever before, television showed the terrible human suffering and sacrifice of war, whatever the intention behind such relentless and literal reporting of the war, the result was a serious demoralization of the home front, raising the question whether America would never again be able to fight an enemy abroad with unity and strength of purpose at home.

(Nixon 1978)

their government. Overall, these developments in media (24-hour, real-time news) and global politics (the ending of the Cold War) have been understood by some as ushering in an era of unequalled media power (e.g. Entman 2000).

Further impetus was given to the CNN effect claim by an increase in interventions during humanitarian crises (see Key quotes 9.2). Following the 1991 Gulf War, when the USA led a UN-authorized war to reverse the invasion of Kuwait by Iraq, uprisings occurred in northern and southern Iraq aimed at the overthrow of Saddam Hussein's regime. When these were suppressed by Saddam Hussein a major humanitarian crisis developed and, in northern Iraq, Iraqi Kurds became trapped in the mountainous region of northern Iraq attempting to escape Saddam's forces. Following weeks of critical media coverage, the USA intervened by creating safe areas in northern Iraq. For many this represented an unprecedented instance where the USA had been moved by media and public pressure to intervene in the internal affairs of another state in order to protect human rights (e.g. Shaw 1996). Further US involvement during crises in Somalia in 1991–2 (see Box 9.1), Bosnia in 1995, and Kosovo in 1999, all of which received extensive attention from the US media, seemed to confirm the power of media to drive foreign policy formulation (Robinson 2002).

Overall, the idea of the CNN effect dovetails with liberal-democrat arguments (see Major debates and their impact 9.1) that favour a democratic and open foreign policy agenda shaped by media and public opinion. Furthermore, for some liberal advocates of humanitarian intervention, media are a source of power in terms of helping build public support for humanitarian operations. At the same time, many realists who oppose US involvement in humanitarian operations perceive this influence as damaging to US interests. But how true is the CNN effect?

In fact, rather than confirming the impression of an all-powerful media, a large body of research into the CNN effect conducted over the last fifteen years has suggested the existence of a far more subtle range of effects, most of which indicate that claims of a media-*driven* foreign policy are exaggerated (e.g. Gowing 1994). It is to a discussion of these types of effect that we now turn.

Routes of influence and types of effect

We can identify two routes by which media coverage may influence policy (Livingston and Riley 1999). The *indirect route* refers to the process by which media reports influence public opinion, which in turn can then influence policy makers who are sensitive, via

> **KEY QUOTES 9.2:** Michael Mandelbaum on humanitarian intervention

For the United States, however, what lies behind intervention in the post-Cold War era is neither gold, nor glory, nor strategic calculation. It is, rather, sympathy. The televised pictures of starving people in northern Iraq, Somalia, and Bosnia created a political clamor to feed them, which propelled the US military into those three distant parts of the world.

(Mandelbaum 1994)

BOX 9.1: Case study: US intervention in Somalia, 1992–3

The US intervention (Operation Restore Hope) during the crisis in Somalia 1991–2 was a seminal event both in terms of intervention during a humanitarian crisis and the role of media in US foreign policy formulation. The crisis in Somalia had developed due to civil war, the collapse of central government, and ensuing mass starvation. By 1992, the crisis was attracting a significant degree of international attention and the USA started to become increasingly involved. By December 1992, 28,000 US troops were deployed in Somalia in order to support the provision of aid. As well as apparently cementing a new norm of humanitarian intervention, the intervention was a major news event remembered perhaps most for the graphic images of starvation and conflict in Somalia and the images of US marines being greeted on the beeches of Mogadishu, not by hostile gunmen, but by the world's press. By the end of the operation, with the worldwide broadcast of a dead US marine being dragged through the streets of Mogadishu, the intervention was indelibly etched on US memory. As a case study in media, public opinion, and US foreign policy, the intervention highlights the various roles media and public opinion might play. In terms of the initial intervention, many have argued that the decision to intervene was caused by the CNN effect whereby graphic and emotive images of starving people created a cry to 'do something' from the American public, thereby compelling US policy makers to take action (e.g. Kennan 1993). Others have claimed that the attention of US media to the suffering in Somalia helped to build a domestic constituency for the interven-

tion which policy makers were then able to draw upon to support the intervention (Robinson 2002: 59–62). As such, the media and public opinion had an enabling effect with respect to the decision to intervene. Once the intervention was under way, US media coverage helped to mobilize support amongst the US public for the operation by portraying US actions in a positive light, emphasizing the role US soldiers and aid workers were playing in saving Somali lives (Robinson 2002: 59–62). By mid-to-late 1993, however, the operation had evolved beyond supporting aid delivery to include military action against specific factions within Somalia. The now infamous 'Black Hawk Down' incident, which involved the deaths of 18 US soldiers and up to 1,000 Somalis, was a pivotal moment vis-à-vis the perceived failure of the intervention and US withdrawal from the country. In particular, images of a dead US combatant being dragged through the streets of the Somali capital Mogadishu were broadcast on US media and generated, according to some (e.g. Kennan 1993), a political imperative to withdraw from the country. As such, at this stage of the intervention, media may have come to have an impediment effect on policy makers whereby images of dead US soldiers turned public opinion against involvement in Somalia. Beyond the specifics of the intervention and withdrawal, and any role public opinion and media played in these, the Somalia intervention and its ignominious end have become embedded in US foreign policy thinking as an example of US military failure in the context of humanitarian intervention.

the democratic process, to public opinion. The *direct route* refers to the process by which policy makers are directly affected by what they see and read in the media. So, for example, when images of civilian deaths during the Bosnian conflict were broadcast by CNN, some senior policy makers would react to such images on a personal level and be moved to 'do something' to prevent further loss of life.

With respect to types of effect, four distinct categories of effect can be identified; a *CNN effect*, an *accelerant effect*, an *enabling effect*, and an *impediment effect* (Livingston 1997; Robinson 2002). The CNN effect

occurs when media coverage plays a direct role in causing policy makers to adopt a particular policy. This does not mean that media were the only reason that policy makers chose a particular policy option, but it does mean that without media pressure, the policy would not have been adopted. Generally, when academics talk of media influence, it is the CNN effect they have in mind. For example, George Kennan (1993) argued that it was emotive images of starvation that caused US policy makers to intervene in Somalia (see Box 9.1). In the absence of those images, no intervention would have occurred. In fact, evidence for the CNN effect has been hard to find. For example, a decade of research into this phenomenon has failed to provide consistent evidence of strategic foreign policy initiatives (for example humanitarian intervention) being caused by media pressure (Gilboa 2005). More commonly, research has found evidence of an accelerant effect, whereby the decision-making process is speeded up by media attention. However, whilst often cited by both policy makers and academics, the accelerant effect does not entail media causing a particular policy outcome; rather this type of effect suggests that policy makers respond more quickly to a particular issue, but do so in precisely the same ways they would have done without media attention. For example, in relation to the crisis in northern Iraq 1991, media attention to the Kurdish crisis might have speeded up the US decision to intervene, but that decision would have, in any case, been made at some later point. Another effect is that media can enable policy makers to pursue a policy by building public support for that policy (Wheeler 2000: 165). For example, it could be argued that the 9/11 attacks on the USA, and the fact they were communicated to the US public in horrific real-time reporting, were crucial in helping to mobilize public support in favour of the Bush administration's war on terror and military action in Afghanistan and Iraq. The attacks, and their mass-mediated nature, therefore helped to build a constituency amongst US citizens for a more interventionist foreign policy. Finally, the impediment effect is linked to the Vietnam Syndrome. Here, it is a fear over negative media coverage of US casualties and its impact on public opinion that constrains policy makers and prevents them pursuing a policy. For example, during the air war against Serbia in 1999, the Clinton administration limited military options to air strikes in order to avoid US casualties. A factor in this decision was the desire to avoid negative publicity of US casualties during an already politically controversial operation.

Procedural criticism versus substantive criticism

In concluding our discussion of pluralist accounts, it is important to note that whilst claims about the

influence of public opinion and media abound, academic research suggests actual influence wielded is more subtle and nuanced than is commonly assumed. As discussed, the influence of public opinion upon foreign policy, whilst receiving empirical support, needs to be moderated by the acknowledgement of the multitude of factors influencing policy making. At the same time, notions of a CNN effect need to be moderated through acknowledgement that a more subtle range of effects (e.g. the enabling effect) are occurring most of the time. Whilst it would be churlish to argue that media and public carry no influence, the question of whether that influence is sufficient from a liberal-democratic perspective is debatable.

More significantly, much research on media influence suggests that media influence occurs most often at the procedural level, rather than at a substantive level (Althaus 2003). The term *procedural* describes criticism and influence that relates to debate over the implementation of foreign policy. The term *substantive* is used to describe criticism and influence that relates to the underlying justification and rationale for particular foreign policies. For example, the Vietnam War was criticized by US media and public more often at a procedural level whereby the central question revolved around whether the USA was winning or losing the war. Criticism, however, rarely raised the more substantive question of the justification for US involvement in Vietnam. Again, returning to the example of the 1999 air war against Serbia, most of the controversy within US media related to whether or not air power was enough to win the war. At the same time, debate over whether intervention could be justified at all remained marginal (Robinson 2002: 93–110). As we shall see in the next section, when we discuss elite/critical accounts of the public opinion/media/foreign policy nexus, the primary focus of concern is precisely this lack of substantive debate over US foreign policy.

Criticisms of the pluralist model

The claim that the relationship between US public opinion, media, and foreign policy can be described as pluralist is often subject to four major criticisms. The first relates to the tendency of pluralists to overestimate agency, that is the ability of individuals to influence and change politics, whilst underplaying the importance of political and economic structures that serve to constrain and direct individuals. For example, whilst US journalists are 'independent' and guaranteed the right to free speech, both the political system within which they operate and the commercial company their media are a part of are likely to exert an influence upon what the journalist thinks and writes. Second, the pluralist model can be criticized for overplaying both the knowledge levels of the US public vis-à-vis foreign affairs as well as the actual responsiveness of the US government to public and media influence. Here, a tendency to measure the more plentiful procedural-level criticism and influence, as opposed to the rarer substantive-level criticism, leads to overestimates regarding the pluralist credentials of the US system. A third and related problem is a tendency for advocates of the pluralist model to focus on relatively rare events, such as the Watergate scandal, as evidence of public and media power when, in fact, these are very much exceptions to the rule. Finally, the pluralist model tends to ignore the financial and material resources that are employed by the US government in order to influence media and public opinion. Here, a substantial public relations apparatus serves to promote official viewpoints via press briefings, information packs, off-the-record briefings, and the careful packaging (or 'spin-doctoring') of policy. As such, the flow of information between government and public is not a two-way street, as assumed by the pluralist model, but heavily weighted in favour of the US government.

> **KEY POINTS**
>
> ❏ The liberal-democratic perspective maintains that public opinion and media should influence foreign policy.
> ❏ The pluralist model argues the public are capable of both rationally assessing foreign policy and influencing foreign policy.
> ❏ The pluralist model argues media have a significant impact upon foreign policy formulation.
> ❏ Media criticism of, and influence upon, foreign policy can be categorized according to procedural and substantive categories.

The elite model

Compared to the pluralist model, the elite model of the public opinion/media/foreign policy nexus works with different assumptions. Whilst the pluralist model assumes that power is dispersed throughout the political system and society, the elite model argues that relatively small groups within the USA wield power. With respect to US foreign policy, groups with power include the combination of foreign policy officials, think tanks, and representatives of large business interests. Those who are not included, according to the elite model, are the bulk of the American public. Consequently, the political process, including media debate and public opinion formation, is the outcome of elite interests and agendas that dominate media and public debate. Specifically, the elite model maintains the US public are not only influenced by what they see and hear in the news, but are also directed to think about issues in a way congenial to elite interests. Following on from this, the elite model maintains that media are closely located to elite groups in both political and financial terms. Consequently media are a propaganda tool for elites. Finally, the elite model maintains the US political system is immune from non-elite influence.

Having introduced the elite model, and following the section on the pluralist model, I will first examine elite accounts of the relationship between public opinion and foreign policy, and then discuss elite accounts of the relationship between media and foreign policy. But first, we need to briefly discuss the differing normative stance of realist and critical perspectives.

Realists and critical perspectives

Unlike the liberal-democratic perspective, which advocates public involvement in foreign policy formulation, realist approaches caution against allowing public opinion to influence foreign policy (see Major debates and their impact 9.1). Beyond the realist perspective, critical accounts share a similar empirical position to that of the realist; i.e. that elites control the foreign policy process and are immune from public influence. The critical perspective, however, does not share the normative assumption of the realist perspective that this state of affairs is right. Rather, critical accounts develop a moral critique of elite domination of US foreign policy (see Controversies 9.1). To recap, both realist and critical perspectives maintain that foreign policy is conducted by elites, largely free from the pressures of public opinion. Where the two perspectives differ is on whether this is right, as argued by realists, or wrong, as is claimed by critical approaches.

Public opinion and foreign policy

It was largely early research that laid the ground for realist hostility toward the US public. Gabriel Almond's (1950) *The American People and Foreign Policy* argued that only a small proportion of the US public, which he labelled as an 'attentive public', possessed knowledge sufficient to hold a valid position on foreign policy issues. The broader mass public held non-attitudes whereby individuals responded irrationally to foreign affairs issues and held unstable, rapidly changing opinions. Associated with Almond's position was a significant stream of research maintaining public opinion had little impact on foreign policy. Together, the idea that public opinion was both irrational and possessing of little influence became known as the 'Almond–Lippman Consensus' (see Key quotes 9.3). For example, Bernard Cohen's (1973) *The Public's Impact on Foreign Policy* asserted that foreign policy officials discounted public opinion and maintained that public opinion should rather be shaped by government. Whilst pluralist challenges have emerged (as discussed in the previous section), plenty of examples abound to support the Almond–Lippman Consensus. For example, in relation to knowledge levels of the US public and the 2003 Iraq War, some opinion polls showed that a significant number of the US public believed the Iraqi President Saddam Hussein was involved with Osama bin Laden in conspiring to attack the USA.[1] An example that policy elites regard US public as something to be led is that of President Bush's speech writer Michael Gerson who asserted the 9/11 attacks provided the Bush administration with a 'plastic, teachable moment' (Woodward 2004: 84) whereby the US public could be persuaded to support Bush's war on terror and other foreign policy initiatives. With respect to the impotence of public opinion, one can also highlight the case that, whilst US public opinion has increasingly turned against the war in Iraq, there has apparently been no decision by the US government to withdraw from Iraq.

Whilst the realist perspective highlights the inadequacy of public knowledge and understanding, critical accounts point toward the ways in which public

---

 KEY QUOTES 9.3: Walter Lippman on public opinion

The people have impressed a critical veto upon the judgements of informed and responsible officials. They have compelled the government, which usually knew what would have been wiser, or was necessary, or what was more expedient, to be too late with too little, or too long with too much, too pacifist in peace and too bellicose in war, too neutralist or appeasing in negotiations or too intransigent . . . It has shown itself to be a master of indecision when the stakes are life and death.

(Lippman 1955)

knowledge and understanding are shaped by mainstream media. Contrasting with pluralist accounts, critical accounts argue the extent to which US public are able to consume news and form independent opinions is more limited than suggested by the pluralist model. Here, the concepts of *agenda setting* (McCombs and Shaw 1972), *priming* (Iyengar and Kinder 1987), and *framing* (Entman 1991) clarify the ways in which public opinion can be shaped. In his seminal study *The Press and Foreign Policy*, Bernard Cohen (1973) argued, '[t]he press may not be successful much of the time in telling people what to think, but it is stunningly successful in telling its readers what to think about'; that is to say, media are able to set the agenda by getting the public to think about certain issues and not others. Priming refers to the ability of media to direct publics to the issues upon which they should judge their leaders, whilst framing refers to the ways in which the presentation of news information helps to shape how people think about specific issues. For example, analysing the 1991 Gulf War, Iyengar and Simon (1994) demonstrate that media focus on the Gulf crisis led to the public defining the crisis as the most important political issue at the time. Media had set the agenda and directed the public as to what was the most important issue to think about. Their analysis also demonstrated that US public were, accordingly, primed to judge US President George Bush Sr. on how well he handled the war. Finally, Iyengar and Simon argue that media coverage of the war was framed in terms of event-driven news (*episodic news*) that focused upon military matters, such as military technology and the progress of the war, and tended to downplay *thematic news* dealing with diplomatic issues and issues related to the rationale and justification for war. According to their analysis this framing of news increased viewers' support for military action, as opposed to alternative diplomatic solutions.

Thus far, it is clear that elite accounts (both realist and critical) perceive the US public as either ill informed, a 'bewildered herd' as the famous political commentator Walter Lippman (1922) once asserted, or as dependent upon media in terms of their opinion formation. But what role do US media play in creating this state of affairs? With this in mind, it is to elite accounts of media we now turn.

Media and foreign policy

At the core of elite accounts of mainstream US media lies the claim that the media agenda, and the framing of issues, is usually highly compatible with the agenda and perspective of US political and social elites. A significant and powerful early critique of US media was developed by Daniel Hallin (1986) in his analysis of US media coverage of the Vietnam War, *The Uncensored War*. Directly challenging claims (noted earlier) that US media adopted an adversarial stance toward the war, Hallin's analysis found that coverage was actually very supportive of the war right up until 1968. At this point, however, communist forces launched the Tet Offensive, and fighting that had, hitherto, been confined to rural parts of the country spilled over onto the streets of major cities including the capital Saigon. Whilst this event produced some of the most graphic and infamous images of the war, and did precipitate an increase in media criticism, Hallin finds that this only occurred after the US political establishment had become divided over whether or not the war in Vietnam could be won at a cost that was bearable for the United States. Importantly, according to Hallin, media rarely reported in positive terms the views of the US anti-war movement which maintained that the war was immoral and unjustified. As such, US media,

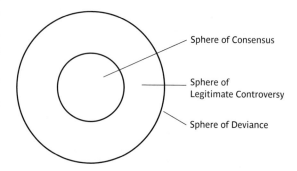

Fig. 9.1 Spheres of consensus, controversy, and deviance

Source: By permission of Oxford University Press Inc. Originally published in Daniel C. Hallin (1986), *The Uncensored War: The Media and Vietnam* (New York: Oxford University Press), 117.

throughout the war in Vietnam, merely followed the contours of elite opinion as journalists relied upon, and privileged, Washington-based news sources. Consequently, when the US establishment was in agreement on policy, media operated within a *sphere of consensus* and coverage was supportive of the war. When the US establishment became divided over the war, US media reflected this debate by reporting within the *sphere of legitimate controversy*. However, US media rarely reported upon those with views outside the boundary of legitimate controversy (such as the anti-war movement) which, according to Hallin, lay within a *sphere of deviance*. As such, media criticism of the Vietnam War remained at a procedural and tactical level, reflecting debate over whether current policy was winning the war, and did not extend to substantive questioning of the legitimacy of US involvement in Vietnam.

Further conceptual clarification of the elite model came with Bennett's influential *indexing hypothesis*. According to Bennett (see Key quotes 9.4), media deference to US elites can be explained through the propensity of journalists to index news coverage to public officials in Washington. In part this is because journalists see it as their democratic responsibility to consult publicly elected officials when reporting the news. But it is also a function of the tremendous quantity of information (press briefings, public statements, etc.) that is produced by US centres of government which helps to feed media demands for a constant flow of news stories. Perhaps most significantly, Bennett notes that the indexing norm helps to keep 'news compatible with the shifting political and economic interests of the state' (Bennett 1990: 109).

Overall, the net result of the close proximity between US mainstream media and the foreign policy establishment is, according to elite perspectives, that the US public is rarely presented with news information that does anything other than 'manufacture consent' (Lippman 1922; Herman and Chomsky 1988), via processes such as *agenda setting* and *framing*, for policy-making preferences that are decided in Washington. Even when the news *appears* to be critical and adversarial, it is kept within the bounds of elite-legitimized controversy. As Bennett describes: 'the media have helped create a world that is, culturally speaking, upside down. It is a world in which governments are able to define their own public and where "democracy" becomes whatever the government ends up doing' (Bennett 1990: 125). Of course, for realists, this state of affairs is to be welcomed as it ensures that foreign policy remains debated and decided by those who have the skills to do so. From this perspective, a compliant and therefore supportive public and media become a source of power for US foreign policy with media helping to mobilize the US public in support of US foreign policy objectives. From the critical perspective, this state of affairs is to be challenged as an affront to the democratic principles of the United States and its claimed commitment to human rights and justice (see Controversies 9.1).

Criticisms of the elite model

The empirical claims put forward by advocates of the elite model are subjected to five main criticisms. First, that they overemphasize the idea that political and

---

❝ KEY QUOTES 9.4: Lance Bennett and indexing

In this ironic twist on the democratic ideal, modern public opinion can be thought of as an 'index' constructed from the distribution of dominant institutional voices as recorded in the mass media. By adopting such an opinion index, the media have helped create a political world that is, culturally speaking, upside down. It is a world in which governments are able to define their own publics and where 'democracy' becomes whatever the government ends up doing.

(Bennett 1990)

CONTROVERSIES 9.1: Herman and Chomsky's (1988) propaganda model

In *Manufacturing Consent: The Political Economy of the Mass Media*, Herman and Chomsky set out their propaganda model: a provocative and controversial elite model explanation of why, in their view, mainstream US media function as a tool to mobilize public support for elite policy preferences (see Key quotes 9.5). According to this model, five filters function to shape news media output. First, the 'size, ownership and profit orientation of mass media' and their shared 'common interests . . . with other major corporations, banks, and government' create a clash of interest between the media's supposed role as a watchdog of the elite and the interests of that elite (Herman and Chomsky 1988: 3, 14). Consequently, news stories that run contrary to those vested interests are less likely to surface than those consistent with the world view of major corporate conglomerates. Second, media reliance on advertising revenue introduces a further constraining link between the news media and the interests of commerce. This reliance shapes media output in order to appeal to affluent audiences, in whom the advertisers are most interested. It also limits the amount of critical and controversial programming because advertisers generally want 'to avoid programs with serious complexities and disturbing controversies that interfere with the "buying mood"' (Herman and Chomsky 1988: 17). Third, journalists rely heavily on official sources when constructing the news. The need to supply a steady and rapid flow of 'important' news stories combined with the vast public relations apparatus of government and powerful interests more broadly means that journalists tend to become heavily reliant on public officials and corporate representatives when defining and framing the news agenda. Fourth, whenever controversial material is actually aired it generates a disproportionate degree of 'flak' from individuals connected with powerful interests

including 'corporate community sponsored . . . institutions' (Herman and Chomsky 1988: 27) such as the Center for Media and Public Affairs, and Accuracy in Media (AIM) and government 'spin doctors'. Such criticism serves to caution editors and journalists against putting out news stories that are 'too' controversial. Finally, Herman and Chomsky highlight the importance of an ideology of 'anti-communism as a control mechanism' that provided journalists, at least during the Cold War, with a ready-made template with which to 'understand' global events, and provided the political elite with a powerful rhetorical tool with which to criticize as unpatriotic anyone who questioned US foreign policy (Herman and Chomsky 1988: 29). At the core of the critique developed by Herman and Chomsky (1988) is the claim that mainstream US media perpetuate an image of the United States as inherently benign, peaceful, and committed to high moral standards when, in fact, its foreign policies are riddled with self-interested economic and political objectives that often lead the USA to support violent and illiberal policies. As such US media are not free and autonomous but, rather, mobilize—through deception—US citizens in support of the actions of their government. For instance, in support of their case, Herman and Chomsky (1988) document how US media functioned to promote anti-communism by highlighting human rights abuses committed by communist states and downplaying similar abuses committed by allies of the United States during the 'struggle against communism'. Overall, Herman and Chomsky present a profound and forcefully argued thesis that raises fundamental questions about the democratic credentials of US society and politics.

For discussions sympathetic to the propaganda model see 'Forum on Chomsky' (2003). For critical discussion of the propaganda model see Lang and Lang (2004).

KEY QUOTES 9.5: Edward Herman and Noam Chomsky on manufacturing consent

The mass media serve as a system for communicating messages and symbols to the general populace. It is their function to amuse, entertain, and inform, and to inculcate individuals with the values, beliefs, and codes of behaviour that will integrate them into the institutional structures of the larger society. In a world of concentrated wealth and major conflicts of class interest, to fulfil this role requires systematic propaganda.

(Herman and Chomsky 1988)

economic structures limit the autonomy and agency of both journalists and the US public. Here, the argument is advanced that journalists and citizens actually have a good deal of independence from political and economic power and are capable of forming opinions that are distinct from the viewpoints of elite groups. Associated with this is a second criticism, based upon audience reception studies, that individuals have been shown to be capable of resisting dominant messages and frames promoted by political elites. For example, whilst US elites, and indeed media, promoted the value of the Vietnam War, some claim that significant sections of the US public rejected the legitimacy of the action throughout the war. Third, elite accounts are criticized for exaggerating both the level of agreement and the consistency of shared interests that exists between elite groups in society. Here, the idea is advanced that, in reality, there are divergent interests between, for example, US government and big business, which means that elite groups as a whole are far weaker than implied by the elite model, often 'fighting' amongst themselves and rarely succeeding in promoting a unified dominant message to media and public. Fourth, the elite model is also sometimes criticized for treating 'the media' as a unified and monolithic entity, effectively acting as a well-honed propaganda wing of the US state when, in fact, there is a good deal of diversity across different US media outlets. For example, Matthew Baum (2003) has argued that new forms of light entertainment channels are

---

BOX 9.2: Beyond the elite/pluralist dichotomy: new approaches to theorizing the public opinion/media/foreign policy nexus

Whilst elite and pluralist perspectives continue to influence academic debate, recent research has attempted to develop models that capture both these theoretical perspectives and, therefore, provide a more nuanced and differentiated understanding of media–state relations. For example, many academics now argue that both elite dissensus (Hallin 1986) (when there exists disagreement within the political and foreign policy establishment), and unexpected events (Lawrence 2000) that occur beyond the control of governments, can considerably open up the boundaries of media criticism and influence. So, for example, during the build-up to and the invasion of Iraq in 2003, widespread debate raged amongst politicians and within the foreign policy community in the UK over the justification for the war. As a consequence, media coverage was much more critical and perhaps influential in terms of shaping public and elite perceptions of the war (although, of course, the fundamentals of UK policy in Iraq appear to have remained unchanged to date). At the same time, unexpected or uncontrolled events (such as the abuse of Iraqis by coalition forces) that spread through the world's media meant that the UK and US governments were subjected to varying levels of criticism and dissent from their respective domestic medias. Other recent accounts that attempt to bridge the elite/pluralist divide include Wolfsfeld's (1997) *political contest model* and Robinson's (2002) *policy-media*

interaction model. These models emphasize variables such as levels of policy certainty (Robinson 2002) and control over the political environment (Wolfsfeld 1997). For example, when a government is uncertain over policy, media and public opinion can exert greater influence on policy formulation. Alternatively, when policy is set in place, the potential for media influence wanes. Wolfsfeld argues that sometimes a government can lose control of the political environment which in turn leads to a more critical media and space for non-elite challenges. He demonstrates how the Israeli government lost control over the political environment during the 1987 Palestinian uprising, the *intifada*; as a consequence media mobilized support for the Palestinians and criticized Israeli policy (see Key quotes 9.6). Finally, focusing upon public opinion, Douglas Foyle (1999) argues that public influence on foreign policy in the USA is dependent upon the normative position of the president regarding the desirability of public influence on their policy, and their need for public support in order to carry through a policy. Some US presidents, who Foyle labels as 'delegates', believe that public opinion is desirable and necessary and thus are indeed influenced by public opinion. Other US presidents, labelled as 'guardians', believe that the public should never be considered when formulating foreign policy and, therefore, are not influenced by public opinion.

> **❝ KEY QUOTES 9.6:** Gadi Wolfsfeld and political contest

The competition between authorities and challengers over the news media is as fascinating and unpredictable as politics itself. In some ways the central arena resembles the modern sports facility that can be converted into several structures, each designed for a different type of event. Sometimes the arena is used for lavish spectacles in which officials show off their most colourful costumes and weapons. At other times it is a place for fierce contests in which challengers and authorities square off in brutal combat. And at yet other times it becomes a theatre-in-the-round putting on tragic morality plays about the plight of the oppressed and the need for social change.

(Wolfsfeld 1997)

actually important conveyors of political information for the broader public. Finally, the elite model is sometimes criticized for failing to pay attention to circumstances where elite influence might be disrupted and spaces opened up for a more critical and independent media. For example Regina Lawrence (2000) argues that unexpected and newsworthy events that occur beyond the control of government can lead to opportunities for previously marginalized, non-elite, groups to influenced media reporting (see Box 9.2).

KEY POINTS

- ❏ The realist perspective argues that media and public opinion should not influence foreign policy.
- ❏ Critical accounts argue that the failure of media and public opinion to influence foreign policy is wrong.
- ❏ The elite model argues that public are ignorant of international affairs and have little influence.
- ❏ The elite model argues that media mobilize support for government policies.

Public and media diplomacy

Thus far, the focus of this chapter has been the relationship between foreign policy, media, and public opinion with respect to the United States and domestic politics. An important area of research, however, has analysed the ways in which the US government attempts to project power and influence by both influencing non-US public opinion, or world opinion, and shaping news agendas of non-US media. At the heart of these policies lies the concept of *soft power* (Nye 1990), a term that refers to non-coercive (and non-military) approaches to projecting US power and influence in the world. At this point in time, with the Bush administration's global war on terror and desire to 'win hearts and minds'; particularly amongst non-Western and Muslim audiences, the role of public and media diplomacy is perhaps more central than ever to US foreign policy.

Public diplomacy has a long history. For example, *Voice of America* first started radio broadcasts in 1942 aimed at promoting democracy and, in time, came to be broadcast in forty-five languages with over 100 million listeners worldwide (Gilboa 1998: 58). Again, in 1953, the United States Information Agency was created in order to 'coordinate the combat against the spread of communist ideas' (Taylor 2006: 5). Overall the aim of public diplomacy has been to attempt to influence the citizens of foreign nations in ways conducive to US interests so that they can in turn influence their respective governments accordingly. As Gilboa (1998: 58–67) describes, public diplomacy (conducted through both media and other fields including cultural and educational initiatives) has been aimed at long-term influence of target audiences around the world, functioning very much at an ideological level by both promoting US values (such as democracy, human rights, and capitalism), and attempting to persuade peoples of the world that the USA is the leading example of such values. Media diplomacy, conversely, has been more narrowly focused upon both promoting US interests vis-à-vis specific issues, such as peace initiatives, and attempting to promote a US agenda throughout the world's media. More recently, the intensity and resources committed to these aspects of US diplomacy have increasingly adopted the style and approach of the marketing industry, whereby policies are packaged and sold as if they were commercial products. For example, following the toppling of Saddam Hussein's regime in 2003, President George Bush alighted upon a US aircraft carrier against a banner that read 'Mission Accomplished'. Whilst the details behind the organization of this event are unknown, it is likely that the event was carefully crafted so as to produce images that offered a symbol of success to the America public and send a powerful signal vis-à-vis US military prowess to the governments and peoples of the world.

The belief amongst many is that the development of political marketing (or spin as it is commonly described) techniques is a central tool in promoting US interests in today's world of global media. Moreover, the prevalent belief by those involved with public and media diplomacy is that, so long as the message is correctly packaged and communicated, the USA can indeed project power through winning the hearts and minds of world opinion. The extent to which this is true, given the rise of non-US-based global media such as the Arab-based Al-Jazeera and the nature of the current war on terror, is a question to which we now turn.

KEY POINTS

❏ *Soft power* refers to the power to influence international affairs via persuasion.
❏ The US government devotes considerable resources to the projection of soft power.
❏ Soft power is projected through the promotion of US culture and values, in part, to non-US publics and global media.

Conclusion: new technology and US power

Pluralist and elite models of the public opinion/media/foreign policy nexus, and attendant liberal, realist, and critical debates, continue to dominate academic discussion. However, recent debate has increasingly revolved around new developments in communication technology and both their potential and actual impact upon these existing theoretical frameworks and debates. In this closing section, I set out the key features of this debate which are, principally: (1) the extent to which developments in communication technology have empowered US public opinion and media and (2) the impact of these technological developments on global US power and influence, in particular in the context of the current war on terror.

The rise of the internet and global media

On the one hand, the proliferation of new communication technology, such as portable satellite broadcasting equipment and, now, the emergence of digital cameras contained within mobile phones, appears to create a degree of transparency of events around the world that is unprecedented. Potentially, any event can be captured on 'camera' and that information then passed around the world instantaneously via the internet or global media. In addition, the rise of global media, such as CNN and now the Arab-based network Al-Jazeera as well as the internet, means that such images (and their story) can be communicated both to US citizens and to the peoples of the world. Received wisdom claims that such developments have a radically pluralizing effect by bringing information and news to people quicker and, in turn, creating greater difficulty for the US government to influence (or manipulate) news agendas.

These developments offer, at first glance, evidence to suggest that the pluralist model has greater validity today. That is to say, developments in communication technology have indeed increased the independence, and therefore power, of the US media and public. Following on from this, the elite model is less valid and cogent, as the US government has found it harder to direct news agendas and to mould US public opinion. For realists, who advocate elite control of foreign affairs, this is a worrying and perhaps catastrophic development which means that the ability of the USA to protect and promote its interests is being undermined by increased media and public criticism of US foreign policy. From the liberal-democratic perspective, these developments could be seen as potentially positive in terms of strengthening the quality and quantity of both public and media input into the foreign policy-making process. And yet, even liberal US scholars often appear to believe that perhaps too much power and influence has been handed over to US media and public (see Key quotes 9.7). Overall, if the thesis that developments in communication technology have indeed transformed the US public sphere is correct, then a question can be raised as to the ability of US foreign policy elites to both communicate important issues to the US public and maintain support for US foreign policy (the realist position). As we shall see next, current evidence suggests that claims of a transformation in the US public sphere are exaggerated, and that it is important to differentiate between domestic US audiences and global audiences.

In fact, the argument that US public/media/foreign policy relations have been significantly pluralized is very much open to challenge (Domke 2004; Bennett, Lawrence, and Livingston 2006; Livingston and Bennett 2003). Since 9/11, and the emergence of the war on terror as the primary framework within which US foreign policy is formulated, US media and public opinion has been remarkably supportive of the US executive. For example, during the run-up to the 2003 invasion of Iraq, the US government was apparently successful at persuading most of the US media and public of the relationship between Saddam Hussein's regime and al-Qaeda (even though the majority of expert opinion challenged such a link). Again, in what could be seen as a public relations disaster for the Bush administration, the dreadful images of Iraqi prisoners detained by the US military at Abu Ghraib in Iraq were, according to recent research (Bennett, Lawrence, and Livingston 2006), in fact reported in a manner conducive to the official White House line. This was done by the US media echoing the White House line that the events represented abuses by a few soldiers rather than the result of a policy of torture. Finally, whilst public opposition to, and media criticism of, the war in Iraq has escalated as the number of US casualties has increased, the jury is still out as to the extent to which this has reflected the increasing elite dissensus over the course of the war that has emerged across both the Republican and Democrat divide. Overall, the question of whether traditional patterns of media–PO–state relations really have been dramatically transformed, and in doing so reduced the ability of US elites to coordinate US foreign policy in the war on terror, is very much open to contestation.

❝ KEY QUOTES 9.7: Joseph Nye on the impact of new communication technology

The free flow of broadcast information in open societies has always had an impact on public opinion and the formulation of foreign policy. But now the flow has increased in volume and shortened news cycles . . . The so-called CNN effect makes it hard to keep items that might otherwise warrant a lower priority off the public agenda. Now, with the added interactivity of groups on the Internet, it will be harder than ever to maintain a consistent agenda.

(Nye 1999)

Less contentious, however, is the impact of technological developments in terms of global media and public opinion. Here, the USA has arguably suffered a public relations or propaganda disaster certainly in terms of winning 'hearts and minds' in the war on terror. In part this is due to the 'problems' surrounding the invasion of Iraq in 2003 and the diplomatic crises that have emerged as the Bush administration attempted, unsuccessfully, to persuade the governments and global public opinion of the legitimacy of their actions. The material fact that the aftermath of the toppling of Saddam Hussein has not led to a peaceful, democratic, and flourishing Iraq has increased hostility and resentment toward the USA.[2] At the same time, US public diplomacy and media diplomacy is significantly challenged by the rise of new global media such as Al-Jazeera which effectively limit the degree to which the USA can influence broader global opinions. Put quite simply, non-Western audiences will access news sources that are largely independent of the influence of Western governments. Moreover, the internet further compromises influence over global communication flows and, for example again, the infamous images from Abu Ghraib flow freely through the internet and world media who, unlike the US media, will often use such images without qualification with the White House line.

Overall, transformations in the global information environment of today mean that there is a significant shift in the balance of soft power which poses a direct challenge to the ability of the USA to project power internationally. Perhaps of greater importance is the fact that, as I have discussed, at the domestic level media and public debate tends to remain limited to a procedural level, rarely questions the fundamentals of US foreign policy, and significant capability lies with US foreign policy elites in terms of leading public and media debate. And yet opinion outside the US domestic public sphere (i.e. global public opinion within the global public sphere) is increasingly disillusioned, in particular, with America's war on terror. Whether these two increasingly isolated public spheres can be bridged, especially in a time when US public and media diplomacy are compromised by the emerging forms of media, and mainstream US media is reluctant to facilitate debate beyond the procedural level, remains to be seen.

? Questions

1. What influence, if any, does the US public have on foreign policy formulation?
2. In what ways, and to what extent, can media influence public opinion?
3. Assess the relative cogency of elite and pluralist models of media–state relations.
4. To what extent do you agree with the realist perspective on media and public opinion?
5. To what extent do you agree with the liberal-democratic perspective on media and public opinion?
6. Critical accounts argue that US mainstream media and public opinion are manipulated by elite interests. To what extent do you agree?
7. What impact has new technology had on the public opinion/media/foreign policy nexus in the USA?
8. To what extent *should* public opinion and media shape US foreign policy?

» Further Reading

Entman, R. (2004), *Projections of Power: Framing News, Public Opinion and US Foreign Policy* (Chicago: University of Chicago Press).
  Comprehensive introduction to the concept of framing, detailing its impact upon both public and foreign policy.

Foyle, D. (1999), *Counting the Public In: Presidents, Public Opinion and Foreign Policy* (New York: Columbia University Press).

A good example of a contemporary account arguing that that public opinion can influence policy.

Herman, E., and Chomsky, N. (1988), *Manufacturing Consent: The Political Economy of the Mass Media* (New York: Pantheon).

Provocative and widely read example of the elite model, arguing that US media function to mobilize support for elite interests.

Robinson, P. (2002), *The CNN Effect: The Myth of News, Foreign Policy and Intervention* (London: Routledge).

Provides a contemporary theoretical and empirical analysis of the CNN effect debate highlighting the contrasting roles media can play in policy formulation.

Wolfsfeld, G. (1997), *The Media and Political Conflict* (Cambridge: Cambridge University Press).

A rich and nuanced analysis of how media can come to act as champions for non-elite groups, and how at other times media serve the interests of governments.

 Endnotes

1. For opinion poll data on US belief in an al-Qaeda–Hussein link see Milbank and Deane (2003).
2. For extensive information on changing international attitudes toward the USA, see the Pew Global Attitudes Project, http://pewglobal.org/.

 Visit the Online Resource Centre that accompanies this book for web links to accompany each chapter, and a range of other resources: www.oxfordtextbooks.co.uk/orc/cox_stokes/

10 Identities and US foreign policy

Christina Rowley and Jutta Weldes

Chapter contents

Introduction

Conventional explanations of foreign policy, especially realist ones, invoke national—that is, state—interests as the primary factor driving US foreign policy. In contrast, this chapter examines the central role of identity in the construction of US foreign policy. It adopts a critical social constructivist approach—one that takes social realities to be constituted through discursive practices—and argues that particular conceptions of US identity constitute US interests, thus providing the foundations for US foreign policy. After introducing central analytical concepts, including interests, identity, discourse, articulation, and representation, the chapter examines US presidents' articulations of US state identity and US foreign policy during the Cold War and post-Cold War eras, as well as in the war on terror.

On 20 September 2001, in discussing the 11 September attacks on New York and the Pentagon, US President George W. Bush (2001c) raised the question of US identity—of who or what 'the USA' is.[1] In a major address to Congress and the US public, Bush asked: 'Why do they hate us?' Couched as it is in terms of 'us' ('Americans') and 'them' ('the terrorists'), this question places identity at the centre of US foreign policy. Bush's answer is also about US identity: 'They hate what they see right here in this chamber—a democratically elected government. . . . They hate our freedoms—our freedom of religion, our freedom of speech, our freedom to vote and assemble and disagree with each other.' 'They'—'terrorists', 'murderers', 'enemies of freedom'—hate 'us' for who 'we' are. Bush's narrative graphically highlights the importance of identity to US foreign policy. To illustrate more concretely what we mean by identity, we begin with three (mental) exercises.

Exercise one: If you had to describe yourself, what would you say? Would you mention your gender, religion, ethnicity, citizenship, social class, family tree, fashion sense, favourite food, or film genre? Would your answers be the same if you were talking to a prospective employer, a new room-mate, an elderly

neighbour, a blind date? If not, how might they differ? How might your answers change over the course of your life?

Exercise two: Now think about the country in which you live. How would you describe its 'national' identity? Which features do you think are characteristic, or important? What words, concepts, images, and sounds do you associate with it?

Our identities constitute our sense of self. They are literally what makes us who we are, how we think and act. This is true of collective as well as individual identities. We feel a sense of belonging with fans of 'our' football team or with others who enjoy the same music. We join churches or political parties. We celebrate and commemorate important events with our closest friends and relatives. Often we feel that we share a sense of identity and belonging—a 'history in common'—with people of the same nationality, and it is common to generalize about 'national character', of both our own and others' states. Benedict Anderson (1991) has referred to nations as 'imagined communities'. Nationalists often claim that nations (should and do) share a certain degree of homogeneity, or sameness.

Exercise three: Think about the other, someone unlike yourself or people in your country. For instance, imagine a refugee. What do they look like? What are they like? (Think about your answers to exercises one and two.) Where does this image come from? Is it from meeting 'real' immigrants? From talking with family and friends? From news media, films, the internet?

As we discuss in more detail below, the self is never constituted solely in relation to itself. Rather, it is always constituted in relation to others. Self and other are relational terms. Sometimes these relations are oppositional, like 'democratic' versus 'totalitarian' or 'freedom loving' versus 'terrorist'; sometimes they are complementary, like 'us' and 'our allies' or 'our friends'. In all cases, they underpin individual, state, and other collective identities.

Interests and US foreign policy

The concept of interest—the preferences held by individual or collective actors—has long been central to explanations of state action in general and of US foreign policy in particular because the term 'interest' is thought to capture the motives that drive states to act. Accounts that cite interests as an explanatory factor in foreign policy analysis vary widely.[2] Here, we briefly examine the most prominent one as a counterpoint to our focus on identity.

States' interests—generally, but incorrectly, labelled 'national interests'[3]—are central to a theoretical approach called political realism. Realism prides itself on addressing the 'hard truths' of power and (in)security in world politics. In realist accounts, international politics differ from domestic politics primarily in their anarchic character. Anarchy—the absence of a supra-state authority—places states in a security dilemma (Herz 1951): an inevitable, perpetual, and potentially deadly competition for survival. The most basic and fundamental interest of any state is thus always to protect its sovereignty—its independence and decision-making authority—and its territoriality—its physical control over its territory—against encroachments from other states.

A state rationally and objectively assesses the threats it faces and, because power supplies the means necessary for states to protect sovereignty and territoriality in a world in which other states are actual or potential threats, decision makers and analysts must realistically assess power relations in order to determine their interests. Every state, in short, must pursue its national interest 'defined in terms of power' (Morgenthau 1993: 5). For realists, then, interest plays a pivotal role in foreign policy explanation. Through the need for sovereignty and territoriality, it connects the nature of world politics—anarchy and the ubiquitous search for power and security—with the policies and actions of states.

The concept of a rational actor is a key assumption of interest-based explanations. Briefly, a rational actor can be a state, an organization, an individual, which ranks its interests and preferences in order of priority and calculates costs and benefits in order to maximize its outcomes for the least amount of effort. The central problem with interest-based explanations is that they treat interests as exogenous—as predetermined, given, and external to the explanation being offered. In realism, the basic interest in preserving sovereignty and territoriality is determined by the anarchic nature of the international sphere. Interests are assumed to be obvious—they follow from external and objectively identifiable threats and are thus directly accessible to policy makers and analysts alike, who behave as rational actors when assessing these threats and deciding on appropriate courses of action.

The difficulty with this assumption is that objects and events do not present themselves transparently to the observer, however 'realistic' she or he may be. Determining what particular situation a state faces, what (if any) threat a state faces, and what the 'correct' interest with respect to that situation or threat is, always requires interpretation. Rather than being self-evident, threats, and states' interests in the face of threats, are fundamentally matters of interpretation. For example, it is not the physical fact that nuclear weapons can pulverize whole cities that makes them threats to US security. US and British nuclear weapons are not seen as threats. Only when such weapons are interpreted as dangerous—because they are wielded by communists or 'rogue states', for instance—do they become a threat, and only then does it become in the US 'interest' to prevent their development or seek their removal.

This critique notwithstanding, 'interest' remains central to accounts of US foreign policy because 'national interest' is the language of state action (Hollis and Smith 1990: 166). Interests are thus important to understanding US foreign policy in two ways. First, it is through 'the national interest' that US policy makers understand the goals to be pursued by US foreign policy. In making US foreign

> **KEY QUOTES 10.1:** Interests and foreign policy

On realism and interests

The main signpost that helps political realism to find its way through the landscape of international politics is the concept of interest defined in terms of power. This concept provides the link between reason trying to understand international politics and the facts to be understood. . . . We assume that statesmen think and act in terms of interests defined as power, and the evidence of history bears that assumption out. . . . Thinking in terms of interest defined as power we think as he does. . . . The concept of interest defined as power imposes intellectual discipline upon the observer, infuses rational order into the subject matter of politics and thus makes the theoretical understanding of politics possible.

(Morgenthau 1993: 5)

On national interests

[Political] actors have found . . . the concept [of interest] useful both as a way of thinking about their goals and as a means of mobilising support for them. That is, not only do political actors tend to perceive and discuss their goals in terms of the national interest, but they are also inclined to claim that their goals *are* the national interest, a claim that often arouses the support necessary to move toward a realisation of the goals. Consequently, even though it has lost some of its early appeal as an analytical tool, the national interest enjoys considerable favor as a basis for action and has won a prominent place in the dialogue of public affairs.

(Rosenau 1968: 34; emphasis in the original)

policy, decision makers explicitly talk in terms of 'the national interest'. It thus forms the basis for US state action. Second, the national interest functions as a rhetorical device for generating the legitimacy of, and political support for, US foreign policy. As former US Secretary of State Henry Kissinger put it, '[w]hen you're asking Americans to die, you have to be able to explain it in terms of the national interest' (in Kelly 1995: 12). In the next section we examine how state interests are constructed in relation to state identity.

KEY POINTS

- ❑ Realists assume that states are the central actors in world politics and that states' interests are determined by the objective threats states face.
- ❑ Interest-based explanations assume rational actors with given (predetermined) interests.
- ❑ The threats and problems facing states are products of interpretations. Interests are also products of interpretation.
- ❑ The concept of 'national interest' remains central to explanations of US foreign policy because it is the language of foreign policy decision making and thus of state action.

Critical social constructivism

Rather than taking interests as exogenously given, critical social constructivism understands interests as constituted in relation to identity. Critical constructivism foregrounds the role of identity— itself understood as constituted in and through

representations—in the construction of state interests and thus of state action. This approach has three central analytical commitments: (1) 'reality' is socially constructed, (2) constructions entail naturalized power relations, and (3) naturalized power relations can and should be denaturalized (Weldes et al. 1999: 13–21). We discuss these commitments as the theoretical framework for introducing discourse and the role of processes of articulation and representation in constituting identity. We then discuss the conceptualization of identity in more detail, briefly consider possible data sources for investigating state identity, and highlight the importance of insecurity, threats, and crises to the (re)production of state identity/identities.[4]

The social construction of reality

Critical social constructivism assumes that 'reality' is socially constructed. All 'things'—states, subjects, objects, feelings, interests, processes, practices, relationships—only come to have meaning through the linguistic, visual, and other symbolic signifiers—words, photographs, sounds, signposts, musical notes—that we use to describe, represent, and understand these things (Hall 1997a: 1; Shapiro 1986: 193). As Terrell Carver puts it, 'we use language

to inscribe meanings into the world—whether into or onto objects, or experiences—and then we read those meanings back to ourselves as if they had always resided in the objects or experiences' (2002: 50).

This means that the world is constituted (constructed) through meaningful practices and that people act on the basis of the meanings that 'things' have for them. These meanings are fundamentally cultural: they are made possible by discourses—systems of meaning production (see below)—which provide the categories through which the world is understood. There is no universal or objective 'view from nowhere' from which we can view the world. We are always already situated within (many) different discourses. Meaning is a social (intersubjectively constituted) phenomenon: meaning resides in the practices and categories through which people engage with each other and with the world.

One such discursively constituted category is 'terrorist'. Rather than being self-evident, a 'terrorist'

> **KEY QUOTES 10.2:** Identity and foreign policy

On power

If power were never anything but repressive, if it never did anything but to say no, do you really think one would be brought to obey it? What makes power hold good, what makes it accepted, is simply the fact that it doesn't only weigh on us as a force that says no, but that it traverses and produces things, it induces pleasure, forms knowledge, produces discourse. It needs to be considered as a productive network which runs through the whole social body, much more than as a negative instance whose function is repression.

(Foucault 1980: 119)

Definitions of discourse

[D]iscourses ... [are] practices that systematically produce the objects of which they speak.

(Foucault 1972: 49)

The fact that every object is constituted as an object of discourse has *nothing to do* with whether there is a world external to thought, or with the realism/idealism opposition. An earthquake or the falling of a brick is an event that certainly exists, in the sense that it occurs here and now, independently of my will. But whether their specificity as objects is constructed in terms of 'natural phenomena' or 'expressions of the wrath of God', depends upon the structuring of the discursive field. What is denied is not that such objects exist externally to thought, but the rather different assertion that they could constitute themselves as objects outside any discursive condition of emergence.

(Laclau and Mouffe 2001: 108; emphasis in the original)

(continued)

> **KEY QUOTES 10.2:** (continued)

Now, turning to the term discourse itself, we use it to emphasise the fact that every social configuration is *meaningful*. If I kick a spherical object in the street or if I kick a ball in a football match, the *physical* fact is the same, but *its meaning* is different. The object is a football only to the extent that it establishes a system of relations with other objects, and these relations are not given by the mere referential materiality of the object, but are, rather, socially constructed. This systematic set of relations is what we call discourse. . . . [T]he discursive character of an object does not, by any means, imply putting its *existence* into question. The fact that a football is only a football as long as it is integrated within a system of socially constructed rules does not mean that it thereby ceases to be a physical object. A stone exists independently of any system of social relations, but it is, for instance, either a projectile or an object of aesthetic contemplation only within a specific discursive configuration. . . . For that same reason it is the discourse that constitutes the social position of the social agent, and not, therefore, the social agent which is the origin of the discourse—the same system of rules that makes that spherical object into a football, makes me a player.

(Laclau and Mouffe 1987: 82, emphasis in the original)

Discourses are best conceptualised as . . . sets of sociocultural resources used by people in the construction of meaning about their world and their activities. It is not simply speech or written statements, but the rules by which verbal speech and written statements are made meaningful. Discourses enable one to write, speak, listen and act meaningfully.

(Ó Tuathail and Agnew 1992: 92–3)

On articulation and representation

[T]he term [articulation] has a nice double meaning because 'articulate' means to utter, to speak forth, to be articulate. It carries that sense of language-ing, of expressing, etc. But we also speak of an 'articulated' lorry (truck): a lorry where the front (cab) and back (trailer) can, but need not necessarily, be connected to one another. The two parts are connected to each other, but through a specific linkage, that can be broken.

(Stuart Hall, quoted in Grossberg 1986: 53)

In language, we use signs and symbols—whether they are sounds, written words, electronically produced images, musical notes, even objects—to stand for or represent to other people our concepts, ideas and feelings. Language is one of the 'media' through which thoughts, ideas and feelings are represented in a culture. Representation through language is therefore central to the processes by which meaning is produced. . . . [W]e give things meaning by how we *represent* them—the words we use about them, the images of them we produce, the emotions we associate with them, the ways we classify and conceptualise them, the values we place on them. . . . These elements . . . construct meaning and transmit it. They signify.

(Hall 1997a: 1–5; emphasis in the original)

On identity

[A]ll identity is relational.

(Laclau and Mouffe 2001: 113)

An identity is established in relation to a series of differences that have become socially established. These differences are essential to its being. . . . Entrenched in this indispensable relationship is a second set of tendencies, themselves in need of exploration, to congeal established identities into fixed forms, thought and lived as if their structure expressed the true order of things. When these pressures prevail, the maintenance of one identity (or field of identities) involves the conversion of some differences into otherness, into evil, or one of its numerous surrogates. Identity requires difference in order to be, and it converts identity into otherness in order to secure its own self-certainty.

(Connolly 1991: 64)

[B]oth subject and object gain their meaning and intelligibility by reference to their location in a system of meaning . . . As a consequence, 'absolute' objectivity—*no* interference from value-laden subjectivity—is an incoherent claim. To make a *meaningful* claim, one is always already in a value-laden (intersubjective) context that necessarily includes power relations. The relationship between knowledge and power becomes central—and political . . . producing the codes of meaning and intelligibility that govern how we think, communicate and produce knowledge claims.

(Peterson 2003: 28 emphasis in the original)

A fundamental principle of constructivist social theory is that people act toward objects, including other actors, on the basis of the meanings that the objects have for them. States act differently towards enemies than they do toward friends because enemies are threatening and friends are not. Anarchy and the distribution of power are insufficient to tell us which is which. . . . It is collective meanings that constitute the structures which organise our actions. Actors acquire identities . . . by participating in such collective meanings. . . . The commitment to and the salience of particular identities vary, but each identity is an inherently social definition of the actor grounded in the theories which actors collectively hold about themselves and one another and which constitute the structure of the social world. Identities are the basis of interests. Actors do not have a 'portfolio' of interests that they carry around independent of social context; instead, they define their interests in the process of defining situations.

(Wendt 1992: 396–8)

On insecurities and danger

[I]nsecurities, rather than being natural facts, are social and cultural productions . . . insecurity is itself the product of processes of identity construction in which the self and the other, or multiple others, are constituted. . . . The constitution of identities is often a reciprocal process. As each subject seeks to perform its identity, it threatens others, whose identities are consolidated in response.

(Weldes et al. 1999: 57–9)

Danger is not an objective condition. It [*sic*] is not a thing which exists independently of those to whom it may become a threat. . . . [D]anger is an effect of interpretation. . . . Modern society contains a veritable cornucopia of danger; indeed, there is such an abundance of risk that it is impossible to objectively know all that threatens us. Those events or factors that we identify as dangerous come to be ascribed as such only through an interpretation of their various dimensions of dangerousness. . . . The ability to represent things as alien, subversive, dirty, or sick, has been pivotal to the articulation of danger in the American experience. . . . The boundaries of a state's identity are secured by the representation of danger central to foreign policy.

(Campbell 1998: 1–3; 'sic' insertion in the original)

must be discursively constructed as such. While much twentieth-century US discourse constituted the Irish Republican Army (IRA) as patriotic nationalists valiantly fighting a foreign (British) occupation, British state (and media) discourse constituted the IRA as terrorists. These two discourses constitute the same object differently. Similarly, George W. Bush's statements in the war on terror constitute the USA as rational, as an innocent victim of Islamic terrorism, and as fighting a virtuous struggle, and construct the al-Qaeda network as murderous and irrational barbarians with whom one cannot do anything except fight, while Osama bin Laden's statements, on the other hand, construct Muslims as innocent victims of the USA's terrorist foreign policy, and the USA as murderous and irrational barbarians against whom one can do nothing but fight (Agathangelou and Ling 2004: 521–4).

Discourse

The concept of discourse is essentially open ended; it can be used to refer to a variety of levels and types. There are academic, legal, medical, and cinematic discourses. More narrowly, we might refer to sociological or anthropological discourses within academia, specific genres within cinema, or neo-realist or feminist discourses of world politics. There is more than one US foreign policy discourse, depending on the perspective from which US foreign policy is understood. Institutions are often seen as having their 'own' discourses, such that we may talk of World Bank discourse(s). At a broader level, we can apply the term discourse to Western philosophy, science, modernism, Islam, or Judaeo-Christianity.

Discourses are both structures and practices; this means that they comprise the rules that govern what can be said (language as structure), as well as instances of what *is* said (language as practice) that can lead to changes in those rules (Laffey and Weldes 2004: 28). ('Language' is used here as a metaphor for communication, rather than in the narrow sense of languages such as English or Arabic.) Every occurrence of language use has the potential to change the rules about how language is used but most of the time language use adheres to and thus reinforces these rules. Discourses both constrain what we can say/think/imagine and enable us to speak/think/imagine. Furthermore, although we are always (whether consciously or not) manipulating discourses and signifiers when we communicate, in order to tell a persuasive story, or to find the most accurate or expressive verbs and adjectives, discourses can also be deployed more instrumentally—spin doctoring, public relations exercises, and speech writing are some examples that occur in the construction of US foreign policy (see Box 10.4).

Articulation

Articulation refers to the process through which meaning is produced from these extant socio-cultural and linguistic resources, the terms, symbols, and ideas that are already present within a culture. Extant linguistic resources are articulated (connected together, discursively linked) to produce contingent—non-necessary, historically and contextually specific—representations of the world. In this way, meaning is created and temporarily fixed, on which action is then based. Phenomena, whether objects, events, or social relations, come to connote, or invoke, one another and are thereby welded into associative chains. '9/11' is an example of articulation, functioning as a kind of cultural 'shorthand' that stands for a series of discursively linked concepts: 'World Trade Center', 'New York', 'aeroplanes',

have been articulated with 'Islamic', 'terrorists', 'war', as opposed to, say, 'murder', 'crime', and 'police', such that the attacks of 11 September 2001 appear *inevitably* to require a military response in Afghanistan rather than a domestic and/or international policing effort to apprehend the criminals responsible for planning the attacks. Conversely, deaths from road traffic accidents each year in the USA far outnumber the deaths caused by terrorist attacks, but road safety is rarely if ever articulated as a national security concern.

With their successful repeated articulation, these representations come to seem as though they are inherently or necessarily connected and the meanings they produce as natural and an accurate description of reality. Despite this apparent naturalness, however, the chains of association established are socially constructed and historically contingent rather than logically or structurally necessary. The non-necessary, contingent character of any particular articulation means that these connections can be contested. This contestability has two important consequences. First, it means that specific articulations are never simply produced once and for all. Instead, to prevent them from becoming unglued, or from being forcibly pried apart, they have always to be reproduced. Second, it means that any articulation can be uncoupled and the resulting component parts rearticulated in different, and perhaps even novel, ways. Put simply, alternative representations are always possible.

To the extent that such a rearticulation is successful—i.e. persuasive—the result is a very different description of US foreign policy. A different articulation of 9/11 might focus on the Pentagon as one of the targets, the attacks as an act of 'war', or the USA funding bin Laden and other 'freedom fighters' against the USSR in Afghanistan in the 1980s. If the events of 11 September are contextualized through the decades of interventionist US foreign policy in the third world (Blum 2003), or the USA's role in funding and supplying the Israeli state and thus sustaining the occupation of Palestinian territory (Chomsky 2003), then 9/11 may appear as 'retaliation', a violent *reaction* to US foreign policy, not a 'beginning' to which US foreign policy responds.

Discourses as productive

Power

Social constructions reflect, enact, and reify—treat as natural—relations of power. Discourses are sites of social power in at least two important ways. First, discourses bring with them the power to define and thus to produce or constitute the world. Representations of reality provide both the conditions of possibility and limits on possibility. Such constructions successfully become common sense when they are treated as naturally or transparently reflecting reality. In this way social constructions are naturalized, and both their constructedness and their specific social origins are obscured. Conversely, anything outside this common sense is rejected as implausible, 'ideological',[5] or spurious. When US discourse successfully articulates the IRA as patriotic nationalists fighting a passé European empire, funding them makes sense—despite the 'special relationship' between the USA and the UK—and condemning them as 'terrorists' becomes unsustainable.

Likewise, articulating al-Qaeda or Iraqi insurgents as irrational Islamic fanatics who simply hate 'American' freedoms creates a situation in which military force is appropriate and necessary. In contrast, articulating them as rational Arab militants who use a 'tactic of the weak' in order to oppose US foreign policy, and make intelligible political demands—e.g. withdrawal of US military forces from Iraq and Saudi Arabia, and of Israeli forces and settlers from Palestinian territory in the West Bank (Barkawi 2004)—would

reconfigure them as political actors with whom one could potentially negotiate.

Second, some discourses are more powerful than others because they partake of institutional power. Certain elites, or powerful institutional actors, play privileged roles in the (re)production of discursive constructions. State foreign policy discourses are a prominent example. State officials'—policy elites'—representations have immediate prima facie plausibility because these officials are themselves constructed as speaking for 'us' and 'our state'. They have legitimacy, especially in the construction of foreign policy, since the 'national interest' is understood to be quintessentially the business of the state and the identification of threats to state interests is thus a task rightly belonging to its officials. US presidents are, in this sense, the USA's interpreters-in-chief (Stuckey 1991) (see Boxes 10.3 and 10.4). Dominant discourses, like those of the state, become and remain dominant because of the power relations sustaining them. When there is little or no challenge to dominant discourses, they become hegemonic—that is, they receive assent from most, if not all, of the public.

Identity

One hegemonic discourse in relation to identity is liberal individualism. It is 'common sense' in Western society that each body houses one self-contained individual with a stable and coherent identity. However, identity is a complex concept. Think back to the exercises at the start of this chapter: we listed several subject positions, or 'identity markers': race, class, gender, sexuality, ethnicity, and so on. Although we assume the stable, single, and unitary 'I' when we speak about ourselves, individuals are embedded in many identities; the notion of a singular 'core identity' is in fact a complex interplay of multiple subject positions. Marysia Zalewski (2000: 23) uses apples and onions as metaphors representing these opposing liberal and constructivist views of identity: an apple has a vital core, but when you peel away the layers of an onion, there is nothing there at the end. Our accounts of ourselves as gendered beings look very different from an account in which we privilege our racial or class identities; no aspect of identity is more 'fundamental' than any other. We also tend to assume that identities are only relevant when they deviate from the white, masculine, heterosexual, able-bodied, middle-class norm (Hearn 2004). We often act as though only non-white people have ethnic identities, and only female bodies are gendered.

Similarly, analysing identity in US (or, indeed, any state's) foreign policy requires undermining the notion that the nation-state is a natural phenomenon or possesses a unitary identity. An immense amount of ideological labour goes into constructing nations (Smith 1991) and the notion that the state is 'an' or 'the' actor in international relations (Enloe 1996). Other identities must be marginalized, silenced, or denied: 'America, love it or leave it' is an illustration of how any dissent from dominant US foreign policy discourse is considered 'un-American' or even 'anti-American', despite the belief that free speech is a cornerstone of US identity. Dissent is almost always understood in terms of aiding and abetting terrorists. In the statement 'support the troops', what is denied/silenced is the argument that withdrawing US troops *is* a form of support, by removing them from potential danger and terminating an immoral occupation.

Furthermore, identities are not fixed and stable but are constantly in flux, changing as people grow older (as states change over time) and experience new things. Thus interests, which derive from identities, are not fixed, exogenous, or permanently given, but are also dynamic and unstable. The US detention

facility at Guantánamo Bay (on the island of Cuba) provides an excellent example. The psychological intimidation and imprisonment of 'terror suspects' without trial in the name of preserving liberty and justice undermines these very notions. On the one hand, it is warranted by the juxtaposition of an irredeemably evil terrorist threat with US leadership in the fight for Western freedoms. On the other hand, it contrasts starkly with the US identity as freedom-loving, committed to the rule of law, and opposed to cruel and unusual punishments.

We emphasize different aspects of our identities—perform our identities differently—depending on who or what we are identifying with (and against). The claim that we perform our identities, while sharing some connotations with actors in the theatre, is not exactly the same. Actors consciously choose to perform certain roles, whereas performance of identity is inescapable, occurring all the time, and usually at a much less conscious level. Nor do we have complete control over how we are defined—our identities are also largely constituted for us by others. For example, the USA and its allies have the power to construct other state identities: Afghanistan and Somalia thus become 'failed states' (Rotberg 2002), and Iraq and North Korea become 'rogue states' or 'rogue regimes' (Klare 1996; Rice 2000) or 'states of concern' (BBC News 2000). The USA and the international community, rather than the states themselves, construct their identities for them.

Representation

To represent means to symbolize, to stand for (Hall 1997b: 16); representations can be pictures, models, signs, words. Discourses and discursive articulations manifest themselves—and identity is produced—in concrete representations. However, representation is also a discursive *practice*. Thinking of representation as a practice reminds us that representation only takes place when interpretative labour is being performed. When we generalize about other people or cultures, we represent them in particular ways. We decide that certain features are important and others are less valid or relevant. The notions that women in

CONTROVERSIES 10.1: Identity and academic scholarship

In 2006, author David Horowitz published a book enti-tled *The Professors: The 101 Most Dangerous Academ-ics in America*, in which he claims that some academics employed in US colleges and universities have introduced 'political' agendas into the classroom and abandoned tra-ditional academic notions of objectivity and impartiality. In particular, he argues that 'anti-American' and left-wing 'radicals' have 'set about re-shaping the university curric-ulum to support their political interests. . . . New depart-ments began to appear with objectives that were frankly political' (2006: p. x).

Among the examples he gives are 'Black Studies' and 'Women's Studies', which are 'really devoted to Black Nationalism, feminism and similar ideological programs' (2006: p. x). Peace Studies, Gay and Lesbian Studies, Post-Colonial Studies, Queer Studies, Whiteness Studies, and Cultural Studies are similarly indicted, all of these being disciplines and subdisciplines which have as their explicit focus the problematization of 'identity'. Critics of US for-eign policy—such as Noam Chomsky and Juan Cole—are also cited among the 101 'Most Dangerous Academics'.

Horowitz has previously published articles such as 'Unholy Alliance: How the Left Supports the Terrorists at Home' (2004b) and 'How the Left Undermined Ameri-ca's Security before 9/11' (2004a), in which he argues that 'radical legal groups [in the USA] assumed decep-tive names like the Center for Constitutional Rights and passed themselves off as "civil liberties" organizations [while t]heir terrorist clients . . . frequently presented themselves as "humanitarian groups"' (2004b) and that the Clinton administration's response to the events in Somalia in 1993 'telegraphed a clear message to his nation's enemies: We are unsure of purpose and unsteady of hand; we are self-indulgent and soft; we will not take

risks to defend ourselves; we are vulnerable' (2004a). He also criticizes 'Washington liberals', as well as universities and the mainstream media, for their belief that 'terrorism was not the instrument of political fanatics and evil men, but was the product of social conditions—poverty, racism and oppression—for which the Western democracies, including Israel, were ultimately always to blame' (2004a).

The notion that academics should remain impartial is not a new one; however, critical social constructivists argue that impartiality is an unattainable (and undesir-able) aim because it is impossible to 'be' from 'nowhere': one's identity is always already implicated in the consti-tution of one's interests. The notion of 'bias' and that stu-dents should hear 'both' sides of the story itself contains the political position that there are only two sides to every story, and the implication that the 'correct' answer and attitude must lie somewhere in the middle. For example, some people believe that God created the planet in seven days, while others believe that Earth took approximately 4.5 billion years to evolve to its present state. It is nonsen-sical to suggest a 'compromise' of 2.25 billion years.

Furthermore, what is notable about the links that Horowitz makes between academia and activism is that he considers only left-wing academics to be political, and that his understanding of 'political' is rather narrow (i.e. it is acceptable for academics to critique US foreign policy for not being effective enough, but not to challenge its moral legitimacy). He also does not pick up on the politi-cization of academia in other ways—e.g. the 'revolving door' of academic analysts who become state advisers and vice versa (a long list which includes, among others, Zbigniew Brzezinski, Francis Fukuyama, Samuel Hunt-ington, Henry Kissinger, Joseph Nye, Condoleezza Rice, and Walt Rostow).

burkas are necessarily oppressed and that US women are necessarily liberated are two examples. Generali-zations, simplifications, abstractions—all are inher-ently *political* processes of representation.

Often, representations take the form of narratives. Narratives are basically stories: fairy tales, this chap-ter, history, the 'good versus evil' storyline articulated by George W. Bush after 9/11—these are different types of narrative. Tropes, devices such as figures of

speech, metaphors, and analogies, are also common representational practices. The repeated references, explicit and implicit, to the lessons of Munich 1938 and the dangers of appeasement drawn from the Second World War that can be seen in Cold War and post-Cold War US foreign policy rhetoric are tropes. Examples of hegemonic foreign policy tropes and narratives can be seen in Boxes 10.3 and 10.4, and are discussed in more detail below.

BOX 10.1: Strategies of representation

Infantilization

Attributing childlike or immature characteristics and behaviours to individuals or groups. Roxanne Doty discusses this strategy of representation in the context of US–Filipino relations: 'Filipinos were regarded as precocious children who had assimilated the superficial aspects of US culture but had failed to grasp its more fundamental implications. . . . The ostensibly nurturing relationship invoked by the parent/child opposition obscured and justified practices of domination' (1996: 88–9). This metaphor can also be seen in representations of 'developing' states as politically immature.

Feminization

Attributing feminine characteristics to something or someone. As Susan Jeffords discusses with regard to some of the Vietnam War films of the 1980s, '[w]hat is different about these films and the cultural revisionism that accompanies them is the depiction of the US government as feminine. And it is precisely its femininity that is seen to have caused the loss of the Vietnam War' (1986: 189; see also Jeffords 1989). Processes of *masculinization*—attributing masculine characteristics to something or someone—occur in similar ways (see, e.g., Hooper 2001: ch. 3).

Naturalization

Making something appear natural, unquestioned, or unchangeable, as 'just the way things are'. Critics of realism argue that realists naturalize the concept of anarchy (Wendt 1992; Linklater 1998) and notions such as the

state and insecurity (Weldes et al. 1999). Feminists argue that gender is often naturalized—e.g. 'boys will be boys' (see Peterson and Runyan 1999: ch. 2).

Bestialization

Attributing animal characteristics to, or using animal metaphors to describe, objects, individuals, or groups. President George W. Bush has used this strategy in his speeches in the war on terror (Jackson 2005: 5), when referring to Afghan and Iraqi militants as 'parasites' that 'leech' onto 'host' countries (2001d, 2002a, 2004, 2005b) and depicting 'suicide bombers' as *burrowing* into our society' (2001b (emphasis added), 2006a). It is also sometimes used when naming military weapons and operations, e.g. Operation Mongoose, the name for covert CIA operations aimed at overthrowing and assassinating Fidel Castro (Drinnon 1990: 434). Mongooses are animals renowned for their skill in killing venomous snakes, thus this articulation discursively links Castro with (identifies him as) a snake.

Demonization

Representing someone or something as monstrous, demonic, or evil. Rogin (1987: p. xiii) argues that the 'creation of monsters [h]as [been] a continuing feature of American politics'. This strategy was used by President Reagan in speeches about Nicaragua and the Soviet 'Evil Empire' in the 1980s (1987: p. xv and *passim*) and in President George W. Bush's 2002 State of the Union Address on the 'Axis of Evil' (Bush 2002a) which articulates a concept from the Second World War ('Axis' powers) with the war on terror.

Just as individuals are assigned gendered identities, gendered characteristics can also be assigned to states, institutions, and concepts. Peterson and Runyan (1999: ch. 2) discuss how stereotypes of men's and women's behaviours, roles, and preferences are organized around binaries that link the concepts male/female, strong/weak, active/passive, rational/emotional, international/domestic, public/private, such that in each binary the first term is masculine and privileged over the second, feminine term. Laura Shepherd (2006) has demonstrated how articulations of US identity and foreign policy after 11 September

were explicitly gendered. US identity was coded masculine in contrast to both the hyper-masculinity of al-Qaeda and the Taliban and the feminization of the 'Afghan women', who, in needing to be 'saved', provided justification for the intervention. The US self-image was heroic, embodied in the fire-fighters and policemen repeatedly photographed assisting 9/11 victims and in authority figures such as George W. Bush and New York Mayor Rudy Giuliani.

Examples of representational strategies that can be deployed in discursive articulations are outlined in Box 10.1.

KEY POINTS

- Constructions entail naturalized power relations. Constructions successfully become common sense when treated as transparently reflecting reality.
- Elites play privileged roles in the (re)production of discursive constructions. When there is little or no challenge to dominant discourses, they become hegemonic.
- Individuals and states are embedded in many identities; the notion of a singular 'core identity' masks a complex interplay of multiple subject positions.

- Identities are subject positions constituted in discourse. Discourses manifest themselves in representations.
- Representation is a process: generalizations, simplifications, abstractions are inherently political processes.

Critical social constructivism as critique

Denaturalization

'Critique' is not synonymous with 'criticism' or negativity. Critical social constructivism is expressly 'critical' in that it assumes dominant constructions can be, and ought to be, denaturalized. The process of denaturalization seeks to defamiliarize—literally, to make strange—common-sense understandings and so to make their constructedness apparent. Exposing 'what-goes-without-saying' (Barthes 1973: 11) exposes the ideological labour that is required to produce and maintain such meanings. Constructivist approaches examine the ways in which representations, themselves products of specific discourses, constitute (among other things) state identity and thus interests and actions. This leads, in turn, to possibilities for the transformation of common sense and facilitates the imagining of alternative worlds and ways of being.

It ought to be emphasized that discourses are not '*merely* rhetoric', nor is critiquing them about 'political correctness'. 'Rhetoric' is sometimes used to mean ornamental or strategic language designed to persuade, rather than describe reality; 'political correctness' is usually invoked in order to imply that language is unimportant. It should be clear from the above discussion that a constructivist approach is committed to the view that *all* language is rhetorical—all language use is designed to persuade; the linguistic

constructions we use *matter* (Weldes 1999a: 117). Language is the medium through which we think and act. Thus, linguistic constructions are not merely a 'veneer' covering the 'truth', and critiquing these representations does not mean stating that they are false.[6]

The idea that social 'facts'—identities like 'terrorist' and 'freedom fighter'—are constituted in discursive representations implies neither artificiality nor dispensability (Griffin 2007: 227). Constructions are not 'false', nor can we do without them. Social facts exist only within wider discourses and through power relations and, importantly, they can be transformed. The UK state thus made considerable, partially successful, efforts to transform US discourse about the IRA in order to undercut moral and financial support for it among the US public. Soon after taking office, UK Prime Minister Gordon Brown announced a shift in UK foreign policy: he declared that the UK would no longer pursue a war on terror, but would instead treat terrorism as a criminal issue (*Independent* 2007).

Elite discourse and popular culture

What data sources[7] are best for finding and analysing the identity/identities that drive US foreign policy? Most analysts turn immediately to the statements and actions of states or, more accurately, the decision makers who act in their name. Elite representations of US identity and interests are contained in formal policy documents—like the *National Security Strategy of the United States of America* (White House 2002), speeches and other statements by decision makers, congressional hearings, white papers, government department reports, and the like. Such elite representations generally provide the dominant interpretation of US identity and interests, but sometimes, in times of crisis and controversy, provide alternative interpretations as well (Hallin 1989). Data abounds in other elite sources, including the news media—magazines, newspapers, television news—which both reproduce and occasionally contest these official discourses (Herman and Chomsky 1988).

Often neglected in foreign policy analysis, but central to the discursive constitution of state identity, is popular culture. As Box 10.2 shows, meanings for 'self' and 'other' underpinning US foreign policy are constituted in television programmes, e.g. legitimizing torture on *24*; in magazines, e.g. constructing the Soviet enemy and US leadership in *Reader's Digest*; in

photography, e.g. *National Geographic*'s exoticization of the third world. Hollywood films notoriously construct enemies, whether Arab or otherwise, like those prominent in contemporary foreign policy discourse (e.g. Chapman 2000; Shaheen 2001).

Such representations in popular culture, *precisely because* they are treated primarily as just 'entertainment', contribute to the background knowledge through which we understand and represent state identities and foreign policy. When policy makers want to persuade the public of the validity or importance of a particular foreign policy decision or action, they construct their arguments from the cultural resources already present in society. These understandings 'are produced not only in state officials' rhetoric but also, and more pervasively, in the mundane cultures of people's everyday experiences. This then implicates popular culture' in the manufacture of consent for states' foreign policies (Weldes 1999b: 119). Conversely, in order to be plausible, popular cultural texts also need to resonate with people's prior expectations about the 'real' world.

KEY POINTS

- ❑ Naturalized power relations can and should be denaturalized.
- ❑ Claiming that the world is socially constructed does not mean it is false or that the world does not exist.
- ❑ The social construction of reality means that although the world exists independently of our knowledge of it, we cannot access this knowledge except through discourse(s).

- ❑ Analysing and critiquing discourses is not about political correctness; language is not 'merely rhetoric'.
- ❑ Language matters because it is the primary medium through which we make sense of the world.
- ❑ Representations of identity and foreign policy can be investigated using official/elite and popular cultural discourses.

BOX 10.2:   Articulations of US identity in popular culture

[A]lthough it would appear that simple matters of taste drive the production and consumption of both high and popular culture, it is the case, rather, that, with the exception of some resistant forms, music, theatre, TV weather forecasts, and even cereal box scripts tend to endorse prevailing power structures by helping to reproduce the beliefs and allegiances necessary for their uncontested functioning.

(Shapiro 1992: 1)

BOX 10.2: (continued)

'Diamonds from Sierra Leone'

In the lyrics to this song, KanYe West articulates the 'bling' culture of US hip hop with both drugs and the illegal smuggling of diamonds out of Sierra Leone that finances the civil war in that country: 'Though it's thousands of miles away, Sierra Leone connect to what we go through today, over here [USA] it's the drug trade, we die from drugs, over there [Sierra Leone] they die from what we buy from drugs, the diamonds, the chains, the bracelets.' This song neatly encapsulates how actions that seem connected only to one's personal identity may have international repercussions. These connections also highlight how international relations are about much more than merely states' official foreign policy interactions with each other.

24

The popular counter-terrorism drama *24* routinely shows its hero, Jack Bauer, torturing terrorist suspects, a practice justified by *24*'s classic 'ticking time bomb' narrative. In 2006 US Army Brigadier General Patrick Finnegan met with the show's creative team to express concern that the show's 'central political premise—that the letter of US law must be sacrificed for the country's security'—influenced US soldiers—cadets at West Point as well as troops in Iraq, for instance—to view torture, illegal in US law, as nonetheless both legitimate and efficacious (Mayer 2007).

Independence Day

The Hollywood blockbuster film *Independence Day* (1996, dir. Roland Emmerich) not only reconstitutes US identity, it generously endows the rest of the planet with it. As Jan Mair has argued, '*Independence Day* explicitly delivers the apotheosis of the American Dream. In this movie, all that is not America . . . gets totally eradicated courtesy of aliens. What results from this apocalyptic conflict is a new global Fourth of July that subsumes every terrestrial being in Pax Americana. . . . Here aliens underline the total supremacy of America, their onslaught demonstrates the impregnability of American supremacy and its rightful leadership of the globe' (2002: 34; see also Rogin 1998).

National Geographic

Catherine A. Lutz and Jane L. Collins examine 'the making of national identity in popular photography' in *National Geographic* (1993: 1). 'Taking the photograph as a central feature of modern life', they ask '*how* photographs signify' (4). Because 'identity formation draws on images of the other', Lutz and Collins examine the ways in which photographs of (and accompanying texts about) peoples and cultures in the 'third world' are exoticized and appropriated in the West—specifically in *National Geographic*, a popular 'high middlebrow' magazine (6)—and thus how they contribute to defining Western, and US, identity.

The West Wing

Despite its seemingly liberal slant, the award-winning TV series *The West Wing* legitimizes the Bush administration's war on terror. Its representations of that 'war' are based upon three themes central to US war on terror discourse and US identity as constituted in it: 'Islamic fundamentalism as the root of the problem, terrorism as a phenomenon that cannot be handled through traditional means of international law and diplomacy, and . . . support for Israel in its responses to terrorism' (Gans-Boriskin and Tisinger 2005: 100).

Reader's Digest

Joanne Sharp argues that *Reader's Digest*, the largest-circulation general-interest magazine in the USA, 'might offer the single most important voice in the creation of popular geopolitics in America in the twentieth century' (2000: p. ix). The magazine created an imagined geography of the world and the US place therein by creating, and then reifying and therefore naturalizing, representations of 'America' in opposition to the Soviet 'evil empire'. During the Cold War, *Reader's Digest* constructed models for people in the USA 'of how the world works, of what America could and should do as a major player in this international political geography, and of what the individual American could and should do to help this national mission' (p. xv).

Star Trek

Analysing the discourse of *Star Trek* (notably the original series and *The Next Generation*) in relation to US

BOX 10.2: (continued)

foreign policy exposes striking parallels between *Star Trek*'s superficially liberal world—defined by benign exploration, liberal multiculturalism, and individualism—and the less savoury underlying constitutive themes on which it rests—namely, the same racism, interventionism, and militarism characteristic of US foreign policy. The ideological effect of the *Star Trek* narrative is to naturalize racial hierarchy, interventionism, and militarism (Weldes 1999b).

Identity in US foreign policy

US identity and the Cold War

In the dominant narrative, the bipolar Cold War conflict—intense rivalry between the two superpowers—is understood as a global struggle: the USSR vs. the USA, 'East' vs. 'West', 'Communism' vs. 'the free world', 'totalitarianism' vs. 'democracy'. During the Cold War, US foreign policy revolved around the grand strategy of containment (Gaddis 1982): the USA led 'the Free World' in preventing Soviet/communist expansion into non-communist regions of the world, preserving freedom—free markets, free elections, and, later, human rights—through interventions particularly, although not exclusively, in the so-called third world ('less developed' countries).

However, another story can be told about the Cold War. In this alternative narrative, the Cold War was largely an enterprise of US empire, through which US (and Western) neo-imperial relations—that is, domination through unequal exchange rather than through colonial administration—were extended to ever larger parts of the world. On this view, the USA established an empire in Latin America with the 1823 Monroe Doctrine, broadened it in wars against Spain (1898) and the Philippines (1899–1902), and sought to expand its domination into Europe and elsewhere, through a globalizing free trade system, global US military deployments, and global alliance structure. US empire was driven not by anti-communism, but by the underlying US drive to establish a capitalist—private property-based—global free market (Cox 1984; Williams 2004).

How does one story—global US intervention in the Cold War to contain communism and preserve freedom—become hegemonic (i.e. accepted as true) and the other marginalized? In the remainder of this section we provide an introductory discourse analysis[8] of the tropes and narratives of US identity articulated by US presidents (Boxes 10.3 and 10.4), to show how these representations continually operate to reinforce and naturalize the state-centric 'freedom' Cold War narrative while marginalizing representations of US imperialism.

One of the most significant representations articulated in US presidential speeches is historical parallels and references/analogies to the Second World War. Kennedy refers to the USA having fought for Berlin before, and Kennedy, Carter, and Truman all invoke the clear 'lesson' of history learned from the 1930s and the rise of Nazism. Truman uses the word 'appeasement' in describing policy alternatives with regard to the conflict in Korea. The Second World War has been constructed as the most noble war ever waged (at least, by the USA and its Allies) and 'Munich conditioned the thinking of every Cold War administration from Truman to George H. W. Bush' (Record 2007: 165). Articulating Cold War events with the Second World War, then, served to legitimize US intervention and provided continuity for the USA's role as leader of the 'free world' against all forms of 'totalitarianism'—previously fascism, now communism.

When 'totalitarianism' is invoked, through its association with Nazism, it simultaneously carries with it connotations of 'expansion' and 'aggression'. The main enemy/threat to the USA, its allies, and global stability in US Cold War discourse is 'communism', whether embodied in the Soviet Union, other communist states like China and Cuba, or an 'international communist conspiracy' guided from the Kremlin. The identity of the communist 'other' is represented as a threat in several ways. Kennedy, Reagan, Carter, and Truman all emphasize the USSR's massive size in comparison with the small countries it threatens. Eisenhower, Kennedy, Johnson, and Carter use words such as 'aggressive' and 'hostile', while Nixon refers to 'massacres' perpetrated by Vietnamese communists. The dominant theme, occurring in almost every Cold War speech in Boxes 10.3 and 10.4, is a communist conspiracy based on betrayal and deception (Kennedy), undertaken by an enemy who violates agreements and whose claims are false (Johnson, Carter), whose methods are ruthless and insidious (Eisenhower), and whose aims are subversion, infiltration, and world conquest (Truman, Johnson, Nixon).

The USA is constituted in opposition to this evil and dangerous 'other'. US actions are always represented as benign and defensive, and only ever as *responses to* objective and external (communist) threats; the USA is never the aggressor. The predicates (qualities) most commonly articulated with the USA are leadership, freedom, strength, and commitment. The USA is represented as decisive and united;[9] it has 'moral stamina', 'courage', 'determination', shoulders 'responsibilities', carries 'burdens', and makes 'sacrifices' in order to preserve freedom and fulfil its commitments to protect other (weaker) states. US credibility is based on this role as the world's policeman: an attack on any state is an attack on the USA (Carter, Johnson, Kennedy) and nations look to the USA for leadership in international affairs (Nixon, Truman), thus providing a clear moral basis for US intervention. However, the USA also works in partnership with other states to defend liberty (Carter, Johnson, Truman).

Constructing the USA as strong, benign, determined, and defending freedom, in contrast to the USSR defined as 'a slave state, duplicitous and secretive, despotic and aggressive' (Laffey and Weldes 2004: 29), creates a warrant for action in US foreign policy. It makes some policies and actions possible, legitimate, and necessary, while rendering others unlikely or even unthinkable. It 'permits the US to engage in certain practices, e.g., "noble causes," and precludes others, e.g., "aggression" or "coercion"' (Doty 1993: 310–12).

This accounts for the US construction of the 1962 Cuban missile crisis as a scenario in which it defended 'the free world' from the Soviet missiles placed in Cuba with the purpose of creating a communist bridgehead to the Americas. It was not possible to understand the missile deployment—as the Cubans and Soviets did—as a legal and internationally acceptable defensive measure protecting a small and vulnerable island from sustained US imperial aggression (Weldes 1999a: 21–40).

BOX 10.3: Articulations of US identity in foreign policy crises

Crises are social constructions in that they are fundamentally the outcome of particular social practices, including, centrally, practices of representation. . . . The construction of crises . . . occurs in tandem with the construction and reconstruction of state identity. Crises are typically understood to issue from outside of the state and to disrupt its normal functioning. I have suggested instead that crises are internal to the functioning of states because they are inextricably intertwined with state identity in two complementary ways: first, state identity enables crises; second and conversely, crises enable state identity. . . . Because state identity is always potentially precarious, it needs constantly to be stabilised or (re)produced. Crises present important opportunities for that reproduction.

(Weldes 1999c: 57–9)

1961: the Berlin Wall

The immediate threat to free men is in West Berlin. . . . We are there as a result of our victory over Nazi Germany—and our basic rights to be there . . . include both our presence in West Berlin and the enjoyment of access across East Germany. . . . But in addition to those rights is our commitment to sustain—and defend, if need

(continued)

BOX 10.3: (continued)

be—the opportunity for more than two million people to deter-mine their own future and choose their own way of life. . . . [W]e have given our word that an attack upon that city will be regarded as an attack upon us all. For West Berlin . . . has many roles. It is more than a showcase of liberty, a symbol, an island of freedom in a Communist sea. It is even more than a link with the Free World, a beacon of hope behind the Iron Curtain, an escape hatch for refu-gees. . . . [A]bove all it has now become—as never before—the great testing place of Western courage and will. . . . We do not want to fight—but we have fought before. . . . The strength of the alli-ance on which our security depends is dependent in turn on our willingness to meet our commitments to them. . . . We recognise the Soviet Union's historical concern about their security in Cen-tral and Eastern Europe, after a series of ravaging invasions, and we believe arrangements can be worked out which will help to meet those concerns, and make it possible for both security and freedom to exist in this troubled area. . . . [But t]he world is not deceived by the Communist attempt to label Berlin as a hot-bed of war. There is peace in Berlin today. The source of world trouble and tension is Moscow, not Berlin.

(Kennedy 1961)

1962: the Cuban missile crisis

This secret, swift, extraordinary build-up of Communist missiles in an area well-known to have a special and historical relationship to the United States and the nations of the Western Hemisphere . . . is a deliberately provocative and unjustified change in the status quo which cannot be accepted by this country if our courage and our commitments are ever to be trusted again, by either friend or foe. . . . The nineteen thirties taught us a clear lesson. Aggressive conduct, if allowed to go unchecked and unchallenged, ultimate-ly leads to war. This nation is opposed to war. We are also true to our word. . . . That is why the latest Soviet threat . . . must and will be met with determination. Any hostile move anywhere in the world against the safety and freedom of peoples to whom we are committed including in particular the brave people of West Berlin will be met by whatever action is needed. Finally, I want to say a few words to the captive people of Cuba to whom this speech is being directly carried by special radio facilities. . . . I have watched and the American people have watched with deep sorrow how your nationalist revolution was betrayed and how your fatherland fell under foreign domination. Now your leaders are no longer Cuban leaders inspired by Cuban ideals. They are puppets and agents of an international conspiracy which has turned Cuba against your friends and neighbors in the Americas. . . . The path we have chosen for the present is full of hazards. . . . But it is the

one most consistent with our character and courage as a nation and our commitments around the world. The cost of freedom is always high, but Americans have always paid it.

(Kennedy 1962: 66–8)

1964: the Gulf of Tonkin (Vietnam)

Our policy [in Vietnam] has been consistent and unchanged since 1954. . . .

1. American keeps her word. Here as elsewhere, we must and shall honor our commitments.

2. The issue is the future of southeast Asia as a whole. A threat to any nation in that region is a threat to all, and a threat to us.

3. Our purpose is peace. We have no military, political, or territo-rial ambitions in the area.

4. This is not a jungle war, but a struggle for freedom on every front of human activity. Our military and economic assistance to South Vietnam and Laos in particular has the purpose of helping these countries to repel aggression and strengthen their independence.

The threat to the free nations of southeast Asia has long been clear. The North Vietnamese regime has constantly sought to take over South Vietnam and Laos. This Communist regime has violated the Geneva accords for Vietnam. It has systematically conducted a campaign of subversion, which includes the direc-tion, training, and supply of personnel and arms for the conduct of guerrilla warfare in South Vietnamese territory. . . . In recent months, the actions of the North Vietnamese regime have become steadily more threatening. . . . I should now ask the Congress on its part, to join in affirming the national determina-tion that all such attacks will be met, and that the United States will continue in its basic policy of assisting the free nations of the area to defend their freedom. . . . We must make it clear to all that the United States is united in its determination to bring about the end of Communist subversion and aggression in the area.

(Johnson 1964)

1993: Somalia

This past weekend we all reacted with anger and horror as an armed Somali gang desecrated the bodies of our American soldiers and displayed a captured American pilot—all of them soldiers who were taking part in an international effort to end the starvation of the Somali people themselves. . . . A third of a million people had died of starvation and disease. . . .

BOX 10.3: (continued)

Meanwhile, tons of relief supplies piled up in the capital of Mogadishu because a small number of Somalis stopped food from reaching their own countrymen. Our consciences said, enough. In our nation's best tradition, we took action with bipartisan support. President Bush sent in 28,000 American troops as part of a United Nations humanitarian mission. Our troops created a secure environment so that food and medicine could get through. We saved close to 1 million lives. . . . [N]one of this could have happened without American leadership and America's troops. . . . So now we face a choice. Do we leave when the job gets tough, or when the job is well done? . . . I want to bring our troops home from Somalia. . . . But we must also leave on our own terms. We must do it right . . . even as we prepare to withdraw from Somalia, we need more strength there. We need more armor, more air power, to ensure that our people are safe and we can do our job. . . . For, if we were to leave today, we know what would happen. Within months, Somali children would again be dying in the streets. Our own credibility with friends and allies would be severely damaged. Our leadership in world affairs would be undermined at the very time when people are looking to America to help promote peace and freedom in the post-Cold War world. And all around the world, aggressors, thugs, and terrorists will conclude that the best way to get us to change our policies is to kill our people. It would be open season on Americans. . . . [I]f we take the time to do the job right . . . we will have lived up to the responsibility of American leadership in the world. And we will have proved that we are committed to addressing the new problems of a new era.

(Clinton 1993)

2001: the 9/11 attacks

The deliberate and deadly attacks which were carried out yesterday against our country were more than acts of terror. They were acts of war. . . . Freedom and democracy are under attack. The American people need to know that we're facing a different enemy than we have ever faced. This enemy hides in shadows, and has no regard for human life. This is an enemy who preys on innocent and unsuspecting people, then runs for cover. But it won't be able to run for cover forever. . . . This enemy attacked not just our people, but all freedom-loving people everywhere in the world. The United States of America will use all its resources to conquer this enemy. We will rally the world. We will be patient, we will be focused, and we will be steadfast in our determination. This battle will take time and resolve. But make no mistake about it: we will win. . . . The freedom-loving nations of the world stand by our side. This will be a monumental struggle of good versus evil. But good will prevail.

(Bush 2001a)

US identity and the New World Order

The fall of the Berlin Wall and collapse of the USSR signalled the Cold War's abrupt and unexpected demise. The disappearance of the Soviet/communist 'other'/threat and US containment policy's resultant irrelevance triggered a crisis in US identity and foreign policy. As they had after the Second World War, policy makers understood the interventional system as fundamentally altered. On 11 September 1990, President George Bush Sr. announced a 'New World Order' that would be free from old Cold War threats and insecurities (Box 10.4). Multilateralism—working in concert with the international community and international organizations—and humanitarian intervention—the threat or use of military force to prevent human rights violations—were the new strategy for the New World Order. President Clinton's 1993 speech about

the downing of a Black Hawk helicopter in Somalia (Box 10.3) provides an explicit example.

Alternative narratives continued to construct US foreign policy as imperialist. Post-Cold War foreign policy, on this view, was about the defence and expansion of empire. The New World Order was a unipolar system—dominated by a single global power—and the USA was intent on expanding its political and economic reach into former Soviet and communist bloc areas. The Persian Gulf War (1990–1), for instance, was an imperialist war in which the USA sought to maintain Western access to Middle Eastern oil (Chomsky 1991; Said 1991). Through what representational mechanisms did the conventional narrative become hegemonic and the imperial alternative marginalized?

Despite the post-Cold War world being 'quite different', the New World Order is also immediately represented as sharing continuities: 'the world

MAJOR DEBATES AND THEIR IMPACT 10.1: Samuel Huntington's 'Clash of Civilisations'

In 1993, former adviser to President Carter Samuel Huntington (1993, 1996) hypothesized that post-Cold War world politics would be characterized by a 'clash of civilizations': '[t]he great divisions among humankind and the dominating source of conflict will be cultural' (1993: 1). His 'civilisations' are the West, Latin America, the 'Orthodox' (Christian) world, Islam, Hindu civilization, 'Sinic' (Chinese) civilization, and Japan (1996: 45–6). His argument launched a debate about the nature of post-Cold War world politics and contributed to debates about the importance of culture and identity in world politics. Critics charge (among other issues) that Huntington essentializes cultural identities/differences and is unreflective about the processes constituting them. Although some elements of this rhetoric appear in early US statements in the war on terror, the US 'War on Terror' discourse is more accurately characterized as 'good versus evil' rather than 'the West versus Islam' (Kline 2004).

remains a dangerous place' (Bush Sr.). US foreign policy discourse proliferates threats and insecurities. 'In the post-Soviet era', Les Aspin, then chairman of the US House Armed Services Committee, argued, 'threats to American security will be broader and more diverse, and the security environment will be murkier, more ambiguous, and more fluid' (1992: 4). These include residual threats from the USSR/Russia, regional aggressors (Iran, Iraq, Syria, Libya, North Korea, China, Cuba), the proliferation of nuclear weapons and other weapons of mass destruction, terrorism, hostage taking, and drug trafficking, among others. Post-Cold War 'others' are 'renegade regimes and unpredictable rulers', 'rogue states', 'aggressors, thugs, and terrorists', and 'cynical leaders' full of 'poisonous' 'hatred', who engage in systematic terror, repression, brutality, aggression, and mass killing (Bush Sr., Clinton).

Threats are 'launch[ed]', 'unleash[ed]', and 'arise suddenly, unpredictably, and from unexpected quarters', which 'require' responses and to which 'we all react' (Bush Sr., Clinton). The USA is represented as benign and defensive, acting decisively and effectively, creating security, and saving lives. Unlike Somali men, who starve children, the USA distributes food. Unlike Yugoslavia, oppressing Kosovar Albanians, the USA has 'shed racism' and its 'sense of superiority'. The 'New World Order' is a place where 'freedom and democracy have made great gains', where nations can 'prosper and live in harmony' (Bush Sr.) and pursue 'economic progress' (Clinton) because the USA is doing the 'morally right thing' by protecting freedom.

The USA is strong and committed in the face of these threats. Strength is equated with military force, and military intervention is presented as inevitable, the only way in which these threats can be countered. Both Clinton and Bush refer to international cooperation and shared responsibilities, and Clinton emphasizes that US intervention in Somalia is part of a UN humanitarian mission, but US leadership continues to be presented as natural: 'people are looking to America', 'American leadership and America's troops', to get the job done (Clinton).

References to the Second World War continue to appear in post-Cold War US foreign policy representations. At a ceremony commemorating Second World War veterans, Clinton articulates the impending NATO intervention in Kosovo with the Allied struggle against the Nazis. In the 1990–1 Gulf War, representations of Iraq/Saddam Hussein are (as with representations of the USSR during the Cold War) modelled on narratives and tropes about the Nazis/ Hitler/Second World War (Record 2007). However, all history of US and Western imperialism in the Middle East is erased. Through the rhetoric of humanitarian intervention and discursive articulation with the Second World War and the Cold War, the USA continues to construct world politics in such as way that it is authorized to act in defence of freedom, democracy, and human rights. In contrast, the US imperialist narrative, in which the USA continues to engage in exploitative economic practices, political intervention, and military action in and against other states, is obscured (Blum 2003).

US identity and the war on terror

9/11 was represented as another major rupture in world politics and US foreign policy, creating a new geostrategic reality that directly challenged US identity. In the face of the ongoing transnational terrorist threat, the grand strategies of multilateralism and humanitarian intervention were replaced by the war on terror, a global battle between good and evil, civilization and barbarism. The non-state version of this narrative, focusing on an amorphous network of terrorist organizations and cells, was quickly replaced by a more conventional state-centric narrative, one that manifested itself in the wars in/on Afghanistan and Iraq.

Alternatively, the war on terror can be represented as the further expansion of, and a new guise for, US imperialism. The events of 11 September provided a tool for the implementation of an imperial US strategy for the twenty-first century, previously articulated by the Project for the New American Century (www.newamericancentury.org/; Bennis 2003), in which the Bush administration has used 9/11 to legitimize the broadening of US empire as the means for securing long-term global US military and economic supremacy.

BOX 10.4: Presidents articulate US identity through foreign policy

2002: President George W. Bush on the axis of evil

Our nation will continue to be steadfast and patient and persistent in the pursuit of two great objectives. First, we will shut down terrorist camps, disrupt terrorist plans, and bring terrorists to justice. And, second, we must prevent the terrorists and regimes who seek chemical, biological or nuclear weapons from threatening the United States and the world. . . . States like these, and their terrorist allies constitute an axis of evil, arming to threaten the peace of the world. By seeking weapons of mass destruction, these regimes pose a grave and growing danger. They could provide these arms to terrorists, giving them the means to match their hatred. They could attack our allies or attempt to blackmail the United States. In any of these cases, the price of indifference would be catastrophic. . . . Our war on terror is well begun, but it is only begun. This campaign may not be finished on our watch—yet it must be and will be waged on our watch. . . . History has called America and our allies to action, and it is both our responsibility and our privilege to fight freedom's fight.

(Bush 2002a)

1999: President Bill Clinton on US intervention in Kosovo

[W]e [are] work[ing] with our allies to reverse the systematic campaign of terror, and to bring peace and freedom to Kosovo. . . . Kosovo is a crucial test: Can we strengthen a global community grounded in cooperation and tolerance, rooted in common humanity? Or will repression and brutality, rooted in ethnic, racial and religious hatreds dominate the agenda for the new century and the new millennium? The

World War II veterans here fought in Europe and in the Pacific to prevent the world from being dominated by tyrants who use racial and religious hatred to strengthen their grip and to justify mass killing. . . . Some have questioned the need for continuing our security partnership with Europe at the end of the Cold War. But in this age of growing international interdependence, America needs a strong and peaceful Europe more than ever as our partner for freedom and for economic progress, and our partner against terrorism, the spread of weapons of mass destruction, and instability. . . . Serbs simply must free themselves of the notion that their neighbors must be their enemies. The real enemy is a poisonous hatred unleashed by a cynical leader, based on a distorted view of what constitutes real national greatness. The United States has become greater as we have shed racism, as we have shed a sense of superiority, as we have become more committed to working together across the lines that divide us, as we have found other ways to define meaning and purpose in life. And so has every other country that has embarked on that course. . . . This is the right vision, and the right course. It is not only the morally right thing for America, it is the right thing for our security interests over the long run.

(Clinton 1999)

1990: President George H. W. Bush on the New World Order

We stand today at a unique and extraordinary moment. The crisis in the Persian Gulf, as grave as it is, also offers a rare opportunity to move toward an historic period of cooperation. Out of these troubled times . . . —a new world order—can emerge: a new era—freer from the threat of terror, stronger in the pursuit of

(continued)

BOX 10.4: (continued)

justice, and more secure in the quest for peace. An era in which the nations of the world, East and West, North and South, can prosper and live in harmony. A hundred generations have searched for this elusive path to peace, while a thousand wars raged across the span of human endeavor. Today that new world is struggling to be born, a world quite different from the one we've known. A world where the rule of law supplants the rule of the jungle. A world in which nations recognise the shared responsibility for freedom and justice. A world where the strong respect the rights of the weak.

(Bush 1990a: 1219)

1990: President George H. W. Bush on the persistence of threats

Even in a world where democracy and freedom have made great gains, threats remain. Terrorism, hostagetaking, renegade regimes and unpredictable rulers, new sources of instability—all require a strong and engaged America. The brutal aggression launched last night [by Iraq] against Kuwait illustrates my central thesis: Notwithstanding the alteration in the Soviet threat, the world remains a dangerous place with serious threats to important US interests wholly unrelated to the earlier patterns of the US–Soviet relationship. These threats . . . can arise suddenly, unpredictably, and from unexpected quarters.

(Bush 1990b: 1092)

1986: President Ronald Reagan on US aid to Nicaraguan counter-revolutionaries

I must speak to you tonight about a mounting danger in Central America that threatens the security of the United States. I am speaking of Nicaragua, a Soviet ally on the American mainland only two hours flying time from our own borders. . . . Using Nicaragua as a base, the Soviets and Cubans can become the dominant power in the crucial corridor between North and South America. . . . Gathered in Nicaragua already are thousands of Cuban military advisors, contingents of Soviets and East Germans and all the elements of international terror—from the P.L.O. to Italy's Red Brigades. [T]he Sandinistas are transforming their nation into a safe house, a command post, for international terror. . . . The Sandinistas not only sponsor terror . . . they provide a sanctuary for terror.

(Reagan 1986)

1979: President Jimmy Carter on the Soviet invasion of Afghanistan

Massive Soviet military forces have invaded the small, non-aligned, sovereign nation of Afghanistan, which had hitherto not been an occupied satellite of the Soviet Union. Fifty thousand heavily armed Soviet troops have crossed the border and are now dispersed throughout Afghanistan, attempting to conquer the fiercely independent Muslim people of that country. The Soviets claim, falsely, that they were invited into Afghanistan to help protect that country from some unnamed outside threat. . . . This is a callous violation of international law and the United Nations Charter. . . . The United States wants all nations in the region to be free and independent. If the Soviets are encouraged in this invasion by eventual success, and if they maintain their dominance over Afghanistan and then extend their control to adjacent countries, the stable, strategic, and peaceful balance of the entire world will be changed. This would threaten the security of all nations including, of course, the United States, our allies, and our friends. . . . [N]either the United States nor any other nation which is committed to world peace and stability can continue to do business as usual with the Soviet Union. . . . These actions will require some sacrifice on the part of all Americans, but there is absolutely no doubt that these actions are in the interests of world peace and in the interest of the security of our own nation, and that they are also compatible with actions being taken by our major trading partners . . . Neither our allies nor our potential adversaries should have the slightest doubt about our willingness, our determination, and our capacity. . . . History teaches, perhaps, very few clear lessons. But surely one such lesson learned by the world at great cost is that aggression, unopposed, becomes a contagious disease. . . . The United States will meet its responsibilities.

(Carter 1980)

1969: President Richard Nixon on 'Vietnamization' of the war in Vietnam

[T]he question before us is not whether some Americans are for peace and some Americans are against peace. . . . The great question is: how can we win America's peace? . . . For the South Vietnamese, our precipitate withdrawal would inevitably allow the communists to repeat the massacres which followed their takeover in the North 15 years before. . . . For the United States, this first defeat in our Nation's history would result in a collapse of confidence in American leadership, not only in Asia but throughout the world. . . . A nation cannot remain great if it betrays its allies and lets down its friends. Our defeat and humiliation in South Vietnam without question would promote recklessness in the councils of those great powers who have not yet abandoned their goals of world conquest. This would spark violence wherever our commitments help maintain the peace—in the Middle East, in Berlin, eventually even in the Western Hemisphere. . . . The defense of freedom is everybody's business—not just America's business. . . . This [American] withdrawal will be made from strength and not from weakness. . . . Two hundred years ago this

BOX 10.4: (continued)

Nation was weak and poor. But even then America was the hope of millions in the world. Today we have become the strongest, richest nation in the world. And the wheel of destiny has turned so that any hope for the survival of peace and freedom will be determined by whether the American people have the moral stamina and the courage to meet the challenge of free world leadership. Let historians not record that when America was the most powerful nation in the world we passed on the other side of the road and allowed the last hopes for peace and freedom of millions of people to be suffocated by the forces of totalitarianism.

(Nixon 1969: 901–9)

1961: President Dwight D. Eisenhower on the Cold War

We face a hostile ideology—global in scope, atheistic in character, ruthless in purpose, and insidious in method. Unhappily, the danger it poses promises to be of infinite duration. To meet it successfully is called for not so much the emotional and transitory sacrifices of crisis but rather those which enable us to carry forward steadily, surely, and without complaint the burdens of a prolonged and complex struggle—with liberty at stake.

(Eisenhower 1961: 236)

1950: President Harry S. Truman on the Korean War

These men of ours are engaged once again in an age-old struggle for human liberty. Our men, and the men of other free nations, are defending with their lives the cause of freedom in the world. They are fighting for the proposition that peace shall be the law of this earth. . . . Two months ago Communist imperialism turned to the familiar tactics of infiltration and subversion to a brutal attack on the small Republic of South Korea. When that happened, the free and peace-loving nations of the world faced two possible courses. One course would have been to limit our action to diplomatic protests, while the

Communist aggressor went ahead and swallowed up their victim. That would have been the course of appeasement. If the history of the 1930s teaches us anything, it is that the appeasement of dictators is the sure road to world war. If aggression were allowed to succeed in Korea, it would be an open invitation to new acts of aggression elsewhere. . . . It is your liberty and mine which is involved. What is at stake is the free way of life—the right to worship as we please, the right to express our opinions, the right to raise our children in our own way, the right to choose our jobs, the right to plan our future and to live without fear. . . . We cannot hope to maintain our own freedom if freedom elsewhere is wiped out.

(Truman 1950: 609–10)

1947: President Harry S. Truman on aid to Greece in the early Cold War

At the present moment in history nearly every nation must choose between alternative ways of life. The choice is too often not a free one. One way of life is based upon the will of the majority, and is distinguished by free institutions, representative government, free elections, guarantees of individual liberty, freedom of speech and religion, and freedom from political oppression. The second way of life is based upon the will of a minority forcibly imposed upon the majority. It relies upon terror and oppression, a controlled press and radio, fixed elections, and the suppression of personal freedoms. I believe that it must be the policy of the United States to support free peoples who are resisting attempted subjugation by armed minorities or by outside pressures. . . . The free peoples of the world look to us for support in maintaining their freedoms. If we falter in our leadership, we may endanger the peace of the world—and we shall surely endanger the welfare of our own nation.

(Truman 1947)

Interestingly, this imperial argument is no longer the sole preserve of the left (Hardt and Negri 2000; Ignatieff 2003; Panitch and Gindin 2004; Stokes 2005), and is no longer easily dismissed or entirely marginalized. Conservative politicians and commentators have begun to rearticulate the notion of 'American empire' as a fundamentally positive goal of the right (rather than a critique from the left), and, further, as a necessity in a dangerous world (Boot 2002; Mallaby 2002). 9/11 and the war on terror have

brought new and overt support for US empire from policy makers, analysts, and media pundits alike.

In US discourse after September 2001, terrorists, and their allies and sponsors, rogue states, are claimed to be unlike anything the world has ever seen, forming an irredeemable axis of evil. They are barbaric and brutal, fanatical extremists who operate through totalitarianism, tyranny, and aggression (Bush 2001b, 2001e, 2005b, 2006b; Boxes 10.3, 10.4). They are both cowardly and predatory: plotting in secret, running for cover, retreating, hiding; and resorting to propaganda, blackmail, and terror whenever and wherever the opportunity arises (Bush 2005b; Box 10.4). In their lack of 'regard for conventions of war or rules of morality', they are 'outlaw regimes' (Bush 2003, 2002a), and the USA must again respond to this new and unprovoked attack and ongoing threat from a ruthless enemy (Bush 2004).

Similar to Cold War and New World Order rhetoric, this threat is posed not just to the USA, but to the whole world: the enemy struck at all 'freedom-loving people' (Bush 2001b). US identity is conflated with both the 'innocent and unsuspecting' victims of the 9/11 attacks and with 'freedom and democracy' everywhere. As in previous eras, the USA has the 'responsibility' of being the leader of a global coalition fight for freedom, defending itself, its friends, and allies. The USA 'continue[s] to be steadfast', 'patient', 'persistent', and 'focused', with strength, commitment, determination, and resolve to 'pursue' its objectives and defeat the terrorists (Bush 2001d, 2001e, 2004, 2005b, 2006a; Boxes 10.3, 10.4).

Bush also invokes historical parallels, articulating 9/11 with Pearl Harbor and the Holocaust (2006a, 2001e), the war on terror with the fight against fascism, Nazism, and the Japanese, as well as against communism in the Cold War (2001c, 2002b, 2005a, 2006b). He claims that the terrorists cannot be 'appeased' (2001e, 2006a), and the rhetoric of the axis of evil is itself a reference to the Axis powers of Germany, Japan, and Italy in the Second World War.

The pervasive rhetoric of good vs. evil, dark vs. light, civilization vs. barbarism, that underpins US policy in the war on terror makes possible both interstate wars in/on Afghanistan and the global torture system—manifest in Abu Ghraib and Guantánamo—of disappearances, extraordinary renditions, indefinite incarceration without trial, psychological intimidation and abuse of prisoners, and the undermining of civil rights in the USA and UK, all in the name of 'freedom'. The articulation of 'we' the USA as 'innocent and unsuspecting' erases the history of US actions in the Middle East, its complicity in the imperial origins of most Middle Eastern states and in

repeated military and covert political operations, and its support of Israel against the Palestinians.

This rhetoric also serves to construct a 'fundamental' difference between, on the one hand, intentionally targeting civilians in the World Trade Center, a Bali nightclub, or car bombs in Iraqi towns and cities, and, on the other, killing many tens of thousands of civilians as a 'side effect' of security measures in Iraq and Afghanistan. The terrorists' attacks are 'deliberate and deadly', in contrast to allied-caused deaths, which are merely 'collateral damage'.[10] Crucial to US identity is the notion that these latter deaths are unplanned and unavoidable, and that the USA is just as morally blameless for these deaths as for those in September 2001.

Within the hegemonic narrative, 9/11 is constructed as a radical disjuncture in US foreign policy. Seen in the context of US imperialism, however, 9/11 represents a continuation of the rhetoric, tropes, and narratives—most prominently, analogies with the Second World War—identifiable in US foreign policy discourses from earlier eras.

KEY POINTS

- ❑ Constructions of identity in dominant US foreign policy discourse obscure and marginalize other interpretations of US identity and foreign policy such as the USA as imperialist and interventionist.
- ❑ In all three eras the primary characteristics associated with 'the USA' are leadership, freedom, strength, and commitment/determination.
- ❑ The predicates most commonly attached to the 'other' in Cold War US discourse represent the USSR as totalitarian, aggressive, deceitful, and subversive.
- ❑ In the post-Cold War era, the dominant threat is articulated as 'rogue states', often through the use of analogies to Hitler/Nazism/Second World War.
- ❑ In the war on terror, terrorists are articulated as evil and irrational, while the USA continues to be represented as defensive, strong, and committed to defending freedom.
- ❑ The USA's and others' identities interact and constitute discourses of US foreign policy in complex and multifaceted ways.

Conclusion

In this chapter we have shown how processes of identity construction and representations of foreign policy are mutually constitutive. US identity is a complex phenomenon, and is constantly being articulated and rearticulated, maintained, contested, and transformed in the face of revised representations of supposedly external and objective threats. These articulations occur in discourses and manifest themselves in representations. Each new articulation of US identity in US foreign policy is based on recurring themes and signifiers that have been articulated by previous generations of policy makers.

Transformations in world politics—e.g. the shift to the Cold War, its subsequent evaporation, 9/11—generally appear to policy makers and analysts as fundamental challenges to US identity and the attendant US role in the world. Such developments force policy makers to rearticulate the nature of threats and insecurities so as to be able to reconstitute a (seemingly) stable US identity. As we have argued here, this has meant reproducing and representing US leadership in a global fight for freedom against a variety of mutating threats.

We have also presented a different narrative, that of US imperialism, in order to demonstrate how both of these discourses are socially constructed. If we examine US foreign policy from different vantage points, other aspects of US identity come to the fore. Scholars have examined how models of masculinity influenced US Cold War policy makers (Dean 2001), how religion and 'family values' are articulated through Bush's war on terror discourse (Kline 2004), how gender and race were deployed in the build-up to the 1991 Gulf War (Farmanfarmaian 1992; Niva 1998) and after 9/11 (Kimmel 2003; Shepherd 2006; Nayak 2006).

Countless other stories remain untold about identity and US foreign policy in this chapter. In particular, it should be evident that we have chosen to focus on the USA's own constructions of (US and others') identities in articulations of US foreign policy, and have not examined other states' representations. No doubt an analysis of identities in US foreign policy from the perspective of, say, the Iranian state would look very different from what we have outlined here, not to mention the interstate and supra-state organizations, as well as non-state actors, who also construct representations of (their own and others') identities.

We have also only briefly discussed how these representations also exist outside official policy discourses, in music, films, TV shows, and other popular cultural sites. However, while it is impossible to give a comprehensive account of all of the facets of identity in US foreign policy, we hope we have provided some insights into what such analyses might look like and, more importantly, we have unpacked the assumptions upon which these analyses are based and the concepts with which such analyses can be conducted.

Finally, we want to point out that, as well as political and cultural/media elites constructing representations of US identity, academic elites (lecturers, authors, researchers) are also involved in these processes of identity construction.

Exercise four: how are US and other identities articulated and represented in the approaches and chapters in this book?

? Questions

1. What is identity?
2. How is the concept of identity useful in understanding US foreign policy?
3. In what ways is social constructivism a useful framework for analysing US foreign policy?
4. How does identity relate to values and interests?
5. Has US identity changed or remained constant over time?

6. What is the relationship between identity, insecurity, and threats?

7. How are 'others' represented in discourses of US foreign policy?

8. What roles do race and religion play in representations of US foreign policy?

9. How are narratives and representations of US foreign policy gendered?

10. What is the relationship between capitalism, US identity, and US foreign policy?

11. Think about your own foreign policy preferences; in what ways are these values constituted through, and connected with, your identity?

》 Further Reading

Campbell, D. (1998), *Writing Security: United States Foreign Policy and the Politics of Identity*, rev. edn. (Minneapolis: University of Minnesota Press).

In this classic study, which helped to introduce identity into the study of international relations and US foreign policy, Campbell argues that the identities and foreign policies of states are performatively constituted in representations of danger.

Dean, R. (2001), *Imperial Brotherhood: Gender and the Making of Cold War Foreign Policy* (Amherst, Mass.: University of Massachusetts Press).

Dean argues that US foreign policy has been shaped by gender and class. Examining the McCarthy era and the war in Vietnam, Dean shows how elite conceptions of male identity—particularly a deeply ingrained sense of upper-class masculinity—fashioned the course of US foreign policy in the Cold War.

Doty, R. L. (1996), *Imperial Encounters: The Politics of Representation in North–South Relations* (Minneapolis: University of Minnesota Press).

Doty examines US–Philippine and UK–Kenya relations, demonstrating that the representational practices of policy makers, scholars, journalists, and others in the global north constitute the identities, and thus the relations between, diverse peoples, states, and regions.

Drinnon, R. (1990), *Facing West: The Metaphysics of Indian-Hating and Empire Building* (New York: Schocken Books; 1st pub. 1980).

Drinnon's searing critique examines the interconnection between racism—'Indian-hating'—and territorial and commercial expansion—'empire building'—as central factors explaining the history of Anglo-American expansion across North America and beyond, from the first Puritan confrontation with Native Americans through twentieth-century US interventions in the Philippines and Vietnam.

Hunt, M. (1987), *Ideology and US Foreign Policy* (New Haven: Yale University Press).

Hunt argues that US foreign policy has, since its inception, been based on a persistent ideology comprised of three components: an extroverted conception of national greatness, a detailed racial (and racist) hierarchy, and an abiding hostility toward social revolution.

Jackson, R. (2005), *Writing the War on Terrorism: Language, Politics and Counter-Terrorism* (Manchester: Manchester University Press).

Jackson critically examines US war on terror discourse—defined by evil terrorists and good Americans—to illuminate how it has become the dominant political narrative in the USA, justifying and normalizing a global counter-terrorist campaign.

Lipschutz, R. (2001), *Cold War Fantasies: Film, Fiction, and Foreign Policy* (Lanham, Md.: Rowman and Littlefield).

Lipschutz illustrates how popular media both reflect and constitute understandings of identity and threat by examining US Cold War domestic and foreign policies in light of contemporaneous films and novels.

Weber, C. (2006), *Imagining America at War: Morality, Politics, and Film* (London: Routledge).

Weber examines the political functions of film in the 'War on Terror', arguing that filmic representations are intimately connected to US identity and foreign policy.

Weldes, J. (1999), *Constructing National Interests: The United States and the Cuban Missile Crisis* (Minneapolis: University of Minnesota Press).

Weldes re-examines the Cuban missile crisis from a critical constructivist perspective.

Williams, W. A. (2004), *The Tragedy of American Diplomacy*, new edited edn. (New York: W. W. Norton; 1st pub. 1962).

Williams examines US–Cuban relations 1898–1961 in order to defend the thesis that the USA has long had an expansionist and economically imperialist foreign policy, thereby undermining US claims to defend self-determination and democracy abroad.

 # Endnotes

We would like to thank Ana Jordan for providing editorial assistance and Mick Cox and Doug Stokes for their helpful comments on earlier drafts of this chapter.

1. Using the noun 'America' for the USA or the adjective 'American' to describe its citizens or inhabitants is problematic because these terms refer to the entire American continent, comprising North, Central, and South America. People from Chile, Mexico, and Cuba are also 'American'. Throughout this chapter, we use 'USA'/'US' as noun and adjective to describe the state, its citizens, and inhabitants.

2. Other interest-based explanations focus on the rational decision making of various sorts of actors—whether bureaucrats (Allison and Zelikow 1999), interest groups (Terry 2005), public opinion (Entman 2004), or electoral politics (Gaddis 1982).

3. 'Nation' and 'state' are commonly hyphenated together to form the concept 'nation-state', based on the assumption that these two terms are interchangeable. However, the notion that states contain an ethnically or culturally homogeneous population is empirically unsustainable. There are no 'true' nation-states.

4. We use the terms '(re)produce' and '(re)production' to emphasize that processes of discursive constitution are dynamic, temporary, and unstable. Meaning is always being both produced and reproduced (as well as being contested and transformed). We also use the term 'identity/identities' to highlight that identity is never singular.

5. The term 'ideological' is commonly used pejoratively (negatively), to connote something that is based on ideas about how the world works, rather than on the 'truth'. We problematize this notion in the section 'Critical social constructivism as critique'. See Purvis and Hunt (1993) for a discussion of the relationship between 'ideology' and 'discourse'.

6. Maps provide a useful way for us to think about these issues because maps are neither 'true' nor 'false', but rather are ways of *representing* the world. Different maps serve different purposes and they represent (construct) the world in different ways.

7. As scholars we do not simply 'find' data waiting for us in the world, even in the natural sciences. Data sets are always *constructed*: the boundaries between what is interesting/relevant and what is to be discarded as unimportant are defined by the analyst, in the theoretical assumptions underpinning the research design and methods.

8. See Jennifer Milliken's (1999) critical overview of discourse analytical research for examples of other concepts and approaches that can be applied to the study of discourses and representations in world politics.

9. A common theme in US politics is that, however the two political parties (and the public) may be divided on domestic issues, the country must unite behind its foreign policy, which should enjoy bi-partisan support (survival and national security are 'prior to' domestic politics).

10. See Collins and Glover (2002) for a discussion of language in the war on terror, and Cohn (1987) for an analysis of the rhetorical function of terms such as collateral damage in US nuclear decision making.

 Visit the Online Resource Centre that accompanies this book for web links to accompany each chapter, and a range of other resources: www.oxfordtextbooks.co.uk/orc/cox_stokes/

Section 3

The United States and the World

11 US foreign policy in the Middle East

Toby Dodge

Chapter contents

Introduction

This chapter assesses the main dynamics that have transformed United States foreign policy towards the Middle East over the last eighty-five years. First it discusses the applicability of realist, Marxist, and constructivist theories of international relations. It will then assess the role that the Cold War, oil, and Israel have played in shaping American foreign policy. In each of these three areas the United States' tactical approach to the Middle East has produced unintended consequences that have increased resentment towards America, destabilized the region, and undermined its long-term strategic goals. The chapter concludes by discussing the Bush Doctrine, launched after 9/11 and the resultant invasion of Iraq. The Bush Doctrine certainly represented a major change in US policy but its application to Iraq has been disastrous and will damage the United States' ability to influence politics in the Middle East long after Bush has left office.

BOX 11.1: Important dates and events in relations between the states of the Middle East and the United States of America

1917	April: the United States of America enters the First World War. 2 November: the Balfour Declaration. British Secretary James Balfour in a letter to Lord Lionel Walter Rothschild says Britain (with US acquiescence) would support the creation of a Jewish homeland in Palestine.
1918	8 January: the American President, Woodrow Wilson issues the 14-point statement of its reasons for joining the war and what it expects the peace to look like.
1919	January–June: the Paris Peace Conference draws up the international agreement to run the world after the First World War. It results in the formation of the League of Nations.
1947	12 March: US President Truman addresses Congress and launches the Truman Doctrine, asking for permission to aid Greece, Turkey, and then Iran against the Soviet threat.
1948	May: the founding of the state of Israel. The first Arab–Israeli War.
1955	24 February: the formation of the Baghdad Pact: an anti-communist regional alliance with Iraq, Turkey, Iran, and Pakistan as members. September: Egypt's arms deal with Czechoslovakia.
1956	26 July. Nasser announces the nationalization of the Suez Canal.

	July–November: Suez crisis and the second Arab–Israeli War. Britain, France, and Israel collude to invade Egypt and attempt to remove President Nasser. US President Eisenhower refuses to offer military, diplomatic, or financial support, thus forcing a humiliating withdrawal.
1958	15 July: the first Lebanese civil war erupts; 15,000 US troops are sent to Beirut to stop radicals taking control of the country.
1962	September: left-wing officers in Yemen overthrow Imam Mohammed al-Badr and invite Nasser to send troops to help them consolidate power.
1966	22 February: the British government announces a large-scale reduction of troops in the Middle East, drawing their military out of territory east of Suez Canal in Egypt.
1967	5 June: the third Arab–Israeli War. Israel launches a pre-emptive strike against Egypt, Syria, and Jordan as they prepare for war. The 'Six-Day War' ends with Israel occupying the Sinai Peninsula and the Gaza Strip previously held by Egypt, the Golan Heights formerly held by Syria, and the West Bank previously held by Jordan.
1972	September: the Munich Olympics massacre. Seven Palestinian terrorists belonging to the

BOX 11.1: (continued)

	Black September group kill eleven Israeli athletes during the Olympic games in Germany.
1973	6 October: the fourth Arab–Israeli War. Egypt and Syria launch a surprise attack against Israel during the Jewish holiday of Yom Kippur. In retaliation for United States support of Israel during the war, the Organization of Arab Oil-Producing States impose an oil embargo on exports to America, to try and force territorial concessions from Israel. It lasts until 1974 by which time oil prices have quadrupled.
1974	16 June: Richard Nixon is the first US President to visit Israel.
1977	19 November: Egyptian President Sadat flies to Israel in an attempt to make peace.
1978	April: the communists seize power in Afghanistan in a bloody coup.
1979	March: Egyptian President Sadat and Israeli Prime Minister Begin sign a peace treaty in Washington. Israel agrees to withdraw from Sinai and to commence Palestinian autonomy talks within three years in exchange for a formal peace treaty with Egypt. February: the Shah of Iran is overthrown by the Islamic revolution. 24 December: the Soviet Union invades Afghanistan.
1980	22 September: the Iraqi air force attacks Iran and a land invasion begins at several points along the Iran–Iraq border.
1981	6 October: Anwar Sadat gunned down in Cairo by the 'Islamic Group'.
1982	June: Israel invades Lebanon and lays siege to its capital Beirut in what becomes a bloody military stalemate.
1983	23 October: the US marine compound at Beirut airport is destroyed by a suicide bomber: 241 are killed.
1984	7 February: President Ronald Reagan announces the retreat of US forces from Lebanon to American warships offshore.
1987	December: the Palestinian uprising or *intifada* begins in the West Bank and Gaza Strip.
1988	July: the eight-year Iran–Iraq War ends.
1990	2 August: Iraq invades Kuwait.
1991	16 January: Operation Desert Storm. Allied air attacks against Iraqi troops in Kuwait begin. 24 February: the Allied ground offensive against Iraq begins. 27 February: President George Bush announces hostilities with Iraq will cease at midnight, hours after the liberation of Kuwait City.
1993	September: the Oslo Accords are signed between the PLO and Israel.
2000	September: the second Palestinian uprising or *intifada* begins. 12 October: USS battleship *Cole* is attacked by al-Qaeda in Aden harbour, Yemen, killing 17 US sailors.
2001	11 September: Al-Qaeda uses passenger planes to attack the World Trade Center in New York and the Pentagon in Washington, DC.
2003	20 March: the invasion of Iraq begins shortly after a 48-hour deadline for Saddam Hussein to leave the country expires. 9 April: US marines help crowds to topple a giant statue of Saddam Hussein in Firdous Square, central Baghdad. Widespread looting breaks out unhindered in the Iraqi capital.

The evolution of the United States' early relationship with the Middle East was shaped by the demise of both the Ottoman and the British empires. The Ottoman Empire collapsed in the wake of the defeat it suffered during the First World War. The United States consequently intervened to limit the imperialist ambitions of both the French and British. In the aftermath of the Second World War, America was increasingly drawn into the Middle East, first to replace the rapidly declining power of the British Empire but also to counter the military and ideological influence of the Soviet Union. The end of the Cold War has seen

American foreign policy dominated by the Middle East, especially since the attacks of 11 September 2001 and the invasion of Iraq in March 2003. The region currently sits at the top of Washington's list of grave concerns.

The growing importance of the Middle East to US foreign policy since 1945 has been driven by geo-strategic, economic, and domestic concerns. Geo-strategically the region sits at the junction of three continents, in close proximity to the Mediterranean, the Persian Gulf, and America's main rival during the twentieth century, the Soviet Union. As the Cold War intensified, the USA came to regard the Middle East as second in order of strategic importance to Europe. Economically the region supplies 32 per cent of the world's oil and has 58 per cent of the globe's proven reserves (Shlaim 1995: 35). Although the United States' own dependence on Middle Eastern oil has slowly increased during the twentieth century, American policy towards the region has been shaped by a keen appreciation of the global economic significance of its oil reserves. The creation of the state of

 CONTROVERSIES 11.1: The influence of the 'Israeli Lobby' on United States foreign policy

In March 2006, two respected professors, John Mearsheimer and Stephen Walt, published the 'Israeli Lobby' in the *London Review of Books* (Mearsheimer and Walt 2006). The article caused an explosion of controversy and debate across the United States. Mearsheimer and Walt, two of the most influential realists working in international relations, argued that America's support for Israel ran counter to US national interests. They examined Israel's role as an ally in the war against terrorism, its vulnerability to attack by its neighbours, and the moral case for American support. They concluded that after the Cold War, Israel had become a strategic and political burden and US support for it had directly damaged American interests.

They went on to examine why, given what they saw as the high costs of this support, it continued. They concluded that an Israeli lobby, a 'loose coalition of individuals and organisations who actively work to steer US foreign policy in a pro-Israel direction', were responsible. Mearsheimer and Walt went on to detail the ways this lobby influenced Congress, the president, and shaped public opinion to ensure US support of Israel remained unquestioned. This support, they suggest, shaped the decision to invade Iraq and was not only bad for America but also for Israel.

Given the highly polemical nature of debates in the United States surrounding the Middle East in general and Israel in particular, it was no surprise that the article ignited an extended and at times bitter response. Amongst their most trenchant critics was Alan Dershowitz, along with Walt a professor at Harvard (Dershowitz 2006). Dershowitz argued that the paper was 'filled with errors and distortions', with quotations 'wrenched out of context', facts mis-stated, and 'embarrassingly poor logic'. Given what he saw as the poor quality of the scholarship and analysis, Dershowitz went on to question Mearsheimer and Walt's motives, implying that they were driven by anti-Semitic motives.

The controversy that the 'Israeli Lobby' caused indicates the passions and sensitivities surrounding the issue in US foreign policy circles. However, some sections of Mearsheimer and Walt's arguments were factually incorrect. They also attributed a unity of viewpoint to an ideologically diverse set of organizations. One of the central accusations of the article, that the Israeli lobby played a key role in driving the USA to invade Iraq, takes a complex and multifaceted issue and reduces it to a single cause. This is not an academically sustainable explanation. However, Michael Massing, in a much stronger and more thoughtful paper, sets out in detail the manner and extent of the influence those organizations seeking to persuade the US government to pursue a pro-Israeli policy have (Massing 2006). It is Massing's reasoned and well-sourced argument that needs to be debated in a calm and analytical fashion at the heart of US foreign policy making. One of Mearsheimer and Walt's key criticisms was that anyone seeking to question the American–Israeli special relationship was intimidated by accusations of anti-Semitism. Dershowitz's response went a long way to proving that point at least.

Israel in 1948 and its long-running conflict with its Arab neighbours has likewise dominated US foreign policy. For strategic, ideological, and domestic political reasons, Israel has enjoyed a very strong alliance with the USA. Strategically it has been perceived as a reliable ally at the centre of the Middle East from the Cold War onwards. In domestic American politics, lobby groups supporting Israel have always had the ability to organize public support in favour of a very close and supportive relationship.

Within Washington, the president is primarily responsible for shaping America's policy in the region. However, both houses of Congress, the Senate and the House of Representatives, are empowered to oversee foreign policy and have historically provided an influential point of access for those individuals, companies, lobby groups, and countries seeking to shape US policy. Washington is overflowing with think tanks and policy experts whose sole purpose is to influence the US government's development of foreign policy generally and Middle Eastern policy specifically (Hudson 2005: 296). The high level of politically motivated intra- and interstate violence in the region has forced it to the forefront of US media coverage. This in turn has caused Middle Eastern politics to loom large in the foreign policy concerns of the educated and mobilized section of American public opinion. Middle East policy is hence developed in the full glare of the media spotlight, subject to intense discussion, lobbying, and analysis. A US president neglects this fact at his or her electoral peril.

The transformation of US foreign policy towards the Middle East: from Wilson to Bush

KEY POINTS

- ❑ US foreign policy towards the Middle East has been dramatically transformed over the twentieth century.
- ❑ President Woodrow Wilson, in 1918, organized US foreign policy around the promotion of self-determination for previously oppressed people.
- ❑ President George W. Bush, after 9/11, sought to constrain the sovereignty of Middle Eastern states in an attempt to promoted democracy and limit the spread of weapons of mass destruction and terrorism.
- ❑ Woodrow Wilson's foreign policy greatly enhanced the standing of the USA in the Middle East.
- ❑ The Bush Doctrine and the invasion of Iraq have fuelled the rise of a powerful anti-Americanism across the region.

 MAJOR DEBATES AND THEIR IMPACT 11.1: Islam and democracy

President George W. Bush's promise to commit the USA to democratizing the Middle East has focused attention on why the region has so few democracies. Some pundits argue that the dominance of Islam, the major religion in the Middle East, has hindered the spread of democracy. They call for the equivalent of the Protestant Reformation in Europe to 'free' individuals to rationally pursue their own best interests. A more historically nuanced approach would point out that Sunni Islam does not have a powerful clerical hierarchy, so that calls for a reformation are misguided. Instead it is the comparative autonomy of Middle Eastern states from their own societies, delivered by oil wealth, the evolution of their economies, and the size of their secret services and armies, which explains the lack of democracy.

The United States' relations with both the states and societies of the Middle East have been transformed during the twentieth century. The extent and nature of this change can be gauged by comparing the tone, content, and reception of two landmark speeches that have had far-reaching consequences for the region. On 8 January 1918, as the First World War drew to an end, American President Woodrow Wilson addressed a joint session of the United States Congress in Washington, DC (Wilson 1918). The USA, under Wilson's leadership, had been drawn into the war against its better judgement and the president was determined to shape the peace settlement in a way that would make another world war impossible. Wilson faced two major obstacles in securing this goal. The first was the conflict's main protagonists; the European states themselves. For Wilson, they represented all that was wrong with international relations; indulging in secret, even conspiratorial, agreements amongst themselves while simultaneously competing to expand the territorial extent of their non-European empires to dominate other nations for their own benefit. The second emerging challenge was represented by the new ideology of Bolshevism, personified by the Russian Communist Party's seizure of power in Moscow.

Wilson's attempt to meet these challenges, combined ambition with idealism. He outlined a fourteen-point agenda that would shape America's post-war diplomacy. The speech called for transparent public diplomacy, open markets, and collective security. However, it was the twelfth point of Wilson's speech that led directly to the transformation of the Middle East. He demanded that the non-Turkish-speaking nationalities which had been ruled by the now defeated Ottoman Empire 'should be assured an undoubted security of life and an absolutely unmolested opportunity of autonomous development'. These words were seized upon by Arab nationalists across the region. Wilson's promotion of self-determination for previously oppressed nations became a touchstone for those Arabs seeking to escape the imperial ambitions of the Ottomans, then the British and French troops who controlled the region. The subsequent formation of the League of Nations under Wilson's direction placed direct limits on the imperial ambitions of both France and Britain. In effect, Wilson can be seen as the father of the modern independent state in the Middle East (Dodge 2005b: pp. xii–xix).

Eighty-four years later on 29 January 2002, President George W. Bush addressed Congress, giving his annual State of the Union Address. It had only been four months since al-Qaeda launched its devastating attacks on the World Trade Center in New York and the Pentagon in Washington. Like Wilson before him, Bush invoked the powerful imagery of a nation at war, a 'war against terror' which 'is only beginning'. Bush stressed that America faced two enemies in this war, the 'terrorist underworld' responsible for 9/11 and the allied states who were seeking to develop weapons of mass destruction. These allies were grouped in 'an axis of evil' whose 'regimes pose a grave and growing danger' (Bush 2002a). Two of the three members of this axis, Iraq and Iran, were key Middle Eastern states.

This speech heralded what developed into the Bush Doctrine, a potentially revolutionary approach to international relations. It forged weapons of mass destruction and terrorism into one homogeneous threat to the continued security of the American people that was primarily located in the Middle East. George W. Bush, unlike Woodrow Wilson, saw the best way to meet this threat was to restrict the right to sovereignty of errant Middle Eastern states. All means necessary were to be deployed to ensure rogue regimes did not support terrorism or develop weapons of mass destruction. In a startling contrast to Woodrow Wilson's fourteen-point speech and his promotion of self-determination, the Bush Doctrine was greeted with widespread hostility across the Middle East. President Bush's attempt to link the fight to the promotion of democracy was largely dismissed and the Bush Doctrine rejected as a new form of American imperialism (Harvey 2003; Bush 2002b). The logic of the Bush Doctrine led directly to the invasion and regime change in Iraq. The ongoing insurgency and ensuing civil war this caused has greatly destabilized the Middle East and all but dissipated the genuine empathy felt for the American people in the wake of the 9/11 attacks. Whereas Wilson's ambitious and idealist approach to the Middle East increased the prestige and standing of the United States in the region, the Bush Doctrine and the cataclysmic aftermath of the Iraqi invasion has driven anti-American sentiment to new levels of hostility.

International relations, United States foreign policy, and the Middle East

KEY POINTS

❑ Given the length of time under consideration and the diversity of states in the Middle East, International Relations theory is needed to understand US foreign policy towards the region.

❑ Realism stresses the instability of the international system with states maximizing their power in competition with each other. This helps scholars understand the Middle East as dominated by interstate war and conflict.

❑ Marxism perceives the international system as structured by hierarchy not anarchy. US foreign policy in the region is designed to defend its economic and political dominance and access to oil.

❑ Constructivism stresses the role that ideas and norms play in foreign policy making. US interaction with the Middle East is thus structured by its own self-image and what policy makers see as the 'backwardness' of Middle Eastern societies.

The period between these two momentous speeches encompasses sixteen American presidents and their relations with a diverse group of states that spread from Morocco in North Africa, west to Iran, and from Turkey south to Yemen. The radically different policies towards the Middle East pursued by Wilson and Bush indicate how the United States' relations with the region have been transformed over the twentieth century. International relations theory needs to be deployed to assess what has driven this changing policy agenda. This theory is both descriptive and prescriptive. It allows those studying the actions of decision makers to investigate their motivations and perceptions. In addition, different approaches to international relations guide or constrain the politicians and diplomats themselves, offering the categories and units of analysis used to understand a complex world.

Realism, the USA, and the Middle East

Three different and competing approaches to international relations can be usefully deployed to assess the United States' changing relations with the Middle East: realism, Marxism, and constructivism. Against the background of the Cold War realism rejected any appeal to morality as a dangerous diversion. It stresses the anarchical nature of international relations, ungoverned as it is by any higher power to adjudicate between competing states, all seeking to maximize their power in an uncertain world. For Hans Morgenthau decision makers 'think and act in terms of interest defined as power', allowing for predictability and a common understanding of state behaviour (Morgenthau 1985: 5). Morgenthau stressed that state competition would ultimately result in a balance of power between two or more states as they reached a rough and ready equilibrium (Keohane 1986: 13). Morgenthau's approach appeared to explain the evolution and comparative stability of the Cold War, a world divided into two multi-state alliances, where each superpower dominated its weaker allies. Realism's descriptive and predictive abilities apply equally to the Middle East with one of the longest running conflicts in modern diplomatic history, the Arab–Israeli dispute, the eight-year Iran–Iraq War, and Iraq's invasion of Kuwait in 1990.

The Marxist approach

However, a series of damaging critiques of the methodological assumptions underpinning realism have shaped two useful alternatives, constructivism and Marxism. Marxist approaches to international relations argue that the states that realists see as their central unit of analysis have to be placed in a much wider context. This stresses the socio-economic dynamics within which the state and the international system itself were formed. Marxists argue that there are three levels of analysis operating within international relations (Cox 1986: 220). The determinant level shows how a society organizes its economic production. This, Marxists argue, shapes power relations within societies: who owns the means of production and who they employ to work for them. This in turn frames how political and military power is structured to protect the economic organization of society. It also defines how people within that society think about their lives and roles.

From a Marxist perspective, the Cold War was not primarily about two states maximizing their own power but a clash of two very different modes of production attempting to impose their specific economic model on the rest of the world (Halliday 1994: 103). Marxists certainly recognize the importance of the political and military power of the state, but argue that it has been created within a specific set of socio-economic circumstances, determined in the last instance by the mode of production. First, states are dominated and act in the interests of those who own the mode of production; in advanced capitalist countries it is the bourgeoisie. It is these economic entrepreneurs who, in search of new markets and resources, use state power to move across the world, imposing a capitalist mode of production upon weaker societies as they travel.

Finally, Marxists argue that the international system is structured by hierarchy not anarchy, by the dominance of a hegemon. Woodrow Wilson's speech

---

BOX 11.2: US Presidential doctrines and the Middle East

Doctrines are developed by specific presidents to map out a grand strategy to deal with pressing foreign policy issues. The aim is to focus governmental resources on the most serious problem or threat the president believes is facing the United States.

The Truman Doctrine

Announced on 12 March 1947, in a speech before Congress, it committed the USA to defend Turkey and Greece against Soviet aggression.

The Eisenhower Doctrine

Announced on 9 March 1957, it offered US military and economic aid to any Middle Eastern state threatened by international communism.

The Nixon Doctrine

On 25 July 1969, faced with the growing cost of the war in Vietnam, the USA aimed to develop regional allies to act as proxies in the Cold War struggle against the Soviet Union. In the Middle East these proxies were Israel, Iran, and Saudi Arabia.

The Carter Doctrine

Announced in the January 1980 State of the Union Speech, as a response to the invasion of Afghanistan, it committed the USA to deploy military force to counter Soviet intervention in the Persian Gulf.

The Clinton Doctrine

Announced by Martin Indyk, a senior official on the National Security Council, on 18 May 1993, it committed the USA to 'dual containment', placing sanctions on both Iran and Iraq.

The Bush Doctrine

Developed in response to the attacks of 9/11 and set out in the January 2002 State of the Union Address and *The National Security Strategy of the United States*, published in September, it promised to fight terrorism, countries that developed weapons of mass destruction, and encourage democratization in the Middle East.

in front of Congress in January 1918, heralded the United States' bid to take over from Britain as the new international hegemon. Marxists would argue that Wilson, in calling for open markets and the end of European imperial domination, was attempting to reorder international economic and political relations in a way that would be of primary benefit to the United States. From this perspective, US policy in the Middle East is designed to defend its economic and political domination of the region. United States policy towards the Middle East and its deployment of military forces in the region is primarily driven by the desire to protect its access to oil and keep in power governments who facilitate this access.

A Marxist approach to international relations provides powerful insights into the motivation of the US government and the vulnerability of regimes in the region to American power. However, they have a propensity to overstate the economic rationale shaping US policy to the exclusion of other incentives. There is a tendency to assume that the US government is always acting to further the interests of their multinational corporations. This can lead to a focus on oil and a reduction in the influence of ideology, belief, and perception in shaping the policy making. It is this tendency to neglect the influence of ideas and perceptions that has given rise to the final approach to international relations, constructivism.

Constructivism

Constructivism places great explanatory weight on the role that ideas, culture, and norms play in the policy decisions of politicians and diplomats. Preconceived ideas about the situation statespeople find themselves in then become a crucial variable that shapes how the policies are chosen. For constructivists, belief systems constrain and ultimately direct those at the pinnacle of state power. A state's collective understanding of its own identity is a key factor in how diplomats perceive their national interests (Wendt 1999: 20; Ruggie 1998: 14).

In the context of the United States' relations with the Middle East, American politicians' perceptions of the region are a crucial factor. Douglas Little persuasively argues that US policy towards the Arab world has been decisively shaped by three ideological dynamics. First, the United States' own collective self-image that perceives America as selflessly reaching out to the region to share with it the benefits of its own political and economic system. Secondly, Little argues American popular culture has, over many years, perceived the Middle East to be backward looking, prone to violence, and dangerously unstable. Finally this negative perception is reinforced by a contrastingly positive perception of Israel. Little argues this has fuelled a mutual incomprehension between the Middle East and the United States that has given rise to mistrust and violence (Little 2002: 2–33).

The United States, the Cold War, and the Middle East

KEY POINTS

❑ The Cold War acted as the dominant issue shaping US relations with the Middle East. However, seeing the region simply as an arena for a global struggle had profound unintended consequences.

❑ The Cold War meant that ideologies originating from within the region, Islamic radicalism and Arab nationalism, were either seen as tools of Soviet influence or weapons with which to fight Soviet power.

❑ In 1947, as the Cold War took hold, President Truman announced his doctrine to meet the challenge of Soviet expansionism in the region. However this overestimated Moscow's interest in the Middle East.

❑ The Eisenhower Doctrine of 1957 went further, promising direct military support to any state facing communist aggression. This fuelled growing Arab nationalist resentment towards the USA.

(continued)

KEY POINTS (continued)

❑ President Nixon in 1973 faced the tension between the regional Arab–Israeli conflict and the Cold War, when the Soviet–American rivalry in the Middle East brought the world to the brink of a nuclear confrontation.

❑ President Carter's support of anti-Soviet forces fighting in Afghanistan inadvertently lent American financial and military aid to Islamic radicals who went on to strike at the USA itself on 9/11.

The dominant global dynamic shaping the United States' relations with the Middle East has been the Cold War, from its origins in the aftermath of the Second World War to the collapse of the Soviet Union in 1989. On one level, realists would argue, the demands of the Cold War simplified diplomacy for the United States. The preferences and even personal morality of individual statespeople could be subsumed within what Henry Kissinger has termed 'the ethic of responsibility'. United States interests under this rubric were straightforward: it must maximize its interests, defined as power, in the face of the Soviet threat (Gaddis 1987: 221). The Middle East became one of many arenas within which global struggle ensued. It was divided between the two superpowers as they each struggled to build the largest stable alliances possible.

However, the realist simplicity of rolling the Middle East into a global struggle for allies and dominance had a number of unintended consequences. The complexities of struggles based within the Middle East subsystem itself did not always sit well within the Cold War mindset that dominated thinking in Washington. Often ideologies originating within the region, Arab nationalism and Islamic radicalism for example, were either co-opted into the struggle against the Soviet Union, which had profound ramifications for the domestic politics of the Middle East. Alternatively, they simply misdiagnosed as a tool or product of Soviet interference. The unintended consequences and misperceptions of US foreign policy during the Cold War still haunt the region's politics today.

The Middle East became an early venue for the opening stages of the Cold War. The Soviet Union had stationed troops in Iran during the Second World War but had agreed to withdraw them at the end of hostilities. However, by 1945 it looked increasing reluctant to do so. In addition it encouraged locals to establish an autonomous government in the Iranian province of Azerbaijan, north-west of Tehran. US alarm increased when Stalin's attention focused on Turkey, attempting to pressure Ankara into sharing control of

---

BOX 11.3: US military interventions in the Middle East

Lebanon, July 1958

President Eisenhower sends 14,000 US marines to Lebanon to stop a civil war. In its aftermath President Camile Chamoun is replaced by General Fu'ad Shihab, a less divisive figure.

Lebanon, August 1982

President Reagan sends US marines to Lebanon as part of a multinational peacekeeping force. The US embassy, the embassy annexe, and a marine compound are attacked by suicide bombers, causing US troops' withdrawal in February 1984.

Kuwait, February 1991

President Bush Sr. launches a ground war to liberate Kuwait from the Iraqi invasion. Iraqi troops are pushed out of Kuwait in 100 hours. However Saddam Hussein survives the war and over a decade of harsh sanctions in its aftermath.

Iraq, March 2003

President Bush Jr. invades Iraq to remove Saddam Hussein from power. US troops reach Baghdad in 20 days. However the country descends into violence and then an insurgency kills thousands of American soldiers and tens of thousands of Iraqi civilians.

shipping through the Dardanelles. The US administration concluded that the Soviets' central aim in the region was to gain control of Turkey. Their unease increased when evidence came to light of Soviet meddling in the Greek civil war. President Truman sought to meet this challenge in March 1947, by announcing the Truman Doctrine, a $400 million package of economic and military aid for Greece and Turkey. However, Truman appears to have overestimated Stalin's interests and goals in the region. Stalin regarded Arab nationalist politicians as unreliable bourgeois nationalists (Brown 1984: 199). The Soviet Union under Stalin treated the Middle East as a sideshow.

Eisenhower and the Middle East

United States–Soviet competition over the Middle East and the problems this caused increased with Stalin's death and the Eisenhower presidency. Nikita Khrushchev, the new leader of the Soviet Communist Party, announced a new policy towards the third world during the Congress of the Communist Party in 1956 at which he denounced Stalin (Westad 2005: 68). It resulted in 'rubble diplomacy', a substantial programme of economic aid directed at third world states, including Egypt.

The Eisenhower administration, developing Truman's fears of Soviet encroachment through Turkey, colluded with Britain to organize the 'northern tier' of the Middle East in an anti-Soviet alliance, the Baghdad Pact. This grouped Iraq, Turkey, Iran, and Pakistan in a mutual defence agreement, strengthened by US military assistance. Eisenhower further escalated US involvement and Cold War tensions in the Middle East in 1957. Worried that a reduction in British influence in the region would be exploited by the Soviet Union, he countered with a promise of direct US military intervention and economic aid in support of any state which felt under threat from communist aggression. Congress voted to support what become known as the Eisenhower Doctrine in 1957. However the only intervention sanctioned was to send marines to stop the eruption of the Lebanese civil war of 1958. This was a purely regional conflict, remotely connected to the Cold War.

Increasing US involvement in the Middle East under Eisenhower drove growing resentment amongst Arab nationalists who were battling to defend their newly won independence and minimize outside interference in the region. In spite of US political rhetoric stressing freedom from Soviet domination, Arab politicians found it increasingly difficult to distinguish between the dying days of a British imperialism justified in terms of progress and development and a militarized US presence promoting capitalism and democracy. It was this sentiment that caused the Baghdad Pact to be denounced by both Syria and Egypt as an attempt to sustain foreign domination rather than the protection of its members.

It was a bloody military coup in Iraq in July 1958, orchestrated in the name of Arab nationalism and freedom from foreign domination, that overthrew the British-installed monarchy and broke the Baghdad Pact. The rising tide of Arab nationalism, primarily driven by the remnants of British imperialism, was continuously mistaken by Washington during this period as a stalking horse for international communism. Egypt's radical president, Gamal Abdul Nasser, became the personification of this problem. In 1955 he struck a major arms deal with Czechoslovakia. However, this transaction had more to do with his military confrontation with Israel than a desire to join the Czechs as a member of the Communist International. When the US government reversed a promise to help fund the building of the Aswan dam in 1956, Nasser announced the nationalization of the Suez Canal. This triggered a wave of economic nationalism across the third world that was driven by a desire for economic sovereignty and development, not international communism.

Britain and France in a secret compact with Israel attempted to reverse the nationalization of the Suez Canal and remove Nasser from power by invading Egypt in October 1956. Public opinion across the Middle East saw the Suez crisis as the personification of European imperialism, an illegal conspiracy using military force to reverse Arab independence. For President Eisenhower the invasion of Egypt coincided with Soviet tanks crushing the Hungarian uprising in Budapest. In a nationwide television broadcast he angrily insisted that there 'can be no peace without law': the United States would not support and thus be associated with Anglo-French colonialism in the Middle East (Little 2002: 177). Instead it deployed financial and diplomatic pressure to force France and Britain into a humiliating withdrawal, turning Nasser into a hero across the third world and making Arab nationalism the dominant ideology in the Middle East.

Nixon, Kissinger, and the 1973 war

The next presidential doctrine to have significant consequences for the Middle East was developed by Richard Nixon. Inheriting an increasingly unpopular and costly war in Vietnam from his predecessor President Johnson, the Nixon Doctrine's goal was the empowerment of proxy states in the third world to replace the already overstretched United States. The application of the Nixon Doctrine to the Middle East encouraged Saudi Arabia and especially Iran and Israel to become regional policemen, enforcing an American policy agenda at second hand. The Shah of Iran seized upon his new-found responsibilities with gusto, demanding larger and larger amounts of sophisticated weaponry from Washington in return. Any doubts this raised within the US administration were placated, temporarily at least, by the Shah's help in destabilizing the Ba'athist regime in Iraq, who were in receipt of Soviet weaponry. The Shah's support for the Cold War reached its peak when he agreed to send 1,200 troops to support the Sultan of Oman in his struggle against a Soviet-supported uprising in the restive province of Dhofar in 1973.

However, the nexus between an essentially regional conflict and a global Cold War created a crisis with the Arab–Israeli War of 1973–4. During 1969–70, the Soviet Union dramatically increased its military support for Egypt in the aftermath of the cataclysmic defeat of 1967. Twenty thousand Soviet military personnel served in Egypt during this period, with pilots and artillery crews directly involved in combat

with Israel. Although Egyptian President Sadat distanced himself from Moscow in 1972, the Soviets felt compelled to threaten direct intervention in the face of massive US support for Israel in the 1973–4 war. Nixon responded by putting US nuclear forces on DEFCON 3, the stage preceding all-out war. Although the Soviet Union backed down and the Arab states suffered another defeat at the hands of Israel, Cold War manoeuvring in an essentially regional conflict had very nearly brought the superpowers into direct confrontation in the Middle East.

Carter, Iran, and Afghanistan

It was Democratic President Jimmy Carter who inherited the fallout from Nixon's decision to give unconditional backing to the Shah of Iran. Throughout the 1970s, the Shah had become increasingly detached from Iranian society. His oil-fuelled development strategies and land reform backfired, causing rapid unplanned urbanization, inflation, and unemployment. US support for an increasingly autocratic and corrupt monarch only increased his unpopularity. This allowed the opposition to combine a powerful Iranian nationalism that portrayed the Shah as an American stooge with a religious moralism which focused on his family's decadence and corruption. It resulted in the 1979 Islamic revolution which brought Ayatollah Khomeini to power and mobilized the population behind a radical manifesto of Islamism and anti-Americanism.

The Carter administration was further engulfed in a crisis of Middle Eastern origin when the Soviet Union airlifted thousands of troops into Afghanistan on Christmas Eve 1979. The invasion was almost certainly defensive, attempting to limit the threat that political Islam posed for the USSR's own Muslim population. However, Carter saw it in terms of the Cold War's balance of power. Afghanistan had always been seen as a buffer between the Soviet Union and the Middle East. On 23 January 1980, during his State of the Union Address, the president announced the 'Carter Doctrine'. Consciously modelled on the Truman Doctrine before it, Carter announced that 'the implications of the Soviet invasion of Afghanistan could pose the most serious threat to the peace since the Second World War'. The Middle East contained two-thirds of the world's oil reserves and the Soviet invasion of Afghanistan brought its troops 'close to the Straits of Hormuz, a waterway through which most of the world's oil must flow'. Carter concluded by placing the region at the heart of the Cold War and stressing its centrality to US interests: 'let our position be absolutely clear: An attempt by an outside force to gain control of the Persian Gulf region will be regarded as an assault on the vital interests of the United States of America, and such an assault will be repelled by any means necessary, including military force.' In order to turn Afghanistan into the Soviets' Vietnam, the USA quickly built an unwieldy alliance of convenience. It brought together the logistical capacity of Pakistan's military intelligence with funding for the Arab Gulf states and, most damagingly, a motley group of Afghan and Arab Islamic radicals. It certainly succeeded in trapping the Soviet army in Afghanistan, fighting a long, costly, and unwinnable war of attrition. Their eventual ignominious defeat and withdrawal hastened the end of the Cold War and America's victory. However, the unintended consequence of Afghan war was to empower a transnational network of Islamic radicals, who, having defeated one superpower, were on 9/11 emboldened to strike at the other.

Reagan and Lebanon

If the empowerment of al-Qaeda under the auspices of the Carter Doctrine represents the worst unintended consequence of the United States Cold War policy in the Middle East, then the Reagan administration's involvement in Lebanon in the early 1980s indicates how a Cold War prism could distort the basis to policy making. With his focus on combating the 'evil empire' of Soviet communism, President Reagan placed the military threat of the Soviet Union at the core of his foreign policy. This threat

was greatest in western Europe, but the Middle East's vulnerability came a close second. The Arab–Israeli conflict and regional dynamics more generally were downgraded in the face of a renewed Cold War. The Reagan administration's unquestioned support for Israel meant it backed Prime Minister Begin and Defence Minister Sharon's plans to invade Lebanon in June 1982 and drive Yasser Arafat's Palestine Liberation Organization from the Middle East. Ariel Sharon sold the plan to Washington by claiming it would bring in its wake a new political order across the region: weakening two of the USSR's main clients, the PLO themselves and Syria (Shlaim 1995: 55). However, the US military were drawn into the resultant conflict as peacekeepers. By analysing the violence in Lebanon through a Cold War lens, US military power was deployed to back one side of a largely indigenous civil war against another. As a result the USA became party to an increasingly bloody civil war. In retaliation a suicide bomber attacked US facilities in Beirut in 1983, killing 241 American marines and forcing the USA to leave Lebanon in trauma and defeat.

The realist approach to international relations that shaped US policy on the Cold War assumed that the conflict was global and that 'interests defined as power' could be deployed in a bipolar struggle. However, in the Middle East this approach led to profound miscalculations about which regimes to support and the consequences of that aid. The USA, under different presidents, twice intervened in the Lebanese civil war using the Cold War as justification. They took sides in a bitter and bloody civil war, paying a terrible price, and exacerbated the violence. In creating the coalition that funded a disparate group of Islamic radicals in Afghanistan, the country simply became another arena for the Cold War. Once the Soviets had left, the USA turned its back on Afghanistan and the organizations it had created, with tragic consequences. Afghanistan, largely ignored by the USA and the international community, become the launch pad from which the attacks of 9/11 were planned and executed, providing the most traumatic example of Cold War blowback in the history of US diplomacy.

The United States and Israel

KEY POINTS

- The United States' supportive relationship with Israel is most often cited as a cause of Arab and more generally Muslim anger towards American foreign policy.
- Constructivist explanations of this relationship focus on the empathy generated by the horrors of the Holocaust, the pioneering spirit of Israeli state builders, its democracy, and an affinity between US Christians and Jews returning to the Holy Land.
- As the Cold War escalated President Eisenhower became increasingly aware of the damage America's relations with Israel were causing in the Arab Middle East and attempted to constrain Israeli foreign policy in the Suez crisis of 1956.
- During the Arab–Israeli War of 1967 President Johnson, on the other hand, saw the victory of America's ally Israel over Arab states supported by the Soviet Union as beneficial to US power.
- President Nixon's extended support for Israel in the 1973 war resulted in the Arab oil embargo that quadrupled the world price of oil.
- It took the end of the Cold War to see a major breakthrough in Israeli–Palestinian relations with the Oslo agreements of 1993 that delivered limited self-rule to the Palestinians.
- US policy remains focused on maintaining Israel's military superiority in the hope that this will give them the confidence to negotiate a substantive peace deal with both the Palestinians and Syria.

The United States' alliance with Israel has grown progressively closer from the founding of the state in 1948 until today. The American government now gives Israel $3 billion a year in military assistance and economic aid (Hudson 2005: 289). However, it is the United States' supportive relationship with Israel that is most often cited as a cause of Arab and more generally Muslim anger towards American foreign policy. The founding of the state of Israel led to the dispossession of tens of thousands of Palestinians and six major wars. It is both the continued exile of a large diaspora of Palestinian refugees along with Israel's occupation of the West Bank of the Jordan River and the Gaza Strip that fuel violent resentment towards both Israel and the United States. Despite the cost, in terms of Arab public opinion and diplomatic censure, the American–Israeli relationship shows no sign of weakening. Both realist and constructivist explanations can be usefully deployed to examine the enduring nature of this alliance.

Constructivism and the special relationship

Constructivist explanations focus on the ideas and perceptions that the American public and more importantly their politicians have about Israel. This, they argue, is the key to explaining the strength and durability of the alliance. The relationship is deeply anchored into both history and cultural affinity. First, the murder and suffering that the Jewish population of Europe were subjected to during the Holocaust forms the backdrop against which the Israeli state was built. The empathy generated by such horrors is the bedrock upon which the American–Israeli relationship is constructed. The argument that the Israeli state was founded as a safe haven for all Jews, both the survivors of the Holocaust and those facing persecution elsewhere, meets with deep approval in the United States. In addition Israel's supporters argue that since 1948 it has been surrounded and outnumbered by hostile neighbours bent on its destruction. These arguments in favour of American support of Israel are strengthened by the perceived similarities the US public sees between their own history and that of Israel. The USA, like Israel, is a settler nation created by waves of mass immigration from Europe. At the core of America's own myth of nationhood is a pioneering spirit. This self-perception of pioneers building a state and society from scratch is very close to Israel's own myth of formation. Central to America's identity in the wider world is its democracy, a democracy that Israeli politicians are keen to stress they share. Added to these cultural affinities are religious ones. Various forms of Christianity dominate American society and the idea of Jews returning to the holy land resonates with their own reading of the Bible. This potent mix of history, national self-identity, and religion has been carefully cultivated and deployed by those mobilizing pubic opinion and lobbying the American government to pursue policies that favour Israel.

> **KEY QUOTES 11.1:** The Middle East through American eyes

Because of their own pioneer heritage, Americans were even more apt than Europeans to identify with lurid images of brave, outnumbered settlers of European stock taming an arid land in the face of opposition from ignorant, fanatical nomads—wildly distorted and unrealistic (albeit lasting) though these images were.

(Khalidi 2004: 119)

From the dawn of the Cold War through the twilight of the twentieth century, US policy makers insisted time and again that Islamic radicals, Israeli prime ministers, and Iraqi dictators had merely misunderstood America's good intentions and that better understanding would produce better relations. Over the years, however, critics from Tel Aviv to Tehran have retorted that they understood those intentions all too well and that the peculiar blend of ignorance and arrogance that characterised US policy would effectively prevent American from ever truly understanding the region and its people.

(Little 2002: 2–3)

. . . America saw the world in rather simple terms: on one side was the Soviet Union and militant Third World nationalism, which America regarded as a Soviet tool; on the other side was political Islam, which American considered an unqualified all in the struggle against the Soviet Union.

(Mamdani 2004: 120)

This, I think, is where Saddam Hussein comes in: Iraq is the most feasible place where we can strike the next blow. If we can topple this tyrant, if we can repeat the Afghan Agincourt on the banks of the Euphrates, then we can accomplish a great deal. We can complete the task the Gulf War left unfinished. We can destroy whatever weapons of mass destruction Saddam Hussein may have accumulated since. We can end whatever support he's providing for terrorists elsewhere, notably those who act against Israel. We can liberate the Iraqi people. We can

ensure an ample supply of inexpensive oil. We can set in motion a process that could undermine and ultimately remove reactionary regimes elsewhere in the Middle East, thereby eliminating the principal breeding ground for terrorism. And, as President Bush did say publicly in a powerful speech to the United Nations on September 12, 2002, we can save that organization from the irrelevance into which it will otherwise descend if its resolutions continue to be contemptuously disregarded.

(Gaddis 2002)

Iraq provided a blank screen on which Americans were free to project anything they wanted, and because so few Americans had anything directly at stake there, many of them never saw more than the image of their feelings. The exceptions of course, were the soldiers and their families, who carried almost the entire weight of the war.

(Packer 2005: 382, 385)

The failure of state-building in Iraq raises a series of profound questions about US foreign policy in the wake of 9/11. The decision to invade and remove Saddam Hussein was meant to signal a new approach to international relations. The 'war against terror' was constructed in the broadest possible terms, uniting the disparate themes of terrorism with weapons of mass destruction and the instability of postcolonial states. By justifying the invasion in terms of democratising the Middle East, President Bush evoked a renewed, if supercharged, spirit of Wilsonian idealism. The sovereignty of states in the so-called 'developing world' was now dependent upon their ruling elites meeting US-defined responsibilities. It was only after these responsibilities had been met that the right to non-intervention would be granted. Regime change in Iraq was meant to herald the beginning of this new era of international relations. As the violence and instability in Iraq continues unabated this new 'grand strategy' must

(continued)

> **KEY QUOTES 11.1** (continued)

now come into question. In the future the lessons taken from the invasion should at least mean that the promises made to the peoples of the states being intervened in, the population of the intervening state and indeed the international community will not be based, as they were in 2003, on unblinking ideology, wishful thinking and blithe assertions of ahistorical universalisms.

(Dodge 2006: 198)

The realist explanation of US–Israeli relations is much more straightforward. It downplays or even discounts ideological influences. Instead it stresses Israel's role as a staunch ally during the Cold War and its aftermath. Surrounded by Arab regimes with ties to the Soviet Union, realists would argue that Israel has provided a reliable partner in an unstable region. The United States' interests were continually furthered by giving the strategic, diplomatic, and economic support Israel needed to prosper. Realists examine the strength of US–Israeli relations in terms of the geostrategic utility to America of Israel's position in the Middle East.

The final argument seeking to explain the longevity and strength of the alliance would point to domestic electoral calculations. There is a very well-organized lobby designed to ensure US policy is very supportive of Israel. The leading organization in this lobby, the American Israeli Public Affairs Committee (AIPAC), has a membership of 100,000 and a yearly budget of $47 million (Massing 2006). By deploying both realist and constructivist arguments and tactics AIPAC has successfully mobilized American public opinion in support of Israel.

A second electoral calculation is the Jewish section of American society. Although estimated to number only between 2 and 3 per cent of the electorate, as a group they have one of the highest voter turnouts, with 89 per cent living in electorally key states, with enough votes to return a president (Bard 1994: 81). However, it is easy to overstate the electoral significance of the Israeli lobby. The majority of Jewish voters have a tendency to vote Democrat, reducing their tendency to change their preference on the basis of Israeli policy. Secondly, a broad consensus exists in mainstream politics around the issue of Israel.

Harry Truman, the US president in 1948, set a pattern for the way future American presidents dealt with Israel. In reaction to the horrors of the Holocaust, Truman pushed for Jewish emigration to Palestine. He also deployed diplomatic pressure at the United Nations in favour of dividing Palestine between a Jewish and Arab state and authorized the recognition of Israel as soon as it declared statehood on 15 May 1948. Truman, clearly influenced by a close presidential election that year, ignored State Department warnings about the negative effect recognition would have on US influence in the wider region.

Eisenhower and Israel

As the Cold War escalated, Truman's successor President Eisenhower became increasingly aware of the damage America's relations with Israel were causing in the Arab Middle East. This alarm reached its peak with the Suez crisis in October 1956. Eisenhower, because the Anglo-French-Israeli invasion of Egypt coincided with US presidential elections, came face to face with the electoral mathematics surrounding Israeli policy. Eisenhower, casting these concerns aside, pushed the United Nations to condemn the invasion and was re-elected with a landslide over the Democrats. He then went on to push for UN sanctions against Israel. Faced with a concerted public campaign to overturn this decision he confronted the issue directly in a television broadcast which resulted in an Israeli climb-down (Little 2002: 92).

Eisenhower, in the run-up to and during the Suez crisis, decided that US interests in the Middle East and its Cold War foreign policy more generally were directly harmed by its relations with Israel. With this foremost in his mind, he ignored the potential electoral risks, and took his argument directly to the American people, over the heads of the American–Israeli lobby, defending his policy. Eisenhower subsequently implemented the approach he thought best served America's interests and Israel was forced into a compromise.

The Arab–Israeli conflict descended into open warfare for the third time in 1967 under Lyndon B. Johnson's presidency. The stunning victory that Israel inflicted on its Arab neighbours confirmed in American public opinion the David and Goliath image of Israel fighting to win against all the odds. Johnson, who believed that Eisenhower had been far too lenient on Egypt during the Suez crisis, saw the discrediting of Nasser by the Israeli military as a welcome retort. The victory of America's ally Israel over Arab states supported by the Soviet Union was similarly perceived as beneficial to US power. The aftermath of the Six-Day War left Israel in occupation of Jordanian, Egyptian, and Syrian territory. It also cemented American–Israeli diplomatic and military relations, removing any ambiguity from the partnership.

Nixon and Yom Kippur

The Nixon Doctrine of developing regional proxies had strengthened Israel's status as a key ally in the fight against Soviet influence. The surprise attack launched by Syria and Egypt over the Jewish holiday of Yom Kippur placed that policy in doubt. The Arab armies made early gains, with Egyptian tanks crossing the Suez Canal and the Syrians threatening to retake the Golan Heights. Israeli Prime Minister, Golda Meir made a desperate plea to Nixon for help and the president responded with a massive airlift of 11,000 tons of military equipment and munitions that gave the Israeli military yet another victory. However, such sustained US support for Israel's success triggered a united Arab response; the oil embargo against America and western Europe.

For the Nixon administration, the 1973 war highlighted the destabilizing effect of the ongoing Arab–Israeli conflict on the region and America's interests. Nixon's foreign policy guru, Henry Kissinger, was assigned the task of defusing the conflict. Through 1974 and 1975 Kissinger flew back and forth to the region, first brokering a disengagement agreement and then persuading Israel to undertake a limited redeployment of troops in return for even greater American military assistance, oil supplies, and economic aid.

Following the Yom Kippur War, Kissinger was unable to secure a sustainable peace settlement because Israel was unwilling to embark on further territorial compromise. It was regional diplomacy that broke the stalemate, with Egyptian President, Anwar Sadat boldly flying to Jerusalem in November 1977. By this time Jimmy Carter was in the White House and he had to structure a peace process that would capitalize on Sadat's statesmanship. It created the first sustainable peace settlement between Israel and one of its Arab neighbours. The signing in Washington of the March 1979 Treaty of Peace between Egypt and Israel ended thirty-one years of hostility between the two states and was built around the 'land for peace' formula originally suggested by the UN in 1967. Israel agreed to withdraw its troops from the Sinai Peninsula that it had seized from Egypt. In return America compensated Israel economically and committed itself to continued generous financial and military support for both Israel and Egypt. Thus the United States underwrote the peace treaty with considerable economic incentives for both sides. However, for the hawkish Israeli Prime Minister, Menanchen Begin, this was not the beginning of a comprehensive peace deal with the Palestinians or Israel's Arab neighbours but the splitting of the Arab front. Vague references in the treaty to Palestinian self-rule were never acted upon and Israel was free to continue building houses for Israelis in the territory on the west bank of the Jordan River it had seized in 1967.

James Baker and the Oslo peace process

It took the ending of the Cold War in 1989, Iraq's invasion of Kuwait, and then defeat in 1990–1, to trigger another sustained American attempt to solve the Arab–Israeli conflict. President Bush's Secretary of State, James Baker, came face to face with Arab resentment at the continuing stalemate with Israel when building the diplomatic and military coalition needed to eject Iraq from Kuwait. In the aftermath of that victory he applied economic pressure to Israel and shuttle diplomacy to the wider region to set up a multinational peace conference in Madrid in October 1991. Despite the diplomatic fanfare surrounding the talks in Spain and the subsequent Palestinian–Israeli negotiations in Washington, no breakthrough was achieved. Like Sadat's initiative in 1977, it was direct interaction between the main protagonists, the Palestinians and Israelis, which delivered a breakthrough in 1993. The negotiations were hosted by Norway, who were judged a more neutral arbiter than the United States. The resulting Israel–PLO Declaration of Principles was signed in Washington under the watchful eye of President Clinton. But this was not a fully-fledged peace treaty but a set of guidelines and aspirations for further negotiations. Those negotiations delivered restricted Palestinian self-rule in Gaza and parts of the West Bank, but the turbulent and violent history of Palestinian–Israeli relations since 1993 shows the profound limitations of the Oslo process. The Oslo process was followed by a separate peace treaty between Jordan and Israel. Again, however, the deal was basically bilateral, representing the work of the two states who signed it, not the success of muscular American diplomatic intervention (Shlaim 1995: 120–40).

The presidency of George W. Bush has proved to be just as pro-Israeli as the presidencies of Clinton and Reagan before him. US policy towards Israel after the Cold War has been based on similar if not identical foundations to those which guided policy since 1948, with Israel's military superiority being maintained at all costs. This, it is hoped, will give Israel the confidence to negotiate with the Palestinians and the Arab states from a position of unchallengeable strength. However, with the brief exception of James Baker in 1991, US diplomacy has proven to be chronically unable or unwilling to put enough pressure on Israel to deliver the compromises needed to reach sustainable peace settlements. This would involve implementing the United Nations Security Council Resolution 242, passed in November 1967. Israel would give up enough land on the West Bank for the Palestinians to create a sustainable state. It would also give back to the Syrians all of the territory of the Golan Heights it seized in 1967 in return for a peace settlement.

Now that the dynamics of the Cold War are well and truly in the past it is the constructivist argument, stressing an ideological affinity between US policy makers, their population, and Israel, which best explains American–Israeli relations. US opinion, both at a policy-making level and across the public in general, favours Israel to such an extent it appears diplomatically unable to apply the pressure needed to force the Israeli government to compromise. With US backing, Israel is militarily and diplomatically strong enough not to have to enter into sustained or meaningful negotiations with either the Palestinians or Syria, facilitating an ongoing conflict with no end in sight. The United States' continued support for Israel has certainly fuelled resentment amongst Arab and wider Muslim public opinion. It also prohibits any viable solution to a violent conflict at the heart of the Middle East. The direct costs of this conflict to the United States have been the destabilization of a region of great geostrategic importance to them and a continued sense of resentment and anger. It is this anger that al-Qaeda and Islamic radicals have continued to exploit for recruitment and justification.

The United States and oil

KEY POINTS

❑ United States support of Israel has often been in conflict with its policy of obtaining oil from the Gulf at the
lowest possible cost.

❑ As the American economy's dependence upon oil
increased after 1945, US government policy became
concerned with the stability and pliability of the main
oil-producing states in the region.

❑ In 1953 the USA supported a coup in Iran aimed at
stopping the nationalization of the Iranian oil industry.

❑ In the aftermath of Iraq's invasion of Kuwait in 1990,
the USA put together a multinational coalition to liberate Kuwait and stop Saddam Hussein dominating oil
supplies from the region.

❑ The USA has repeatedly intervened in the Middle East
to secure its economic advantage but its policy cannot
be reduced to a focus solely on oil.

There is a tension at the heart of United States' policy towards the Middle East between two of its primary interests: first the almost unquestioning support for Israel, but secondly to maintain the flow of oil at the lowest price from the Gulf region. The Arab Gulf states have been historically the leading financial backers of the struggle against Israel. The USA, when faced with the deep antipathy between Israel and the Arab Gulf states, has struggled to keep its relations with the two separate and the Arab–Israeli conflict confined to the front-line states surrounding Israel.

In examining America's relations with the oil-rich states of the Middle East the Marxist approach to international relations provides a series of power-ful insights. As the American economy's dependence upon oil increased after 1945, US government policy increasingly became concerned with the stability and pliability of the main oil-producing states in the region. US military power, both overtly and covertly, has been repeatedly deployed to remove troublesome governments or support those whose ruling elites are close to Washington. Marxists would argue this is a clear example of the United States' political and mili-tary power being deployed to further the economic interests of American multinational corporations.

The interests of major American oil companies in the Middle East have slowly grown since the First World War. President Wilson's 'open door' policy was perfectly suited to their needs, giving access to the oil-rich former territories of the Ottoman Empire cov-eted by British and French companies. As the United States economy rapidly expanded during and after the Second World War, the US government came to view access to Middle East oil fields as a crucial issue for national security. Diplomacy and the military power of the American state would be deployed to ensure US oil companies could operate in the region on the best possible terms. With the rise of strident Middle Eastern nationalisms demanding economic sovereignty, this aim often clashed with the policies of regional governments.

The USA, Iran, Iraq, and oil

Two post-1945 examples show the extent and nature of US government attempts to shape the Middle East oil industry to its own advantage. In April 1951, the Iranian parliament, dominated by nationalists led by Mohammed Mosaddeq, passed a law nationalizing the Iranian oil industry. This triggered a clandestine intelligence operation by the US Central Intelligence Agency and the British. In August 1953, this operation reached its peak when the Iranian army, trained and advised by the American military since the Second World War, launched a coup that removed Mosad-deq and placed the pro-American Shah back on his throne. In the aftermath of the coup, nationalization was halted and the American oil company ARAMCO gained a 40 per cent share in the industry (Khalidi 2004: 90–1, 104).

Similar motives drove US interference in Iraq between 1958 and 1963. In 1958, a coup by army officers, led by Colonel Abdel Karim Qassim, seized power in Baghdad in the name of Arab nationalism. The new government set about drafting a law to nationalize the Iraqi Oil Company which was jointly owned by British and American businesses. The Kennedy administration saw in Baghdad a dangerously radical government with increasing ties to Moscow seeking to reduce American control and profits from Middle Eastern oil. The American embassy in Baghdad established ties with dissident officers in the Iraqi army and a second coup in February 1963, ousted Qassim, just before the nationalization of oil took place.

US interference in both Iranian and Iraqi politics may have postponed oil nationalization but had dramatic unintended consequences. In Iraq, the 1963 coup and a counter-coup later that year sparked off a series of violent military takeovers, which resulted in the Ba'ath party coming to power in 1968. They eventually nationalized the oil industry and were only removed in April 2003, by a US invasion. In Iran, once reinstalled, the Shah ruled until 1979 but was similarly removed from power, this time by a violent revolution inspired by Islamism and anti-Americanism.

OPEC and Israel

The United States' ability to keep the Arab–Israeli conflict separate from its relations with the oil-producing states of the region also dramatically broke down in 1973. The growing influence of nationalism across the region began to define the oil policies of the Arab Gulf states. During the 1960s, these countries became increasingly disgruntled by the low price of oil on the world market. This frustration resulted in the formation of the Organization of Oil Exporting Counties (OPEC) in 1960. During the Arab–Israeli Yom Kippur War of 1973, the Gulf states became increasingly outraged at the United States' large-scale and overt

support for Israel. In retaliation, OPEC's Arab members deployed the oil weapon against America. The price of oil was increased by 70 per cent and production was cut by 5 per cent a month with an embargo placed on exports to America until Israel made major territorial concessions. By December 1973, the price of oil was four times what it had been in October. After twenty-five years of support for Israel, America's policy had finally caused it a direct and painful economic cost.

President Nixon sent Henry Kissinger to the Middle East to directly intervene in the conflict and he persuaded Israel to make some limited territorial compromises. Even though he convinced OPEC to lift its embargo in 1974, the price of oil continued to rise, reaching a new height when the news broke that another staunch American ally, the Shah of Iran, had been removed by an Islamic revolution in 1979. The USA, in an attempt to limit the damage of Islamic radicalism in Iran, supported Iraq in the eight-year Iran–Iraq War. But Iraq's invasion of Iran in 1980 further pushed up the price of oil.

Oil prices did not substantially fall until 1985 but United States oil policy towards the Middle East is still haunted by the unintended consequences of its actions. This was personified on 2 August 1990, when Saddam Hussein, previously supported by the United States in his war with Iran, invaded Kuwait. President George Bush Sr.'s response to this breach of international law summed up over fifty years of US policy towards the Gulf:

" An Iraq permitted to swallow Kuwait would have the economic and military power, as well as the arrogance, to intimidate and coerce its neighbours—neighbours who control the lion's share of the world's remaining oil reserves . . . We cannot permit a resource so vital to be dominated by one so ruthless. And we won't. (Bush 1990) **"**

Although the war to liberate Iraq was launched in the name of democracy and a post-Cold War New World Order, the region and its ruling regimes looked very similar in the aftermath of the invasion to before. US policy, focused amongst other things on the security of its oil supplies, had once again chosen to back the regimes it was familiar with, in the hope that conservative stability would deliver oil at the best possible price. With this in mind, Marxist explanations of US policy do have strong analytical purchase. The USA has clearly and repeatedly intervened in the region to secure economic advantage. However, the danger of this approach is that economic motivations are promoted to the exclusion of all others. Clearly America's relations with the Middle East cannot simply be reduced to the quest for cheap oil and the creation and defence of pliant regimes to deliver it.

Conclusions: the Bush Doctrine and the invasion of Iraq: continuity or change in US foreign policy towards the Middle East?

KEY POINTS

❏ In the wake of 9/11 the Bush Doctrine committed the United States to fighting a global war against terror, stopping the spread of weapons of mass destruction in combination with the muscular promotion of democratization across the Middle East.

❏ The invasion of Iraq launched in March 2003 by George W. Bush appeared to combine all three motives.

❏ The majority of realist academics were against the invasion, arguing that it was a miscalculation driven by ideology not a rational assessment of US interests.

❏ It was the overtly ideological promotion of democracy that set the Bush Doctrine aside from previous US foreign polices toward the Middle East.

❏ The US invasion of Iraq resulted in the collapse of the state, a violent civil war, and tens of thousands of deaths. It will almost certainly be viewed as a major defeat for the USA.

The attacks on the United States by al-Qaeda on 11 September 2001 gave rise to an intense debate about the causes and consequences of America's relations with the Middle East; where had this radical ideology of violence come from? Who or what was to blame? The removal of the Taliban in Afghanistan, because they gave sanctuary to the senior leadership of al-Qaeda, was undertaken with speed. However, the longer-term goals of the Bush administration in the wake of 9/11 took some time to emerge. Eventually the Bush Doctrine committed the United States to fighting a global war against terror, stopping the spread of weapons of mass destruction in combination with the muscular promotion of democratization across the Middle East. The invasion of Iraq launched by George W. Bush appeared to combine all three motives. Saddam Hussein had defied United Nations sanctions for over a decade, was falsely thought to be committed to building weapons of mass destruction, and was undoubtedly a bloody dictator.

Marxist scholars were quick to identify the economic logic of oil underpinning the decision to unseat Saddam (Harvey 2003: 24–5). One realist, John Lewis Gaddis, supported the invasion, calling for a 'repeat of the Afghan Agincourt on the banks of the Euphrates' (Gaddis 2002). Interestingly, however, many more notable realists very publicly set themselves against the invasion, arguing that it was a miscalculation driven by ideology, not a rational assessment of US interests (Mearsheimer 2005; Bacevich 2005). It was the overtly ideological content of the Bush Doctrine which sets it aside from previous US foreign policies toward the Middle East. Repeatedly before and after the invasion itself, George Bush committed his government to spreading democracy throughout the Middle East. Bush, in stating that 'it would be reckless to accept the status quo' in the Middle East and pursuing 'a forward strategy of freedom', was clearly and overtly attempting to distance himself from previous American policy (Bush 2003). The realist approach adopted by his predecessors, which supported dictators because they were allied with Washington, was jettisoned. Instead the goal was a transformation of the governing systems throughout the Middle East, if necessary using American military power to democratize the region. This represented a major point of departure from traditional US policy guided by the principles of realism, with its focus on the amoral maximization of power.

However, the dangers of US policy soon became apparent; there was a backlash from those who did not want to be dictated to by the world's sole remaining superpower. George Bush's vision of what Iraqis needed collided violently with realities on the ground in Baghdad. US troops were not, as predicted, greeted as liberators when they reached Baghdad in April 2003. Instead what started off as sullen suspicion soon descended into violent opposition (Dodge 2005a). One of the most far-reaching and bold attempts to change US foreign policy towards the Middle East since Woodrow Wilson has resulted in tens of thousands of people dying and the almost certain defeat of the United States military in Iraq (Dodge 2007). The Bush Doctrine and the subsequent invasion of Iraq stand as a stark warning to future American presidents developing policy for the Middle East. The miscalculation at the heart of America's debacle in Iraq was driven by a potent mix of ideology and hubris, creating a catastrophic defeat for the United States when it should have been at the peak of its post-Cold War power.

? Questions

1. What has been the balance between interests and ideology in the evolution of the United States' relations with the Middle East since the First World War?

2. What accounts for the differences of approach to the Middle East between President Wilson after the First World War and George W. Bush after 9/11?

3. Does a realist or constructivist approach best explain US foreign policy towards the Middle East?

4. What accounts for President Eisenhower's policy towards Israel?

5. What accounts for President Eisenhower's reaction to the Suez crisis of 1956?

6. Can the application of the Nixon Doctrine to the Middle East be judged a success?

7. Was the Carter Doctrine an overreaction to the Soviet Union's invasion of Afghanistan?

8. Was Ronald Reagan right to see the Lebanese civil war as an extension of the Cold War?

9. What accounts for the durability of America's special relationship with Israel?

10. Is Marxism the best approach to explaining the United States policy towards oil in the Middle East?

11. Did the OPEC oil embargo of 1973 represent a failure of US policy towards the Middle East?

12. To what extent is the Bush Doctrine a major departure from previous US foreign policy towards the Middle East?

» Further Reading

Cooley, John (2002), *Unholy Wars: Afghanistan, America and International Terrorism* (London: Pluto Press).
   A detailed discussion of the United States' relations with radical Islam.

Khalidi, Rashid (2004), *Resurrecting Empire: Western Footprints and America's Perilous Path in the Middle East* (London: I. B. Tauris).

A trenchant critique of the United States' relations with the Middle East by a renowned historian.

Little, Douglas (2002), *American Orientalism: The United States and the Middle East since 1945* (London: I. B. Tauris).

A detailed diplomatic history of the United States' relations with the Middle East, written from a constructivist point of view.

Packer, George (2005), *Assassins' Gate: America in Iraq* (New York: Farrar, Straus and Giroux).

The best book yet written on the reasons for the US invasion of Iraq and its failure.

Quandt, William B. (2005), *Peace Process: American Diplomacy and the Arab–Israeli Conflict since 1967* (Berkeley and Los Angeles: University of California Press).

A diplomatic history of America's role in trying to solve the Arab–Israeli conflict.

Shlaim, Avi (1995), *War and Peace in the Middle East: A Concise History* (Harmondsworth: Penguin).

A wide-ranging historical account of US–Middle East relations.

Westad, Odd Arne (2005), *The Global Cold War: Third World Interventions and the Making of our Times* (Cambridge: Cambridge University Press).

A very detailed historical work on the relationship between Cold War and the third world, stressing the role of ideology.

 Visit the Online Resource Centre that accompanies this book for web links to accompany each chapter, and a range of other resources: www.oxfordtextbooks.co.uk/orc/cox_stokes/

12 The USA and the EU

Mike Smith

Chapter contents

Introduction

This chapter explores one of the key relationships in which the USA has been involved since the end of the Second World War: the transatlantic relationship with the 'European integration project'. This is a relationship not with a single state, but with a densely institutionalized region, which has itself grown and become markedly more prominent in the world arena over the past half-century. American foreign policy makers have generally been consistent in their support for the integration project, but it has challenged US foreign policy in a number of important areas. The focus of the chapter is thus on the ways in which US policy makers have developed images of the European Community (EC) and now the European Union (EU), on the challenges posed by European integration for US policy processes and the uses of US power, and on the ways in which these challenges have been met in the very different conditions of the Cold War and post-Cold War periods.

The United States was present at the creation of the 'European integration project' and has remained central to the process ever since. In the immediate aftermath of the Second World War, the presence of US power and the availability of US support for economic and social reconstruction played a key role in the establishment of the European Coal and Steel Community (ECSC, 1951), and the Eisenhower administrations of the 1950s showed consistent support for the further development of the integration process. This was reflected in their acceptance of the idea for a European Defence Community (EDC) in the early 1950s—even though that idea eventually ran into the sand because of opposition in Europe itself—and of the Treaty of Rome, which in 1957 set out the framework for the European Economic Community (EEC) and the European Atomic Energy Community (Euratom). American foreign policy makers have remained generally supportive of the developing project as it has enlarged from its original six member states to the present twenty-seven (after the enlargements of 2004 and 2007), and as it has expanded its scope—particularly in the post-Cold War period—from the organization of a common market and customs union into a largely common economic and monetary policy, a common foreign and security policy, a European security and defence policy, and common policies in the area of justice and home affairs.

This very brief summary shows that this is a relationship with a history, and also one that has seen considerable change, both in the context within which it is conducted and in the content with which it is concerned. In terms of the context, US policies towards European integration have spanned both the Cold War and the post-Cold War periods, and have also contended with the growth of globalization and its consequences. In terms of content, US policy makers have had to adapt to a European project that has expanded both in scope and scale, and which has become a central feature in the foreign policies of individual European Union member states, some of whom are among the USA's oldest and closest allies.

The purpose of this chapter is to explore the ways in which American foreign policy makers have promoted or responded to these changes, and to point out some of the key areas of tension that have emerged from the changing relationship between the USA and European integration. The chapter begins with a review of key factors in the evolution of the relationship within US foreign policy up to the end of the Cold War, focusing especially on US images of the European integration processes and on responses to change. This is followed by an analysis of key trends and tensions during the period. The third part of the chapter then focuses on the ways in which the post-Cold War period has thrown up new changes and challenges, and the ways in which these have been dealt with by US policy makers, again with attention to images and responses. As with the analysis of the Cold War period, this is followed by an evaluation of trends and tensions in the period since 1990. The conclusions raise a number of questions about the capacity of the USA to shape and adapt to European integration, and thus about the future of the USA–EU relationship.

US foreign policy and European integration

This section deals with the ways in which US foreign policy makers formed their images of the European integration process between 1945 and 1990, the ways in which they responded to the evolution of the project, and with a number of key trends and tensions reflected in the evolution of US policies. In particular, it focuses on the balance in US policies between economic, political, and security priorities, and on the balance between underlying trends in US policies towards 'empire', 'alliance', and 'interdependence'. By taking this focus, we should be able to clarify the place occupied by European integration in US foreign policy, and understand the nature of the changes and challenges that have emerged in the post-Cold War period, to be dealt with later in the chapter.

Images and adaptation

As shown elsewhere in this volume (Chapter 4), the end of the Second World War ushered in a period of uncertainty in US foreign policy. The emergence of the US 'liberal order' was not a preordained outcome, and indeed the initial US position on continued involvement in western Europe was shaped by the desire to retreat to the American homeland. But the development and definition of the Soviet threat between 1945 and 1947 led to a redefinition of US policies towards Europe that had a profound effect on European integration (DePorte 1986; Grosser 1982; Heller and Gillingham 1996).

Central to this reorientation of US foreign policy was the Marshall Plan—the system of financial and other assistance that contributed to the recovery and stabilization of the western European countries, and thus, it can be argued, to the initiation of European integration itself. Secretary Marshall's speech made at Harvard University in June 1947 concentrated on the need for immediate economic assistance, but also had an explicitly political aim: to stabilize (or in some cases, to create) democratic institutions and free markets, which were seen as two sides of the same coin. Between 1947 and 1950, the European Recovery Programme channelled

$19 billion of US aid to those countries that accepted the ground rules, and by so doing also accentuated the Cold War division of Europe by excluding the countries of the developing Soviet bloc (Hogan 1987; Milward 1984). Because the aid was given explicitly on the basis that the European recipients would cooperate in its distribution and the associated planning processes, it is possible to see this as the seed of the eventual European integration process. When in 1950 Robert Schuman and Jean Monnet proposed the 'Schuman Plan' for the creation of a European Coal and Steel Community, this was generally welcomed in the US administration as a further step in the recovery and consolidation process. The ERP and the ECSC together, it can be claimed, expressed the US position in the political economy of western Europe, and led to the 'Americanization' of large parts of European industry.

But this was not the whole story. Alongside the ECSC, US policy makers had come—in some cases reluctantly—to the conclusion that they needed a long-term commitment to European security, not just to economic and political recovery. This was what lay at the bottom of the North Atlantic Treaty signed in 1949 by the USA and fourteen other members (western European plus Canada). It is important to note here that the NAT and subsequently the North Atlantic Treaty Organization (NATO) are not strictly 'European integration'—they were explicitly transatlantic, with a dominant US presence expressed in military and political structures. One immediate consequence, though, was a focus on the need to rearm West Germany in order for it to play its part in the defence of the 'western alliance'. This led the French to propose a further and dramatic step in European integration: the creation of a European Defence Community with a multinational structure and a common military command. Whilst not sponsored by the Americans, this was eventually accepted as a way to create a robust European 'pillar' of the Atlantic alliance. When in 1954 it was defeated, ironically by the French National Assembly, the Americans and the British stepped in to provide an alternative structure through which the West Germans could eventually join NATO and be rearmed as part of the Atlantic alliance (Fursdon 1980).

By the mid-1950s, therefore, it could be argued that the Americans had achieved all of their key goals in respect of European integration. They had fostered European cooperation in key industries, and had managed to get the West Germans integrated into the NATO command and political structure. Led by the State Department, US foreign policy elites saw European integration as an unquestioned and positive contribution to western security, and also to the development of a liberalized 'western' world economy centred on the Atlantic area. The Eisenhower administration wanted this to go further, through the entry into European institutions of Britain and other key NATO allies. Thus, when the original six member states of the ECSC set out in 1955 to create a European Economic Community, US policy makers saw this as positive, despite the fears of some that it might constitute a protectionist economic bloc which would damage American agricultural and industrial interests (Winand 1993).

It is important to note, though, that this position was not aligned with some of the emerging realities of life in the 'new Europe'. The British proved strangely reluctant to immerse themselves in what they saw as a second-rank organization, partly because of their perceived 'special relationship' with the USA itself. At the same time, the French saw US enthusiasm for British membership as a sign of a malign hegemony, which led them ever more strongly to emphasize the EEC's role as a point of resistance to US policies. President Charles de Gaulle, who held power in France from 1958 to 1969, was especially sensitive to the American threat, and made constant efforts to turn the West Germans and others away from their Atlanticist orientation. As a result, when in 1962 John F. Kennedy made a major speech calling for the development of a true 'Atlantic partnership' between the United States and a uniting Europe, this became a major point of friction rather than a rallying point. Throughout the remainder of the 1960s, the discourse among US policy makers about 'Atlantic partnership'

or 'Atlantic community' was countered by calls from Paris for resistance to US domination and for the use of the EEC as a means of fighting back (Calleo 1970; Cleveland 1966). Ironically, this was accompanied by a substantial flow of US foreign direct investment into the EEC—a factor that was to contribute greatly to integration at the transatlantic level, and to become a significant influence on US foreign economic policy (Krause 1968).

The late 1960s, therefore, saw contradictory trends in US policies towards European integration. On the one side, there was the continuing rhetoric of 'Atlantic partnership' as part of the broader Cold War system—a rhetoric which defined the EEC as part of the 'western system' and as the economic equivalent of NATO. This rhetoric was strongly dedicated to the leading role of NATO in western security, and incidentally as a major source of US leverage over the countries of western Europe. On the other side, there was the rhetoric of 'adversarial partnership', focusing on the challenge posed by the French and on the danger of a developing 'third way' which might turn into a European form of neutralism or non-alignment. This second rhetoric was given added force by the economic turbulence of the late 1960s, by the loss of dynamism in the US economy, and by the feeling that the Europeans had profited from US financial and military support without playing their full part in return.

In this context, the Nixon–Kissinger foreign policy conducted between the late 1960s and the mid-1970s played a crucial catalytic role. In economic terms, Nixon and Kissinger subscribed to the view that the USA was an 'ordinary country' which needed to defend its national economic interests and to protect itself against those who took advantage of the liberal international economy (Rosecrance 1976). In security terms, the 'Nixon Doctrine' implied that America's allies would have to do far more to protect themselves and pay far more towards the costs of alliance, both in Europe and elsewhere. For European integration, this policy stance held important implications. It meant that they could no longer rely on the USA as a benign hegemonic force in the global economy, and that they could no longer count on the unqualified support of the USA for European defence. US policy makers came to see European integration as much more of a problem than a solution; the EEC's development of foreign policy cooperation, with its insistence that the Community was a 'civilian power', implied to US policy makers that the Community was a means of hiding from international obligations and developing a form of the non-alignment that they feared and despised. The entry of the British into the EEC in 1973 thus could be defined not as a triumph for US policy but as a worrying move that could lead to the loss of their most trusted ally. The Nixon–Kissinger response was characteristic: Kissinger proclaimed 1973 'the year of Europe' and called for the conclusion of a new Atlantic treaty in line with the administration's idea of the global 'structure of peace' (Cromwell 1978). But this initiative, which had not been discussed with any European governments, fell on stony ground in a year when the combination of EEC enlargement, conflict in the Middle East, and an accompanying oil price crisis preoccupied European policy makers.

US policies towards European integration during the early 1970s might thus be summarized as a form of wary containment, but this misses the point that the EEC had become a genuine economic rival to the USA in a number of major areas. Although the Community's plans for economic and monetary union and political union by 1980 came to little or nothing, the 1970s as a whole gave evidence of the fact that the Americans needed the Community as much as the Community needed them. Thus the process of adjustment in US policy positions and policy rhetoric could be observed especially during the Carter administration between 1976 and 1980: Europeans were seen as partners in interdependence and as a focus for cooperation within international institutions, although this was not without its own difficulties in a period of economic stagnation (Hoffmann 1978). European foreign policy cooperation was a source of worry, for example over the Middle East where the Community members were much more pro-Palestinian than was Washington, but as it became clear that European declarations would lead to little substantive policy change, this suspicion moderated (Allen and Smith 1983).

Much of this apparent reconciliation was dissipated by the events of the 'second cold war' and by the arrival of the Reagan administration in 1980. Reaganism attacked the Europeans on two fronts. First, it politicized and 'domesticized' American foreign economic policies, leading to a concentration on the needs of the US economy but also to a strong emphasis on the sin of 'trading with the enemy', in this case the Soviet bloc in particular. For some Europeans, this rhetoric and the subsequent application of 'extra-territorial' measures to restrict trade with the Soviet bloc was evident of US unilateralism and a form of imperialism; for others, such as the British, it was defined much more positively as a reassertion of US leadership. That is certainly the way the US administration saw it: the USA was the leader of the free world, and was assuming its responsibilities (Allen and Smith 1989).

The second area in which US foreign policy challenged European integration was in the development of the fledgling 'European' foreign and security policies. Here, we can see again the 'containment' aspect of the US stance vis-à-vis European integration. US policy makers felt strongly that they did not want the Community to develop in such a way as to erode NATO, or to reduce their capacity to form 'special relationships' with individual EEC member states. In pursuit of this stance, Washington was prepared to use its connections with the British and others to ensure that any new developments in the Community were moderated and always made subject to the primary role of NATO in ensuring European security (Treverton 1985; Joffe 1987). Thus during the late 1980s when the revival of the Western European Union created a platform for a distinct European defence identity, the White House was quick to emphasize the dire consequences of any attempt to duplicate or to undermine NATO.

By the end of the 1980s, then, US policies towards the European integration project continued to manifest a series of tensions and contradictions. Washington supported European integration in general, but was never short of reasons for opposing it or criticizing it in particular contexts. US policy makers wanted a strong European partner both within Europe and the Atlantic area and in the broader global arena, but

> **KEY QUOTES 12.1: US policy makers and European integration in the Cold War**

The Marshall Plan speech, 1947

It is evident . . . that, before the United States Government can proceed much further with its efforts to alleviate the situation and help the European world on its way to recovery, there must be some agreement among the countries of Europe as to the requirements of the situation and the part those countries themselves will take in order to give proper effect to whatever action might be undertaken by the Government. It would neither be fitting nor efficacious for this Government to undertake to draw up unilaterally a program designed to place Europe on its feet economically. This is the business of the Europeans. The initiative, I think, must come from Europe. The role of this country should consist of friendly aid in the drawing up of a European program and of later support of such a program so far as it may be practical for us to do so. The program should be a joint one, agreed to by a number, if not all, of Europe's nations.

(Marshall 1947; George C. Marshall was US Secretary of State)

The 'Declaration of Interdependence'—John F. Kennedy, 4 July 1962

The nations of Western Europe, long divided by feuds more bitter than any which existed among the Thirteen Colonies, are joining together, seeking, as our forefathers sought, to find freedom in diversity and unity in strength. The United States looks on this vast new enterprise with hope and admiration. We do not regard a strong and united Europe as a rival but as a partner. To aid its progress has been the basic objective of our foreign policy for 17 years. We believe that a united Europe will be capable of playing a greater role in the common defense, of responding more generously to the needs of poorer nations, of joining with the United States and others in lowering trade barriers, resolving problems of currency and commodities, and developing coordinated policies in all other economic, diplomatic, and political areas. We see in such a Europe a partner with whom we could deal on a basis of full equality in all the great and burdensome tasks of building and defending a community of free nations.

. . . I will say here and now on this day of independence that the United States will be ready for a 'Declaration of Interdependence', that we will be prepared to discuss with a united Europe the ways and means of forming a concrete Atlantic partnership, a mutually beneficial partnership between the new union emerging in Europe and the old American Union founded here 175 years ago.

(Kennedy 1962)

The 'Year of Europe' speech: Henry Kissinger, April 1973

The problems in transatlantic relationships are real. They have arisen in part because during the fifties and sixties the Atlantic community organised itself in different ways in the many different dimensions of its common enterprise. In economic relations, the European community has increasingly stressed its regional personality; the United States, at the same time, must act as part of, and be responsible for, a wider trade and monetary system. We must reconcile these two perspectives. In our collective defense, we are still organised on the principle of unity and integration, but in radically different strategic conditions. The full implications of this change have yet to be faced. Diplomacy is the subject of frequent consultation, but is essentially being conducted by traditional nation states. The United States has global interests and responsibilities. Our European allies have regional interests. These are not necessarily in conflict, but in the new era neither are they automatically identical. In short, we deal with each other regionally and even competitively in economic matters, on an integrated basis in defense, and as national states in diplomacy. When the various collective institutions were rudimentary, the potential inconsistency in their modes of operation was not a problem. But after a generation of evolution and with the new weight and strength of our allies, the various parts of the construction are not always in harmony and sometimes obstruct each other.

(Kissinger 1973; Henry Kissinger was US Secretary of State)

'The transatlantic relationship: a long-term perspective'

I have often discussed with European friends the different requirements for a nation with global responsibilities to those with more regional concerns. The use of the word global is not meant in any arrogant fashion. Nor is it to deny the interests that several European nations retain in

(continued)

> ❝ **KEY QUOTES 12.1:** (continued)

areas of the world beyond their continent. But the sheer scope of American interests engages us in a different set of perspectives and imperatives. I am persuaded that despite periodic inconsistencies (mainly on our part) and even more frequent crises of policy disagreement (emanating frequently from the European side) members of the alliance can still forge a strong consensus on most issues of importance . . . [but] . . . now may well be the appropriate moment for all of us—Europeans and Americans—to take a new look at where we should be going together and how we should get there . . . The two pillars of a 'smarter' relationship, in my opinion, are: increasing respect for the differences in our alliance; and a more coordinated approach—across the board—to all political, economic and security issues with our European allies.

(Eagleburger 1984; Eagleburger was US Under Secretary of State for Political Affairs)

they did not want it to be so strong that it developed a mind of its own. They valued the prosperity and stability of the EEC, not simply as a contribution to broader global stability but also as a source of economic gains for Americans, but they found difficult in accepting the Community as a 'partner in leadership' within the global economy. US hegemony over the Community, if it had ever fully existed, was fragmented and fraying at the edges in the late 1980s, and subject to question not only in the core economic domain but also in political and security terms.

Trends and tensions

The review of US attitudes towards European integration up to the end of the 1980s reveals that the relationship as a whole was characterized by a number of overall trends and a number of persistent tensions. For US foreign policy, a key trend was the move from apparently unqualified hegemony to a position where leadership had to be justified and legitimized. Another associated trend was what might be called the problem of leadership and followership: by the end of this period, EC member states had become far less inclined simply to follow where the USA led, but at the same time there were areas where they could not collectively follow. A third trend was in the adaptation of US policy makers' images of the EC: not surprisingly, these images often said more about the needs and priorities of US foreign policy than they did about the evolving realities of the European project, and they were also 'sticky', that is, resistant to change. Finally, US policy makers' approach to European integration was clearly

conditioned to significant degrees by events in US–Soviet relations, as Cold War tensions fluctuated and evolved in periods of détente or 'new cold war'. Thus, the European project could be seen as a pillar of the western alliance, as a breeding ground for neutralism or non-alignment, or as a source of often intense economic competition. In reality, of course, it was often all three of these at once, with consequent implications for the focus and direction of US policy.

Alongside these trends and tensions in the images held by US policy makers went another set of significant connections and interactions. From the outset, relations between the USA and European integration were an uneasy combination of the political, the economic, and the security related. Between 1950 and 1990, the balance and linkages between these three components of the relationship grew, shifted, and evolved, and this was a key issue for policy makers in Washington. Thus, during the 1950s and 1960s, it was tempting to see the integration process as somehow separate from the political and security dimensions of the relationship, and as somehow subordinate to the demands of NATO and of superpower diplomacy. In many ways this was never true, but the 1970s disposed of the myth in no uncertain terms. The politicization of economic issues (especially in the energy crisis), the use of economic sanctions (for example against Iran, or the Soviet bloc in the 'new cold war'), and the increasing attention to issues of high technology as matters of foreign or national security policy, all meant that US views of the 'economic' integration process needed to change. As noted above, these images were often 'sticky', and

American policy makers found it difficult to adjust to the world of economic power, in which the preconditions for what later came to be termed globalization were being established. By the end of the 1980s, with the initiation of new stages of European integration through the Single Market Programme, and with discussion of economic and monetary union in the EC, the tensions were still observable and if anything more severe than before.

A third set of trends and tensions, strongly related to those described above, was in the stance of US foreign policy overall, as affected by and expressed in their relationship to European integration (Smith 2000). It can be argued that three central trends are observable in US policies towards the integration project. The first can be termed 'imperial': the integration project was subsumed willingly or unwillingly within the creation and maintenance of an American empire, in which transatlantic relations were a central component (Lundestad 1998). A subset of this trend is the exercise of hegemony, and the holding of hegemonic assumptions about the nature of US–EC relations, whether these relate to trade, to monetary relations, or to foreign and defence policies (Calleo 1987). In this trend, US policy makers assumed that the European project was essentially dependent, that they held the power to make the rules within which integration proceeded, and that they could also detach key EC member states when the need for 'special relationships' overrode the need for a relationship with the EC as a whole.

Alongside the 'imperial' component of US policies towards European integration went two other, not always compatible, trends. One was what might be termed 'alliance', according to which the relationship with the EC was a part of the broader Western system and subject to rules and conventions about leadership and followership (Sloan 2005). As we have seen above, this dimension of US policy was consistent throughout the 1950–90 period, and the Europeans came increasingly to make their collective voices heard within the alliance structure. But this dimension was of course in tension with persistent 'imperial' tendencies, which might admit of the need for alliance but also emphasize American structural dominance in all of the areas that really mattered. Both 'imperial' and 'alliance' trends were in tension with the third dimension of the relationship: that of 'interdependence'. The growth of transactions, exchange, and institutions in the Atlantic area during the 1950s and 1960s created a dense region of interdependence, in which the actions (both domestic and external) of each of those involved had implications for all of the others (Cooper 1968). During the 1970s and 1980s this reality became more apparent, and US policy makers were faced with the need to incorporate interdependence thinking into their approach to European integration. Not only this, but they were compelled to go beyond interdependence into the realm of what some observers called 'interpenetration'—where US and European societies and economies were so closely linked that it was difficult to work out 'who is us' and 'who is them'. Not surprisingly, these views were more strongly rooted in some parts of the US administrations than others, and in some administrations than others. Thus the Carter administration in the late

---

BOX 12.1: Trends and tensions in US–EU relations, 1945–80s

- *Images and reality*: move from US hegemony to questioning of leadership and legitimacy; problems of 'leadership and followership'; 'stickiness' of adjustment of images and expectations in US policy making; influence of fluctuations in US–Soviet relations.

- *Politics, economics, and security*: shifting balance and linkages; intersection of the three areas, and consequent 'politicization' of economic issues especially

in the 1970s (Middle East, 'new cold war'); impact of intensification of European integration in the 1980s.

- *Empire, alliance, and interdependence*: challenges to US assumptions of European dependence; US capacity to 'divide and rule' through 'special relationships'; tensions between 'imperial' assumptions, those of 'alliance', and those of 'interdependence', affecting policies, institutions, and 'rules of the game'.

1970s played heavily on the interdependence theme, but this was not welcomed by those within the political system and US society more broadly who believed in the restoration of US dominance. Equally, the Reagan administrations of the 1980s emphasized the 'imperial' or hegemonic aspects of the relationship, but found themselves confounded at times by the impact of alliance politics and interdependence.

US–EC relations by the end of the Cold War displayed the effects of a forty-year history, and of the trends and tensions that arose within it. It is logical to see 1990, and the end of the Cold War, as a major break in this history, and as posing new challenges for US foreign policy. The next section turns to this problem, and to the question 'what has changed during the 1990s and in the new millennium?'

KEY POINTS

- ❑ In the early years of the Cold War, the US position in Europe was consolidated, and the European integration process was part of this consolidation.
- ❑ Nonetheless, there were tensions in US policies about the extent to which on the one hand the European project should be part of the Cold War system and the 'western alliance', and on the other hand the basis for a more independent Europe. US policy makers' images were shaped not only by relations with the EEC, but also by Cold War priorities and by domestic needs.

- ❑ From the late 1950s onwards, US policy makers had to respond to change within the EEC, especially its continuing economic growth and the beginnings of political assertiveness. This created a kind of 'containment' policy on the part of the USA, alongside continuing support for the integration process as a whole.
- ❑ As a result, there were continuing tensions involving issues of US leadership, the linkage between political, economic, and security factors, and three strands in US policies: 'empire', 'alliance', and 'interdependence'.

The United States and the European Union

As noted above, it is tempting to see the end of the Cold War as a key point of transformation in US policies towards the European integration project. If the European Community is seen as a key component of a US 'empire' or as a key element of the 'western alliance', the collapse of the Soviet Union and the Soviet bloc are clearly likely to have fundamental implications for the terms on which US–EC relations were conducted. The picture is somewhat less clear if one sees US–EC relations in terms of economic and social interdependence, since major changes had been occurring in these domains for years if not decades. The purpose of this section is to explore the ways in which the changing European integration project interacted with changes in US foreign policy after 1990, and thus to arrive at an assessment of the ways in which the central trends and tensions in the relationship changed during that period. As before, the chapter looks first at images and responses in US foreign policy, and then at trends and tensions.

Images and responses

As with the end of the Second World War, the end of the Cold War ushered in a period of uncertainty and fluctuation in US foreign policy. As shown in Chapter 5, the tension between triumphalism and caution in Washington, and in the country as a whole, was a key feature of the early 1990s, as was the tension between internationalism and 'domesticism'. These tensions were still present in the early years of the new millennium, as the search for an effective 'grand strategy' in US foreign policy evoked painful and often highly partisan debates. Our interest here is in the ways in which the EC and after 1993 the European Union took their place in these debates, and in the images that US foreign policy makers deployed in their efforts to meet the challenge of renewed European dynamism.

For the George H. W. Bush administration that presided over the end of the Cold War, a number of key factors played into their redefinition of relations with European integration. One was that the end of the Cold War was a European process—albeit one with global reverberations. In consequence, it was tempting for the administration to see the European Community as playing a new and special role in stabilizing and assisting the reconstruction of the eastern half of the continent (Smith and Woolcock 1993; Treverton 1992). James Baker, the Secretary of State, made this abundantly clear as early as December 1989, in the immediate aftermath of the fall of the Berlin Wall, when he underlined the EC's role in the 'New World Order'. For Baker, the EC should enlarge to the east, and quickly, to provide the anchor for the newly liberated states of the ex-Soviet bloc. This did not mean that the US position in Europe, and especially NATO, should be abandoned; it did mean, though, that the EC was seen as a major 'subcontractor' in the establishment of a new European order. Thus the Americans were willing to give the EC a lead role in providing aid to the ex-Soviet states and in coordinating the provision of reconstruction assistance at the continental level. They were also willing to envisage a new diplomatic and security role for the EC, giving it responsibility for more of the 'hard security' issues that were likely to emerge in the 'new Europe' and also for the broader range of 'soft security' issues arising from such areas as migration or the development of human rights regimes.

This US perception was buttressed to a large degree by the evident willingness of leading European states to take the lead in the new European order. During 1990 and 1991, the negotiations that led to the Treaty on European Union and to the establishment of a Common Foreign and Security Policy for the EU led many to believe that a new era of political and defence integration was just over the horizon. As during the Cold War, the development of these new areas of integration was broadly welcomed by Washington, for reasons especially of 'grand strategy' (see above), but the EC and its members proved rather less able (or in some cases, willing) to follow through with dramatic initiatives. One of the problems for Washington in dealing with the EC and then the EU has always been the question attributed to Henry Kissinger during the early 1970s: 'if I want to talk to Europe, who do I call?' In the conditions of Europe immediately after the end of the Cold War, this question was if anything more pressing than before but the answer was still not easy to discern.

For US policy makers, therefore, the early 1990s were years of frustration as well as expectation where the EU was concerned. The Europeans had agreed a treaty, but it took two years to get it ratified, and there were also strong limitations on the extent of EU collective action built into it. When the federation of Yugoslavia collapsed during 1991–2, with fierce fighting first between Serbia and Croatia and then between warring groups in Bosnia-Herzegovina, there were European leaders prepared to proclaim that 'this is the hour of Europe, not of the United States', and to call for a European solution to a European problem—a sentiment supported by a number of key figures in Washington (Smith and Woolcock 1993). But as the war in former Yugoslavia continued and intensified, it became apparent that the EU and its member states were singularly unprepared to deploy the 'hard power' that might have brought an early end to the conflict. As a result, the Clinton administration was eventually led to intervene, using NATO as a vehicle for the use of force against the Bosnian Serbs in 1994–5 and against the Milosovic regime in Belgrade during 1999 when the Serbs attempted a forcible solution to the problem of Kosovo.

US policy makers thus had good reason by the late 1990s to be cautious about claims of EU responsibility for major international conflicts, even when they took place in the Europeans' backyard. They also had their doubts about the speed with which the EU moved to enlarge its membership and thus contributed to the emerging new European order. The Clinton administration's National Security Strategy focused on 'engagement and enlargement' (see Chapter 5), and the EU was assigned a key role in this process with particular reference to the continent of Europe itself. But a combination of the complexities of the enlargement process, together with the reluctance of some member states to go for a 'big bang' enlargement to at least ten new members, created an understandable frustration in Washington as the 1990s unfolded (Peterson 1996; Smith and Woolcock 1994). Here there is a key cultural difference between

US foreign policy and the nature of policy making at the European level: for Europeans, the process is at least as important as the result, whereas for Americans the result is what matters. This basic difference underlines the key fact that all US foreign policy makers need to remember when dealing with the EU: despite its impressive institutional apparatus and economic weight, the Union is not a state. Nor would most US policy makers want it to be a state, since that might very well mean that it would be much more difficult to deal with on an everyday basis as well as on matters of grand strategy.

The Clinton administrations also had to deal with the impact of the EU's changing economic structure, and with its increasing influence in the global political economy. The Treaty on European Union consolidated the gains made in the EU's Single Market Programme, which by the mid-1990s had taken market integration to new levels (Hocking and Smith 1997). It also had to deal with the approach of economic and monetary union, which eventually led to the establishment of the 'Eurozone' and of the euro as a major international currency at the beginning of the new millennium. Alongside these 'internal' developments, the EU also became more active in leading international trade initiatives, in pursuing trade disputes with the USA in particular, and in taking on issues in the 'new agenda' of environmental issues, human rights, and the like. The fact that these were often intractable issues within the USA itself, and within the administration, frequently meant that the USA seemed less sure-footed than policy makers in Brussels—who were not slow to comment on this shift.

Towards the end of the Clinton years, a further challenge emerged from the EU. Partly as a result of the failures in Bosnia and Kosovo, in 1998 and 1999 the British and the French led a move to establish a European Security and Defence Policy. Whatever the motivations and expectations of those involved within the EU, the importance of this move for the discussion here is clear: this was a challenge to the idea that US priorities and NATO would automatically take precedence in matters of 'western security', and it promised the establishment of a second centre of military power within the western system (Howorth

2000, 2005). The response of the Clinton administration, through Secretary of State Madeleine Albright, was to caution the Europeans in terms of the 'three Ds'—no duplication of capabilities, no discrimination by Europe between third countries that would be unacceptable to the USA, and no decoupling of Europe from the USA. At the same time, the administration continued to nurture its 'special relationships' with some of the EU member states most closely involved, especially Britain, who was its closest ally in the continuing confrontation with Iraq.

By the end of the 1990s, there was thus a dynamic and somewhat confused picture in US–EU relations. Since 1995, there had been a formal institutional link between the USA and the EU in the shape of the New Transatlantic Agenda and its extensive action plan—an initiative taken by the USA and agreed by the Europeans for a combination of political and economic reasons, but which covered a very large number of 'new agenda' items with a global dimension (Philippart and Winand 2001; Pollack and Shaffer 2001; Steffenson 2005). But this formal link did not comprehensively or consistently cover key emerging areas of security policy, and for US tastes was rather limited in terms of the commitments made to support US policies outside Europe. Indeed, as time went on, the NTA captured less and less of what was important to key US policy-making groups, and covered more and more of those areas where the USA and the EU diverged quite strongly—for example, the environmental issues surrounding the Kyoto Protocol. When this was combined with glacial progress on enlargement and the concerns aroused by the development of ESDP, there was much to be cautious about in US–EU relations (Gompert and Larrabee 1997).

The George W. Bush administration initially pursued policies much like those of the Clinton administration towards the EU, with some crucial differences in policy areas that 'flanked' but did not form part of the core of relations at the European level—for example, ballistic missile defence, or policies towards Russia. There was also a 'hardening' of policies on the environment and other areas where the Clinton foreign policy had attempted to soften the edge of US domestic opposition. But the key event in shaping US policies towards the EU in the early part of the new millennium was—as in so many other areas of US foreign policy—the attack on New York and Washington on 11 September 2001. The implications of this event, and of the neo-conservative influence on subsequent US policies, are dealt with elsewhere in this volume (see Chapter 5), but it is vital for the purposes of this chapter to recognize that together with subsequent US policies on Iraq and the war on terror it had a major shaping influence on US–EU relations.

The immediate impact of 9/11 was to encourage EU member states collectively to support the USA, but it soon became very clear that the EU did not feature large in US policies undertaken on a predominantly unilateral basis or with key allies (many of them member states of the EU itself). US policy makers, led by Vice-President Cheney and Secretary of Defense Rumsfeld, simply did not see the use of an organization that depended so heavily on the generation of internal consensus, and which could mobilize almost nothing in the way of 'hard power'; whilst the Department of State and Secretary of State Powell were less resistant to the notion of 'civilian power' and multilateral diplomacy, their voices were much less loud and insistent. As a result, the initial stages of the war on terror in Afghanistan and elsewhere were predominantly led and coordinated by the USA and a few close allies. In the words of Donald Rumsfeld, 'the mission determines the coalition, not the coalition the mission', and the EU as a major focus of intense coalition politics was largely out of the game. Things were different, however, when the war on terror touched areas in which the EU had a substantial presence, such as financial sanctions, border security, and post-conflict reconstruction—all key elements in counter-terrorism cooperation; here, the Americans could not do without the EU and had to accept in large measure the complexities of dealing with Brussels (Pollack and Peterson 2003; Rees 2006).

When the Bush administration decided to move against Iraq in 2002–3, it was clear that the EU would not be a major factor in their deliberations. But a number of key long-standing EU member states were, including Britain, Italy, and Spain, as were a number of the eastern European states that were due to join in 2004. For US foreign policy makers, attention focused naturally on those who were either strongly with Washington, or—as in the case of France and to a lesser extent Germany—against it (Gordon and Shapiro 2004; Lindstrom 2003). During 2003–4, US policies were aimed essentially at dividing the EU, and at isolating the French whose demands for fuller use of the United Nations process grated with the administration. The fact that the French lined up with the Russians to thwart US aims at crucial points only increased the tension. In this atmosphere, with Rumsfeld encouraging intra-EU frictions with talk of the division between 'old' and 'new' Europe, it was easy to draw a stark contrast between US unilateralism and EU multilateralism, and between the US role as a 'warrior' state and the EU's qualities as a 'trading state' and 'civilian power' (Smith 2004).

The argument earlier in this chapter should warn us against making sweeping and stark distinctions, though. Alongside the open conflicts of 2003–4, a great deal of US–EU cooperation persisted, disputes were managed, and the transatlantic networks in economic and social affairs were maintained. The definite change of style that the George W. Bush administration had brought to the relationship softened during 2005 and 2006, as a 'new multilateralism' seemed to spread in transatlantic relations (Andrews 2005; Zaborowski 2006). By 2007, the Americans even seemed to be warming to the EU's position on global environmental change, and to be more ready for compromise on a number of key trade and commercial issues. For US foreign policy, a number of questions remained open: how would the USA relate to the European Security and Defence Policy in 'normal' times rather than in the heat of war against Iraq? Could the political partnership between the USA and the EU be restored on the basis of mutual respect and awareness of each other's distinctive priorities and internal constraints? Could American policy makers accommodate the nature of the EU's 'normative power' with its focus on human rights and conflict prevention, as opposed to the US focus on hard power and pre-emption? Could the USA and the EU operate as 'partners in leadership' to address some of the most pressing questions

> **KEY QUOTES 12.2:** US policy makers and European integration after the Cold War

James Baker's Berlin speech in December 1989

As Europe changes, the instruments for western cooperation have got to adapt. Working together, it is up to us to design and generally to put into place what I refer to as a new architecture for this new era . . . The future development of the European Community will also play a central role in shaping the new Europe . . . As Europe moves toward its goal of a common internal market, and as its institutions for political and security cooperation evolve, the link between the United States and the European Community will become even more important. We want our transatlantic cooperation to keep pace with European integration and with institutional reform. To this end, we propose that the United States and the European Community work together to achieve, whether it is in treaty or some other form, a significantly strengthened set of institutional and consultative links . . . We propose that our discussions about this idea proceed in parallel with Europe's efforts to achieve by 1992 a common internal market, so that plans for U.S.–EC interaction would evolve along with changes in the Community. The United States also encourages the European Community to continue to expand cooperation with the nations of the east. The promotion of political and economic reform in the east is a natural vocation for the European Community . . . We see no conflict between the process of European integration and an expansion of cooperation between the European Community and its neighbors to the east and west. Indeed, we believe that the attraction of the European Community for the countries of the east depends most on its continued vitality. And the vitality of the Economic Community depends in turn on its continued commitment to the goal of a united Europe envisaged by its founders—free, democratic and closely linked to its North American partners.

(Baker 1989; James Baker was US Secretary of State)

Madeleine Albright's warning to the EU on the 'three Ds' in 1998

Our . . . task is working together to develop a European Security and Defense Identity, or ESDI, within the Alliance [NATO], which the United States has strongly endorsed. We enthusiastically support any measures that enhance European capabilities. The United States welcomes a more capable European partner, with modern, flexible military forces capable of putting out fires in Europe's own backyard and working with us through the Alliance to defend our common interests. The key to a successful initiative is to focus on practical military capabilities. Any initiative must avoid pre-empting Alliance decision-making by delinking ESDI from NATO, avoid duplicating existing efforts, and avoid discrimination against non-EU members.

(Albright 1998; Madeleine Albright was US Secretary of State)

Donald Rumsfeld on 'old' and 'new' Europe in 2003

Q: Sir, a question about the mood among European allies . . . If you look at, for example, France and Germany . . . it seems that a lot of Europeans rather give the benefit of the doubt to Saddam Hussein than President George Bush. These are US allies. What do you make of that?

A: What do I say? Well, there isn't anyone alive who wouldn't prefer unanimity. I mean, you just always would like everyone to stand up and say, Way to go! That's the right [thing] to do, United States . . . Now, you're thinking of Europe as Germany and France. I don't. I think that's old Europe. If you look at the entire NATO Europe today, the center of gravity is shifting to the east. And there are a lot of new members . . . They're not with France and Germany on this, they're with the United States.

(Rumsfeld 2003; Donald Rumsfeld was US Secretary of Defense)

George W. Bush on US–EU relations during his 2005 visit to Brussels

Today, America and Europe face a moment of consequence and opportunity. Together we can once again set history on a hopeful course—away from poverty and despair, and toward development and the dignity of self-rule; away from resentment and violence, and toward justice and the peaceful settlement of differences. Seizing this moment demands idealism: we must see in every person the right and the capacity to live in freedom. Seizing this moment requires realism: we must act wisely and deliberately in the face of complex challenges. And seizing this moment also requires cooperation, because when Europe and America stand together, no problem can stand against us. As past debates fade, as great duties become clear, let us begin a new era of transatlantic unity.

(Bush 2005)

in the global political economy, such as those linking environment and development?

Such questions are by definition impossible to answer, but they encapsulate the kinds of dilemmas faced by US foreign policy makers in dealing with the EU in the new millennium. They also provide us with the cue to return to the other key element of this chapter: trends and tensions in US–EU relations.

Trends and tensions

When we explored the nature of US policies towards European integration in the Cold War period, we uncovered three sets of trends and tensions that shaped ideas and actions. The first set was related to the images held by US policy makers of the European integration project—and importantly, of the US role in relation to Europe. To put it simply, US views of European integration told us a lot about US views of themselves and of US foreign policy. The second set of trends and tensions related to the interaction of political, economic, and security forces within the 'Atlantic community', and the ways in which these defined and redefined the nature of the what might be termed the 'Euro-American system'. The shifting balance between these three forces seemed by the end of the Cold War to have changed the terms of the Atlantic partnership, but in uneven and often unexpected ways. Finally, there was a set of trends and tensions surrounding the modes of US behaviour and the style and structure of US policies: a shifting mix of 'empire', 'alliance', and 'interdependence' which arose from the other two sets of interactions and which allowed us to assess the ways in which the relationship itself was structured and maintained. What can we now say about the changing nature of the US–EU relationship since the end of the Cold War, using these sets of trends and tensions as our starting point?

A first observation is that US policy makers have found it very difficult in the period since 1990 to generate settled images either of European integration or of the USA's own role in that process. At one end of the spectrum, US leaders have feared being excluded from the 'new Europe' as a result of decreased threat from the east and the declining need for US military involvement. As a result, there has been a desire to maintain both presence and leverage in the security affairs of Europe, and to resist the apparent threat of exclusion. At the same time, however, the progress of European integration has actually increased the American stake in Europe in the economic and political domains. The Single Market Programme and its successors have stimulated ever greater US foreign direct investment (matched, it must be noted, by major increases in investment by EU companies in the USA). The image of the EU held by major US corporations has often been at odds with that of the US administration, and in many ways this is not surprising.

But perhaps the greatest challenge to US images of European integration, and their own role in relation to it, has come from the increasing international assertiveness of the EU itself. In an increasing number of policy domains, especially those of the 'new agenda' such as environment or human rights, the EU has asserted its right to be heard and to take a leadership role. This exertion of 'soft power' and a form of 'EU exceptionalism' has been accompanied by persistent EU failings in the area of 'hard power' and military security—failings given added prominence in American eyes by the lack of collective support from EU member states over Iraq and in certain parts of the 'War on Terror'. This issue of power has come to be seen in terms of two key interrelated images, largely but not entirely propounded by US policy makers or their close advisers. The first is the 'Mars/Venus' debate, in which European unwillingness to resort to or collectively deploy 'hard power' is seen as part of a fundamental cultural disconnect between the USA and Europe (Kagan 2003; Lindberg 2005). The second is the 'unilateral/multilateral' debate, through which the Europeans' commitment to multilateral institutions and rules of conduct in the international arena is contrasted to US unilateralism and willingness to take hard national decisions (Pollack 2003). In terms of US policy, it can readily be seen that these two areas of imagery express American ambivalence and uncertainty about the status and future of their EU partners, and to this extent they express starkly ideas that have been around in US–EC and US–EU relations for decades. The post-Cold War period may have highlighted and focused them, but it did not entirely create them.

The same can be said of the second set of trends and tensions: those between political, economic, and security dimensions of the US–EU relationship. There is no doubt that the post-Cold War period has both intensified and reshaped these forces, but the question is, how and with what effects? As we have seen, the breakdown of the Soviet bloc and of the Soviet Union itself was not merely a political event; it has had profound implications for economic and security processes, and has brought together the need for 'comprehensive security' alongside that for purely military security. These trends were reinforced (but not created) by the events of 9/11 and the war on terror. As noted above, one consequence for US policy makers was that they found themselves having to deal more and more with the EU, on matters of economic and financial sanctions, on questions of counter-terrorism, and on problems of what has been termed 'societal security', involving social and environmental standards (Pollack and Peterson 2003). This has been a challenge both for the institutional structure of US foreign policy and for the substance of policy itself. At the level of institutions, the EU poses the challenge of working across departmental boundaries and of coordinating policies at the transnational or the supranational level—a challenge to which not all US government departments have been fully responsive, and which has caused frictions within and between parts of the foreign policy community. At the level of policy substance, the EU demands close control of what is being said and done by US officials at the national and at the EU levels within Europe, and a strong capacity to undertake multidimensional negotiations with a variety of partners. This has not come easily to US policy makers even where they have wanted to pursue this kind of policy approach; others have rejected this kind of policy style, in favour of strong action by the USA and certain favoured allies, but it is not clear that this has been successful in anything but the short term.

Finally, what can we say about the balance in US policies towards European integration between the underlying structures of 'empire', 'alliance', and 'interdependence' since the end of the Cold War? Discussion of the ways in which US foreign policy since 1990 has expressed a kind of liberal imperialism is of course much more broadly based than in US–EU relations alone (see many other chapters), but the rise of the EU has had its own distinctive impact. Indeed, there is some ground for the argument that the new continental scale of the EU has created or expressed a form of 'EU imperialism' based on its structural power within the continent and on its dominance of what the European Commission calls the 'new neighbourhood' (Zielonka 2006; Smith 2007). American policy makers have found this difficult to pin down or to deal with, since it is based on the form of 'civilian power' that is at least at odds with if not alien to US thinking about world order. Whilst Washington had been able to continue its overall support for the stabilizing role and the economic benefits of EU enlargement, it has found itself at odds with the Europeans over how far this can be pushed. The most obvious example is that of Turkey, which American policy makers want to see as a member state of the EU but to which both the EU's enlargement processes and some existing EU member states are resistant. The EU has also been resistant to US pressure to deal more forcefully with the Russia of Vladimir Putin as it has become more assertive within and outside Europe. Alongside these primarily political contradictions, the EU has gained strength through the consolidation of the Eurozone and of the euro as an international currency. But the example of the euro (to which in 2007 only thirteen of twenty-seven member states belonged) does still point to the lack of a fully collective EU policy in many areas—a feature that can be and has been exploited by American policy makers.

The jury is thus still out on the persistence of 'empire' or hegemony in US–EU relations. Equally, the 'alliance' dimension must be seen as still valid but still inconclusive. At times in the post-Cold War period, US–EU relations have appeared as a form of 'adversarial partnership', with structural constraints preventing a divorce but plenty of disputes and tensions within the transatlantic 'family'. The formal institutional commitments of the New Transatlantic Agenda are not legally binding, but they do form a powerful set of shaping factors in all but the hardest of 'hard security' areas. The development of the European Security and Defence Policy has also provided a new channel for communication on matters of military security, although this is often still mediated through NATO, using the so-called 'Berlin plus' arrangements for coordination of resources and planning (Howorth 2005). Yet there is no common perception of a transatlantic 'grand strategy' either for the global political economy or for the areas of 'hard security' that proved so troublesome in the early years of the new millennium (Sloan 2005). What there is, is a form of institutional pluralism in which mechanisms to adjust and deal with differences have grown up over the post-Cold War period, rather than a new 'transatlantic bargain' covering all areas of US–EU interaction. From a US foreign policy perspective, and from the point of view of Washington preoccupied with the rise of China, India, and other emerging regional or global powers, this may be the best that can be hoped for.

The forces of 'empire' and 'alliance' are thus still intermingled in US policies towards the EU. The same can be said for 'interdependence', the third of our underlying factors. The intensification of globalization, and the consistent growth of transactions between the USA and the EU, have been persistent shaping factors since the 1960s. But since the end of the Cold War, there has been a growing tension between the various approaches to the management of these issues. The EU is the most highly developed form of regional interdependence—in fact, it goes beyond interdependence because of its dense institutionalization and the legal structures that sustain it, especially in economic activities. For US policy makers, this makes the EU a key partner in the management of interdependence not only in the North Atlantic area but also at the global level. US–EU competition and convergence strongly shape such bodies as the World Trade Organization, the International Monetary Fund, and the World Bank, not to mention a vast range of more specialized organizations within the global political economy (McGuire and Smith 2008). They also increasingly influence what goes on in a wide variety of newly 'securitized' organizations dealing with migrations, asylum, transport, and other areas central to the war on terror. US policy makers have thus had to adapt to dealing not with a number of independent interlocutors in Europe, but with governments and other groups who are themselves constrained by membership of the EU. US foreign policy has thus faced conflicting pressures in dealing with the growth of interdependence between the USA and the EU—on the one hand, a pressure to act unilaterally and make others adjust to US preferences, on the other hand a realization that in the EU, this is not as

---

BOX 12.2: Trends and tensions in US – EU relations, 1989 – 2007

- *Images and reality*: difficulty of generating settled images of European integration; fears of exclusion, desire to retain leverage; increasing assertiveness of the EU, debates over nature of EU and US power and over unilateralism/multilateralism.

- *Politics, economics, and security*: linkages intensify, assisted by collapse of Soviet bloc and processes of globalization; pressures on new dimensions of security, including 'societal security'; need for complex policy mix to match growing scope of EU.

- *Empire, alliance, and interdependence*: US as 'only superpower'—liberal imperialism; growing continental power of the EU; links to issues of European and world order; pressures on alliance from changes in EU, US, and world arena; new challenges of global governance created by globalization and interdependence; 'securitization' and institutionalization of many international issues, with implications for exercise of power in US – EU relations.

easy as it might appear and that multilateral methods might be more effective. It would be too much to claim that dealing with the EU has changed the culture of US foreign policy, but there can be no doubt that the development of the EU since 1990 has provided a concentrated form of the interdependence to which all US foreign policies have had to adjust since the 1960s.

KEY POINTS

❑ The end of the Cold War had a major impact on US views of European integration, but has to be seen alongside other and more long-lasting factors in shaping US policies.

❑ US policy makers engaged in a redefinition of their views of European integration during the 1990s, especially in light of the change from European Community to European Union, but this was subject to a series of uncertainties and contradictions.

❑ Tensions between the USA and the EU over matters of European order (conflict in former Yugoslavia, enlargement) were a key feature of the 1990s.

❑ The EU also posed a broader challenge to US policy in the global political economy (through the Single Market and monetary union), and in matters of security and defence (through the European Security and Defence Policy from the end of the 1990s).

❑ Although there was a growth of new 'partnership' institutions between the USA and the EU, these did not eliminate tensions—rather they assisted with their management.

❑ The impact of 9/11 was substantial, but did not change everything in US–EU relations. Rather, it meant that existing issues were cast in a new light and given additional point. Longer-term processes such as globalization and new types of conflict were crystallized in 9/11 and later by Iraq.

❑ By the early 2000s, the tensions in US–EU relations caused by US policy makers' redefinition of their images, by linkages between political, economic, and security issues, and by underlying trends towards 'empire', 'alliance', and 'interdependence' were still apparent, but in radically changed conditions.

 MAJOR DEBATES AND THEIR IMPACT 12.1: US policies towards European integration

The 'Mars/Venus' debate of the early 2000s

The controversies centring around US and EU responses to the war on terror and the war in Iraq during 2002–4 generated debate not only in policy circles but also in academic analysis. One of the key figures in this debate was the American policy analyst Robert Kagan, who in 2003 published his book *Of Paradise and Power: America and Europe in the New World Order*. Kagan's argument was that there was a deep difference over the interpretation and the uses of power between the United States and Europe, and that this reflected long historical experience as well as current events. To put it simply, the United States had evolved with a strong orientation towards the use of 'hard' military power and a strong position both on sovereignty and national security, as the result of its geopolitical location, its industrial and technological development, and the growth of an official culture in which military force was a central means of implementing foreign policy. On the other side, Europe—best represented by the 'civilian power' promoted by the EU—had grown to focus on the use of 'soft power' and the building of institutions for the solving of international problems. This too reflected the relevant historical and cultural experiences: the disastrous history of the use of force in Europe up to 1945, and the conclusion drawn by ruling elites that military force was to be constrained and subjected to rigorous rules. But according to Kagan, it also effectively reflected the weakness of Europe, since if the EU or individual European countries had been able to match the USA in military terms, they would not have had to adopt this rationalization of their own inadequacies. This debate was of course centred on the war in Iraq, and it also adopted a sweeping view of both US and European positions—but how much can it be seen as reflecting a permanent underlying set of differences?

Conclusion

As noted in the Introduction, this chapter has explored one of the key relationships in which the USA has been involved since the end of the Second World War: the transatlantic relationship with the 'European integration project'. This is not a relationship with a single state, but with a densely institutionalized region, which has itself grown and become markedly more prominent in the world arena over the past half-century. American foreign policy makers have generally been consistent in their support for the integration project, but it has challenged US foreign policy in a number of important areas. The focus of the chapter has thus been on the ways in which US policy makers have developed images of the European Community (EC) and now the European Union (EU), on the challenges posed by European integration for US policy processes and the uses of US power, and on the ways in which these challenges have been met in the very different conditions of the Cold War and post-Cold War periods.

The chapter has shown that US foreign policy makers have consistently placed European integration at the core of their policies, but that this has not prevented persistent tensions, many of which express issues about the nature of US foreign policy itself and the US role in the world arena. We have seen that US policy makers have needed to develop an image of European integration, but that this has been made difficult by the nature of the integration process itself, by the 'stickiness' of US assumptions about the status and the role of the EC and then the EU, and by changes in the broader world arena, specifically those surrounding the end of the Cold War and the rise of globalization. We have also seen that US policy towards European integration has reflected the complex interaction of political, economic, and security forces, and that the shifting balance between these three elements has made US policy formation problematic. Finally, we have seen that underlying tendencies in US foreign policy, towards 'empire', 'alliance', and 'interdependence', have coexisted more or less easily in dealing with the European integration, and that whilst conflicts between the three elements have been especially clear during the first years of the new millennium this is not the first time that such conflicts have been seen. Such is the nature of US–EU relations that one can safely say it will not be the last.

 CONTROVERSIES 12.1: How has the US responded to European integration?

The US role in European integration: partnership, leadership, or hegemony?

This has been a continuous thread in the development of US–EU relations. US policy makers have found themselves constantly trying to balance their expectations about European dependence and the USA's right to exert its predominance against those that reflect the desire of Europeans to assert themselves—and of course, the Europeans can only really assert themselves against the USA, their 'most significant other'. This controversy also links to the key questions about the nature of power and its exercise that we have encountered at many points in the chapter.

The US adaptation to the development of European integration: adaptation or the pursuit of new dominance?

As the Europeans began to develop their own 'identity' and to strengthen their institutions during the 1980s, this meant that the Americans were forced to adjust. But this was quite a difficult process, because of the 'stickiness' both of images and of institutional cultures in the USA. As a result, during the late 1980s and the 1990s, US policies towards European integration went through a series of partial adjustments, with no overarching grand strategy. This was also affected by the range of global challenges in which US foreign policy became embroiled,

(continued)

CONTROVERSIES 12.1: (continued)

which in many cases deflected their attention from the EU. The George W. Bush administrations of the new millennium attempted to assert a new US predominance, but whilst this was possible in issues of 'hard power' and security, it was less possible in economic, cultural and humanitarian issues.

The US response to the European Union: cooperation or containment?

This is really a continuation of the 'controversies' above. The USA has pronounced its support for European integration from the start, and for the EU since it was established in the early 1990s. But many of the actions taken by US policy makers have accompanied that general support with a desire to contain the specific harm that a growing EU might do to US interests. Economically, this has meant vigorous use of the WTO to raise complaints against the EU; politically, it has meant the desire by many US leaders to contain the development of a 'European foreign policy', and to put the EU in a subordinate position; and in security affairs, it has led to considerable ambivalence about the development of a European Security and Defence Policy. Often, this ambivalence in US policies has led Washington to try and exploit 'special relationships' with EU member states such as the UK, and to pursue a kind of 'divide and rule' strategy either explicitly or implicitly.

The USA, the EU, and the aftermath of 9/11: unilateralism versus multilateralism?

One of the key contrasts that has been drawn between the USA and the EU since the early 1990s has been the alleged preference of US policy makers for unilateral solutions, and thus the contrast with the EU's search for multilateral solutions through a range of international organizations. In the aftermath of 9/11, and especially in the build-up to war in Iraq, this seemed an important distinction to draw, but the question is, how much of this contrast is permanent, and how much is it the product of particular circumstances? Do the EU and the USA really inhabit different 'worlds' of international relations, or are they more alike than they are often presented as being? Certainly, in the economic field, the EU has armed itself with the same range of weapons as the USA, and shows a tendency towards unilateral actions where its 'targets' are relatively weak; the USA, on the other hand, has stuck with multilateral rules for the most part, even where they threaten its short-term interests. Kagan (see Major debates and their impact 12.1) would certainly argue that the EU's apparent promotion of multilateral solutions to political and security problems is a rationalization of its own weakness (although he would also argue that the USA's preference for unilateralism is a reflection of perceived power). Events such as 9/11 and the Iraq War can be seen as those most likely to underline the differences, although it must not be forgotten that the war on terror covers a wide range of activities in which the EU has major strengths, such as international financial and judicial cooperation. It might thus show the EU's strength as well as its weaknesses, and be more challenging to US policy makers than apparently simple issues of military force.

? Questions

1. What motivated US support for the early stage of European integration?
2. What is the importance of John F. Kennedy's 1962 speech on Atlantic partnership?
3. Why were US–EC relations especially difficult in the early 1970s?
4. Why did the 1970s see a new pattern of interaction between political, economic, and security issues in US–EC relations?
5. What was the impact of the 'new cold war' during the early 1980s on US policies towards European integration?
6. What events in the late 1980s created concern in the USA about the future impact of European integration?
7. What role did US policy makers envisage for the EC at the end of the Cold War?

8. What impact has the enlargement of the EU had on US perceptions of the European integration process?

9. Why did American foreign policy makers initially feel that the war in former Yugoslavia was a matter for the EU, and why did they have to change their minds?

10. What effect did the changing agenda of global economic and social issues have on US policies towards the EU in the late 1990s, and why?

11. Has the war on terror strengthened or weakened US support for European integration?

12. Why was it said in the early 2000s that 'Americans are from Mars, Europeans from Venus'?

» Further Reading

There is a vast range of literature on the transatlantic relationship, both from an American and from a European standpoint. The following deal especially with the issues raised in this chapter.

Andrews, D. (ed.) (2005), *The Atlantic Alliance under Stress: US–European Relations after Iraq* (Cambridge: Cambridge University Press).

A strong collection of contributions from Americans and Europeans.

Bujajski, J., and Teleki, I. (2007), *Atlantic Bridges: America's New European Allies* (Lanham, Md.: Rowman and Littlefield).

Deals with the ways in which the new or newly liberated countries of central and eastern Europe relate both to the EU and to the USA.

Heller, F., and Gillingham, J. (eds.) (1996), *The United States and the Integration of Europe: Legacies of the Postwar Era* (New York: St Martin's Press).

Strong collection on the foundations of US policy towards the European integration project between 1945 and 1960.

Hocking, B., and Smith, M. (1997), *Beyond Foreign Economic Policy: The United States, the Single European Market and the Changing World Economy* (London: Cassell Pinter).

Explores American responses to the new challenge of the Single Market, and places this in the context of broader global trends.

Peterson, J., and Pollack, M. (eds.) (2003), *Europe, America, Bush: Transatlantic Relations in the Twenty-First Century* (London: Routledge).

Charts the controversies of the early 2000s with a particular focus on the ways in which 9/11 and Iraq feed into them.

Philippart, E., and Winand, P. (eds.) (2001), *Ever Closer Partnership: Policy-Making in US–EC Relations* (Brussels: PIE-Peter Lang).

Especially useful on the working of the New Transatlantic Agenda, but also on institutional and policy questions more generally.

Pollack, M., and Shaffer, G. (eds.) (2001), *Transatlantic Governance in the Global Economy* (Lanham, Md.: Rowman and Littlefield).

Major collection exploring the growth of institutions and multi-level politics in the transatlantic arena, including US policy responses.

Sloan, S. (2005), *NATO, the European Union, and the Atlantic Community: The Transatlantic Bargain Challenged*, 2nd edn. (Lanham, Md.: Rowman and Littlefield).

Places the US–EU relationship both into its historical context and into the context of security relations through NATO.

Smith, M., and Woolcock, S. (1993), *The United States and the European Community in a Transformed World* (London: Pinter for the Royal Institute of International Affairs).

Focuses on the nature of the transformations taking place in the early 1990s, and covers political, economic, and security dimensions.

Winand, P. (1993), *Eisenhower, Kennedy and the United States of Europe* (Basingstoke: Macmillan).

Substantial historical study of the ways in which US administrations dealt with European integration within their foreign policies between 1950 and 1963.

 Visit the Online Resource Centre that accompanies this book for web links to accompany each chapter, and a range of other resources: www.oxfordtextbooks.co.uk/orc/cox_stokes/

13 US foreign policy in Russia

Peter Rutland and Gregory Dubinsky

Chapter contents

Introduction

The end of the Cold War lifted the threat of nuclear annihilation and transformed the international security landscape. However, that historic shift also involved the collapse of the Soviet Union and its fragmentation into fifteen new independent states. The Russian Federation, which inherited half the population and 70 per cent of the territory of the former Soviet Union, was an unknown quantity. Would it become a friend and partner of the United States, a full and equal member of the community of democratic nations? Or would it slip back into a hostile, expansionary communist or nationalist power?

What would happen to the Soviet arsenal: its 27,000 nuclear warheads, and stocks of chemical and biological weapons? What would Moscow do to defend the interests of the 25 million ethnic Russians who were now living outside the boundaries of the Russian state? Would Russia follow the example of Slobodan Milosovic, who was fighting to carve a 'Greater Serbia' out of the former Yugoslavia?

There was no obvious answer to such questions in 1991. And even fifteen years after the onset of transition, there are still many uncertainties surrounding Russia's present condition and future trajectory, from its domestic political regime to its relations with its neighbours. It would take the US security establishment some time to adjust to a post-Cold War world, and to come up with a grand strategy to replace that of 'containing' the Soviet threat.

US–Russian relations have gone through several distinct phases since 1991. Initially, the hostility and mutual fear of the Cold War was replaced by a feeling of giddy cooperation, but that gradually eroded in the course of the 1990s. That was replaced by a sense of uncertainty about Russia's intentions, following Russia's hostile reaction to the US-led war over Kosovo in 1999 and the accession to power of Vladimir Putin later that year. In 2000–1 both the outgoing and incoming US presidential administration took a wait-and-see posture about the new Russian president. The terrorist attacks on 11 September 2001 led to a renewal of hope that a strategic alliance could be forged between Moscow and Washington. But this third phase was short-lived. Visions of partnership were dashed by the March 2003 invasion of Iraq and Russia's slide into authoritarianism, signalled by the arrest of oil magnate Mikhail Khodorkovsky in October 2003. Mutual recriminations during this fourth phase have led some to talk of a 'new cold war'.

In retrospect, it seems that the heady optimism of the early 1990s was unrealistic. At the same time, the notion of a 'new cold war' appears equally exaggerated. Despite differences of opinion between Russia and the USA—over the handling of regional issues in Iran, North Korea, and the former Soviet states—there continues to be substantial cooperation in areas of common interest, such as nuclear proliferation and the war on terror. The main uncertainty now revolves around the willingness of the United States to deal with a Russia that has an authoritarian political system and that is willing to act assertively in defence of its perceived national interests.

> **KEY QUOTES 13.1:** Condoleezza Rice on the post–Soviet power vacuum

The United States has found it exceedingly difficult to define its 'national interest' in the absence of Soviet power.

(Condoleezza Rice, writing in 2000, shortly before she became National Security Adviser)

The end of an era

The collapse of the Soviet Union on 25 December 1991 abruptly terminated a fifty-year-old struggle for global supremacy between the Soviet Union and the United States. That contest remained a 'Cold War' because nuclear weapons prevented the two superpowers from attacking each other directly. Washington's relationship with Moscow was focused on preventing nuclear war and containing the arms race, while also striving to limit Soviet expansionism in the third world.

The Soviet Union collapsed as a result of Mikhail Gorbachev's efforts to reform the archaic Soviet economy and political system. Historians argue over the extent to which Gorbachev was responding to internal causes, or was reacting to the new aggressive policies of President Ronald Reagan—such as support for the guerrillas fighting the Soviet occupation of Afghanistan and the ambitious 'Star Wars' missile defence programme.

There is also a lively debate over 'Who won the Cold War?' Most Americans see the United States as the clear victor. The Soviet collapse led to the triumph of American ideals of liberal democracy and market capitalism and left the USA as the unchallenged sole superpower. But many Russians believe that *both* sides won the Cold War, since it ended by mutual agreement, and because both countries benefited from the removal of the threat of nuclear annihilation. After all, it was primarily Moscow's initiatives that brought the confrontation to an end. Mikhail Gorbachev's 'New Thinking' in foreign policy led to the unilateral reduction of Soviet troops in eastern Europe and their complete withdrawal from Afghanistan. In this sense, the Cold War had effectively ended in 1989—at the December Malta summit of Gorbachev and President G. H. W. Bush, shortly after the fall of the Berlin Wall on 9 November. That was *two years* before the collapse of the Soviet Union. So the break-up of the USSR and the end of the Cold War can be seen as two different things.

The new understanding between Moscow and Washington paid dividends in August 1990, when Saddam Hussein invaded Kuwait. Secretary of State James Baker persuaded his Soviet counterpart Eduard Shevardnadze to support the US plan to threaten Hussein with military action if he did not withdraw his forces. The Soviet Union's refusal to use its United Nations Security Council veto to protect its old ally Iraq was a clear signal that the Cold War era of superpower confrontation was over.

The Bush administration supported Soviet President Mikhail Gorbachev to the very end and spurned contacts with Boris Yeltsin, the leader of the democratic opposition. Bush did not meet Yeltsin until July 1991, one month after he was elected president of the Russian Federation. The White House and particularly National Security Adviser Brent Scowcroft were the most wary of Yeltsin, while the Pentagon and CIA favoured closer contacts with him. Secretary of State James Baker was a canny but cautious realist, whose attention was focused on the Soviet nuclear arsenal and 500,000 troops still scattered across eastern Europe. In August 1991 hardliners launched an abortive coup in a desperate effort to maintain the Soviet Union. Power then shifted from Gorbachev to Yeltsin, who personally brokered the break-up of the Soviet Union in December 1991.

The USA was delighted to see the end of the Soviet Union, but fearful of its consequences. The dissolution of the Soviet Union and Yugoslavia triggered a number of bloody regional conflicts that needed containing. Above all, the USA was concerned to manage the dismantling of the Soviet nuclear arsenal and to prevent the proliferation of nuclear weapons to third countries or terrorist groups. Already in September 1991 President Bush unilaterally announced that the USA would destroy all its tactical battlefield nuclear weapons, and Gorbachev said the Soviet Union would do the same. Two US senators, Richard Lugar and Sam Nunn, took their own initiative and introduced a bill pledging $400 million to help pay for the dismantling of Soviet nuclear weapons. The Pentagon opposed the idea, but the Senate approved the money in November 1991. This, the Cooperative Threat Reduction programme, would turn out to be one of the most successful US security policies. By the end of the decade the USA had poured $5 billion into the project, helping to destroy nuclear materials and paying Russian nuclear scientists to deter them from selling their expertise abroad.

During 1992 the Bush administration focused on persuading Ukraine, Kazakhstan, and Belarus to give up the nuclear weapons that were located on their territory. In a May 1992 meeting in Lisbon the foreign ministers of those three countries pledged to give up their nuclear weapons. Kazakhstan's willingness to quickly disarm laid the foundation for good relations with the United States. Yeltsin's pro-Western foreign minister, Andrei Kozyrev, urged radical cuts in both sides' nuclear arsenals. Bush and Yeltsin signed the Strategic Arms Reduction Treaty START II in January 1993, under which they promised to reduce their arsenals to 3,000–3,500 strategic warheads each by 2003. Baker had some difficulty persuading the Pentagon to accept such large cuts. The Russians worried that they did not have the money to pay for dismantling the weapons. START II also committed both sides to completely eliminate multiple warheads on land-based missiles. (MIRVs or multiple-warhead missiles were considered destabilizing because there was an incentive to launch them pre-emptively in a crisis, before they could be destroyed on the ground by a single incoming warhead.) START II was ratified by the US Senate in January 1996, but not accepted by the Russian State Duma until April 2000 (with additional qualifications).

Russia experienced a profound economic crisis in the spring of 1992 as the government introduced radical reforms known as 'shock therapy'. Production plummeted while goods disappeared from the shelves and prices spiralled. The Bush administration was criticized for doing nothing as Russia fell into chaos. Former Republican President Richard Nixon wrote a memorandum entitled 'Who lost Russia?' Democratic candidate Bill Clinton talked about the need for a new Marshall Plan—even as he attacked Bush's preoccupation with foreign policy. In response Bush announced in April 1992 a $24 billion international aid package, including $5 billion from the USA. But most of that was money already committed: the administration believed that Russia was too chaotic to make use of a serious influx of funds. Rather than aid, the US Treasury's main concern was the Soviet Union's $65 billion international debts. Russia eventually agreed to take full responsibility for paying back the loans.

KEY POINTS

- ❏ In December 1991, the Soviet Union ceased to exist as a geopolitical entity, and with its demise the post-Second World War central organizing principle for US foreign policy—containing the Soviet threat—no longer existed.
- ❏ During the break-up of the Soviet empire, a revolutionary figure named Boris Yeltsin came to the forefront of Russian politics and promised to lead his new country to a better and brighter future in cooperation with the West.
- ❏ The United States sought to limit the threats posed by the immediate transition, especially by persuading the newly independent states to relinquish their nuclear arsenals.

Bill and Boris

Bill Clinton took office in January 1993 with high hopes that a partnership with Russia could be the linchpin for America's role in the post-Cold War world. The goal was to transform Russia into what

Clinton called a 'market democracy', while integrating it into international institutions. Clinton was influenced by the 'democratic peace' theory, which was experiencing an academic revival. It was in

CONTROVERSIES 13.1: Debates in US – Russia relations

Building market democracy in Russia

Yes: Russia had a good chance of becoming a stable market economy with democratic political institutions, and the United States had a responsibility to do all it could to bring that about.

No: American interference in Russia's domestic politics and economics was bound to fail and cause a negative reaction from Russian elites.

NATO enlargement

Yes: NATO is a defensive alliance and Russia had nothing to fear from its enlargement into eastern Europe.

No: By expanding NATO the Western powers were effectively excluding Russia from the most important international security institution of post-Cold War Europe.

Relations with Putin

Yes: Russia is a great power due to its geographical presence in Eurasia, its seat in the United Nations Security Council, and its role as an energy exporter. The USA has to establish a good working relationship with whoever is in power in Moscow.

No: Putin is a dictatorial leader whose authoritarian rule will only bring instability to Russia. He cannot be trusted as a reliable partner.

America's best interests to ensure that Russia became a democracy, since democracies do not go to war with each other.

Clinton appointed his former Oxford roommate, Russia expert Strobe Talbott, point man for relations with Russia. (Talbott served as counsellor and then Deputy Secretary of State from 1993 to 2000.) Talbott's close personal relationship with Clinton meant that Secretaries of State Warren Christopher and Madeleine Albright had a less prominent role in USA–Russia relations than one might have expected. National Security Adviser Anthony Lake was sceptical about the scope for democratic transition in Russia, but likewise deferred to Talbott.

Yeltsin and Clinton seemed to hit it off at their first meeting in April 1993, backslapping and bearhugging. Both sides declared their readiness to create a 'dynamic and effective Russo-American partnership'. Clinton promised a financial aid package of $1.6 billion (half aid and half credits), predicated on the assumption that Yeltsin was introducing reforms

that would create a market democracy. Clinton visited Russia in January 1994, and by the end of his term the two men had met no less than eighteen times. The 'Bill and Boris' relationship was in full bloom. Clinton was fully aware of Yeltsin's idiosyncrasies, telling Talbott on one occasion that 'Yeltsin drunk was better than most of the alternatives sober'.

The USA clung to this policy despite a series of events indicating that all was not well, such as Yeltsin's shelling of the opposition-controlled parliament in October 1993 and the invasion of the breakaway province of Chechnya in December 1994. New York University Professor Stephen Cohen ridiculed the Clinton administration's approach as a 'failed crusade' that strove to remake Russia in America's image. Russia expert Dmitri Simes argued that the United States was mistakenly treating Russia as if it were a 'defeated enemy'. Many Russians came to blame the chaos of the early 1990s on the capitalist reforms that they believed were forced on Russia at America's insistence.

KEY QUOTES 13.2: The spinach treatment

Behind the façade of friendship, Clinton administration officials expected the Kremlin to accept the United States' definition of Russia's national interests. Talbott and his aides referred to it as the spinach treatment.

(Dmitri Simes, President of the Nixon Institute, 2007)

While Talbott handled diplomatic and security issues, economic relations were handled by Larry Summers and David Lipton at the US Treasury. They focused their attention on macroeconomic stabilization and debt management. Despite earlier pronouncements, by 2001 the USA had sent only about $1 billion in aid to Russia, and two-thirds of that was spent on nuclear-weapon-related programmes, managed by the Pentagon and Department of Energy. The main vehicle for influencing Russian economic policy was International Monetary Fund loans, tied to the introduction of specific reform policies. At the suggestion of the Russians, a special commission was created between Prime Minister Viktor Chernomyrdin and Vice President Al Gore to promote economic cooperation. It also handled some sensitive strategic issues such as Russian missile sales to Iran, cooperation in space launches, and a plan for the USA to process plutonium that had been removed from Russia nuclear warheads for use in civilian reactors.

The 1990s reforms produced few concrete results for US business interests. The privatization programme mostly excluded foreign buyers, and Russia took in only $3.7 billion in foreign direct investment over the decade. The European Union was Russia's main economic partner, accounting for more than half of Russia's foreign trade, while the USA accounted for less than 5 per cent.

After the communist victory in the December 1995 State Duma election, Yeltsin appointed former foreign intelligence chief Yevgenii Primakov as Foreign Minister. Primakov tried to move Russia away from its dependency on the United States, sometimes talking about a strategic triad of Russia, China, and India. But Primakov realized that the USA was the dominant power, and in practice he effected only minor course corrections in the Moscow–Washington relationship. (He even folded in the face of US determination to enlarge NATO.)

Boris Yeltsin faced the daunting task of winning re-election in June 1996. He was deeply unpopular.

The war in Chechnya was ongoing, and the economy was in its sixth year of decline. Many of his advisers urged him to cancel the election, but he went ahead with the vote and managed to win a second term, thanks to a massive media campaign and an influx of IMF loans, used to pay off wage and pension arrears. Washington breathed a huge sigh of relief. A cancelled election—or a communist victory—would have been the end of the road for Clinton's democratic transition paradigm.

Russia was not yet out of the woods, however. The 1997 Asian financial crisis triggered a slump in world oil prices, hitting Russia's export earnings and government revenue. A growing fiscal deficit was covered by reckless external borrowing. Despite a last-minute $22 billion IMF rescue package, the ruble crashed in August 1998, losing 75 per cent of its value. The government went into default on its debts. The crisis forced the resignation of Yeltsin's new liberal Prime Minister, Sergei Kirienko, and his replacement by the conservative Primakov. The crisis shattered any illusions that Russia was in transition to stable market democracy.

KEY POINTS

- ❑ The relationship forged by the two leaders, Bill Clinton and Boris Yeltsin, was cemented by what Clinton saw as Yeltsin's commitment to reforms to modernize the Russian state and economy. The two men thought American assistance and expertise could transform Russia into a 'market democracy'.

- ❑ The reforms failed, and as Russia's economy shrank the quality of life for many Russians plummeted. The economy was dealt a further blow by the August 1998 financial crash.

- ❑ Yeltsin did manage to win re-election in 1996, which enabled the USA to continue in its commitment to building democracy in Russia.

> **KEY QUOTES 13.3:** Russia's democratic prospects

A true and lasting transition to normalcy, democracy, and free markets in Russia is neither inevitable nor impossible.

It is an open question.

(Secretary of State Madeleine Albright, October 1998)

NATO enlargement

The main problem in the USA–Russia relationship was the US plan to expand the North Atlantic Treaty Organization (NATO) into central Europe. NATO had been created in 1949 to deter the Soviet military threat, so Moscow argued that since the Soviet Union and its military alliance, the Warsaw Pact, had dissolved in 1991, NATO should follow suit. Yeltsin withdrew Russian troops from the Baltic countries and eastern Europe—but only after the USA promised funds to build housing for officers relocated to Russia. The USA radically cut its 300,000 troops stationed in Europe, but did not want to dismantle NATO—which it saw not only as a highly successful defensive alliance, but also a vehicle for projecting stability into eastern Europe.

Initially, the USA had hoped that the European Union (EU) would take the lead in integrating the former socialist countries. But it was clear that preparing the central European countries for full EU membership would take many years. A sense of urgency was introduced by the first-place finish of the semi-fascist Liberal Democratic Party, led by Vladimir Zhirinovsky, in the State Duma elections in December 1993. This prompted Clinton to approve NATO enlargement in Prague in January 1994 ('not if, but when'). In September 1994 the enlargement plans were published, leading Yeltsin to warn of a 'cold peace' in a speech in Budapest. Countries that were not candidates for membership in the immediate future would be offered a Partnership for Peace cooperation plan.

The year 1995 saw renewed fighting in Bosnia, culminating in NATO's airpower intervention on the side of the Bosnian Muslims and Croats. The US-brokered November 1995 Dayton Accords brought peace to Bosnia, and Russia was invited to send peacekeepers to join NATO's Implementation Force there.

Clinton delayed NATO expansion until after Yeltsin's hotly contested election battle in June 1996. In October 1996 Clinton set a deadline of 1999 for the first wave of NATO enlargement. In December 1996 the hard-line Madeleine Albright replaced Warren Christopher as Secretary of State. Countries joining the alliance would receive a cast-iron security guarantee: Article V of the NATO Charter pledges all signatories to come to the aid of a fellow member under attack. In July 1997 NATO's Madrid summit invited Poland, Czech Republic, and Hungary to join the alliance. The three Baltic countries were worried that they were being excluded, so in January 1998 the USA signed the Baltic Charter pledging to help them in their bid for NATO membership. In April 1998 the Senate approved NATO expansion by 80 to 19. On 12 March 1999 Poland, Hungary, and the Czech Republic joined NATO, bringing the alliance to 19 countries.

Moscow was deeply offended by the alliance's expansion, which stoked fears of 'capitalist encirclement' among communists and nationalists. In protest at NATO enlargement, the State Duma refused to

> ## 66   KEY QUOTES 13.4: 'We had a deal'
>
> I told Yeltsin that if he would agree to NATO expansion and the NATO–Russian partnership, I would make a commitment not to station troops or missiles in the new member countries prematurely, and to support Russian membership in the new G-8, the World Trade Organization, and other international organizations. We had a deal.
>
> (President Bill Clinton, at a meeting in Helsinki in March 1997)

ratify the START II treaty. In September 1996 Clinton and Yeltsin did initial a Comprehensive Nuclear Test Ban Treaty (including a ban on underground tests), but the US Senate rejected the treaty in 1999. In 1997 Russia started deploying a new intercontinental missile, the SSX-27 Topol-M, and introduced a new National Security Concept—one that seemed to show a greater willingness to be the first to use nuclear weapons.

In order to mitigate Russia's feeling of exclusion, in May 1997 the NATO–Russia Founding Act created a Permanent Joint Council in Brussels. Also, in June 1997, Yeltsin was invited to attend the Group of Seven (G7) annual meeting of leaders of the foremost developed democracies. Russia would be granted full membership in the G8 in June 2002, one of the few Western organizations it was allowed to join. There was no progress with Russia's application to enter the World Trade Organization (WTO), which it commenced in 1993. Russia did join the Council of Europe in 1996, where its actions in Chechnya were sharply criticized. It continued as a member of the Organization for Security and Cooperation in Europe, which tried ineffectively to resolve the 'frozen conflicts' in Moldova, Georgia, and Azerbaijan.

For Clinton, NATO enlargement was an insurance policy that protected US interests in case Russia 'went bad'. National Security Adviser Lake favoured rapid NATO expansion, while Talbott was more cautious, fearing a hostile Russian response. But the Kremlin realized that it was powerless to stop the alliance, and tried to make the best of a bad situation. US–Russian relations soon faced the most severe test of the entire post-Soviet period, the Kosovo crisis.

> ### KEY POINTS
>
> ❑ The Russians were severely disappointed by the US decision to expand the NATO alliance into countries that had once been part of the Soviet Union's Warsaw Pact security organization.
> ❑ To placate Russia it was allowed to join the G7 group of leading democracies, and the 1997 NATO–Russia Founding Act created a Permanent Joint Council in Brussels.
> ❑ In March 1999, Poland, Hungary, and the Czech Republic joined NATO.

The Kosovo crisis

On 24 March 1999, just two weeks after the three new members joined the alliance, NATO planes started bombing Yugoslavia. The West wanted President Slobodan Milosovic to accept international peace-keepers to halt violence in the rebellious province of Kosovo. The bombing commenced as Prime Minister

Primakov was flying to the USA to ask for more financial aid. Primakov ordered his aircraft to turn around mid-Atlantic and head back to Russia: a step that became symbolic of a new chill in US–Russian relations. Russia also withdrew from participation in the NATO Permanent Joint Council. Russia was incensed that the United States was using brute force to advance its political agenda in Europe—over Russian objections.

Moscow saw itself as having close historical ties with the Serbs. But in reality the relationship had been dormant since the Second World War, and in practice Moscow had little interest in tying itself to the sinking ship of Slobodan Milosovic. During the run-up to the bombing campaign Moscow's policy vacillated from one of limited support for the NATO pressure on Milosovic to vocal opposition. When the opportunity arose to play the peacemaker in June 1999, Moscow seized the chance. Ex-Prime Minister Chernomyrdin was sent to Belgrade to deliver the bad news—that NATO was preparing to launch a ground invasion, and Milosovic could not expect any more Russian support. If Milosovic agreed to withdraw his troops from Kosovo, he could ensure Russian participation in the military occupation of Kosovo, and preserve Yugoslavia's formal sovereignty over the province. In a curious footnote to the crisis, several hundred Russian peacekeepers drove down from Bosnia to seize the Kosovo airport before advancing British troops arrived. An armed clash was only averted thanks to the cool head of the British commander at the scene.

KEY POINTS

❏ The US decision to use military force against Yugoslavia met strong opposition from Moscow. The latter saw it as an unjustified use of force in its sphere of influence, and felt embarrassment at its seeming impotence in the face of US military might.

The 'Great Game' revisited

The USA had a clear strategic interest in securing the viability of the newly independent states, and preventing their possible reabsorption into a revived Soviet Union. US advisers and aid flowed into the region. The first priority was securing the removal of nuclear weapons from the non-Russian states. With that task accomplished, the Clinton administration turned to promoting the same kind of transition to 'market democracy' that was being attempted in Russia. The task was straightforward in the three Baltic states, but was much more challenging in the other countries, which had weak states and weaker economies, and lacked a tradition of self-rule. Civil wars raged in Tajikistan, Moldova, Azerbaijan, and Georgia, conflicts in which Russia was heavily involved. Former Communist Party leaders stayed on as authoritarian presidents in every Central Asian country except Kyrgyzstan, where a reformist president came to power.

The oil and gas reserves of the Caspian basin were seen as the key to securing the long-term development of the newly independent states. Building pipelines to export Caspian oil and gas through Georgia and Turkey would increase the flow of hydrocarbons to world markets, while containing the influence of Iran and Russia. Moscow regarded the region as part of its exclusive sphere of influence, and despite US assurances it saw the rivalry for Caspian oil as a zero-sum game in which US advances would come at Russian expense.

Azerbaijan and Kazakhstan opened the doors to Western investors. In 1993 Texaco (now Chevron) entered Kazakhstan to develop the giant Tengiz field, and through the Caspian Pipeline Consortium built a new export pipeline to the Russian Black Sea port of Novorossiisk. (Russia subsequently delayed the planned expansion of the pipeline's capacity.) In September 1994 BP signed 'the contract of the century' with Azerbaijan to develop some offshore fields in the Caspian. Production started in 1997. BP wanted to build a 1,100-mile export pipeline from Baku through

Tbilisi to Ceyhan on Turkey's southern coast. A complicating factor was the 1992–4 war over the disputed province of Nagorno-Karabakh, which left 15 per cent of Azerbaijan's territory in Armenian hands. The Armenian-American lobby persuaded the US Congress to enact section 907 of the Freedom Support Act, effective January 1993, which barred direct US aid to the Azerbaijani government so long as it maintained a blockade and state of war with Armenia. (President Bush lifted section 907 in January 2002, in return for Azerbaijan's cooperation in the war on terror.) Work started on the BTC pipeline in 2002 and it became operational in 2006.

Energy exports brought strong economic growth to Azerbaijan and Kazakhstan, though democracy is lacking in both countries, and Azerbaijan's stand-off with Armenia remains unresolved. The West would also like to export Kazakh oil and Turkmen gas by building pipelines across the Caspian Sea to Baku. But Russia used a dispute over the legal status of the Caspian to block plans for an undersea pipeline. In the meantime, Central Asian oil and gas must be exported through Russian pipelines (although Kazakhstan has already completed one export pipeline to China).

Under the Partnership for Peace programme, NATO held joint exercises in Uzbekistan in 1998, followed by extensive military assistance programmes in Georgia and Azerbaijan. The latter countries looked to Western help to regain control over breakaway regions that had established de facto independence with Russian military support. Incursions by Islamic guerrillas into Uzbekistan and Kyrgyzstan in 1999–2001 threatened the stability of those regimes, and stimulated Russia into a more proactive security role in the region. China also became involved, through the Shanghai Five, a multilateral security framework that with the addition of Uzbekistan became the Shanghai Cooperation Organization (SCO) in 2001. In recent years, US relations with some Central Asian states, especially Uzbekistan, have faltered in the face of human rights violations and political crackdowns.

For most of the 1990s Ukraine showed considerable enthusiasm for closer ties with NATO and the EU, but corruption and economic stagnation limited the scope for real reform and closer Western ties. President Leonid Kuchma, who came into office in 1996, tried to follow a balanced course between Russia and the West, aware of Ukraine's dependence on Russian gas imports and the presence of 12 million ethnic Russians in east Ukraine. The scandal which erupted in 2000 after the murder of crusading journalist Heorhy Gongadze damaged Kuchma's credibility in the West, while Moscow remained loyally supportive.

KEY POINTS

- ❏ The United States was quick to establish a diplomatic and economic presence in the new states of the Caucasus and Central Asia. This paid dividends in the form of lucrative commercial contracts to develop oil and gas fields in the region.
- ❏ Russia resented the projection of US influence into what it regarded as its own sphere of influence and tried to block US initiatives.
- ❏ The rise of the Shanghai Cooperation Organization, a multilateral security framework including China and Russia, has dealt a blow to US influence in Central Asia.

A new face in the Kremlin—and the White House

Fighting broke out again in Chechnya in August 1999, which had been de facto independent since the withdrawal of Russian troops in 1996. That was followed by several terrorist apartment bombings in Moscow a month later. Yeltsin appointed as Prime Minister Vladimir Putin, a seventeen-year KGB veteran who was heading the Federal Security Service. Putin launched a second full-scale invasion of Chechnya. Yeltsin resigned on New Year's Eve and appointed Putin 'acting president'. That cleared the way for Putin to win election as president in March 2000.

The United States watched these developments with resigned detachment. Washington no longer thought it could influence the outcome of Russian elections. Moscow was looking increasingly irrelevant to global affairs, saddled as it was by economic instability, corruption, and political instability. Russia was seen as incapable of providing domestic order, still less projecting power abroad.

Putin was an unknown quantity to Western leaders. His KGB background and ruthless prosecution of the war in Chechnya gave cause for concern. On the other hand, in personal meetings he impressed European leaders with his charm and intelligence. In his public statements, Putin signalled that he was well aware of Russia's debilitated condition. While moving quickly to restore the Kremlin's control over Russian society, Putin realized that integration within the global economy was essential to rebuild Russian state power. Europe's economic strength and America's military muscle left Russia with no choice but to cooperate with these twin powers.

Arms control was the main item on the agenda during President Clinton's farewell visit to Moscow in June 2000. The USA pushed for modifications in the 1972 Anti-Ballistic Missile Defense (ABM) treaty so it could begin testing a national missile defence system (NMD). Washington argued it needed NMD to counter a possible nuclear strike from a rogue state like Iraq or North Korea. Moscow was sceptical, fearing a hidden strategic agenda. Successful deployment of NMD would lock in US global dominance. Also, the Kremlin worried that the number of Russian nuclear weapons would steadily diminish due to lack of funds for maintenance, perhaps to the point at which they would be unable to guarantee second-strike retaliation against a US first strike. The US Senate approved the development of theatre missile defence in March 1999. In a bid to head off NMD, Putin persuaded the State Duma to ratify START II, signed in 1993, which they dutifully did in April 2000.

Clinton could not offer deep cuts in strategic missiles in return for Russian approval of NMD: influential Senate Republican Jesse Helms made it clear that he would block approval of any such treaty. Clinton signed two minor agreements: to cut each country's weapons-grade plutonium reserves, and to create a joint early warning centre in Moscow to reduce the risks of an accidental nuclear launch. (The centre never opened.) After the disappointing June summit, US–Russian relations went into a stall as the Russians waited to see who would succeed Clinton.

USA–Russia relations were not a prominent issue in the November 2000 election campaign, although the Republicans attacked the Clinton administration for its naive and costly pro-Yeltsin policy. For example, in October 2000 it was revealed that Russia had agreed to terminate arms deliveries to Iran by 1999 in a confidential deal struck with Vice-President Al Gore back in 1995. Presidential candidate Bush denounced Russia's pervasive corruption—in one presidential debate he even charged former Prime Minister Chernomyrdin with pocketing Western loan money. In an autumn 2000 essay in *Foreign Affairs* Condoleezza Rice, Bush's top foreign policy adviser, laid out a blunt assessment of the Clinton-era Russia policy, in a section entitled 'Russian weakness'.

❝ KEY QUOTES 13.5: Time for a new approach

The Clinton administration's embrace of Yeltsin and those who were thought to be reformers around him has failed . . . Support for democracy and economic reform became support for Yeltsin. His agenda became the American agenda. The United States certified that reform was taking place where it was not, continuing to disburse money from the International Monetary Fund in the absence of any evidence of serious change. The realities in Russia simply did not accord with the administration's script about Russian economic reform . . . There is no longer a consensus in America or Europe on what to do next with Russia. Frustrated expectations and 'Russia fatigue' are direct consequences of the 'happy talk' in which the Clinton administration engaged . . . U.S. policy must concentrate on the important security agenda with Russia. First, it must recognize that American security is threatened less by Russia's strength than by its weakness and incoherence.

(Condoleezza Rice, Bush's top foreign policy adviser, November 2000)

> **KEY QUOTES 13.6:** Bush's impression of Putin

I found a man who realizes his future lies with the West, not the East, that we share common security concerns, primarily Islamic fundamentalism, that he understands missiles could affect him just as much as us. On the other hand he doesn't want to be diminished by America.

(President George W. Bush, talking of Vladimir Putin in July 2001)

US–Russian relations did not get off to a good start with the new Bush administration. Until the two leaders met in Slovenia in June 2001 it appeared that Washington was assuming that Moscow was not a serious player on the global stage. Condoleezza Rice, Bush's national security adviser, argued that 'It would be foolish in the extreme to share defenses with Moscow as it either leaks or deliberately transfers weapons technologies to the very states against which America is defending.' In a February 2001 interview in *Le Figaro*, Rice commented that 'I believe Russia is a threat to the West in general and to our European allies in particular.'

As the USA was ignoring Moscow, Putin was flexing his diplomatic muscles. In July 2000 on his way to the G8 summit in Okinawa Putin stopped off in Pyongyang and tried to pull off a diplomatic coup by securing a pledge from North Korea to discontinue its missile programme—a 'pledge' it later denied. Iranian President Muhammad Khatami visited Russia in March 2001 to discuss arms sales, and Putin reiterated Russia's intention to help complete the long-stalled Bushehr nuclear power plant. Putin also stepped up military and political cooperation with China. A huge scandal erupted following the February 2001 arrest of FBI agent Robert Hanssen, who had spied for the Russians for fifteen years. In response, the USA ejected fifty Russian diplomats: the largest number of expulsions since 1986. The Russians reacted by expelling an equivalent number of American officials.

It was not until June 2001 that the two leaders finally met, in Ljubljana, Slovenia. President Bush famously 'looked the man in his eye' and 'was able to get a sense of his soul'. Bush said, 'I am convinced that he and I can build a relationship of mutual respect and candor', and promised support for Russia's entry into the WTO. Putin said he and Bush had forged a 'very high level of trust', and referred to the American president as a 'partner' and 'a nice person to talk to'. But the drama and sense of historical importance that characterized the past two presidential relationships was gone; in the new century, Russia simply did not capture the focus of the US strategic mind. The Ljubljana summit did prepare the ground for closer US–Russian cooperation. And then came 11 September.

KEY POINTS

- ❑ The ailing economy, the war in Chechnya, and the weakness of the state were the priorities on Vladimir Putin's agenda as he assumed power in 1999.
- ❑ President George W. Bush saw Russia as in a weakened state, and relations with Moscow were not a priority for the new administration.
- ❑ The United States and Russia attempted to find common ground on arms control, but Putin was opposed to the US national missile defence effort.

A strategy for a New World

The terrorist attacks on the World Trade Towers and the Pentagon had a major impact on US–Russian relations. Putin was the first leader to telephone Bush with condolences and an unequivocal condemnation of the terrorist act. Putin, still embroiled in the second Chechen war, saw 9/11 as powerful vindication of his warnings about the threat of militant Islam.

Putin decided to share intelligence and aid Washington's campaign against the Taliban regime in Afghanistan, despite opposition from some in the Russian military. According to some reports, Putin only agreed to US bases in Central Asia after Uzbek President Islam Karimov said he would cooperate with the Americans whatever Moscow's position. Russia was not pleased by the prospect of an indefinite US military presence in the region. After the defeat of the Taliban, the USA was able to forge a viable coalition government for Afghanistan in the Bonn conference, without Russian interference. Russia declined to send peacekeepers, in light of its role in the Afghanistan War. In August 2003 NATO took over the International Security Assistance Force in Afghanistan—the alliance's first deployment outside Europe. Some Russian foreign policy elites thought that 11 September would weaken the US proclivity for unilateral action by demonstrating America's vulnerability. In this they were sorely mistaken.

Putin's visit to the presidential ranch in Crawford, Texas, in November 2001 symbolized the return of the feel-good factor in US–Russian relations, but failed to produce any specific rewards for Moscow. The USA and Russia released a joint statement declaring that the Cold War legacy had been overcome and announcing that 'neither country regards the other as an enemy or threat'.

At Crawford, Bush promised to ask Congress to lift the 1974 Jackson–Vanik amendment, which required Russia to go through annual vetting of its emigration policies to maintain normal trade relations with the USA. (But Congress did not budge.) Hopes that the summit would produce some kind of deal to bridge the gap between the two sides on NMD were dashed. The USA was now suggesting that the whole concept of formal treaties defining strategic arsenals was an irrelevant relic of the Cold War. In December 2001, Secretary of State Colin Powell travelled to Moscow to report that the USA would withdraw from the ABM treaty in six months' time. Putin's response was surprisingly muted: he merely stated that Russian security was not threatened by the development. In return for Putin's acquiescence, in May 2002 Bush signed the Strategic Offensive Weapons Reduction Treaty in Moscow, under which each side promised to cut its strategic weapons from 6,000 warheads to 1,700–2,200 over ten years. But the treaty, unlike START II, did not mandate the destruction of warheads and had no on-site verification procedures. It was ratified by the State Duma in May 2003.

It still looked as if a strategic partnership based on mutual security interests might be a realistic goal. The May 2002 Rome summit saw the creation of a new NATO–Russia Council (19 plus 1) to give Russia a new voice in the alliance. In November 2002 the NATO summit in Prague invited Estonia, Latvia, Lithuania, Bulgaria, Romania, Slovakia, and Slovenia to join. Those seven countries subsequently entered NATO in March 2004, and five of them joined the European Union alongside Poland, Hungary, and the Czech Republic in May 2004. (Bulgaria and Romania joined in January 2007.) Russia's relations with Poland, Estonia, and Latvia remain fractious. As of 2007 Russia still did not have ratified border treaties with Estonia and Latvia. The Baltic countries would probably not have been allowed into the EU had they not already been in NATO, because the EU would have been wary of the unresolved security issues with Russia.

❝ KEY QUOTES 13.7: Partners in the war on terror

We affirm our determination to meet the threats to peace in the 21st century. Among these threats are terrorism, the new horror of which was vividly demonstrated by the evil crimes of September 11 . . . We have agreed that the current levels of our nuclear forces do not reflect the strategic realities of today. . . . We support the building of a European-Atlantic community whole, free, and at peace, excluding no one, and respecting the independence, sovereignty and territorial integrity of all nations.

(Joint US – Russian statement after the presidential summit in Crawford, Texas, November 2001)

> **KEY QUOTES 13.8:** Relations cool

When they met in Moscow in mid-2002, President Bush and President Putin could justly claim that they had created a bilateral relationship marked by greater mutual confidence, greater symmetry of goals and expectations, and greater practical cooperation than Russia and the United States had ever enjoyed. And they could count on far greater domestic support for such cooperation than we had seen before. But it didn't last.

(Stephen Sestanovich, former US diplomat, to the House Foreign Affairs Committee in May 2007)

The USA even grew interested in Russia as a possible source of energy supplies. The fact that fifteen of the nineteen 11 September hijackers were Saudis raised doubts about the political stability of Saudi Arabia, the linchpin of US energy policy. Perhaps Russia, the world's no. 2 oil exporter, could be used to break the OPEC stranglehold on the global oil market. Russian oil output had recovered since 1998, accounting for half the increase in world oil supply between 1998 and 2004.

US business interests were also bullish. Since 1999, the Russian economy had been growing strongly, boosted by the rise in the world oil price. The oligarchs who controlled most of Russia's oil industry were looking for Western partners. In September 2003 the TNK oil company merged with BP, and Mikhail Khodorkovsky's Yukos, Russia's largest oil corporation, seemed to be preparing for a merger with Exxon. It was argued that the oil oligarchs were a new, pro-Western elite that would take control of Russia once Putin, a transitional post-Yeltsin figure, had stepped down. Khodorkovsky himself promoted such a scenario, and he became a well-known figure in Washington.

In this new spirit of cooperation, a joint US–Russian Energy Working Group met in Washington in April 2002, and an energy summit convened in Houston in October 2002. Russian producers hoped for access to the US market, and there was talk of creating a US–Russian Strategic Energy Reserve, whereby the USA would pay for reservoirs of Russian oil that could be released in the event of a global market squeeze.

KEY POINTS

❑ Putin's support for the USA in the wake of 11 September revived hopes for a strategic partnership between Russia and the United States.

❑ Presidents Bush and Putin managed to strike up a warm personal relationship at their summit meetings in Slovenia and in Crawford, Texas, in 2001.

A reversal of course

The tide of USA–Russia relations turned decisively for the worse in the course of 2003, for three reasons: the US-led war in Iraq; Putin's crackdown on political opposition; and the wave of 'colour revolutions' that brought regime change to three post-Soviet states.

The looming Iraq War was a major challenge for Putin. In November 2002 Russia reluctantly accepted United Nations Resolution 1441 forcing Iraq to accept weapons inspectors. On 5 March 2003 the leaders of France, Germany, and Russia publicly stated they would block UN approval for war against Iraq. The USA went ahead with the invasion anyway, and after the conquest of Baghdad Secretary Rice decided to 'punish France, ignore Germany and forgive Russia'. The fact that the USA went ahead with the invasion despite the warnings from international leaders was taken in Moscow as demonstration that the US administration was a loose cannon and an unreliable ally. Russia was also aggrieved that it lost $8 billion that Iraq owed for past arms deliveries and its old contracts to develop Iraqi oil fields.

Revelations in 2002 of Iran's secret nuclear enrichment programme led to renewed pressure from the USA for sanctions against Tehran. Moscow agreed with the USA that Iran should not acquire nuclear weapons, but was firmly opposed to sanctions and wanted to complete construction of Iran's Bushehr reactor for commercial reasons. Since 2005 Moscow has been pushing a compromise under which it would supply fuel for Bushehr but reprocess the spent fuel back in Russia.

In 2003 Putin moved against the ambitious oligarch Mikhail Khodorkovsky—the richest man in Russia, with an estimated net worth of $16 billion. The arrest of several Yukos executives in July was followed by the detention of Khodorkovsky himself in October. He was sentenced to eight years' imprisonment on charges of tax evasion and fraud. Khodorkovsky's arrest was connected to the upcoming December 2003 State Duma elections. Khodorkovsky was funding parties across the political spectrum. A victory for the opposition in the parliamentary election could serve as a launch-pad for a candidate who could challenge Putin for the presidency in the March 2004 election. After Khodorkovsky's arrest, the pro-Kremlin United Russia Party won a sweeping victory in the Duma election. In September 2004, in the wake of the Beslan school siege, Putin announced the abolition of direct elections for regional governors. A new law on political parties made it even more difficult for opposition groups to enter parliament. Russia's return to a centralized, authoritarian system of power seemed complete. The US human rights group Freedom House downgraded Russia from 'free' to 'partly free' that same year.

Meanwhile, Putin was moving to extend Kremlin control over the Russian economy. Yukos assets were seized for tax arrears and sold off to state-owned Rosneft. The independent oil company Sibneft was forced to merge with state-owned Gazprom. Putin oversaw the creation of a network of state-owned corporations in energy and engineering and appointed Kremlin officials to chair their boards. Foreign oil companies were forced to give up majority control in the handful of joint ventures that had been allowed to start in the 1990s.

In November 2003 a US-backed opposition movement swept Mikheil Saakashvili to power in Georgia's 'Rose Revolution'. That set off alarm bells in the Kremlin, which perceived a US plot to encircle Russia's borders with pro-Western governments. The same month a last-minute US intervention derailed a Russian plan for a settlement between Moldova and the breakaway province of Transnistria. In response, Putin dragged his feet in withdrawing troops from Georgia and Moldova.

In March 2004 veteran diplomat Sergei Lavrov replaced Igor Ivanov as Foreign Minister: he reportedly has testy relations with Secretary Rice. In his May 2004 State of the Union Address, Putin warned Western groups not to meddle in Russia's domestic politics. A new law was introduced in November 2005 cracking down on foreign-financed NGOs. (The US Peace Corps had already been expelled from Russia in December 2002.) In an angry speech after the Beslan tragedy in September 2004, Putin publicly referred to Western threats against Russia, for the first time since 2001. 'We showed weakness,' Putin said, 'and weak people are beaten.'

Putin's clumsy efforts to influence the Ukrainian presidential election of November 2004 backfired, helping to spark an 'Orange Revolution' that replicated the victory of pro-Western forces in Georgia the previous year. That was followed by a 'Tulip Revolution' in Kyrgyzstan in March 2005, ousting President Askar Akayev. Russia's testy reaction to these developments; military incidents in Georgia; a series of diplomatic confrontations with Estonia; and a sharp increase in Russian defence spending were all fodder for those who argued that Russian imperialism was once more on the march. US criticism of Uzbek President Islam Karimov in the wake of the Andizhon massacre in 2005 caused him to terminate the US lease on its base in Uzbekistan, while moving closer to Russia. In a memo to National Security Adviser Stephen Hadley in July 2006, Defense Secretary Donald Rumsfeld warned that the USA was 'getting run out of Central Asia' by the Russians.

> **KEY QUOTES 13.9:** Cheney speaks out

In Russia today, opponents of reform are seeking to reverse the gains of the last decade. In many areas of civil society the government has unfairly and improperly restricted the rights of her people . . . No legitimate interest is served when oil and gas become tools of intimidation or blackmail, either by supply manipulation or attempts to monopolize transportation. And no one can justify actions that undermine the territorial integrity of a neighbor, or interfere with democratic movements.

(Vice President Dick Cheney, speaking in Vilnius, Lithuania, in May 2006)

The interruption of Russian gas supplies to Ukraine in January 2006, dramatic and highly publicized, was a serious blow to Putin's international image. Russia was selling natural gas to Ukraine for $47 per 1,000 cubic metres while European customers were paying $230. Ukraine rebuffed a proposed price hike. Russia's main gas export pipeline crosses Ukraine, so Moscow could not cut deliveries to Ukraine without interrupting supplies to Europe, which gets one-quarter of its gas from Russia. In January 2006 Gazprom did close the pipeline for two days, alarming its Western customers. After the Ukrainian shutdown, and as oil prices climbed above $80 a barrel, commentators started talking of Russia as an 'energy superpower'.

A bipartisan Council of Foreign Relations task force issued a report in 2006 that expressed fears about Russia's backsliding from democracy and its international assertiveness, but still urged the administration to continue engaging with Russia in order to deal with urgent issues such as the threat of nuclear proliferation in Iran and North Korea. 'The real question that the United States faces in this period is not how to make a partnership with Russia work, it is how to make selective cooperation—and in some cases selective opposition—serve important international goals.'

One positive development was the US acceptance of Russia's bid for entry to the WTO in November 2006. The USA had been holding out for Russian concessions on food imports, liberalization of financial services, and improved intellectual property rights. But with 150 countries now members of the WTO, Russia's exclusion was increasingly anomalous. Russia had signed bilateral agreements with nearly all the other member countries: the USA was the main holdout. After the two sides failed to close a deal at the G8 summit in Petersburg in June 2006, Russia's patience was exhausted. Moscow slapped a ban on US chicken imports, citing sanitary concerns, and passed up a $3 billion option to buy twenty-two Boeing 787 airliners. These Russian actions triggered the shift in the US government's position.

The Kosovo problem resurfaced in 2007, with the Kosovo government stating that it will declare independence from Serbia with or without UN approval. Russia warned that such an action would have dire but unspecified consequences, implying that it would alter its policy of denying recognition to breakaway regions such as Abkhazia and Ossetia in Georgia, Karabakh in Azerbaijan, and Transnistria in Moldova. The USA effectively delegated responsibility for dealing with Kosovo to the Europeans.

Putin's second and final term as president expires in March 2008. In preparation for the political transition, Putin stepped up the nationalist political rhetoric. In a May 2007 speech he implicitly compared the USA to the Third Reich. Putin told an election rally in November 2007 that 'Those who confront us need a weak and ill state. Regrettably, there are those inside the country who feed off foreign embassies like jackals and count on support of foreign funds and governments, and not their own people. If these gentlemen return back to power, they will again cheat people and fill their pockets.'

By the end of 2007, there were few advocates of a conciliatory course towards Russia in the USA. Republican Senator John McCain suggested in November 2007 that Russia should be barred from the G8 because of its 'diminishing political freedoms' and 'efforts to bully democratic neighbors, such as Georgia'. Referring to President Bush's 2001 comment that he had 'looked into Putin's soul', McCain said, 'I looked into Mr. Putin's eyes and I saw three things—a K and a G and a B.'

Conclusion

The influx of petro-dollars has clearly facilitated the consolidation of a new authoritarian regime under President Putin. Russia is no longer begging for extensions on its foreign debts, as it was throughout the 1990s. In 2006 it paid down its entire $22 billion debt to the IMF ahead of schedule. The Kremlin wants to preserve the territorial integrity of the Russian Federation (threatened by the war in Chechnya) and to maintain its sovereignty in the face of foreign subversion (the perceived menace of a Western-sponsored 'colour revolution'). Russia also wants to insure itself against military intimidation—hence the wariness at NATO's eastward expansion; the desire to hold onto the naval base in Sevastopol, Ukraine; the chafing at Conventional Forces in Europe arms limitations; and hostility to the US plans to build missile defences in eastern Europe. Moscow wants to protect itself against such threats by building up its military muscle and by trying to use its energy exports as a political weapon. Hostile countries will be punished by price hikes and even denial of energy supplies, while friendly powers will be rewarded by investments in joint projects.

The weight of this new Russian assertiveness falls most heavily on neighbouring countries, and on Russia's European energy customers. Given that the USA imports no oil or gas from Russia, these actions are not of vital importance to US national security. The European Union countries are divided in their approaches to Russia, leaving the USA as the dominant player shaping Russia's relations with the West.

The past fifteen years have seen the rise and fall of hopes for a breakthrough to partnership in US–Russian relations. The switchbacks in US policy reflect the fact that Russia was in the throes of a major historical transition whose outcome was bound to be uncertain. US policy cycled between exaggerated optimism and wary dismissal. The same cycle was repeated twice: through the liberal idealism of the Clinton administration; and then through the realism of the post-11 September Bush administration. In each case American perceptions of Russia's national interests diverged from the world view of the Kremlin. Strobe Talbott's faith in Russia's democratic transition foundered in the messy realities of post-Soviet Russia. Bush was determined to wage the war on terror according to American priorities, and Putin was not content to be a silent partner. The USA was slow to recognize the extent of Russia's decline in the 1990s, then slow to realize its rise after 1999.

One striking continuity through the whole period is the tendency to personalize US–Russian relations. Clinton's belief that he could understand and manage the mercurial Yeltsin came to dominate Washington's relations with Moscow, focusing on Yeltsin's personal commitment to reform rather than on Russia's larger geopolitical situation. A similar dynamic occurred, on a more limited scale, between Bush and Putin.

Nevertheless, the USA was able to pursue its desired policies over Iraq, NATO expansion, and the former Yugoslavia without Russia playing a spoiler role. None of the truly nightmare scenarios has come to pass, such as Russia invading one of the Baltic countries or trying to annex parts of Kazakhstan or Ukraine. To our knowledge there has been no significant leakage of nuclear weapon materials out of Russia.

The USA failed to transform Russia into a trusty and reliable strategic partner. But that was probably an unrealistic goal—whether it was based on a weak Russia or a strong Russia.

? Questions

1. What were the priorities for US foreign policy during the break-up of the Soviet Union?
2. Would it have served US national interests to launch a Marshall Plan-style aid programme for Russia in 1992?
3. Was it wise for President Bill Clinton to tie US policy so closely to the figure of Boris Yeltsin?
4. What were the main achievements of US policy towards Russia in the 1990s?
5. Was it a good idea for the USA to pursue NATO expansion over Russian objections?
6. How did 9/11 change US–Russian relations?
7. How did personal relations between the national leaders affect US–Russian relations in the Clinton and Bush administrations?
8. What should be the principles shaping US policy towards Russia under the authoritarian rule of President Vladimir Putin?
9. What are the areas of common interest and conflicting interests between Russia and the United States?
10. What are the issues of cooperation and conflict between the United States and Russia in the states of the former Soviet Union?

» Further Reading

Council on Foreign Relations Task Force (2006), *Russia's Wrong Direction: What the United States Can and Should Do*.

A bipartisan task force that assessed the options for US policy towards Russia in the wake of the Khodorkovsky affair.

Goldgeier, James, and McFaul, Michael (2003), *Power and Purpose: US Policy toward Russia after the Cold War* (Washington, DC: Brookings Institution).

An authoritative account of US–Russian relations based on extensive interviews with leading US and Russian officials.

Kanet, Roger (ed.) (2007), *Russia: Re-emerging Great Power* (New York: Palgrave).

A collection of essays looking at Russia's changing security agenda.

Rice, Condoleezza (2000), 'Campaign 2000: Promoting the National Interest', *Foreign Affairs*, Jan.–Feb.

A blunt assessment of Russian weakness from candidate George W. Bush's foreign policy adviser.

Simes, Dimitri K. (2007), 'Losing Russia: The Costs of Renewed Confrontation', *Foreign Affairs*, Nov.–Dec.

An argument in favour of continued engagement with Russia despite its turn to authoritarianism.

Talbott, Strobe (2002), *The Russia Hand* (New York: Random House).

A thorough and occasionally candid description and defence of Clinton's Russia policy, by the man who was primarily responsible for it.

 Visit the Online Resource Centre that accompanies this book for web links to accompany each chapter, and a range of other resources: www.oxfordtextbooks.co.uk/orc/cox_stokes/

14 The USA and Asia-Pacific

Michael Cox

Chapter contents

Introduction

At the end of the Second World War the United States faced three historic tasks as the dominant capitalist power in a world that had for the past thirty years been convulsed by a successful communist revolution in one country (the USSR), two global wars (claiming over a hundred million lives), and a major economic depression (that annihilated the world economy as a functioning system). The first was to recreate the conditions that would over time lead to the reconstitution of an open, and hopefully increasingly prosperous international economy. The second was to limit, and if possible defeat, the ambitions of those who after 1945 were pressing to push the world in a radically different direction from that favoured by America and its market allies. And the third was both to incorporate old enemy states while balancing the rising power of others whose interests were diametrically opposed to those of the USA.

Nowhere in the world did the challenge to the United States appear so great as it did in East Asia after the war. Here the legacy of European colonialism, Japanese rule, and economic collapse combined together to make for a most uncertain future from Burma to Indonesia, Korea to Indochina. But it was in China where all the tensions within Asia seemed to converge to produce a series of conflicts that left the country in tatters and by 1949 the communists in power. Whether communist success in China was the result of superior organization, social discontent, the successful manipulation of nationalist sentiment or the backing of communist USSR has long been debated by different generations of historians. There has been very little debate however about the known consequences of the Chinese revolution. In effect, China's particular brand of revolutionary communism not only brought the Cold War to Asia while guaranteeing a permanent American presence in the region—one that still endures to this day; it also compelled the USA to intervene militarily on at least two occasions to stop what many in Washington viewed, somewhat simplistically, as Chinese communist expansion: first in Korea between 1950 and 1953 (a war that cost millions of lives) and then later in Vietnam, an extended conflict that finally ended with America's most humiliating defeat in the 1970s.

This chapter is not so much a history of the Cold War in Asia but an attempt to explain what in global terms must be seen as one of the great transformations of the modern era: that which turned one of the most disturbed and bloody regions in the world after mid-century into one of the more stable and prosperous by century's end. As we shall see the process of transition did not occur overnight. Nor did it take place without a mighty struggle being waged between competing ideologies and rival states. But in the end East Asia underwent a massive change and did so, in large part, because of the role played by the United States. Critics will no doubt question how this was done—often very brutally and more often than not with little regard for democracy. And no doubt they will say it might have been done better with fewer casualties along the way (the coup against the communists in Indonesia in 1965 cost 750,000 lives while two million died in the Vietnam War). Still, in the brutal world of international politics, the United States proved to be a most successful hegemon.

To make good on this claim the chapter has been divided into several sections. In the first section we look at perhaps the most critical metamorphosis of all: that experienced by Japan, a nation that in the 1930s and 1940s was wreaking havoc throughout the region while a few years later—following defeat at the hands of the United States—was playing an increasingly constructive role alongside its American benefactor and protector. In the next part we go on to explain the equally important change that was to take place in USA–China relations. As we shall see, the increasingly close ties between the United States and a state still formally led by a Communist Party (admittedly one with increasingly 'capitalist characteristics') has not merely transformed East Asia since the 1970s but the wider international order as well. In the third part we will then examine one of the great unsolved legacies of the Cold War: that posed by a still divided Korea and North Korea's apparent determination to acquire nuclear weapons. Next we shall ask a question that many experts have been seeking to answer since the end of the Cold War: namely whether or not the Asia-Pacific region can overcome its unsettled past. As our analysis indicates, though the region as a whole still contains many problems, there are more reasons to be optimistic than pessimistic about its future. To this extent, Asia-Pacific is not bound for new and dangerous rivalries as some have claimed.

Finally, in the last section we try to assess America's long-term prospects in the region. Here we take issue with those who have been arguing for some time that the region is either drifting away from the USA or that a rising China is likely to displace it over the next few decades. In our view, the United States will almost certainly remain a key player in East Asia for some time to come. This is not to imply that it will not face major challenges in the years ahead. Nor is to suggest that other actors will not play more of a role. There are however powerful factors—American as well as local—that will keep the US embedded in East Asia for the foreseeable future. There is still some way to go before we can talk of a new Pacific Century.

Japan, the United States, and the new Asian order

As an emerging world power in the nineteenth century whose western frontier ended where the Pacific Ocean began, it was almost inevitable that the United States would early view the great stretch of shining water to its east as an American lake whose sea-lanes it should control and resources it should exploit to the full. At a very early date in its history therefore the United States pursued an expansionist eastward policy that brought it into conflict with Japan by the middle of the nineteenth century and imperial China by the end. Certain in the knowledge that its own brand of muscular Christianity and robust enterprise were superior to anything on offer in Asia itself, Americans, like most 'normal' imperialists, viewed the nations with whom they came into contact with a mixture of contempt—the Chinese according to one American observer were 'cold, snaky, slow, cowardly, treacherous, suspicious, deceitful people'—laced with a large dose of nineteenth-century racism. The peoples of Asia offered little by way of inspiration it seemed, and the best one could do was either convert them to the Christian faith (which might help explain why missionaries later fell foul of most Asian revolutionaries) or conquer them and hope that one day, after years of careful tutelage (as in the cases of Hawaii and the Philippines), they would become as civilized as Americans themselves.

If expansion and the declared policy of maintaining an open door defined the American purpose in East Asia, it was rising Japan as much as disintegrating China that shaped its long-term thinking. Initially though its view of Japan was by no means a hostile one. In fact whereas Americans generally tended to regard other Asians as being either inferior or quaint, they viewed Japan at first with some regard. Indeed, like the Japanese themselves, the United States looked at this modernizing nation from the late nineteenth century onwards as being almost, though not quite completely, Anglo-Saxon in its outlook. Nor was Japan without its uses. Initially a bulwark against imperial Russia (whose powerful navy Japan had defeated in 1904), later a counter to the USSR (after the revolution of 1917), and in possession of an altogether more developed material civilization than that of decadent (and, after the Boxer rebellion of 1900, collapsing) China, the country against which the United States later waged such a devastating war was for a while at least viewed with some respect.

All this was to change, albeit very slowly, as Japan began its own imperial conquest of Asia, beginning with its annexation of Korea in 1910 (about which the United States hardly protested at all), its invasion of Manchuria in 1931 (which again did not provoke much by way of a US response), its attack on China six years later, through to its conquest of much of the rest of East Asia in 1941 followed shortly thereafter by its attack on the US Pacific fleet at anchor in Pearl Harbor. This 'day of infamy', as President Roosevelt was to call it, not only drew the United States into what turned into a bloody Pacific war with deeply racist overtones but turned it, in time, into a permanent part of the Asia-Pacific strategic landscape and a major actor in Japan itself. Indeed, for at least seven years after the Second World War, the United States effectively governed Japan alone, and did so with a degree of political acumen—made all the more necessary by the onset of the Cold War—that left an indelible and generally positive imprint on the minds of many Japanese.

Critical to the success of the post-war relationship was the making of a series of unspoken but well-understood bargains between the two countries. The first was an acceptance by the Japanese ruling elite that Japan would accept its subordinate position within an American-led Pacific order in exchange for an American guarantee of its security. This in turn assumed low military spending by Japan and a declaration that it would never possess, or even seek to acquire, weapons of mass destruction. Japan in effect would neuter itself so long as the United States was prepared to protect it. There was a second, more specifically economic aspect to the bargain: namely one struck between a United States keen for Japan to concentrate most of its efforts on developing its not inconsiderable economic assets—critical if East Asia was ever to recover after the war—in exchange for Japan's privileged access to the US market. Finally, underpinning the relationship was a recognition that while Japan might pursue certain external policies

of its own, these would never be at the expense of regional order or US leadership.

No relationship remains entirely unchanged and at times this very special relationship was to come under some strain, most notably in the 1980s when high Japanese exports to the USA began to create genuine economic disquiet in the United States itself. There were also a few on the Japanese right who continued to resent Japan's dependent status, and during the 1990s argued that Japan should now begin to say 'No' to its powerful patron across the Pacific. Greater assertiveness however was not something that generally tended to recommend itself to Japan. First, there was the simple, but important political fact that the Liberal Democratic coalition that had governed Japan for so long had no interest in challenging an America with which it had become intimately associated. It also had a good deal to do with political economy: the relationship had brought nearly forty years of sustained growth (with a blip in the 1990s) and most Japanese had no desire to upset something upon which their future prosperity continued to depend. Finally, it had more than a little to do with the still problematic region within which Japan happened to find itself. Some Japanese may have yearned for greater autonomy. Most however recognized that the road to their own security still ran through Washington—and for good reason. Relations with China remained strained. There were unresolved tensions on the Korean peninsula. And post-communist Russia continued to hold on to territory that Japan regarded as its own. For all these reasons (and no doubt a few more) Japan continued to insist that it was altogether much safer to remain close to an ally whose support remained crucial.

KEY POINTS

❑ Historically, the outcome of the war in the Pacific determined the fate of East Asia in the post-war period.

❑ Defeat by 1945 was followed by an American occupation that integrated a reformed Japan into a US-led Asian Pacific security system.

❑ In spite of certain calls on both sides since the end of the Cold War to change the terms of the relationship, the 'bargain' that was struck between the USA and Japan after the Second World War looks likely to endure for the foreseeable future.

BOX 14.1: Japan: chronology

1945	Japan surrenders.
1947	A new constitution establishes a parliamentary system. Japan renounces war and pledges not to maintain land, sea, or air forces for that purpose.
1951	Japan signs peace treaty with the USA and other nations.
1952	Japan regains its independence. The USA retains several islands for military use.
1955	Liberal Democratic Party (LDP) formed. Apart from a brief interlude in the early 1990s, the party governs almost uninterruptedly for the rest of the century and beyond.
1956	Japan joins United Nations.
1972	Japanese Prime Minister visits China and normal diplomatic relations are resumed. Japan subsequently closes its embassy in Taiwan.
1989	Emperor Hirohito dies, succeeded by Akihito.
1998	Keizo Obuchi of the LDP becomes prime minister.
2000	Obuchi suffers a stroke and is replaced by Yoshiro Mori. Obuchi dies six weeks later.
2001	A US submarine executes an emergency surfacing manoeuvre off Hawaii and collides with a Japanese training vessel. Nine Japanese are missing after the incident. Junichiro Koizumi becomes new LDP leader and prime minister. Trade dispute with China after Japan imposes import tariffs on Chinese agricultural products. China retaliates with import taxes on Japanese vehicles and other manufactured goods. Koizumi visits Seoul and offers an apology for the suffering South Korea endured under his country's colonial rule.

2002	Koizumi becomes the first Japanese leader to visit North Korea. North Korean leader Kim Jong-il apologizes for abductions of Japanese citizens in 1970s and 1980s. Five Japanese nationals kidnapped by North Korea return home to emotional family reunions.
2003	Government announces decision to install 'purely defensive' US-made missile shield.
2004	Non-combat soldiers arrive in Iraq in first Japanese deployment in combat zone since Second World War. Japan launches an application for a permanent seat on the UN Security Council. Dispute with North Korea over the fate of Japanese citizens kidnapped by North Korea during the Cold War. Pyongyang says any imposition of sanctions by Tokyo will be treated as declaration of war.
2005	Relations with Beijing deteriorate amid sometimes-violent anti-Japanese protests in Chinese cities, sparked by a Japanese textbook which China says glosses over Japan's Second World War record.
2006	Japan, China fail to reach a breakthrough at talks in Beijing over the issue of who controls oil and gas reserves in disputed areas of the East China Sea. The last contingent of Japanese troops leaves Iraq. Parliament approves the creation of a fully-fledged defence ministry, the first since the Second World War.
2007	Wen Jibao becomes the first Chinese prime minister to address the Japanese parliament. Mr Wen says both sides have succeeded in warming relations.

BOX 14.2: An alliance upon which the sun never sets?

The United States' long-standing alliance with Japan has been the pillar of US policy in the Pacific for over half a century.

(Calder 2006: 135)

As Japan extends its security profile to become more of a global player, it is doing so wholly within the context of a US–Japanese alliance . . . This should be comforting to other states in the region.

(Cha 2007: 103)

China comes in from the cold

If the foundational building block of America's post-war position in Asia-Pacific was its relationship with a one-time enemy, its greatest challenge was a nation with whom it had been formally allied until the late 1940s. This challenge was partly ideological, partly strategic, and partly conditioned by American domestic politics following China's entry into the Korean War against US forces on the Korean peninsula in the winter of 1950. Indeed, even as late as the 1960s many Americans continued to view China through a distinctly Cold War lens, a perspective reinforced at the time by the sheer turmoil through which China itself was then passing—the so-called Cultural Revolution—and by an increasingly desperate struggle America was waging in Vietnam against a communist enemy supported and armed in part by the Chinese. To make matters worse, American conservatives in particular remained closely allied with the Republic of China (Taiwan) whose leaders had every interest in continuing to foster distrust between policy makers in Washington and political leaders in mainland China.

The great strategic shift that initially broke the diplomatic deadlock and subsequently saw the United States open up formal relations with Beijing has been described in great detail by both historians and students of international politics, including some of those who were involved in this most remarkable of diplomatic reversals. It has also given rise to a lively debate as to why it happened. Hence, according to one school of thought, the new deal was the product of Chinese and American recognition that their greatest enemy was less each other and more the USSR. Others have stressed America's effort to decamp as quickly as possible from Vietnam using China's diplomatic clout as at least one way of covering its retreat. Some have even suggested a longer-term American goal of opening up China and by so doing enticing it back into the Western fold. No doubt all these factors played a role, though what now seems to have been near inevitable looked anything but at the time. Indeed, it is just possible that if Mao Tse-Tung had not died in 1976, or if

the Chinese economy had not been so weakened by his earlier policies, or the USSR had not acted with such ineptitude in the late 1970s by invading Afghanistan and thus increasing Cold War tensions, the new relationship might have taken much longer to mature or might not have happened at all. But in the end it did, transforming the international scene and drawing China closer to its former 'imperialist' enemy.

The US rapprochement with Beijing, followed in close order by China's implementation of far-reaching economic reform and ready acceptance that its own modernization required an ever closer association with the global economy, set China on a new course that over the next twenty-five years would have a major impact on the rest of the world and the United States. For the USA the benefits were tremendous. First, by abandoning the path of revolution in Asia, China helped reinforce America's temporarily weakened international position in Asia following its defeat in Vietnam. China also played a significant role in helping contain America's main Soviet rival (some would even argue that by playing the China 'card' the USA accelerated the end of the Cold War too). Lastly, by helping ease China's move towards the market and away from state control of the economy, the United States opened up a new chapter in the history of world capitalism. Certainly, China's adoption of the market was to have a huge ideological impact. As the well-known American theorist Francis Fukuyama later noted in 1989, the global 'crisis of socialism' in the 1980s occurred for several important reasons including its own failure to produce efficient economies that could compete under world market conditions. However, it was the effective abandonment of planning in China that did as much as anything else to undermine Marxism as a global political project.

Naturally, the Chinese leadership continued to proclaim its own socialist credentials, all the time arguing that it was not taking China down the capitalist road but rather building its own form of socialism with 'Chinese characteristics'. Even Chairman Mao was not rejected in his entirety (the official line now was that he had been 70 per cent correct and 30 per cent wrong). But this was so much window dressing. China was now rushing headlong down the path to modernity and nothing would be allowed to stand in its way. Drawing upon a mass of foreign capital, a steady supply of cheap Chinese labour, ready access to Western markets, and a system of political controls that permitted neither organized trade unions nor strikes, China was to undergo in twenty years what it had taken many countries in Europe two or three generations to achieve. The economic results were impressive; dazzling even. Every year its productive power grew by around 10 per cent, turning it by the beginning of the twenty-first century into one of the most significant players in the global economy. The United States in particular had much to be grateful for it seemed: not only was China acting as another—most welcome—motor for the world economy but by buying up the American debt with its vast accumulation of surplus dollars (over $1.3 trillion by 2007) it was helping keep US inflation down as well.

Still, in spite of these critical changes, the relationship between the United States and the new China was never free of problems. Most obviously the Chinese leadership remained doggedly determined to ensure that economic change was not accompanied by a loss of control by the Communist Party, something many Americans found deeply distressing (most especially in the wake of the Tiananmen Square massacre of 1989). There was in addition the outstanding issue of Taiwan, once the United States' key ally in the early Cold War, now a democracy whose very existence posed a very real problem for a Chinese leadership committed to a 'one China' policy.

Finally, there remained the very real long-term problem of the impact of China's speedy rise on America's position within the wider international system. Optimists could claim, and of course did, that an increasingly integrated and dynamic Chinese economy was good for the American consumer (cheap imports), good for the American economy, and good for regional economic growth (critically important following the Asian financial crisis of 1998). They could also point to China's willingness to support the USA on a number of big strategic issues such as North Korea and the war on terror. All this though could not allay some deeper American worries, and there were more than just a few in Washington who wondered where all this might lead one day. As more than one observer was to note, the real issue was not whether China was trying to rise peacefully but rather what would happen once it had finally achieved its ascent. As the first decade of the twenty-first century drew to an end, few Americans seemed to have a clear answer to this difficult question.

KEY POINTS

- ❑ The rapprochement between China and the United States in the 1970s not only altered the relationship between Beijing and Washington but transformed world politics while making economic reform in China possible.
- ❑ China's entry onto the modern world stage has been brought about by its rapid transition to economic giant in less than two decades.
- ❑ China's rise has generated a feeling of opportunity in Washington tempered by fears.

BOX 14.3: The China puzzle

China is a threat, China is a customer, and China is an opportunity. . . . You cannot ignore it.

(Kenichi Ohmae, quoted in Friedman 2005: 117)

The challenge is going to be how to create a framework where successful models different from the United States' can be incorporated . . . The future institutions are going to have to deal with the fact that China may be rich and non-democratic.

(Donald C. Hellmann, director of the Institute for International Policy at the University of Washington, quoted in Zissis 2007)

There has emerged the view that China can be part of a structure of cooperation among the great powers to address the major foreign policy changes of our time.

Richard C. Bush III, director of Northeast Asian Policy Studies at the Brookings Institution, quoted in Zissis 2007)

BOX 14.4. China: chronology

1949	Communist victory, founding of the People's Republic of China. Nationalists retreat to the island of Taiwan and set up a government there.
1950	China intervenes in the Korean War on the side of North Korea. Tibet becomes part of the People's Republic of China.
1953	Eisenhower ends US naval blockade of Taiwan.
1954	First Taiwan Straits Crisis.
1955	US signs mutual defence treaty with Taiwan.
1958	'Great Leap Forward'.
1959	Chinese forces suppress large-scale revolt in Tibet.
1962	Brief conflict with India over disputed Himalayan border.
1964	China's first atomic test.
1969	Differences with USSR culminate in border skirmishes.
1972	US President Richard Nixon visits China. Both countries declare a desire to normalize relations.
1976	Mao dies.
1979	Diplomatic relations established with the USA.
1989	Troops open fire on demonstrators in Tiananmen Square, killing 200. International outrage leads to sanctions.
1992	Russia and China sign declaration restoring friendly ties.
1993	Clinton policy of 'constructive engagement' launched at summit with President Jiang Zemin.
1994	China abolishes the official renminbi (RMB) currency exchange rate and fixes its first floating rate since 1949.
1995	China tests missiles and holds military exercises in the Taiwan Strait, apparently to sway Taiwanese voters against pro-independence presidential candidate Lee Teng-hui. Lee wins by a large margin.
1997	Hong Kong reverts to Chinese control.
1999	NATO bombs the Chinese embassy in Belgrade. Macao reverts to Chinese rule.
2000	US Congress grants permanent normal trade relations.
2001	Diplomatic stand-off over the detention of an American spy plane and crew after a mid-air collision with a Chinese fighter jet. China joins the World Trade Organization.
2003	China, India reach de facto agreement over status of Tibet and Sikkim in landmark cross-border trade agreement.
2004	China signs a landmark trade agreement with ten South-East Asian countries; the accord could eventually unite 25 per cent of the world's population in a free-trade zone.
2005	New law on Taiwan calls for use of force should Taipei declare independence from mainland China. China and Russia hold their first joint military exercises. Taiwan's National Party leader Lien Chan visits China for the first meeting between Nationalist and Communist Party leaders since 1949.
2006	China–Africa summit in Beijing results in the signing of business deals worth nearly $2bn and China promises billions of dollars in loans and credits.
2007	Reports say China has carried out a missile test in space, shooting down an old weather satellite. The USA, Japan, and others express concern at China's military build-up.

The United States, Korea, and the legacy of the Cold War

If the Chinese leadership revealed a shrewd appreciation of how effectively a formally communist state could take advantage of the global economy without conceding any of its power at home, its neighbour and formal ally North Korea demonstrated an equally shrewd understanding of how to survive under conditions where the tide of history was moving against it following the collapse of communism in Europe. Indeed, like South Korea, the North drew some very important lessons from the collapse of one very special communist state in particular: namely East Germany. But whereas the leaders in the South drew what seemed at the time the not unreasonable conclusion that the regime in the North was destined to change (its policy then being how to ensure this occurred without causing instability) those in the North concluded that everything had to be done to ensure that the communist state they had built at such cost since 1945 did not change at all.

The method adopted by the North to maintain the regime was a crude but simple one: to use nuclear brinkmanship and its controversial nuclear programme as a way of extracting concessions from its various opponents—most obviously South Korea—while forcing the wider international community to come to terms with the North. Fearful that its very survival was now in doubt, North Korea—whose nuclear programme had been raising some very real concerns in Washington since the late 1980s—began to act in an increasingly aggressive way, such that by 1993 it was even threatening to withdraw from the Nuclear Non-Proliferation Treaty (NPT). Not surprisingly, this set a series of loud alarm bells ringing in Washington which forced policy makers to look at their very limited options, including the appalling (and impossible) one of conventional war. After much soul searching a decision was arrived at: the so-called 'Framework Agreement' of 1994, a compromise solution that made a series of concessions to the communist regime—including delivery of large amounts of oil and aid—in exchange for a promise that they would remain party to the NPT. Few believed the agreement was perfect. But hardly anybody could see any serious alternative, including a highly nervous South Korea whose leaders by now were desperately keen to maintain some kind of relationship with a regime whose rhetoric they seemed to fear a good deal less than its collapse.

The adoption of what many in the United States regarded as a flawed policy forced upon them by North Korean intransigence on the one hand, and a South Korean desire to maintain a détente-style relationship with the North on the other, soon came under attack within Washington. The 1994 deal, it was now regularly argued by critics on the right, was little more than a modern-day form of appeasement whose only consequence would be to preserve a regime already doomed by history. It would also allow the communists to play a game of divide and diplomatic rule between the United States and its once steadfast South Korean ally. It also did very little in the opinion of critics to slow down the North's nuclear programme. Thus the Agreement was a failure in nearly every conceivable way. Naturally, no serious policy maker wanted confrontation for its own sake. But there had to be a more robust approach to the North Korean problem, one that weakened this hideous regime rather than strengthening it, that punished it rather than rewarding it for its various transgressions, only one of which was having a highly destabilizing nuclear programme.

It was perhaps only a matter of time before there was a serious policy review, and this finally came in 2001 following the election of the more conservative president, George W. Bush. Initially, North Korea was not a policy priority and little was done therefore. The attack of 9/11 followed by President Bush's announcement of an altogether tougher policy towards all 'rogue' regimes quickly changed all this. Indeed, by early 2002, Bush was already counting

North Korea as part of a wider 'axis of evil', stating that the policy of the United States towards it could be nothing less than regime change. Inevitably this provoked a response by the North Koreans who once more threatened to withdraw from the Nuclear Non-Proliferation Treaty (which they did in 2003) while pushing ahead again with their stalled nuclear programme. Thus began what looked to many observers like a rather dangerous diplomatic game conducted between all the interested parties (going under the official title of the Six-Party talks), one however that failed to prevent the North acting in an increasingly aggressive fashion, exemplified in 2006 when it conducted its own missile tests and confirmed that it had, at last, exploded a small nuclear device. This provocation had the intended effect of once more forcing its enemies to the negotiating table and in 2007 nuclear inspectors were once again admitted into North Korea while Pyongyang committed itself—yet again—to the NPT. Finally, in November 2007, North and South Korea's prime ministers met for the first time in fifteen years.

North Korea thus posed many significant challenges for US foreign policy in the years following the collapse of communism in other parts of the world. Certainly, it revealed that the end of the Cold War was just as likely to create new difficulties as opportunities. What North Korea also illustrated was that critical issues such as nuclear weapons would not necessarily wither away once the Cold War had come to an end. If anything, the end of the Cold War era made these problems even more difficult to resolve. Finally, in attempting to deal with the policies of a hostile regime on a divided Asian peninsula, the United States discovered something that many Americans seemed to have underestimated in the unipolar age: that however much power the USA happened to possess, it could not avoid talking to those whom it disliked intensely. As former Secretary of State James Baker pointed out, 'it's not appeasement to talk to your enemies'.[1] Furthermore, since there was no problem more difficult to solve than North Korea, it required the United States to 'get serious' (Moltz and Quinones 2004) about multilateralism and recognize that one had a much greater chance of solving these problems by acting with others rather than acting by oneself.

KEY POINTS

- ❑ The end of the Cold War in Europe was to make the political situation more rather than less problematic in Korea.
- ❑ North Korea has used nuclear weapons to gain diplomatic and economic concessions form its enemies.
- ❑ US policy towards North Korea has veered between engagement and regime change.

BOX 14.5: North Korea and nuclear weapons

What must be avoided is to leave a beleaguered nuclear nation convinced that it is permanently excluded from the international community, its existence threatened, its people suffering horrible deprivation and its hard-liners in total control of military and political policy.

(Carter 2006)

Why won't the Bush administration talk bilaterally and substantively with North Korea as the Brits (and eventually the US) did with Libya? Because the Bush administration sees diplomacy as something to be engaged in with another country as a reward for that country's good behavior. They seem not to see diplomacy as a tool to be used with antagonistic countries or parties, that might bring about an improvement in the behavior of such entities, and a resolution to the issues that trouble us. Thus we do not talk to Iran, Syria, Hizballah or North Korea. We only talk to our friends—a huge mistake.

(Gregg 2006)

BOX 14.6: Korea: chronology

1945 End of war leaves Korea divided between communist North and pro-American South Korea.

1948 Anti-communist Syngman Rhee elected President of the Republic of (South) Korea in UN-sanctioned elections and assumes control of the South; in the North, Kim Il-Sung is installed as President of the Democratic Republic of Korea.

1949 US troops depart from South Korea, leaving only a small military advisory force.

1950 North Korean troops cross the border on 25 June, initiating the Korean War. The United Nations provides the United States with a mandate to assist in the defence of the Republic of Korea.

1953 A 27 July armistice brings fighting to a halt and restores the previous border along the 38th parallel. US troops remain stationed in Korea and will contribute to significant military build-up along the demilitarized zone at the border.

1957 The United States begins deployment of nuclear weapons to the Korean peninsula.

1968 North Korean vessels capture the surveillance ship the USS *Pueblo*.

1969 US EC-121 surveillance aircraft shot down over the Sea of Japan.

1972 North and South Korea announce an agreement to seek cooperation and eventual unification. This agreement breaks down in the following year and initiates a decade-long suspension of relations between the two countries.

1976 Two US officers serving with the United Nations Command mission in Korea are killed by North Korean soldiers following an altercation at the DMZ.

1985 North Korea joins the Nuclear Non-Proliferation Treaty (NPT).

1988 The United States places North Korea on the list of state sponsors of terrorism on 20 January following the involvement of North Korean agents in the in-flight destruction of Korean Airlines Flight 858 in November 1987.

1991 The United States withdraws the last of its nuclear weapons from South Korea, prompting an agreement between North and South Korea to denuclearize the peninsula. Both countries join the UN.

1993 International Atomic Energy Authority (IAEA) refused access to inspect nuclear site; North Korea threatens to withdraw from the Non-Proliferation Treaty.

1994 North Korea announces its withdrawal from the IAEA. Kim Il-Sung dies and is succeeded by his son, Kim Jong-Il. Agreement between North Korea and the United States establishes 'Agreed Framework'.

1995 Korean Peninsula Energy Development Organization (KEDO) formed—North and South Korea, the United States, and Japan are its founding members.

1996 Talks between North Korea and the United States end with US sanctions and the deployment of US warships to Japan following North Korean declaration that it will conduct missile tests. North Korea announces its abandonment of the 1953 armistice and sends troops into the DMZ.

1998 South Korean President Kim Dae-Jung reveals his 'Sunshine Policy' to seek improved relations and reconciliation with Pyongyang.

1999 USA – North Korea talks produce a suspension of missile testing by North Korea.

2000 Progress towards a normalization of relations continues as sanctions are reduced; North and South Korea agree to 'resolve' the issue of reunification.

2001 President Bush makes statements implying a new, tougher policy towards North Korea, and a repudiation of Kim Dae-Jung's Sunshine Policy, provoking an angry reaction from Pyongyang and cancellation of reconciliation talks in South Korea.

(continued)

BOX 14.6: (continued)

2002	President Bush labels North Korea part of an 'axis of evil' and implies the regime has the desire and intention to support terrorism. USA announces that North Korea admitted to having a nuclear weapons programme, in violation of the 1994 Agreed Framework. Pyongyang denies having made such an admission but admits to possession of a uranium enrichment programme.
2002	Ship carrying North Korean-made Scud missiles bound for Yemen is intercepted by US and Spanish forces but released due to lack of legal authority to seize its cargo. North and South Korean naval vessels wage a gun battle in the Yellow Sea, the worst skirmish for three years. Thirty North Korean and four South Korean sailors are killed.
2003	North Korea withdraws from NPT, hints at a resumption of long-range missile testing,

and declares it has enough plutonium to start making nuclear bombs. North Korea withdraws from the 1992 agreement to denuclearize the Korean peninsula.

2005	Six-Party talks initially produce an agreement for North Korea to rejoin the NPT and cease all nuclear activity, but then break down.
2006	UN Security Council approves sanctions in response to North Korean missile tests. North Korea detonates what it claims to be a nuclear weapon, and US intelligence officials confirm that the test was in fact of a small nuclear device.
2007	Inspectors readmitted to North Korea; Pyongyang commits to disable three nuclear facilities and declare all its nuclear programmes by year-end. In November, North and South Korea's prime ministers meet for the first time in fifteen years.

Asia-Pacific: primed for rivalry?

The continued division of Korea and the many problems it has posed for the United States over several decades points to something more general about East Asia: that the region as a whole appears to contain within it many serious fault lines that are not easily amenable to simple diplomatic solution. Here the contrast with Europe could not be more pronounced as scholars of international relations have been quick to point out. As they note, whereas Europe after the Second World War managed to create some form of a 'liberal security community', East Asia for a whole host of reasons did not. More worryingly, there is little chance that it will be able to do so now. In fact, according to at least one school of influential American thought, East Asia, far from being primed for peace since the end of Cold War, has been 'ripe' for new rivalries. As Aaron Friedberg noted in an influential and much quoted article published in

1993, Europe's very bloody past between 1914 and 1945 could easily turn into Asia's future. Uncertainty about the future of North Korea, unresolved tensions between China and Taiwan, Japanese suspicion of China, China's historical dislike of Japan, the persistence of authoritarianism, and the legacy of a very bloody Cold War history, taken together meant that the world in general and the United States in particular should remain deeply concerned abut East Asia.

This pessimism (inspired as much by philosophical realism as by a deep knowledge of the region itself) has over the past few years given way to an altogether less bleak assessment by American analysts and policy makers. Few think that Asia-Pacific will be without its fair share of difficulties in the twenty-first century. That said, there is now probably more to look forward to than dread. There are four reasons why.

First, the region has turned into one of the most materially dynamic in the world. Indeed, in global terms, Asian Pacific countries now account for nearly 30 per cent of world economic production. Nor does there seem much likelihood that they will slip backwards any time soon. On the contrary, the region overall appears to be economically 'blessed', not so much in terms of raw materials but with other, more intangible, but important assets including a culture of hard work, a system of entrepreneurial values, a plentiful supply of labour, a huge reservoir of capital, and a set of political and economic structures that allow the state to play a critical role in engineering successful economic outcomes. Nor in this lengthy list should one ignore the part played by the United States itself. Indeed, by opening up its market to East Asian goods while providing the region with security on the cheap, the USA has played what some would see as a very important part in generating growth throughout the region.

Secondly, though many states in the region continue to have powerful and emotionally charged memories of past conflicts, in and of themselves these are not enough to generate new conflicts in the present, especially in circumstances where regional trade and investment is rapidly rising. Asia-Pacific certainly carries more than its fair share of historical baggage. The fact remains that economic pressures and material self-interest are increasingly driving countries in the region together rather than apart. The process of East Asian economic integration may have been slow to develop. ASEAN after all was only formed in 1967. Nor has integration been accompanied by the formation of anything like the European Union. However, since regionalism began to take off during the 1990s it has showed no signs of slowing down.

A third reason for greater optimism is Japan itself. Unwilling to apologize unambiguously for past misdeeds, Japan nonetheless has played a most positive role in the region. Indeed, having adopted its famous peace constitution while renouncing force as a means of achieving its goals abroad (Japan still remains one the strongest upholders of the original Non-Proliferation Treaty) it has demonstrated no interest at all in upsetting its suspicious neighbours by acting in anything other than a benign manner. Furthermore, by spreading its not inconsiderable economic largesse in the form of aid and large-scale investment it has gone a very long way to fostering better international relations in the region. Even its old ideological rival China has been a significant beneficiary and by 2003 was home to over 5,000 Japanese companies.

Finally, there is China itself. As we have already indicated, much American ink has already been spilt worrying about 'rising China' and the possible threat this may (or may not) pose to US interests in the region. Once again however there may be more cause for optimism than pessimism, China after all has not only theoretically committed itself to rising peacefully but has taken several concrete measures to ensure the status quo is not undermined in any serious way. This has not only involved being as cooperative with the United States as it is possible to be, but constructively engaging with the East Asian region as a whole—first and foremost economically but also in other 'softer' ways such as working responsibly within regional institutions. The strategy seems to be paying off. Indeed, whereas in the 1990s there was deep concern about China in East Asia, this has now given way to a more positive view of its role. As a more recent study has pointed out, what China's neighbours now seem to fear more is not so much a confident China actively cooperating with others from a position of economic strength but a weak and insecure China whose economy can no longer act as the motor of the region.

KEY POINTS

- As a region East Asia is quite different from Europe and has never formed a genuine 'security community'.
- According to one school of thought East Asia is likely to remain a highly disorderly region.
- The evidence over the past fifteen years however suggests that several factors—including China's economic rise—are leading towards a more stable Asia.

BOX 14.7 Asia-Pacific: bound for conflict?

In the long run it is Asia that seems far more likely to be the cockpit of great power conflict . . . for better or for worse, Europe's past could be Asia's future.

(Friedberg 1993–4)

Most of the structural features . . . [that have been] identified as promoting instability in East Asia actually point in the other direction towards greater regional stability. The balance of power favours the maintenance of the status quo. Economic interdependence is on the rise. . . . There has been a steady growth of international institutions of all sorts.

(Berger 2000)

The United States: hegemonic still?

As we have seen, the United States has been a major actor in the Pacific region for a very long time, especially so since 1941, the year coincidentally when the famous American publisher Henry Luce announced the onset of an 'American Century'. Nowhere over the next fifty years however did this bold and optimistic vision come under such sustained attack as it did in Asia-Pacific: first in China in 1949, then in Korea in 1950, and finally in Vietnam where the United States committed itself fully to the defence of the 'free world' only to be ejected ignominiously in the 1970s. Even then the challenge did not disappear entirely. Its character though now changed from being revolutionary and ideological to economic, so much so that twenty years after the fall of South Vietnam, pundits were speculating that the new century would be neither communist nor American but increasingly Pacific. Japan's economic rise, the dynamism displayed by capitalist South Korea and a variety of other Asian tigers, and of course the emergence of China, all seemed to point to a great shift in power away from the United States to the countries along the Pacific Rim.

Speculating about the future is of necessity fraught with danger. Nonetheless, it continues apace and over the past few years it has become increasingly popular (once again) to lament the future demise of US influence in Asia. As one American official has noted, critics not only think that the world in general is moving outside the US sphere of influence but that

Asia-Pacific is becoming a region more likely to listen to Beijing than Washington, more inclined to resolve its own problems rather than look across the Pacific for American-made solutions (Cha 2007). Nor have recent events in the Middle East made the situation any better. Indeed, with the USA mired down in Iraq and Afghanistan, many feel that this will only accelerate America's decline in East Asia. As has been observed by many writers, the ultimate strategic effect of the Iraq War will be to hasten the arrival of the Asian Century.

Such prognoses are difficult to evaluate and perhaps even more difficult to prove one way or another. Still, we should beware predictions about the US future in East Asia based on America's difficulties in other parts of the world. We should also be sensitive to the specificities of the region itself and note first how much the American presence is desired by local actors themselves. Thus China views a continued US role as being critical to stability, Japan looks to Washington for guidance and protection, South Korea remains dependent on the USA for its protection, and a host of other states maintain important bilateral ties with Washington which they have shown little inclination of giving up. Nor do other states appear willing to play the wider role America plays. Indeed, Japan cannot play it because of its history, while China is unable to play it because it remains formally wedded to an ideology that has too many echoes of the Cold War.

Secondly, there is really very little popular agitation to get America out of Asia. In fact, while other countries in the world have been experiencing an upsurge of anti-Americanism over the past few years, in East Asia—with the obvious exception of the two Koreas—the mood has remained positive. This is even true in Vietnam, a country the United States fought until 1975, while in China the United States appears to be remarkably popular, in part because of the close relationship the two countries have had over thirty years but also because the Chinese economy needs access to the US market. Evidence from Japan shows a very similar set of views.

The position of the United States is likely to endure finally for the simple reason that many in Asia-Pacific have fewer doubts about its intentions than they do about their neighbours. Asia-Pacific may be in the process of shedding part of its bloody history. Nonetheless, the legacy of the past lives on in many concrete ways. Thus so long as Taiwan worries about China, China has its differences with Japan, Japan fears a rising China, and Korea remains divided, there are few in the region willing to contemplate a future without the United States. Many may denounce the United States as being an 'Empire' in East Asia; but if it is, then it is one which remains a welcome guest in nearly every capital in most countries in the region. The days when the USA was the sole focus of activity might have gone. But for the foreseeable future it will remain—as one observer has noted—the 'number one' player in the region.[2]

BOX 14.8: East Asia and the end of the American Century?

The Pacific Century has not arrived and is not likely any time soon . . . the American century that Henry Luce first pointed to in 1941 has not yet run its course.

(Foot and Walter 1999)

? Questions

1. For how long and why has the United States had interests in East Asia?
2. Why was the war in the Pacific so critical for the United States?
3. How did the Chinese revolution of 1949 impact on US foreign policy?
4. How would you characterize the post-war relationship between Japan and the USA?
5. Why were the Korean and Vietnam wars important for the United States?
6. Why did the United States and China re-establish a diplomatic partnership in the 1970s?
7. What is the connection between nuclear weapons and the end of the Cold War in North Korea?
8. Should the United States fear or welcome China's rise?
9. Is East Asia the prisoner of its past?
10. Can the United States remain hegemonic in East Asia for ever?

» Further Reading

Hemmer, C., and Katzenstein, P. J. (2002), 'Why is there no NATO in Asia? Collective Identity, Regionalism and the Origins of Multilateralism', *International Organization*, 56: 4575–607.

Argues that the failure by the United States to establish genuinely multilateral bodies in Asia such as NATO was the result of an American perception of potential Asian allies—unlike those in Europe—as being alien and in important senses inferior. Absent a collective identity, bilateral rather than multilateral arrangements became the norm.

Ikenberry, G. J., and Tsuchiyama, J. (2002), 'Between Balance of Power and Community; The Future of Multilateral Security Co-operation in Asia -Pacific', *International Relations of the Asia-Pacific,* 2: 69–94.

Insists that there is little chance of moving beyond the current ad hoc security system in East Asia which reflects the absence of shared identity within the region itself. The liberal hope of moving beyond this system may not be fulfilled any time soon.

Van Ness, P. (2002), 'Hegemony, Not Anarchy: Why China and Japan are not Balancing US Unipolar Power', *International Relations of the Asia-Pacific,* 2: 131– 50.

What the author terms the 'passive influence of US structural power' continues to shape Chinese and Japanese thinking and makes likely their continued bandwagoning rather than balancing behaviour towards the United States. Indeed, participation in an American-led hegemonic system provides substantial benefits they would be loathe to give up.

Ross, R. S. (1999), 'The Geography of the Peace: East Asia in the Twenty-first Century', *International Security,* 23: 81–118.

Argues against the notion that a combination of history and geography increase the prospects for regional tension; if anything the geography of East Asia creates the possibility of order by minimizing the likelihood of a power transition and conflict.

Buzan, B. (2003), 'Security Architecture in Asia: The Interplay of Regional and Global Levels', *The Pacific Review,* 16: 143–73.

There is a distinct and long-standing regional structure in East Asia that is of at least as great an importance to the global level in shaping the region's security dynamics. The US though remains a key player and cannot risk withdrawing from the region. On the other hand it is not easy to calculate the longer effect of the US being and staying engaged in Asia's security.

Christensen, T. J. (1999), 'China, the US–Japan Alliance and the Security Dilemma in East Asia', *International Security,* 23: 49–80.

If the security dilemma theory is applied to East Asia the chance for spirals of conflict in the region seems great. Perhaps one factor more than any other makes this outcome less likely: the strength of the US relationship with Japan. US strategy must be to continue to reassure Japan while not triggering concerns in Beijing.

Acharya, A. (2003–4), 'Will Asia's Past be Its Future?', *International Security,* 28: 149–64.

Asia, the author contends, is increasingly able to manage its insecurity through shared regional norms, rising economic interdependence, and growing institutional linkages. The 'ripe for rivalry' thesis outlined by Aaron Friedberg in 1993 is thus misconceived'

Mastanduno, M. (2000), 'Models, Markets and Power: Political Economy and the Asia-Pacific, 1989–1999', *Review of International Studies,* 26: 493–507.

Broad survey of the decade after the Cold War which concludes that while the United States seeks to preserve its dominant position in the region, to do so it will have to act with great diplomatic skill. The US must through its actions seek to avoid the rise of challengers and serious challenges to the US conception of international and regional order.

Bisley, N. (2006), 'Neither Empire nor Republic: American Power and Regional Order in the Asia-Pacific', *International Politics,* 43: 219–40.

The regional order of East Asia is not, and is unlikely in the foreseeable future, to be a rules-based or an institution-led order. Rather it is the product of a series of relationships between states including the most important one that each state in the region has with the United States. The United States, however, is not an imperial overlord nor even a hegemon in the region. Its power is real but it should not be overstated.

Foot, R., and Walter, A. (1999), 'Whatever Happened to the Pacific Century?', *Review of International Studies*, 25: 245–69.

    Argues that predictions suggesting the emergence of a new Pacific Century were based on a flawed political economy whose illusions were exposed by the East Asian economic crisis of 1997–8. The American Century has not yet run its course in East Asia.

 ## Endnotes

1. Comments of James Baker on ABC News, 6 Oct. 2007.
2. David C. Kang, Dartmouth University, quoted in Zissis 2007.

 Visit the Online Resource Centre that accompanies this book for web links to accompany each chapter, and a range of other resources: www.oxfordtextbooks.co.uk/orc/cox_stokes/

15 US foreign policy in Latin America

James Dunkerley

Chapter contents

Introduction

This chapter surveys the historical evolution of US relations with Latin America. The contemporary geopolitical balance of power within the western hemisphere is highly asymmetrical. US policy has usually been determined under various doctrines and was only partly affected by the Cold War. So, the post-Cold War period has seen only some changes to the historical pattern. The second section surveys that historical background from the Monroe Doctrine and manifest destiny, which sought to contain European expansion and to justify that of the USA under an ethos of hemispherism. The third section covers the projection of US power beyond its frontiers in the early twentieth century. Direct intervention in Central America and the Caribbean was common until the depression of the 1930s, when a less unilateral approach was adopted. After 1945 the implementation of policy was often routed through the multilateral institutions set up after the Second World War. However, the Cuban Revolution prompted an aggressively ideological approach. The chapter traces policy towards the left in Central America, where armed conflict prevailed in the 1980s, and that for South America, where the 'Washington Consensus' brought an end to the anti-European aspects of the Monroe Doctrine by promoting globalization. The failure of this free trade platform to provide sustained growth contributed to regional disenchantment and the emergence after 2001 of a political current unsympathetic to Washington's renewed unilateralist tendencies.

Immediately after his inauguration, President George W. Bush declared, 'The best foreign policy starts at home. We've got to have good relations at home.' He meant relations inside the western hemisphere, and particularly with the twenty-one countries of Latin America and the thirteen independent states of the Caribbean. Latin America has sometimes been referred to as the 'backyard' of the United States—an inferior section of 'home'. This attitude has prompted an uncomfortable coexistence of attitudes in Anglo and Latin America, the former exhibiting a presumption of hegemony (Lowenthal) or the assumption of overwhelming superiority. Latin Americans, by contrast, have often adopted a geographical fatalism in recognition of their proximity to a state of far greater resource and ambition. For no other part of the world has the term 'US empire' been employed for longer or with greater justification. Yet, Latin America, almost by virtue of 'being at home', has also been overlooked and sidelined by US policy makers, except in secondary disputes or as proxy forces for antagonistic extra-hemispheric powers, which is the principal way in which the Cold War affected hemispheric relations.

On 6 September 2001 President Bush had invited Mexican President Fox to a joint session of Congress, declaring that Mexico 'is our most important relationship'. Within a week the attacks of 11 September meant that this relationship was downgraded for over five years. According to Michael Shifter, 'at least in the short-term no other country in the world was as deflated [as Mexico] by the new configuration brought about by September' (Shifter 2002: 52). Latin America as a whole felt the shift nearly as acutely.

Although Bush dutifully attended several of the regular regional summits for heads of states after 9/11, he did not give them priority and he undertook no tour of Latin America until March 2007. By then a third of the governments of the region had been elected on platforms which questioned the US invasion of Iraq, its enthusiasm for free trade, and its approaches to the environment, the International Criminal Court, energy, drugs control, and immigration. Led by the long-term but ailing Cuban leader Fidel Castro and the energetic Venezuelan President Hugo Chávez, the new movement reflected Washington's failure to retain the considerable initial sympathy over 9/11.

Bush's tour of 2007 to six countries of South and Central America proved less of a failure than some had anticipated in view of the fact that only seven of the regional states had supported the invasion of Iraq (all of them had been in the midst of trade negotiations or, in the case of Colombia, in receipt of annual military aid of $600 million). The tour was less triumphant than the famous visit to South America by

Franklin Roosevelt in 1936, when non-intervention and a new-found sense of good neighbourliness was at its peak. On the other hand, Bush's presence never excited the popular venom provoked by Richard Nixon's visit of 1958, when the physical safety of the Vice-President was put at risk. Unsurprisingly, given his treatment, Nixon told Donald Rumsfeld in 1971, 'Latin America doesn't matter . . . People don't give a damn about Latin America now' (Reid 2007: 1). Even during the Cold War, Washington has seen the region as one of limited costs and risks.

Reactions to the presidential tour of 2007 illustrate an enduring feature of US–Latin American relations: the profound ambivalence on both sides about the qualities and behaviour of the other. Although many Latin Americans thought that the inevitable asymmetry of the relationship too often took the avoidable form of US supremacism and inequitable treatment of the societies in the southern part of the continent, they also admired and envied the material wealth and civic freedoms prevailing in North America. Equally, Washington has not conducted its policies towards the region with a consistent and absolute unilateralism, oscillating between intervention on ideological and humanitarian grounds and a principled respect for sovereignty. Moreover, it has sometimes accepted suggestions from a south which recognizes that 'ignoring America is not an option' and that some form of cohabitation must be contrived (Grandin 2006: 11–51). Even whilst he criticized Bush, Chávez continued to supply 15 per cent of US oil imports. A major poll in 2005 found that two-thirds of Latin Americans looked positively on US society as a whole.

Since the Second World War the emergence of global and multilateral institutions has broadened the channels for the development of US policy towards the rest of the hemisphere. This has reduced the image of the unilateralism of the early twentieth century, and it has provided Latin American states with some subordinate voice in hemispheric affairs.

Table 15.1 depicts the hemispheric asymmetry in economic resources and state capacity between the twenty-one states of Latin America and the USA. Latin America is not the poorest continent on the globe, but it displays huge internal inequities in wealth and power. Of its constituent countries only Brazil, Mexico, and Argentina could be said to be middle-level states of international standing. Yet even those countries have not developed as was anticipated. In 1966 Mexico was richer than Portugal and Brazil than South Korea, but by 2002 Portugal and South Korea were twice as rich in income per capita terms as Mexico and Brazil. US production was ten times that of Mexico and Brazil combined and six times that of all Latin America.

One result of this asymmetry has been the widespread conviction within the region that development policies promoted by Washington and its allies have yielded, at best, very modest results. Although two-thirds of foreign direct investment in Mexico is of US origin and the USA is Mexico's largest trading partner, every year a million Mexicans migrate to the USA. This raises doubts as to the qualities of contemporary globalization and how far the formal bilateral relations between the two states matter in the lives of ordinary Mexicans. Many of these immigrants are returning to territory that was Mexican before 1848, and the issue of national sovereignty and pride remains a key issue in popular culture as well as public policy on both sides of the border.

Brazil, the region's only Portuguese-speaking country and a state of semi-continental proportions, has had no tradition of anti-Americanism. However, since the onset of democratic government in the 1990s, Brazil has increasingly sought to develop a South American bloc of states and to negotiate over Washington's free trade policies on a regional basis rather than the individual bilateral basis preferred by the USA. For the Brazilian foreign ministry there is no such thing as 'Latin America' because Mexico's membership of NAFTA since 1994 has placed that country firmly within the North American economic circuit. At the 2003 World Trade Organization (WTO) summit at Cancún, Mexico, Brazil took the regional lead in contesting the US and European limited versions of free trade, particularly over agricultural production and intellectual property. Brazil, by virtue of its size and regional role, has avoided the need of many states to seek out 'the greatest and most powerful ally'

Table 15.1 Latin America: basic indicators, *c.*2000

	Pop. (m)	GNP per cap. ($)	LA rank	Urban (%)	Primary goods % exps.	Life expect.	Military (000)
Argentina	37.1	7,695	1	89.4	67.9	70.3	69
Bolivia	8.3	994	17	64.8	72.9	63.4	33
Brazil	170.4	3,494	7	81.3	42.0	68.0	290
Chile	15.2	4,638	5	84.6	84.0	75.8	90
Colombia	42.3	1,922	13	74.9	65.9	71.8	158
C. Rica	3.8	4,159	6	51.9	34.5	78.4	—
Cuba	11.2	2,030	12	75.3	N/A	76.2	46
Dom. Rep.	8.4	2,349	9	65.0	N/A	67.2	24
Ecuador	12.7	1,076	16	62.4	89.9	69.4	50
El Salv.	6.3	2,105	10	46.4	51.6	70.2	18
Guatemala	11.4	1,668	14	40.4	68.0	64.5	32
Haiti	8.0	509	19	35.7	N/A	48.5	—
Honduras	6.4	924	18	46.9	64.4	68.5	8
Mexico	98.0	5,864	3	74.4	16.5	73.2	200
Nicaragua	5.1	473	20	64.7	92.5	69.2	15
Panama	2.9	3,463	8	57.7	84.1	73.5	—
Paraguay	5.5	1,369	15	56.0	80.7	62.9	20
Peru	25.7	2,084	11	72.8	83.1	68.8	110
Uruguay	3.4	5,908	2	91.3	58.5	75.2	24
Venezuela	24.1	4,985	4	87.4	90.9	73.1	45
Lat. Am.	506.0	3,879		75.4	66.4		
USA	282.0	34,320				77.0	1,466

or to accept that 'the USA is our best friend, whether we like it or not'. Yet, even under the Workers' Party governments led by the radical Lula da Silva, Washington has generally found Brasília to be a reasonable regional partner with which differences over distinct policies have not descended into ideological conflict.

Although it has performed economically below expectations since the 1970s, Brazil has rarely exhibited strategic illiteracy. This has been recognized in Washington, but the State Department has expressed only limited appreciation of a third world country with nearly 200 years of independent existence and as rich a popular and sporting culture as any on earth. Brazil possesses as much soft power as any non-hegemonic state in the modern era.

Cuba, along with Puerto Rico, remained a colony of Spain throughout the nineteenth century. Despite frequent US efforts to purchase the prosperous slave-based plantation island up until the Civil War, it was not overtly threatened by the Monroe Doctrine, which was aimed at new European colonies. Although in 1898 Washington invaded Cuba, it did so with the explicit objective of halting the brutal Spanish campaign against the Cuban independence movement. As a result of this and the domestic anti-colonial lobby, it proved impossible to annex the country, which in 1902 acquired the status of an independent republic. However, the Platt Amendment to the US Army Appropriations Act of 1901 restricted Cuba's freedom to trade or form military alliances as well as permitting US intervention should its citizens or their property be threatened. An example of both conditionality and the use of Congress to formulate foreign policy, the Amendment effectively reduced Cuba to informal colonial status until it was withdrawn in 1934 following a revolution in the island.

The Cuban Revolution, which took state power in 1959 and remained in force nearly fifty years later, sealed that country's exceptional status on a number of grounds. It became and long remained the sole communist state in the western hemisphere; for thirty years it was a highly dependent client of the USSR and so drew the region more tightly into Cold War strategic culture than would otherwise have been the case. Throughout that period Cuba was subject to a US embargo, widespread diplomatic isolation, and exclusion from many regional organizations. The Missile Crisis of October 1962 was a moment of huge international consequence in the nuclear age, and Washington understandably formulated policy towards Cuba with its eyes set on eastern Europe before the rest of the hemisphere. However, within Latin America Cuba increasingly came to stand as a symbol of nationalist resistance, small-state solidarity, and a Spartan critique of the North American consumerist ethos that many Latin American governments had sought and failed to emulate.

From the abortive Bay of Pigs invasion of April 1961 onwards US administrations have both openly called for and covertly planned 'regime change' in Havana (although after the Missile Crisis they pledged not to enforce this unilaterally). In the wake of the collapse of the USSR in the early 1990s and with Castro's severe illness in 2006 such change seemed close at hand, but it did not come about. Nor, indeed, was it broadly supported in a region long suspicious of interventionism. Many Latin Americans who harboured little sympathy for communism recognized the prophecy of Simón Bolívar in 1830 that the United States 'seems destined by providence to plague America with torments in the name of freedom'. Familiar with the core US policy motifs of promoting freedom and democracy, the Latin American response has often been to accept this idealist rhetoric as a constant and to question its practical application in discrete cases on realist grounds. In the case of Cuba, even the pro-US and quite conservative OAS Secretary General José Miguel Insulza felt constrained to advise Condoleezza Rice, 'There is no transition, and it is not your country.'

Jorge Domínguez has argued that the Cold War did not in many respects affect US–Latin American relations: 'The United States had faced military, political and economic competition in the Americas from extra-continental powers before the Cold War, just as it did during the Cold War' (Domínguez in Bulmer-Thomas and Dunkerley 1999: 33). However, he also shows that the Cold War did introduce a strong ideological element that sometimes disturbed Washington's 'normal' interest-based or realist approaches, and this continued to be the case for Cuba even after 1991. So, despite strong evidence that the embargo fortified Castro, the hard-line policy of antagonism was retained. This was in good measure because the vocal and electorally powerful Cuban émigré communities of Florida and New Jersey were able to hold all administrations to account over commitments made from the 1960 election campaign and during the Kennedy administration. Nowhere else—not even in Mexico during the revolution or in Nicaragua under the Sandinistas—has such an unbending policy been sustained for such a time. For this reason it is best seen as exceptional and not representative.

Although Brazil, Cuba, and Mexico may be treated as exceptional in certain key aspects, they have still been subject to the broad conditions of US policy making towards the region described by Lars Schoultz:

> For nearly two centuries, three interests have determined the content of US policy toward Latin America: the need to protect US security, the desire to accommodate the demands of US domestic politics, and the drive to promote US economic development. Each generation's specific policies have changed with the times and the circumstances, as one year's fear of communist adventurism yields to next year's dismay over human rights violations, as the Big Stick transmutes into Dollar Diplomacy and then Good Neighborliness, as democracy and free trade vie for attention with drug trafficking and immigration . . . (Schoultz 1998: 367)

Within these parameters we can identify three unique and enduring features. First is the prominence of the doctrinal format, from Monroe, through Theodore Roosevelt's 'Corollary', F. D. Roosevelt's 'Good Neighbour Policy', and John F. Kennedy's 'Alliance for Progress', to a doctrine that seemed almost ashamed of its status—the Washington Consensus.

The second feature is the cultural tension between the two sectors of the hemisphere, and particular the frequent Anglo-American disparagement of Hispanic Catholic tradition. We shall return in the final section to this theme in the section with respect to the exceptionalist claims about Latin America's present 'threat' to the social and moral fabric of the USA (Box 15.9). We should also note the more prevalent commitment to a modernization theory within US policy circles, non-governmental organizations, and development agencies. This perspective often assumes that the USA's own path of development provides the natural model for the rest of the continent, overlooking significant historical differences. US policy makers frequently misunderstand indigenous cultures or the outlook of poor peasants, who are often key constituents in Latin America but never formed part of the mainstream historiography of the USA.

The third special feature is the degree to which US–Latin American relations have impacted upon the territory and population of the USA itself, from the Louisiana Purchase, through the annexation of half of Mexico's territory in the 1840s, to the mass immigration from the 1990s.

Taken together, these aspects have meant that the relationship cannot either be managed or understood simply in terms of bilateral state-to-state interactions. From the start it involved cultural competition and the often conflictive relations between transnational civil societies.

Latin America and the formation of the modern USA

'Latin America' is a term that first appeared in the 1850s and was in regular use before the 1930s. In 1783, when the thirteen colonies had won independence from Great Britain as the United States, Spain controlled a very great part of what would become over the following century the modern, continental USA. As Table 15.2 shows, US expansion was as much by purchase as by conquest.

Map 15.1 shows how conflicts involving European powers enabled Washington to expand its new 'empire', most notably through the Louisiana Purchase of 1803, when Napoleon, facing defeat at the hands of the ex-slaves of St Domingue (Haiti) turned his attentions back to European expansion and sold the Spanish-administered mid-section of North America to the USA. Napoleon's subsequent invasions of Portugal (1807) and Spain (1808) removed their monarchies, the first relocating to Brazil, which declared itself an independent empire in 1822, and the second going into exile. As a result, Spain's American colonies began to agitate for self-government.

The Latin American experience of national liberation and decolonization had no precedent other than that of the USA itself from Great Britain. Following the Treaty of Vienna (1814–15), London had sought to restore its ties with Washington and to distance itself from the resurgent absolutism of the European

Table 15.2 Major US territorial acquisitions, 1803–98

Date	Treaty/Act	Property	Acquired from	Area (acres)	Price ($)	Price per acre (cents)
1803	Louisiana Purchase	Louisiana	France (Spanish-administered)	559,513,600	15 mn.	3
1819	Adams-Onís	East Florida	Spain	46,144,640	15 mn.	33
1846	Oregon territory	Pacific north-west beneath 49th parallel	Great Britain	192,000,000	—	—
1848	Guadalupe-Hidalgo	Texas, California, New Mexico etc.	Mexico	338,680,960	20 mn.	6
1850	Texas cession	New Mexico	Texas	78,926,720	10 mn.	13
1853	Gadsden Purchase	Southern Arizona	Mexico	18,988,800	10 mn.	53
1867	Alaska Purchase	Alaska	Russia	375,296,000	7.2 mn.	2
1898	Treaty of Paris	Philippines	Spain	74,112,000	20 mn.	27

monarchies of the Holy Alliance. As a result, in mid-1823—when Mexico, Central America, and much of South America were free of Spanish rule but unrecognized by the major powers—Foreign Secretary Canning inquired of the Monroe administration whether it would consider a joint statement on policy towards the region. What became known as the Monroe Doctrine was Washington's response to that overture. However, its twin precepts of non-colonization (including the 'non-transferability' of colonies between European powers) and 'two spheres' (the Americas and Europe) proved to be far more consequential than the initial pragmatic rationale for the diplomatic recognition of the ex-Spanish colonies as republics.

Within fifteen years it was plain to the new Latin American states that Washington would not detain its rising and highly mobile population from moving west and south. On the one hand, this involved the dispossession of the traditional lands of the Native American peoples and their relocation to the western territories. On the other, it embodied the idea of manifest destiny, whereby providential powers were invoked to justify expansion into lands held both by indigenous tribes and the successor states to the Spanish empire.

Although fought 160 years ago, the Mexican–American War is still sharply recalled south of the new border established in 1848–53. Mexican national pride was assaulted by a series of defeats inflicted by US troops. The idea that the USA might simply conquer new territory from other republics was anathema to some sections of opinion in New England, whilst many in the slaveholding South felt that Catholic, Spanish-speaking peoples could not be incorporated into the USA without damaging its constitutional balance over the institution of slavery. Today those millions of Mexicans who have migrated to US states west of the Mississippi are moving to lands that were

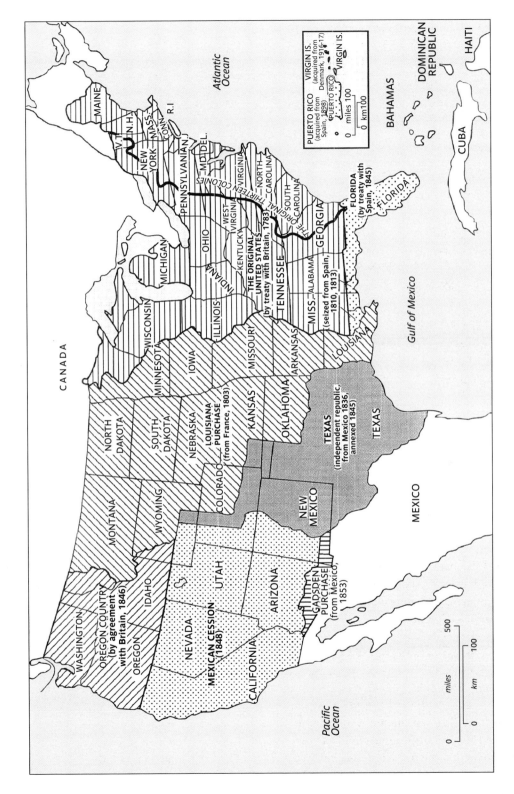

MAP 15.1: Territorial growth of the United States, 1783–1853

BOX 15.1: Monroe Doctrine and manifest destiny

We owe it . . . to candor and to the amicable relations existing between the United States and those [European] powers to declare that we should consider any attempt on their part to extend their system to any portion of this hemisphere, as dangerous to our peace and safety. With the existing colonies or dependencies of any European power we have not interfered and shall not interfere. But with the governments who have declared their independence and maintained it, and whose independence we have a great consideration in and on just principle, acknowledged, we could not view any interposition for the purpose of oppressing them or controlling in any other manner their destiny, by any European power in any other light than as the manifestation of an unfriendly disposition toward the United States.

(President James Monroe, 2 Dec. 1823)

Other nations have undertaken to intrude themselves . . . for the avowed objective of thwarting our policy and hampering our power, limiting our greatness and checking the fulfilment of our manifest destiny to overspread the continent allotted by Providence for the free development of our yearly multiplying millions . . . Whatsoever may hold the balance, though they should cast into the opposite scale all the bayonets and cannon, not only of France and England, but of Europe entire, how would it kick the beam against the simple solid weight of the 250 or 300 millions—and American millions—destined to gather beneath the flutter or the stripes and stars, in the fast hastening year of the Lord 1945?

(John O'Sullivan, July–Aug. 1845)

---

held for far longer by Madrid than they have been by Washington. From one perspective, 'the United States came to us, not we to it'.

If the Mexican War contributed to the origins of the US Civil War, that country also suffered sharply through the collapse of the Union—an experience which served to revive the apparently moribund Monroe Doctrine. With the USA unable to sustain its foreign ambitions in the early 1860s, the European powers returned momentarily to regional affairs, most notably in the effort to administer Mexico under the European Prince Maximilian, sponsored by the French Emperor Louis Napoleon. That tragic adventure presaged the European 'Rush for Africa' over the following decades, but it was already an anachronism in a western hemisphere where the culture of colonialism had been comprehensively repudiated.

Maximilian's nemesis, Benito Juárez, the first indigenous head of an American state, showed some signs of forming with Abraham Lincoln the kind of 'special relationship' sought by Presidents Fox and Bush. However, assassination and the unforgiving course of Mexican political life meant that whilst US Reconstruction was accompanied to the north by self-government in Canada, to the south it coexisted with the long-term dictatorship of Porfirio Díaz (1876–1910). For decades, US talk of democracy in Mexico was rare and

empty, and a steep price would be paid for that 'benign neglect' in the revolutionary era that followed. But a pattern was emerging—Washington favoured political stability and economic opportunity in Mexico above all else, including political freedom, for reasons of national security.

With the construction of the trans-continental railroad in 1869, the wars against the Native Americans of the Plains states over the following decades, and the simultaneous intense industrialization, the USA was reaching the limits of a 'home-based' policy towards the rest of the hemisphere. Washington's rising interest in the potential of a Pan-American strategy failed to develop into an enduring hemispheric initiative until the start of the 1890s, when trade and investment had grown to such a level that financial arrangements, particularly currency exchange rates, and the rules of international commerce required agreement on a continental scale.

The 1898 intervention in Cuba occurred, then, at a time when the US frontier had been closed for almost a decade, when Washington was concerned about European economic competition rather than colonial expansion in the rest of the hemisphere, and when overseas opportunities for trade and investment were being avidly sought. Now pledged to a 'two ocean' strategy involving the capacity to operate simultaneously in the Atlantic and Pacific,

Washington was industriously building up its naval strength. Extra-continental projection of force had become imaginable by dint of intra-hemispheric supremacy (see Box 15.2). Nonetheless, this first real experience of regional asymmetry brought fast in its wake the problems of conflict management in constitutionally and culturally foreign settings. The unilateral deployment of great power resources proved necessary but insufficient for maintaining prolonged and legitimate leadership.

KEY POINTS

❑ The Monroe Doctrine was not a charter for US expansion but for containing European territorial intervention in the Americas.

❑ Manifest destiny' was a popular ideology that justified expansion and assumed the cultural superiority of Anglo-America.

❑ Aside from the Mexican War, the USA was primarily involved in expansion within continental North America until 1898.

❑ US–Latin American relations in the nineteenth century were much stronger in Central America than South America.

A reluctant superpower

If the United States truly became an 'empire' in 1898, it certainly did not do so in the European manner of acquiring colonies. Not only was Cuba retained on a protectorate basis under the Platt Amendment but the Supreme Court ruled in 1901 that Puerto Rico 'was foreign to the United States in the domestic sense'. (US citizenship was granted to the population of Puerto Rico in 1917, and the island became a self-governing commonwealth in 1952. Puerto Ricans may travel freely in and out of the USA.)

In 1905 Theodore Roosevelt declared that 'the United States has not the slightest desire for territorial aggrandizement at the expense of any of its southern neighbors'. This was no mere rhetoric: Washington wanted not more land but markets. Between 1870 and 1900 Great Britain had added 4.7 million square miles to its empire and France 3.5 million, but US territories grew by only 125,000. Yet Roosevelt feared European intrusion in the hemisphere. When, in 1902–3, Germany and Britain tried through naval strength to enforce financial claims on Venezuela, Roosevelt sought to clarify strategy by issuing a 'corollary' to the Monroe Doctrine. He recognized that European intervention would now probably take the form of enforcing commercial agreements and that the failure of Latin American states to meet their international obligations was the most likely cause of such intrusion. In a December 1904 message to Congress, Roosevelt so qualitatively expanded the meaning and application of the 1823 message that many saw it as a total break with the original Monroe Doctrine.

Roosevelt's 'corollary' retained the notion of the two spheres, but these were now between 'civilized' and 'uncivilized' states. Whereas Monroe had effectively been supporting revolutions, Roosevelt was resolutely opposed to them, and while Monroe had urged non-intervention, Roosevelt reserved that right to the USA, assuming US control over markets, wherever they were located. Above all else, the Roosevelt corollary represented a declaration of conditionality of US policy upon the behaviour of regional states as much as it was a manifesto towards Europe.

The corollary was encouraged by the accelerated and conflictive manner in which Washington had acquired the rights to build an inter-oceanic canal through Panama. Until 1903 Panama had been a province of Colombia, but the Senate of that country refused to ratify the treaty with the USA over the canal since it surrendered so much sovereign power. As a result, Washington supported a Panamanian

---

BOX 15.2: The rights and responsibilities of the mighty: Olney and Roosevelt

Today the United States is practically sovereign on this continent, and its fiat is law upon subjects to which its confines its interposition. Why? It is not because of the pure friendship or good will felt for it. It is not simply by reason of its high character as a civilized state, nor because wisdom and justice and equity are the invariable characteristics of the dealings of the United States. It is because, in addition to all other grounds, its infinite resources combined with its isolated position render it master of the situation and practically invulnerable as against any or all other powers.

(Secretary of State Richard Olney to Thomas Bayard, 18 May 1895)

Chronic wrongdoing, or an impotence which results in a general loosening of the ties of civilized society, may in America, as elsewhere, ultimately require intervention by some civilized nation, and in the western hemisphere the adhesion of the United States to the Monroe Doctrine may force the United States, however reluctantly, in flagrant cases of such wrongdoing or impotence, to the exercise of an international police power.

(President Theodore Roosevelt to Congress, 9 Dec. 1904)

---

revolution, recognized the new country's independence in record time, and over the following decade undertook a quite remarkable piece of civil engineering for strategic purposes, allowing two-oceanic naval planning, and providing an awesome example of North American industrial vision and capacity.

When the canal opened in August 1914, it appeared as if Washington had truly achieved the means to make its disavowal of armed intervention in other countries a reality since it now apparently possessed the logistical capacity to deter unfriendly activity. However, it was precisely in the first three decades of the twentieth century, when the USA secured such manifest superiority over both the local states and its European competitors, that it intervened most often, and to widespread criticism at home and abroad. Roosevelt, always disposed towards belligerence, started this process, but his successors Taft and Wilson failed to replace 'the big stick' with non-violent 'dollar diplomacy' (Taft) and 'peace between equals' (Wilson).

Between 1898 and 1930 US gunboats were sent into Latin American ports more than 6,000 times; marines were deployed in Cuba, Mexico, Guatemala, Honduras, Dominican Republic, Nicaragua, Haiti, and Panama; elections were supervised in six states; anti-government rebels actively supported in four countries; loans obligatorily renegotiated in six states;

and governments in fourteen countries refused diplomatic recognition (Grandin 2006: 3; Dunkerley in Bulmer-Thomas and Dunkerley 1999: 10). Almost all this activity occurred in Central America and the Caribbean, and most was undertaken under governments which insistently repudiated intervention as their preferred policy.

What happened? Basically, US economic ties with Latin America had widened and deepened to such an extent that it was no longer possible for an administration to determine precisely how it would respond to circumstances driven by market forces beyond its direct control. US investment overseas had risen from $700 million in 1897 to $3.5 billion in 1914, over half of it in Latin America. With the First World War severely reducing European trade and capital flows, the USA had by the 1920s come to dominate the commercial and financial life of the Caribbean basin. Such economic dominance brought with it political complications, and not all of them were readily negotiable.

The small and unstable states of the Caribbean constituted a particular sphere of influence, the Dominican Republic being governed directly under occupation by the US Marine Corps from 1916 to 1924, whereas US forces were deployed in Haiti from 1915 to 1934, when that country was administered as a protectorate. However, as in the nineteenth century, it was Nicaragua and Mexico which presented Washington with the greatest challenge.

In the case of Nicaragua, the logical site for an alternative trans-isthmian route to that in Panama, continued feuding between liberal and conservative forces required every administration from Roosevelt to Hoover to dispatch marines, support or suppress local revolts, administer the collection of customs in order to secure repayment of loans, and seek to broker local political peace. By 1928 Washington had been enmeshed for over a dozen years in the complex conflicts of a small and poor country far beyond any reasonable demand of strategic need or economic interest.

In the 1890s criticism of 'the northern colossus' had taken a largely literary or cultural form—in the campaigning journalism of the Cuban martyr José Martí or the essays of the Uruguayan José Enrique Rodó, whose polemic *Ariel* depicted the USA as a vulgar, materialist democracy dominated by the mob and counterposed to the classical tradition. By the 1920s, anti-Americanism was taking a more activist form, with calls for the internationalization of the Panama Canal and widespread support for Augusto César Sandino, who from 1928 led an effective guerrilla campaign against US military occupation of Nicaragua. By 1933 this opposition contributed not only to the withdrawal of the marines but also a major shift in US policy to the region as a whole.

In Mexico the economic, strategic, and diplomatic issues were of a greater order since US interests in the neighbouring country were the largest in the region and so placed in considerable jeopardy by the revolution (1910–20). After the prolonged and highly profitable US alliance with the pre-revolutionary Díaz regime, the prominent role of US ambassador Henry Lane Wilson in the assassination of President Madero in 1913 became infamous and set the two countries on a twenty-year course of tense contestation. In 1914 US forces attacked and occupied Veracruz for several months, reviving memories of the 1847 war. Two years later General Pershing invaded the state of Chihuahua in pursuit of the rebel leader Pancho Villa.

In 1917 the new Mexican Constitution reserved to the state all rights over the subsoil, raising doubts over the property rights of US mining and oil companies. However, it was only in 1938 that Mexico finally expropriated all foreign oil companies, and then it promised compensation. Even before the Second World War this nationalist attitude was being extended to manufacturing, the larger Latin American states adopting policies of import-substituting industrialization in order to reduce what would later be termed dependency on the advanced northern economies.

Washington had been prey to corporate and press accusations that the Mexican government was emulating Moscow if not itself actively Bolshevik. The charge never stuck, though. Even Woodrow Wilson, deeply anti-revolutionary, perceived a certain logic in the evolving Mexican political process, and thereafter no US administration promoted ideological accusation above a cool appraisal of national interest, allowing the PRI a full seventy years of one-party rule until the election of President Fox in 2000.

By the time of the 1932 presidential election, a dictatorship in Cuba was enjoying US patronage by default under the Platt Amendment, and this demanded that Washington rethink and eventually repudiate the Roosevelt corollary. The fall in 1933 of the Machado regime in Cuba gave the new administration of F. D. Roosevelt (FDR) a good opportunity to proclaim the Good Neighbour Policy, reversing the Roosevelt corollary, reducing tariffs, and making a virtue out of what many saw as the necessity of isolationism in the Great Depression.

Designed to be high-minded and restore the legitimacy squandered through thirty years of 'gunboat diplomacy', the Good Neighbour Policy did not surrender US national interest. The tariff reductions that revived trade were conditional upon reciprocity from Latin American states. However, the policy did suspend the 'Americanist' vocation to promote freedom abroad. When it was enunciated, of the twenty-one states of the region only Colombia was ruled by a government that had come to power through an open election. Now the policy of non-intervention—or what some would call 'benign neglect'—effectively

---

BOX 15.3: Burying the big stick: the Clark memo and Good Neighbour Policy

The so-called 'Roosevelt corollary' was to the effect, as generally understood, that in case of financial or other difficulties in weak Latin American countries, the United States should attempt an adjustment lest European Governments should intervene, and intervening should occupy territory—an act which would be contrary to the principles of the Monroe Doctrine . . . it is not believed that this corollary is justified by the terms of the Monroe Doctrine, however much it may be justified by the application of the doctrine of self-preservation . . . So far as Latin America is concerned, the Doctrine is now, and always has been, not an instrument of violence and oppression, but an unbought, freely bestowed, and wholly effective guaranty of their freedom, independence, and territorial integrity against the imperialistic designs of Europe.

(Undersecretary of State Reuben Clark, to Secretary Frank Kellogg, Dec. 1928)

The essential qualities of a true pan Americanism must be the same as those which constitute a good neighbour, namely, mutual understanding, and, through such understanding, a sympathetic appreciation of the other's point of view . . . the independence of each republic must recognize the independence of every other republic.

(President Roosevelt, speech to Pan American Union, Apr. 1933)

---

endorsed the existence of the many dictatorships installed in the wake of the 1929 Crash. In Brazil, Washington's closest ally, party politics was suspended and the authoritarian *Estado Novo* set up by Getúlio Vargas in 1935–7 in emulation of Salazar's Portuguese dictatorship.

The outbreak of the Second World War in Europe in September 1939 found the republics of the western hemisphere less politically invigilated than for fifty years but also tied to the US market to an unprecedented degree. War between European powers posed the long discussed issue of a regional defence treaty that would make the Monroe Doctrine both practical and pluralistic. Although agreements on reciprocal defence were signed in 1940, it was only with the Japanese attack on Pearl Harbor in December 1941 that regional states were obliged to take hard decisions. Very few themselves upheld FDR's four freedoms—of speech and religion, from want and fear—but fewer still could rely on extra-hemispheric alternatives to trade with the USA. Authoritarian Brazil provided troops which engaged with Nazi forces in Italy, but most of Latin America had only to confront the diplomatic and economic consequences of the conflict. All the Caribbean and Central American republics immediately followed Washington in declaring war on the Axis. However, the bi-oceanic nature of the conflict, caution, and ideological sympathies meant that several countries remained neutral until weeks before the end of the war: Chile, Venezuela, Uruguay (February 1945), Argentina, and Paraguay (March 1945).

The prominent anti-fascist profile of the Allied campaign restored a long suspended ideological element to hemispheric politics, and this would feed fiercely into the Cold War era. Yet in the immediate post-war years the region underwent an intense transitional experience whereby the populist Argentine government led by General Perón was targeted as fascistic and intent upon expanding its influence throughout South America. Perón, however, positively flourished on the nationalist backlash against ill-judged accusations, survived, and came to find a sober *modus vivendi* with Washington based on shared anti-communism.

The conflict with Perón presaged policy issues that would dominate US–Latin American relations until the 1990s. How was Washington to distinguish between state-based development policies and 'crypto-communism'? How could it promote liberal capitalism through social reform without undermining anti-communist allies? How were the NATO and traditional hemispheric security needs to be reconciled in the context of ideological challenges from Moscow, Beijing, and the third world movements against imperialism and colonialism?

KEY POINTS

❑ The 'Roosevelt corollary' of 1904 made US policy conditional upon the behaviour of Latin American states—a significant shift from the Monroe Doctrine.

❑ The growth of US economic interests in the region not only surpassed its European competition but also complicated a foreign policy based purely on political considerations.

❑ US interventionism in Central America and the Caribbean was extensive in the early twentieth century although Washington preferred to avoid deployment of military forces.

❑ The Good Neighbour Policy introduced by F. D. Roosevelt in 1933 consolidated prior efforts to reduce direct US intervention but also suspended the promotion of democracy.

Cold War coexistence

The Cold War had a partial and uneven effect on US policy towards Latin America. Sometimes ideological aggression and interventionist impulses were given full rein (Guatemala, 1954; Cuba, 1961; Dominican Republic, 1965; Chile, 1970–3; Nicaragua, 1979–90; Grenada, 1983; Panama, 1989), but sometimes a more circumspect policy was applied (Venezuela, 1945–8; Bolivia, 1952–64; Peru, 1968–75; Honduras and Panama, 1972; Mexico, throughout). Washington could tolerate high levels of commerce with the USSR (Argentina) or even extensive arms purchases from it (Peru), provided a fundamental anti-communism was sustained at home. Equally, agrarian reform was encouraged in some countries (Bolivia, Venezuela, Chile, and El Salvador) for its counter-insurgency potential, whereas it was deemed anathema in others (Guatemala, Cuba, Brazil) where it was seen to encourage popular radicalism. On occasion, such as the Falklands War of 1982, even a staunch anti-communist ally would be deserted for an older alliance (although forces within the Reagan cabinet resisted this).

Grandin suggests that one reason for this mixed record was that Washington used the hemisphere as a laboratory for testing the techniques of neo-colonial anti-communism in the third world. Domínguez, on the other hand, uses the destabilization of the Allende government in Chile to question the logic and true usefulness to US national interest of such activity (in Bulmer-Thomas and Dunkerley 1999).

Two factors stand out in this period. First is the regular use by Washington of the new multilateral treaties and organizations. Of particular importance were the regional defence agreement signed at Rio in 1947 and the Organization of American States (OAS) in 1948. Sometimes described as a 'meeting of pigeons presided over by a cat', the OAS was preferred to the UN for its malleability—it proved unproblematic to suspend Cuba's membership in 1962—but by the 1970s it had become more independent.

As befitted an era of competition between liberal and collectivist development models, the institutions set up at Bretton Woods in 1944, such as the IMF, and related bodies like the World Bank, also became valuable channels for imposing economic discipline and making loans conditional upon fiscal austerity. By the 1980s such policies were no longer enforced in the unilateral manner of the 'Roosevelt corollary' and were accepted as part of a capitalist regime that extended beyond narrow US national interests.

The second distinctive feature of late twentieth-century regional relations has already been noted—the importance of the Cuba revolution. Before 1959 regional anti-communism had either, as Grandin suggests, to experiment or to draw its repertoire of fears, soft-power, and counter-insurgency techniques

---

BOX 15.4: The case against Guatemala

That the domination or control of the political institutions of any American state by the international communist movement, extending to this hemisphere the political system of an extra-continental power, would constitute a threat to the sovereignty and political independence of all the American states, endangering the peace of America, and would call for appropriate action in accordance with existing treaties.

(Draft US resolution on Guatemala, OAS Conference, Caracas, Mar. 1954)

---

from extra-hemispheric experiences. Once the rebels took power in Havana, US policy was transformed by a tangible foe occupying state power. Containment was not enough since Cuba initially urged emulation of its example, creating 'two, three Vietnams' in Che Guevara's provocative phrase, which did nothing to persuade Washington that domino theory was neater in theory than practice.

Havana, viewed throughout as a loyal but erratic client of Moscow, preferred supporting guerrilla groups to communist parties, several of which it helped to split. By the 1970s Castro displayed greater pragmatism and urged caution on the Sandinistas after they took power. Often Washington recognized these features but under the Reagan administration (1981–9) its invective was virulent. Moreover, the existence of a communist regime in the hemisphere sharpened the anti-communism of Latin American conservative forces, which increasingly embraced the ideology of the national security state, militarizing political power and suspending all civil liberties, which sometimes led to the mass murder of citizens by their own states (particularly Chile and Argentina in the 1970s, Guatemala and El Salvador in the 1980s).

The destabilization of the reformist government of Jacobo Arbenz in Guatemala was approved at the highest levels of the Truman and Eisenhower administrations, orchestrated by the CIA, and favoured the interests of the United Fruit Company whose lands had faced expropriation. Arbenz had been elected president in a fair poll and had adopted a modest programme of reforms. Yet Washington put his close ties to the country's small Communist Party at the heart of a propaganda campaign designed for its deterrent effects elsewhere as well as to destabilize a state that lacked the resources to match its radical rhetoric.

The June 1954 overthrow of Arbenz by a band of US-trained rebels was not seriously opposed in the OAS although it was recognized as Washington's work. That success encouraged a repeat of the combination of diplomatic isolation with covert action by local proxy forces against the Sandinistas in the 1980s.

There was scant criticism of the Guatemalan operation in the USA at the height of the McCarthy era, but when the rebels took power in Cuba five years later the debate over how Washington should respond was sharper. In the 1960 election campaign Kennedy attacked Nixon as weak on the issue, and his new government readily accepted plans for a Guatemalan-style invasion by counter-revolutionaries at the Bay of Pigs in April 1961. That operation was a disaster that helped to radicalize the Castro government, which not unreasonably supposed that it needed a superpower patron if it was to survive for long and so assiduously developed an alliance with a sceptical but enticed Moscow. Within eighteen months this process had led the world to the verge of a stand-off between the world's leading nuclear powers. Kennedy opted for a naval blockade to prevent the USSR from siting missiles within 100 miles of the North American mainland, and Moscow stepped back once promises were secured that Cuba would not be invaded.

Again, criticism was slight since Kennedy's policy upheld the Monroe Doctrine, anti-communism, and regional security. However, by 1962 it was plain that the USA needed more than reactive policies to deal with the influence of Cuba. Military aid rose, counter-insurgency operations were continuously developed and planned—in 1965 the Johnson administration did not hesitate to invade the Dominican Republic—but they were now accompanied by North American calls for agrarian reform, institutional modernization,

---

BOX 15.5: The Cuban Revolution

1952	Batista seizes power and establishes dictatorship.	1959	January: rebels take Havana after a general strike brings down military junta; Fidel Castro takes control; agrarian reform starts (May).
1953	Castro launches abortive assault on Moncada barracks, Santiago.	1960	May: Cuba establishes diplomatic relations with USSR.
1954	Che Guevara observes overthrow of Arbenz government in Guatemala.		June: US oil companies nationalized; further expropriation of foreign-owned property.
1955	Castro and other surviving rebels amnestied, go into Mexican exile.		October: US imposes trade embargo.
1956	Rebel yacht *Granma* lands in southern Cuba; guerrilla operations begin.	1961	January: US breaks diplomatic relations with Cuba.
1957	Second guerrilla column set up under Che Guevara.		April: abortive counter-revolutionary landing at Bay of Pigs.
1958	Raúl Castro establishes new front in north. Washington imposes arms embargo on Batista government following human rights violations; Batista removed in military coup.	1962	October (22–8): Missile Crisis.

---

increased foreign investment, and political liberalization, all under the mantle of an Alliance for Progress.

Very much moulded in the idealistic style of the Kennedy government, the Alliance was driven more by rhetoric than hard cash. Once Kennedy was gone, the policy lost priority, and by the end of the 1960s Washington had relegated reformist responses to radicalism. Johnson and Nixon welcomed a clutch of right-wing military dictatorships in South America without great concern for their anti-democratic character.

The rapid shift away from encouragement of liberal modernity back towards a threat-driven anti-communist strategy was most marked in the case of Chile. Although President Allende was a socialist and Santiago had diplomatic relations with both Havana and Moscow, the Chilean government was a weak constitutional coalition and did not seek ties with the Soviet bloc like those held by Cuba. Yet beneath a now familiar veil of secrecy, Nixon and Kissinger authorized the CIA to stop Allende's election and then, when that failed, to destabilize his government. The eventual coup of September 1973, in which Allende died, needed no direct US intervention, but the sixteen-year dictatorship of Augusto Pinochet owed much to Washington's support.

Washington's role in destabilizing the Allende government aroused controversy at home, prompting a congressional investigation into US covert operations in the region. In the wake of defeat in Vietnam, this current of criticism helped to reanimate support for the multilateral approach developed by the Carter White House. Carter's deliberate adoption of a 'low profile' included negotiating return of the canal to Panama and criticizing the violation of human rights violations of the dictatorships, which, in a new form of conditionality, lost military aid. This was most telling in Central America.

The radical movements of Central America in the 1980s have been described as 'inevitable revolutions' (LaFeber 1983) because they sprang out of prolonged poverty and political oppression. The movement was most advanced in Nicaragua, where the FSLN (Sandinistas) challenged the sixty-year rule of the Somoza family. When, late in 1978, the FSLN threatened to take power, Washington sought OAS support for multilateral intervention but this was rejected, not least because several dictatorships wanted to avoid a precedent that might be used against them. Carter had to harden his policy, but he came under fierce criticism. Reagan's 1980 election campaign made much of the 'loss' of Central

BOX 15.6: The destabilization of the Allende government in Chile

One in 10 chance, but save Chile!
worth spending
not concerned risks involved
no involvement of embassy
$10,000,000 available, more if necessary
Full-time job—best men we have
Game plan
Make the economy scream
48 hours for plan of action.

(CIA Director Richard Helms, notes after meeting of 15 Sept. 1970, with Pres. Nixon, Henry Kissinger, and John Mitchell; photocopy published by Senate Select Committee on Intelligence Activities, 94th Congress, 4 and 5 Dec. 1975)

Once Allende comes to power we shall do all in our power to condemn Chile and Chileans to utmost deprivation and poverty.

(US Ambassador Edward Korry, Santiago, to Kissinger, 21 Sept. 1970)

I don't see why we have to let a country go Marxist just because its people are irresponsible.

(Attributed to Kissinger, *New York Times*, 11 Sept. 1974)

Our hand doesn't show on this one.

(Nixon to Kissinger, 11.50 a.m., 16 Sept. 1973)

America, and his government subsequently adopted the ideas and services of the Democrat academic Jeane Kirkpatrick, who defended the 'moderate repression' of the Argentine dictatorship (under which at least 15,000 people disappeared) as far more acceptable than the communist alternatives that she saw Carter's policies as encouraging.

Once in office, Reagan sought not just to contain the Sandinistas but to 'make them say Uncle'. At the same time, he provided military aid to El Salvador,

BOX 15.7: The Cold War revived in Central America

Human rights is the soul of our foreign policy.

(Pres. Jimmy Carter, 1978)

What did the Carter administration do in Nicaragua? It brought down the Somoza regime . . . acted repeatedly and at critical junctures to weaken the government of Anastasio Somoza and to strengthen his opponents . . . hurried efforts to force complex and unfamiliar political practices on societies lacking the requisite political culture, tradition, and social structures not only fail to produce the desired outcomes; if they are undertaken at a time when a traditional regime is under attack, they actually facilitate the job of the insurgents.

(Kirkpatrick 1979)

Let's not delude ourselves . . . the Soviet Union underlies all the unrest that is going on. If they weren't engaged in this game of dominoes, there wouldn't be any hotspots in the world.

(Ronald Reagan, quoted in *Wall Street Journal*, 3 June 1980)

. . . the national security of the Americas is at stake in Central America. If we cannot defend ourselves there, we cannot expect to prevail elsewhere. Our credibility would collapse, our alliances would crumble, and the safety of our homeland would be put in jeopardy.

(Pres. Ronald Reagan, 2 May 1983, *Weekly Compilation of Presidential Declarations*, 613–14)

Many of our citizens don't fully understand the seriousness of the situation, so let me put it bluntly: There is a war in Central America that is being fuelled by the Soviets and the Cubans. They are arming, training and supplying, and encouraging a war to subjugate another nation to communism, and that nation is El Salvador. The Soviets and the Cubans are operating from a base called Nicaragua. And this is the first real Communist aggression on the American mainland.

(Reagan 1983: 1044)

where the FMLN guerrillas were strong. These forces were certainly supported by Managua and Havana, but their resilience owed more to popular support, strategic ability, and the unpopularity of the regimes they were fighting. Washington recognized this, held back from close association with the Guatemalan regime, which had a particularly bad record of repression, and forced the Salvadorian government to accept agrarian reform and elections as key counter-insurgency tactics.

Yet Reagan's Central American policy rested on vocal accusations of communist conspiracy. Domestic concern at the renewed threat of covert operations against the government of Nicaragua led to congressional amendments which aimed to avert a repetition of the Chilean experience. However, the CIA and officers of the National Security Council sought to circumvent constitutional restrictions imposed by Congress. They clandestinely raised cash to fund their counter-revolutionary forces based in Honduras and Costa Rica by selling missiles to Iran, then at war with Iraq. When this doubly illegal operation was revealed, a major political scandal—the Iran-Contra Affair—broke out.

The guerrilla wars in Guatemala and El Salvador were eventually settled by UN- and European-brokered peace accords in the 1990s. The Sandinistas were removed from office in 1990, but by the Nicaraguan electorate. The Reagan policy had yielded some success—it had certainly stopped national conflicts combining into a Central American regional war. But it did so at very high costs to its support and legitimacy elsewhere.

KEY POINTS

❏ The Cold War did not have a uniform impact on US–Latin American relations after 1947.

❏ Washington retained a pragmatic or 'realist' approach to the region where it did not perceive a serious radical challenge.

❏ The Cuban Revolution changed US–Latin American relations, introducing the only communist regime in the western hemisphere.

❏ Although Cuba initially sought to encourage other revolutions and was always sympathetic to radical causes, after 1973 it displayed a quite pragmatic policy in the western hemisphere.

❏ After the Cuban Revolution US policy alternated between hard-line, military-led approaches (Johnson/Nixon/Reagan) and those that included a significant element of 'soft power' (Kennedy/Carter/Bush Sr./Clinton).

The Washington 'Consensus' questioned

KEY POINTS

❏ The Washington Consensus was a set of orthodox liberal policies designed to stabilize the performance of Latin American economies and open them to international markets after the debt crisis of the early 1980s.

❏ The Consensus was a doctrine supported by the US government but practically implemented by multilateral organizations such as the IMF and World Bank, so it represented an end to the 'hemispherism' of both the Monroe Doctrine and the Roosevelt corollary.

❏ Aside from Central America, the Consensus replaced anti-communism as Washington's prime concern in Latin America.

❏ The economic recession of the 1980s and 1990s, in part prompted by the Consensus, prompted a regional rise in drug production and emigration to the USA, issues that by 2000 had firmly displaced ideology as the key US concerns relating to Latin America.

In August 1982 Mexico effectively went bankrupt by defaulting on its sovereign debt. Other countries had likewise sought to subsidize national industries and welfare systems by borrowing on the international markets in the wake of the oil crises of the 1970s; they were barely less vulnerable. The governments and the private banks that had lent so generously to them in uncertain times now faced demands from the IMF for stabilization of trading accounts and strictly balanced budgets, which usually meant a substantial reduction in 'public goods' such as health and education—all with the objective of securing growth, and with the alleviation of poverty a strictly secondary issue. Under this 'neo-liberal' agenda, the economies were to be opened up as much as possible to international trade since this would, according to the classical economic theories dominating the multilateral institutions, produce growth, and the results of growth would, sooner or later, 'trickle down' to the benefit of the poor.

In fact, the poor of Latin America grew in number, as did income inequality as a whole. The only tangible benefit of neo-liberalism for the millions under the poverty line was the severe reduction in inflation. Everywhere, the post-war 'boom' was over, and multilateral institutions were enforcing orthodox capitalist policies and management. Almost everywhere public spending was slashed, companies went broke, and employment fell. What failed to follow for over a decade was sustained growth and renewed investment in the public services. Even private foreign investment was cautious, after an upsurge in the late 1990s proved short-lived.

As the larger economies opened up under what became known as the Washington Consensus, they became exposed to the erratic movements of international finance, with the result that Mexico suffered a severe monetary crisis in 1994–5, Brazil in 1998–9, and Argentina in 2001–3. Liberalization had brought its own problems, even if it had lessened the problems of import-substituting industrialization, mixed economies, and unorthodox fiscal policies. What had been sold in the early 1980s as a foolproof 'one-size-fits-all' solution was shown to be very uneven. Even in Chile, where the Pinochet regime introduced an early adjustment programme designed with advice from the University of Chicago, it proved necessary to bale out banks and limit the movement of foreign finance.

Elsewhere, in a very poor country like Bolivia or a medium-sized oil state such as Venezuela, 'stabilization' sparked mass unemployment and enduring social discontent. The most modern form of 'conditionality' had proved to be an insensitive instrument in itself and Washington was not always able to micro-manage a controversial 'consensus' founded in its own name. Only in the case of the Mexican crisis of 1994–5 did the Clinton administration act directly to bale out its neighbour—for fear of the consequences for the USA of a second hemispheric debt crisis south of the border.

The free trade policy that stood at the heart of the Washington Consensus attracted much controversy, but one relatively neglected consequence of this endorsement of globalization was its opening of the region to all markets, including those of Europe. In a post-colonial age, this may represent the true termination of the Monroe Doctrine, especially since Washington and the European Union were alike reluctant to allow the opening up of their own more protected markets to competition from the south.

As a result of the recession of the 1980s and the free competition of the 1990s the 'informal economy' of Latin America grew, and nowhere more so than in the illegal production of drugs, overwhelmingly destined for the US market. Drugs policy became a leading policy item from the early 1980s, particularly affecting the Andean countries producing the coca plant used to manufacture cocaine and the Central American and Caribbean countries, used as conduits into the USA. From a Latin American perspective, US drug policy was consistently 'supply led' in that it prioritized eradication at source and interdiction over reducing demand, providing few real economic alternatives to the poor farmers who supplied the mafia with their illicit goods. From the US perspective reduced supply increased the costs and so shrank demand; the imposition of conditionality was reasonable, given the aid that Congress was financing. However, Washington did move in the 1990s to reduce the attention given

---

BOX 15.8: The 'drugs war': asymmetry or inequity?

. . . [Bolivian President Evo Morales] is right to complain about American imperialists criminalizing a substance that's been used for centuries in the Andes. If gringos are abusing a product made from coca leaves, that's a problem for America to deal with at home . . . America makes plenty of things that are bad for foreigners' health—fatty Big Macs, sugary Cokes, deadly Marlboros—but we'd never let foreigners tell us what to make and not make. The

Saudis can fight alcoholism by forbidding the sale of Jack Daniels, but we'd think they were crazy if they ordered us to eradicate fields of barley in Tennessee.

(John Tierney, *New York Times*, 23 Sept. 2006)

---

to government 'certification' of compliance by Latin American states since this plainly wounded pride and was counterproductive. Whether judged by the state of bilateral relations or flows of contraband narcotics from the region, the policy was not a success.

When President Fox visited Washington in September 2001, he did so in search of a solution to the mutual problem of mass and rising immigration to the USA. When President Bush visited Mexico City in March 2007 he had the same issue at the top of his agenda. In the intervening period some five million Mexicans had crossed the border, there being nearly 50 million people of Hispanic descent living in the USA. One in six babies now born in the USA has a Hispanic mother, and the total Hispanic population is projected to be 100 million in 2050.

There is a positive side to this new reality. Hispanic GDP within the USA is now $700 billion—bigger than those of Spain and Mexico—and a significant amount of it is returned to the region in the form of private remittances. However, it is arguable how economically efficient and equitable this is. Moreover, many immigrants are undocumented—both illegal and unable to secure the support of the US welfare system. Within the USA Hispanics are disproportionately poor and overly represented in the armed forces, even if they have avoided the poor health and crime profiles of the African-American population they overtook as the largest minority group early in the twenty-first century.

For some conservative thinkers, such as Harvard Professor Samuel Huntington, this Hispanic diaspora posed a uniquely acute threat to the traditional US 'melting pot' and represented a 'clash of cultures' within the very borders of the USA.

Others expected this fast-developing scenario to provide a beneficial impact on both sides of the border: Hispanic middle-class employees of the State Department would introduce knowledge and sensitivity into bilateral relations, and US politicians would be more responsive to the rising Hispanic electorate. But progress has only been patchy, since those

---

BOX 15.9: The great fear: Latin America *within* the USA

Americans, to varying degree, have defined the substance of their identity in terms of race, ethnicity, ideology and culture. Race and ethnicity are now largely eliminated: Americans see their country as a multiethnic, multiracial society. The 'American Creed', as initially formulated by Thomas Jefferson . . . however, was the product of a distinct Anglo-Protestant culture of the founding settlers of America in the 17th and 18th centuries. Key elements of that culture include: the English language; Christianity; religious commitment; English concepts of the rule of law, the responsibility of rulers, and the rights of individuals; and dissenting Protestant values of individualism, the work ethic, and

the belief that humans have the ability and the duty to try to create a heaven on earth, a 'city on a hill' . . . In the late 20th century, however, the salience and substance of this culture was challenged by a new wave of migrants from Latin America and Asia, the popularity in intellectual and political circles of the doctrines of multiculturalism and diversity, the spread of Spanish as a second language and the Hispanization trends in American society . . .

(Huntington 2004: pp. xv–xvi)

Hispanics who have not grown up in Latin American countries speak the same language but often underestimate the power of nationalist sentiment. Equally, many Hispanics in the USA are not on the electoral registers, and their political profile reflects neither a blanket poverty—there is a distinct Hispanic middle class—nor the traditional social sensibilities of a society unused to Catholic values, which, for example, promote with equal energy the right to life and the right to join a trade union.

In the meantime, the new, independently minded governments elected in the first years of the new century showed every sign of moving away from the Washington Consensus, choosing which of its economic instruments they wished to maintain—largely control of inflation—and which they repudiated—largely open access for foreign companies to strategic resources. They had few extra-hemispheric options with which to test Washington, and whilst the Chinese market helped to underpin economic recovery, it did not represent an enduring alternative to the USA. So, even the more radical regimes recognized the continuing continental asymmetry, but they refused to accept the existing political terms—and particularly the presumption of hegemony – through which this had long been expressed.

Conclusion

If in 1803 Thomas Jefferson was seeking to develop the USA into a truly continental power by expanding into lands occupied by Native Americans and Mexicans, in 2003 George W. Bush was concerned to limit the arrival of Latin American people in the assured continental power that the USA had been for over a century. Markets and jobs had replaced land. The colonization feared in the early nineteenth century had not occurred. Large parts of Mexico were annexed after the war in 1846–8, but the Monroe Doctrine was not exploited to extend direct US control and administration of the Latin American republics. When this was sought after 1898 in order to secure and guarantee commercial advantage, it caused a backlash at home and abroad, embarrassed governments formally pledged to the principles of non-intervention and sovereignty, and it yielded insufficient economic advantage to justify the political and diplomatic costs. By 1930 the USA had already out-competed the European economies and readily dominated the political economy of the hemisphere. FDR's Good Neighbour Policy restored an earlier attachment to non-intervention, and it was only moderated in the Second World War in terms of the need for logistical cooperation. The onset of the Cold War saw a return to a much more ideological and interventionist approach, which was strengthened by the Cuban Revolution. Yet under the Kennedy and Carter administrations, some important variation of approach and style was undertaken. At no time was anti-communist language more virulent than under Reagan, but after the Cold War equally pressing problems of economic failure, drugs, and immigration proved just as difficult to manage.

? Questions

1. Has US policy towards Latin America been consistent over the nineteenth and twentieth centuries?
2. To what degree has Europe determined the pattern of US–Latin American relations?
3. Is the USA an empire based on neo-colonialism in the western hemisphere?
4. What have been the main consequences of the Monroe Doctrine?
5. To what degree has the Latin American policy of the USA been 'idealist' in the twentieth century?

6. Have Latin American countries consistently been the passive subaltern states of the western hemisphere?

7. To what extent have multilateral organizations affected US–Latin American relations since 1945?

8. Has there been a consistent Latin American anti-Americanism?

9. To what degree is Cuba as 'exceptional' as the USA itself?

10. Has globalization finally ended the era of the Monroe Doctrine?

» Further Reading

Bemis, Samuel Flagg (1943), *The Latin American Policy of the United States* (New York: Harcourt Brace).

    The standard or 'official' version of regional policy up to the Second World War. Still worth reading for an insight to mainstream attitudes and accounts.

Bulmer-Thomas, V., and Dunkerley, J. (1999), *The United States and Latin America: The New Agenda* (Cambridge, Mass.: David Rockefeller Center for Latin American Studies/Institute of Latin American Studies, University of London).

    A collection of essays covering the historical background, drugs and immigration, and a focus on Cuba as well as the main themes of the relationship in the 1990s.

Carothers, Thomas (1991), *In the Name of Democracy: US Policy toward Latin America in the Reagan Years* (Berkeley and Los Angeles: University of California Press).

    A critical survey that is detailed and well informed.

Grandin, G. (2006), *Empire's Workshop: Latin America, the United States, and the Rise of the New Imperialism* (New York: Metropolitan Books).

    A radical reinterpretation of the twentieth-century relationship that argues for a deliberate use of the region by Washington to experiment and develop techniques for wider application.

Joseph, G., Legrand, C., and Salvatore, R. (eds.) (1998), *Close Encounters of Empire: Writing the Cultural History of US–Latin American Relations* (Durham, NC: Duke University Press).

    A wide-ranging collection of detailed cultural case studies on both hard and soft power.

LaFeber, W. (1983), *Inevitable Revolutions: The United States in Central America* (New York: W.W.Norton).

    An historical survey of the origins and development of the social conflict of the 1970s and 1980s that stresses local inequities and is sceptical about Soviet influence.

LaRosa, M., and Mora, F. (eds.) (1999), *Neighborly Adversaries: Readings in US–Latin American Relations* (Lanham, Md.: Rowman and Littlefield).

    A broad selection of excerpts from primary materials, mostly from the twentieth century.

LeoGrande, William M. (1990), 'From Reagan to Bush: The Transition in US Policy towards Central America', *Journal of Latin American Studies*, 22/3: 595–621.

    A comprehensive synopsis of how the hard-line Cold War approach to the region was upheld in moderated form.

——(2007), 'A Poverty of Imagination: George W. Bush's Policy in Latin America', *Journal of Latin American Studies*, 39/2: 355–86.

    A short but comprehensive survey of the policy of George W. Bush Jr. towards Central and South America, laying stress on the resurgence of interventionist elements already in place under Clinton.

Lowenthal, A. (1976), 'The United States and Latin America: Ending the Hegemonic Presumption', *Foreign Affairs*, 55 (Oct.): 199–213.

    A succinct statement about the long-standing 'culture' of US approaches to Latin America and an argument for how policy might be changed.

——(ed.) (1990), *Exporting Democracy: The United States and Latin America,* (Baltimore: Johns Hopkins University Press).

A balanced collection that surveys the experience of different countries at the end of the Cold War.

Schoultz, Lars (1998), *Beneath the United States: A History of US Policy toward Latin America* (Cambridge, Mass.: Harvard University Press).

A survey of the entire period since independence based overwhelmingly on primary documentation. Less detailed on the last two decades but a vital source for the earlier years.

Smith, Peter (1996), *Talons of the Eagle: Dynamics of US–Latin American Relations* (New York: Oxford University Press).

A useful liberal survey up to the Clinton presidency, aimed at students.

Suárez-Orozco, Marcelo, and Páez, Mariela M. (2002), *Latinos: Remaking America* (Berkeley: David Rockefeller Center for Latin American Studies, Harvard).

The best series of essays covering the Hispanic community from the perspective of the social sciences.

 Visit the Online Resource Centre that accompanies this book for web links to accompany each chapter, and a range of other resources: www.oxfordtextbooks.co.uk/orc/cox_stokes/

16 US foreign policy in Africa

Robert G. Patman

Chapter contents

Introduction

Despite historic ties with the continent, US policy toward Africa has in general been marked by indifference and neglect. Throughout the Cold War, Africa was treated as a pawn in the battle between the USA and the Soviet Union, as both sides attempted to limit the influence of the other. Since the end of the Cold War, Africa has been increasingly racked by internal conflict, state failure, famine, poverty, and disease. Despite initial hopes for a USA-led 'New World Order' after the Cold War, in which the international community could work together to tackle such issues, the withdrawal of US troops from Somalia in 1994 marked a period of considerable disengagement from the continent. While limited re-engagement occurred during the second half of the 1990s, it was the events of 9/11 and the fear of state failure in Africa, acting as a breeding ground and safe haven for terrorists, that triggered a fresh American strategic focus on Africa. Emerging Chinese influence in Africa, and growing competition for African oil, is further stimulating renewed interest. Nevertheless, relatively little headway is being made in tackling Africa's biggest problems.

US policies toward Africa, particularly since the end of the Second World War, exemplify many of the themes already discussed throughout this book. American exceptionalism, the foreign relations of a global hegemon, Cold War dealings with periphery states, the American post-Cold War search for a new foreign policy purpose, and the post-9/11 war on terror are all themes which have been played out in the relationship between the USA and Africa. Throughout the Cold War, Africa was an 'active bystander'— on the one hand periphery to the conflict, and yet on the other a stage on which the USA and the Soviet Union could play out their global struggle while minimizing the risk of nuclear confrontation. In the early post-Cold War period, President George H. W. Bush's New World Order meant a change in policy toward Africa as the USA went in search of a new mission, yet this quickly changed as humanitarian intervention in the Somali conflict led to the loss of

American lives. However, the early twenty-first century has seen another sharp change in policy. The events of 9/11, the recognition that in a globalized world internal problems have external ramifications, and China's increasing challenge to the USA's interests in Africa, are all driving a new-found US interest in African affairs.

One of the hallmarks of President George W. Bush's foreign policy has been the steady re-emergence of Africa as an area of strategic importance for the USA. An indication of this new thinking appeared in 2005 when North Atlantic Treaty Organization (NATO) commander Marine General James L. Jones said that NATO should be called the US, European, and African Command (Cobb 2006). While Africans might take exception to being cast as part of Washington's global strategic network, several concerns have framed the new approach of the Bush administration. These include the post-9/11 recognition that failed states constitute a potential threat to US security, and the corresponding concern that America must not allow African states to be infiltrated by terrorist organizations such as al-Qaeda. At the same time, Washington remains concerned about internal conflicts in African nations such as Chad and Sudan, the spread of HIV/AIDS, increasing US dependence on African oil, and the growing role of China in Africa.

All this seems a far cry from President George W. Bush's pre-9/11 approach towards Africa. In 2000, as a presidential candidate, Bush indicated a lack of strategic interest in Africa and expressed his strong opposition to what he called 'nation-building', a reference to the use of US forces for the purpose of re-establishing a viable state in countries where such structures are weak or failing states. President Bush's position seemed to firmly entrench a policy retreat from Africa that had actually begun under the previous Clinton administration. In May 1994, following the profoundly disappointing US–United Nations (UN) humanitarian intervention—the attempt by an actor or a combination of actors to intervene in the internal affairs of a state to realize a humanitarian objective(s)—in Somalia, President Clinton passed Presidential Decision Directive (PDD) 25. Amongst other things, PDD 25 specified that the USA would only participate in UN peacekeeping operations if they were deemed to be in the direct national interest (Ward 1994: 23–5). Thus, in the wake of the Somali debacle, Washington was anxious not to cross the so-called 'Mogadishu line' and engage in humanitarian actions that ran the risk of US casualties. It was 'the Mogadishu line' mentality which largely paralysed US decision making in the face of a brutal genocide in Rwanda that killed 800,000 people in mid-1994. But while the Clinton administration subsequently moderated its post-Somalia national interest stipulation for humanitarian engagement, the arrival of the Bush administration in 2001 seemed to confirm Africa's status as something of a foreign policy 'backwater'.

This chapter proceeds in four stages. The first part considers US engagement with Africa in historical terms, particularly during the Cold War era of US–Soviet Union superpower rivalry. The second part examines the immediate post-Cold War era, in which a New World Order—a vision in which the USA and the UN could combine to establish freedom and respect for all nations—held out the possibility of positive US involvement in Africa. This section also assesses the post-Somalia period when US policy retreated to a more realist approach that linked America's engagement to perceived strategic or national interests. The final part of the second section outlines the renewal of limited US engagement between 1996 and 2001. The third section considers US Africa policy after 9/11. Finally, the concluding section contends that unless the Bush administration moves from its narrow view of American national security interests in Africa, it is difficult to see how it can become effective in the struggle against terrorism on that continent.

USA – Africa relations: history and the Cold War

Despite deep historic linkages between the USA and Africa, there is general agreement that US Africa policies from the founding of the Republic in 1789 to the present have been marked by indifference at worst, and neglect at best. Africa has very often been treated as a foreign policy 'backwater' in official policy-making circles, compared to the time and resources allocated to other regions considered to be of greater concern (Schraeder 1993: 776). The United States did establish an independent Liberia on the west coast of Africa in the 1840s as a possible resettlement option for liberated slaves and others of African descent residing in the United States but exerted little effort to treat Liberia as an official US colony.

However, US engagement with Africa did increase with the onset of the Cold War. The Cold War brought about a fundamental change in American foreign policy. From 1947, the USA had to become organized for a long-term political struggle with the Soviet Union and the real prospect of war in order to protect its national interests. This development was shaped by two key ideas of American post-war foreign policy, namely, anti-communism and a new doctrine of national security that went well beyond the concept of national defence. These ideas clearly framed US foreign policy toward Africa. In a policy of 'selective engagement', Washington essentially treated African countries as pawns in a global strategic contest with the Soviet Union (Keller 2006: 3–4). Republican and Democratic administrations alike supported American allies on the African continent and sought to undermine African countries that were friendly towards Moscow. Economic and military assistance was directed to key allies, such as President Mobutu Sese Seko of Zaire, the apartheid regime in South Africa, and Emperor Haile Selassie of Ethiopia, as well as anti-communist rebel organizations, like Jonas Savimbi's UNITA in Angola.

But while US engagement in Africa was largely defined by Cold War competition, developments in Africa did play a part in actually shaping Washington's containment policy, aimed at preventing the spread of communism. Nowhere was this truer than in the Horn of Africa, on the east of the continent, comprising the states of Ethiopia, Djibouti, Eritrea, and Somalia. Having been displaced in Ethiopia by the Soviet Union, the USA (under President Jimmy Carter) was left as a bystander as Moscow launched a massive military intervention to determine the outcome of the Ethiopian–Somali war of 1977–8 (Patman 1990: 204–54). That experience helped to end the era of superpower détente, a short period in which tensions had eased and exemplified by the signing of the Strategic Arms Limitation (SALT) treaties aimed at reducing nuclear arsenal build-ups. 'SALT', President Carter's National Security Adviser, Zbigniew Brzezinski, once noted, 'lies buried in the sands of the Ogaden' (Brzezinski 1983: 187–9). The very success of the Soviet–Cuban intervention prompted the Carter administration to establish a 'rapid intervention' capability in the Horn of Africa, the Red Sea, and the Indian Ocean region and propelled the USA towards a 'second cold war' in the early 1980s, through a re-emergence of intense rivalry.

The new strategic significance of Africa during the Cold War period received some institutional expression in Washington. In 1958, the State Department created a separate Bureau of African Affairs (Schraeder 1994: 16). Then, in 1960, the CIA established its own separate Africa Division within the Deputy Directorate of Operations (DDO) which had responsibility for mounting covert actions throughout the globe. However, the Defense Department was relatively late among the national security bureaucracies in acknowledging the importance of Africa. In 1982, the Office of International Security Affairs (ISA) appointed a Deputy Assistant Secretary of Defense to head the newly created Office of African Affairs (Schraeder 1994: 18). At the same time, a number of other executive agencies became involved in the making of US Africa policy during this period. These included the United States Agency for International Development (USAID), the Departments of Treasury and Commerce, and the US Information Agency (USIA). Sitting on top of this constellation of loosely allied organizations was the president.

BOX 16.1: Presidential leadership

As in other areas of foreign policy, the president has been the dominant influence on US policy towards Africa. At least four variables have affected the presidential interest in Africa:

1. *Low level of attention paid to African issues.* Although contacts between the USA and Africa have expanded in both quantity and quality during the post-Second World War period, presidents from Harry Truman to George W. Bush traditionally have been the least interested in, and subsequently have paid the least amount of attention to, Africa, relative to other regions of the world.

2. *American assumption of European responsibility for Africa.* All presidents (although in varying degrees) traditionally have looked upon Africa as a special area of influence and responsibility of the former European colonial powers. This perception has sometimes manifested itself in relatively slow American responses to some African conflicts such as Somalia (1988–91), Rwanda (1994), and Sierra Leone (1999).

3. *East–West dimension of the Africa situation.* The Cold War dimension was another element that influenced presidential attention to African issues. The threat posed by the Soviet Union and its allies to US interests in Africa was of concern to presidents from Truman to Bush Sr. Although there were variations in the assessment of the Soviet threat, all presidents during this period sought to limit Soviet influence in Africa.

4. *African-based threats to US national security.* After 9/11, the Bush administration publicly acknowledged that weak or failed states in Africa could provide a sanctuary for terrorist groups, like al-Qaeda, that seek to target the USA. As a consequence, Africa now finds itself classified by Washington as a potential battleground in the war on terror.

(Adapted from Schraeder 1994: 12–15)

KEY POINTS

- ❏ Historically the USA has had little interest in Africa, despite the deep historical linkages shared.
- ❏ During the Cold War US engagement with Africa increased, as the USA attempted to stop the spread of Soviet Influence on the African continent, while increasing US influence.

- ❏ During the Cold War incidents in Africa also helped to shape the USA's policies toward the Soviet Union.
- ❏ A number of US departments set up divisions focused on Africa during the Cold War.

The USA and Africa in a post-Cold War world

Bush's 'New World Order' and Africa

The end of the Cold War in the late 1980s seemed to offer an extraordinary opportunity for a policy of positive US engagement with Africa. While some uncertainty over the new international environment existed, three distinctive features were immediately apparent. First, there were no longer military confrontations of a system-threatening kind. After 1989, a nuclear conflict between Washington and Moscow seemed inconceivable. Second, the USA emerged from the Cold War as the world's only superpower with no real geopolitical or ideological competitors in sight. In terms of interstate relations, the relative power of the USA had sharply increased. Third, the post-Cold War world was subject to deepening globalization. The latter could be broadly defined as the intensification of technologically driven links between societies, institutions, cultures, and individuals on a worldwide basis.

At the beginning of the new era, the George H. W. Bush and Bill Clinton administrations appeared confident about constructing a New World Order. For many observers, the decisive military victory of the US-led coalition in the Persian Gulf War of 1990–1, during which the USA led a coalition which successfully repelled Iraq's invasion of Kuwait, seemed to affirm the reality of this new order. Three elements appeared central to Bush's new vision (Sloan 1991: 21–2). First, the conviction that the new order should

guarantee security, defend freedom, promote democracy, and enforce the rule of law. Second, the belief that the key diplomatic and political institution for operating and managing the new order was the UN. It should be noted that the UN was the forum in which international opinion against Saddam Hussein's invasion of Kuwait was mobilized. Third, the Bush administration anticipated an active leadership role for the USA, in partnership with the UN, in creating and maintaining this new order. The model of the Persian Gulf crisis was one of strong US leadership, albeit one underpinned by UN-authorized coalition diplomacy.

During the period 1989–92, Africa featured in Washington's vision of a New World Order. In the area of conflict resolution, the USA, Russia, Portugal, Cuba, and South Africa began working together to broker a negotiated settlement to the Angolan civil war (Lawson 2007: 1). At the same time, the USA and Russia worked closely through the UN to bring an end to the civil war in Mozambique and facilitate the independence of Namibia. Political reform was also emphasized. After Mengistu Haile Mariam's exit from Addis Ababa in May 1991, Washington played a crucial role in establishing transitional arrangements in Ethiopia by backing an Ethiopian People's Revolutionary Democratic Front (EPRDF) takeover of the country and endorsing the Eritrean People's Liberation Front (EPLF) proposal for a UN-supervised referendum to decide the issue of Eritrean independence (Dagne 1991: 3). Meanwhile, the USA, Britain, and France each announced that future foreign aid to Africa would be contingent on democratization. Between 1990 and 1992, the USA delivered on this pledge by cutting off assistance to long-time Cold War allies, like Zaire, Liberia, and the Sudan, which resisted political liberalization, and redirecting its resources to countries such as South Africa, Ethiopia, and Mozambique that were actively engaged in the democratization process.

Intervention in Somalia

However, the most visible expression of a new American approach to Africa was the 1992–3 humanitarian intervention in Somalia. In 1992, constant civil war and drought had combined to produce a catastrophic famine killing an estimated 300,000 Somalis. On 3 December 1992, the UN Security Council, in its capacity to decide on matters of international peace and security, recognizing that the situation in Somalia had become 'intolerable', authorized a US-led Unified Task Force (UNITAF) to use 'all necessary means to establish as soon as possible a secure environment for humanitarian relief operations' (UNSCR 794, 3 Dec. 1992).

The intervention was a landmark decision for both the UN and the USA. It was the first time the Security Council had sanctioned a major enforcement action under Chapter VII of the UN Charter, which legally binds all members, in a theoretically sovereign state. For the USA, the offer by an outgoing administration of President George H. W. Bush to lead a UN-backed force in Somalia was an abrupt departure from previous American policy. The turnaround followed a 'heated debate'[1] within the US government and President Bush's (belated) recognition in July 1992 that 'something must be done'[2] about Somalia. In any event, the US decision was virtually unprecedented. It was the first time in recent memory that the USA explicitly justified sending its troops to a foreign country, not to safeguard US strategic interests, but to perform a humanitarian mission. At the same time, Bush's decision to intervene in Somalia marked a major change in US policy toward UN peacekeeping. The administration indicated before the humanitarian intervention even began that a sizeable portion of US forces deployed in Somalia would stay on to serve as full members of the UN peacekeeping force which would replace the US-led coalition. Thus, in a clear break from the past, the USA was prepared

---

> **❝ KEY QUOTES 16.1:** Africa and the US national interest

No other continent has been so consistently ignored by our policy-makers, and yet none but Europe has been so continually connected to important developments in America, from the founding of the Republic in the era of the Atlantic slave trade to the inauguration of training exercises for the new Rapid Development Force.

(Jackson cited in Schraeder 1994)

Africa does not fit into the national security interest.

(George W. Bush cited in Cameron 2002)

In Africa, promise and opportunity sit side by side with disease, war, and desperate poverty. This threatens both a core value of the United States—preserving human dignity—and our strategic priority—combating global terror. American interests and American principles, therefore, lead in the same direction: we will work with others for an African continent that lives in liberty, peace, and growing prosperity.

(Bush 2002)

The first concern, of course, would be to make sure that Somalia does not become an al-Qaeda safe haven, it doesn't become a place from which terrorists can plot and plan.

(George W. Bush cited in Aljazeera.Net 2006)

in principle to allow its forces to operate under UN military command.

The Somali crisis highlighted seven key features of the emerging post-Cold War security environment. First, weak or failed states—that is states with little to no legitimate or functioning government and/or a government with little to no control over its territory—were now the main source of threat and instability in the world; second, these new civil conflicts were typically characterized by the absence or inadequacy of legitimate governance; third, many of the 'new wars' were driven by issues of identity and often involved the mobilization of movements along ethnic, tribal, racial, and religious lines; fourth, civil conflicts such as Somalia served to stimulate calls for higher standards of governance, including the spread of democracy; fifth, the globalized mass media now had the ability—the so-called 'CNN effect', the ability to use their influence through raising awareness—to help internationalize internal conflicts; sixth, the potential for economic and military overspill from intrastate conflicts challenged the old sovereign distinction between domestic and external policy in the field of security; and finally, the capacity of the international community to respond to major security challenges was largely determined by the stance of the USA, the sole superpower.

The retreat to 'the Mogadishu line'

But if Somalia was a paradigm for post-Cold War security, the Bush and Clinton administrations struggled to come to terms with it. The US-led UN operation ran into problems almost immediately and ultimately proved to be a profound disappointment. Nation building was not written into the Unified Task Force's (UNITAF) mandate and instead of striving to stabilize Somalia through political reform, UNITAF concentrated largely on short-term humanitarian needs.

When its successor mission, the United Nations Operation in Somalia (UNOSOM II), became embroiled in major hostilities with the warlord General Aideed's faction, Clinton's handling of the Somali crisis was singled out for fierce criticism by Republicans, like John Bolton and Charles Krauthammer, and conservative Democrats, such as Senator Robert Byrd. They claimed the Clinton administration had abandoned the hard-headed approach of former President George Bush, and taken a multilateralist line that had 'no conceivable connection to the US national interest' (Bolton 1994: 56–66). These observers simply did not believe that the typical failed or failing state was geostrategically important to the USA. Other critics were concerned that state failure could only be fixed by nation building, and that was seen as beyond the scope of what US foreign policy could and should do.

Having warned it would be 'open season' on Americans all over the world if the USA pulled out of Somalia in the wake of the bloody confrontation with General Aideed's forces on 3 October 1993, President Clinton nevertheless proceeded to quickly announce a scheduled withdrawal of US troops by March 1994. That decision effectively ended the US–UN experiment with peace enforcement in Somalia and eventually led to the humiliating withdrawal of all UN troops from the country in March 1995 (Patman 2001: 59).

Reeling from the Somali fiasco, President Clinton sought to quell domestic unease over US participation in future UN operations. In May 1994, the Clinton administration passed Presidential Decision Directive (PDD) 25. This directive said the USA would only participate in UN peacekeeping missions if they were in the US national interest. Moreover, PDD 25 listed seven factors that American officials would review before approving UN operations to be carried out by non-Americans. PDD 25 signalled a clear shift away from Bush's New World Order vision and what Clinton called 'Assertive Multilateralism' towards a more unilateral, state-centred approach to international security (Lawson 2007: 2).

Thus, in the wake of the unsuccessful US–UN operation in Somalia, there was a determination in Washington not to cross 'the Mogadishu line' and

MAJOR DEBATES AND THEIR IMPACT 16.1: The responsibility to protect?

By the early 1990s a wave of brutal internal conflicts was enveloping much of eastern Europe and the developing world. In reaction a challenge to state sovereignty soon arose—the responsibility to protect citizens facing brutal oppression, insurgency, state failure and genocide was seen by many as giving the right to undertake humanitarian interventions in such countries. International humanitarian law, scholarly opinions and influential leaders all had a role to play. However this concept was not without detractors, many in the developing world saw the doctrine of the responsibility to protect as a direct threat to

their sovereignty, and for this reason the idea has never been universally accepted. The obligation to protect has been applied in US policies toward Africa in a very on-again off-again fashion. While Somalia was a humanitarian intervention, its consequences led to PDD 25, and in the aftermath the Tutsi population of Rwanda suffered genocide. Many other instances across Africa have shown that the responsibility to protect is a doctrine which is accepted but not often applied by the developed world (see International Commission on Intervention and State Sovereignty 2001).

engage in peace operations that had the potential to expand into armed nation-building actions containing the attendant risk of US casualties. The first major test of the new policy would be genocide in Rwanda, which began to unfold as PDD 25 was released. Reluctant to do anything that might draw the USA in, the Clinton administration blocked the idea of an early deployment of UN troops in Rwanda in the Security Council (Johnston and Dagne 1997: 191). Requests from General Romeo Dallaire, the commander of UN forces in Rwanda to oversee the implementation of the Abuja Accords ending the war between the government and the Rwandan Patriot Front, for reinforcements to forestall the prospect of genocide were declined, and when the genocide duly began all UN forces were quickly withdrawn. But while the Clinton administration could use PDD 25 to reject pleas for humanitarian intervention, there was the problem of the obligation to act against genocide under the Geneva Conventions, which govern the laws of war and the treatment of civilians. Consequently, the Clinton administration refused to classify the slaughter in Rwanda as genocide until events had taken their course, and 800,000 people had been killed in the most barbaric circumstances. The only response from the international community to the Rwandan genocide was a very late UN-authorized intervention by France.

US concerns about conflicts in Africa, and the perceived risk of becoming involved when no American national interests were deemed to be stake, had several

other consequences. PDD 25 called for regional organizations to take on more of the peacekeeping burden, with UN Security Council endorsement. This move served to reduce US engagement in Africa where many of the UN peacekeeping missions were deployed. The USA and the UN were already supporting the peacekeeping efforts of the Economic Community of West African States (ECOWAS) in Liberia. US direct support to the ECOWAS Monitoring Group (ECOMOG) between 1991 and 1996 averaged about $15 million annually. The costs of the operation, around $1 billion, were largely shouldered by Nigeria (Malan 1999). While the ECOWAS peacekeeping operation was beset by difficulties, the Clinton administration could point to ECOWAS as an example of Africa trying to take more responsibility for its own security problems.

The period of retreat from Africa also affected US support for democratization on the continent. While the Clinton administration did apply some serious pressure on the autocratic regimes in Sudan and Nigeria to move towards political reform in 1995, there was a tacit recognition in Washington that political liberalization was associated with security problems in several countries in the mid-1990s. These included the Central African Republic, Congo-Brazzaville, Lesotho, and most strikingly Rwanda's neighbour Burundi. In July 1996, the democratic government in Burundi was overthrown in a military coup which returned former president Major Pierre Buyoya to power. But the Clinton administration supported the new military government in the expectation that Buyoya would be able to establish greater security in the country. Interestingly, this occurred while several East African states tried to apply sanctions against the non-democratic government in Burundi (Lawson 2007: 3).

Furthermore, US assistance to Africa continued to decline. The decline had begun in the late 1980s with the virtual elimination of Security Assistance and Economic Support Funds to former Cold War allies. In 1995, the US Congress sought to reorganize and substantially trim the existing US foreign assistance programmes. Some members of Congress questioned the logic of assisting Africa in the post-Cold War era. They argued that three decades of US aid had done little to promote economic performance, democratization, or US political interests. But congressional supporters of African aid opposed the restructuring initiative and managed to limit the severity of the proposed new cuts (Copson 2004).

The renewal of limited US engagement in Africa

A period of renewed but limited US engagement in Africa began in the first year of Clinton's second term of office. It reflected the gradual recognition that in a globalizing world the USA could not afford to strictly condition its involvement in Africa according to PDD 25 criteria. The lessons of Somalia, Rwanda, and Liberia were that the civil wars of the 1990s could be major international security problems; the USA could not be seen to do nothing in the face of such challenges; and the USA could not realistically expect African states to contain instability entirely on their own.

Clinton's second term brought some important changes in his foreign policy team. Madeleine Albright, who, as US Ambassador to the UN, had been critical of the Pentagon's lukewarm attitude towards humanitarian intervention, replaced Warren Christopher as Secretary of State. In addition, Susan Rice succeeded George Moose as Assistant Secretary of State for African Affairs. Rice was a political appointee rather a career foreign service officer, and she seemed to be attuned to what Clinton wanted to do in Africa (Keller 2006: 6).

Re-engagement in African security

In its second term, the Clinton administration followed a two-pronged approach to Africa that occupied a middle-ground position somewhere between the narrow confines of PDD 25 and a broader conception of human security that sought to reconcile the security and welfare of the individual (including their economic well-being) with more traditional security concerns. First, the Clinton administration sought to address security threats emanating from Africa, including conflicts between and within states, terrorism, the HIV/AIDS pandemic, trafficking in drugs, and illicit arms. Confronted with the possibility that Burundi would follow Rwanda's descent into civil war, the Clinton administration proposed in October 1996 the establishment of an African Crisis Response Force (ACRF) (Howe 2001: 248–51). It was proposed that ACRF would consist of a standing force of 5,000 African troops, trained and equipped by Western countries, which would be capable of rapid deployment for UN-authorized peacekeeping operations. But the plan received a very cool reception from virtually all quarters in Africa. To countries like South Africa and Nigeria, ACRF seemed to be a case of the Clinton administration seeking to exercise power in Africa without accepting responsibility in the process.

Consequently, the ACRF concept was replaced in late 1996 by the African Crisis Response Initiative (ACRI). This new initiative was essentially a bilateral training programme, which was intended to improve the capabilities of African forces participating in peacekeeping. While South Africa and Nigeria showed little interest, other countries, starting with Malawi, Senegal, and Uganda, agreed to accept US training and equipment. However, critics charged that ACRI-provided equipment was often used against internal and external adversaries rather than in peacekeeping. During the transition from the Clinton to the George W. Bush administration, ACRI evolved into the African Contingency Operations Training and Assistance (ACOTA) programme. The latter focuses on 'training the trainer', delivering programmes to meet the needs of specific recipient countries, and training for peace enforcement as well as peacekeeping. Between 1997 and 2005, the USA spent $121 million to train 10,000 troops from

Benin, Botswana, Ethiopia, Ghana, Kenya, Malawi, Mali, Mozambique, and Senegal (Lawson 2007: 4).

Despite these measures, the security threats faced by Africa, and the USA in Africa, worsened. In August 1998, the US embassies in Tanzania and Kenya were bombed by al-Qaeda terrorists, killing 253 people. The al-Qaeda terrorists suspected of involvement were believed to have had links with Somalia and the Sudan (Rothchild 2006: 250). Further, a bloody border dispute between two US allies, Ethiopia and Eritrea, erupted in 1998 and killed more than 70,000 people over the next two years. The civil war in Angola resumed; and a civil war in the Democratic Republic of Congo (DRC) escalated, killing more than one million people and eventually involving seven African countries supporting the government of the DRC or its opponents. Moreover, in 1999 at a time when the Clinton administration endorsed a humanitarian intervention by NATO in Kosovo, Sierra Leone endured a brutal civil war involving rebel groups opposed to a democratically elected government. Eventually, the British, not the USA, intervened militarily to re-establish some semblance of order in Sierra Leone (Keller 2006: 7–14).

Re-engagement in poverty, trade, and health

As Box 16.2 shows, President Clinton's administration was crucial in bringing the AIDS pandemic into the global political arena. However President Clinton's policies in regard to the socio-economic plight of the African continent went beyond this. The Clinton administration sought to accelerate Africa's integration into the global economy. A key political initiative in this area was the Africa Growth and Opportunity Act (AGOA). This was passed in 2000 despite opposition from domestic constituencies in the USA that feared increased textile exports from Africa. AGOA provided $500 million in support of economic development to African countries embracing free market principles, the rule of law, and political pluralism. It also provided preferential access to the US market for African countries deemed eligible. Both Presidents Clinton and Bush designated most African countries as AGOA eligible.

As a policy instrument, AGOA was the embodiment of the 'trade not aid' rhetoric of the mid- to late 1990s in which American and African leaders, such as Yoweri Museveni of Uganda, agreed that enhanced access to the American market would prove more effective in facilitating economic growth and development in Africa than decades of foreign assistance.

While the Office of the US Trade Representative hailed the success of AGOA after its implementation, critics charged there was little cause for celebration. The provisions of AGOA included numerous protections for American producers who might be harmed by competition from Africa. At the same time, oil exports have always accounted for the majority of African exports to the USA. Although the USA has a clear interest in increasing its international market share in African oil exports, the oil sector by itself is unlikely to stimulate more broad-based economic growth and development in Africa, especially when non-oil African exporters find it so hard to break into the American market. In other words, critics argue that AGOA served more than anything as a vehicle for the USA to consolidate its own strategic interests around Nigeria and South Africa, two of the bigger economic players in Africa, and, to a lesser degree, mineral-rich countries like Angola, Uganda, and the Sudan (Cheru 2006: 219–22). To a degree, the numbers back up such claims. Records show a remarkable rise in US imports of products from four African nations in particular since the implementation of AGOA, with only slight changes for the remainder of the continent. The total value of imports from Nigeria, Algeria, Angola, and South Africa almost tripled between 2000 and 2006. For Algeria alone imports increased almost sixfold, while Nigerian imports make up well over one-third of all US imports from Africa as of 2006 (source: US Department of Trade and Commerce).

Re-engagement on an official level

Another sign of renewed American interest was the flurry of visits to Africa by high-level officials from Washington. President Clinton spent two weeks in Africa in August 1998; Madeleine Albright, the Secretary of State, visited the continent three times

---

BOX 16.2: Presidential initiatives on HIV/AIDS

Presidents Bill Clinton and George W. Bush have taken a proactive role in combating HIV/AIDS, a disease which has decimated the African continent. According to a report produced by the National Intelligence Council (NIC) in 2000, sub-Saharan Africa accounted for four-fifths of the 22 million deaths from AIDS since the beginning of the epidemic around 1980. The report added that AIDS was devastating African countries, depriving them of the educated and skilled individuals required to build democratic governments, professional militaries, and free market economies.

The Clinton administration was instrumental in moving the HIV/AIDS pandemic onto the international agenda. AIDS in Africa was the focus of the US presidency of the UN Security Council in January 2000. Vice-President Gore emphasized that 'AIDS is not just a humanitarian crisis. It is a security crisis—because it threatens not just individual citizens, but the very institutions that define and defend the character of a society' (Al Gore in Cam-

eron 2002: 168). Before Clinton left office, he signed the Global AIDS and Tuberculosis Relief Act.

President Bush announced in September 2001 a $200 million contribution to the UN AIDS campaign and committed the USA to an active role in fighting the disease (Cameron 2002: 168–9). Prior to his 2003 visit to Africa, Bush announced a $15 billion package to tackle this disease. Then, in May 2007, Bush requested a doubling of funding to fight AIDS, with up to an extra $30 billion being invested over the next five years (Office of the US Global AIDS Coordinator 2007). While there are of course, humanitarian and security grounds for Bush's desire to improve the well-being of those on the African continent, there are also political underpinnings to his commitment. The president wants to demonstrate that the USA is not neglecting the welfare of the world's poor while waging the war on terror, but perhaps more importantly, the battle against HIV/AIDS is a response to his conservative and religious constituency.

---

between 1997 and 2000; Richard Holbrooke visited the continent in December 2000 in his capacity as US Ambassador to the UN; and Colin Powell, the Secretary of State for the first George W. Bush administration, paid an official visit to Africa within five months of assuming his new position in January 2001. To some extent, the increased political engagement with Africa reflected the lobbying efforts of the congressional Black Caucus and other Afro-American groups. Indeed, Clinton took several members of the Caucus with him on his 1998 trip to Africa when he made a major effort to build bridges with the continent (Cameron 2002: 170). He was the first US president to publicly admit that 'the United States has not always done the right thing by Africa', and in a brief visit to Rwanda, Clinton apologized for American inaction during the 1994 massacres, implying that US military power could be deployed to prevent future genocides (Schabas 1999: 6–7). It should be added that the Clinton administration had firmly supported the establishment of a UN tribunal charged with the indictment and prosecution of individuals accused of crimes against humanity and genocide in Rwanda.

Despite the increased US involvement in Africa, there was little sign that President George W. Bush would carry on where the Clinton administration left off. US national interests were central to Clinton's policies in Africa after the Somali fiasco, but he demonstrated, particularly in his second administration, a certain flexibility to balance US needs and objectives with an African environment that had been profoundly changed by the end of the Cold War. But while Bush appointed Afro-Americans as his main foreign policy advisers, he did not seem to see Africa as a priority for US foreign policy. Initially, President George W. Bush strongly rejected the notion of 'nation building', embraced the traditional view that security was fundamentally determined by the military means of sovereign states and advocated 'a distinctly American internationalism'. In 2001, the US Congress authorized $1.6 billion in aid to Africa which, as Fraser Cameron points out, was less than Americans spend each day on health care (Cameron 2002: 170).

KEY POINTS

❑ The end of the Cold War gave rise to the opportunity to drastically reassess US policy toward Africa.

❑ At the beginning of the 1990s President George H. W. Bush envisioned a New World Order, in which the UN (with strong leadership by the USA) would take a more proactive role, particularly in conflict resolution and peacekeeping.

❑ This New World Order came to a dramatic halt after the USA's disastrous intervention in Somalia, and President Clinton's issuing of PDD 25.

❑ By President Clinton's second term (1996–2000) the USA began to re-engage with Africa as it became clear that failing states were a threat to international security. During this time a series of training programmes for African troops were undertaken by the USA, and the AGOA Act was implemented in the hope of integrating Africa into the world economy.

The USA and Africa after 9/11

9/11, failed states, and African insecurity

After the terrorist attacks of 11 September, the Bush administration revised its approach towards Africa and acknowledged that the continent was a major strategic concern for the USA in the war on terror, in which the USA and its allies sought to reduce the ability of terrorist organizations to function and carry out terrorist activities. Previous opposition to nation building was quietly de-emphasized as the Bush administration now recognized that weak or failing states could be a security threat to the USA. Such societies were perceived as potential safe havens for terrorist groups to plan, prepare, and launch attacks against Western targets. The 2002 National Security Strategy (NSS) asserted that 'America is now threatened less by conquering states than we are by falling ones' (Bush 2002: 1–31). Africa was seen as a prime target for terrorist organizations. According to a Pentagon official forty out of forty-eight countries in sub-Saharan Africa are not in control of their borders and could harbour terrorists (Malan 2002). Consequently, the former US Assistant Secretary of State for African Affairs, Susan Rice, considers 'Africa is the soft underbelly for global terrorism' (Susan Rice in Carmody 2005: 97–120). The belief

that Africa is susceptible to terrorist penetration also brought a new but narrowly based recognition that poverty and injustice could play a part in this situation.

With respect to the perceived threat of international terrorism in Africa, there have been two main Bush policy initiatives: the deployment of the Combined Joint Task Force-Horn of Africa (CJTF-HOA) in December 2002, and the Pan-Sahel Initiative/Trans-Sahel Counter-Terrorism Initiative, which also began in late 2002. CJTF-HOA, staffed by about 1,500 US troops in Djibouti, has the mission of 'detecting, disrupting and ultimately defeating transnational terrorist groups operating in the region—denying safe havens, external support and material assistance for transnational terrorism in the region' (US Central Command in Lawson 2007: 7) The Pan-Sahel Initiative (PSI) was a more indirect effort to boost the border defence capabilities of countries to the west of the Horn: Chad, Niger, Mali, and Mauritania. Beyond this specific counter-terrorism strategy, the 2006 National Security Strategy sets out three interlocking strategies for Africa: giving 'focused attention' to anchor states like South Africa, Nigeria, Kenya, and Ethiopia, coordinating with European allies and international institutions for constructive conflict mediation and peace operations, and strengthening Africa's capable reforming states and sub-regional organizations as the primary means of addressing transnational threats, which adds up to essentially to more 'African solutions to African problems'.

Case study: Somalia and the war on terror

In concert with formal initiatives, the USA has also stepped up its assistance to non-state actors. In Somalia, a country without an internationally recognized functioning government for sixteen years, the Bush administration became alarmed by the political rise of the Islamic Courts Union (ICU). Supported originally by members of the Somali business community and some professional groups in the mid-1990s, the clerical courts gained legitimacy and popular support through an ability to provide a semblance of judicial order based on Shari'a law.

In early 2006, the Bush administration began to secretly fund and arm the Alliance for the Restoration of Peace and Counter-Terrorism (ARPCT), a coalition established by secular warlords to counter the ICU in Mogadishu. But the ARPCT was no match for the ICU's own militias. On 5 June 2006, the battle for Mogadishu ended in the routing and dispersal of the warlords. For the first time since the fall of the Siad Barre dictatorship in 1991, Somalia's capital was firmly under the control of one group.

However, in July 2006 several thousand Ethiopian troops moved into Somalia to protect the fragile but internationally recognized Transitional Federal Government (TFG). The ICU leadership reacted by threatening 'a holy war' against Somalia's traditional enemy, Ethiopia, and 'traitors' like the TFG.

Ethiopia, a traditionally Christian state, fears an Islamist state on its doorstep with aspirations to create a Greater Somalia incorporating Ethiopia's ethnically Somali Ogaden region. In December 2006, Ethiopia sent additional troops, backed by a small number of US special operations forces, into Somalia to help oust the ICU. US warplanes carried out at least two air strikes in January 2007 to kill suspected al-Qaeda members.

Far from buttressing the internationally recognized TFG, the presence of Ethiopian troops on Somali soil sparked national outrage and enabled Eritrea—a foe of Ethiopia's since their border war of 1998–2000—to help coordinate and arm an insurgency in Somalia fronted by remnants of the ICU and disgruntled militiamen of the prominent Hawiye clan. Fighting between Ethiopian troops and insurgents in March and April killed nearly 1,500 people, and an estimated 400,000 residents fled Mogadishu.

Moreover, the insurgency in Somalia appears to be spreading to the relatively peaceful north-east of the country, In June 2007, foreign fighters, Somali militants, and international terrorists, including British, American, Swedish, Pakistani, and Yemeni nationals, were killed in military operations by local officials and US Navy forces.

In short, the conflict in Somalia now threatens to become a Horn of Africa-wide conflict, and embroil the Bush administration in a new strategic crisis.

Because the Horn of Africa holds the key to much of the global oil and cargo trade through the Red Sea and Suez Canal, it is clear why the Bush administration does not want Somalia to fall into the hands of the Islamists. However, for many Somalis, the ICU remains a more attractive alternative than the warlords, who are widely blamed for the crime and chaos of the post-1991 era, or the feeble TFG, which is viewed as beholden to Somalia's traditional enemy, Ethiopia, for its political survival.

Some US officials, such as Michael Ranneberger, US Ambassador to Kenya, recognize the dangers of current US policy and have publicly called on the TFG to hold talks with moderate members of the ICU. But Somali reconciliation talks have been repeatedly postponed.

If the TFG continues to ignore calls for national dialogue, the Bush administration could find its counter-terrorist approach to Somalia coming under severe strain. Without an inclusive national reconciliation process in Somalia there will not be a functioning government, and without a functioning government there will not be an end to the conditions of chaos and lawlessness that breed extremists and terrorists (Patman 2007).

Conflict resolution, aid, and trade

As for active support for conflict resolution in Africa, the response of the Bush administration to the Liberian crisis in 2003 and to what it called 'genocide' in Darfur, Sudan, in 2004 could be described as cautious. According to Latitia Lawson, these two cases indicate 'some recovery from the Somalia Syndrome, but also [demonstrate] its continuing influence' (Lawson 2007: 5). In the case of Liberia, the Bush administration came under heavy pressure internationally to intervene as rebel forces began surrounding Monrovia in summer 2003. The Bush administration eventually agreed to send a peacekeeping force but only after President Charles Taylor resigned and left the country. Despite the historical connection between the USA and Liberia, the Bush administration only committed a small number of US peacekeepers and then only briefly. However, it did provide monetary and other forms of support for Nigeria to take a lead peacekeeping role, which reflected the administration's commitment to assisting African states in leading regional peacekeeping endeavours. The crisis in Darfur began in 2003 with a local uprising against what many in the province felt were biased policies and neglect by the government in Khartoum. Consequently 'Arab' *janjaweed* militia forces began methodically evicting 'African' farmers from their land, with widespread reports of killing, raping, and the burning of villages. Within a year, Secretary of State Colin Powell went to Sudan to investigate the situation and declared upon his return that genocide had indeed occurred in Darfur. But as a contracting party to the Geneva Conventions, US action was largely confined to demanding a full UN investigation into Darfur and providing diplomatic and financial support for the African Union (AU) to facilitate a negotiated settlement to the conflict (Lawson 2007: 5).

Meanwhile, the Bush administration launched the Millennium Challenge Account (MCA) initiative in 2003. It called for economic and political reforms in developing countries as a precondition for new additional aid. The USA pledged to increase its core development assistance by 50 per cent over the next three years, resulting in a projected annual increase of $5 billion by 2006 (White House 2002). While the Millennium initiative represents a step in the direction of recognizing the link between poverty, weak governance, and terrorism, it was slow to actually begin committing funds and to date falls far short of what is required. By the end of 2006, 25 countries were eligible for MCA funding, of which 11 were African, and the MCA had actually signed agreements with just 4 African countries (Madagascar, Cape Verde, Benin, and Ghana). Judging by these figures, the impact of the MCA initiative in Africa may be limited by the strict political conditions attached to it (Carmody 2005: 97–120).

Two other factors have shaped the Bush administration's strategic engagement with Africa. One is America's increasing dependence on African oil. In August 2001, the Assistant Secretary of State for African Affairs, Walter Kansteiner, declared that African oil 'has become a national strategic interest' (Kansteiner in Lawson 2007: 8). African oil currently accounts for 15 per cent of US imported oil and major new American investments are at present under way in Nigeria, Angola, São Tomé, and Equatorial Africa. Within a decade, African oil is expected to climb to about 25 per cent of US oil imports (Keller 2006: 8). Nigeria is currently the fifth largest crude-oil exporter to the USA; Angola is ninth. Because of oil, the USA now trades more with Africa than the former Soviet Union and eastern Europe combined.

Just as the USA is recognizing the importance of African oil to its interests, China is actively seeking to expand its own market share. But China's economic (and thus political) engagement of Africa since the turn of the century goes far beyond the hunt for energy. China's overall trade with Africa doubled from 2002 to 2003, and then doubled again between 2003 and 2005. This 400 per cent growth in three years comes atop a 700 per cent growth in the decade of the 1990s, and there is no end in sight. China is now

Africa's third largest trading partner, behind the USA and France, and ahead of former colonial power Britain. Chinese foreign direct investment in Africa has grown equally dramatically from about $50 million annually between the mid-1990s and 2002, to $100 million in 2003 and $430 million in 2004 (Saunders 2006: 38–54). This budding economic relationship is supported by the China–Africa Cooperation Forum, established by China in 2000 to bring Chinese and African leaders together every three years, much as the France–Africa summit had done throughout the post-colonial period. In stark contrast to the USA's approach to Africa, China maintains a policy of strict non-interference in the internal affairs of its African partners, and seeks mutually beneficial engagement, not humanitarian paternalism. Thus Chinese engagement in Africa threatens to substantially reduce the leverage of the USA and its Western allies, and perhaps undermine the political and economic reform agendas the West has been pushing in Africa for two decades.

> **KEY POINTS**
>
> ❑ After 9/11 the Bush administration revised its policies toward Africa, with the recognition that weak or failing states could be potential safe havens for terrorist organizations.
>
> ❑ This revision of policy led to two main security initiatives: GJTF-HOA and PSI.
>
> ❑ The situation in Somalia exemplifies the threat of failed states; however US policy there has possibly exacerbated the situation.
>
> ❑ Increased significance of Africa also led to the MCA; however the political requirements of membership have led to a very small take-up. HIV/AIDS has also been targeted by President Bush.
>
> ❑ The USA is becoming increasingly dependent on African oil; however growing Chinese influence in Africa is perhaps threatening US interests.

Conclusion

While Africa has generally been on the periphery of the USA's foreign policy agenda, the events of 11 September significantly enhanced the strategic importance of Africa in President Bush's foreign policy. Amongst other things, Washington established a new military base in Djibouti and has bolstered the military capabilities of some state and non-state actors on the African continent. But to date the Bush administration has shown little real inclination to come fully to terms with the globalization of the security environment that became evident in Africa in the early 1990s.

In a partial realignment of US Africa policy, the Bush administration has persisted with essentially a neorealist conception of national interest that has encouraged a disproportionate reliance on the military in US foreign policy. It is a selective or compartmentalized form of engagement that can include moral considerations, such as poverty relief or resisting the African AIDS pandemic, providing they are seen to serve US national security interests. In other words, the Bush administration has shown a marked reluctance or inability to move to a more integrated, holistic view of security—a human security perspective that understands security as multidimensional and recognizes that the requirements of development and global security are interdependent (UNDP 1994: 229–35).

Thus, there is something of a mismatch between the current tendency towards US unilateralism and the security environment of Africa, where people face multiple interlinked threats of hunger, disease, lawlessness, terrorism, and war. In many ways, President Bush's recent counter-terrorist strategy in Somalia highlighted these problems. Far from weakening the position of radical Islamists in that

CONTROVERSIES 16.1: Trade, pharmaceuticals, and humanitarian interventions

While Presidents Clinton and George W. Bush have taken measures to combat HIV/AIDS, and integrate Africa into the world economy, a number of controversies and stumbling blocks remain.

Today drug cocktails are available, which if taken appropriately can transform HIV/AIDS from a virtual death sentence into a chronic disease—in the developed world HIV patients' lifespans have improved exponentially. However, these drugs are costly; as of 2002 the average cost of annual treatment in the USA was $14,000—$34,000 per patient depending on the stage of the disease (CNN 2002), which is wholly unaffordable for the majority of regions where HIV/AIDS is most prevalent, particularly the least developing countries. While prices have steadily dropped since then, pharmaceutical companies (many based in the USA) are resistant to further reducing prices in developing countries, given the high cost of research and development. Thanks to a loophole in international trade law an industry of generic anti-retroviral drugs has sprung up and developing countries are able to access these treatments at far lower prices. Despite this, for the majority of Africans treatment is still unaffordable. As of 2005 only 1 in 6 of those in need of anti-retroviral therapy in Africa were receiving it (UNAIDS 2006: 151).

At the same time US trade policy has been heavily criticized, in regard to access and fairness for developing countries. Despite steps forward such as AGOA, protectionist policies remain and developing nations find it impossible to compete and gain access to US markets for many of their primary products. Without a dramatic transformation in US and EU trade policies, and the successful end to the current Doha round of trade negotiations on trade liberalization, developing countries in Africa will have little chance of improving their economic situation through trade.

Finally, the question of humanitarian interventions by the USA in African conflicts has been highly controversial. The cases of Somalia and Rwanda exemplify this. Major debates and their impact 16.1 outlines some of the issues at stake; however, a number of questions remain: (1) should the USA intervene to protect the lives of civilians in other countries when it is not deemed to be in 'the national interest'? (2) Does the USA and the international community have the right to intervene against the wishes of the government of a sovereign state in order to protect the lives of civilians? (3) Should the USA intervene without the authorization of the UN Security Council?

country, the Bush administration may have actually boosted them by first backing a coalition of warlords against the ICU and then, when that did not work, endorsing the intervention of Ethiopia, a traditional adversary of Somalia, to prop up the TFG government that has very little popular support in the country.

All this points to the fact that the Bush administration's post-9/11 engagement in Africa is unlikely to achieve its security goals. Bush's current war on terror strategy lacks political legitimacy in the eyes of many Africans because it seems too unilateralist and does not do enough in the short term to improve the socio-economic position of those on a continent where there is so much deprivation. Unless the Bush administration moves from its rather narrow view of US national security interests to a broader,

more comprehensive and inclusive human security approach, it is difficult to see how it can become more effective in the struggle against terrorism in Africa.

KEY POINTS

❑ While 9/11 led to a change in US Africa policy, the Bush administration is struggling to come to terms with the realities of the African security environment.

❑ The US unilateralist approach to security and Africa's multiple obstacles in regards to human security are fundamentally mismatched.

❑ The current Bush administration is unlikely to achieve its security goals in Africa unless it reconsiders its approach to the continent.

? Questions

1. Why was Africa important during the Cold War?
2. How did Africa shape the course of the Cold War? What particular incidents were important in this?
3. How did US policies toward Africa change in the immediate aftermath of the Cold War?
4. Why did the USA choose to intervene in Somalia?
5. What were the implications of the Somali intervention for US policy toward Africa and its foreign policy more generally?
6. Why did the USA begin to re-engage with Africa by the start of President Clinton's second term?
7. How did the USA re-engage with Africa in the mid- to late 1990s? Give specific examples, and do you think it was successful in its efforts?
8. Why did the events of 9/11 change President Bush's attitude toward Africa, and how was this manifested?
9. Using the example of Somalia explain why/how weak and failing states are a security threat to other states. Can you think of any other examples?
10. What are some of the deficiencies in policies under Presidents Clinton and George W. Bush to reduce poverty through the dual mechanisms of trade and aid?
11. How is China challenging American interests in Africa?

» Further Reading

Clapham, Christopher (1996), *Africa and the International System: The Politics of State Survival* (Cambridge: Cambridge University Press).

A solid and thoughtful assessment of the survival challenges facing African states in a radically reshaped international environment.

Magyar, Karl P. (ed.) (2000), *United States Interests and Policies in Africa: Transition to a New Era* (London: Macmillan).

A useful source for understanding the origins of modern American policy making in relation to Africa.

Morrison, J. Stephen, and Cooke, Jennifer G. (2001), *Africa Policy in the Clinton Years: Critical Choices for the Bush Administration* (Washington, DC: Center for Strategic and International Studies).

This volume focuses on evolving challenges in Africa, examines Clinton's policy toward Africa, and offers some balanced policy recommendations to the new Bush administration.

Rothchild, Donald, and Keller, Edmond J. (eds.) (2006), *Africa – US Relations: Strategic Encounters* (Boulder, Colo.: Lynne Rienner Publishers).

An authoritative and multifaceted edited volume of US – African relations in the era defined by both globalization and 9/11.

Schraeder, Peter J. (1994), *United States Foreign Policy toward Africa: Incrementalism, Crisis and Change* (Cambridge: Cambridge University Press).

An impressive theoretical and empirical treatment of US policy towards Africa in the Cold War and early post-Cold War period.

Taylor, Ian, and Williams, Paul (2004), *Africa in International Politics: External Involvement on the Continent* (London: Routledge).

This book provides a reasonably comprehensive and critical analysis of the policies of the major external actors, including the USA, toward Africa after the Cold War.

Endnotes

I wish to acknowledge and thank Ms Marjolein Righarts, a Ph.D. student in the Department of Political Studies at the University of Otago, for her excellent research assistance in the preparation of this chapter.

1. Ambassador Frank G. Wisner, former Under Secretary of State for International Security Affairs, interview with the author, 1 Nov. 1999.

2. Walter Kansteiner, former Director of African Affairs on the National Security Council staff, interview with the author, 8 Nov. 1999.

Visit the Online Resource Centre that accompanies this book for web links to accompany each chapter, and a range of other resources: www.oxfordtextbooks.co.uk/orc/cox_stokes/

Section 4

Key Issues

17

Global economy

Peter Gowan

Chapter contents

Introduction

For a century the United States has had the largest economy in the world and since 1945 it has also possessed the most powerful state, a status enhanced since the collapse of the Soviet bloc. It has thus been in a position to shape the structures of the world economy to a greater degree than any other power. This chapter is designed to introduce you to some of the central debates on how we should understand the efforts of the American state to reshape international economic relations since the 1940s.

We begin by exploring debates on the sources and mechanisms of American policy on the world economy. We then turn to debates about the substance of American efforts to shape the world economy. And we will conclude with a brief assessment of current debates about how successful American efforts in this field have been from the angle of sustaining American economic strength within international capitalism.[1]

The actors and mechanisms of American economic strategy

Despite continual executive efforts to assert institutionalized control over American external economic policy since 1945, the Congress retains an extraordinary degree of power over the conduct of this aspect of American foreign policy. In comparison with other legislatures, the Congress is supremely well equipped for defending specific domestic interests in this field.

Its members are acutely sensitive to the business interests of their constituencies and Congress possesses not only constitutional blocking power in this area but also an extraordinary degree of legislative initiative. So groups within it have repeatedly mounted campaigns in this field and especially in trade policy at odds with official opinion in the executive.

 CONTROVERSIES 17.1: Controversies within the United States

- Over the Clinton and Bush administrations' efforts to sign free trade agreements with other countries, for example in Central America, Latin America, and East and South-East Asia. Protectionist business and labour interests, usually most influential in the Democratic Party, tend to be suspicious of the impact of these agreements on companies and jobs in the USA.

- Over linkage between commercial agreements and environmental standards, labour rights, and more general human rights in countries of the global south. Champions of such linkage, strongest in the Democratic Party, wish to bring environmental standards and labour rights into the policies of the WTO and view such standards as both good on principle and necessary to prevent unfair competition with American producers. At the same time there is a long tradition of

human rights movements in the USA calling for trade sanctions against regimes judged to be serious human rights violators, and these movements have, on occasions, become powerful, as at the start of the 1990s on China trade following the crushing of the protest movement in Beijing in 1989.

- Over the strong tendency on the part of American companies to outsource jobs and relocate production to countries with much cheaper labour in the south, notably China. Opponents of this trend, mainly centred in the American trade unions and in the Democratic Party, seek measures to limit this flow of jobs outside the United States.

- Over countries whose governments are judged to be manipulating their currencies' exchange rates against the dollar to gain export advantages. At the present

CONTROVERSIES 17.1: (continued)

time the main focus of such campaigns is the Chinese government's policy on the renminbi. The campaign on this is powerful in the Congress where its leaders demand the imposition of large, penal tariffs against Chinese exports to the United States insofar as China does not allow the renminbi to rise sharply against the dollar. But in the past, notably in the mid-1980s, the large swings in the dollar exchange rate against other main currencies have led to intense political debate over US Treasury policy on the exchange rate.

- Over foreign investment by companies based outside the OECD in sectors and assets judged sensitive from a national security angle by some powerful groups within the United States. One such recent case concerned a state-owned company in Dubai which attempted to buy a number of port facilities in the USA. A more general concern in the same field is currently focused upon so-called Sovereign Wealth Funds: state-owned companies, mainly in East Asia and in oil-producing countries, seeking to use their large dollar reserves to buy a range of assets in the American economy, rather than confining themselves, as in the past, to buying US Treasury bonds.

- Over American aid policies and policies in the international financial institutions. The political right, mainly in the Republican Party, has a tradition of hostility towards substantial aid programmes for the global south, arguing that free markets will solve problems in the south and the aid is usually wasted, while it could better be spent tackling problems within the USA. Similar arguments have been advanced against American support for the IMF and the World Bank, with an added twist that the IMF has been used by Wall Street as little more than public insurance for their irresponsible drives for risky and speculative profit seeking abroad. This line from the right has produced a curious link-up in Congress with left-wing critiques of the IMF, resulting in the blocking of administration moves for greater financial support for various IMF initiatives. Under the Bush administration a further campaign by the Christian right over aid policy has gained strength and administration support: a drive to ensure than no American aid funding goes to programmes that support abortion or even, for some groups, contraception. Heated debates over these issues have centred on American aid for tackling AIDS in Africa and elsewhere.

- Over the more general strategic emphasis in American trade policies between sectors which consider themselves to be fully competitive in world markets and sectors which feel threatened by foreign competition. The former want the strategic focus of trade policy to be on opening the markets of other countries, rather than on closing American markets to foreign competitors. The latter wish a more protectionist stance on imports. The Clinton administration generally adopted the former approach; the Bush administration has been more inclined towards a defensive, protectionist stance, notably in the cases of steel and of agricultural subsidies. The more protectionist constituencies have available to them a large range of policy instruments still on the statute book for penalizing countries for alleged dumping and for other sorts of supposedly unfair trade practices, and these anti-dumping instruments continue to be used, though they are widely viewed among proponents of free trade as rather transparently protectionist weapons.

All matters pertaining to America's external commercial relations fall squarely within the jurisdiction of Congress. Since the Reciprocal Trade Act of 1934, presidents have repeatedly won negotiating authority from Congress on trade matters, but always only on temporary bases (Pastor 1980). And congressional pressure ensured that from the early 1960s onwards, trade policy was taken out of the hands of the State Department and placed in those of two agencies much more directly sensitive to congressional (and domestic business) influence: the Commerce Department and what is now known as the US Trade Representative (USTR). The latter's role, defined in congressional legislation both as having exclusive responsibility for trade policy advice to the President and as being directly accountable to Congress, ensures congressional leaders a powerful influence over the USTR's work (Low 1993).

Congressional influence is also great in other areas affecting external economic relations. Its role in fiscal policy remains central. And even in the field of monetary policy the US Treasury and the Federal Reserve (the central bank) remain far more accountable to Congress than is the case in most other countries: legislators can in principle rewrite the Federal Reserve's mandate through ordinary legislation, if they wish. Thus, tracking the details of American foreign economic policy since 1945 requires exploring the politics and policies of the US Congress.

The other main institutional actor in the field is, of course, the executive branch, and its roles include attempting both to set the agenda in external economic policy and to maintain the policy initiative against potential opponents in Congress and beyond. Within the executive, external economic policy is handled by a wide array of agencies in addition to Commerce and the USTR: most crucially the US Treasury as well as the White House and the National Security apparatus and its satellite bodies particularly focused on economic aspects of American national strategy.

Battles by the executive to win on foreign economic policy issues in the Congress have frequently figured amongst the most dramatic tussles in the American policy-making system. Recent examples of such battles were the successful efforts of the Clinton administration to win the passing of NAFTA—the North Atlantic Free Trade Agreement—in the early 1990s and to gain acceptance of China's entry into the WTO.

Conventional accounts of US external economic policy making then explore how various domestic groups and influences seek to capture the levers of decision-making power within the executive and Congress (Verdier 1994). Both pluralist and public choice theorists stress the predominant role of market-based groups with narrowly focused, intensely held preferences, pitted against broader groups with diffuse interests. Others give weight to the interests of election candidates and elected officials seeking funding and other kinds of electoral support through appealing to groups concerned about external economic policy. What Thomas Ferguson has called the 'investment theory of American politics' suggests that both domestic and external economic (and political)

policy is strongly influenced by the specific sectors and even companies which have produced large, early funding for the victorious presidential candidate: Ferguson himself stresses those who contribute large funds before the start of the primary races. More generally, this perspective views US foreign economic policy as driven by conflicts between different US business sectors. A consequence of this approach is to read different administrations as favouring specific and rather narrow sectors, such as Wall Street, the military industrial sector, the pharmaceutical industry, or ICT companies (Cox and Skidmore-Hess 1999). Yet others give weight to broad trends in public opinion concerning economic ideologies and doctrines, such as free trade or mercantilism (Goldstein 1988). What all such theories have in common is a stress on the centrality of electoral politics and a suggestion of the predominant role of its interaction with various domestic business interests.

Others who stress policy capture by special interest groups offer a more elitist perspective, outside the purely electoral arena. Bichler and Nitzan, for example, argue that those business groups which can offer the highest rates of return tend to gain policy dominance. From this angle they see a conflict over the last fifteen years in external economic (and political) policy between what they call the Technodollar–Merger Dollar coalition, broadly reflected in the Clinton administration, and the Petro-dollar–Weapon Dollar coalition, represented by the Bush administration since 2001 (Bichler, Rowley, and Nitzan 1989). A similar stress on elitist links between business groups and groups within the American state apparatus has been advanced by others like Robert Wade who has written about the role of what he calls a Wall Street–Treasury–IMF Complex in the foreign economic policies of the Clinton administration (Wade and Veneroso 1998). These kinds of analysis are in some ways reminiscent of earlier debates of the 1960s and 1970s over the extent to which American state policy had been captured by a 'power elite' combining state managers and the managers of powerful business organizations (Wright-Mills 1959).

All these approaches yield fruitful insights on nuances and conflicts within US external economic policy. The electoral and institutional dimensions of the politics of external economic policy are certainly inescapable realities. But so too are the elitist dimensions of the policy-making system. Yet much of the work on these elitist dimensions is either devoted to stressing elite divisions or inclined towards a rather managerial conception of elites as leaders of big powerful organizations.

The work of Gabriel Kolko, drawing upon the Marxist tradition, has combined a stress on the class divisions within American society with an emphasis on the centrality of the leaders of the American business class in the formulation of American foreign economic policy. He thereby stresses a number of features of the American policy-making system which have been downplayed by other authors. In the first place, he emphasizes the centrality of the power of this business class in American politics since the days of McKinley at the end of the nineteenth century: business funds politics at all levels and business interests predominate in the mass media. Secondly, he stresses the informal mechanisms through which the American business class throws up and establishes its own leaderships in the field of strategy and policy. Thirdly he stresses the zones of consensus within the business class on fundamentals of domestic and international policy despite differences on tactics and style. Fourthly, he stresses the way in which the leaders of the American business class seek to treat politics and economics as an integrated field, rather than as two separate spheres with autonomous logics. And finally Kolko stresses the mechanisms through which strategic conceptions for American foreign economic policy amongst the leaders of the American business class are translated into state policy in Washington (Kolko 1976: chs. 7 and 8).

The dominance of the interests of the American business class in American society and politics is expressed in the set of core values embodying the organizing principles of the American state and American capitalism. These principles have remained remarkably unchanged within the American business class despite the inflections produced by the New Deal: what Philip Bobbitt has called the principle of the 'market state' in which individuals determine

their own future in the marketplace and the state's role is largely confined to organizing and policing the market (as well as, often, underwriting it) rather than making large social policy commitments to citizens (Bobbitt 2002); in which the needs of business should come first in the fashioning of state policy since a thriving capitalism is the key to people's welfare; and for which American capitalism needs a secure and friendly environment through the preservation and enlargement of a capitalist world outside the United States sympathetic to the distinctive values of American capitalism.

What these distinctive, business-dominant values imply for the strategy of American capitalism in any given period depends upon the perceptions of this class of how these values can be defended and enhanced in the given environment. Grappling with these problems is achieved through the work of a dense and sophisticated network of institutions facilitating what may be called strategic debate and research amongst policy-making elites. The fact that these institutions form what might be called an informal ensemble, with a centre of gravity outside government, makes them no less important as vehicles for strategic policy making. One label for the ensemble of institutions is the 'think tank' networks: bodies like the Brookings Institution, the American Enterprise Institute, the Heritage Foundation, and the Council on Foreign Relations. But more important are informally selected, recognized leaders from powerful law firms in Washington and New York, investment and commercial banks, and some CEOs from leading corporations. Leaders of the major economic interest groups are involved and so too are media leaders, worldly wise academics, and leading figures from American politics, including members of Congress. Such leaders meet and discuss strategic issues in a wide range of fora outside government and interact with specialist researchers from the think tanks and leading academic institutes. Thus we may view these elite networks as the 'organic intellectuals' of the American business class: men and, increasingly, women who have through their work won the confidence of the broader business class as people who can be trusted to give a lead conceptually or operationally in the management of America's longer-term global economic interests (Gramsci 1971).

These continuing debates in elite networks are geared towards integrating the array of pressures and interests into unified strategic conceptions for guiding the American state's approach to external economic policy. And such strategic integration is not achieved through such elites lobbying government. It is achieved through their *staffing* government. They are transferred into government through the distinctive American mechanism of the so-called Inner-and-Outer system by means of which incoming presidents appoint thousands of policy people from such elite networks to policy-making posts in government. When presidents change, these same officials leave their posts, but typically return both to jobs in the non-governmental institutions from which they came into executive posts and to the ongoing elite discussions on American strategy.

The origins of the contemporary form of this elitist element in American policy making can be traced back to the Roosevelt wartime coalition and to the people from it who played such a large part in the formation of the American-centred post-war order: early leaders who were, in Dean Acheson's striking, biblical metaphor, 'Present at the Creation' of that order: men like Robert Lovett, John McCloy, and Paul Nitze (Isaacson and Thomas 1986). These elite figures have given extraordinary continuity to American strategic thinking—a figure like Nitze served no less than nine presidents. Many have pointed out that this post-war elite fractured during the Vietnam War. But the extent of this split should not be exaggerated. More significant have been the shifts in strategic thinking that have taken place, especially about international economics, across the whole elite since the 1970s (Davis 1984). Extraordinary continuities of personnel within this policy elite continue as can be seen in the career paths of such figures as Paul Volcker and Alan Greenspan. And the degree of partisan divisions of an ideological kind amongst such leaders should also not be exaggerated, again especially in the economic field: it is, for example, hard to imagine a major split on strategic outlook between Robert Rubin, Clinton's Treasury Secretary, and Henry Paulson, the Treasury Secretary of George W. Bush.

At the same time, the self-understanding of the policy elite since 1945 has been that their task is to do more than to champion American interests within the given world economy: it is to shape that world economy itself as a more or less integrated, America-centred order. It is this standpoint which has marked out the role of these elites and which has given rise to distinctive labels for their approach to policy making since 1945. One such label has been that they are 'globalists'. Another is that they have had a 'hegemonic' agenda, rather than a narrowly and immediately America-first agenda. Whichever label is used, American foreign economic policy making since 1945 has thus been marked by a dialectic between two poles: one pole has been that of immediate, focused interests within American society, articulated within the Congress; the other has been that of American strategic elites, preoccupied with shaping and sustaining an American-centred world economic order. The outputs of the American foreign economic policy-making system have been the result of the often conflictual interaction of these two poles.

This dialectic has also provided Washington's policy elites with their central policy-making dilemma in handling foreign economic strategy. The drive for preponderant American global power to reshape the world in an American-friendly way will, if successful, enable the American state to impose its will on others for direct and immediate American interests in economic as well as other fields. And this will, in turn, generate resistance and hostility elsewhere to American power. Yet building a world order in which other centres can flourish under American tutelage may require the United States to sacrifice its own direct interests in favour of the interests of other centres. Paul Nitze expressed this dilemma clearly in the late 1950s: 'The most difficult problem facing the formulators of United States foreign policy is that of relating and bringing into some measure of convergence policies appropriate to the coalition of free nations, the alliance system, and the United States as an individual nation' (Nitze 1959).

The central task of America's policy elites since 1945 has been to find ways of managing this contradiction. While Congress may be the sounding board for those demanding the defence of immediate American interests first, America's strategic elites must find ways of mediating between such nationalist pressures and the requirements of the American-centred world order as a whole: they must be American globalists, putting first the needs of a global economic order, fashioned to suit American long-term interests. This mission may, on occasion, require action which breeds strong hostility amongst America's subaltern allies, raising charges of American empire; but it may also, on occasion, require reshaping domestic American arrangements and sacrificing some immediate American interests for the sake of the longer-term gains that can be harvested from an American-friendly global economic and political order.

Against this background, in the second part of this chapter we will explore debates about how the American state has actually defined and pursued its goals in the world economy.

KEY POINTS

Sources of American foreign economic policy

❏ Pluralists and public choice analysts, who view public policy as the outcome of decentralized group politics involving coalition building and conflict linked to electoral politics, see this arena, centred on Congress, as the key source of foreign economic policy.

❏ Elitists, who view state and business elites as the shapers of public policy, downplay the role of broad electoral influences and view policy as being shaped in and around the executive.

❏ Writers in the Marxist tradition, like Kolko, have argued that both the American state and American society have been shaped as a distinctive type of capitalist social system with distinctive values and institutions which shape approaches to foreign economic policy. And business-funded mechanisms for debating foreign economic strategy have helped overcome both institutional fragmentation and group conflicts of interest, thus providing continuity and a large measure of consensus on fundamental, strategic issues. This third approach enables us to integrate the insights of both the pluralists and the elitists.

The big strategic dilemma

❏ Since 1945 America has had the power to shape and reshape the world economy.

❏ This power presented the leaders of the American business class and state with a central strategic dilemma: how to be a global order that would both favour American economic interests and gain sustained support from other centres of the world economy.

Perspectives on American economic strategy since 1945

We approach the debates about the substance of American external economic policy since 1945 by classifying varying perspectives on this question in three alternative images. The first such image is that of America as the promoter of a cooperative, multilateral order in international economics. This implies that the United States is not predominantly seeking either its own immediate advantage or its own one-sided long-term strength vis-à-vis other economic centres. Instead it is promoting change in the collective interests of world prosperity. We will call this the 'multilateral' image of American economic strategy.[2] Proponents of this image would tend to view the various deviations from multilateralism as being both secondary and generated by domestic protectionist or mercantilist lobbies using their domestic political power to undercut a multilateral mainstream to some extent on some issues at various times.

The second image is that of an American economic nationalism: a drive to both protect important American domestic business interests and rather aggressively champion key American business interests abroad, in particular through opening other markets to American operators and through structuring international markets to favour American businesses over their competitors. Those who adhere to this image tend to view evidence of an American commitment to multilateralism as hollow: an ideology for promoting free commerce primarily in fields where American businesses are likely to lead.

Both these first two images assume that American external economic strategy is focused rather exclusively on economics as opposed to international politics, although supporters of both images would concede that international power politics has been present as an external constraint on economic strategy. But the third image is what we will call that of an American empire. This implies that American external economic policy has been part of a larger project of constructing and sustaining an American-centred international political order embracing more than economics and within which the purely economic aspects must be understood. It also implies that American policy in the economic field is driven neither by multilateralism nor by economic nationalism but by the goal of maintaining and expanding a zone of both politics and economics covering the main centres of capitalism and under effective American leadership. Proponents of this image would view instances of American multilateralism and American economic nationalism as being merely aspects of a larger American project.

Each of these three images includes scholars working within different normative and analytical perspectives. Thus those who view American external economic policy as having been broadly multilateral include many liberal economists, but also others who reject liberal—or neoclassical—economics. Those who view American economic strategy as having

been marked by nationalist mercantilism may themselves be normative liberals or indeed mercantilists or Marxists. And those with an American world empire image stretch from neo-conservative theorists on the right to Marxists of various kinds on the left. We will briefly explore each of these images, before suggesting some conclusions of our own.

The multilateral image

The image of American external economic policy as being predominantly multilateral since 1945 rests above all on two simple but powerful indicators: levels of protectionism in the field of goods and services; and levels of America's international economic integration, in particular the growth of the share of imports as a percentage of GDP. On both these indicators, American policy since 1945 would seem to have broadly favoured economic multilateralism: both tariff and non-tariff barriers, historically high in the United States throughout the nineteenth and first half of the twentieth century in the industrial field, have, in aggregate, been dramatically reduced since 1945 and the American economy has become progressively more integrated into the world economy, its trade rising rapidly as a percentage of GDP notably in the last quarter of a century.

A third indicator supporting the multilateral image is the discourse of American administrations and of the broader American policy-making community in the post-war period. This has been couched overwhelmingly in the language of international liberalism and multilateralism. And even where Washington has adopted policies contradicting liberalism, as in the case of the Nixon administration in the early 1970s or, for that matter, the Reagan administration in the 1980s, it has justified its backsliding always on the grounds that it has been driven to protectionism by the economic nationalism of others, notably the Japanese government.

The case for this multilateral image would seem to be especially strong for the quarter of a century after 1945, paradoxically because Washington did not, at that time, use its enormous power resources to force open the markets of the rest of the capitalist world in a wrenching way, as a strategy of economic nationalism would have suggested, given American business's economic ascendancy at that time. Instead, Washington scaled back its earlier plans for a radically open post-war world economy and placed first the economy revival of both western Europe and Japan.

At the same time the United States' goal for the world economy was not in doubt: a liberal, open world economy as envisaged in the Bretton Woods agreements and in the early discussions of an International Trade Organization. The Bretton Woods regime was eventually put into full operation in 1958 and the General Agreement on Tariffs and Trade—a regime that gave other countries wide scope for resisting radical free trade measures but that was also clearly committed to multilateral freer trade—led to significant reductions in tariffs in the 1960s, not least on the part of the United States, especially through the Kennedy Round, completed in 1967.

Those adhering to this multilateral image of American post-war economic strategy acknowledge a turn away from multilateralism on the part of the Nixon administration, notably with the closing of the Gold Window in 1971 and with the linked imposition of a 15 per cent import surcharge. These steps were followed by others, indicating a mounting turn in a protectionist direction on trade matters through the 1970s and 1980s. Yet these shifts can be, and often are, explained not as a strategic shift amongst economic policy elites in the USA but rather as a consequence of the effectiveness of rent-seeking special interest politics within the American Congress. At the same time, the claim was often made that the revival of European and Japanese industry posed such a radical competitive challenge to American business that Washington was no longer willing or able to play the role of a multilateralist, liberal hegemon, paying the costs of leading the world economy in a more open direction. Thus the argument was made that the American shift was more from that of playing the role of hegemonic stabilizer of the international economy than a shift from a commitment to multilateralism as such.

Proponents of the multilateral image argue that despite the strength of protectionists and mercantilists in the 1980s and early 1990s, the basic thrust of American economic strategy remained that of building an open, multilateral order in that the main effort was directed towards domestic restructuring

---

 MAJOR DEBATES AND THEIR IMPACT 17.1: US foreign economic policy

The 1940s

- Over the Bretton Woods project for international monetary arrangements, especially the roles of the International Monetary Fund and restrictions on the movements of private finance.

- Over the Truman administration's plan for an International Trade Organization.

The late 1960s and early 1970s

- Over the future of the dollar and of the Bretton Woods monetary system.

The 1980s

- Over the high dollar and rising US trade deficits in the first half of the 1980s.

- Over whether the US government should adopt a sectorally targeted industrial policy in the early 1980s.

- Over more aggressive trade policy action against industrial competitors like Japan and the Asian Tigers and over European agricultural protectionism.

The 1990s

- Over Strategic Trade Theory as a guide to foreign economic policy.

- Over the North American Free Trade Agreement (NAFTA).

- Over the World Trade Organization.

Since 2000

- Over outsourcing jobs to China and to other emerging market economies.

for competitive revival, rather than using American power to undermine competitors. On this view the decisive steps along the multilateral path were the abandonment of Keynesian mercantilism with the Volcker Shock and the turn to the primacy of anti-inflationary goals at the end of the 1970s, the readiness to face the serious recession of 1982, and the readiness of the Reagan administration to confront trade union militancy in the early 1980s. The liberalization of finance then ensured that financial forces were able to punish companies which failed to prioritize shareholder interests and ensured that a massive restructuring of American capitalism could take place, transforming its efficiency and productivity for the better. All these actions showed that American political and business leaders were prepared to do what economic liberalism required: use market disciplines to put your own house in order, allowing inefficient business to go to the wall, penalizing overpriced labour, and creating strong incentives on managers to make their companies more profitable (Krugman 1994).

The other side of this story is Washington's long campaign for a further and more radical opening of the world economy, through the battle for the Uruguay Round and through the campaign to end capital controls and thus free the international movement of private finance. The triumph of these two campaigns is then often viewed as the triumph of a new, more radical opening of the world economy in a liberal direction, often known as 'economic globalization'. Many commentators then view the long boom which began in 1994 and continued until 2001, followed by a shallow recession in 2002 and renewed growth up to 2007, as the fruits of this continuing commitment to liberal multilateralism. They point to the faster rise in productivity indicators in the USA during the second half of the 1990s. They have also viewed 'economic globalization' as broadly beneficial on a world scale (Wolf 2004).

The final and perhaps most decisive argument for the multilateral image of American foreign economic policy is the extraordinary degree of acceptance on the part of other governments of the American-led projects for the Uruguay Round and the WTO as well as for the liberalization of private finance and many other aspects of characteristically American conceptions of capitalism. If there is continuing hostility to aspects of this programme in parts of the global south, its widespread acceptance within the OECD countries suggests that the multilateral image fits better than the mercantilist one, at least as regards the main thrusts of American policy towards the advanced capitalist core over the last fifteen years.

⊚ CONTROVERSIES 17.2: Controversies between the USA and other countries

- All the issues listed above have generated controversy between the United States and other governments. Particularly prominent have been battles in the WTO's current Doha Round over American subsidies for domestic agriculture. This issue, along with similar hostility to EU agricultural subsidies, has been at the centre of the deadlock over the Doha Round.

- A major international controversy over current American foreign economic policy has concerned how the large US current account deficit and rising US foreign debt should be dealt with. While American opinion has generally favoured a solution through the foreign exchange markets lowering the exchange rate of the dollar, other governments have favoured domestic US measures to tackle the very low (or negative) levels of US household and government saving.

- Another set of arguments between American official opinion and some governments abroad as well as left-oriented political movements abroad concerns both the free movement of private finance and the unregulated nature of activities by many financial operators, notably 'hedge funds'—operators seeking to exploit price differences in markets for financial gain—mainly centred in the USA. The activities of such hedge funds were a major issue in disputes concerning the East Asian crisis of 1997–8 and they continue to cause controversy, notably between the German government and Washington.

The mercantilist image

Yet a large group of students of American foreign economic policy view it as having a much more strongly national-mercantilist edge, which cannot be dismissed as the work of scattered special interest lobbies managing to use their political influence to blunt a mainly multilateral thrust. Those who stress this mercantilist bent are themselves diverse, ranging from liberal international economists to conservatives and Marxists.

A number of writers on the history of American international economic policy in the century and a half before 1945 have stressed the centrality of mercantilism in traditional American foreign economic policy, most especially in the field of industrial trade. As Paul Bairoch has put it, the USA and most particularly the industrial North-East became, in the nineteenth century, the 'mother country and bastion of modern protectionism' (Bairoch 1993). Even in 1925 in the middle of inter-war trade liberalization, US tariffs on industrial goods were 37 per cent of total import value. As Rune Skarstein puts it, 'No other country in history has accomplished a more protectionist policy during industrialisation than the United States' (Skarstein 2005). And if the rhetoric shifted under Cordell Hull in the 1930s,[3] American wartime planning for the post-war economic order was rather aggressively focused upon opening up the European empires, especially the British, to American capital and upon reorganizing the world economy under American, rather than European, dominance. Evidence of American restraint on opening the trade regimes of other countries in the post-war decades overlooks the centrality of foreign direct investment (FDI) rather than exports in American expansion and the way in which, by ensuring that West Germany was entirely open to American FDI, American capital could deeply penetrate European markets in the 1960s and thereafter.

There is an increasingly influential trend amongst historians of America's twentieth-century foreign policy to stress the centrality of Washington's drive to open other markets to American capitals. Associated with the work of William Appleman Williams and his followers, this school has stressed the economic expansionist dynamic in American foreign policy and the drive for what Williams called an 'Open Door world'.[4] On this reading, the language of liberal free trade has supplied a legitimizing discourse for a strategy devoted to opening the markets of others to American capital.

This theme has also been expressed at times by figures on the right of the political spectrum like Samuel Huntington, who argued that in the post-war period America used its military power as a bargaining lever, offering to protect governments with it provided that they 'permit access to their territory by a variety of U.S. governmental and non-governmental organizations pursuing goals which those organizations considered important. . . . The "Pax Americana," as I. F. Stone put it, "is the 'internationalism' of Standard Oil, Chase Manhattan, and the Pentagon"' (Huntington 1973: 344). David Rothkopf argued similarly that 'If a country depended on the United States for security protection, it dealt with the United States on trade and commercial matters' (Rothkopf 1998: 1).

Proponents of the mercantilist image also argue that the liberal characteristics of the international trade regime which emerged in the 1950s and 1960s were a reflection not of a strategic commitment to multilateralism on the part of American leaders but instead of their confidence in the competitive ascendancy of American industry. Thus when that ascendancy faced evident challenges in the 1970s, American economic strategy turned against liberal principles.

At the top of the charge list over this mercantilist turn would come Washington's abandonment of the gold-linked international monetary regime from the time when the Nixon administration closed the Gold Window in August 1972.

A cardinal principle for an open international economy since the mid-nineteenth century was that business operators should have a stable unit of account for calculating the profitability of their international ventures and for giving monetary security and predictability to their international operations. The Bretton Woods system fulfilled this function, with the dollar as the key unit of account, at a fixed, though in principle adjustable, exchange rate to gold. This system required the American Treasury to adjust American macroeconomic policy to ensure the stability of the dollar against gold. Yet by breaking the link with gold, Washington refused to allow American national economic policy to be constrained in this way, thus subordinating the stability of international monetary relations to purely American national interests. Since that time the dollar has swung wildly up and down against the other main currencies and the world has lacked a stable international monetary unit and indeed any universal and homogeneous international monetary system (Williamson and Milner 1991).[5] This move was a staggering blow to the efficient functioning of the international capitalist economy, often creating dramatic swings in the macroeconomic conditions facing other countries, swings which have frequently plunged one country or another into financial crises. At the same time, businesses engaged in international operations across currency zones have faced extremely volatile and risky conditions, surviving through transfer pricing, paying the costs of hedging, and abandoning trade wherever possible in favour of transplant operations in other centres. But Washington was able to maintain the dollar as the main global vehicle currency, partly as a result of the continued centrality of the American market but also in large part because of the American state's political hegemony as the protector of the main centres of the capitalist world. Such security dependence on the USA also encouraged the Saudis both to keep the international oil trade denominated in dollars and to recycle the resulting petro-revenues through the American banking system as dollars (Spiro 1999). And the whole system was powerfully supported by the dollar zone's London satellite, acting as an offshore financial market.

The success of this dramatic American strategic manoeuvre to make the fiat dollar the world's vehicle currency ensured that the American national economy could remain central to the global capitalist economy. It enabled the USA to run progressively larger current account deficits and thus keep its market open as a vital revenue source for capitals around the world. It enabled the USA to let its foreign debt rise to ever larger heights without strain and to fund the American state's overseas operations without difficulty. Dollar dominance has ensured that imports, debts, and overseas military-political operations could all be paid for with greenback paper produced by the American state. The regime has also allowed the US Treasury and Federal Reserve the unique privilege among states of being able to gear its domestic macroeconomic management exclusively to domestic conditions within the USA without a significant external constraint.

While many promoters of the multilateral image of American external economic policy view the scrapping of capital controls and the emergence of free movement of both finance and financial services as an indicator of deepening international economic liberalism, some liberal theorists strongly disagree. Jagdish Bhagwati, for example, a passionate advocate of liberal free trade, considers that the liberal argument applies to trade in goods but does not necessarily apply to financial services or require untrammelled free movement of private finance (Bhagwati 2001). Instead the large, fast, and unpredictable flows of funds in and out of small economies, particularly in the south, have been viewed by many as extremely dangerous and indeed as a potential source of vulnerability for the entire international economic system. Yet both the free movement of finance and freedom for financial services to extend their reach internationally has been enormously profitable for the American financial sector, while financial crises in the south as well as the East Asian crises of 1997 have been widely viewed as offering opportunities for the US Treasury to pursue policies restructuring crisis-ridden economies to the advantage of American capitals (Wade and Veneroso 1998). The free movement of finance has also been an essential prop both to the preservation of the fiat dollar and to the capacity of the American national economy to sustain chronic current account deficits with the rest of the world.

Supporters of the mercantilist image are able to provide powerful evidence of a sharp and deep turn in American trade policy from the 1970s to the mid-1990s towards aggressive forms of industrial mercantilism which took extreme forms in some high-tech sectors.[6] Jagdish Bhagwati dubbed this turn a move towards 'aggressive unilateralism' in American trade policy (Bhagwati and Patrick 1990). It was also in the late 1980s and early 1990s that for the first time in the post-war period, influential voices at the level of American policy elites mounted an open and vigorous attack on liberal principles in international economics, arguing that these principles were flawed since they rested on factual premises which were false: above all the foundational assumption that firms face constant or decreasing returns to scale (Lawrence and Schultze 1990). Given that in most industrial sectors, not least high-tech sectors, firms face increasing returns to scale, the logic of maximizing efficiency must push them towards gaining monopoly power over markets. In such circumstances states should rationally opt for so-called 'strategic trade theory' in which their task is to assist their companies in key sectors to gain maximum international market power: in other words, the USA should adopt a mercantilist strategy in key, high-tech sectors. Leading proponents of this view were subsequently brought into senior positions in the Clinton administration.[7] And that administration also established a new National Economic Council with the explicit goal of ensuring American economic security, widely viewed as, in fact, a vehicle for assertive economic nationalism on the part of the Clinton team.

Proponents of the mercantilist image view much of the substance of the Uruguay Round as having strong mercantilist accents, not least in such fields as intellectual property rights and the field of services, while at the same time American (and European) policy makers have continued to maintai n heavily protected agricultural sectors despite their promises to dismantle these protections when the Uruguay Round was signed.

While it is true that the penchant for what Bhagwati called 'aggressive unilateralism' has dramatically declined since the WTO came into existence, some see it as continuing in a somewhat different guise, through the drive by both the Clinton administration and its Bush successor for so-called free trade agreements (FTAs).[8] Bhagwati has argued strenuously that these should be viewed as new forms of protectionist preferential trade arrangements which threaten to undermine the liberal multilateral system. Meanwhile the end of confrontation with Japan in high-tech sectors like ICT can be viewed not as the result of a change of strategy by Washington but rather as the result of a recognition that the USA had won the battle for leadership in ICT against the Japanese challenge.

The world empire image

Though not new, the image of American external economic strategy as integrally linked to a world empire project has emerged strongly over the last decade, particularly since the arrival in office of the Bush administration in 2001. As in the case of the other two images we find proponents of this view amongst very diverse schools of thought from neo-conservatives close to the Bush administration itself to realists, liberals, and various kinds of Marxists on the left. We will take as the distinguishing feature of proponents of this image a series of shared ideas. First, that external economic policy is internally linked to the projection of American military-political power outwards. It is this link between political expansionism and economic strategy which requires the concept of 'empire' as a political term. Second, in marked contrast with earlier European empires, this American empire stretches out over the other core centres of industrial activity with a telos of stretching across the main centres of Eurasia, rather than concentrating on what World System Theorists have called the periphery and semi-periphery. Thirdly this empire involves restructuring politics and culture as much as economics. And finally the proponents of this empire image do not necessarily believe either that empire is a project for the benefit of all American citizens or that it is disadvantageous to all social groups outside the United States but within the empire zone. Yet it is, at the same time, an *American* empire not only in its geographical origins but in the interests which it serves and the goals which it pursues.[9] Authors as diverse as Andrew Bacevich, Christopher Layne, and neo-conservatives have then argued that the American drive to expand its sphere of influence into Eurasia after 1945 was not merely a negative, reactive response to Soviet threats but a positive, empire-construction project. The distinctive feature of the political side of this project was that Washington effectively took over the security functions of other main capitalist centres, turning them into members of an American-managed security zone, most directly in the cases of Germany and Japan; in a more attenuated way for, say, France and Britain. What had been a central, crucial attribute of such states in the pre-1945 world—defence of their realm and of their external sphere of influence—was effectively transferred to the United States. In the jargon of American grand strategy this American takeover of its allies' security is known as 'Primacy'—a concept of direct security management of allies rather than a looser posture of 'offshore balancing' of the sort practised by Britain towards the continent of Europe in the nineteenth century. And it also forms the essential background, in American strategic thought, for the construction of an integrated capitalist world economy.

The American commitment to supplying security for its core capitalist allies has extended beyond protecting them from major powers outside the security zone (like the Soviet Union during the Cold War or China today) and protecting them from each other to guaranteeing their sources of supply of strategic materials from the south, above all oil, and where possible also protecting their markets and investments in the south. Thus, insofar as the United States could deliver on such commitments, the only rational grounds for any other core capitalism to break out of the security zone would be to make an anti-American challenge for regional dominance and their own sphere of influence.

Nevertheless, this American approach to organizing world order has entailed significant costs to its subaltern allies, since they have been required to forgo substantial independent economic linkages with states outside the zone. Particularly wrenching in the early post-war years was Washington's insistence that the other core centres cut their economic links with the Soviet bloc and China. Thus West Germany had to be turned round from what would have been its spontaneous tendency to build economic linkages with the Soviet bloc and with the USSR itself. It was offered instead a west European economic base for its industrial strength and also plentiful energy supplies and other raw materials from within the

American sphere. Japan also was even more strictly banned from pursuing what would otherwise have been its spontaneous tendency to establish strong economic linkages with communist China. Until the 1970s it had been required to sever all such ties and turn its national capital accumulation strategy towards the American market and towards a non-communist South-East Asia, policed and kept open by American power. And this requirement has continued to cause tensions between the United States and its core allies in the post-Cold War period, whether over German energy dependence on Russia, South Korean dependence on the Chinese market, or efforts by allies to build independent links with oil states such as Iran.

If states outside the security zone have faced exclusion to a greater or lesser degree from access to major markets and from legal protections for their international economic activities, states within the zone have been supplied with economic rules largely, though by no means entirely, protected in international law, and managed through inclusive international institutions. This regime has been legitimized by liberal international economic theory, with its stress on multilateral free trade.

It is worth stressing the geopolitical and geo-economic dimension of the American empire perspective. It privileges the inclusion of the rich, advanced capitalist centres and while bringing them under American military-political control it has simultaneously drawn their governments into cooperative strategies towards the global south, through the various multilateral institutions like the IMF/World Bank, the WTO, etc. In the context of strains and tensions within the advanced capitalist core, common strategies can be developed for opening economies in the south for the collective benefit of the rich centres, notably through the so-called Structural Adjustment Programmes for opening the south in the 1980s and 1990s.

And the American global empire image does not exclude the possibility of a rather strongly multilateral economic regime within the security zone. Indeed, neo-conservative supporters of this image justify it precisely on the grounds that within the borders of the empire, the American record has been an overwhelmingly benign one in the field of economic relations. At the same time, the largest businesses within the zone find, in American military-political power, a welcome protector of their markets and investments.

Proponents of the American empire image on the left have a less benign view of the role of the American state in structuring market and state institutions both within the security zone and outside it. They generally view this role as one of transforming the internal regimes of other states in the direction of Philip Bobbitt's notion of a 'market state': a brand of capitalism very much along the lines favoured by the American business class in which the lives of citizens are decided by their ability to cope with unfettered market imperatives. Yet this can also be a source of strength for a strategy of global empire since these very values of the American business class should win strong support from the wealthiest and most powerful social groups within the other states of the global empire—the business classes of those states.

As the protector of all the main centres of capitalism and of an open, integrated international market, the American state can claim special privileges to enable it to preserve the zone effectively. One such special privilege is certainly the fiat dollar system, despite its dysfunctionality as a monetary system. Others may include a self-assigned right to ensure American dominance in what Washington considers to be strategic economic sectors, as in the case of ICT and the confrontation over it with Japan. And the consequences of the political empire dimension for American bargaining capacity over the rules of the world economic order are immense. Students of international economic diplomacy have long recognized the important role of military-political capacities in international economic bargaining (Odell 2000; Meunier 2005). Thus a perspective on American external economic policy which recognizes the existence of an American imperial political dimension in relations with other main economic centres will stress the special capacity which this dimension gives Washington to shape procedures and outcomes in the world economy. And it also suggests that narrowly economic frameworks for analysing American external economic policy, whether liberal-multilateral or mercantilist-nationalist, may miss central aspects of that policy and also central preoccupations of the framers of that policy.

Conclusions on the debate about the three images

Debate between proponents of these different images of American foreign economic policy rests not only on disputes about empirical evidence but on differing concepts and theories, not least in the field of economics itself. Many of those favouring a multilateral image of American external economic policy identify the economics of capitalism very closely with the idea of market exchanges. Within this perspective, the United States has fairly consistently championed the spreading and deepening of such exchanges both within and across national economies and this trend has evidently accelerated since the collapse of the Soviet bloc.

At the same time champions of the mercantilist image can draw strength from strategic trade theory which gives much more weight to the industrial dynamics of capitalism and to the consequences for capitalist competition of pervasive increasing returns to scale. When such trends are present, companies are driven to strive for market power so that they can defeat their rivals through maximizing their returns to scale. In such a world, the national economy with the biggest domestic market can hope to generate the most powerful companies capable of competing effectively on a global level. And that national economy has been, and will remain for some time, the United States. In such circumstances, an American insistence on an international level playing field for interfirm competition would actually favour those companies with the largest home base—American companies.

At the same time proponents of New Growth Theory have emphasized the crucial role of non-market-generated factors in economic growth, above all 'human capital'—the knowledge and competences of workforces. Since state budgets play a central role in the development of human capital an international economic order which opens markets but allows states with very large budgets to spend freely on developing their human capital would be a regime which would favour the countries with the richest budgets over those without the resources for building such infrastructures.

And proponents of the American global empire image, particularly those with sympathy for Marxist conceptions of capitalism, tend to follow Joseph Schumpeter's insistence that 'the social process is really one, indivisible whole' (Schumpeter 1934: 3), and thus view capitalism not as a purely economic system but as a whole social system in which arrangements in the economic field are profoundly conditioned by social and political context. In such a system business classes are as much concerned about their security and well-being as about more technical economic matters and may be ready to accept an American leadership of a distinctive kind of security-zone empire in exchange for being provided with a politically safe environment for prospering. Within such a perspective American external economic strategy should be seen as being only one aspect of a more holistic strategy for maintaining and managing the entire capitalist order within its zone.

It is this last image which we favour as the most fruitful one for exploring the many different aspects of American external economic strategy which are otherwise so seemingly contradictory. But this empire image in turn raises questions about the new challenges faced by the United States as a result of the Soviet bloc collapse and of the turn by Russia and China towards capitalism and integration into the world economy. The political and indeed economic configuration of the American empire was, after all, structured in large measure through the Cold War exclusion of these states. Thus American external economic and political strategy since the start of the 1990s should be seen in the context of US efforts to reconstruct an American empire zone on a global scale—a task by no means completed.

KEY POINTS

Three alternative images of American foreign economic policy since 1945:

❏ The multilateralist view: Washington has prioritized the collective interests of the capitalist world fairly consistently, on the whole resisting domestic pressures to privilege particular US interests over those of other centres, despite America's great political power.

❏ the mercantilist view: the USA has increasingly sought to reshape the world economy for its own benefit, especially since the crisis of the 1970s. This has been most evident in its reshaping of monetary and financial arrangements but also in its efforts to ensure that the USA retains dominance in the new growth sectors at the summit of the international division of labour.

❏ the Global Empire view: the American state has pursued external economic policies within a broader perspective of ensuring its effective political control over the other centres of capitalism: this empire goal, not just economics, has driven US external economic policy. The empire involves shaping other societies to fit with the distinctive features of American capitalism and it offers benefits to the business classes of other centres in exchange for their acceptance of American predominance.

While favouring this last perspective, we conclude that it raises important questions about America's current position and challenges after the Soviet bloc collapse and with the turn of China and Russia towards capitalism.

Has the strategy worked?

Within the scope of this chapter, we cannot hope to draw a detailed balance sheet of the success of US strategy in international economics, far less risk confident predictions on the future. But we can, at least, briefly address some of the main current debates about the strength of American capitalism in the world economy.

One school of thought holds that since the mid-1990s American capitalism has regained the dynamism which it had lost in the 1970s and 1980s and that its global ascendancy is as great as it has ever been. Others question this and some argue that American capitalism faces very grave structural weaknesses threatening its position at the centre of the world economy.

America's macroeconomic performance

Official figures for American gross domestic product (GDP) show that since 1994 the American economy has grown at a significantly faster rate than during the previous fifteen-year period and has also grown substantially faster than the other main advanced capitalist centres, the Eurozone and Japan. Growth declined sharply in 2001 and remained low in 2002 but has since recovered strongly if not quite to the growth rates of over 4 per cent a year from the start of 1997 to 1999. Thus, according to these figures, the relative weight of the US economy in the total output of the advanced capitalist countries has increased substantially (BEA 2007). Thus, if we look at the US share in total output of the G7 countries, we find that it has risen from 46.6 per cent of the total in the period 1989–95 to 49.6 per cent during the period 2000 to 2004.[10] These GDP growth figures have been widely interpreted, particularly in the United States, as demonstrating that the US economy has discovered new structural sources of growth which have so far eluded the other main OECD centres. The key evidence for this claim lies in the official statistics for productivity growth in the USA since the mid-1990s, figures which seem to show that this has risen sharply in contrast to experience in other advanced economies.

But there are problems with all these claims. In the first place, GDP figures for growth exclude patterns of indebtedness. US growth has been strongly driven by high levels of household consumption, yet much of this has been funded by rising indebtedness, both in the household and government sectors. In the long term this pattern of growth is not sustainable and is likely to entail a phase of stagnation or much slower growth in the future.

A second set of criticisms refer to the technical inadequacy both of GDP statistics in general and of the methodologies used in the United States for calculating GDP and productivity trends. GDP statistics rest on national accounting systems which count as production all market-based activity except personal consumption. Thus, police and defence agencies, all kinds of financial services, and the retail and wholesale sectors all fall within the sphere of 'production' in the calculation of GDP. This accounting system thus casts recent American growth in a particularly favourable light since so much of this growth has been in financial services and in the retail sector.

The basis for this kind of accounting lies in neoclassical economics, which uses a subjectivist way of measuring value and thus argues that all exchanges which people enter into are subjectively valuable to them and thus should be judged to be socially necessary and productive. But both classical economists and Marxists, using an objective concept of value, define production much more narrowly, arguing that it should be confined to the output of use values. Using this approach, American growth since the mid-1990s would appear much less impressive (Sheikh and Tomak 1994).

To these criticisms we should add criticisms of the specifically American accounting rules adopted in the USA since the mid-1990s. At this time, the USA decided to treat all military investment and production as productive, while other OECD countries have generally treated as productive only military investments which have at least potentially a dual use—such as military hospitals. This shift may add as much as 0.5 per cent annually to US GDP growth figures since the mid-1990s. The USA also calculates output in its financial services in a way which makes US GDP growth about 1 per cent greater per annum than the EU, which calculates its financial services output more conservatively (Giles 2006). And finally, since 1995 the US Bureau of Economic Analysis, which calculates US GDP, has used a controversial technical device known as the Hedonic Price Index for calculating the value of output in the ICT (Information and Communication Technology) sector. This technique, not used in other countries, has been implemented in such a way as to greatly enlarge the calculated value of output in this field, which has been a key growth sector in the USA since 1995. Thus there are grounds for suggesting that the US boom since the mid-1990s has been much less impressive than its GDP statistics imply.

Similar problems beset official American claims about labour productivity—taken by most economists to be a key indicator of the underlying strength of a national economy. Reputable American research bodies like the Conference Board have claimed that from 1995 through to about 2003, US productivity grew significantly more rapidly than that of other advanced countries (McGuckin and Van Ark 2005). They claim that since 1995 output per hour grew 1 per cent per year faster in the USA than in EU Europe and also exceeded Japan's growth in output per hour, by a somewhat smaller margin.

Yet these claims have also been challenged. The main areas of US productivity growth have been financial services and the retail sector (including firms such as Wal Mart). For those who use a narrow definition of production, productivity gains in these sectors do not have great significance. Furthermore, the method used to calculate productivity gains, again using hedonic indicators for ICT, is challenged by many for it involves making assumptions about increased productivity in sectors using more powerful computers which are open to challenge.

For all these reasons assessments of the real performance of the US economy since the mid-1990s are controversial. For some, this performance signals the triumphant return to dynamism of the American economy, assuring it global ascendancy in the early twenty-first century. They also suggest that the revival expresses the superiority of the US free market model. For others, the underlying trend in the US economy since the 1980s has been one of a weakening of its industrial competitiveness and a trend towards 'financialization' in which short-term financial speculation and unsustainable asset price bubbles in securities or the housing market block long-term investment in the productive sector.

Structural flaws?

Linked to these debates are others about American capitalism's underlying international competitiveness. Here the focus has been on the USA's current account deficits and its mounting international indebtedness. Critics of America's economic performance see these trends both as signs of underlying weakness and as harbingers of long-term structural problems. Their opponents are inclined to argue that the current account deficit derives from currency misalignments and can be corrected by a fall in the dollar against East Asian currencies. They will thus often tend to blame the deficits on manipulation of exchange rates by East Asian central banks, especially by China.

The argument that the deficit and foreign debt is the result of currency misalignments focused on East Asia lacks credibility since less than half of the US trade deficit derives from East Asian export surpluses with the USA. Furthermore, the notion that there is a tight correlation between trade patterns and currency values, though true in the Bretton Woods era, is open to challenge today, in the age of free movement of private finance. An alternative reading would suggest that the deficit and foreign debt are driven by the collapse of saving in the United States. On this reading, the solution should lie in a domestic austerity drive in the USA, cutting US budget deficits and constraining households to save more—a policy mix that would entail a large recession in the USA and a reduction in American living standards.

But behind these debates lies a deeper set of issues concerning America's overall position in the world economy, issues which raise questions about the units of analysis that we use for discussing such matters. The activities of the American business class are no longer largely confined within the frontiers of the American national economy and within the field of exports from that base. They derive a large share of their profits from activities around the world, centred on their ability to establish operations in other countries. An increasingly large segment of these activities is in the financial field and in the various asset markets around the world. And the sustainability of these international activities depends upon the jurisdictions of other states being open to American operators, an ultimately political matter. Insofar as the American state has the political capacity to shape market rules to further the operations of American capitals in such markets, there is every reason to believe that an American capitalism centred on financial operations can continue to flourish.

Secondly, both the American current account deficit and American foreign debt must be viewed in the context of the continued dominance of the dollar and the linked centrality of US asset markets. In this light the deficits, however large, can be funded in dollars. If the dollar ceased to be the dominant currency, this would change and the US national economy would be in serious deficit and debt difficulties.

But the dollar's ascendancy is not seriously under threat at the present time. One key reason lies in the fact that American asset markets remain by far the largest and most liquid in the world. This is especially true of the huge Treasury bond market, a safe haven for the reserves of the rest of the world's central banks, but it applies also to other US asset markets, from agency bonds, through stocks and shares, to other types of securities. There is no integrated market for euro-denominated government bonds in Europe—arrangements in this field remain fragmented along national lines.

None of this means that the state elites of the rest of the capitalist world consider the fiat dollar to be a satisfactory world currency: with the wild swings of the dollar against other main currencies it is in many ways a dysfunctional system. Yet paradoxically this same system, in combination with free movement of short-term private finance, creates great opportunities for financial arbitrage and speculation, offering extraordinarily high returns to the richest segment of the world's population insofar as they gain access to the top American investment banks and the hedge funds linked to them.

And the sheer size of the American economy as a product market makes it an important magnet for capitalisms in the rest of the world, particularly if their growth strategy centres on exports. This encourages other centres, particularly the East and South-East Asians, to accept the American-centred international economic regimes and to cooperate with American economic policy managers.

The dollar will not cease to be the dominant currency unless it is replaced by a positive alternative and such an alternative does not exist at the present time. It would have to be created by political decisions, above all by decisions to create an East Asian currency zone that would link up with the euro, uniting Eurasia as a stable, independent monetary zone. Such a set of moves, conceivable if China's currency became fully convertible and became the key currency in East Asia, would mark a serious threat to the dollar and thus to the sustainability of US deficits and foreign debt.

It is also possible to conceive of a grave international economic crisis leading the governments of major centres to reimpose capital controls, breaking with the current regime allowing the free movement of short-term funds. This would also constitute a serious challenge to the ascendancy of the increasingly financialized American capitalism. But such moves again should be seen as political steps in which American political power would be in play.

Thus, the ascendancy of American capitalism within the world economy is not simply the result of the industrial dynamism of the domestic American economy. It is also crucially related to the political ascendancy of the United States over the capitalist world and its ability to use its political power to shape the regimes of the world economy and to block political decisions in other centres that would disfavour key sectors of American business strength. In the wake of the Soviet bloc collapse, the American state was extraordinarily successful in using its political influence to reshape market rules internationally to favour the ascendancy of American business. Whether it will retain that political capacity in the future in the face of potentially contagious economic shocks remains to be seen. Thus the ascendancy of American capitalism within the world economy is as much a question about American success in constructing a global empire in the post-Soviet world as it is a question about economics.

And in this context, the effects of the Soviet bloc collapse and the turn by China and Russia towards capitalism and integration have been ambivalent in their effects. The political cohesiveness of the post-war capitalist core under American security protection in the Cold War has weakened. And China, as well as, to a lesser extent, Russia, seem likely to acquire substantial influence over both economic trends and the rules of the world economy while rejecting a role of geopolitical subordination to the United States. At the same time, the scale of the Chinese market as it deepens and grows offers scale economies that could dwarf those currently enjoyed with the American market. Thus for those who adopt an American empire perspective on American external economic policy and for those who stress the centrality of economies of scale in international competition, the political and economic challenges to American global ascendancy in the twenty-first century may seem formidable.

KEY POINTS

❏ The appropriateness and reliability of the indicators of American economic revival since the mid-1990s.

❏ The significance for American economic ascendancy of its current account deficits and its mounting foreign debt.

❏ The continued grounds for arguing that the USA is likely to maintain its economic ascendancy over the next two decades.

❏ Challenges on the horizon.

? Questions

1. Research American political debates and press opinion on any free trade agreement between the United States and another country in order to establish why the America government has promoted this agreement and why some powerful groups in Congress have opposed the agreement. Who do you think was right and why?

2. What sectors of the American civilian economy, if any, should be protected from foreign takeover and why?

3. In what ways does America's enormous military-political strength and reach make a major contribution to enabling the United States to shape the rules of the world economy?

4. During the 1980s and much of the 1990s successive American administrations perceived a serious industrial threat from Japan and imposed managed trade and managed production on some high-tech and medium-tech Japanese industrial sectors. Were they right about the threat and in the actions they took against Japan during this period?

5. Do you view America's chronic current account deficits as beneficial for the world economy or an irresponsible exploitation of American power in world affairs?

6. Does the readiness of American corporations to outsource jobs abroad and to relocate production in countries with cheap labour enhance or undermine the welfare of ordinary Americans? And what, if anything, could be done to stop such moves?

7. What have been the main driving forces of protectionist political pressures in the United States since the 1980s?

8. To what extent do you think there is a broad, bipartisan elite consensus on the main lines of American external economic strategy at the present time?

9. What do you consider to have been the major disagreements on foreign economic policy between the Bush administration and the Democratic Party in Congress since 2001?

10. Some authors have stressed the importance for American external economic policy of special interest coalitions such as a 'military-industrial complex' or a 'Wall Street – Treasury complex'. Do you consider that such authors are right about the power of such coalitions?

11. Do you think those authors who talk about competitive threats to the American economy and about the need for strong external action against such competitive threats from other economies are right?

》 Further Reading

On the sources of US foreign economic policy

Cox, Ronald W., and Skidmore-Hess, Daniel (1999), *US Politics and the Global Economy: Corporate Power, Conservative Shift* (Boulder, Colo.: Lynne Rienner).

Dam, Kenneth W. (2004), *The Rules of the Global Game: A New Look at US International Economic Policymaking* (Chicago: University of Chicago Press).

Goldstein, Judith (1988), 'Ideas, Institutions and American Trade Policy', *International Organisation*, 42/1 (Winter): 178–218.

Kolko, Gabriel (1976), *Main Currents in Modern American History* (New York: Harper & Row), chs. 7 and 8.

Verdier, Daniel (1994), *Democracy and International Trade* (Princeton: Princeton University Press).

On debates over what US economic strategy should be

Bhagwati, Jagdish N. (2001), *The Wind of the Hundred Days: How Washington Mismanaged Globalization* (Cambridge, Mass.: MIT Press).

Foreign Affairs (1994), *Competitiveness: An International Economics Reader* (New York: Foreign Affairs).

Lawrence, Robert Z., and Schultze, Charles L. (eds.) (1990), *An American Trade Strategy: Options for the 1990s* (Washington, DC: Brookings Institution).

On the politics of international economics

Gilpin, Robert (1987), *The Political Economy of International Relations* (Princeton: Princeton University Press).

Meunier, Sophie (2005), *Trading Voices: The European Union in International Commercial Negotiations* (Princeton: Princeton University Press), ch. 2.

Odell, John S. (2000), *Negotiating the World Economy* (Ithaca, NY: Cornell University Press).

Endnotes

1. Our focus in this chapter is on American policy for international economics. It therefore does not discuss American 'economic statecraft'—the ways in which the American state uses its economic and political resources to influence other states for political purposes, but altering their economic environment. On this important field of American external economic policy see Baldwin (1985).

2. Neo-Gramscian theorists would call this image a hegemonic one in Gramsci's sense of hegemony as leadership of others rather than a corporatist form of dominance. On Gramsci and hegemony, see Cox (1996).

3. Hull's influence on the international policy of the Roosevelt administration was, in fact, small. See, for instance, Hathaway (1984).

4. See Williams (1970, 1972). Other American historians who have been linked with Williams's perspective include Walter LaFeber and Lloyd C. Gardner. On the school's influence, Michael Hogan writes that it 'constitutes perhaps the most creative contribution to our field in the last century and the only contribution to frame a grand, master narrative for American diplomatic history' (Hogan 2004: 13).

5. John Williamson has aptly called the monetary arrangements since 1971 a 'non-system' (Williamson and Milner 1991: 387).

6. See Major debates and their impact 17.1.

7. Notably, Laura D. Tyson, who became chair of Clinton's Council of Economic Advisers from 1993 to 1995 and director of the National Economic Council between 1995 and 1996.

8. FTAs are bilateral agreements giving preferential trade treatment outside multilateral frameworks such as those of the WTO. The economic case for this 'bilateralist' strategy was made in the 1990s by Rudiger Dornbusch. See his contribution in Lawrence and Schultze (1990).

9. Thus we exclude from this group those like Negri and Hardt who argue that the empire is not distinctively American in our sense. See Negri and Hardt (2000).

10. All such statistics are matters of significant debate. Here we are using those of Jorgenson and Khuong Vu (2006).

 Visit the Online Resource Centre that accompanies this book for web links to accompany each chapter, and a range of other resources: www.oxfordtextbooks.co.uk/orc/cox_stokes/

18 Global terrorism

Paul Rogers

Chapter contents

Introduction: the 9/11 attacks

This chapter discusses the nature of terrorism and examines the US experience of terrorism, especially in relation to the 9/11 attacks and the resulting global war on terror. It assesses the conduct of the war in the context of regime termination in Afghanistan and Iraq, the survival and evolution of the al-Qaeda movement, and the problems that arose for the United States over the first six years of the conflict. It concludes by discussing possible changes in US policy towards terrorism, especially in the Middle East

At 8.46 a.m. on 11 September 2001, American Airlines Flight 11, a Boeing 767, crashed into the North Tower of the World Trade Center in New York. The immediate belief was that this was a horrifying accident, not least because there had been a similar incident in 1945 when a military aircraft crashed into the Empire State Building. However, sixteen minutes after the North Tower was struck, United Airlines Flight 175, also a Boeing 767, struck the South Tower. This was followed at 9.37 a.m. by American Airlines Flight 77, a Boeing 757, crashing into the Department of Defense headquarters, the Pentagon, in Washington.

Just under half an hour later, United Airlines Flight 93, also a Boeing 757, crashed into a field in Pennsylvania, after passengers had attempted to take over the plane from hijackers. Both of the World Trade Center towers collapsed and the toll in New York, Washington, and Pennsylvania was 2,973 people killed and 24 missing presumed dead.

Within minutes of the North Tower being struck, live television coverage was available throughout the United States and the rest of the world, and tens of millions of Americans saw the towers collapse. The impact has been compared with the Japanese attack on Pearl Harbor in December 1941, but many would argue that it was substantially greater (see Box 18.1). The administration of President George W. Bush responded to the atrocity with great vigour, starting what was termed the 'global war on terror'. All four planes had been taken over by people associated with the radical Islamist group al-Qaeda, and the Bush administration made clear its intention to bring those behind the attacks to justice. This would clearly involve punishing the Taliban regime in Afghanistan

---

BOX 18.1: 9/11 and Pearl Harbor

The shock of the 9/11 atrocities to the people of the United States was so great that many commentators compared it to the only other surprise attack of any magnitude—the Japanese attack on the US naval base at Pearl Harbor in Hawaii on 7 December 1941. The Pearl Harbor attack left over 2,400 people dead and more than a thousand injured, and brought the United States into the Second World War, but it had less impact in at least four respects. The first was that the attacker was another country with which there was already a state of tension, with a fear of a war against Japan widespread, whereas the 9/11 attacks were a complete surprise and involved non-state actors.

Secondly, the Japanese attack was directed against a major naval base and, however much of a shock, could be understood as a traditional if particularly shocking act of war against military forces. Although 9/11 included an

attack on the Pentagon, the much greater impact came from the targeting of the World Trade Center towers in New York. These were hugely well known across the United States and beyond, and represented the success of the country as the leading trading state in the world.

Finally, the 9/11 attacks were witnessed live on television by tens of millions of Americans, whereas Pearl Harbor had a much slower impact, given the virtually non-existent TV systems at that time. Television coverage gave 9/11 an immediacy that was particularly shocking, as so many Americans witnessed the collapse of the two towers as they actually happened, knowing that thousands of people were being killed. In all of these respects, the impact of 9/11 was much greater than Pearl Harbor, and, given the nature of the Bush administration, a war was inevitable even if it was to be against an enemy that was far more amorphous and dispersed than was imperial Japan.

if it did not cooperate, since it was harbouring the leaders of al-Qaeda.

Although the Bush administration was confident in its determination to destroy the al-Qaeda movement, early progress in the war on terror, including the termination of the Taliban regime, was not matched by the subsequent developments—six years after the 9/11 attacks the United States remained mired in protracted conflicts in Afghanistan and Iraq which had cost the lives of over 100,000 civilians and the al-Qaeda movement was still very active and seen in many countries as a persistent threat. The war on terror, especially the US occupation in Iraq, had by this time become deeply controversial across the world and was even losing support in the United States itself. More generally, the 9/11 attacks and the robust American response were raising questions over the nature of terrorism in the early twenty-first century and whether the approach of the Bush administration was either effective or even appropriate.

This chapter begins by discussing definitions of terrorism and then examines US experience of terrorism prior to 9/11 as well as the political environment in Washington at the time of the attacks. It then analyses the response of the Bush administration in Afghanistan and Iraq as well as the nature and aims of the al-Qaeda organization. After making an assessment of the conduct of the war on terror in the first six years it concludes by discussing the options available to the United States in what has come to be called the 'Long War against Islamofascism'.

Terrorism and the background to 9/11

Defining terrorism

A commonly used definition of terrorism is:

> **"**the threat of violence and the use of fear to coerce, persuade, and gain public attention. **"**

A more widely used definition, and one that is regarded as being particularly helpful, is that of Wardlaw:

> **"**Political terrorism is the use, or threat of use, of violence by an individual or group, whether acting for or in opposition to established authority, when such action is designed to create extreme anxiety and/or fear-inducing effects in a target group larger than the immediate victims with the purpose of coercing that group into acceding to the political demands of the perpetrators. (Wardlaw 1982)**"**

This definition is particularly useful in several respects. First, it specifically focuses on 'political terrorism' as distinct from criminal use of terror, as in enforcing protection rackets. Referring to political terrorism does not mean that terrorists should not be considered criminals. Indeed, many analysts argue that doing so reduces their perception of themselves as fighting for a political cause.

Secondly, it specifically refers to state terrorism as well as substate terrorism, a distinction that is largely lacking in most post-9/11 studies on terrorism where almost the entire emphasis is on substate terrorism. This is important because the overwhelming majority of the victims of terrorism, certainly in recent decades, have been the victims of terror instituted by their own governments. Such terror has involved the deaths and detention of many millions of people in almost all regions of the world. It includes major terror campaigns in Stalin's Soviet Union, Nazi Germany, and post-war China and the actions of many governments across Africa, Latin America, and Asia. It also includes the use of terror in many late colonial conflicts by the colonial powers. Almost all of this is lost in current terrorism studies, where the emphasis may extend to state sponsorship of substate groups, but rarely acknowledges the activities of states, including some democracies.

Finally, Wardlaw's definition is useful because it places emphasis on a key aspect of terrorism, the determination to cause fear in a wider community than those immediately targeted. This, too, applies to state terrorism, where detention without trial, torture, disappearances, and death squads have been employed and are still employed in many countries. While the concern of this chapter is specifically the American experience of substate terrorism, especially since the 9/11 attacks, it is necessary to remember this wider context, particularly as there is a persistent tendency to apply the terms 'terror' and 'terrorist' in a pejorative sense, embracing a wide range of opponents, many of whom cannot easily be declared to be terrorists.

The American experience before 9/11

Western European countries experienced paramilitary violence in the 1970s and 1980s from politically motivated groups such as Brigate Rossi in Italy, Action Direct in France, and the Baader Meinhof gang or Red Army Faction in West Germany, and there have been sustained paramilitary actions in Northern Ireland, from the Provisional IRA and loyalist groups, and in Spain from the Basque Separatists, ETA. Across the Middle East, prior to 9/11, there were numerous paramilitary groups, many of them associated with the Palestinian cause. These were particularly active in the years between the Six-Day War of 1967 and the Yom Kippur/Ramadan War six years later, with the phenomenon of aircraft hijacking first becoming significant at that time.

Elsewhere in the world, the Liberation Tigers of Tamil Elam (LTTE) in Sri Lanka have used political violence repeatedly, although they would claim in response to government violence against the Tamil community. Many other countries have experienced terrorist activity, although the great majority of those killed, injured, or traumatized have been victims of state terrorism rather than the activities of substate actors.

Prior to 9/11, the American experience of terrorism was relatively small, at least in terms of the conventional understanding of the term. At a time of political unrest in Europe in the 1960s and early 1970s, there were small-scale equivalents in the United States, including the left-wing Weathermen and the Symbionese Liberation Army, the latter famous for the kidnapping of the heiress Patty Hearst in

February 1974. In parallel with these were the right-wing Minutemen, and it was from the political right that the worst individual act of terrorism came with the bombing of the Alfred P. Murrah Federal Government building in Oklahoma City on 19 April 1995. In this atrocity, a large bomb combining ammonium nitrate and fuel oil was detonated in a truck at the front of the building, killing 168 people, injuring more than 500, and collapsing much of the building. Timothy McVeigh was convicted of the crime and subsequently executed. His associate, Terry Nichols, was convicted of conspiracy and sentenced to life imprisonment. McVeigh was associated with various right-wing militia groups and the Oklahoma bombing resulted in a much wider appreciation of the extreme nature of some of the groups.

Although less serious than the Oklahoma bombing in terms of casualties, the first attack on the World Trade Center, on 26 February 1993, was potentially catastrophic. In that incident, a powerful truck bomb was placed in an underground car park in the complex, close to the support columns for the south side of the North Tower. The intention was to collapse the tower over the Vista Hotel, which connected the two towers, and then into the South Tower, completely destroying all three buildings. If it had succeeded, the death toll would have been of the order of 30,000 people. The North Tower's structure proved to be too strong and survived the blast, although part of the Vista Hotel came close to collapse and was only saved by some extraordinary emergency engineering work. In the attack, six people were killed and over a thousand were injured, although most of these involved relatively minor instances of smoke inhalation. Although some of those responsible had already left the country, a number of others were detained and later imprisoned for long terms.

The Oklahoma and 1993 World Trade Center bombings are generally considered to be the main examples of terrorist action in the United States prior to 2001, although many people would argue strongly that there had been highly significant examples of systematic terrorism directed against minorities. These would include many incidents involving First Nation (Native American) groups during the mid- and late

1800s, some involving massacres on a considerable scale. The argument from a First Nation perspective was that these should be properly described as acts of terrorism as they were intended to use large-scale fear for direct political purposes. Similarly, the innumerable examples of beatings, torture, and lynchings of black Americans, especially in Southern states well into the mid-twentieth century, have been described as systematic terrorism—the deliberate use of violence to instil fear into a wider community, ensuring their compliance with their allotted and subservient position in society.

More problematic in terms of foreign relations and as controversial with regard to perceptions of terrorism was the widespread support among Irish Americans for the activities of the Provisional IRA in Northern Ireland and Britain, especially in the 1970s and 1980s. The Irish Northern Aid Committee (NORAID), which drew particular support from Irish American communities in Boston and Chicago, was regarded by its members as engaged in providing legitimate financial support for groups opposed to British control of Northern Ireland. Such groups, especially the Provisional IRA, were rightly working for a united Ireland. To the British government of Margaret Thatcher, NORAID was simply supporting a terrorist organization that was responsible for widespread destruction.

Even more controversial has been the question of US government support for paramilitary groups and what has been described as state terrorism in Latin America. The arguments revolve around direct or indirect support for anti-leftist paramilitary groups in countries such as Nicaragua, El Salvador, and Guatemala, as well as for autocratic regimes such as that of General Augusto Pinochet in Chile, the main period being the 1970s and 1980s. Frequent claims were made of the training of military and paramilitary personnel at sites such as the School of the Americas, with training including the use of torture and other forms of terror. The counter-argument was that support for such groups did not extend to terrorism and was, in any case, necessary in the context of the intense Cold War competition with the Soviet Union.

US foreign policy and the Bush administration

The election of George W. Bush to the White House resulted in an administration that developed its foreign and security policy in a particular direction. This was largely due to the influence of a group of neo-conservative opinion formers, backed by a wider circle of politicians and advisers from an assertive realist background. Following the collapse of the Soviet Union at the end of the Cold War, the post-Cold War world was seen as a vindication of free market liberal democracy, and many in the Bush administration were convinced of the possibility of envisaging a New American Century for the twenty-first century. In such a global environment, the United States would play a worldwide civilizing role, ensuring an era of peace and security for humankind.

One particular concern was that what was seen as an excessive involvement in multilateral initiatives and negotiations could limit freedom of action, to the detriment both of the United States and its role in the New American Century. As a consequence, a number of early moves by the Bush administration signalled a desire to avoid such limits. It was clear that a Comprehensive Test Ban Treaty would not be ratified by the United States, there would be a withdrawal from the Anti-Ballistic Missile Treaty, there were grave doubts about aspects of the planned International Criminal Court and proposals to control arms transfers between states, and the United States would be highly unlikely to support negotiations to prevent the weaponization of space. Of particular concern to a number of western European states was the decision of the Bush administration to withdraw from the Kyoto climate change protocols, but there was also concern that the administration might not back the complex negotiations under way in Geneva to strengthen the 1972 Biological and Toxin Weapons Convention.

From the perspective of the Bush administration, however, all of these policy changes fitted in with the idea that the United States, as the world's sole superpower, had the right to determine its future. Furthermore, it had a historic responsibility to promote its political and social ideals in a manner that was confidently expected to make the world a better place. By the late summer of 2001, the mood in Washington was one of ebullience as it appeared that the administration really could further the idea of a New American Century, with little prospect of any serious opposition. It was in this mood that the United States was to respond to the 9/11 attacks, and it was perhaps inevitable that the response would be very robust, given the sudden perception of vulnerability at a time when the future had looked so bright.

KEY POINTS

❑ Most terrorist acts are carried out by states against their own people, but most of the research emphasis is on substate terrorism.

❑ The United States had limited experience of domestic terrorism before the 9/11 attacks.

❑ The Bush administration believed that the United States was facing a worldwide threat and that a robust military response to the 9/11 attacks was essential.

The war on terror I

9/11 and the start of the war

Prior to the 9/11 attacks, the United States had already experienced a number of paramilitary attacks on facilities in the Middle East and North Africa. These included the killing of a number of US soldiers in Riyadh in Saudi Arabia in the mid-1990s, and the much more substantial attack on the Khobar Towers accommodation block at the US Air Force's King Abdul Aziz Air Base at Dhahran in eastern Saudi Arabia on 25 June 1996. In that attack, 19 US service personnel were killed and 500 people injured when a large truck bomb concealed in a sewage disposal tanker was detonated in front of the building, collapsing a large part of the structure. The US Air Force subsequently relocated its main Saudi facilities to the remote and easily secured Prince Sultan base some 50 miles south of Riyadh. The bombing was claimed to have been down to internal Saudi paramilitaries, possibly linked to the al-Qaeda movement, but some investigators pointed to a possible connection with Iran.

Even more costly than the Khobar Towers attack were the bombings of the US embassies in Nairobi and Dar es Salaam on 7 August 1998. The Dar es Salaam attack killed ten Tanzanians, with one American employee wounded, but the Nairobi attack was far more devastating as it caused the collapse of an office building alongside the embassy. The huge blast killed twelve US citizens and wounded six more, but the cost in lives for Kenyans was even higher than the Oklahoma bombing a year earlier, with 279 Kenyans killed and around 5,000 injured. Even so, neither the Khobar Towers nor the embassy bombings were sufficient to prepare Americans for the impact of the 9/11 attacks.

The immediate response of the Bush administration to the atrocities was to demand that the Taliban regime in Afghanistan cease harbouring the leadership of the al-Qaeda movement or risk the use of US military force to do so, implying the termination of the regime if it did not comply. In the wake of the attacks the United States had strong support from people and governments in western Europe, with the French newspaper *Le Monde* famously using the headline 'We Are All Americans Now' the day after the attack. Support in much of the rest of the world was far more muted. It ranged from a degree of satisfaction, especially among many people in the Arab world, that the United States was on the receiving end of a violent attack, to a much more nuanced concern that a resultant worldwide war on terror might be deeply counterproductive (see Box 18.2).

In the absence of the required response from the Taliban regime in Kabul, the United States then moved rapidly to destroy the regime and the al-Qaeda militias in Afghanistan. Although the al-Qaeda movement might have hoped for a full-scale

---

BOX 18.2: 9/11 and the majority world

One of the most astute analysts of the immediate aftermath of the 9/11 attacks from a perspective away from the North Atlantic community was the academic and activist Walden Bello, a former academic at the University of California and later a professor at the University of the Philippines and director of the influential Focus on the Global South non-government organization in Bangkok. In a remarkably prescient analysis written barely two weeks after the 9/11 attacks, Bello pointed to the risk of an endless war if the United States concentrated almost exclusively on a military response. He was forthright in condemning the attacks themselves but counselled against a response that ignored the widespread view of the United States across much of the majority world, pointing to the massive use of force in Vietnam and the bitter mood of opposition to US policies in the Middle East, not least in terms of US support for Israel and for elitist and autocratic regimes in countries such as Saudi Arabia and Egypt.

According to Bello, a quite different response was required:

The only response that will readily contribute to global security and peace is for Washington to address not the symptoms but the roots of terrorism. It is for the United States to re-examine and substantially change its policies in the Middle East and the Third World, supporting for a change arrangements that will not stand in the way of the achievement of equity, justice and genuine national sovereignty for currently marginalized people. Any other way leads to endless war. (Bello 2001)

Some indication of the radically different responses to the 9/11 attacks is that such a view would be roundly condemned in most political circles in Washington, just as it struck a loud chord with many opinion formers in the world away from the countries of the North Atlantic community.

US military occupation of Afghanistan, a rather different route to regime termination was taken, involving three elements. The main one was the decision to rearm and resupply the Northern Alliance forces, at that time the participants in the Afghan civil war that were in retreat. Supplies came largely from former Soviet states, although funded by the United States. Secondly, the United States used extensive air power, both to destroy specific targets of value to the Taliban, and also to use area impact munitions to kill Taliban units when they could be caught in any sizeable concentrations. Finally, the United States made extensive use of special forces, partly for target acquisition but also for direct support of Northern Alliance forces. US conventional military units were deployed in due course, principally troops from the Marine Corps in the south-east of the country especially around Kandahar.

The Afghan War initially appeared to have been a conspicuous success, with the Taliban regime terminated by the end of November 2001, little more than six weeks after the start of the war, but this was somewhat misleading. In many cases, most notably

in Kabul, the Taliban militia simply melted away, with their armaments intact, to towns and villages in Afghanistan and western Pakistan. Very few of the al-Qaeda militia were killed or detained, with most of the training camps found to be deserted when US troops eventually entered them. There were some instances when US troops came under intensive attack, especially in the Tora Bora mountains, but for the most part both the Taliban and al-Qaeda simply dispersed.

Even so, many hundreds were detained and there was an immediate controversy over the Bush administration's decision to detain large numbers of suspected terrorists at a camp established at the Guantánamo Bay military base in Cuba. This was out of the area of the US judiciary but was not under the control of the Cuban judiciary and, as a result, the detainees were fully under the control of the Pentagon and were widely seen outside the United States as being illegally detained. This was strongly disputed by the administration in Washington and there was initially little opposition to the Guantánamo detention centre within the United States.

The State of the Union and West Point speeches

The first six months of 2002 can be said to have marked the high point of the success of the war on terror and are particularly significant for the manner in which the early achievements in Afghanistan led on to a significant expansion of the war aims, an expansion that was expressed in two key addresses by President Bush, the 2002 State of the Union Address in January and the Graduation Address at the West Point Military Academy five months later. The State of the Union Address was delivered to both Houses of Congress in the manner of a victory speech, with numerous rounds of applause. While signalling the extent of the victory in Afghanistan it went much further in extending the concept of the war on terror well beyond retaliatory action against the al-Qaeda movement in two specific ways.

The first of these was to make it clear that the enemy in the war on terror was not just limited to the al-Qaeda movement but included other Islamic radical organizations such as Hezbollah, Hamas, and Islamic Jihad. President Bush cited US operations in Bosnia, Somalia, and the Philippines, and placed particular emphasis on the need to destroy training camps wherever they might be, 'in remote jungles and deserts, and hides in the centres of large cities' (Bush 2002). He made it clear that it was essential for all legitimate states to control such movements and went on to emphasize that if some governments chose not to act, then the United States would do so.

The second extension announced in the Address was even more significant. The global war on terror was to be extended well beyond the issue of substate terror groups to include a number of rogue states that were defined as working against US security interests, both by their support for terrorist organizations and by their determination to develop weapons of mass destruction. Using the key phrase an 'axis of evil', President Bush expanded the war to include such states as Iraq, Iran, and North Korea and made it clear that these states would not be allowed

to threaten the United States. Either they gave up their activities in relation to terrorism and pursuit of weapons of mass destruction or they would face regime termination.

This major extension of the war was generally popular in the United States in early 2002, and there was specific support for possible action against the Saddam Hussein regime in Iraq. At the same time, it gave rise to considerable unease in other countries that were otherwise sympathetic to the American predicament after 9/11. This was reflected in the cautious response of some western European governments to the speech, but much more so in terms of adverse public opinion, even in countries such as Britain where the Prime Minister, Tony Blair, was fulsome in his support for the Bush administration.

Five months after the State of the Union Address, President Bush's speech at the West Point Military Academy went even further, making it clear that the United States had the right to take pre-emptive action against an enemy that might be a future threat to US security. This clearly included military action against states, with key members of the axis of evil such as Iraq and Iran being obvious candidates for enforced regime change if there were not internal transformations. In the intervening period between the two addresses, there were many indications that the Saddam Hussein regime in Iraq would be the first candidate for pre-emptive military action because of its support for terrorism and its pursuit of weapons of mass destruction.

The Iraq War

Following discussions and a relatively weak resolution at the United Nations, a coalition of states led by the United States began a military campaign to terminate the Saddam Hussein regime. Within three weeks this had been achieved and there was an expectation that Iraq would make a rapid transition to a stable pro-Western country, with the coalition forces welcomed as liberators. This proved to be a gross misreading of the situation on many counts. The first was that weapons of mass destruction were not found, despite this being the primary stated motive in going to war. Secondly, little evidence emerged of any relationship between the Saddam Hussein regime and the al-Qaeda movement. This was hardly surprising given that Iraq had had a largely secular regime under Saddam Hussein, a form of governance anathema to the al-Qaeda movement.

In the immediate aftermath of the termination of the regime, there was widespread public disorder, extensive looting, and rampant criminality as the coalition forces proved hopelessly inadequate to maintain control. Furthermore, the intentions of the US-appointed Coalition Provisional Authority (CPA), answerable to the Pentagon and not the State Department, failed almost from the start. A plan to establish a free market economy with a flat rate tax and wholesale privatization of state assets was made almost impossible to achieve by the decision to terminate the employment of public service officials who had been members of the Ba'ath Party of the old regime. Such membership was a prerequisite for most posts and did not necessarily imply strong support for Saddam Hussein, and the loss of a huge cohort of technocrats, managers, and administrators meant that much of the state apparatus ceased to function. A further mistake was the wholesale dismissal of the Iraq Army, throwing several hundred thousand trained soldiers onto the streets where many could join an evolving insurgency.

That insurgency developed rapidly within four months of the start of the war, one of the most notable examples being the bombing of the UN headquarters in Baghdad. The killing of Uday and Qusay Hussein in July 2003 and the capture of Saddam Hussein himself five months later had no discernible effect on the insurgency, which continued to develop over the next three years. By early 2007, the United States military had lost nearly 3,500 people killed and over 25,000 injured, with many of those injured being maimed for life. Countering a largely urban insurgency by determined paramilitary groups proved very difficult, and there was a marked tendency for US forces to use their immense firepower advantages, often resulting in considerable collateral damage and civilian casualties.

By the third year of the war the situation was becoming complicated by the development of sectarian conflict between the Shi'a majority and the Sunni minority that was responsible for most attacks against coalition forces. There were, though, many occasions when Shi'a militia groups also fought coalition troops, not least the British contingents attempting to gain control of Iraq's second city, Basra, with its substantial Shi'a majority. Although Iraqi civilian casualties were difficult to measure with any accuracy, at least 100,000 were killed in the first four years; at times in the fourth year of the war, the monthly civilian casualties in Iraq were as great as the entire loss of life in the 9/11 attacks.

Although the Iraq War was primarily against insurgents who were Iraqis, there were also paramilitary elements drawn in from other states, with some of them loosely connected to the al-Qaeda movement. Partly on this basis, the Bush administration persistently represented the Iraq War as an essential part of the overall war on terror, seeking to establish it within the United States as part of the justified response to the original 9/11 attacks. Even so, support for the war decreased markedly during 2006, leading to the loss of control of Congress by the Republican Party. Furthermore, even as this was happening, developments in Afghanistan and in the capabilities of the al-Qaeda movement were such that more general aspects of the war on terror were becoming pertinent to any assessment of its progress.

KEY POINTS

❏ The immediate response to the 9/11 attacks was the termination of the Taliban regime in Afghanistan.

❏ In 2002 the Bush administration extended the war on terror to include an 'axis of evil' of rogue states such as Iraq, Iran, and North Korea.

❏ The Saddam Hussein regime in Iraq was terminated in April 2003 but an insurgency against US occupation developed almost immediately.

The war on terror II

Afghanistan

When the US-led coalition successfully terminated the Taliban regime in Afghanistan, the Bush administration was confident that the al-Qaeda network had been substantially disrupted and that Afghanistan would make a rapid transition to a stable pro-Western state, increasing US influence in Central Asia. At the time, though, some of the most experienced analysts, especially senior UN personnel, expressed the need for very substantial aid for Afghanistan, in addition to the immediate deployment of a peacekeeping force of around 30,000 troops to ensure stability. Given that the country had experienced decades of war, it was considered wholly unrealistic to think that it could achieve a peaceful transition without substantial external help. There was also a particular concern, largely ignored by the Bush administration, that the Taliban militias had disappeared from sight rather than had been defeated, and that they and their al-Qaeda associates had substantial scope for redeveloping their capabilities given that the frontier districts of Pakistan such as north and south Waziristan were areas where there was little or no central Pakistani control.

In spite of these warnings, the United States was already preoccupied with preparing for regime termination in Iraq, and European states were very slow in providing aid or security assistance for the country. As a result, Taliban and other militias began to regain influence and control especially in the south and south-east of Afghanistan so that within five years of regime termination a substantial insurgency was developing. Insurgents were aided by a substantial increase in opium poppy cultivation, with record harvests being declared in 2006. Moreover, far more of the raw opium was now being refined into heroin and morphine within the country rather than exported in its raw form. This greatly increased the illicit finances coming into the country. During the period 2002–7, NATO's International Security Assistance Force (ISAF) was eventually increased to around 30,000 troops, together with many thousands more US combat troops not under NATO command. While much of northern and western Afghanistan made slow progress, large areas of the south and east of the country were mired in conflict between coalition forces and a resurgent Taliban.

The Taliban capabilities were greatly aided by the lack of Pakistani government control of frontier districts. With the Taliban and other militias drawing largely from ethnic Pashtuns, and with the Pashtun community stretching well into Pakistan, the result was that the border districts were secure areas in which paramilitary groups were relatively safe from attack, could train recruits, and feed supplies into Afghanistan. Furthermore, although the al-Qaeda movement was substantially dispersed, it too could treat areas of western Pakistan as safe havens. Given a strong mood of anti-Americanism across much of Pakistani society, it was not feasible for US forces to extend the war against the Taliban or al-Qaeda elements to Pakistan.

The al-Qaeda movement

In the 1980s, there was vigorous opposition to the Soviet occupation of Afghanistan that came mainly from radical Islamic paramilitaries known as the *mujahidin*. Aided by the Inter-Services Intelligence Agency in Pakistan and strongly supported by the CIA, the *mujahidin* were eventually successful and the Soviet armed forces withdrew in some disarray. The Afghan defeat was one of the reasons for the collapse of the Soviet system, although some Islamic radicals believed that it was almost entirely due to the resistance.

One significant member of the *mujahidin* was a young Saudi of Yemeni extraction, Osama bin Laden. His main role was in logistics and he had considerable wealth stemming from his father who had run the leading construction company in Saudi Arabia, although he also had support from the CIA. Osama bin Laden and others, especially the Egyptian intellectual Ayman Zawahiri, regarded the Soviet withdrawal from Afghanistan as a great achievement but were subsequently rebuffed by the Saudi authorities when they offered their expertise to help safeguard the Kingdom of the Two Holy Places (Mecca and Medina) when the Saddam Hussein regime occupied Kuwait in 1990.

After the 1991 Iraq War, bin Laden and others were horrified at the continuing US military presence in Saudi Arabia, regarding it as an utter affront to Islam that such 'crusader' forces could be entrenched in the heart of the Islamic world. Their opposition resulted in bin Laden's exile to Sudan during the 1990s and later to Afghanistan where the radical Taliban regime enabled him and his associates to develop training camps and build a radical paramilitary movement known as al-Qaeda ('the base'). While the al-Qaeda movement tends to be regarded as a nihilistic terrorist organization that cannot be considered in any way a political entity, this is a fundamental misreading of a movement that is an unusual combination of fundamentalist religious belief with very clear-cut political aims that stretch from a few decades through to a century or more.

Al-Qaeda is therefore best seen as a revolutionary movement with a religious belief rather than a specific political ideology at its root. In the short term it seeks the expulsion of all 'crusader' (i.e. Western) forces from the Islamic world, commencing with Saudi Arabia, and the termination of what it sees as elitist, corrupt, unrepresentative, and pro-Western regimes in countries across the Islamic world, especially Saudi Arabia and Egypt. The movement also supports some separatist groups such as those in southern Thailand and Islamic radicals in Kashmir and Chechnya. It is bitterly anti-Zionist and supports the Palestinian cause, even though most Palestinians do not want to be associated with the movement.

All of these aims are regarded as achievable over a timescale measured in several decades, with the removal of US military forces in Saudi Arabia already having taken place. In the long term, the movement seeks to establish a radical Islamist caliphate, centred on the Middle East, but this is an aim that may take 50 to 100 years to achieve. Four aspects of the movement are particularly important. One is that it works on an entirely different timescale from that of Western political systems. They may look four to five years ahead whereas al-Qaeda measures its progress in decades. Secondly, and related to this, the al-Qaeda leadership does not envisage its long-term aims being achieved in its lifetime. This is quite different from most revolutionary movements in the last three centuries, where the revolutionaries have depended on support generated substantially from the prospect of short-term success.

A third feature of the movement concerns its dispersal since the 9/11 attacks and the remarkable manner in which this has been combined with an increase in support. Regime termination in Afghanistan and the killing or detention of significant elements of the leadership might have been expected to have hugely weakened the movement but this has not proved to be the case. It has transformed itself into a very loose connection of groups, with some modest degree of centralization, primarily in western Pakistan. It has been hugely aided by the coverage of the wars in Afghanistan and Iraq, especially the reporting of large numbers of civilian casualties on channels such as Al-Jazeera (see Box 18.3). Such reporting has combined with overtly propagandistic videos, DVDs, and internet communications to produce a sense of Islam under attack that has powerfully aided support for the movement.

The value of Iraq

Finally, the greatest single advantage to the al-Qaeda movement has been the American occupation of Iraq. This has benefited the movement in two quite different ways. The first is that it can be readily represented as a 'crusader' occupation of a key Arab/Islamic state and, as such, an affront to Islam as a whole. This may be the direct opposite to a view still common in the United States that the Iraq war was a war of liberation of the Iraqi people from a dangerous and brutal dictatorship. The second benefit has been for Iraq to become what might be described as a jihadist combat training zone, steadily producing an accumulation of young paramilitaries who have travelled to Iraq from across the Middle East and North Africa and have gained combat experience in the cities and towns of central Iraq.

The proportion of foreign paramilitaries in Iraq may be small, perhaps barely a tenth of the insurgents,

---

BOX 18.3: Television and terrorism

One of the reasons for the very robust response of the Bush administration to the 9/11 attacks was that there was tremendous support from across the United States, partly because of the manner in which the atrocity had been witnessed live on television by many tens of millions of Americans. In the months that followed, television footage of the war in Afghanistan on US TV networks showed little of the civilian casualties of the war, but this was not the case for audiences across the Middle East and the majority world. In Afghanistan and even more so in Iraq, a new generation of 24-hour satellite TV news channels was covering the wars not from an American perspective but from the position of civilians who were on the receiving end of US firepower. Two of the most significant channels were Al-Arabiya, based in Dubai, and, even more so, Al-Jazeera, based in Qatar.

Al-Jazeera, in particular, developed a reputation for technical competence and professionalism, but took a much more robust approach to broadcasting images of casualties, showing dead and injured people in a far more graphic manner than was common among Western networks. A few months into the Iraq War, Al-Jazeera was getting audiences for some of its prime-time bulletins of some tens of millions of people across the Middle East. Moreover, it acquired a reputation for authenticity because it also screened debates about major Arab themes, some of them covering thorny questions such as corruption, with implied criticisms of some of the elites controlling countries such as Egypt and Jordan.

When the United States was fighting its ten-year war in Vietnam, television was still a young medium, but coverage of the war did much to reduce domestic support for it. Al-Jazeera, Al-Arabiya, and other Middle Eastern news stations had the opposite effect in that they showed the costs of the US and coalition wars in Afghanistan and Iraq in terms of the human impact, leading to an increase in support not just for the insurgents fighting the United States but for the wider al-Qaeda movement as well.

---

but as they move in and through Iraq they make up a growing cohort. Moreover, their experience is more significant than that of an earlier generation of paramilitaries in Afghanistan in the 1980s. They were opposing a Soviet occupation primarily by young conscripts in a largely rural environment. Jihadist paramilitaries in Iraq are gaining combat experience against professional and exceptionally well-equipped US forces in a largely urban environment. Given that the wider al-Qaeda movement is concerned with terminating regimes across the Middle East over a period of several decades, such an evolving cohort of paramilitaries is of extraordinary value.

The status of al-Qaeda

More than a decade after it first evolved, and several years after the 9/11 attacks, the al-Qaeda movement was still developing and was attracting substantial support from across the Middle East and beyond. In terms of its direct capabilities and leaving aside the substantial involvements in Afghanistan and Iraq, by mid-2007 the movement could be said to have been far more active in the six years following the 9/11 attacks than in a similar period before. This alone is enough to suggest that the conduct of the US-led war on terror had not achieved its anticipated aims.

Over the period 2002–7, the al-Qaeda movement or its loose affiliates undertook attacks in many countries. They included major incidents in London, Madrid, and Bali, and many other attacks against Western or Israeli targets or against local elites. Examples included a number of attacks on US interests in Pakistan, two double bombings against Jewish and British targets in Istanbul, the bombing of the Marriott Hotel and the Australian Embassy in Djakarta, a synagogue in Tunisia, and four Western-oriented targets in Casablanca. Israeli interests were attacked at the Paradise Hotel in Kikambala, Kenya, the attempt to shoot down an Israeli tourist jet, also in Kenya, and the bombing of the Taba Hilton and a campsite in Sinai, both popular with Israeli tourists. In addition to other attacks in Sinai, there was an attempt to damage an American warship in Aqaba Harbour in Jordan, the bombing of three Western hotels in the Jordanian capital of Amman, and several attacks in Saudi Arabia, including an attempt to disrupt oil exports by bombing the Abqaiq oil-processing plant.

Many other planned attacks in London, Paris, Rome, Singapore, and elsewhere were disrupted, but the overall situation, six years after 9/11, was of a movement that was not in retreat and of a United States military predicament in Iraq and Afghanistan that did not lend itself to easy solutions unless there were major changes in policy. Although domestic support for the Iraq War had declined by 2007, a major reassessment of the strategy of the war on terror seemed unlikely, given that both participants, the United States and the al-Qaeda movement, had reasons to be engaged for the long term.

KEY POINTS

❏ In Afghanistan, Taliban militia regrouped after 2001 and, combined with revenues from burgeoning opium production, ensured enduring insecurity across much of the country.
❏ The al-Qaeda movement remained active across many countries, with little sign that the war on terror was having the success originally expected.
❏ Iraq became particularly valuable to the al-Qaeda movement as a paramilitary combat training zone against well-armed US troops.

Rethinking the war on terror

In the first six years of the war on terror the United States and its coalition partners terminated two regimes, in Afghanistan and Iraq, took action in Yemen, Pakistan, and Somalia, and engaged with intelligence and security agencies across the world. During this period it did not experience another major paramilitary attack on its own territory. At the same time, the al-Qaeda movement engaged in many actions against Western interests, including attacks on US facilities such as diplomatic missions and US-owned business including hotels. Planned attacks on the United States were reportedly prevented, including an intended bombing in Los Angeles and hijacking of aircraft.

During the first six years of the war, well over 100,000 people were detained without trial for varying periods, with some detained for over five years, not least at Guantánamo in Cuba. At any one time, around 20,000 people were in detention, mainly in Iraq and Afghanistan. At least 100,000 civilians were killed in Iraq and Afghanistan, possibly many more. A confrontation with Iraq was possible. Across the Middle East and much of the majority world, there was a measured increase in anti-American attitudes and the coalition of states that supported the United States in Iraq was reduced to a handful. US military casualties were high, with 3,500 killed and well over 25,000 injured in Iraq. Because of improvements in body armour and battlefield medicine, many of the injured who survived had grievous wounds, frequently likely to have lifetime effects. In spite of many changes in tactics, more than four years of war in Iraq showed little sign of ending, and prospects for a stable peace with an organized withdrawal of US forces seemed remote. Stability in south and south-east Afghanistan was proving difficult to achieve.

Long-term changes in the conduct of the war on terror are constrained by two factors. One is that the al-Qaeda movement is working on a very long timescale, certainly measured in decades rather than years. From its own perspective there is unlikely to be any major change in strategy or tactics, given that it remains highly active and benefits both from the US occupation of Iraq and from the Taliban revival against coalition operations in Afghanistan. The other factor is that while US domestic politics may be subject to short-term change, the enduring significance of the Persian Gulf for the security of oil supplies means that any future US administration will have difficulty in withdrawing military forces from Iraq. To do so would mean that US influence in the region would decline markedly. Indeed, abandoning Iraq would be seen by many in the United States as a foreign and security policy disaster at least as great as the defeat in the Vietnam War.

BOX 18.4: Terrorism and oil security

The war on terror has been substantially complicated by the strategic importance of the Persian Gulf region as the location of most of the world's remaining proved oil reserves. While the argument that the United States occupied Iraq in 2003 for this reason is at best tenuous and at worst no more than a conspiracy theory, there certainly has been a long-term US concern with Persian Gulf security, not least with the establishment of the Joint Rapid Deployment Task Force in 1979 and its expansion into US Central Command four years later. From a US perspective, ensuring Persian Gulf security is a necessary part of the US defence posture for two reasons. One is the sheer concentration of reserves (see table) and the other is the increasing dependence of both the United States and China on imported oil as they run down their small remaining domestic reserves. In 2000, the United States imported about 58 per cent of its oil requirements and this was expected to grow to 74 per cent by 2020. China's import dependency is increasing even faster—it was self-sufficient in 1993 but will need to import half its requirements by 2010.

World oil reserves 2005 (billion barrels)

Saudi Arabia	264.2
Iran	137.5
Iraq	115.0
Kuwait	101.5
United Arab Emirates	97.8
Venezuela[a]	79.7
Russia	74.7
Kazakhstan	39.6
Libya	39.1
Nigeria	39.1
United States	29.3
Canada[a]	16.5
China	16.0
Qatar	15.2
Mexico	13.7

[a] Venezuela and Canada also have large reserves of low-grade heavy oil and tar sands.

Source: BP Statistical Review of World Energy, June 2006.

It can certainly be argued that there are circumstances in which the al-Qaeda movement, and likeminded groups, could lose support, but these would involve major changes in US and coalition policies. They would include withdrawal from Iraq, successful support for an enduring and just settlement of the Israeli–Palestinian conflict, support for political and social emancipation in Saudi Arabia, Egypt, Pakistan, and some other Islamic states, and a policy of counterterrorism rooted primarily in policing and criminal investigation rather than vigorous pursuit of military solutions. The problem is that this would involve a fundamental shift in US attitudes towards paramilitary movements such as al-Qaeda. This can best be exemplified by the radically different perceptions of the Fallujah assault in November 2004, not just to the

US and al-Qaeda leaderships but to the supporters of al-Qaeda and the electorate in the United States (see Box 18.5). To the former, Fallujah was an atrocity by invading forces, whereas to the latter it was a fully justified military action against a terrorist entity with which any kind of compromise is impossible. Negotiations with al-Qaeda may well be beyond any near-term possibility but that is not the point. What is relevant is that the effects of the Fallujah assault go far beyond the al-Qaeda leadership or its most dedicated and determined supporters to reach out to many tens of millions of people and increase their sense of antagonism to the United States.

In one sense this goes back to the issue of defining terrorism. If viewed purely as a substate phenomenon, then there is no way that an American

BOX 18.5: Case study: Fallujah—whose terrorism?

In November 2004, with the war in Iraq barely eighteen months old, the US Army and Marine Corps launched a combined assault on the city of Fallujah, west of Baghdad, believing it to be the epicentre of the insurgency that was proving so difficult to counter. To the Bush administration, the Fallujah assault was an entirely necessary part of countering the terrorism that lay at the heart of the insurgency. As a result, considerable access was given to TV channels to record the assault, from the American side, as it progressed. To Muslims across the Arab world, the assault on Fallujah, which killed thousands of people, was nothing less than terrorism, and was widely compared to the 9/11 attacks. There was therefore a complete discontinuity in how the events were seen, and exploring this throws some light on the vexed question of why the war on terror has lasted so long.

Origins

A year after the termination of the Saddam Hussein regime, the insurgency in Iraq was developing rapidly, with American forces already losing scores of soldiers killed and hundreds wounded every month. The city of Fallujah was in the heart of central Iraq and was very largely populated by Sunni Muslims, many of whom had supported the previous regime of Saddam Hussein and were bitterly opposed to what was widely seen as a US occupation of their city and country, not a liberation from an oppressive regime. In April 2004, Fallujah was not under the control of the US forces, but a major attempt was made to change that in the wake of a particularly violent incident. On 31 March, five US marines were killed when their armoured personnel carrier was blown up and on the same day four American private security contractors were seized by insurgents and killed. Their bodies were then mutilated and burnt before being hung from the girders of a bridge by a large angry crowd.

The subsequent attempt by the US Marine Corps to gain control of the city was partly in reaction to this atrocity, but US military units frequently found themselves engaged in bitter fights in an enclosed urban environment. On one notable occasion, a group of marines was ambushed in the city by insurgents, suffered injuries, took refuge in nearby buildings, and was only rescued by a heavily armed and armoured convoy after many hours

of fighting. While Marine Corps representatives spoke proudly of the marines' code of leaving no one behind, tensions in the city were exacerbated by an intensive reprisal raid on the area of the fighting by US AC-130 gunships several hours later. This destroyed several city blocks.

In spite of the level of firepower available to the US forces, the abilities and determination of the insurgents were such that the marines were not able to gain full control of Fallujah in April 2004, and sought to enforce a degree of order by negotiating with local leaders. This policy failed, and six months later the city was considered to be such a centre of insurgency that a much larger assault and takeover of the city was thought likely to cause the insurgency irreversible damage. As a result, a large force of around 15,000 troops and marines was assembled for an all-out assault on the city. This would involve a systematic takeover, neighbourhood by neighbourhood, using the overwhelming firepower advantage to destroy any centres of insurgent activity that showed resistance.

The taking of the city

Over a protracted operation lasting more than two weeks the city was indeed brought under control. The full extent of Iraqi casualties remains unknown but appears to have been several thousand people killed. US sources stated that most civilians had left the city and that all that were left were insurgents. This was disputed by Iraqi sources and it is certainly the case that of the 1,450 suspected insurgents detained during the assault, a third were released almost immediately as non-combatants, suggesting that there were many civilians present at the time of the assault. About half of the 39,000 houses in Fallujah were either destroyed or badly damaged during the conflict, as well as most of the schools and other public buildings.

What was particularly notable about Fallujah was the remarkably contrasting images of the conflict as seen on US and Middle Eastern television channels. In the United States there was copious coverage of the artillery, tanks, and other weapons used in the assault. Particularly graphic images were broadcast of tracer bullets arcing over the river and into the town. Other images showed mosques and other buildings being hit as US troops systematically moved through the city. All of them demonstrated the

(continued)

BOX 18.5: (continued)

power of the US military and they were generally well received by many Americans as proof of the progress of the war. Here was a clear example of US forces taking the war to the enemy and taking control of the heartland of the insurgency—a city in which atrocities had been carried out against Americans earlier in the year. Throughout the assault, the administration repeatedly described the insurgents as terrorists. For the United States, Fallujah was a major success in the war in Iraq, and since this was seen as part of the wider war on terror, then the Fallujah attack could be seen as a battle won in that difficult war.

Even as the images of US military success were being broadcast, regional stations such as Al-Jazeera were showing graphic and uncensored images from within the city, with corpses and body parts strewn across the streets, and with women and children critically wounded and waiting in understaffed and under-equipped medical centres. The image for Arab and Muslim audiences was almost a mirror image of the view from Washington. Fallujah was known as 'the city of mosques' and the American attack was seen as a direct assault by 'crusader' forces on what was almost a holy city. Furthermore, both the US TV footage of the firepower directed into the city, and the regional coverage from within the city, strongly reinforced this view. In particular, the US TV images of the heavy firepower being used to great effect may have gone down well in the United States but had the directly opposite effect in the Middle East. Whatever the value of the taking of Fallujah to the US military, its propaganda

value for the insurgents, and, indeed, the wider al-Qaeda movement, was very much greater.

Aftermath

Moreover, Fallujah did not turn out to be in any sense a turning point for the United States in Iraq. In the months that followed, the city was garrisoned by US and Iraqi government troops and was subjected to very high levels of security. These included a cordon around the entire city, with all vehicles subject to search and all adult males searched with particular diligence. In spite of this, improvised explosive devices were being manufactured in the city and used against American forces within months of the original attack.

Across Iraq as a whole, the insurgency gathered pace in the following months. Indeed at the very time that the US forces were engaged in the assault on Fallujah, the insurgency moved north to the city of Mosul. Such was the intensity of the sudden outbreak of fighting there that the United States had to move in 2,400 troops to reinforce the units there. Not only did the November 2004 assault on Fallujah fail to stem the insurgency, it almost certainly increased antagonism to the United States in Iraq and beyond, a result directly counterproductive to the original aim of the operation. What remains most significant, though, is the directly opposite views of the same events. For many Americans it was a reassuring demonstration of military capabilities in a bitter war against uncompromising terrorists but for millions of people across the region it was proof of the ruthlessness of a foreign invader.

---

perspective can even begin to embrace the idea that the Fallujah operation was an example of state terrorism. The problem is that this is precisely how it was seen by tens of millions of people, many of them not especially supportive of the al-Qaeda movement. There is no easy solution to these radically divergent views. Moreover, there seems little prospect of any changes in US policy along the lines suggested above. This does suggest, however, regrettably that the 'Long War against Islamofascism' may be a conflict measured in decades rather than years.

KEY POINTS

- ❑ Given the strategic importance of the Persian Gulf oil resources to the United States, a withdrawal from Iraq is unlikely for some years.
- ❑ The al-Qaeda movement is also operating on a decades-long timescale.
- ❑ Undercutting support for the al-Qaeda movement through changes in US foreign policy is necessary, but prospects for such changes are low.

? Questions

1. What were the main examples of terrorism in the United States before the 9/11 attacks?
2. Why did the Bush administration extend the war on terror to include an 'axis of evil'?
3. What are the aims of the al-Qaeda movement?
4. Why was the termination of the Saddam Hussein regime and the subsequent occupation of Iraq of value to the al-Qaeda movement?
5. What were the different perceptions of the US attack on Fallujah in November 2004?
6. Why is the strategic significance of the Persian Gulf oil reserves relevant to the conduct of the war on terror?

» Further Reading

Aldis, Anne, and Herd, Graeme P. (eds.) (2007), *The Ideological War on Terror* (London: Routledge).

A comprehensive analysis of ideological counters to the al-Qaeda movement and its associates.

Allen, Charles (2006), *God's Terrorists: The Wahhabi Cult and the Hidden Roots of Modern Jihad* (London: Abacus).

Places the development of the al-Qaeda movement in a broad historical perspective.

Bergen, Peter (2002), *The Holy War Inc.: Inside the Secret World of Osama bin Laden* (Phoenix, Ariz.: The Free Press).

A perceptive analysis of the movement.

Burke, Jason (2007), *Al-Qaeda: The True Story of Radical Islam* (London: Penguin Books).

This remains the best account of the origins and development of the movement.

George, Alexander (ed.) (1991), *Western State Terrorism* (Cambridge: Polity Press).

A robust analysis of Western involvement in political violence.

Gregory, Shaun (2007), 'The ISI and the War on Terrorism', *Studies in Conflict and Terrorism*, 30/12 (Dec.): 1013–31.

A seminal paper on the role of the Pakistani Inter-Service Intelligence Agency in Afghanistan.

Horgan, John (2005), *The Psychology of Terrorism* (London: Routledge).

A wide-ranging study of the motivations and behavioural traits relevant to political violence.

Lawrence, Bruce (ed.) (2005), *Messages to the World: The Statements of Osama bin Laden* (London: Verso).

A translation of Osama bin Laden's main speeches and writings, with a succinct introduction to the al-Qaeda movement by Bruce Lawrence.

Rogers, Paul (2007), *Global Security and the War on Terror: Elite Power and the Illusion of Control* (London: Routledge).

Seeks to place the war on terror in the wider context of trends in global insecurity.

 Visit the Online Resource Centre that accompanies this book for web links to accompany each chapter, and a range of other resources: www.oxfordtextbooks.co.uk/orc/cox_stokes/

19

Global environment

Robyn Eckersley

Chapter contents

Introduction

This chapter critically explores the evolution of US foreign policy on environmental issues from the administration of Richard Nixon to that of George W. Bush Jr. It shows that while the USA was widely regarded as an environmental leader during the Cold War period, it has increasingly become an environmental laggard in the post-Cold War period. This has occurred at the same time as international environmental problems have moved from the periphery towards the centre of international politics. The decline in US leadership is attributed to the USA's new status as the sole superpower, the more challenging character of the new generation of global environmental problems that emerged in the late 1980s, the structure of the US economy and political system, and key features of US grand strategy, which include the ways in which US foreign policy elites frame and prioritize security threats and risks.

During most of the period of the Cold War, the environment was widely regarded as a matter of 'low politics' for state foreign policy makers as well as International Relations scholars (Smith 1993). When the Cold War came to an end, however, some observers looked forward to the possibility that the new world order would not only be more peaceful but also more ecologically sustainable. Lester Brown, in the 1991 *State of the World Report*, went so far as to suggest that 'the battle to save the planet will replace the battle over ideology as the organizing theme of the new world order' (Brown 1991: 3). The signs did appear promising. The increasing prominence of trans-boundary and global environmental problems in the 1980s, the proliferation of environmental non-government organizations (NGOs), and the publication of *Our Common Future* by the World Commission on Environment and Development (the Brundtland Report) (WCED 1987) helped generate the momentum for the spectacular 1992 Earth Summit held in Rio de Janeiro—the largest ever gathering of heads of state at the time. The emergence of local and transnational environmental networks behind the Iron Curtain had played a role in the transformations that led to the collapse of the Soviet Union while the leader of the world's emerging sole superpower, US President George H. W. Bush Sr., declared himself 'the environmental president' when he came to office in 1989. Yet despite the unprecedented rise in international environmental concern in the 1980s, the environment proved not to be a central foreign policy priority for George Bush Sr., or indeed any previous or subsequent US president (as distinct from vice-president). Indeed, the neo-liberal New World Order that Bush championed after the demise of the Soviet Union has become less, rather than more, hospitable to environmental concerns.

Yet as the Cold War period recedes, both foreign policy makers and International Relations (IR) scholars are increasingly recognizing that environmental problems can no longer be quarantined from, or relegated as secondary to, security and economic concerns. Growing rates of species extinction, land degradation, deforestation, natural resource depletion, pollution, and, above all, the multiple risks to life-support systems and human communities from human-induced climate change are now being reframed as sources of potentially catastrophic risk that pose major 'threats' to human health, economic stability, and physical security while also challenging traditional strategies of territorial defence. In the wake of four, increasingly serious assessment reports by the Intergovernmental Panel on Climate Change (IPCC), the problem of climate change has gradually moved from the periphery towards the centre state of international politics and foreign policy concerns. The much publicized, and appropriately titled, *Stern Review on the Economic Costs of Climate Change* (Stern 2007), released in October 2006, argued that the economic costs of mitigating global warming are minuscule when set against the longer-term economic costs of failing to take action. In April 2007, the UN Security Council held its first meeting to discuss the international security implications of climate change.

This chapter provides a historical survey and critical evaluation of the United States' shifting response to international environmental problems. It begins with the administration of President Richard Nixon, which is the period when international environmental problems first rose to international prominence, and tracks the USA's involvement in major international environmental summits and environmental treaties up to and including the administration of George W. Bush Jr. (to mid-2007). It will be shown that the USA was regarded as a leader in both domestic and foreign environmental policy making in the 1970s and to some extent in the 1980s, but by 1992 it had lost this international leadership mantle and by the mid-2000s it was widely regarded as a laggard, especially in relation to the world's most significant global environmental challenge—climate change.

The central puzzle raised by this history is: why has US leadership tended to wane at a time when global and trans-boundary environmental problems have become more rather than less serious and threatening to both US and global security? In order to address this question, the chapter seeks to locate the evolution of US foreign environmental policy in the context of the evolution of domestic environmental policy, on the one hand, and the evolution of US grand strategy in response to key geopolitical developments, on the other hand. It will be shown that both of these developments have shaped the negotiating context for US foreign environmental policy making, but that US grand strategy is emerging as an increasingly significant barrier to US environmental leadership in the post-Cold War period in the context of more demanding global environmental challenges. Finally, the chapter offers a critical analysis of theories of foreign policy making and argues that critical constructivist interpretations provide a more satisfying account of the decline in US international leadership in the environmental policy domain than the materialist and rationalist explanations offered by realists, traditional Marxists, and neo-liberal institutionalists.

Environmental multilateralism and the USA

The late 1960s are typically singled out as the birth of the modern environmental movement as a widespread and persistent social movement. The long period of economic boom and population growth following the end of the Second World War produced a range of mass-produced goods but also a mass of ubiquitous ecological problems, an increasing number of which crossed state boundaries. Although most political leaders rejected the doomsday scenarios generated by the limits-to-growth advocates of the early 1970s, a steady stream of studies of global environmental trends has continued to underscore the increasing gravity of the global ecological crisis, culminating in the biggest global environmental challenge of all—human-induced climate change.[1] In response to these broad developments, the post-Second World War period also witnessed a spectacular increase in environmental lawmaking at the national and international levels. Yet the spectacular rise in environmental multilateralism, punctuated by three major earth summits—in Stockholm in 1972, in Rio de Janeiro in 1992, and Johannesburg in 2002—has also brought into relief a range of tensions between developed and developing countries over environment and development priorities, the meaning of sustainable development, environmental justice, and environmental security, and the assignment of environmental international responsibilities and burdens. Throughout this period, the world has looked to the USA for environmental leadership as the world's richest country, with the largest per capita ecological footprint. However, for a complex range of reasons, the US response to global environmental problems has been uneven, and since the early 1990s the USA has been less inclined to assume a leadership role. Under the second Bush administration, the USA has increasingly sought to avoid the entanglements of environmental multilateralism.

From environmental leader to environmental laggard

In the early 1970s, the USA stood out as a world leader in domestic environmental law and policy (much of which has since been emulated by other states), and under the presidency of Richard Nixon, the USA pursued a relatively proactive role at the 1972 Stockholm Conference on the Human Environment. Indeed, Richard Nixon (along with Lyndon Johnson) has received the strongest rating in a survey of the environmental records of the ten presidents from Truman to Clinton (Soden and Steel 1999: 347–9). Yet Soden and Steel (1999: 347–8) suggest that even the greenest presidents were 'merely caught in the tide of congressional efforts, public support, and environmental realities that demanded a federal response to a growing number of programs'. They conclude that the credit for US domestic and international environmental leadership in the 1970s must go to the environmental movement (which generated a major momentum for environmental concern in American society), to their lobbyists, and to Congress, which displayed mostly bipartisan support for environmental initiatives during this period.

As the following brief history shows, although the US president is chief diplomat and chief executive officer, US foreign environmental policy decisions have been largely shaped by domestic environmental politics, and the president is merely one, albeit one very significant, player in a complicated set of political processes in the deeply fragmented US political system. While there has never been a 'substantial "environmental president"' (Soden and Steel 1999: 349) there have certainly been some substantial and unapologetic *anti*-environmental presidents, most notably Ronald Reagan and George Bush Jr. No president has yet exploited the full capacity of their constitutional or leadership powers to promote, as distinct from obstruct or compromise, environmental goals.

The Nixon years: setting the pace

President Richard Nixon was not known for his environmental sympathies but he nonetheless presided over one of the most innovative periods of environmental policy making and lawmaking in US history, which included the enactment of the National Environmental Policy Act (NEPA) in 1969 that established the Council on Environmental Quality (CEQ) within

the White House, and the Environmental Protection Agency, set up in 1970. The 1960s had seen the spectacular growth of environmental organizations and public environmental awareness in the USA, culminating in the first nationwide 'Earth Day' in 1970. Nixon had assumed office in 1968 on a tide of rising environmental concern and he signed a range of new environmental treaties relating to fisheries and the protection of Antarctic seals, which was consistent with a history of long-standing US leadership in the protection of marine resources and marine mammals. He also signed a treaty designed to protect the seabed from nuclear testing.

However, it was the 1972 Stockholm Conference where the USA sought to develop a green reputation. During the period 1968–72 the Nixon administration was facing a major crisis over its intervention in Vietnam, including international criticism for the 'ecocide' resulting from the use of Agent Orange by the US military, along with international criticism for its atomic testing. Against this broader background, both Nixon and his advisers saw Stockholm as a significant opportunity to reassert moral leadership, gain electoral advantage, and divert attention from 'that war'. Preparations for the conference were dominated by the executive, particularly the State Department and the CEQ, with very little involvement by US environment or business organizations. Hopgood attributes this lack of involvement to the relative insulation of the State Department and CEQ from domestic social pressures, and also the relative lack of international focus of US environmental organizations at that time (Hopgood 1998: 87). However, Stockholm acted as a major catalyst for the development of both domestic and international environmental NGOs, which have played an increasingly significant role in subsequent international environmental negotiations.

The USA's two most prominent initiatives at Stockholm were support for the establishment of the United Nations Environment Program to coordinate environmental matters within the UN, and a pledge to contribute 40 per cent of a $100 million voluntary fund to support UNEP. The USA also used the occasion to promote the development of a convention on ocean dumping, the establishment of a World

Heritage Trust, and a ten-year moratorium on whaling. These were relatively ambitious initiatives when judged by the standards of the day. Yet they also provide a good illustration of the limited scope of environmental policy making at the international level (Hopgood 1998: 79). For example, the USA rejected calls for additional funding to developing countries to assist them with meeting their environmental commitments.

Nixon pursued fewer environmental initiatives in his second term of office, which coincided with the energy crisis of 1973–4 and the Watergate scandal, which led to his resignation. Nixon's successor, President Gerald Ford, was largely preoccupied with the political fallout from Watergate (including his pardoning of Nixon) and an economy suffering from stagflation. Although Ford had once worked as a park ranger at Yellowstone national park, he took very few domestic or international environmental initiatives during his brief tenure, and his international efforts largely involved follow-up work arising from previous administrations. This period saw the signing of the two conventions dealing with ocean pollution, the ratification of the Convention on Trade in Endangered Species of Wild Fauna and Flora (CITIES) in 1974 and the signing of a treaty on the conservation of polar bears (Long, Cabral, and Vandivort 1999: 207).

The Carter years: the well-intended but under-achieving president

President Jimmy Carter is widely regarded as the first US president to adopt a global environmental perspective, evidenced by his commissioning in May 1977 of the *Global 2000 Report to the President* (CEQ and DoS 1980), which was released in 1981. Through this report, Carter sought a comprehensive overview of global environmental trends on population, resources, and the environment. Although Carter's international environmental concerns may have been more sincere and noble than those of Nixon, his international environmental record turned out to be more modest. Confronted with an ongoing energy crisis and an ailing economy at home, and the Iranian hostage crisis abroad, the Carter administration was unable to play any concerted leadership role in addressing the alarming global environmental trends that were revealed in the *Global 2000 Report to the President*. Nonetheless, he began the difficult process of addressing the USA's growing dependence on imported energy. He introduced the Public Utilities Regulatory Policy Act, which included energy conservation measures, appointed a White House Task Force on National Energy Policy, placed the Department of Energy in the presidential cabinet, and introduced a major energy bill (which failed to pass Congress), and a bill establishing a Synthetic Fuels Corporation, which passed Congress (Long, Cabral, and Vandivort 1999: 208). Two further major domestic environmental initiatives were the Superfund Act (later signed off by Reagan), to regulate the clean up of toxic waste sites, and the protection of vast areas of Alaskan wilderness.

On the international front, Carter extended the application of the NEPA to US government activities abroad (Executive Order 12114 in January 1979) and he banned the export of toxic waste to other countries in 1981 (Executive Order 12264). He initiated negotiations with Canada on acid rain and signed the Convention on Long Range Transboundary Air Pollution 1979. Shortly before leaving office, he ensured US participation in the World Climate Conference 1979, which contributed to the growing international research effort on climate change. However, Carter's most significant environmental legacy was his preparedness to question America's dependence on imported oil and his efforts to promote energy conservation and a renewable energy industry in America. Yet he also saw Persian Gulf Oil as vital to US interests and created a new military command structure in the region, which eventually became the United States Central Command.

The Reagan years: winding back the clock

Ronald Reagan's first official act in coming to office was to dismantle the solar panels that Carter had installed on the roof of the White House (Hartmann 2003)—an act that set the environmental tone of his presidency. As the first US president with an explicit anti-environmental agenda, Reagan embarked upon a comprehensive effort to reduce, and where possible eliminate, many of the environmental regulations that had been enacted over the previous decade. His Economic Recovery Act 1981 sought to reduce taxation and wind back spending on social and environmental programmes, including Carter's tax incentives for renewable energy, and to make way for the efficiency of the market. Reagan also devolved environmental responsibilities to the states and local governments and screened all senior appointments to environmental agencies to ensure their conformity with his anti-environmental agenda (Vig 2006: 105). Although his attempt to abolish the CEQ failed to gain congressional approval, he succeeded in sidelining the agency by cutting its staff and ignoring its advice (Vig 2006: 105). Reagan's budget cuts also made it impossible for federal environmental agencies, such as the EPA and the Department of the Interior, to implement their mandates. However, Reagan's anti-environmental campaign slowed down considerably in his second term as a result of growing public opposition. Indeed, Reagan's efforts to demonize environmentalists provoked a surge in the funding and membership of US environmental organizations (Dryzek et al. 2003: 34).

Although Reagan's anti-environmental agenda was mainly directed toward US domestic policy he made it clear that he would not sign any international environmental treaties that would compromise US economic competitiveness (Long, Cabral, and Vandivort 1999: 211). Reagan reversed Carter's 1981 executive order banning the export of toxic waste to other countries, declined to sign the 1989 Basel Convention which regulated the trans-boundary movement of hazardous waste, and stalled the acid rain negotiations with Canada. His administration rejected the United Nations Convention on the Law of the Sea (UNCLOS III) on the ground that the USA should not be made to share its technological capabilities regarding seabed mining and offshore fishing with other nations. Reagan also ceased funding US population projects and withdrew from UNESCO, although his attempt to end US contributions to UNEP was successfully resisted by Congress (Hopgood 1998: 125–6). However, Reagan did support a number of international environmental initiatives, such as the Convention on the Conservation of Antarctic Marine

Living Resources 1982 and the International Tropical Timber Agreement 1985.

Yet it is no small irony that the most significant foreign environmental policy development that occurred during Reagan's second term—US ozone diplomacy—also stands out as the most significant example of US environmental leadership and multilateral engagement in the twentieth century. Scientists had discovered the link between the release of chlorofluorcarbons (CFCs) and the thinning of the earth's ozone layer in the early 1970s, and the USA had phased out non-essential CFC aerosols as early as 1978 under its Clean Air Act. The USA also played a leading role in pushing for a complete phase-out of ozone-depleting substances (compared to the weaker proposal for a 30 per cent cut proposed by the European Union (EU)) in the negotiations leading to the 1985 Vienna Convention for the Protection of the Ozone Layer. The discovery of the so-called Antarctic ozone hole in 1985 had prompted a concerted push for a phase-out by the US EPA. Moreover, in response to EU resistance, the US State Department mounted a major international consensus-building campaign to persuade other countries to agree to a worldwide phase-out of ozone-depleting substances, including ongoing periodic assessment of the list of ozone-depleting substances (Sitaraman 2001: 123–4). This campaign required all US embassies to explain the US negotiating position, beginning with like-minded countries and then extending to reluctant countries (Benedick 1991: 55–67). Domestically, the State Department worked closely with all branches of the US government, the major environmental and science agencies, and the CFC producers.

Although US CFC producers initially formed a united front against EPA regulatory proposals for a unilateral phase-out, they shifted their stance to support the international harmonization of regulations following the signing of the Vienna Convention in 1985 (which supported the principle of protecting the ozone layer, but without specific commitments). Key producers such as DuPont and Allied Chemical had invested in new production facilities for CFC substitutes and the US negotiators supported the industry's commercial interests in the negotiation for the Montreal Protocol 1987, which introduced a mandatory phase-our regime (DeSombre 2000: 93–4). The establishment of a multilateral fund has assisted developing countries with the financial and technical resources to meet the costs of compliance with the regime.[2]

Many analysts of US ozone diplomacy have argued that the USA's international leadership role can be understood as an attempt by the USA to internationalize its domestic environmental regulation. According to Elizabeth DeSombre (2000) this situation arises when there is a set of domestic environmental regulations in place and an agreement between US environmentalists and US industry that international regulation would be both environmentally and economically advantageous. On this analysis, the Reagan administration's ozone diplomacy is consistent with its position that it would not support any international environmental treaty that would compromise US economic competitiveness.

Bush the elder: the failed 'environmental president'

In the wake of public criticism of Reagan's anti-environmentalism, the resurgence of the US environment movement during the 1980s, and growing international concern over global warming, George Bush Sr. chose to badge himself 'the environmental president' in the 1988 presidential race. Once elected, Bush surprised his critics by appointing key environmental advocates to head the EPA and CEQ and he supported the further strengthening of the Clean Air Act in 1991, which included more stringent reductions in sulphur dioxide emissions. These amendments also pioneered the system of tradable pollution permits in sulphur dioxide and prepared the ground for the negotiation of an acid rain treaty with Canada in 1994 to reduce sulphur dioxide emissions by 50 per cent by 1994. Bush also agreed to amendments strengthening the ozone treaty in 1992.

Yet despite this promising start, and the significant opportunity for environmental leadership presented by the 1992 Earth Summit, George Bush Sr. failed to live up to his promise to be America's environmental president. Having served for eight years as Reagan's vice-president, which included actively supporting his campaign of environmental deregulation, Bush reverted to type in negotiations over the two biggest international environmental challenges confronting his administration: climate change and biodiversity protection. Indeed, President Bush negotiated his presence at the 1992 Earth Summit on the condition that the United Nations Framework Convention on Climate Change (UNFCCC) include no specific targets or timetables for greenhouse gas (GHG) reductions on the ground that this would place an intolerable burden on the US economy. Bush also declined to sign the Convention on Biological Diversity (CBD), bowing to pressure from the US biotechnology and pharmaceutical industries which argued that the provision requiring royalties to be paid to developing countries for the use of their native genetic diversity did not provide adequate patent and copyright protection for US industry. President Bush also attracted international condemnation for his oft-quoted declaration at the summit that 'America's lifestyle is not up for negotiation'.

The Bush administrations' early initiatives on domestic environmental policy were overshadowed by a reassertion of his conservative economic ideology in the last eighteen months of his presidency, when he installed Vice-President Dan Quayle as head of the Council on Competitiveness to respond to industry complaints of excessive regulation, including environmental regulation (Vig 2006: 107).

The Clinton years: unfulfilled promises

Bush's failure as an environmental president served as a key target in Bill Clinton's presidential campaign in 1992. Clinton, and his green Vice-President Al Gore, received strong endorsement from the US environment movement, and their Democratic campaign included a wide range of environmental promises, including signing the CBD, committing to quantitative targets to reduce US carbon dioxide emissions (i.e. to return to 1990 emissions levels by 2000), raising the corporate average fuel economy (CAFE) standard for motor vehicles, promoting renewable energy research and development (Paarlberg 1999; Vig 2006: 108). The Clinton–Gore team also emphasized the economic advantages that would flow from an increased investment in more environmentally friendly technologies as an antidote to the traditional discourse of 'environment versus the economy' that had characterized the Reagan and Bush administrations. On winning office, Clinton abolished the Council on Competitiveness, appointed a number of well-known environmental professionals to key executive positions, and established an Office for Environmental Policy to ensure the integration of environmental policies in all departments (Vig 2006: 108). This push for integration also extended to foreign policy. Vice-President Al Gore was a key advocate of enlarging the USA's security framework to include environmental concerns (see Key quotes 19.1) and Secretary of State Warren Christopher announced in 1997 that the Clinton administration would 'put environmental issues where they belong: in the mainstream of American foreign policy' (Christopher 1998: 412). Indeed, Long, Cabral, and Vandivort (1999: 218) assert that Clinton had 'assembled one of the most environmentally friendly (greenest) administrations in American history'.

Despite this initial enthusiasm, the Clinton administration faced a number of significant obstacles in promoting a new environmental agenda. The 1992 presidential race had taken place in the context of a declining economy, declining public interest in environmental issues, and falling funding and membership of environmental organizations. Even before the 1994 congressional elections, which gave control of both houses to the Republicans, Clinton suffered a major congressional defeat over his proposal to introduce a broad-based tax on fuels, which was his major initiative for fulfilling his commitment to reduce US carbon dioxide emissions to 1990 levels by 2000. The initiative was eventually replaced with a much more modest tax on gasoline. Moreover, his Climate Change Action Plan, which relied on voluntary measures, bore little relationship to his climate pledge.

Although Clinton signed the CBD in 1993 (subject to certain reservations), he failed to secure ratification from a highly partisan Senate, despite gaining the approval of representatives from the US biotechnology and pharmaceuticals industry as a result of the reservations based on side agreements with industry (Paarlberg 1999: 239). A similar fate befell the USA's signing of the Kyoto Protocol in 1997. Prior to the negotiations at Kyoto, the Republican-dominated Senate—sensitive to the concerns of coal-producing states in the USA—had unanimously passed the Byrd–Hagel resolution making any support by the Senate conditional on developing states also taking action within the same time period (see Key quotes 19.2). This was followed by a $13 million advertising campaign by the US fossil fuel industry in the lead-up to the Kyoto meeting that warned Americans of the economic costs of implementing the mooted Protocol (Oberthur and Ott 1999: 72). The US delegates at Kyoto were initially constrained by a limited mandate: to accept only a zero growth emissions reduction target, and only if developing countries also accepted emissions reductions targets in the same time period. However, last-minute intervention by Al

> ### 66 KEY QUOTES 19.1: Letter from Vice-President Al Gore
>
> We have moved beyond Cold War definitions of the United States' strategic interests. Our foreign policy must now address a broad range of threats including damage to the world's environment—that transcend countries and continents and require international cooperation to solve.
>
> Environmental problems such as global climate change, ozone depletion, ocean and air pollution, and resource degradation—compounded by an expanding world population—respect no border and threaten the health, prosperity, and jobs of all Americans. All the missiles and artillery in our arsenal will not be able to protect our people from rising sea levels, poisoned air, or foods laced with pesticides. Our efforts to promote democracy, free trade, and stability in the world will fall short unless people have a livable environment.
>
> (Letter from Vice-President Albert Gore Jr. attached to US Department of State 1998)

Gore to break a deadlock in the negotiations resulted in the USA agreeing to cut emissions by 7 per cent by 2008–12 from 1990 levels without developing country participation. Although this diplomatic shift by the USA was hailed as a major breakthrough in the international climate negotiations, it was clear that the Clinton–Gore administration would be unable to win Senate ratification. Indeed, Clinton avoided such a confrontation with the Senate by not submitting the Protocol for approval, despite the fact that the USA had successfully negotiated a range of so-called flexibility mechanisms under the Kyoto Protocol (such as carbon trading, joint implementation, and the clean development mechanism) that would make it easier for the USA to reach its target.

In the negotiations for the Cartagena Protocol on Biosafety 2000, under the CBD, the USA led the so-called Miami group of nations that opposed trade restrictions on the trans-boundary movement of genetically modified organisms. Moreover, Clinton's negotiation of the North American Free Trade Agreement with Canada and Mexico attracted strong criticism from US environmental organizations for setting off a 'race to the bottom' in environmental regulation and enforcement, which he sought to allay through the inclusion of new environmental provisions and side agreements. A concerted campaign by US

environmental organizations against the environmental limitations of the GATT also prompted the USA to play a role in ensuring the inclusion of the objectives of sustainable development and environmental protection in the 1994 Marrakesh Agreement establishing the World Trade Organization.

In the end, the Clinton administration failed to make any significant progress on climate change, failed to secure the ratification of the Kyoto Protocol or CBD, and declined to sign the Cartagena Biosafety Protocol. This may be attributed largely to a well-organized industry opposition and a hostile Congress, which gave considerable airing to the views of global-warming sceptics (McCright and Dunlap 2003: 361), but also to Clinton's pragmatic disposition, which included a readiness to compromise environmental goals, and an overriding concern to maintain the competitiveness of the US economy. Nonetheless, the Clinton administration did seek to grapple with the challenge of policy integration by promoting the discourses of ecological modernization and introducing environmental security as a component of US foreign policy and defence planning (White House 1996). However, critics such as Barnett (2001: 84) have pointed to the Clinton administration's mostly narrow framing of environmental problems as direct or indirect 'threats' to US interests, as if environmental

---

❝ KEY QUOTES 19.2: Byrd–Hagel Resolution

Resolved, That it is the sense of the Senate that—

(1) the United States should not be a signatory to any protocol to, or other agreement regarding, the United Nations Framework Convention on Climate Change of 1992, at negotiations in Kyoto in December 1997, or thereafter, which would—

(A) mandate new commitments to limit or reduce greenhouse gas emissions for the Annex I Parties, unless the protocol or other agreement also mandates new specific scheduled commitments to limit or reduce greenhouse gas emissions for Developing Country Parties within the same compliance period, or

(B) would result in serious harm to the economy of the United States; and

(2) any such protocol or other agreement which would require the advice and consent of the Senate to ratification should be accompanied by a detailed explanation of any legislation or regulatory actions that may be required to implement the protocol or other agreement and should also be accompanied by an analysis of the detailed financial costs and other impacts on the economy of the United States which would be incurred by the implementation of the protocol or other agreement.

(Byrd–Hagel Resolution, sponsored by Senator Robert Byrd (D-WV) and Senator Chuck Hagel (R-NE), 25 July 1997, available at www.nationalcenter.org/KyotoSenate.html)

problems were a danger emanating from outside the USA. Such a framing obscured the USA's own complicity in, and responsibility for, the production of environmental problems.

Bush Jr.: the fossil fuel president

The election of George Bush Jr. to the White House in 2001 following his narrow victory over Al Gore in the 2000 presidential race saw the return of a strong pro-business agenda and a corresponding roll-back and revision of many domestic environmental regulations that was reminiscent of the Reagan years (Vig 2006: 115–17). However, whereas the Reagan administration had led the world in the negotiations to protect the ozone layer, the Bush administration attracted widespread international criticism for its rejection of environmental multilateralism in general, and its repudiation of the Kyoto Protocol in particular (despite the fact that US public opinion was in favour of ratification in early 2001).[3] As the world's biggest aggregate GHG emitter and second highest per capita emitter, the USA stands alongside Australia (the highest per capita emitter) as the only two developed countries that have refused to ratify the Kyoto Protocol.[4]

The Bush administration's major reasons for repudiating Kyoto have been that the 7 per cent emission reduction target negotiated by the Clinton–Gore administration would harm the US economy, and that the Protocol is flawed and ineffective because it does not require major developing country emitters to commit to mandatory emissions reduction targets in the same time period. Although the USA has continued to play a major role in climate change research, the Bush administration has, at least up until 2005, remained deeply sceptical of the science of climate change. On the domestic front, the Bush administration has rejected prescriptive legislation such as mandatory emissions reductions targets (including a national carbon trading scheme), carbon taxes, or mandatory renewable energy targets. Instead, through its Climate Change initiative, it has sought to reduce the GHG emissions intensity of the US economy by 18 per cent by 2012, largely through voluntary measures and technology development (White House 2002). However, GHG intensity reflects the amount of GHG produced per unit

of GDP, not aggregate emissions, and by the Bush administration's own admission, the GHG intensity of the US economy has been in long-term decline and the 18 per cent target is only slightly above forecasts based on a business-as-usual scenario (Depledge 2005: 23).

More significantly, the Bush administration's climate change strategy has been overshadowed by its National Energy Strategy, which was based on recommendations from an Energy Task Force chaired by Vice-President Cheney. Drafted in secrecy by representatives from the fossil fuel and related industries, the report of the Task Force (concluded in May 2001) sought to step up the supply of energy (primarily, but not exclusively, fossil fuels) rather than reduce demand. Many of the report's recommendations were incorporated into the Energy Policy Act, which passed Congress in 2005. The Act provided greater subsidies to the oil and gas industries to encourage exploration and drilling, the streamlining of environmental regulations to accelerate increased energy production, the opening up the Alaskan National Wildlife Refuge to exploration and drilling, and low-interest loans and research grants for the development of nuclear power plants (White House 2006). Although President Bush has acknowledged America's vulnerability arising from its addiction to oil in his 2006 and 2007 State of the Union Addresses (Bush 2006, 2007) his response has been primarily technology driven and concerned to secure supply rather than reduce demand in order to maintain a cheap energy supply for America.

Vice-President Cheney's energy strategy has proved to be the single most important initiative shaping the Bush administration's domestic and international climate change policy. It also underpins the Bush administration's insistence on developing country commitments, which reflects a concern that a rapidly growing China would gain a significant competitive advantage over the USA while competing with the USA for the world's dwindling supply of oil. The USA's dependence on externally sourced oil rose to 56 per cent in 2006, almost half of which came from the Middle East. China became a net oil importer in 1993 and by 2005 was importing over 40 per cent of its oil (IEA 2005). China is the world's second biggest

CONTROVERSIES 19.1:   The multiple risks of the USA's oil addiction

President Jimmy Carter was the first US president to demonstrate serious concern about the risks of US dependency on imported oil. In his famous 'crisis of confidence speech' televised to the nation on 15 July 1979 during the second energy crisis he declared that 'In little more than two decades we've gone from a position of energy independence to one in which almost half the oil we use comes from foreign countries, at prices that are going through the roof' (Carter 1979). In response to soaring inflation and gasoline queues he announced a range of measures, including import quotas, significant investment in developing domestic sources of energy (including renewables and coal), and domestic energy conservation.

Between 1979 and 2007, the risks associated with America's dependence on imported oil have increased. Alongside the problem of rising oil prices from any future disruption of supply are the risks of climate change from the burning of fossil fuels, the predicted onset of peak oil, and the deteriorating security situation stemming from US military presence in the oil-rich Persian Gulf. This confluence of risks has prompted calls for a new US energy strategy based on aggressive demand management and the promotion of renewables and low-carbon energy alternatives.

However, the Bush–Cheney energy strategy has continued US dependence on oil. Although President Bush has acknowledged America's vulnerability arising from its addiction to oil in his 2006 and 2007 State of the Union Addresses (Bush 2006, 2007) his administration has provided major tax breaks to the US oil industry and avoided aggressive demand management or a major switch to renewables. On the foreign policy front, the Bush administration strongly resisted efforts at the Johannesburg Summit in 2002 to seek agreement on an international renewable energy target and it has continued to use oil as a strategic resource in pursuing its general foreign policy objectives. Although the Bush administration has denied that oil was a motivation behind the US invasion of Iraq in 2003, gaining access to Iraq's oil fields for foreign multinationals has nonetheless emerged as the only significant pay-off from the war. However, the Bush administration is unlikely to justify a continued occupation of Iraq on the grounds that it will secure an unsustainable energy resource for Americans, especially given that the US presence in the region has fanned anti-Americanism and Islamic fundamentalism.

In a provocative essay on the Greening of Geopolitics, *New York Times* journalist Thomas Friedman argued that since 11 September 2001, the USA has been financing both sides of the war on terrorism. As he puts it: 'We were financing the US military with our tax dollars; and we were financing a transformation of Islam, in favour of its most intolerant strand, with our gasoline purchases' (Friedman 2007). According to Friedman, the next president will have to rally America with a new green patriotism: 'green' must become 'the new red, white and blue' because it is the only agenda that can simultaneously address the challenges of 'jobs, temperature and terrorism'.

Since the congressional elections in November 2006, the US legislature has increasingly recognized the limitations of the Bush–Cheney energy strategy. On 4 August 2004 the House of Representatives passed (241–172) a new energy bill that requires energy utilities to produce 15 per cent of their power from renewable sources (solar, wind, geothermal, and other non-fossil fuel sources) by 2020. Power utilities are responsible for about one-third of the USA's domestic carbon dioxide emissions. The passage of this bill had been a top priority of Nancy Pelosi, as the new Leader of the House after the November 2006 congressional elections. Twenty-six Republicans crossed party lines to vote for the bill, while nine Democrats opposed it.

The House also passed a bill to repeal the tax breaks for the oil industry, enacted in the Bush–Cheney energy bill of 2005. Part of this money is to be redirected towards research grants and projects to improve energy efficiency, the development of alternative fuels, and further research on carbon capture and storage from coal-fired utilities. The bill also requires the US federal government, including the Pentagon, to be 'carbon neutral' by 2050.

The Senate passed a more conservative version of the bill in June but which (unlike the House bill) calls for increased fuel efficiency standards in cars and light trucks. Democrats have claimed that if the best of the House and Senate bills were combined, then it would be 'the most significant energy legislation ever enacted' (Broder 2007). However, President Bush has vowed to veto the bill on the grounds that it does not encourage domestic production of oil and gas, while the tax bill unfairly singles out the oil industry.

aggregate emitter and will soon overtake the USA as the world's largest aggregate emitter, but its per capita emissions are only around one-eighth of the USA's (WRI 2001). This massive gap underlies China's insistence that developed countries take the lead in tackling climate change in accordance with their historical responsibility for past cumulative emissions and their greater capacity to absorb emission cuts. This burden-sharing principle is embodied in the principle of common but differentiated responsibility enshrined in Article 3 of the UNFCCC.

The mutual dependence on fossil fuels by the USA and China underpins the Bush administration's promotion of the Asia Pacific Partnership in Clean Development and Climate 2006 (the AP6), which is the centrepiece of the USA's international response to climate change. The AP6 is a non-binding framework for cooperation to promote the development and diffusion of new 'clean' technologies to reduce pollution and greenhouse gas (GHG) emissions and to promote economic development, poverty alleviation, and energy security. The six partners—the USA, Australia, Japan, China, South Korea, and India—are collectively responsible for around half of the world's GHG emissions.[5] However, the AP6 is consistent with the USA's preference for voluntary, market-friendly initiatives on the domestic front, and its general proclivity to promote 'bottom-up, coalitions of the willing on specific issues' on the international front (Depledge 2005: 24). The AP6 provides no targets or timetables, no price signals, no new carbon markets, and no enforcement mechanisms. The initiative also fails to address the problem of rising aggregate emissions and it encourages its partners toward a continued reliance on fossil fuels as a primary source of energy (Christoff and Eckersley 2007). The AP6 is based on market-friendly procedural norms of equality of commercial opportunity rather than the UNFCCC's principles of equity and common but differentiated responsibility (McGee and Taplin 2006: 188). In focusing only on future emissions, the AP6 fails to address the significant disparities in responsibility for past emissions, per capita emissions, institutional capacity, and environmental vulnerability

between developed and developing countries. These considerations have been central to the environmental justice norms in Article 3 of the UNFCCC and explain why the Protocol requires only developed countries to undertake mandatory emissions reductions in the first commitment period.

Indeed, the Bush administration's refusal to take the lead in combating GHG emissions stands as one of the major stumbling blocks to the participation of China and other major developing country emitters in the negotiation for the second commitment period under the Kyoto Protocol. In contrast to the USA, the EU has committed itself to its Kyoto target of an 8 per cent reduction in emissions by 2012 and is pursuing a target of a 30 per cent cut by 2020 for developed countries in the second round of Kyoto negotiations (EurActiv.com 2007).

According to the World Bank (2007), the EU's emissions have grown by 3 per cent between 1990 and 2003 whereas emissions in the USA have grown by 20 per cent during the same period.

The Bush administration has also turned its back on other environmental agreements and follow-up work arising from the 1992 Earth Summit. It has declined to press for ratification of the CBD and declined to sign or ratify the Cartagena Protocol on Biosafety 2000. President Bush also declined to attend the World Summit on Sustainable Development in Johannesburg in 2002 and his administration has not pursued any integrated sustainability planning at the national level. The USA exacerbated transatlantic environmental differences in 2003 by bringing a legal action in the WTO against the EU's moratorium on the approval of GM products in the EU. Although the EU claimed that its moratorium was consistent with its commitment to the precautionary principle and its obligations under the Cartagena Biosafety Protocol, the USA successfully argued in the WTO dispute panel that this was irrelevant because the USA was not a party to the Protocol and the EU's actions constituted an unwarranted restriction on trade under the WTO rules. Throughout this period the US environmental movement has had negligible influence on the executive and legislative branch of government, prompting two environmentalists to proclaim the 'death of environmentalism' in the USA in a widely circulated critique that argued the movement had lost its way in focusing on technical fixes at the expense of developing a broad vision that is commensurate with the magnitude of the crisis of climate change (Schellenberger and Nordhaus 2004).

In all, the Bush administration's foreign policy has been overwhelmingly preoccupied with the war on terror. While the USA remains the largest financial contributor to the IPCC and UNFCCC it has rejected a precautionary approach on climate change and biosafety while pursuing an aggressive policy of prevention and pre-emption in addressing terrorist threats, including military intervention in the territories of states that harbour terrorists. By 2006, the costs to the USA of the Iraq War had exceeded the anticipated costs of conforming to the stiff Kyoto targets negotiated by the Clinton–Gore administration (Sunstein 2007).

Key trends and puzzles in US foreign environmental policy

Table 19.1 provides a summary of the USA's involvement in the most significant international environmental treaties negotiated since the 1970s, showing the date of the USA's signature and subsequent ratification, accession, or acceptance, and which political party controlled Congress at the time of formal acceptance. Although Table 19.1 is not intended to provide a comprehensive coverage of all environmental treaty activity or all US foreign environmental policy activity (it excludes amendments to protocols, and the negotiation of minor protocols of a technical nature which follow on from the negotiation of major conventions), it does provide a reasonable indication of general trends in US involvement in twenty-three major treaties over three and a half decades. One striking trend emerges from this history, which is depicted in the bar graph in Figure 19.1: if we take the 1992 Earth Summit as marking the beginning of the post-Cold War period then the USA has ratified or acceded to ten of the thirteen major

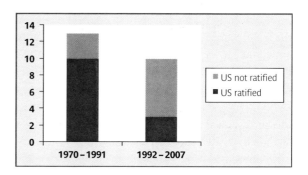

Fig. 19.1 Proportion of major environmental treaties ratified by the USA

treaties (i.e. 77 per cent) negotiated in the previous two decades (and has led the whaling moratorium in 1982) but has ratified only three of the ten major treaties (i.e. 40 per cent) that have been negotiated in the post-Cold War period. A systematic count of US ratifications of all environmental treaties negotiated in the period 1970–2004 and listed on the United Nations Environment Program's register of international environmental treaties is consistent with this pattern, although slightly less favourable to the USA. That is, the USA ratified 71 per cent of treaties in the period 1992–2004 and 33 per cent in the period 1992–2004.[6] Another noteworthy feature of this history is that a Republican-controlled Congress is considerably more hostile to environmental treaty obligations than a Congress controlled by the Democrats. Indeed, all of the major treaty ratifications prior to 1992, and the three ratifications in the period after 1992, were by a Democrat-controlled Congress.

The foregoing history of US environmental foreign policy making since the 1970s raises two interesting puzzles. First, why has US leadership tended to wane as global and trans-boundary environmental problems have become more, rather than less, serious and threatening to both US and global security? Second, why has the USA devoted so many resources and adopted a risk-averse posture to tackling terrorism yet rejected a precautionary approach to climate change and the trans-boundary movement of GM products?

Table 19.1 US involvement in major environmental treaties, 1970–2007

Convention	US position	Parties to Convention	US President (at Convention creation)	Congression-al control
Convention on Wetlands of International Importance especially as Waterfowl Habitat (Ramsar) 1971	Signed 2 Feb. 1971, ratified 18 Dec. 1986	154 states	Nixon	Democratic
Treaty on the Prohibition of the Emplacement of Nuclear Weapons and other Weapons of Mass Destruction on the Sea-bed and Ocean Floor and in the Subsoil Thereof 1971	Signed 11 Feb. 1971, ratified 18 May 1972	66 states	Nixon	Democratic
Convention on the International Trade in Endangered Species 1972	Signed 3 Mar. 1973, ratified 14 Jan. 1974	169 states	Nixon	Democratic
London Convention on Ocean Dumping 1972	Signed 29 Dec. 1972, ratified 30 Aug. 1975	78 states	Nixon	Democratic
United Nations Convention on the Law of the Sea 1972	Not signed or ratified	153 states	Nixon	Democratic
World Heritage Convention 1972	Signed 16 Nov. 1972, ratified 7 Dec. 1973	183 states	Nixon	Democratic
Geneva Convention on Long Range Transboundary Air Pollution 1979	Signed 13 Nov. 1979, and accepted 30 Nov. 1981	51 states	Carter	Democratic
Convention on the Conservation of Migratory Species of Wild Animals 1979	Not signed or ratified	92 states	Carter	Democratic
Convention on the Conservation of Antarctic Marine Living Resources 1980	Signed 20 May 1980, ratified 2 Feb. 1982	31 states	Reagan	Democratic
Whaling Moratorium 1982	Adopted by IWC 23 July 1982	25 votes for, 7 against and 5 abstentions (USA in favour)	Reagan	Democratic
Vienna Convention for the Protection of the Ozone Layer 1985	Signed 22 Mar. 1985, ratified 27 Aug. 1986	191 states	Reagan	Democratic
Montreal Protocol[a] 1987	Signed 16 Sept. 1987 and ratified 21 Apr. 1988	191 states	Reagan	Democratic

(continued)

Table 19.1 (continued)

Convention	US position	Parties to Convention	US President (at Convention creation)	Congression-al control
Basel Convention 1989	USA signed 22 Mar. 1990 (US Congress has given advice and assent) but has not ratified	163 states	George H. W. Bush	Democratic
Madrid Protocol 1991	Signed 17 Oct. 1991, ratified 1 Nov. 1996	All 26 necessary Antarctic Treaty Consultative Parties have ratified, 43 states in total	George H. W. Bush	Democratic
United Nations Framework Convention on Climate Change 1992	Signed 12 July 1992 and ratified 15 Oct. 1992	160 States	George H. W. Bush	Democratic
Convention on Biodiversity 1992	Signed 4 June 1993 but not ratified	190 states	Clinton	Democratic
United Nations Convention to Combat Desertification 1994	Signed 14 Oct. 1994, ratified 17 Nov. 2000	191 states	Clinton	Democratic
Comprehensive Test Ban Treaty (CTBT) 1996	Signed 24 Sept. 1996 but not ratified	132 states	Clinton	Republican
International Tropical Timber Agreement 1994 (replacing the 1983 Agreement)	Signed 27 Dec. 1988, ratified 14 Nov. 1996	58 states	Clinton	Democratic
The 1996 Protocol to the 1972 London Convention on Ocean Dumping	Signed but not ratified		Clinton	Republican
Kyoto Protocol 1997	Signed 12 Nov. 1998 but not ratified	166 states	Clinton	Republican
Rotterdam Convention on Pesticides and Industrial Chemicals 1998	Signed 11 Sept. 1998 but not ratified	114 states	Clinton	Republican
Cartagena Protocol on Biodiversity 2000	Not signed	140 states	George H. W. Bush	Republican
Stockholm Convention on Persistent Organic Pollutants 2001	Signed 23 May 2001 but not ratified	110 states	George W. Bush	Republican

Note: Table 19.1 focuses only on major environmental treaties and excludes amendments to protocols. However, the pattern of ratifications is consistent with a systematic count of US treaty ratifications 1970–2004, based on the United Nations Environment Program's register of international environmental treaties 1970–2004 (UNEP 2005b). For a fuller explanation, see n. 4.

KEY POINTS

❑ A Republican-controlled Congress is considerably more hostile to environmental treaty obligations than a Democrat-controlled Congress.

❑ US international environmental leadership has waned significantly in the post-Cold War period.

❑ The USA has actively opposed the Kyoto Protocol, which seeks to address the most significant global environmental problem facing the international community since the rise of modern environmentalism.

Explaining US foreign environment policy

Before exploring possible explanations for these puzzles, we can draw together a number of key insights that have emerged from the history of US environmental foreign policy making since the 1970s.

First, it is clear that a single-minded focus on the environmental sympathies or antipathies of successive US presidents or their senior staff in the White House is not sufficient to explain shifts in US foreign environmental policy making. It is also necessary to examine the composition of other agencies in the executive branch (the EPA, the State Department), and other branches of government, most notably Congress. Despite the president's significant executive power and foreign policy prerogatives, it is Congress that passes laws, levies taxation, and controls spending. Moreover, the ratification of treaties rests with the Senate. As we have seen, a pale green president (and dark green vice-president) faced with a hostile Congress can do very little (e.g. the Clinton–Gore administration), while a dark green Congress together with a strong environmental movement and growing public environmental concern can do a great deal to prod an indifferent president (Richard Nixon) to support international environmental initiatives.

Second, different environmental problems (biodiversity loss, ozone depletion, marine mammal protection, climate change) vary considerably in their complexity, gravity, incidence, and lead time; in the degree of certainty of scientific understanding associated with the problem and the causal factors that contribute to it; in their relationship to American culture and values; and in the scale of change that is required

to address the problem, including the associated costs of abatement. Accordingly, different environmental problems present different challenges and opportunities for the USA at home and abroad and help to explain the relative influence of different interest groups. As we shall see, the international environmental challenges of the post-Cold War period have proved to be much more confronting across most of these dimensions than the challenges raised during the Cold War period.

Third, the history of US engagement in environmental treaty making since the 1970s has shown that the USA will not enter into an international environmental treaty if it is incompatible with domestic regulations, or if existing domestic regulations cannot easily be changed without a significant backlash from political elites and key interest groups. While the USA has never been an importer of 'foreign environmental policy' ideas from abroad it has often sought to export its environmental regulations (DeSombre 2000).

Fourth, and flowing on from the previous point, US interest groups tend to have less direct influence on foreign policy than domestic policy, but their influence on domestic environmental initiatives can have significant indirect effects on foreign policy (as demonstrated by the previous insight). Business interest groups have had much more influence on domestic and foreign environmental policy than domestic environmental NGOs (Falkner 2001) when the potential economic costs of international cooperation are high (the Kyoto Protocol, Cartagena Protocol), while environmental NGOs have had relatively more influence when the costs are low (e.g. the whaling moratorium, Montreal Protocol).

Finally, US foreign environmental policy cannot be examined in isolation from broader developments in US foreign policy. As we have seen, President Nixon's leadership at the 1972 Stockholm Conference cannot be understood in isolation from the political fallout from the Vietnam War, while President George Bush Jr.'s international response to climate change cannot be understood in isolation from his preoccupation with the war on terror and the pivotal role played by the national energy strategy in the USA's national security strategy.

Yet none of the foregoing insights explain why US leadership has tended to wane as global and trans-boundary environmental problems have become more, rather than less, serious and threatening to both US and global security. That the end of the Cold War served as a key turning point in the waning of US international environmental leadership is significant in one respect, yet merely coincidental in another. The 'significant respect' is that the end of the Cold War changed the geopolitical context in which international environmental negotiations were to take place. The disintegration of the Soviet Union had removed a major incentive for US cooperation with its allies and others within its sphere of influence. As the sole superpower in the post-Cold War world, the USA has chosen to take full advantage of its greater range of exit options than any other state to avoid entanglement in the increasingly demanding and ever growing international processes of multilateralism. The USA's increasing inclination to act unilaterally, via coalitions of the willing, rather than multilaterally, has affected environmental diplomacy, as it has many other policy domains. Indeed, even when the USA has sought to play a proactive environmental role, it still prefers to act through informal partnerships where it can control the process.

However, added to the changed geopolitical context is the fact that the end of the Cold War happened to coincide with the emergence of a new and more complex set of global environmental problems that have challenged what might be called 'core' US national interests. Most of the US environmental initiatives during the 1970s and 1980s (such as the establishment of the United Nations Environment Program, or protecting natural heritage, whales, oceans, or the ozone layer) were relatively uncomplicated issues, and they bore little relationship to, or otherwise did not directly threaten, US security interests or economic competitiveness. The same cannot be said for the environmental problems confronting world leaders at the 1992 Earth Summit. For the USA in particular, the mitigation of climate change, the management of intellectual property over biodiversity, or the regulation of the trans-boundary movement of genetically modified organisms posed direct challenges to the USA's security, energy, and/or economic interests. Indeed, the more general insight emerging from this foreign environmental policy history after the end of the Cold War is that *international environmental problems have increasingly challenged US grand strategy, and that key elements of US grand strategy have increasingly constrained the ability of the USA to adopt a proactive response to key international environmental problems.*

US grand strategy and the environment

US grand strategy represents an overriding prioritization of US foreign policy objectives and goals, backed up with particular strategies, preferred modes of engagement (multilateral, bilateral, unilateral), and preferred policy tools. As we have seen, US foreign environmental policy has never played a role in shaping US grand strategy (despite the promotion of the discourse of environmental security by President Clinton) and it has generally been accorded low priority in the pecking order of foreign policy objectives and goals. As Robert Falkner has noted, 'unlike trade and monetary policy, environmental policy has never been central to the US effort to create international order' (Falkner 2005: 586). But while environmental policy has had little impact on US grand strategy prior to the end of the Cold War, US grand strategy has increasingly set significant limits on US foreign environmental policy after the Cold War. Indeed, this provides one important key to the puzzle raised above: why has the USA not responded to the security and environmental threats of climate change by reducing the USA's dependence on petroleum? The other keys are the energy-intensive structure of the US economy and the fragmented character of the US political system.

US foreign environmental policy during the period 1970–2007 has been shaped and constrained by significant continuities and changes in US grand strategy. Throughout both the Cold War and post-Cold War periods, US grand strategy has remained committed to securing the military and economic supremacy of the USA, promoting a stable world capitalist system, and promoting the spread of liberal democracy. While the last of these foreign policy goals is generally conducive to environmental social learning, the others stand in a more problematic relationship.

First, to the extent to which the growth of an unreconstructed world capitalist system based on neo-liberal economic ideology remains a central pillar of US grand strategy, then we are unlikely to see the USA emerge as a leader in promoting the meta-environmental strategy of sustainable development endorsed at the 1992 Earth Summit. This strategy requires all policy makers and economic actors to move beyond issue-by-issue environmental problem solving by integrating environmental considerations into all areas of policy making and decision making, including foreign policy. However, the appealing rhetoric of policy integration papers over a set of deep-seated debates over whether a rapidly growing world capitalist system of the kind promoted by the USA is capable of delivering ecological sustainability and intra- and intergenerational equity of the kind defended in the Brundtland Report. Critics point out that while capitalism can deliver improved efficiency of resource and energy use through technological innovations that decrease the amount of environmental degradation produced per unit of GDP, this will not necessarily translate into a decrease in environmental degradation in *absolute* terms. Indeed, in the absence of overarching sustainability parameters at the national and international levels, the environmental productivity gains of technologically driven

ecological modernization invariably serve to fuel more consumption and growth. This is why President Bush's strategy of merely reducing emissions intensity will not address the problem of rising aggregate emissions.

While the 'embedded liberalism' of the post-Second World War era might have been compatible with integrated sustainability planning, the neo-liberal economic ideology promoted by the USA since the 1970s, and especially since the end of the Cold War, is deeply resistant to the kind of 'thick regulation' demanded by proponents of ecological sustainability or 'strong ecological modernization' (Christoff 1996; Eckersley 2004). The high-consumption lifestyles of Americans have remained largely non-negotiable during the period 1970–2007, despite the growth of the green consumer movement. As we have seen, the US presidents' enthusiasm for integrated environmental policy planning has never been high and President Clinton's modest efforts to promote policy integration have been dismantled. In contrast, the European Union emerged in the 1990s as the green leader not only in environmental diplomacy but also in domestic efforts at policy integration through the adoption of sustainable development in the Treaty of the European Union (Article 6).

Second, the USA has remained heavily dependent on a cheap and abundant supply of oil to maintain its economic competitiveness. Cheap and abundant petroleum has, as Michael Klare observes, been central 'to the vigor and growth of the American economy and to the preservation of a distinctly *American* way of life' (2004: pp. xiii–xiv). It has also fuelled the USA's vast military apparatus. Even more significantly, oil has also been used as a strategic resource by the USA during the Cold War in pursuing its strategy of containment and in the overall management of its Western leadership (Bromley 1991; 2005). As Keohane puts it, 'In a material sense, oil was at the centre of the redistributive system of the American hegemony' (1984: 140). These links between US energy policy and foreign policy are entrenched and long standing and may be traced to the end of the Second World War when President Roosevelt offered the Saudi regime military support in return for reliable access to the Saudis' vast oil reserves. US dependence on Middle Eastern oil grew during the Cold War period at the same time as US oil capital shifted 'from a powerful interest in US foreign policy-making into a key arm of US power' (Bromley 1991: 123). The net effect of these developments is that oil (along with the US oil industry) became integrated into the structural components of US hegemony. Indeed, Ran Goel (2004: 478) has characterized the international political economy of oil as a US-led order based on a bargain between the US executive and US oil industry to manipulate the international oil market and secure supply. This special arrangement (or 'petro-military-industrial-complex', after Boal et al. 2005) has seen the executive working to overcome obstacles to US investment and the oil industry providing the investment capital and technologies to extract and transport the oil (Klare 2004: 62). This strategic use of oil has remained central to US grand strategy in the post-Cold War period, despite the predicted onset of peak oil and scientific warnings that the world must move rapidly towards a low-carbon economy. The US oil majors and allied industries have been key players in obstructing domestic efforts to reduce US dependence on oil (Newell and Paterson 1998). They have formed the backbone of US opposition to the Kyoto Protocol, run orchestrated political campaigns to disparage the science of climate change, and served as key participants in the Cheney Energy Taskforce. Most of the US oil majors have negligible investment in non-carbon forms of energy compared to their European counterparts (Goel 2004: 476; Kolk and Levy 2001).

Notwithstanding these continuities in US grand strategy, there have also been some significant shifts that have impinged upon foreign environmental policy. The terrorist attacks on the World Trade Center and Pentagon on 11 September 2001 have profoundly reshaped the USA's threat perceptions and national security strategy. The USA has singled out terrorism and the acquisition of weapons of mass destruction (WMDs) by so-called rogue states or terrorists as the most significant security threats facing the USA. It is no small irony that fifteen of the nineteen hijackers involved in the terrorist attacks on New York and Washington on 11 September 2003 were from Saudi Arabia, the USA's major oil supplier since 1945 and a key base for the USA's military operation during the 1991 Gulf War. The stationing of US troops in Saudi Arabia had generated considerable resentment among many Islamists and has been cited by the Saudi-born leader of al-Qaeda, Osama bin Laden, as one of the main reasons for terrorist attacks on the USA in 2001. The USA withdrew its troops from Saudi Arabia in 2003 and there are growing concerns about the Saudis' role as a reliable 'swing producer'.

Indeed, many observers have drawn connections between these developments and the USA's decision in 2003 to invade Iraq, which is home to the world's third largest oil reserves—despite denials by President Bush and former Secretary of Defense Donald Rumsfield that the invasion had any links with oil. Most Iraqis have interpreted the invasion as an attempt 'to steal their oil' and this has also informed the 'No Blood for Oil' protests in the USA. To be sure, there were multiple motives for the invasion, and there was no threat of oil scarcity or fear of disruption to oil supply as in the 1991 Gulf War. Nonetheless, the invasion has paved the way for the restructuring of Iraq's oil industry, which had been nationalized during the OPEC oil crisis and has been operating well below full production (Boal et al. 2005: 13). The USA's proposed petrochemical bill seeks to install a new legal framework that gives effective control of Iraq's oil fields to multinational oil companies without any formal transfer of ownership.

In all, the USA's ongoing commitment to economic neo-liberalism, its dependence on oil to maintain its economic competitiveness and military supremacy, its use of oil as a strategic commodity to maintain hegemony, and its preoccupation with the war on terror have together significantly constrained the ability of the USA to play a proactive role in responding to the most serious environmental problem of the new millennium.

Making sense of foreign policy

The foregoing analysis concerning the relationship between domestic and US foreign environmental policy, and US grand strategy, highlights the necessity of a multilevelled analysis that incorporates the international system, the state, society, and key individuals in the political elite in order to explain US foreign policy (Barkdull and Harris 2002). Yet the choice of level or levels of analysis does not determine the epistemology, or the explanatory priority accorded to power, interests, and/or ideas/norms. The importance of US security and economic interests in shaping foreign environmental policy might appear at first blush to play into the hands of rationalist and/or materialist explanations of foreign policy, such as realism, neo-liberal institutionalism, and traditional Marxism. Yet these accounts ultimately remain crude and unsatisfactory for several reasons.

First, security and economic constraints do not explain the particular menu of policy choices, or the particular policy responses, selected by the US executive in response to different domestic or international pressures. Realist and traditional Marxist accounts, in particular, attribute minimal autonomy to the state on the assumption that its decisions are essentially a reflection of systemic imperatives that derive from the anarchic structure of the state system, or from particular configurations of economic power. Yet there is no single, obvious path to US military or economic supremacy, and it cannot be assumed that different foreign policy elites would produce the same strategies in response to similar challenges. Indeed, most scholars who have undertaken a detailed examination of US foreign environmental policy making have shown that the domestic institutional landscape plays a much more significant role in explaining these environmental policy choices than international influences (Hopgood 1998; DeSombre 2000, 2005; Falkner 2005). This research has challenged the assumption that states are unitary, rational actors, by pointing to internal divisions within states and their societies. According to Hopgood (1998: 222), the central actors in American foreign policy are state officials, and it is the intrastate struggles within the executive branch of government that are ultimately determinative of policy choices.

Second, materialist and rationalist explanations do not offer sufficiently fine-grained tools to explain the waxing and waning of US environmental leadership. They are better at explaining the absence rather than the presence of environmental leadership. For example, materialists and rationalists can provide plausible accounts of why the USA will not enter into an international environmental treaty if it is incompatible with domestic regulations, the interests of key industry groups, or core security interests. But they cannot explain why the USA would bother to take a leadership role in relation to environmental issues that do not impinge upon security or economic interests. Why, for example, has the USA gone to such great lengths (employing persuasion, economic sanctions, and bribery) to support an international moratorium on whaling if not for a strong normative commitment to the preservation of whales within American society?

Neo-liberal institutionalism, which provides the dominant interest-based analysis of environmental regime formation, predicts whether a state will be a leader, a bystander, or a laggard on the basis of relative ecological vulnerability and relative abatement costs (Sprinz and Vaahtoranta 1994). So, for example, if abatement costs are high and vulnerability is low, then states are likely to be laggards, whereas if abatement costs are low and vulnerability is high then they are likely to be leaders. Yet prediction becomes difficult when both abatement costs and vulnerability are high, as in the case of climate change. More importantly, these predictions assume that states are rational, unitary actors, and that their cost–benefit analyses and strategic calculations can be uncritically transposed from one jurisdiction to another in response to similar external challenges.

Third, since rationalist explanations take the security and economic interests of states as given, they are unable to account for historical and geographical variability in the social construction of these interests. Indeed, the significant differences in foreign environmental policy between the USA and the EU since the end of the Cold War directs attention to the idiosyncratic ways in which US foreign policy elites have constructed their security, economic, and environmental agendas—some of which defy standard realist or rationalist analysis. If climate change is a source of catastrophic risk, why has this not been incorporated into US security policy on the basis of the rational cost–benefit analysis of the Stern Review? If states are rational actors, why has the USA not sought to reduce its dependence on imported petroleum by developing an aggressive domestic demand-management strategy? While there are important differences in the imminence of risks of terrorism compared to climate change, the longer risks of climate change are more pervasive, serious, and certain than the risks of terrorism.

Foreign policy making is, after all, a purposive activity that involves the formulation and pursuit of objectives, goals, and strategies by particular decision makers. Understanding this activity requires locating decision makers in their historical context or 'operating environment', understanding their traditions and cultures, causal ideas, and principled beliefs and how they have interpreted their operating environment by selecting and endowing some phenomenon with significance while screening out others. In the case of the USA, there has been plenty of 'screening out' in the case of the science of global warming. While US scientists have played a major role in the IPCC they have had very little influence on US domestic or foreign policy, until recently. In contrast, the findings and warnings of the IPCC have been much more influential in Europe and climate change scepticism has been much less pronounced among political leaders, the media, and the public (McCright and Dunlap 2003; Boykoff and Boykoff 2004). The social construction of new security risks and new ecological risks by political elites in the USA since the end of the Cold War has remained firmly rooted in the traditional 'high' versus 'low' politics distinction, which rests on particular understandings of the 'core' and 'peripheral' business of the US state. In contrast, the EU has displayed a more risk-averse posture in the

post-Cold War period, particularly in response to the potential risks of not only climate change but also genetically modified organisms (GMOs) (Falkner 2007). In the case of GMOs, whereas the USA has pushed for regulatory harmonization to promote trade liberalization in what it regards as a benign technology, in the EU, NGOs have played a major role in framing the problem as a matter of both sovereign and consumer choice; the right to know and to choose safe food based on the precautionary principle; and resistance to corporate control over the agri-food chain (Levidow 2007: 133).

From a critical constructivist standpoint, the economic, energy, and security interests of the USA are not pre-given and they are always open to redefinition by social agents, including foreign policy elites. As it happens, an increasing number of Americans within both the state and civil society are beginning to rethink the meaning of these interests.

KEY POINTS

- ❑ US foreign environmental policy cannot be examined in isolation from domestic environmental policy, on the one hand, and broader developments in US foreign policy, on the other hand.
- ❑ The USA has never been an importer of 'foreign environmental policy' ideas from abroad but it has often sought to 'export' its domestic environmental regulations.
- ❑ The key international environmental problems of the post-Cold War period have increasingly challenged US grand strategy, while US grand strategy has increasingly constrained the ability of the USA to adopt a proactive response to these problems, especially climate change.

Conclusion

The Bush administration's environmental foreign policies, and its associated discourses of risk and security, have come under increasing scrutiny in the wake of Hurricane Katrina in 2005, Al Gore's

widely screened documentary *An Inconvenient Truth* (released in 2005), the publication of the Stern Review in 2006, growing concern about the 'doctoring' of scientific reports on climate change, and the publication of the IPCC's Fourth Assessment report in 2007. Moreover, the November 2006 congressional elections, which delivered control of the Senate to the Democrats, produced a significant shift in the political landscape on Capitol Hill. The 110th Congress is no longer debating whether climate change exists but instead asking what should be done and debating a range of new bills designed to address the problem. Indeed, a record number of climate change bills have been proposed in the new Congress.[7] Significant

shifts have also occurred at the state and municipal levels (Rabe 2003). The North-Eastern US states have negotiated a regional carbon trading scheme to begin trading in 2009 and Governor Arnold Schwarzenegger has enacted the Global Warming Solution Act 2006, which seeks to reduce California's GHG emissions to 1990 levels by 2020. Ten leading US corporations (including General Electric, BP, and Alcoa) have a formed a coalition with four major US environmental organizations, known as the US Climate

---

MAJOR DEBATES AND THEIR IMPACT 19.1: The EPA's authority to regulate emissions: no more deferral to the president?

Although George Bush Jr. had promised to regulate carbon dioxide as a pollutant under the Clean Air Act during his presidential campaign, he reversed this position shortly after coming to office in 2001. He also made it clear that he would not order the federal Environmental Protection Authority (EPA) to regulate greenhouse gas (GHG) emissions under the Clean Air Act and that his administration would pursue a voluntary approach to mitigation based on technological innovation. The Bush administration's refusal to adopt a more prescriptive approach to reducing GHG emissions has attracted widespread criticism from the Kyoto parties as well as from environmentalists, scientists, and many 'progressive' states and municipal governments within the USA.

However, on 2 April 2007 in the landmark case of *Massachusetts* v. *Environmental Protection Agency*, 548 US (2007) the US Supreme Court ruled by a majority of five to four that the EPA has the power to regulate carbon dioxide emissions from new vehicles, along with other greenhouse gases (GHG), as pollutants under the Clean Air Act.

The ruling overturned a decision of the US Court of Appeals of the District of Columbia Circuit in September 2005.

The case had been brought by twelve states (mostly Pacific and north-east coast states) led by Massachusetts, and a coalition of municipal governments and environmental and public health organizations, claiming that the EPA had abdicated its responsibilities under the Clean Air Act in choosing not to regulate GHGs as pollutants. The case was defended by the EPA, a variety of automobile industry associations, and ten US states, most of which

are significantly dependent on the oil, coal, or motor vehicle production industries.

The Administrator of the EPA had claimed in 2003 that it lacked authority to regulate GHG emissions, and that even if it did have the requisite legal power it had discretion to decide whether to regulate. Among the list of reasons given for declining to act were scientific uncertainty and the fact that regulating GHG emissions might interfere with the president's foreign environmental policy. The EPA believed that regulation 'might impair the President's ability to negotiate with "key developing nations" to reduce emissions'. However, Justice Stevens, who presented the majority opinion of the Court, rejected the argument and ruled that the EPA's decision should be determined on the basis of the requirements of the Clean Air Act and not the executive's foreign policy. The president's broad executive authority was held not to 'extend to the refusal to execute domestic laws' (Supreme Court of the United States 2007).

Under a 1967 law, motor vehicle standards can only be set by the federal government, although an exception exists for California. The decision gives the green light to California's new vehicle emissions laws, enacted in 2002 and phased to start in 2009, which require a waiver from the EPA.

In response to the decision, on 14 May 2007 the Bush administration ordered the EPA to begin drafting new regulations to reduce GHG emissions from cars and trucks. The target date for the new rules is the end of 2008, which is less than a month before President Bush is due to vacate his office (Donnelly 2007).

Action Partnership, which has called for cuts in national aggregate carbon emissions of 10 to 30 per cent over the next fifteen years. In 2007, the Center for Naval Analysis commissioned a report on the national security threats raised by climate change, prepared by a group of retired US generals and admirals, which was released on the eve of the United Nations Security Council's first ever meeting to discuss the international security implications of climate change in April 2007 (CNA Corporation 2007). Finally, the influential *New York Times* journalist Thomas Friedman has argued that US environmental leadership on alternative energy can weaken global terrorism, which has been fanned by the USA's military presence in the Persian Gulf (Friedman 2007).

If there is one major lesson to be learned from the foregoing history of US foreign environmental policy making it is that US international leadership requires a considerable confluence of domestic political forces which, in the case of climate change, means acceptance of the need for an integrated energy, economic, and environmental strategy for sustainable development that guides both domestic and foreign policy making. Ideally, this would require a green president surrounded by a forceful and environmentally sympathetic cabinet, an environmentally sympathetic Congress, a well-funded scientific community, a vigorous environmental movement, and an environmentally proactive business community that cooperates with the environment movement because it sees market advantage in being an environmental pace setter. America has never enjoyed this particular alignment of political and economic forces for environmental change, but if it comes to pass—and there are at least a few promising signs—then US international environmental leadership could be formidable. If it does not come to pass within the next decade, then the outcome for the world's climate could be unthinkable.

? Questions

1. How relevant are the environmental sympathies of the President in accounting for US international environmental leadership?

2. What role has Congress played in US foreign environmental policy making?

3. Why was the USA an international environmental leader in the 1970s?

4. Why did the USA play a leadership role in the Montreal Protocol given the anti-environmental sympathies of the Reagan administration?

5. Why was the end of the Cold War a turning point in US foreign environmental policy making?

6. What was the relationship between US grand strategy and foreign environmental policy before the end of the Cold War? In what ways did this relationship change in the post-Cold War period?

7. Why did President George Bush Jr. repudiate the Kyoto Protocol in 2001?

8. What is the relationship between energy security and environmental security?

9. What theories of foreign policy can best explain the shifts in US foreign environmental policy making from the 1970s?

10. What are the prospects of the USA assuming a leadership role in the climate change negotiations?

》 Further Reading

Bromley, S. (1991), *American Hegemony and World Oil* (Cambridge: Cambridge University Press).

A detailed analysis of US hegemony in the domain of oil politics based on a 'conjunctural' model of world politics that combines the geopolitical economy of the world oil industry and the global power of the USA in the system of states.

Harris, P. G. (ed.) (2000), *Climate Change and American Foreign Policy* (New York: St Martin's Press).

This edited collection explores the role of the USA in the climate change negotiations prior to the election of George Bush Jr.

——(ed.) (2001), *The Environment, International Relations, and US Foreign Policy* (Washington, DC: Georgetown University Press).

This edited collection covers a range of case studies of US environmental policy making.

——(2001), *International Equity and Global Environmental Politics: Power and Principles in US Foreign Policy* (Aldershot: Ashgate).

This book tracks the emergence of environmental equity concerns in the Clinton administration's foreign environmental policy.

Hopgood, S. (1998), *American Environmental Foreign Policy and the Power of the State* (New York: Oxford University Press).

A detailed examination of US foreign environmental policy from the Stockholm Summit to the Rio Summit that rejects realist, pluralist, and Marxist accounts and highlights the core role played by senior members of the US executive in shaping foreign policy.

Klare, M. (2004), *Blood and Oil* (New York: Metropolitan Books).

This book provides a detailed analysis of America's growing petroleum dependence and the ways this has shaped national energy and security strategies and led to the increasing use of the US military to secure supply.

Soden, D. (ed.) (1999), *The Environmental Presidency* (Albany, NY: State University of New York Press).

This edited collection provides a detailed examination of the role of the US president in environmental and natural resource policy, focusing on the different facets of the president's constitutional and leadership powers.

Vig, N., and Kraft, M. (eds.) (2006), *Environmental Policy: New Directions for the Twenty-First Century* (Washington, DC: Congressional Quarterly).

A comprehensive edited collection on all facets of US environmental policy making in the domestic and international context.

Endnotes

I am grateful for the research assistance provided by Aron D'Souza and Gerry Nagtzaam.

1. These include the Brundtland Report (WCED 1987), the United Nations Environment Program's *Millennium Ecosystem Assessment* (UNEP 2005a), the regular State of the World Reports prepared by the Washington-based Worldwatch Institute (e.g. 2007), the UK Stern Report (Stern 2007), and the reports of the Intergovernmental Panel on Climate Change (e.g. IPCC 2007).

2. Major amendments to the Montreal Protocol have since been made (in 1990, 1992, 1997, and 1999) which have expanded the list of ozone-depleting substances covered by the regime.

3. According to Michael Lisowski (2002: 114), an ABC News poll released on 17 Apr. 2001 revealed that 61% of Americans supported ratification of the Kyoto Protocol.

4. Australia ratified the Kyoto Protocol in December 2007.

5. Canada joined the partnership in 2007.

6. The United Nations Environment Program's register of international environmental treaties lists 221 environmental treaties concluded 1970–2004 (UNEP 2005b). However, excluding treaties on occupational health and safety, only around 120 of these treaties are relevant to the USA (the remainder refer to bilateral or multilateral treaties in other regions). A count of the total of these treaties ratified by the USA in the period 1970–89 reveals that 54 out of 76 (71%) were ratified, whereas in the period 1992–2004 the USA ratified only 15 out of 45 (33%). I am grateful to Gerry Nagtzaam for carrying out this exhaustive research.

7. The most adventurous of these bills is Rep. Henry Waxman's (Democrat, California) Safe Climate Act 2007 (HR 1590), which mandates an 80% reduction of GHGs by 2050 from a 1990 baseline. See www.house.gov/waxman/safeclimate/.

 Visit the Online Resource Centre that accompanies this book for web links to accompany each chapter, and a range of other resources: www.oxfordtextbooks.co.uk/orc/cox_stokes/

Section 5

Futures and Scenarios

20 American foreign policy after 9/11

Caroline Kennedy-Pipe

Chapter contents

Introduction

In his book *The Landscape of History* the distinguished Cold War historian John Lewis Gaddis (Gaddis 2002) makes an arresting suggestion: 'If you think of the past as a landscape,' he tells us, 'then history is the way we represent it, and it's that act of representation that lifts us above the familiar to let us experience vicariously what we can't experience directly: a wider view' (Gaddis 2002: 5).

That wider view is what this chapter as a whole seeks to place upon contemporary American foreign policy. By seeing the past and the present of American foreign policy as a 'landscape', in Gaddis's sense, one might be able to suggest certain features of a particular landscape, prominent now, which were also apparent long before 9/11. We might then be able to reflect upon whether the consequences of those features might be similar. In other words, however much the foreign policy of George W. Bush and his neo-conservative agenda might strike us as having led the USA down entirely new avenues in terms of the conduct of American foreign policy—the alleged emphasis upon securing oil resources, for example, or the

desire to remove dictators and 'spread democracy'—as this chapter will suggest, these tendencies are as much a part of certain traditions within US foreign policy as they are in some ways a departure from it.

Thus, this chapter will try to give an outline account of US foreign policy after the 9/11 attacks with a view to looking at continuities as well as the disjunctions of Washington's engagement with the world. The terrorist attacks unquestionably altered the shape and thrust of US foreign policy in the short to medium term and have raised many questions, not just about the direction of US foreign policy but also about the shape of the international system itself. The question, however, is the extent to which they have, can, or should change the direction of US foreign policy in the longer term; and so this chapter will try to assess the extent to which US foreign policy after 9/11 manifests familiar tendencies as well as unfamiliar ones.

To begin with, however, we will need to look at the origins of the post-9/11 foreign policies and the general assumptions that seemed to be governing US foreign policy before 9/11. It is to this, we now turn.

The background

KEY POINTS

- ❏ After the collapse of the USSR in 1991 the United States proclaimed a New World Order.
- ❏ The USA did seem to be the indispensable nation and throughout the 1990s was engaged in a range of activities which ranged from negotiations over world trade, the promotion of democracy in central and eastern Europe, and discussions over the Middle East Peace Process.
- ❏ Despite its engagement with global politics the White House remained after the debacle in Somalia reluctant to actually place troops on the ground. It was only

after prolonged discussion and the failure of European powers to effectively deal with the Balkan Wars that the White House intervened.
- ❏ Throughout the 1990s, the USA displayed a continuing preoccupation with dictators and dictatorships. This led both to the Kosovo War and the ongoing frustration with the recalcitrant behaviour of Saddam in Iraq.
- ❏ The 1990s were marked by tussles over foreign policy between the Republican-led Congress and the Democratic White House.

The period between the mid-1990s and the early twenty-first century was certainly not one that was shy of challenges for the USA. The early euphoria of the immediate post-Cold War world wore off rather rapidly and there was little left of the first President Bush's much vaunted 'New World Order' which he had announced in the aftermath of the Gulf War of 1990–1 in a speech to Congress (Nye 1992). Nonetheless, the Clinton administration had sought to position itself as central to a wide range of mulilateral and bilateral relationships, to be, as Secretary of State Madeleine Albright termed it, 'the indispensable nation' (Albright 2004). Thus the USA was throughout the decade after the Soviet Union collapsed heavily involved in the Middle East, in negotiations over world trade and the replacement of the General Agreement on Tariffs and Trade (GATT) with the World Trade Organization (WTO), in trying to support newly established democracies in eastern and central Europe and Latin America, and in building free trade areas throughout the Americas. It had also become somewhat reluctantly but centrally involved in the conflicts in the former Yugoslavia with the bombing campaign that eventually led to the Dayton Agreement of 1995, and then in the controversial NATO (but US- and British-led, some might say British-inspired) intervention in Kosovo in 1999. This campaign was designed to prevent Serbian ethnic cleansing of the Kosovan Albanians and ended with the removal of the authoritarian leader/dictator Slobodan Milosovic (Halbestam 2003; Holbrooke 1999). It is worth noting however the reluctance of Clinton to deal with the messier aspects of international politics, not least the rapid American withdrawal from Somalia after the death of some eighteen rangers in Mogadishu whilst fighting the soldiers of local warlords, and perhaps more markedly the reluctance of the Clinton administration to take seriously the ongoing genocide in Rwanda throughout 1994. Clinton in 1998 while visiting Rwanda in fact apologized for the shortcomings of the international community in preventing the bloodshed.

The Republican-dominated Congress, from 1994 onwards, had opposed much of the Clinton multilateralism and had challenged the President to change certain key policies, especially with respect to issues such as climate change and his initial and enthusiastic support for an incipient International Criminal Court (ICC), negotiations for which got under way in earnest in 1998. Clinton in 2000 signed the Rome Statute for the ICC but failed to recommend that it be ratified.

Despite the turmoil of the international system and the resurgence of genocide in both Africa and Europe, however, the American presidential election of 2000 was chiefly and somewhat predictably about domestic politics. Foreign policy played little part in the tussle over the White House. The Republican candidate, George W. Bush, son of the forty-first president, was in fact critical of President Clinton's 'overambitious' foreign policy (as he saw it) and the supposed tendency to interventionism. He pressed a range of relatively familiar criticisms of Clinton's policies although he had little knowledge or background in foreign policy. This 'ignorance' was a fact in which he almost seemed to glory and he chose to run in the election as a 'compassionate conservative', focusing on a domestic agenda and issues guaranteed to appeal to his core supporters on the Christian right—such as opposition to abortion, stem cell research, and marriage between gay couples.

To counter charges that he was a relative lightweight in foreign policy terms—a charge the Republicans were concerned might ultimately hurt him, since the Vice-President Al Gore, his Democrat opponent, had been a prominent figure in at least parts of the Clinton foreign policy agenda—Bush surrounded himself with veterans of his father's foreign policy team and announced that his own inexperience didn't really matter since 'I'll be surrounded by good, strong, capable, smart people who understand the mission of the United States is to lead the world to peace' (Mann 2004: 255).

The people who actually did advise the Bush campaign formed the nucleus of the team that became the key foreign policy makers of his administration in 2001. His campaign director of foreign policy was Condoleezza Rice, who became National Security Adviser in the first Bush administration and then Secretary of State in the second. His second campaign adviser, Paul Wolfowitz, later became Deputy Secretary of State and one of the chief architects of the Iraq War. Other key figures in the campaign team who went on to be key players in the post-2001 US government, or advisers to it, included Richard Perle, Richard Armitage, Stephen Hadley, and Robert Zoellick. Perhaps most important of all, Bush's running mate, Dick Cheney, had huge experience of foreign policy, having served in Congress and as White House chief of staff (under President Ford) and having been Defense Secretary under Bush's father. As James Mann has argued, this was an important choice as 'The selection of Cheney was of surpassing importance for the future direction of foreign policy. It went further than any other single decision Bush made toward determining the nature and policies of the administration he headed' (Mann 2004: 252).

Many of these individuals had been heavily involved in conservative foreign policy circles for some years and some, at least, were part of a network of policy intellectuals and activists generally referred to as 'neo-conservatives'. Perle, Wolfowitz, and Cheney especially had ties to this group (Mann 2004). Neo-conservatism is a very broad intellectual movement in American public life and can be traced back to reactions to both communism and liberalism in American life and, in foreign policy terms, to a radical critique of the 'realism' of Henry Kissinger, Richard Nixon's National Security Adviser and Secretary of State. For Kissinger, foreign policy was a matter of accepting that all powers in the world (including the Soviet Union) had legitimate interests, and successful foreign policy consisted, of course, of defending your own interests but also recognizing others' legitimate interests. Thus Kissinger's signature policy was 'détente' with the Soviet Union; a policy which was prepared to resist Soviet power when necessary but was also prepared to deal with the Kremlin when possible (see Kissinger 1982, 1994; Isacson 1996).

The neo-conservatives resisted any such claims. The Soviet Union was, for them—in Ronald Reagan's words—an 'evil empire' and it had to be opposed and, eventually, eliminated. Of course, this did not necessarily require force but Kissinger's 'realism' was, for them, a betrayal of everything America stood for. As one of the major architects of neo-conservatism, Irving Kristol, said, realism had no purchase on the future, because it was simply a defence of the status quo. But, to his mind, modern politics is necessarily ideological since it is, fundamentally, a battle over 'who owns the future' (Stelzer 2005) and changing the shape of global politics.

Not all of the team that came in with Bush were neo-conservatives, of course. Condoleezza Rice was not of that persuasion and Donald Rumsfeld was not. But initially at least, the Republican ascendancy was based on a marriage of convenience between neo-conservatives, realists (like Rice), pragmatists (like Rumsfeld and, in a different way, Powell), and social conservatives. Initially, the alliance held, and, as we shall see, 9/11 put the neo-conservative agenda in pole position as far as foreign policy was concerned. It was only halfway through Bush's second term that that alliance really stared to unravel and the neo-conservatives began to lose their dominance in a wealth of acrimony about the failure in Iraq.

Perhaps the most important figure to play a role in Bush's foreign policy who was not part of the Bush inner circle was in fact Colin Powell. As the chairman of the Joint Chiefs of Staff during the 1990–1 Gulf War, as a highly decorated black American, and as a figure who in many respects stood above politics in the eyes of many Americans, Powell's active endorsement of the Bush candidacy was an enormous boost. Many had expected the soldier to run for President but Powell made a key speech supporting Bush at the Republican convention before the election and actively campaigned with him. His reward was to be appointed Secretary of State.

(In fact, as a number of commentators have pointed out, the actual allocation of foreign policy positions was done in almost breakneck pace in the case of the first Bush administration. This was chiefly because the hugely disputed result of the presidential election was not finally settled until just over five weeks before the inauguration of the president amongst huge controversy and accusations of vote rigging in the constituency of Florida where Jeb Bush (brother of George) was governor. The eventual outcome, that of a Bush presidency, was based on the smallest of margins within the state.) The most surprising appointment was in fact that of Donald Rumsfeld as Secretary of Defense. Rumsfeld, who had been Secretary of Defense before, under President Gerald Ford some twenty-five years previously, had not been part of the circle around the previous President Bush (indeed if anything he and the elder Bush had been rivals) and he was not close to the younger Bush either. But he had experience, ability, and was perceived as 'tough', somebody who the military couldn't overawe, and it was that factor that seemed to clinch his appointment.

The Bush foreign policy team, then, was set. What of the world they would confront? Initially, it looked as though relatively traditional foreign policy issues would be the order of the day. The first major visitor to Washington with serious foreign policy concerns was the South Korean President Kim Dae Jung, and despite Secretary of State Powell's emollient statement that the new administration would be picking up where the last one left off, actually Kim found a distinct toughening of the US stance in relation to North Korea. This coldness was in keeping with a paper that Condoleezza Rice had published in the influential periodical *Foreign Affairs* just before the election (Rice 2000). Entitled 'Promoting the National Interest', the article was a fine example of the latest version of what some might call 'National Security Realism'. It posed a challenge to the type of liberal interventionism which had become associated with Clinton's policy. There was also in that early discussion of policy towards North Korea a hint of the views and debates that were to characterize US foreign policy after 9/11. This was the predilection of Powell and the State Department for negotiation and multilateralism versus an emergent and powerful unilateralist view. It was this latter position which

was supported by Cheney, Rumsfeld, and Wolfowitz at the Pentagon. We might note that George W. Bush and the neo-cons did seem determined to resurrect at least some of the more controversial aspects of Reaganite strategic policy with an early commitment to a ballistic missile defence for the United States based upon the idea of a National Missile Defence (NMD). This would involve a rejection of the 1972 ABM Treaty, a step duly taken by Bush. Both the system and the ideology behind it—to create a 'high frontier' of defence against incoming enemy forces—was built upon Reagan's Strategic Defence Initiative (SDI). Early on therefore a desire was apparent to enhance strategic capabilities regardless of the Anti-Ballistic Treaty or indeed the concerns of states such as Russia over the potential of such systems. We might also note a very public commitment by George Bush to modernize the military capabilities of the United States and his stress on the importance of diversifying US oil supplies.

But these new directions were still during that first year in their infancy. There were many hangovers from the Clinton years. (It was after all as we saw a Clinton decision not to ratify the Rome Statute of the Permanent International Criminal Court and indeed Clinton had despite pressure from Congress deferred the decision over ballistic missile defences, leaving it to his successor.) Aside from Korea, the early months of the Bush administration's foreign policy were concerned with relations with China, now dubbed a 'strategic competitor', and with Russia, no longer a superpower but still a major player in Eurasia and one with an increasingly authoritarian domestic agenda. Washington's relations with its European allies were also something of a priority, especially as sharp differences had emerged over environmental questions and especially the US refusal to ratify the Kyoto Protocol (designed as part of the UN framework convention on climate change for countries to commit to reduce the emissions of carbon dioxide and greenhouse gases). Indeed, it appeared to be business in the US world as usual—how to balance friends and foes with the protection of US interests. And then came the events of 9/11.

Framing 9/11 and its aftermath

KEY POINTS

❑ There is a debate about the extent to which 9/11 changed global politics.

❑ Whatever we think of the claim that 9/11 irrevocably transformed global politics we cannot doubt that for many Americans it was a cataclysmic event.

❑ Bush responded to the events of 9/11 with the war on terror and a New National Security Strategy which was enunciated in 2002.

❑ The war on terror challenged many accepted legal norms such as the prohibition on torture. It also led to the controversial practise of extraordinary rendition.

It is now a commonplace to claim that 9/11 changed everything in world politics. Ken Booth and Tim Dunne in the preface to their discussion of the 9/11 attacks have suggested that 'For years to come, if not decades, the "war on terrorism" will be the defining paradigm in the struggle for global order' (Booth and Dunne 2002).

John Lewis Gaddis has invoked an even more powerful emphasis on the 'newness' and radically transformative character of that autumn day in his meditations on the US experience of the 9/11 attacks. He has written thus:

❝through the days, weeks and months that followed . . . most of us managed to return to an approximation of normality. And yet our understanding of what is 'normal' is not what it once was. Just as New Yorkers go about their familiar activities in the shadow of an unfamiliar skyline, so something within each of us has also changed. It's as if we were all irradiated, on that morning of September 11 2001, in such a way as to shift our psychological makeup—the DNA in our minds—with consequences that will not become clear for years to come. (Gaddis 2004: 4–5) ❞

Whether this is true in general or not—and we will come back to this question at the end of the chapter—it was certainly true at least in the short to medium term in the context of American foreign policy and US cultural politics. The impact of 9/11 on America itself is certainly hard to overstate. Both in intellectual circles and in many arenas 9/11 became central to what one might call the 'cultural shape' of the USA in the early twenty-first century. Films like *United 93* and *World Trade Center* sought specifically to grapple with the events of 9/11 and, as some commentators have argued, the reaction in the USA to film sequences in Peter Jackson's *Lord of the Rings* trilogy owed a good deal to 9/11. So for example in the final film,

BOX 20.1: The war on terror

The phrase 'war on terrorism' is not one that was dreamt up by George Bush. It was used as far back as the nineteenth century to refer to attempts by anarchists to attack and assassinate political leaders. Indeed many anarchists used the term terrorist to describe their actions. The phrase 'war on terrorism' was also used by the British in the 1940s during their colonial campaigns, and more recently President Reagan used the term during the 1980s. After the terrorist attacks of 9/11, George W. Bush resurrected the term and argued that the war on terror would begin with al-Qaeda but not end with al-Qaeda. It has been used not just to justify the use of war in Afghanistan and Iraq but also to underpin a series of controversial activities including extraordinary rendition and torture. See Box 20.3.

the King, Aragorn, gives a speech to his own troops before they engage in battle with the forces of the enemy. He uses the evocative phrase 'Stand, Men of the West'. Presumably his forces are to counter, in war they did not seek, an enemy seeking to undermine and destroy the values of the West.

In particular, the assumptions that have gone to make up the key organizing principle of US foreign policy in the immediate aftermath of 9/11—the so-called 'war on terror' later redefined by the Bush administration as 'the long war'—are incomprehensible without the context of the terrorist attacks of 9/11. How a few men could hijack American planes and launch surprise attacks on US soil against probably the world's greatest military power was quite simply, for many citizens, astounding. No wonder that comparisons with the Japanese attack on Pearl Harbor in 1941 proved compelling and that the shock of these surprise attacks led to an immediate reaction in policy terms. One example of this was the development of what amounts to a preventive war strategy as articulated in the National Security Strategy of 2002. This strategy had at its core the right of the USA to eliminate any challenge (real or perceived) to US global hegemony or indeed US security. Alongside this articulation of American determination came a vibrant propaganda campaign which claimed that Saddam Hussein was himself a clear and present danger to the security of the United States and perhaps even involved in the events of 9/11 (Chomsky 2003). Saddam, for so long a thorn in the side of the USA after the First Gulf War, was obviously at some point going to be a target for US vengeance, something the neo-cons had long sought.

Significant change was also apparent in respect to traditional assumptions about the relationship between law and national security under conditions of threat. This was marked most obviously by the creation of the Department of Homeland Security, the establishment of the highly controversial internment centre at the Guantánamo Bay military base in Cuba, and the activities of the CIA in operating so-called 'black sites' in which suspected enemies of the USA would be held outside of normal legal jurisdiction. (Here we might note that 'black sites' had operated under the Clinton regime but the scale of these operations intensified after 9/11.) Most obviously in the months and years that followed 9/11, the use of war seemingly made a comeback as the tool of choice for those in the White House.

So, on the evening of 9/11, President Bush declared that 'night fell on a different world' (Fawn and Buckley 2003) and in an essay published the following year, Francis Fukuyama, the man who had famously—a short twelve years before—announced the end of history, remarked that 'world politics, it would seem, shifted gears abruptly after September 11th' (Booth and Dunne 2002). As this chapter goes on to argue, yes, 9/11 was a defining moment for the USA and did herald shifts in US behaviour especially allowing the 'neo-cons' to put into policy their specific world view, but as we go on to note there were also constants in the shape of debates about the foreign policy and the place of the USA in global politics.

Before looking at the trajectories of US foreign policy after 9/11, however, we need to look at how that policy was framed: what assumptions fed into its creation and execution and affected the conditions of its reception. I shall suggest that there were three overarching framings for US foreign policy after 9/11; the ideological shape of US politics and the agents/individuals who interpreted that ideology, the impact of previous US policy/decisions taken during both the years of Cold War and after, and the new assumptions about the utility of the use of force/war and specifically the idea that the USA could 'go it alone'. It is on this issue of the utility of war that I argue that the USA has antagonized long-standing allies and foes, Muslim sentiment, and some of its own citizens. Iraq has in fact turned into a Vietnam. The war in Iraq has diminished the Bush presidency and the reputation of the United States. But before we come to the war in Iraq, let me take each of the three categories in turn.

The triumph of ideology: the 'neo-cons' in the ascendant

KEY POINTS

❑ It became common after the events of 9/11 to depict global politics as a battle of civilizations or a competition of competing world views.
❑ The USA became preoccupied after 9/11 with Islamic fundamentalism, its causes, and its ambitions.
❑ It is important to consider how and why ideas and beliefs matter in international relations.

Perhaps the most obvious way in which 9/11 changed US foreign policy, and which has been much commented upon, was the extent to which it created an opportunity for the most overtly ideological elements of the Bush administration to take the initiative: that is to say to allow the 'neo-conservatives' to influence policy (see Box 20.2).

President Bush has emphasized that this period of world history is as much, if not more, a struggle about values as it is about interests. It is hard, indeed, not to come to the conclusion that American politicians and indeed much of the public think of themselves as waging or engaged in some type of a cultural or civilizational war at least as much as a war of any other kind. As Bush himself argued in the autumn of 2001, 'We wage a war to save civilization itself. We did not seek it, but we must fight it and we will prevail.' Current American leaders therefore see this struggle with radical Islam as in part a cultural or civilizational conflict; a war for a certain type of 'civilization' even if it is not a war actually against moderate Islam. Politicians such as Bush make clear for public consumption that al-Qaeda does not actually represent Islamic 'civilization'. This is despite the persistent claims made by Osama bin Laden or indeed some of the suicide bombers who attacked London in 2005 to speak in its name and the broader attempts by al-Qaeda to argue for a very specific type of Islamic global regime.

These complex ideological dimensions of the struggle between certain parts of Islam and what extremists claim are the perils of modernity played into the hands of those who thought, as the neo-conservatives did (and do), that 'all politics is a battle over who owns the future'. It also fed into a view which was widely believed about the 'real' nature of the geopolitical conflicts that faced the USA at the opening of the twenty-first century: to wit that they were fundamentally civilizational, or cultural (and even religious) in character. Amongst the most widely cited (semi-)academic books of the last ten years that sought to emphasize this feature of international politics was Samuel Huntington's controversial *The Clash of Civilizations and the Remaking of World Order* (Huntington 2002).

BOX 20.2: The neo-conservatives

The neo-conservatives were originally liberals but liberal thinkers who had become disillusioned with the so-called New Left culture of the 1960s. These liberals began to take up increasingly conservative positions based on the thinking of Irving Kristol. These neo-conservatives were critical of the failures of liberalism both in domestic and foreign policy. Specifically in foreign policy they were dismayed by the degree of anti-Americanism they perceived in critiques of the Vietnam War and the trend towards the downgrading of defence and military issues. More recently neo-conservative thinkers were critical of Clinton and what they saw as a lack of idealism and patriotism in foreign policy as well as crucially a lack of moral purpose to the conduct of policy abroad. Neo-conservatives wanted Saddam removed after the first Gulf War. This group are entirely cynical about the claims that world government might succeed in promoting peace and believe that part of the US mission must be to defend and promote democracy abroad.

Huntington's thesis is now well known. It is perhaps worth pointing out though just how widely taken up his ideas were. It is perhaps now usual to speak of the inevitable 'clash' of civilizations as a motor of conflict in twenty-first-century world politics, and there are echoes of this language in academic, journalistic, and political commentary of, for example, the collapse and bloody wars of the former Yugoslavia, or the possible emergence of a Chinese 'threat' to American primacy. Indeed some commentators within the United States, such as Robert Kaplan, have expressed concern that in the war on terror, with its ideological concerns, more significant threats to US interests than al-Qaeda or civilizational threats are being ignored. Specifically Kagan has highlighted the very real potential for US confrontation with China.

Yet as some of the language that has been routinely used in the war on terror there are clear ideological claims made by the United States about the battle with the terrorists. The term of preference for the 'Islamic fundamentalism' of Osama bin Laden and his peers, for example, seems increasingly to be 'Islamofascism', a deliberate harking back to an earlier period of ideological struggle in the turbulent years of the 1930s. President Bush himself has also used terms such as Islamic caliphate or militant jihadism, themselves evocative of earlier struggles with non-Christian forces. References to the struggle against communism during the years of Cold War as similar to the current battles with al-Qaeda are also frequently made, especially in the United States.

This is understandable. It is clear that bin Laden and his allies entertain notions of representing a specific type of world view based on a certain reading of fundamentalist Islam. Some—for example Bernard Lewis—have therefore seen these undeniable ideological rigidities and apparent certainties that have characterized world politics after 9/11 as a trend that is new and distinct. One aspect of this that has perhaps been most commented on—and for some years now—is the apparent resurgence of religious sentiment in world and in domestic politics (Thomas 2005). This phenomenon is not of course limited to Islam but it is perhaps most visibly manifested in Islamic cultures and has been since the Iranian Revolution in 1979.

In fact religious conflict was a powerful feature of the shape of politics throughout the twentieth century as Michael Burleigh's work has recently shown (Burleigh 2004, 2006). His term 'political religions' is certainly one useful way through which the current ideological struggles that dominate world politics can be seen. In this respect, the Bush administration itself is a conspicuously religious one, with both Bush himself and many of his closest advisers—for example John Ashcroft the Attorney General in his first term—avowedly and militantly 'born again' Christians. The tendency to see political situations, especially conflict, through explicitly religious lenses was present from the start. President Bush's initial reaction to 9/11 was to speak in terms of a 'crusade' and while that was quickly altered to avoid embarrassing Islamic and Arab allies, it revealed a certain mindset. Therefore the attacks of 9/11 seemed to allow for a resurgence of neo-conservative thinking about the world in which democratic (and Christian) forces are pitted against anti-democratic and Islamic forces at both a state and substate level. The terrorists had to be countered, defied, and defeated by the USA or another 9/11 might occur.

Blowback: US foreign policy against itself?

But the point is that the attacks of 9/11 did not simply come out of nowhere. Clinton himself knew of the attacks on the USS *Cole* in Aden in October 2000 and the earlier bombing of the World Trade Center by radical forces in 1993. There had for many years been those scheming to take a certain type of 'revenge' on the USA. In this respect some of Osama bin Laden's appeal to Muslims worldwide must lie in his skilful use of the very real grievances such as the question of Palestine and humiliations many of his audience have or feel, just as communism as an ideology genuinely appealed to the many who were, or felt themselves to be, at odds with a rich and perhaps decadent West. Although here it is interesting that unlike communism, radical Islam has not found a home with Western intellectuals to anything like the same extent that Stalinism did. We need only recall the likes of H. G. Wells trotting off to the Kremlin to see Stalin. Indeed, as Martin Amis has quite recently written, we seem to have something of a tolerance for a liking for communism (Amis 2002). But for the purposes of this chapter, here of course we come to the debates about the nature of US foreign policy over the last few decades and its ability to create antagonisms that can and have returned to haunt the USA both at home and abroad.

Bernard Henri Levy wrote, shortly after 9/11, that there is a tendency in the West to ignore the voices throughout the developing world antagonized by a succession of American policies over a considerable period. As he has written:

> **❝**There are other kamikazes ready to say to the nations of the world, You ignored us while we were alive: now we are dead: you didn't want to know about our deaths as long as they happened in our own countries; now we throw them at your feet, into the same fire that is consuming you. (Levy, quoted in Chan 2004: 57)**❞**

Perhaps we might add that there have always been the powerless or the disenchanted in local, regional global politics that have in various guises launched individual actions against the bastions of local or regional power. But to repeat: the attacks of 9/11 did not come out of nowhere. The hijacking of aircraft and the deliberate destruction by those terrorists intent on suicide can and perhaps must be seen as part and parcel of longer-term patterns of resistance to established US power. Here contemporary global politics remains deeply affected by the origins and development of the Cold War and by the choices made by earlier generations of 'agents', especially—if not exclusively—the United States. The rise of a variant of militant Islam itself, al-Qaeda for example, can be traced to the emergence of groups like the Muslim Brotherhood in Egypt, groups who were profoundly affected by the revolutionary changes of the inter-war period, and by the emergence of the Cold War, not least the US/British-backed coup against the Iranian leader Mosaddeq in 1953. Events, as the old saying has it, have consequences. The Iranian

Revolution of 1979 was in many respects independent of the Cold War, but the revolutionary methods of the Bolsheviks had been studied to great effect by some of the Iranians, and the passions roused by events that followed it (such as the Iraq/Iran War and the growth of groups like Hamas and Hezbollah) were all framed by the overarching structures of the Cold War and the decisions taken by those in Washington to contest the ideological battles with Moscow on every front, especially those of the Middle East.

Most obviously of all, al-Qaeda itself, and the leadership of Osama bin Laden in particular, was forged in the reaction to the Soviet invasion of Afghanistan in late 1979, and the passions that were subsequently inflamed throughout the Muslim world were themselves an offshoot of the Cold War obsession with spheres of influence (Keppel 2005; Rashid 2001). The *mujahidin* in Afghanistan—including bin Laden and al-Qaeda—were supported by the Pakistani intelligence service (ISI) for largely Islamic reasons, but also supported by the USA and the CIA (Central Intelligence Agency) for geopolitical ones—not least because they were considerable thorns in the side of the Soviet Army. The logic of the Cold War therefore had, in some respects, more than a hand in the creation of al-Qaeda, an irony of history perhaps best summed up in Chalmers Johnson's now infamous term for it: 'blowback' (Johnson 2002). The key question though for those in the White House was how to react to this 'blowback'. Their choice was that of war.

KEY POINTS

❑ We can only understand the events of 9/11 if we understand the history of the Cold War.

❑ The events of 9/11 were preceded by a number of terrorist attacks against US personnel and assets both abroad and at home.

❑ Some elements of al-Qaeda emerged out of the Soviet War in Afghanistan. Most notably Osama bin Laden, a Saudi, was radicalized by his experiences of Soviet–US rivalry in the country.

❑ Blowback is the notion that the USA is now suffering the consequences of its actions, especially its covert actions during the period of Cold War.

The centrality of military power—and 'imperial overstretch'?

KEY POINTS

❑ Although many analysts believed that war had a declining utility in international relations, the war on terror proved then wrong.

❑ The emphasis of the Bush administration on war as an instrument of policy proved problematic for many allies of the USA.

❑ It was Tony Blair's Britain which proved the most robust of the allies in supporting the Bush wars in both Afghanistan and Iraq.

❑ The war in Iraq although initially popular with the American public has increasingly become regarded as the new Vietnam.

One of the areas in the contemporary context that has received most comment is the extent to which the post-9/11 world has given a hefty new impetus to those who have always believed in the central utility of force/war in global politics (Gray 2005). Much of the legacy of the 'nuclear era' had been premised on the idea of the 'declining' utility of force. Deterrence and the logic certainly of nuclear weapons was to consider major war as unthinkable. Certainly within the European Union, militaries lost much of their resonance and even within the United States, despite victory in the first Gulf War, there seemed little enthusiasm for the deployment of troops abroad. None of this meant that wars did not happen, or that states gave up their right to use force in defence of their own interest, but certainly war seemed to be on the wane.

Perhaps the general assumptions governing this were best laid out in the late 1970s by two of the most influential scholars of that generation, Robert Keohane and Joseph Nye. In their now classic study *Power and Interdependence*, they asserted, as one of the three central characteristics of the now dawning age of interdependence, the 'declining utility of military force', an argument repeated most in the third edition of this book in 2000 (Keohane and Nye 2000).

A related argument has been pursued by John Mueller whose *Retreat from Doomesday*, first published in 1989, argued that major-power war had gone the way of slavery and duelling; it was a social practice that had simply for Mueller become 'sub rationally unthinkable'. Despite the obviously violent history of the 1990s, and the multifaceted nature of those conflicts, Mueller has repeated his argument recently (Mueller 1989, 2004).

In the immediate aftermath of 9/11, this trajectory seemed to shift, almost overnight. For many, what 9/11 seemed to demonstrate was not the declining utility of force, but actually its huge importance, a position that the neo-conservatives, along with more traditionally minded realists, had argued for some time. The Bush administration followed up the events of 9/11 not only with the invasion of Afghanistan but also as we noted earlier with the new National Security Strategy, which made it perfectly clear that the United States now saw pre-emptive war as a legitimate form of defence and also expanded and redefined the general assumptions on which defences of pre-emption had rested in the past. The war in Iraq was initially justified, in 2003, by the removal of the dictator but soon morphed into a different set of justifications for the Bush administration. Not the least of these were the supposed linkages between Iraq and the production of weapons of mass destruction (WMD) and Iraq and the encouragement of terrorism. There was also a determined effort to reject the 'supposed' Clintonian optimism over international institutions, multilateralism, and international cooperation and a determination to 'go it alone' in terms of shaping regional politics. This as we will see has had a series of consequences, not the least of which was a rejection of the authority of the United Nations but also a widening gap with its European allies (apart from Britain) and an increasingly difficult period for the USA in the Middle East. France and its leader Jacques Chirac was vocal in the condemnation of the invasion of Iraq and the bypassing of the Security Council. Franco-American relations became characterized by a barrage of diplomatic wrangling and insults. Most notably a number of American journalists and indeed politicians characterized the French nation as a bunch of 'cheese eating surrender monkeys'. (This memorable phrase was actually taken from the American hit cartoon *The Simpsons*.) But beneath this Euro-Atlantic difference of opinion lay the critical issue of the American determination to be unfettered in its choice of war.

Let us therefore now turn to seeing how the USA fared and is faring in its decision to make war central to the conduct of its international politics.

The shape of America's wars

If ideology, the unintended consequences of previous US policy, and the increasing belief in the utility of military power set the parameters of post-9/11 US foreign policy, what were the key decisions and consequences?

The first major decision after the 9/11 attacks was, of course, what to actually do in response. After all, this was like the Japanese attack on Pearl Harbor in 1941, taken as a horrific crime against the USA itself. Very swiftly it became clear that al-Qaeda was responsible for the attacks (Wright 2006), but al-Qaeda itself, unlike Japan, was not a state, but rather a transnational or subnational movement. However, it did have very close ties with the government of a state—the Taliban in Afghanistan, which had sheltered the leadership, provided training and basing facilities for the terrorists, and was openly and ideologically sympathetic. The decision was taken, therefore, to request the Taliban to surrender the leaders of al-Qaeda and, if they did not do so, to launch an invasion to remove the Taliban and eliminate al-Qaeda's infrastructure in Afghanistan. The Taliban refused the US request and so, on 7 October 2001, the USA and the UK initiated military operations against this primitive regime.

To begin with these operations were largely air assaults, the fighting on the ground being largely the work of the anti-Taliban factions within Afghanistan itself, principally the 'Northern Alliance'. There were strong indications that al-Qaeda's leadership expected some response along these lines, as shortly before the 9/11 attacks they had successfully assassinated the Alliance's legendary battlefield commander, Ahmed Shah Massoud, the so-called 'lion of the Panshir' and the greatest of the guerrilla *mujahidin* who had fought against Soviet troops throughout the 1980s.

From 2002, however, US and British troops were present on the ground (special forces had been deployed earlier), where they remain at the time of writing. While the invasion was largely successful in the short term—the Taliban were removed from power and al-Qaeda's infrastructure in Afghanistan was destroyed—the invasion did not succeed in capturing or killing the senior al-Qaeda leadership, who escaped, probably into the wild borderland between Pakistan and Afghanistan, after the battle of Tora Bora at the end of 2001. Moreover, the decision to invade Iraq (of which more in a moment) took forces and resources away from Afghanistan at a crucial time and allowed the Taliban to regroup. At the time of writing, the stability of Afghanistan is still very much in the balance.

In general, the reaction of the international community to the invasion of Afghanistan was muted. Most states understood that the USA was bound to respond to the 9/11 attacks and the Taliban regime had few if any friends in any event. The USA's NATO allies in particular rallied round, with even the sometimes critical French declaring, famously and in light of what we discussed earlier ironically, that after 9/11 'we are all Americans now'. Even sometime opponents and rivals of the United States, such as the Russians and the Chinese, offered support. The Russian leader Vladimir Putin was especially eager to claim that the US war on terrorism had much in common with the Russian war against the radical Chechen terrorists who had carried out a number of terrorist atrocities on Russian soil. (Of course, the claim that world politics was irrevocably disturbed by Islamicist terrorist actions also allowed Putin to continue the extremely bloody war against the Chechens without undue US criticism.) So 9/11, or so it had seemed, united much of the world in support of the USA, and the invasion of Afghanistan was widely viewed as a reasonable, just, and proportionate response to the appalling acts of savagery perpetrated by the terrorists.

Within the USA, support for retaliation against al-Qaeda was almost universal, but it also perhaps played into the hands of those who were, in any event, most prone to want to assert/reassert US power and who had been baulking already at the restrictions on that power they had witnessed the Clinton administration signing up to. After the 9/11 attacks, any fetters upon US power were not only seen as problematic in themselves but they could be painted as being dangerous to the USA 'in a time of war' (Hansen 2002).

This tendency in US foreign policy was visible in President Bush's 2002 State of the Union Address to Congress, perhaps the signature statement of the US intention to wage a 'war on terror'. One phrase in particular from that address became notorious. President Bush proclaimed that, in addition to prosecuting the war on terror, the USA would take action against the spread of weapons of mass destruction. It is worth quoting the passage in full:

   ❝Our second goal is to prevent regimes that sponsor terror from threatening America or our friends and allies with weapons of mass destruction. Some of these regimes have been pretty quiet since September the 11th. But we know their true nature. North Korea is a regime arming with missiles and weapons of mass destruction, while starving its citizens.

Iran aggressively pursues these weapons and exports terror, while an unelected few repress the Iranian people's hope for freedom.

Iraq continues to flaunt its hostility toward America and to support terror. The Iraqi regime has plotted to develop anthrax, and nerve gas, and nuclear weapons for over a decade. This is a regime that has already used poison gas to murder thousands of its own citizens—leaving the bodies of mothers huddled over their dead children. This is a regime that agreed to international inspections—then kicked out the inspectors. This is a regime that has something to hide from the civilized world.

States like these, and their terrorist allies, constitute an axis of evil, arming to threaten the peace of the world. By seeking weapons of mass destruction, these regimes pose a grave and growing danger. They could provide these arms to terrorists, giving them the means to match their hatred. They could attack our allies or attempt to blackmail the United States. In any of these cases, the price of indifference would be catastrophic. (www.whitehouse. gov/news/releases/2002/01/20020129-11.html)**❞**

By expressly linking the 'axis of evil' to the global jihad of al-Qaeda and its affiliates, President Bush was greatly expanding the administration's original mission and, at least arguably, running together problems that were perhaps best kept separate. Most significantly of all, perhaps, it seemed to flag up to many the increasing stridency of US intentions and

---

BOX 20.3: Extraordinary rendition and black sites

Legal rendition has been used by the United States for over two decades as a means of dealing with foreign suspects/defendants. Extraordinary rendition is a different and highly controversial process which has become common after 9/11 and forms a central part of the war on terror. Suspects/alleged terrorists are placed in US custody but then are taken to a third-party state without ever coming before the US judiciary. Commonly suspects are taken to third-party states such as Egypt, Jordan.

Uzbekistan, or certain states in central and eastern Europe. Critics of the process allege that the movement of suspects to such sites allows the CIA to avoid US legislation which prohibits torture and allows CIA operatives to gain evidence/confessions through the physical and mental abuse of suspects over a prolonged period. These are the so-called 'black sites'. Secretary Rice has however denied that the United States would deliver individuals to centres where they would be tortured.

the increasing unwillingness of the administration to act within the parameters that their predecessors had been prepared to accept. It thus put the USA on a collision course even with many of its allies.

A second corollary of the above, which also seemed to flag up a similar trajectory, was the additional policies the USA put in place after 9/11 and the Afghan invasion. The creation of the special detaining centre at Guantánamo Bay, the passing of the Patriot Act, the increasing reports on the use of torture, and the practice of extraordinary rendition all pointed towards a USA that was increasingly going its own way, independent of what even its allies might think (Kennedy-Pipe and Rengger 2006).

All of this came to a head, however, in what was certainly the most controversial decision in post-9/11 US foreign policy, the decision to invade Iraq.

KEY POINTS

❏ After the terrorist attacks of 9/11 parallels were immediately drawn with the shock Japanese attack on Pearl Harbor in Hawaii in December 1941.

❏ It was apparent that the USA would seek to destroy the terrorist groups which had perpetrated the attacks and this was broadly supported by many other states.

❏ Afghanistan and its Taliban rulers were chosen as the target for revenge because of their links to al-Qaeda.

❏ Despite the commentaries of many scholars after the end of the Cold War that war was no longer a feasible policy option, the Bush administration made the military response the central response.

❏ A surge of patriotism and a resolve to support America was apparent in the immediate months after 9/11.

❏ Unilateralism characterized the Bush administration. This is the approach by which the USA avoids any permanent alliance with foreign powers and argues against entanglement with international institutions such as the ICC or the UN. It seeks to avoid prohibitions upon the making of US policy.

Iraq: the new Vietnam?

It is now clear that this decision was one with deep roots in the administration. According to the veteran journalist Bob Woodward, Bush asked Rumsfeld about the status of the military plans for an invasion of Iraq very soon after 9/11 itself (Woodward 2004), and there were many within the administration—not least Wolfowitz and, from outside the formal administration (but still influentially), Perle—who had long advocated further military action to dispose of Saddam. Part of the frustration was that the USA had been for over more than a decade involved in an undeclared war with Saddam in attempting to enforce the two designated no-fly zones put in place after the end of the first Gulf War. The problem, of course, was that while other states accepted the need of Washington to strike back after 9/11, and while the Taliban had few allies, an attack on Iraq, which was unconnected to 9/11 and did have some allies, was bound to be much more difficult diplomatically.

So, indeed, it proved. In the months running up to the invasion in March 2003, the USA found that its policy was opposed by many of the powers that had supported it over Afghanistan. Of its major allies only Britain, Australia, and Spain remained firmly committed and in each of those countries there was substantial political and popular opposition to an invasion of Iraq. Part of the problem was simply that despite many attempts, no link between Iraq and al-Qaeda could be established and, indeed, there was in fact a good deal of evidence of hostility to Saddam from the al-Qaeda leadership (Saddam was, after all, a notorious and very public secularist). That led to a focus on what might be termed the 'axis of evil' rationale for intervention, i.e. the prevention of the spread of weapons of mass destruction (WMD). The difficulty here was that the evidence for Iraq's possession of WMD was at best sketchy, and both the IAEA and the inspectors who had been seeking to verify Iraq's destruction of its previous programmes were saying they needed more time to make a proper assessment.

This, of course, bogged down the USA in the UN timetable. The USA had successfully obtained a first UN resolution criticizing Iraq and had, largely at the insistence of the British, gone back to the UN for a second resolution explicitly authorizing the use of force if Iraq continued to be in 'material breach' of its obligations under the 1991 ceasefire agreement. It very quickly became clear, however, that this would be effectively vetoed by the Russians, the Chinese, and the French. Thus the resolution was never put to the vote.

For many in the USA this confirmed their fears about the restrictions being imposed on US power by the 'multilateralism' of the international system. It was doubtless this in part which fed into Rumsfeld's dismissive comment about 'old Europe' and 'new Europe' (many of the newly emerging eastern and central European states supported Washington in its ambitions). His point was that old Europe was failing to take up its responsibilities for maintaining peace (Kagan 2003).

The official rationale for the Iraq invasion was set out by Secretary of State Powell, in his now famous set-piece presentation to the UN Security Council on 5 February 2003. Hence:

❝We know that Saddam Hussein is determined to keep his weapons of mass destruction; he's determined to make more. Given Saddam Hussein's history of aggression . . . given what we know of his terrorist associations and given his determination to exact revenge on those who oppose him, should we take the risk that he will not some day use these weapons at a time and the place and in the manner of his choosing at a time when the world is in a much weaker position to respond? The United States will not and cannot run that risk to the American people. Leaving Saddam Hussein in possession of weapons of mass destruction for a few more months or years is not an option, not in a post-September 11th world. ❞

We might note the extent to which the statement presents not only an unquestioned attempt to link Saddam to al-Qaeda but also an emphasis that, even in the absence of such a link, indeed even in the absence of clear evidence of Saddam possessing WMD, it is not possible to leave Saddam with possible WMD 'in a post September 11th world'. This is the point at which 9/11 had clearly shaped the priorities of US foreign policy. (The attacks of 9/11 were also rapidly used to justify the need for America to move away from observance of the ABM Treaty and invest in NMD.)

The invasion itself began on 20 March 2003, preceded by an attempted so-called 'decapitation' strike against senior military and political figures (including Saddam himself) that was only partially successful. The initial campaign itself, however, was relatively swift. Unlike previous campaigns (for example the Gulf War of 1990–1 and the Afghan campaign in 2001) there was not a long period of aerial bombardment followed by a ground campaign. Rather there was a combination of both together. The ground campaign lasted just over three weeks and the Iraqi military crumbled quickly, outgunned by allied firepower, skill, and equipment. Baghdad itself fell in April 2003 and President Bush declared (unwisely, as it turned out) 'mission accomplished' on board the aircraft carrier *Abraham Lincoln* on 1 May 2003.

KEY POINTS

❑ The decision to wage war against Saddam and Iraq proved controversial with long-standing US allies.

❑ The USA paid little heed to warnings to abide by the wishes of the Security Council of the UN.

❑ The ground invasion of Iraq was actually a success with Baghdad falling rapidly to US troops.

❑ Debate still continues as to the actual motivations for the US invasion. Was it about revenge on Saddam, WMD, oil, or an attempt to reshape Middle Eastern politics?

❑ Certain neo-conservatives had even before 9/11 advocated the removal of Saddam.

After Iraq: continuity and disjunction in US foreign policy

The problem, however, was not the military campaign itself; the problem which very rapidly became apparent was that there was a less than coherent planning for the post-war scenario. The result of a series of bungled decisions taken in the immediate aftermath of the victory—the decision to disband the Iraqi army, the reluctance to stamp early on local looting, and a host of many others—helped to turn a chaotic and patchwork post-conflict Iraq into a hotbed of dissent and insurgency. This was aside from the anger and emotion at the civilian casualties inflicted by the invading forces. This in turn inflamed Muslim sentiment across the world against the USA and its allies, sucked in Muslims from outside Iraq, and acted as a recruiting sergeant for al-Qaeda, which was, to all intents and purposes, one of the chief beneficiaries of the post-war shambles. The terrorist group established a presence in Iraq for the first time.

A second beneficiary was the USA's other chief opponent in the region, Iran. Benefiting in any event from the downfall of a tyrant it had long detested, Tehran was able to profit from America's increasingly difficult counter-insurgency operation in Iraq. Tehran was also able to thumb its nose at US attempts to restrict the development of an Iranian nuclear capacity (insisting that the programme was in any event wholly peaceful), since effective restrictions would have to come through the UN, and US relations with the

other members of the Security Council were not positive apart from Britain, which under Tony Blair remained loyal to the US agenda. (Tony Blair himself was certainly in terms of reputation badly bruised by the Iraq imbroglio and his unstinting support of the Bush administration despite rising British casualty rates.)

The immediate post-Iraq setting for US foreign policy was, however very bullish. Those in charge in Washington felt that they had achieved a good deal and were keen to continue further with this trajectory. For much of the immediate post-invasion period, even after it became clear that President Bush had been—to put it mildly—overoptimistic when he declared 'mission accomplished', the administration still rallied popular support to it. In the presidential election the following year—unlike in 2000, as we saw—foreign policy and the record of the administration in the post-9/11 climate was the major campaign issue and the incumbent beat his Democratic Party challenger (Senator John Kerry) convincingly.

After the election, however, problems began to multiply for the Bush administration. The situation in Iraq went from bad to worse and popular support for the occupation in the USA began to ebb away. Here we began to see the resurgence of sentiment talking of Iraq as the new Vietnam. Increasing US casualty figures are also beginning to take their toll on domestic opinion (see Box 20.4).

BOX 20.4: Soldiers and the war on terror: the case of Patrick Tillman

Patrick Tillman was killed on active duty whilst serving with the US Army in Afghanistan in May 2002. What has marked out the death of Tillman has been the immense controversy over the manner and nature of his death. In part this has arisen because Tillman was the first professional football player to be killed in combat since 1979. Tillman was already before 9/11 a celebrity. After the terrorist attacks on the United States, however, he volunteered to serve his country. He saw action in both Iraq and in Operation Enduring Freedom in Afghanistan. The actual cause of his death is still disputed. His family was originally informed that he had died as a result of hostile fire from the enemy. But then the Pentagon told his family that in fact he had been fatally wounded in a case of 'friendly fire'. His family dispute this account and even now it is not clear how Tillman did die. One line of speculation is that Tillman may have been criminally killed whilst on duty. The controversy continues.

Most recently in 2007 there have been suggestions that, because of the pressures on the volunteer army and especially on those who are now serving on a regular basis in war zones, the military draft might be reinstated. President Nixon had in the final stages of the Vietnam War abolished the draft in 1973, and in August 2007 when the idea of the military draft was seriously discussed it was felt by Bush that this itself might have proved politically damaging especially in the light of a casualty rate which stood at over 3,000 dead for the USA. Symbolically this number was important as US fatalities on the battlefield now exceeded the official number of those who had perished in the attacks of 9/11.

During the course of the first two years of the second term, a number of key personnel changes weakened the group at the centre of the post-9/11 foreign policy. Colin Powell's replacement by Condoleezza Rice was probably 'ideologically' neutral since, though Rice was very close to Bush, she had never been a card-carrying 'neo-con' and had always been closer to the 'national security realism' of her original promoters. But the loss of Paul Wolfowitz—who left the Pentagon to become (very controversially) for a time the president of the World Bank—certainly had an impact as did President Bush's decision to accept the resignation of Donald Rumsfeld after the disastrous Republican showing in the 2006 mid-term elections for Congress. (In 2006, the Republican Party suffered its biggest defeat in a mid-term election for over a decade—and primarily because of the Iraq issue, although the debacle over Hurricane Katrina and the inadequate presidential response appears not to have helped Bush's popularity.)

There seemed to be a recognition on the part of some that the 'perceived' unilateralism of the first Bush term had hurt US interests in the medium to long term and there began a concerted effort to change the diplomatic 'mood music'. Attempts have been made to come to terms with the new French leader, Sarkozy, who seems at least on an initial showing to be more persuaded by President Bush than his predecessor, even remarking that, like all families, amongst allies there will be arguments, but France remains within the family. But more telling have been the recent and repeated attempts by Bush to persuade the UN to play an enlarged role in post-war Iraq. In August 2007 Resolution 1770 was adopted by the UN Security Council which paves the way for a wider political role for the UN within Iraq. Although the actual number of UN staff within the country will undergo only a modest increase, the UN will have a remit to promote national reconciliation on a number of key issues such as border security, energy, and refugees. Although cynics may argue that the USA is simply using the UN to pick up the pieces of a failed strategy, more optimistically it may reflect the fact that the Bush administration now recognize the complexities of the aftermath of war and the futility of even a superpower attempting alone to shape a complex and dangerous regional problem.

So it is perhaps fair to say, some way through the second Bush administration, that US foreign policy stands at a crossroads. There are still many, most notably neo-conservatives, who believe that, despite the clear mistakes made in Iraq, the basic thrust of US policy post-9/11 has been correct and a shift back to a more accommodationist, multilateral approach (as they would see it) would be a disaster. They believe the failure in Iraq is the result of an unwillingness by Bush to push the ideological agenda to the very limit. There are others who want, certainly, to stand up for US interests, but see those interests as being better served working with rather than against allies, repairing relationships perhaps in Europe which were damaged by the bruising disagreement over Iraq, and so on. It is this latter philosophy that in the last months of the Bush administration seems to be emerging as dominant in some sections of the Republican Party and certainly within the ranks of the Democrats.

The range of issues that await US decisions—from relations with Iran, to the stalled Arab–Israeli peace process, which is badly in need of a new injection of optimism after the Lebanese war, to climate change—will all be shaped by the way this debate falls out. And, of course, it is being held in the context of another hotly disputed contest for the US presidency which will take place in 2008 for the first time in a generation without any 'incumbent' standing (President Bush cannot stand again, and Vice-President Cheney has ruled himself out). The success of the Republican Party in recent presidential elections has been striking: the Republicans have won five out of seven presidential elections since 1980, they have also as we have seen in this chapter really taken the USA into a far more conservative mindset—one that certainly on issues such as stem cell research and abortion might prove difficult to undo—and anyway have played well to the conservative agendas of various important lobbies. One need only think about the right-to-life groups, the evangelical churches, and the gun clubs. In foreign policy although it is tricky to foresee just how a new president of whatever complexion might behave, the portents are perhaps for a less militaristic and a more 'ally-friendly' foreign policy. Not least the failure in Iraq means that any new president will tread warily over going it alone, certainly in major wars. This is a lesson that the Democratic contenders for the White House seem determined to showcase for the electorate. Hilary Clinton (wife of Bill Clinton) has steadily moved her stance away from a pro-war one to a position from which she promises to withdraw troops as 'quickly and responsibly' as possible. She has over many months begun to talk of a 'Third Way' for American foreign policy and the importance of working with, not without, allies. In short she wishes after the turmoil of the Bush years to pursue a more internationalist and multilateralist foreign policy. For Democrats such as Hilary Clinton or one of her Democratic opponents, Senator Barack Obama, it is not whether to pursue a war against the terrorists but how to persuade the electorate that they can be more effective in that task without major war.

So 9/11 emboldened the neo-conservatives to set out a new vision for American foreign policy—a vision of unilateral power, military competence, and the removal of dictators (well, dictators unfriendly to Washington who happened to sit in important regions). It unfettered a degree of arrogance about international law, human rights, and civilian casualty rates. It gave those who wished to see global politics as divided by religion the chance to wage war on other cultures and civilizations. Most crucially of all, though, it allowed the American past in the international system to be wilfully misread and misinterpreted. What America did well during the Cold War was to outlast, outplay, and out-manipulate their communist opponents in concert with willing allies who preferred a democratic version of politics to an authoritarian one. Bush and his neo-conservatives preferred war to vigilance and hot wars to cold wars. Most crucially of all the neo-cons misread the lessons of international politics over the need to create consensus. Their successors are determined to resurrect such past success in international politics, as Hilary Clinton has argued: 'We did not face World War II alone, we did not face the Cold War alone and we cannot face the global terrorist threat or other profound challenges alone either.'

KEY POINTS

❑ The lack of post-war planning for Iraq has led to a situation in which many critics claim that it is now mired in civil war with US and British troops suffering increasing casualties—hence the idea of Iraq as the new Vietnam.

❑ The war in Iraq and its uncertain outcomes has led to a noticeable dent in neo-conservative influence over foreign policy making. This despite claims that neo-conservative thinking could yet resolve US difficulties.

❑ Bush does now appear, despite the rhetoric of earlier years, to appreciate the importance of the UN in rebuilding Iraq. This perhaps signals a return to multilateral solutions.

❑ American politicians and scholars have and are engaged in debate over the future of US foreign policy. Democratic contenders for the White House in 2008 display a preference for working with allies, diplomacy, and a rejection of the war option.

? Questions

1. To what extent did the events did the events of 9/11 alter US foreign policy?
2. What influence has neo-conservatism had on the making of US foreign policy?
3. What has been the impact of George W. Bush on the making of foreign policy?
4. Was the war in Iraq an error for the USA?
5. Do comparisons between the attacks of 9/11 and the assault on Pearl Harbor bear comparison?
6. Is the one success of the presidency of G. W. Bush the promotion of an anti-tyranny agenda?
7. What constitutes the 'axis of evil'?
8. What has been the attitude of the Bush administration towards the UN?
9. Has the use of extraordinary rendition injured the image of the United States?
10. Is the United States now a lonely superpower?
11. Has the Vietnam Syndrome been buried?

Further Reading

Ikenberry, G. John (2001), *After Victory: Institution, Strategic Restraint and the Rebuilding of Order after Major Wars* (Princeton: Princeton University Press).

An analysis of how major states respond to victory after war. It explores the US response to the end of Cold War and its options at the beginning of the twenty-first century.

Kagan, Robert (2003), *Paradise & Power* (New York: Knopf).

Looks at the ideological divide between the European powers and the United States. It explores the transatlantic relationship and provides a lively and concise account of recent troubled times in diplomatic circles.

Ricks, Thomas E. (2006), *Fiasco: The American Military Adventure in Iraq* (New York: Penguin).

This book is an account of the war in Iraq up until the middle of 2006. It is a searing indictment of bad strategic judgements and spares few of the political and military elites.

Woodward, Bob (2004), *Plan of Attack* (New York: Simon & Schuster).

Looks at how those around President Bush actively sought to pave the road to war with Iraq. It demonstrates the increasing enthusiasm for the removal of the Iraqi dictator and the arguments for pre-emptive war.

Endnotes

Some of the ideas in this chapter were first explored in Kennedy-Pipe and Rengger (2006).

 Visit the Online Resource Centre that accompanies this book for web links to accompany each chapter, and a range of other resources: www.oxfordtextbooks.co.uk/orc/cox_stokes/

21 America's 'security trap'

G. John Ikenberry

Chapter contents

Introduction

The United States is the most powerful state in world history—unrivalled in military, economic, technological, and geopolitical capabilities. It stands pre-eminent on the global stage. Yet America's authority—measured in terms of credibility, respect, and the ready cooperation of governments around the world—has declined sharply in recent years. In the aftermath of the Cold War, the world seemed to be going in America's direction. America's vision of international relations and the world's aspirations were remarkably congruent. It was a vision symbolized by the fall of the Berlin Wall and the triumph of the ideals championed by the United States—liberal democracy, global markets, and multilateral governance. Today, America and the world are much more at odds. In a recent survey of western European public opinion, the United States was rated as a greater threat to global stability than Iran or North Korea. America is positioned at the centre of the global system—and its power is unrivalled—but its role as a global leader has never been more controversial, contested, or resisted.

This troubling situation will forever be associated with the Bush administration—and particularly its 'war on terrorism' and the invasion of Iraq. Bush's foreign policy has been extraordinarily unpopular around the world. President Bush himself has few admirers outside America. 'The world hates George Bush more than any U.S. president in my lifetime,' the columnist Thomas Friedman observed recently. But is it really that simple? Are liberals and other Bush critics correct that America's eroded authority is essentially a product of Bush foreign policy? Will a new administration be able to wash away the ill will and eroded relations of the Bush years? Or is the crisis of America's global position rooted in deeper problems?

Bush foreign policy is failing—but it is important to come to grips with why it is failing. To be sure, it is failing because Bush led the country into an epic disaster in Iraq. But the problems are not just about policy incompetence, ideological blindness, or high-risk policy choices gone bad. Bush foreign policy is failing—in the large sense—because it is inconsistent with the realities of a transforming international system that shapes and limits the way the United States can effectively exercise power and—more importantly—assert its authority. These deeper dilemmas and dangers that beset America's global position must be confronted if we are to find a coherent, enlightened, and sustainable post-Bush foreign policy.

Put simply, the geopolitical terrain upon which America's leadership position rests is shifting. The rise of American unipolar power and the erosion of norms of state sovereignty have 'flipped' the Westphalian order on its head, altered the logic of order and rule, and made American power more controversial and contested. They have also made it more difficult for the United States to assert its leadership on the global stage.

Because of this, the Bush administration has run into trouble, or as I would put it, it has got America caught in a 'security trap'. It is a security trap in the sense that as the Bush administration tries to solve the nation's security problems by exercising its power or using force, it tends to produce resistance and backlash that leaves the country more isolated, bereft of authority, and, ultimately, insecure.

The problem is that when liberals take over the reins of foreign policy, they too will fall into this security trap unless they understand the problem and devise a foreign policy that works with rather than against these evolving global realities. For Bush and many Democrats, being the unchecked superpower means that the United States has the freedom to act alone or in whatever coalitions it sees fit. But, ironically, the opposite is true. Unfettered power creates resentment and opposition that makes it more difficult for the United States to act. To turn power into authority, the United States needs to find ways to restrain and reconnect its extraordinary unipolar power to institutions and partnerships that make up the international community.

Accordingly, the next administration—liberal Democrat or otherwise—needs to focus on rebuilding America's authority as a global power. Threats and

CONTROVERSIES 21.1: The war in Iraq

In many ways the war in Iraq captures the dilemmas of the security trap. The war was waged on the back of the terrorist attacks on 9/11. It was argued by key administration figures that Saddam Hussein's regime presented a threat to US national security interests as he might pass weapons of mass destruction (developed in contravention of US Security Council mandates) to terrorist groups who in turn could use them against the United States. In pursuing the war, the Bush administration sought to work through the UN Security Council, but ultimately opted for a 'coalition of the willing' and was disdainful of key allies and states that were critical of the war. This was most famously captured when then US Secretary of Defense, Donald Rumsfeld, dismissed Germany and France's criticism of US policy on Iraq and stated that they were part of 'old Europe'. In pursuing the war, Washington signalled to the world its intent to also bypass the rules-based order in pursuit of its more narrow national security interests. In so doing, the USA changed the world's perception of it from one of a superpower willing to work with others to one of a superpower using its military might to attain its key interests. The war in Iraq also raised key questions about the true motives for going to war in the first place, with senior figures such as former Federal Reserve chairman Alan Greenspan arguing that the war was motivated primarily by the need for control of Iraq's vast oil reserves. In short, the Iraq war highlighted the contradictions between a hegemonic and an imperial foreign policy. Whichever grand strategy the USA pursued, it would need to weigh up key questions and dilemmas: should the USA pursue its national interests regardless of the constraints of international rules and global regimes? Why should the USA be constrained given its overwhelming preponderance of power? How do we respond to global threats in ways that maintain a rules-based order? What is the best strategy for both attaining US national interests whilst also upholding the liberal international order and are the two necessarily in contradiction?

challenges abound around the world. But the United States will struggle in responding to any and all of them unless it rebuilds its political capital. Call it a 'renewal agenda'—the next administration will need to attend to this underlying problem. At the core of this renewal agenda must be a set of proposals for rebuilding global institutions and partnerships that are tied to new political bargains between the United States and other major states. The key to rebuilding America's authority is its commitment to sponsoring and operating within a reformed rules-based international order.

KEY POINTS

- The Bush foreign policy has failed to enhance global security or increase US influence.
- Iraq is the most obvious reason for this twin failure but by no means the only reason.
- The only way to enhance global security and rebuild US prestige in the future will involve a new American commitment to international rules and international institutions.

Transformations in global power

The Bush administration does not fully understand the implications of the two most historic transformations in world politics in half a century—the rise of unipolar power and changing norms of sovereignty.

Unipolarity happened almost without notice during the 1990s. The United States began the decade as the world's only superpower and it had a better decade than the other major states. It grew faster than an inward-looking Europe while Japan stagnated and Russia collapsed. China has grown rapidly in recent years but remains a developing country. America's expenditures on defence are almost equal to half of global spending. Interestingly, the United States did not fight a great power war to become the unipolar state or overturn the old international order. It simply grew more powerful while other states sputtered or failed. This peaceful ascent to unipolarity probably has made the transition less destabilizing and less threatening to other nations. But in the aftermath of 11 September and the recent American wars in Afghanistan and Iraq, American power has been exposed to the light of day.

The rise of unipolarity is fraught with implications for American foreign policy. On the one hand, the fact that the United States is the only superpower gives it unprecedented options and opportunities. It can say no to other states and go it alone more readily than in the past. But it is also the case that other states find it easier to 'free ride' on American policy than in the past which opens up new disputes between the United States and its partners about the provision of global public goods—security, open markets, frameworks for cooperation. Is the United States providing a public good when it stations troops around the world and confronts security threats in Asia and the Middle East? Washington thinks it is—and so it wants and expects the cooperation of others. But other countries are not sure they are beneficiaries of American security protection, and even if they are they have incentives to let the United States handle these threats on its own. In other instances, countries around the world expect that United States to be a public goods provider—for example, leading the way in global environmental protection or settling regional Middle Eastern disputes—but Washington officials do not necessarily see this as an American responsibility. This bundle of contradictory incentives and

calculations makes unipolarity ripe for conflict and misunderstandings, even among long-time allies.

But there is another implication of the rise of unipolarity that is more subtle and utterly critical: a shift in the underlying logic of order and rule in world politics. In a bipolar or multipolar system, powerful states 'rule' in the process of leading a coalition of states in balancing against other states. When the system shifts to unipolarity, this logic of rule disappears. Power is no longer based on balancing and equilibrium but on the predominance of one state. This is new and potentially threatening to weaker states (whether they are friendly to the United States or not). As a result, the power of the leading state is thrown into the full light of day. Unipolar power itself becomes a 'problem' in world politics. As John Gaddis argues, American power during the Cold War was accepted by other states because there was 'something worse' over the horizon (Gaddis 2003: 66–7). With the rise of unipolarity, that 'something worse' disappears.

KEY POINTS

❑ The end of the Cold War led to a shift from a bipolar to an increasingly unipolar world order.

❑ This shift has led to a steady reappraisal of Washington's relationships with a number of other great powers as well as increasing resentment of its power.

The erosion of state sovereignty

The erosion of the norm of state sovereignty makes the problem of unipolarity worse. The gradual decline of Westphalian sovereignty is seen in the triumph of the post-war human rights revolution. We celebrate this accomplishment—Eleanor Roosevelt and the Universal Declaration of Human Rights. The implication is that the 'international community' increasingly is seen to have legitimate interests in what goes on within countries. Over the decades, the international community has added more realms of internal

state activity that it has a stake in. This was encapsulated by the US-led NATO intervention in Kosovo which, it was argued, was designed to protect human rights and to prevent genocide within Europe's borders. More recently, the new threat of transnational terrorism has opened up states even more to outside scrutiny. In short, state sovereignty is increasingly contingent.

The increasingly contingent character of sovereignty in world politics has been a quiet revolution, and it has been pushed forward by a variety of forces. As former State Department Policy Planning director Richard Haass notes:

> **"**sovereignty is being challenged from both within and without. Weak states struggle to exercise legitimate authority within their territories. Globalization makes it harder for all nations to control their frontiers. Governments trade freedom of action for the benefits of multilateral cooperation. And outlaw regimes jeopardize their sovereign status by pursuing reckless policies fraught with danger for their citizens and the international community.**"**

As a result, Haass argues, there is 'an emerging global consensus that sovereignty is not a blank check' (Haass 2003).

This transformation has had two implications. First, the erosion of norms of sovereignty has created a new 'licence' for powerful states to intervene in the domestic affairs of weak and troubled states. In effect, the norms of state sovereignty have less 'stopping power'. There are fewer principled and normative inhibitions on intervention. But second, eroded sovereignty has not been matched by a rise of new norms and agreements about when and how the 'international community' should intervene. After all, who speaks for the international community? This vacuum in which old norms have weakened but new norms have not fully emerged has ushered in a new struggle over the sources of authority in the international community.

This global struggle over the sources of international authority has, in turn, been exacerbated by the rise of American unipolarity. After all, only the United States has the military power to systematically engage in large-scale uses of force around the world. Indeed, the two developments reinforce worldwide insecurity about American power: the United States is the only global political-military power and the revolutions in human rights and transnational terrorism call forth new reasons why intervention—in the name of the international community or global security or hegemonic management—may be necessary.

KEY POINTS

- ❏ The new international system is being shaped by two new factors: the erosion of the norms of state sovereignty and the rise of unipolarity.
- ❏ Together these twin changes have encouraged a greater propensity for intervention by the West.
- ❏ There is however no clear idea yet of how, why, and under what circumstances the USA and its allies should intervene.

❝❞ KEY QUOTES 21.1: US foreign policy in new times

America has major strategic and economic interests in the Middle East that are dictated by the region's vast energy supplies. Not only does America benefit economically from the relatively low costs of Middle Eastern oil, but America's security role in the region gives it indirect but politically critical leverage on the European and Asian economies that are also dependent on energy exports from the region.

(Zbigniew Brzezinski, President Carter's former National Security Adviser)

[Our goal] is to prevent regimes that sponsor terror from threatening America or our friends and allies with weapons of mass destruction. Some of these regimes have been pretty quiet since September the 11th. But we know their true nature. North Korea is a regime arming with missiles and weapons of mass destruction, while starving its citizens.

Iran aggressively pursues these weapons and exports terror, while an unelected few repress the Iranian people's hope for freedom.

Iraq continues to flaunt its hostility toward America and to support terror. The Iraqi regime has plotted to develop anthrax, and nerve gas, and nuclear weapons for over a decade. This is a regime that has already used poison gas to murder thousands of its own citizens—leaving the bodies of mothers huddled over their dead children. This is a regime that agreed to international inspections—then kicked out the inspectors. This is a regime that has something to hide from the civilized world.

" KEY QUOTES 21.1 (continued)

States like these, and their terrorist allies, constitute an axis of evil, arming to threaten the peace of the world. By seeking weapons of mass destruction, these regimes pose a grave and growing danger. They could provide these arms to terrorists, giving them the means to match their hatred. They could attack our allies or attempt to blackmail the United States. In any of these cases, the price of indifference would be catastrophic.

(George W. Bush, 2002 State of the Union Address)

We are living in an extraordinary time, one in which centuries of international precedent are being overturned. The prospect of violent conflict among great powers is more remote than ever. States are increasingly competing and cooperating in peace, not preparing for war. Peoples in China and India, in South Africa and Indonesia and Brazil are lifting their countries into new prominence. Reform—democratic reform—has begun and is spreading in the Middle East. And the United States is working with our many partners, particularly our partners who share our values in Europe and in Asia and in other parts of the world to build a true form of global stability, a balance of power that favors freedom.

At the same time, other challenges have assumed a new urgency. Since its creation more than 350 years ago, the modern state system has rested on the concept of sovereignty. It was always assumed that every state could control and direct the threats emerging from its territory. It was also assumed that weak and poorly governed states were merely a burden to their people, or at most, an international humanitarian concern but never a true security threat.

(US Secretary of State Condoleezza Rice)

I am saddened that it is politically inconvenient to acknowledge what everyone knows: the Iraq war is largely about oil.

(Alan Greenspan, former chairman of the US Federal Reserve)

The democratization paradox

Two other shifts in the global system exacerbate this 'problem' of American power. The end of the Cold War has eliminated a common threat that tied the United States to a global array of allies and it has meant that the United States does not need these allies in the same way as in the past. But it also means that other states do not need the United States as much as in the past. As a result, American power is less clearly tied to a common purpose. This makes American power less intrinsically legitimate and desirable in the eyes of states and peoples around the world.

The other long-term shift is the rise of international democratic community with more countries being led by constitutional, popularly elected governments. The world is increasingly filled with democracies—and together these democracies form a sort of democratic community. This fact of democratic community has paradoxical effects on American foreign policy. On the one hand, this development gives the United States the ready access of partners and the ability to pursue complex forms of cooperation. American power itself is seen—because the United States is a democracy—as more benign and accessible to other democracies. On the other hand, these democratic states are not likely to respond to domination or coercion by the United States. Indeed, they will expect the United States to operate within rules and institutions of the democratic community.

The British diplomat and European Union official Robert Cooper has captured the implications of this global democratic transition.

" We live in a democratic era. . . . This has consequences for the international system. The realist world of rational policy making, equilibrium, alliances of convenience, and the balance of power, worked best when we were governed by rational, oligarchs—Richelieu, Pitt, Palmerston or Bismarck. Democratic ideas mean that policy requires a moral basis. . . . In a democratic world, the use of force becomes more difficult to handle. Wars need greater moral legitimacy than in an autocratic age . . . The balance of power, which calls for the application of power with calculation and restraint, is no longer sustainable in a democratic age. Nor is the exercise of hegemony by force—which has been the other source of stability in the international system. (Cooper 2005) **"**

It is this situation that appears to have caused the Bush administration so much grief. The Bush invasion of Iraq and general disregard for international rules and institutions, which it believed was justified by America's uncontested hegemonic status, has triggered an outpouring of resentment and disapproval across the democratic world. Whatever pressure the United States can bring to bear on its democratic allies and partners is offset by the public opinion within these democratic states. The Bush administration has discovered the limits of its power in the age of democracy. It has got into trouble—losing

credibility, prestige, respect, and political support—when it has been seen to sidestep or disrespect the rules and norms of the liberal order. This shifting geopolitical terrain has thus created a security trap for the United States—when America tries to solve security problems by exercising power and wielding force, it triggers resistance and hostility that ultimately makes it harder for the United States to achieve security goals.

KEY POINTS

- ❏ With the emergence of new international norms on human rights, democracy, and the threat of transnational terrorism, state sovereignty is increasingly contingent.
- ❏ In a global order characterized by democratic states, a realist logic of state power is increasingly irrelevant, and consent becomes more important than coercion.

 MAJOR DEBATES AND THEIR IMPACT 21.1: The challenge of world order

In the context of this chapter, the key debate in relation to American power is whether the most effective means for a stable world order is served by a superpower committed to a hegemonic or imperial form of rule. Within a hegemonic order, the key hegemon—the United States—is both producer of and subject to international norms and rules. The USA becomes deeply embedded within global regimes, and works through these regimes and the rules-based order to attain national interests. The benefit of a rules-based order is that it provides a multilateral framework for the attainment of collective goods for other states. This in turn prevents balancing behaviour whereby key states and allies seek to counter the power of the hegemon as well as maintaining authority and the consent of those subject to that order. By working within a rules-based order, as well as being the key power that underwrites that order, the United States provides a key public good which in turn reinforces US hegemony.

On the other hand, by pursuing a more imperial foreign policy, the United States is in danger of undermining its hegemonic power as well as destroying the very rules-based order that it was instrumental in creating in the post-war period. When the hegemon is no longer subject to rules or global regimes, other states become scared and seek to counter the power of the hegemon. Moreover, in bypassing multilateral forms of governance, the USA has increasingly sought to rely on its overwhelming military superiority and a more coercive power. This in turn undermines the 'soft power' and symbolic importance of the USA as a protector of freedom and democracy, and instead replaces it with a picture of a 'global bully'. This security trap can be avoided by reaffirming the USA's commitment to a rules-based order as well as invigorating and reaffirming the importance of the key multilateral economic, political, and strategic institutions.

Bush and the security trap

The Bush administration has walked right into this security trap and made it worse. The changing structural foundations of world politics have put American power on display. The Bush administration added alarms and flashing lights.

As the world witnessed in the wake of 11 September, the Bush administration eagerly embraced some aspects of the brave new post-Westphalian world of unipolarity and eroded state sovereignty. It did not see America's transformed position as a problem but as an opportunity—indeed a necessity—that would allow it to pursue a bold new approach to global security.

This is surprising. Although the Bush administration came to office signalling its intention to replace Clinton-era foreign policy with a more traditional realist orientation, its view of global relations took a radical turn after 11 September. Secretary of State Rice captured the essence of the Bush administration's new view in a January 2006 speech at Georgetown University:

❝Since its creation more than 350 years ago, the modern state system has rested on the concept of sovereignty. It was always assumed that every state could control and direct the threats emerging from its territory. It was also assumed that weak and poorly governed states were merely a burden to their people, or at most, an international humanitarian concern but never a true security threat. Today, however, these old assumptions no longer hold. . . . The fundamental character of regimes now matters more than the international distribution of power. (Rice 2006)❞

There is a double irony in this statement—it is a profoundly non-realist thesis delivered by an official deeply associated with realist thinking, and the Bush administration is embracing this liberal-style argument about global change and using it in a way that is subversive of the post-war liberal international order.

Put simply, Bush has disconnected American foreign policy and national security from the array of global political, economic, and political institutions that have been used in the post-war era as tools to advance the country's global position and national interests. Bush has brought into his political coalition policy officials who question the basic premises of America's long-standing approach to alliances, multilateral governance, and liberal international order— and it shows. My point is that a unipolar state that operates in an era of eroded state sovereignty—but simultaneously does not believe in rule-based international order—is a recipe for global resistance and disapproval, and America will be caught ever more deeply in the security trap.

Stepping into this post-Westphalian world, the Bush administration articulated a sweeping new vision of America's role in the world tied to new security imperatives and the 'war on terrorism'. Three aspects of the new Bush national security orientation have exacerbated America's security trap.

First is the Bush administration's wholesale depreciation of multilateral governance and cooperative security. The Bush scepticism of international rules and institutions is well established—and it is manifest in the long list of agreements and treaties that the administration resisted in its first years. The Bush administration famously unsigned the International Criminal Court. The United States was also the lone holdout as 178 countries agreed to implement the Kyoto Treaty on climate change. The administration rejected or withdrew from an entire array of arms control treaties—the 1995 Biological Weapons Convention, the 1972 Anti-Ballistic Missile Treaty, and the 1996 Comprehensive Test Ban Treaty (CTBT). The Bush administration has not only refused to participate in new international agreements, but it has failed to live up to obligations under existing treaties, such as the Nuclear Non-Proliferation Treaty (NPT). Some of this resistance to security agreements began during the Clinton administration with its refusal to sign the Treaty Banning Anti-Personnel Mines and the Senate's rejection of the CTBT. But the Bush administration proudly made it a major feature of its foreign policy.

There are unwelcome consequences that flow from this Bush-era disregard of global rules and security regimes. One is simply that when the world's most powerful state signals a reduced willingness to uphold the system of global rules and institutions, the very foundations of order and cooperation built up over the decades are thrown into doubt. The post-war system of rules and institutions has provided functional benefits for states around the world—providing mechanisms for communication, channelling conflict, and establishing rights and commitments. Moreover, this post-war system has been both championed and supported by the United States. It has been integral to the way the United States has asserted its hegemonic leadership in the post-war era. So when the United States steps back from this support for rules and institutions, the basic character of international order is thrown into question—and states start to worry and assess their options.

It might be useful to think of this dynamic this way: the United States is unique in that it is simultaneously both the provider of 'global governance' and a great power that pursues its own national interest. America's hegemonic leadership role is manifest when it champions the WTO, engages in international rules or regime creation, or reaffirms its commitment to cooperative security in Asia and Europe. Its great power role is manifest, for example, when it seeks to protect its domestic steel or textile industry. When it acts as an enlightened hegemon, it is seeking to lead or manage the global system of rules and institutions; when it is acting as a nationalist great power, it is seeking to respond to domestic interests and its relative power position. My point is that the Bush administration has pulled back from its hegemonic leadership role and—at least from the perspective of other states—appears to be attempting to run the global system as a more traditional great power. Resistance and backlash follow.

The other implication is more specific to the Bush administration's demonstrated disregard for treaty-based security cooperation. When commitments to security treaties weaken, the entire structure of arms control and disarmament agreements is called into question. As one authoritative study concludes: 'When a powerful and influential state like the United States is seen to treat its legal obligations as a matter of convenience or of national interest alone, other states will see this as a justification to relax or withdraw from their own commitments' (Deller, Makhijani, and Burroughs 2003: p. xxxvi). The United States risks a dangerous unravelling of the treaty-based cooperative security infrastructure that has helped provide a measure of stability over the decades, doing so by establishing agreements that facilitate monitoring, transparency, and incentives for compliance. If the United States does not uphold this system, the system will not be upheld.

The second aspect of Bush's security doctrine is its emphasis on national security through regime change—certain types of states, just because of their nature, cannot be trusted. These designated states are a security threat simply by being who they are. Only by turning them into rule-obeying democracies can America be secure. The old treaty-based arms control and non-proliferation approach to international security—the cornerstone of which is the NPT—will not work in this new era. States themselves must be overturned and transformed.

In effect, the United States presents itself to the world as a 'revisionist' power. It seeks to overturn and transform—and it does so for reasons that are tied directly to its security. America cannot be safe until threatening despotic states join the democratic world. Columbia University political scientist Robert Jervis captures this new logic: '[A]s long as many countries are undemocratic, democracies elsewhere, including the United States, cannot be secure. President Woodrow Wilson wanted to make the world safe for democracy. Bush extends and reverses this, arguing that only in a world of democracies can the United States be safe' (Jervis 2006: 13). This move by the Bush administration to emphasize regime change and transformation creates two types of problems. One is that it is a double standard vision that plays havoc with the NPT and other security treaties. The invidious nature of the Bush Doctrine erodes the entire project of tying global security to a system of universal rules, treaties, compromises, and bargains. The other problem with this aspect of Bush strategic doctrine is that it generates a paradox. On the one hand, American security is only possible by overturning other states, but on the other hand, this strategy of a US-led transformation agenda—with use of force as its cutting edge—triggers backlash, eroded cooperation, and estrangement between the United States and its partners, and it weakens America's global authority. We are back to the security trap.

The third aspect of the Bush strategic vision that exacerbates America's security trap is the exemptions and special status that America claims for itself. Bush sees a world in which a unipolar America enforces order and provides security as a public good that the world should welcome. Recall President Bush's 2002 West Point speech in which he warned other great powers that the United States would not tolerate a 'peer competitor', and he argued that in doing so the United States was doing everyone around the world a favour. If other states simply accept American unipolar pre-eminence, they can concentrate on trade and economic development. Leave the 'driving' to America and the world can remain peaceful and prosperous. The dangers and competitive costs of great power rivalry are put to an end. But in return for this American-provided 'public good', the rest of the world will need to tolerate American departures from adherence to universal rule-based order. The ICC is a perfect example where the United States claims that it cannot play by the same rules as other states because of its unique global security involvements that make it a special target for political prosecutions. This line of unipolar reasoning leads to what John Ruggie has called American 'exemptionalism'.

The problem is that other states do not really buy this argument. Either they do not quite buy the American claim that it is providing a public good for the world, or they do not think the public good is worth the price of expanded American exemptionalism. The result is disagreement, contested authority, lost cooperation, and reduced American capacity to realize its security goals. Again we are caught in the security trap.

KEY POINTS

- ❏ US foreign policy was central to the creation of a liberal international order, and this order has served its interests well.
- ❏ By pursuing narrow national interests outside of this international rules-based order and various global regimes, Washington increasingly undermines this order and in so doing encourages balancing against it and resentment from key allies.

Conclusion: escaping the security trap

The combination of a shifting global landscape—manifest in the erosion of the Westphalian order—and the post-911 national security strategy of the Bush administration has caught America in a security trap that creates an increasingly inhospitable environment for the United States to pursue its interests. Unipolarity and eroded sovereignty give the United States capacities and a warrant to project power across the world, even as it poses American power as a 'problem' for the rest of the global community. At the same time, the Bush administration's resistance to international rules and institutions, doctrine of regime change, and exemptionalism exacerbate worries about American power. Together, this creates an extraordinary situation—the most powerful state in the world is not a keeper of the status quo but a revisionist hegemon. The United States has the capacity to dominate but not the legitimacy to rule—it has power but not authority.

To escape this security trap, the United States will need to find ways to reassure other states and bind itself to the wider international community. If American power is to regain its lost authority it will need to be reinserted into a reformed system of agreed-upon global rules and institutions.

First, the United States needs to send an unmistakable signal to the rest of the world—that it is again committing itself to promoting and operating within a rule-based international order. This was, after all, what the United States did after the Second World War when it emerged as the pre-eminent global power and found itself in a position to shape the post-war global order. Truman and his colleagues created a far-flung liberal multilateral order and Cold War alliance system that fused American power to institutions and liberal purpose. The restraint on American power and the projection of American power went hand in hand.

A rule-based international order does circumscribe the way power is exercised—and it does, to some extent, reduce America's autonomy and freedom of action. But in return, the United States buys itself a more predictable and legitimate international order. By getting other states to operate within a set of multilateral rules and institutions, the United States reduces its need to continuously pressure and coerce other states to follow America's lead. When the United States makes itself a global rule maker, other states become less concerned with resisting American power and more concerned with negotiating over the frameworks of cooperation. Today, American unipolarity is associated with the erosion of a global system of rules and institutions. This association is not inevitable. The United States can turn itself—as it did in the 1940s—into a rule producer, and its authority will increase accordingly.

Second, the United States needs to look for ways to make decisions on the use of force within wider collective bodies, particularly the United Nations and NATO. America's near-monopoly on the use of force is a worry felt around the world. To the extent that this military power is channelled through widely respected multilateral bodies, the more likely the resulting uses of force will be seen as legitimate. Ideally, the United States should try to gain UN Security Council approval for its use-of-force decisions, gaining the legitimacy that flows from this global venue. But practical political constraints on getting the United Nations to make supportive and timely decisions gives the United States incentives to look for collective approval from other bodies.

Among the alternatives, NATO—which embodies the security interests and capabilities of the major

Western democracies—is the most promising. In committing itself to making strategic military decisions within NATO, the United States would be making a basic bargain with its European partners. The United States opens itself up in various ways to the views of other states and in return it gets their cooperation and the legitimacy that follows. The United States gives up some policy autonomy but gets the benefits of other states contributing to the campaign. As a formal organization, NATO provides the mechanisms to engage in strategic planning and aggregate military capacities. As an informal mechanism, NATO provides a venue for consultation. Washington, in effect, says to others: our door is open, please come in and make your case. In the end, the United States will decide on its own and do what it wants. But it creates a political process where other states get involved in trans-governmental pulling and hauling—and they are given at least the opportunity to influence Washington policy.

In binding itself to other states, the United States makes the exercise of unipolarity more acceptable to the outside world. Acknowledging this logic, Robert Kagan has argued that to regain its lost legitimacy, the United States needs to return to its post-war bargain: giving some European voice over American policy in exchange for their support. The United States, Kagan points out, 'should try to fulfill its part of the transatlantic bargain by granting Europeans some influence over the exercise of its power—provided that, in return, Europeans wield that influence wisely' (Kagan 2004: 86). This is the logic that informed American security cooperation with its European and East Asian partners during the Cold War. It is a logic that can be renewed today to help make unipolarity more acceptable.

Third, the United States needs to articulate a substantive and expansive vision of international order. The Bush administration has offered a very limited and narrow conception of what it sees as the desirable system of international relations. The focus is on America's dominant role in using force to confront terrorists and despotic states. It is a vision of order that emphasizes American military pre-eminence, coalitions of the willing, and the war on terrorism. This is not a vision of order that will elicit the cooperation and normative approbation of other countries.

What is missing in the Bush conception is the embrace of a notion of an international order that embodies and advances common global interests and values. In the 1940s, American leaders connected American power to the building of a liberal international order. This liberal vision of order has several components. One is a commitment to free trade and open markets, creating the conditions for growth and development. Another is a commitment to the social bargain. Open markets create winners—but also losers. So countries within the open system need to develop social protections against economic distress. If the United States wants to see other states buy into this open world economy, it needs to help and support those countries to establish the sorts of Western social support structures that allow for stable democracy to coexist with trade and investment.

Another aspect of the liberal vision of international order is a commitment to the creation of permanent governance institutions. These governance mechanisms facilitate ongoing streams of cooperation needed to manage growing realms of complex interdependence. This is America's commitment to building and operating within a rule-based order. The IMF, World Bank, and WTO are all embodiments of this managed system of economic openness. Finally, the liberal vision entails a commitment to cooperative security. This is a vision of order where the United States ties its security to other states through security alliances. These post-war alliances—NATO and the USA–Japan pact—have been about more than simply deterrence and containment of Soviet communism. The alliances have also performed the function of providing political architecture for the political community that bridges Europe, North America, and East Asia. The alliances provide mechanisms for 'doing business' across the Atlantic and Pacific. They keep the United States engaged in Europe and Asia—and they allow leaders in these regions to be engaged and connected to America.

The specific dimensions of liberal international order are less important than the general message the United States needs to send to the world: it is not just concerned with attacking terrorism and promoting freedom—but it is also helping to bring forth and lead a liberal international order in which countries weak and strong can flourish.

The task of articulating a post-Bush foreign policy must begin with coming to grips with the problem of America's growing security trap—and the resulting erosion of America's global authority. It is an ironic problem, in a sense. After all, the structural sources of this problem follow from the fabulous post-war success of America. Unipolarity is a description of the disproportionate and unbalanced material capabilities that the United States has in relation to other states. America has an extraordinary opportunity today—as it has in the past—to use its power to shape the international order.

In the Bush vision, international order arises exclusively from US unipolar pre-eminence, with America wielding its unchecked power to keep others in line and enforce international hierarchy. In the liberal vision, international order arises from the coupling of America's pre-eminence with its founding principles, with the United States wielding its power to craft consensual and legitimate mechanisms of international governance. With this vision America can rebuild and reassert its authority on the global stage.

? Questions

1. To what extent has American foreign policy been realist in orientation and has it changed in recent years?
2. To what extent is democracy a contested concept in American foreign policy?
3. Do we live in an age of American empire?
4. To what extent did humanitarian intervention signify a change in American foreign policy from the earlier Cold War period?
5. Empire, hegemony, or decline: which concept best captures the state of America in the world today and why?

6. Is the security trap for US foreign policy a self-invented one?

7. What is the best strategy for both maintaining a rules-based order and also preventing terrorism?

8. Did the imperial foreign policy emerge with the Bush administration or are there longer-term continuities in American foreign policy?

9. To what extent is the new war on terror an attempt to ensure an American-centric world order?

10. What were the motivations for the war in Iraq? Relate your answer to the security trap outlined in this chapter.

Further Reading

Chomsky, Noam (1999), *The New Military Humanism* (Monroe, Me.: Common Courage Press).

Clark, Wesley K. (2003), *Winning Modern Wars: Iraq, Terrorism and the American Empire* (New York: Public Affairs).

Cox, Michael, Inoguchi, Takashi, and Ikenberry, G. John (eds.) (2000), *American Democracy Promotion: Impulses, Strategies, and Impacts* (Oxford: Oxford University Press).

Ikenberry, G. John (ed.) (2001), *American Foreign Policy: Theoretical Essays* (Boston: Scott Foresman).

Kolko, Gabriel (2006), *The Age of War: The United States Confronts the World* (Boulder, Colo.: Lynne Rienner).

Panitch Leo, and Gindin, Sam (2003), *Global Capitalism and American Empire* (London: Merlin Press).

Power, Samantha (2003), *'A Problem from Hell': America in the Age of Genocide* (London: HarperCollins).

Endnotes

'The Security Trap' first appeared in *Democracy: A Journal of Ideas*, 2 (Fall 2006).

Visit the Online Resource Centre that accompanies this book for web links to accompany each chapter, and a range of other resources: www.oxfordtextbooks.co.uk/orc/cox_stokes/

22 The future of US foreign policy

Anatol Lieven

Chapter contents

Introduction

This chapter analyses and portrays possible futures for US foreign policy in terms of the interests and ideology of the US elites (and to a lesser extent the population at large); the structures of US political life; the real or perceived national interests of the USA; and future developments on the world stage.

On this basis, it suggests that now that the rougher edges have been knocked off Republican foreign policy, there will not be a really major change in US global strategy whichever party comes to power, since both share the same essential ideology and class interests. The 'global war on terror' will continue to be defined in much the same terms, and serious attempts at reconciliation with key parts of the Muslim world will not be attempted.

Instead, this chapter argues that as a result of the disaster in Iraq and the ongoing crisis in Afghanistan, US foreign policy will become more cautious when it comes to radical actions and especially major interventions, but without necessarily becoming wiser. Interventionism will be replaced by drift, until some major global crisis occurs to upset the entire present international order.

The analysis of possible futures of US foreign policy set out in this chapter will be based on a combination of elements from two different traditions in international relations analysis: the realist tradition, which focuses above all on state interests and the relative power of states; and what in German is called the *Primat der Innenpolitik*, the predominant influence of domestic policy on foreign policy. Domestic policy in this sense is defined not just as domestic political agendas and ambitions, but the constitutional, political, economic, social, and ideological structures of the domestic political order.

Realism dictates that many US 'vital national interests' must at present be regarded as givens, even though historians of the future may see them as not really in the interest of the great majority of Americans. This is because they are defined as vital, unchangeable interests by the great majority of the US political classes, the security establishment, and

the media, and have sunk deeply into the public unconscious in the course of several decades of their constant reiteration by the elites. I argue here that the leaderships of the Republican and Democratic parties are to a great extent drawn from the same US establishment, share the same basic class interests, are subject to the same domestic pressures on key issues, and are shaped by the same nationalist and imperialist ideology, in somewhat different forms.

This being so, it is likely that future US foreign policy will share the same basic contours whether the Republicans or Democrats form the administration at the time. In addition—from a realist perspective—all US administrations will face certain irreducible constraints and imperatives stemming from US external interests, the international balance of power, and the extent of US power or the lack of it.

This US power in turn, to be assessed accurately, has to be judged not in absolute terms—total US military spending, the numbers of US aircraft carriers and warplanes, the size of the US economy, and so on—but in terms of the US power that can actually be mobilized domestically behind a given objective, and applied locally, to a particular place or issues, relative to the power that other states can bring to bear on the same place or issue.

Viewed in these terms, US foreign policy for the foreseeable future will be chiefly defined by two desires: the desire of the US political elites, and a large part of US public opinion in general, for the USA to play a hegemonic role on the world stage; and their equally profound desire, as individuals, not personally to pay or fight to maintain this role.

This creates a severe mismatch between American ambitions and the American power actually to achieve them. The problems stemming from this mismatch are likely to be made considerably worse by two additional factors. The first is the rise of rivals to US power in certain key parts of the world, notably China, Russia, and to a lesser extent India and Iran.

The second is sharpening geopolitical competition over access to vital and increasingly scarce natural resources. At present this refers above all to oil, but if the economic rise of China and India continues, and concerns about oil and global warming continue to fuel the diversion of grain to ethanol production, within a generation the world may also be facing shortages of grain.

In these circumstances, it would seem obvious for the USA to seek to redraw its priorities (or at least choose between them) and reduce its commitments in certain parts of the world that are not in fact central to US vital interests—the strategy pursued by Britain in the generation before 1914. However, this is not easy for any empire; and for reasons that this essay will explore, it is especially difficult for the United States.[1]

Belief in America's mission to lead the world towards freedom, democracy, and progress stems from an American nationalism whose roots stretch back almost 500 years, to the Protestant Reformation in England and Scotland. And for reasons which will be explored in this essay, the US political system has become so cumbersome, so snarled by powerful and even indomitable interest groups, that it may no longer even be capable of making clear decisions that offend any significant domestic lobby. The USA might then come to resemble France under Louis XV and Louis XVI—a country whose immense latent strengths simply could not be mobilized behind an effective foreign policy, without revolutionary domestic change.

The ideological roots of US foreign policy

The great majority of Americans do not believe that they have or should have an empire. At the same time, however, a sense of America's mission to bring democracy, freedom, and progress to the rest of the world is deeply rooted in American culture, and deeply entwined with American civic nationalism. It is connected to a widespread sense of the innate goodness of America's actions on the world stage, and of the US military in particular.

This is a key link between the ideological bases of American civic nationalism (based on general belief in the values of what has been called 'the American Creed') and American imperialism. Insofar as they can use this rhetoric in support of their plans, the imperialists have a tremendous means of seduction as far as many Americans are concerned. This is America's version of the missions of the great civilizational empires of the past: of the duties of Rome and imperial China—as seen by their rulers, elites, and intellectuals—to spread their civilizations to the barbarians beyond their borders; of the Spanish to Christianize the New World; of the *missions civilisatrices* of the nineteenth-century European empires; of the Soviet Union to bring the light of communism to the rest of humanity.

In the words of Russell Nye, 'All nations . . . have long agreed that they are chosen peoples; the idea of special destiny is as old as nationalism itself. However, no nation in modern history has been quite so consistently dominated as the United States by the belief that it has a particular mission in the world' (Nye 1966, quoted in Cobb 1998: 4). So powerful is this form of nationalism, and so continuously reinforced by the media, popular culture in general, much of the school system, many of the churches, and the rhetoric of politicians, that it survived what should have been the searing lessons of Vietnam, and will probably survive what ought to be the equally searing lessons of Iraq. It has played a key part in the rhetoric of the Bush administration in the global war on terror. As the opening statement of the National Security Strategy of 2006 reads:

> **"**The United States must defend liberty and justice because these principles are right and true for all people everywhere. These nonnegotiable demands of human dignity are protected most securely in democracies. The United States Government will work to advance human dignity in word and deed, speaking out for freedom and against violations of human rights and allocating appropriate resources to advance these ideals . . . To protect our Nation and honor our values, the United States seeks to extend freedom across the globe by leading an international effort to end tyranny and to promote effective democracy. (National Security Strategy 2006)**"**

It also however profoundly influences most of the leadership and established intelligentsia of the Democratic Party, including those who call themselves 'liberal internationalists'. This is apparent for example in the Princeton National Security Project, a blueprint for the US administration that takes power in 2009, but is directed principally at the Democrats, and co-chaired by an aspirant for senior office, Professor Ann-Marie Slaughter. This project adopted an originally neo-conservative idea for a global coalition of democracies led by the USA—with no regard to the effects of this on relations with China, Russia, and so on, or indeed for what this alliance would actually do, other than validate US claims to global leadership.

Lines written by C. Vann Woodward during the Vietnam War are no less valid today:

❝The characteristic American adjustment to the current foreign and domestic enigmas that confound our national myths has not been to abandon the myths but to reaffirm them. Solutions are sought along traditional lines . . . Whatever the differences and enmities that divide advocates and opponents (and they are admittedly formidable), both sides seem predominantly unshaken in their adherence to one or another or all of the common national myths. (Woodward 1968: 218)❞

Louis Hartz wrote of the American Creed's 'compulsive nationalism' and the 'fixed, dogmatic liberalism of a liberal way of life' (Hartz 1955: 9, 15, 175, 225–37). According to Samuel Huntington,

❝It is possible to speak of a body of political ideas that constitutes 'Americanism' in a sense in which one can never speak of 'Britishism', 'Frenchism', 'Germanism', or Japaneseism'. Americanism in this sense is comparable to other ideologies and religions . . . To reject the central ideas of that doctrine is to be un-American . . . This identification of nationality with political Creed or values makes the United States virtually unique. (Huntington 1981: 2–3, 25)❞

One result of this ideological conformity is to make it much more difficult for most Americans to imagine America as a country among others, or an 'international community' that includes America as a member rather than a hegemon.[2] It thereby contributes to the shortage of true internationalists in the USA, and indeed to an absence of real debate on key underlying principles of foreign policy.

In the areas of foreign relations and security, a capacity for really open debate on underlying principles has also been discouraged by the close links between government, particular university departments, think tanks, and journalists working in this field. Paradoxically, the American system of political appointments, whereby a president chooses some 4,000 officials from outside the civil service, has worked if anything to limit the advice coming to government. Rather than opening the bureaucracy, it has tended to bureaucratize those sections of academia with a role in the foreign policy debate.

Because they are divided into two political tribes, these para-bureaucrats retain a capacity to criticize specific policies of particular administrations. With very few exceptions, however, like most bureaucrats they lack completely an ability to distance themselves from the myths of the state system which supports them.

As a result of this complex of factors, in the view of Andrew Bacevich, the basic American consensus on foreign policy 'is so deep-seated that its terms have become all but self-evident, its premises asserted rather than demonstrated'. As a result, much of the public and media debate on international issues within the USA is no more than 'political theatre' (Bacevich 2002: 9, 33).

The effects of this ideology and this conformism are twofold. Overall, it is extremely difficult within the US establishment to question whether the USA actually needs to remain the sole global superpower, with all the immense costs and risks that this involves. In specific regions and on specific issues, it makes it much more difficult to propose reasonable compromises with local great powers, because this can always be presented as 'appeasement' and 'betraying American values'. As the examples of Colonel Bacevich and others show, it is of course possible to put forward these ideas in the USA—but the general result is to be excluded from the establishment, and to a great extent from the mainstream media.

Strengths and weaknesses of the USA

At first sight, a really radical shift in US global strategy, and the radical diminution of US commitments, might hardly seem necessary. The United States obviously possesses tremendous latent strength, as both the world's largest economy and the world's greatest military power by far. When it chooses to use its economic weight, the USA can play a decisive role in the management and resolution of international economic crises, as demonstrated repeatedly in the past two decades.

The Chinese economy is gradually eroding the economic lead of the USA, but even if steep Chinese growth continues, it will be a long time before China can match US military technology, especially at sea and in the air. The US military's power to suppress insurgencies and rebuild states has been shown to be extremely limited; but its capacity to project force around the world, and to defeat other armies in the field, remains unparalleled.

Most importantly of all, while the US Navy and Air Force's capacity to inflict catastrophic damage on infrastructure targets is irrelevant to the fight against terrorist and guerrilla enemies, it is a very important latent means of pressure on organized states, as was shown by the Kosovo air campaign of 1989. In contemplating any military confrontation with the USA, the Chinese leadership for example would have to be influenced by the tens of billions of dollars they had spent on the Three Gorges dam—and the consciousness that it could all be knocked to pieces by American missiles.

The problem for the USA then is not its absolute strength, but the twin questions of how to bring that strength to bear on particular issues, and even more importantly, how to persuade the American political classes and population actually to mobilize that strength for foreign policy goals.

The contrast between a desire for imperial glory and an unwillingness to pay or fight for empire is not new in Western history. The British and French empires were conquered very much on the cheap, often largely by native auxiliaries recruited and paid for by the colonies themselves. The outrageous cost (by previous imperial standards) of the Boer War brought about a major revulsion of public feeling in Britain.

Until the First World War, the British always rejected conscription. Concern about the deaths of British conscript soldiers in colonial wars was one reason for the speed with which the British Empire was wound up in the 1950s. The French did have conscription, but this was legitimized to the French public as necessary to fight in Europe, in the defence of France itself. Hence the creation of the Foreign Legion, explicitly for imperial campaigns.

The suggestion that the USA lacks the power to conduct a successful strategy of world hegemony may therefore seem absurd in the face of US military spending that as of 2007 probably exceeds the rest of the planet put together, based on a US economy which remains by some distance the largest on earth. However, military and geopolitical power and influence are not abstract things. In the end, all true power is local, and relative: that is to say, it is power that can actually be brought to bear on a particular place or a particular issue, relative to the power that can be brought to bear on the same place and issue by another power or powers.

Moreover, in concentrating on US military spending, on US high technology, and on the number of US aircraft carriers, warplanes, and tanks, military analysts have too often forgotten an older, but still extremely important measure of military strength: the number of 'bayonets' an army possesses: in other words, the number of its fighting infantry. This too is an old dilemma for Western empires, as Kipling noted in his poem 'Frontier Arithmetic'. Of British troops deployed in India, he wrote, 'the troopships bring them one by one | at vast expense of time and steam | to catch the Afridi where they run . . .'

As the wars in Iraq and Afghanistan demonstrate, while conquering a territory may well require comparatively few troops, holding it afterwards, protecting a client government in the face of local revolt, and ensuring basic local stability, require very large numbers indeed—numbers which probably cannot be generated in the long term, or for multiple such operations, without a resort to conscription. In April 2007, a senior retired general, Barry McCaffrey, warned publicly that the US military was now so overstretched that if faced with a successful North Korean invasion of South Korea it could have to resort to an early use of nuclear weapons (Robberson 2007).

As of 2007, the option of conscription is categorically rejected by the Bush administration, both political parties, and the overwhelming majority of US politicians and the US public. It is just conceivable that it might be agreed to in the public hysteria following a massive new terrorist attack on the USA or the large-scale disruption of oil supplies to the USA; but if so, in the long run anxieties and protests about conscript losses would probably restrain and even end future imperial operations, not enable them.

The number of casualties suffered by the US military in Iraq and Afghanistan is not high by historical standards—though one should be careful to note that as of the spring of 2007, not only had more than 3,600 US servicemen been killed, but more than 24,000 had been wounded. Recent advances in medical technology mean that many of these wounded who in previous wars would have died can now be saved. They are however in many cases disabled, and have to retire from the military. Moreover, extensive disabilities have as great or even greater effects on morale and recruitment as do deaths in action.

As several leading generals and military experts have warned, over time, this level of casualties is therefore incompatible with the maintenance of a volunteer army. This is all the more so since unlike in the nineteenth century, even ordinary soldiers have to be able to master quite complicated military technologies. They also of course have to be able to understand not just orders but manuals in English. This fact, as much as political considerations, renders highly questionable the strategy advocated by Max Boot and others, of recruiting increasing numbers of soldiers from the impoverished masses of Mexico and Central America in return for both pay and US citizenship for themselves and their families.

These constraints make it almost impossible to imagine the USA being able to generate the forces that would be able to defeat and occupy Iran or Pakistan, for example—which in turn places obvious limits on the degree of pressure and influence Washington can exert over those countries. In the past, empires have sought to circumvent such constraints by eschewing outright conquest in favour of punitive expeditions, intended not to replace or rule over another state, or even necessarily to replace a government, but rather to inflict sufficient damage to force the government, country, or people concerned to bow to the will of the imperial power on specific issues; at the milder end of this range of options, the strategy known as 'gunboat diplomacy'.

This was the strategy that the British Empire generally adopted towards Afghanistan and the Pashtun tribes of the Afghan frontier after the crushing British defeat of 1842. On a larger scale, this punitive strategy was essentially the military approach of the British and other Western imperial powers towards China in the nineteenth century; since, unlike the Russians and Japanese, they did not believe that it was possible for them actually to incorporate large parts of China into their empires. Some aspects of the Western military campaigns in China were 'punitive' in the sense of extracting financial compensation. Others, like the infamous destruction of the Summer Palace near Peking in 1860, were directly and crudely punitive in terms of deliberate destruction and vandalism.

This strategy has indeed sometimes been adopted by the USA in recent decades, including the bombardment of Libyan government buildings and military positions in 1988, and the Clinton administration's repeated attacks on Iraq in the 1990s (Peters 2006). US economic sanctions against various countries, a strategy beloved of the US Congress in particular, can also be seen as a non-military version of the punitive approach.

However, as these examples demonstrate, there are many problems with the punitive approach to the exertion of US power. In the case of Libya, the US attack did not deter—and may have provoked— the Lockerbie terrorist attack. Sanctions did have an

CONTROVERSIES 22.1: The Israel 'lobby' debate

In March 2006 Professors John Mearsheimer (University of Chicago) and Stephen Walt (Harvard) published an essay in the *London Review of Books* entitled 'The Israel Lobby', strongly criticizing the role of that lobby in shaping US policy towards the Middle East and suppressing free debate of the issue in the USA. Although their essay was unexceptionable by European standards, and certainly not anti-Semitic, the authors were subjected to a storm of criticism in the USA. However, in a sign that the atmosphere of debate may be very gradually changing, leading journals like *Foreign Policy* did actually invite them to debate their work, rather than—as would have generally been the case in the past—either ignoring it or printing only their critics.

effect, but took a generation to work. They have not worked at all in the cases of Cuba, Syria, or as yet Iran; partly, it has been argued, because by reducing international economic contacts and the usual workings of the market, they actually strengthen the power of ruling elites which control access to key economic resources and goods. In the case of Iraq, a mixture of US economic sanctions and intermittent bombardment had no effect in either taming or bringing down the Ba'athist regime, and their failure helped lead in the end to US invasion, with disastrous consequences for the USA, and much more for Iraq.

The rise of international terrorism as a threat has greatly increased interest in punitive strategies, but has also made them much more problematical. Punitive action always brought with it the risk that rather than coercing the state concerned, it would lead to its collapse. This indeed was the eventual result, in 1911, of seventy years of humiliation of the Manchu Dynasty in China by the Western powers. Collapse may be followed either by the appearance of a new, even more hostile regime, or by anarchy; and either may be seen to necessitate the direct intervention and rule of the imperial power.

The US political order and foreign policy

The difficulty the USA has in mobilizing its wealth for foreign policy goals is shown most glaringly in the area of foreign aid. During the Cold War, both Democratic and Republican administrations saw aid as an absolutely critical part of US strategy in the struggle against communism. Since the end of that conflict, spending on aid has declined precipitously, and even 9/11 has led to no really significant improvement, even in most of the Muslim world.[3] As of 2007, there is little sign that this will increase radically in future, given the state of US public opinion on the subject, and the deference of the Democratic Party to public prejudices.

The indifference to foreign aid has worsened in recent years because of the massive shift of resources and influence from the State Department (including USAID) to the Pentagon. This development was already visible in the 1990s, and contributed to the intense militarization of the US global war on terror—rather than an adoption of the more limited

and targeted intelligence and police strategies that the European states and many US diplomats would have preferred.

This shift reflects not only administration but congressional priorities. Congress will not pay much any longer to build up countries like Pakistan which may emerge as economic competitors of the USA in particular fields, as South Korea and Taiwan did during the Cold War. They will pay for the military, not only because of security paranoia or the allure of military 'pork' for their own states, but because more broadly the US military budget serves as something that, according to its free market ideology, the USA does not have: a massive, and in some areas extremely successful programme of state-subsidized industrial development, heavily slanted towards high technology.

The militarization of the structures of US foreign policy does not necessarily mean a more bellicose stance—on the contrary, the US Army and Marine

Corps have emerged as forces for relative moderation and caution in Washington. It does however naturally mean that more and more of America's significant diplomatic contacts with key states will be military to military, and that less aid will be for development and more is likely to be security related, or at best humanitarian aid administered by the US military, as after the Asian tsunami and the Pakistan earthquake.

As a result, the USA is not merely failing to project influence and goodwill, but is being heavily outspent by rival powers in certain parts of the world. Thus Chinese aid to the Philippines (a former US colony) in 2006 was four times that of the United States. Even after the rise in Russian gas prices at the start of 2006, Russian annual energy subsidies to Ukraine exceed many times over US aid to that country. In several parts of Latin America, a strategic combination of the oil wealth of Hugo Chávez's regime in Venezuela and the numerous, highly trained medical and engineering cadres of communist Cuba are greatly overshadowing limited US aid to the region; indeed, Cuba did more to help Pakistan after its 2005 earthquake than did the USA. As Colonel Larry Wilkerson, former chief of staff of the State Department, remarked in 2007, 'People are beginning to like Cuban public diplomacy and despise ours.'[4]

This is also true of US aid to the Middle East as part of the war on terror. The Millennium Challenge Account is a good idea in principle, but is hopelessly under-funded. As of 2006, only $1.5 billion in new aid had been approved under the MCA—not sufficient to make a serious difference to even one large Muslim country. As to the Middle East Partnership Initiative (MEPI) Congress appropriated just $75 million (half of what President Bush requested) under this programme—to help build political reform, economic reform, educational reform, and women's empowerment across the entire Greater Middle East (cf. Sharp 2005; Wittes and Yerkes 2004)!

The inability to generate more foreign aid reflects the unwillingness of US taxpayers to provide the funds, but also profound structural problems in the US political system, which make it extremely difficult to carry out any radical change of policy—even one supported by a majority of the population and the establishment—if this is opposed by even one really powerful lobby or interest group. From this point of view, the inability to raise spending on foreign aid, the inability to end the utterly counterproductive forty-year-old embargo against Cuba, the pursuit of pointless and dangerous anti-Russian agendas, and unconditional support for Israel all find their echoes in certain domestic failures: for example, the inability to reform America's horribly costly and inefficient private health system, or to introduce restrictions on gun sales, despite the existence of large national majorities in favour of these reforms.

The power of small but determined lobbies is favoured by a number of factors: broad church political parties with little central party leadership or direction; Senators who are enabled by this and by the Constitution to act as virtually autonomous political princes in Washington politics; the need for larger and larger sums in order to fight elections, above all for television advertising; presidential elections which increasingly hinge on a small number of evenly divided states, making the votes of every lobby count. As Jack Snyder has pointed out, without strong control by administrations or party leaderships, different factions in Congress and the bureaucracy manage their differences about foreign and security policy by never confronting them. They simply pursue every expansionist agenda simultaneously (Snyder 1991).

Perhaps the single most important factor of all is the apathy of the wider public which makes it extremely difficult to mobilize large numbers of people behind any broad programme of reform. If this is impossible when it comes to gun controls—even after a series of horrors like the massacre at Virginia Technical University in April 2007—how much more difficult it would seem to get masses of Americans to demand radical shifts in policies towards foreign countries of which most know nothing. As a result, US foreign policy will for the foreseeable future be run by a mixture of an unrepresentative security elite deeply attached to its own agendas and interests (a pattern very familiar in the history of many states in the past) and particular lobby groups with no concern for the wider national interest at all. It is not just difficult to change course with such a system, it is difficult to steer any rational and coherent course at all.

Future foreign policies

On the basis of the above, we can predict with reasonable confidence that for a long time to come the basic contours of US foreign policy will remain the same, under both Republican and Democratic administrations. An unkind summary of the most likely course of US foreign policy is that in the wake of the debacle in Iraq, it will become more cautious without necessarily becoming any wiser.

For US foreign policy to change radically would require a revolutionary shift in the US domestic political and economic systems, the international balance of power, or most likely both simultaneously. In a few generations, such a revolutionary change is extremely probable, as the impact of global warming undermines many of the basic structures of international order. Long before that, it also seems probable that a really severe global economic recession will destroy many of the assumptions on which American power and the international system are now based. When this will happen is however impossible to predict with any certainty.

The rest of this chapter will therefore deal only with US policy over the next generation, not the next century. It will be based on the assumption that during that period, the world situation will continue to develop roughly along existing lines, or at least within the parameters of currently recognized alternatives—for example, either that China will continue to grow in wealth and power, until it becomes a serious global rival to the USA, or that it will suffer a severe setback from some combination of political and economic factors.

The most important features of US foreign policy are likely to remain the following:

- A continued bipartisan determination to remain the world's dominant power, though most probably stripped of the extreme unilateralism and anti-diplomacy of the Bush administration;
- A reliance above all on military structures (including at least one multilateral one, NATO) as the chief vehicles for US global power and influence;
- Continued rhetoric concerning America's role as the leader of the free world, and America's right and duty to spread 'democracy' and 'freedom'. In practice, however, Washington will remain cautious about actually putting this into practice, except in the case of real or perceived enemies;

- A continuation of the global war on terror, defined as a global struggle against Islamist terrorism by military means. However, unless the US mainland once again suffers a massive terrorist attack, future administrations are likely to be more cautious than the Bush administration and seek above all to avoid more wars of occupation;

- A continued effort to manage the relationship with China along basically non-confrontational lines. This however is likely to come under increasing strain from protectionist impulses in the USA, and from rivalry over access to natural resources;

- Strong underlying emotional hostility towards Russia, and a desire to diminish Russian influence wherever possible. In practice, however, this strategy is likely to be severely limited by the already mentioned constraints on America's own power, both military and economic;

- Repeated attempts to validate US global leadership through gaining the formal support of the west Europeans for US strategies, irrespective of the very limited real help that Europe can or will give to the USA on most issues;

- Indifference to Latin America, increased by growing Democratic hostility to open trade, and by growing hostility in US society to illegal immigration; continued strong mutual hostility between the USA and the Chávez administration in Venezuela;

- Growing rivalry over access to key international commodities. This will increasingly overshadow US relations with China, but over time could also lead to increased tension with India and even Europe;

- Because of US dependence on imported oil, and commitment to Israel, for a long time to come, the Greater Middle East will be the most important and dangerous subject of US foreign policy.

BOX 22.1: The central debate on US foreign policy

The central, perpetual public debate on US foreign policy is that between realism and idealism: how far US strategy should be shaped by considerations of national interest, and how far by national values. To a greater or lesser extent, this colours the public discussion on strategy towards most countries, and most issues. Among leading public figures, it ranges 'realists' of the stamp of Henry Kissinger and Zbigniew Brzezinski against 'idealists' like Madeleine Albright and Paul Wolfowitz. These differences, it should be noted, cut across both parties.

But this debate has a very curious feature: the public discussion itself is won over and over again by the idealists: witness the statements of the leading candidates for president in 2008, all of whom have stated their belief that America must pursue its mission of spreading freedom and democracy. At the level of actual policy, on the other hand, an underlying realism overwhelmingly predominates at the expense of ideals and values.

The Bush administration's strategy in the Middle East from 2006 on is only the sharpest and most obvious example of this contrast. Phrased in overblown idealist rhetoric about spreading democracy, by 2007 it had in fact reverted to the traditional crudely realist approach of backing pro-American Sunni dictators.

This contrast does not reflect simple hypocrisy and mendacity. Rather, a generally shared American nationalism insists on America's right to lead the world towards American values. Idealism does also have certain effects on US policy, for better and worse. A good effect is that it does limit to some extent both outright American imperialism and crimes committed in the pursuit of empire, and promote cooperation with other democratic states. On the negative side, idealistic or pseudo-idealistic concerns are continually wheeled out by a range of lobbies which hope to prevent US compromise or rapprochement with particular foreign states. This has been true for example of the advocates of trade protection against China, and advocates of aggressive policies towards Russia.

As has been true in the modern history of many countries, therefore, idealism can work simultaneously to promote on the one hand international peace and progress, on the other national programmes of chauvinist superiority and ambition; and realism can promote not just the harsh expansion of national power, but peace and cooperation through diplomacy and compromise.

The Middle East

To begin with the latter two points: at some point in the future, the USA will cease to be dependent on oil, whether because environmental concerns have finally begun seriously to bite, because competition with China has forced prices up to uneconomical levels, or simply because the oil itself has run out. Until this comes to pass, however, the US establishment will see vital US interests as lying in a maintenance of the open flow of oil from the Persian Gulf, at reasonable prices.

The price, and not the oil itself, is the reason for this interest. The great majority of imported US oil comes from Canada, Latin America, and Africa; but Gulf supplies are essential to world supplies and therefore to the world market price. The only alternative to dependence on the world market would be a strategy of controlling the oil at source through outright

conquest and military occupation, or some form of locked-in relationship of patronage and defence with a local government.

Such a strategy may have partly underlain the decision to invade Iraq. It was discussed by the Nixon administration with regard to the Saudi oil fields during the first oil shock of 1973, and this possibility has been raised again in neo-conservative circles in recent years. Contingency plans to this effect certainly exist in the Pentagon. Leaving aside the question of the security of Gulf supplies, it is possible that in the decades to come, geopolitical rivalry with China will lead the USA (and maybe China too) to intervene militarily in some troubled oil producer to ensure that supplies continue to flow to the USA. Nigeria has occasionally been mentioned as a future candidate in this regard.

However, the miserable example of the US occupation of Iraq, and what is likely to be the ongoing conflict in Afghanistan, will for a considerable time to come act as a deterrent to further military occupations. More likely is continued strong military and political commitment to key oil producers, led of course by Saudi Arabia. This, and the general need to retain the support of local regimes for the US presence in the region and the struggle against Islamist terrorism, will keep US support for democracy at the level of rhetoric, at least as far as its allies are concerned.

Just as there is no sign that the USA will seriously reduce its dependence on oil in the near to medium term, so the bipartisan US political elite seems locked into support for Israel, to the exclusion of any real possibility of a genuine peace settlement with the Palestinians, the Arab world, and Iran. If the twin triumphs of the disappearance of the enemy Soviet superpower and the defeat of Iraq at the start of the 1990s could not persuade most Israelis that it was safe to make peace, then nothing will.

And if the shock of 9/11 could not persuade the present US elites that it was necessary to put real pressure on Israel for the sake of better relations with the Muslim world, then nothing will. To break the grip of the Israel lobby on the US political system would take a tremendous political upheaval, involving either a fundamental transformation of one of the two US political parties, or the replacement of one of them by a new party. This will happen one day—but most probably, not for a considerable time.

Partly in consequence, we can equally confidently predict that the USA will not achieve most of its key objectives in the Greater Middle East, whether in terms of stabilizing Iraq (already a lost cause) and Afghanistan; eliminating Islamist extremism as a serious threat; bringing about the acceptance of Israel by the Muslim states; or bringing a mixture of democracy and acceptance of US hegemony to Iran, Syria, and other states.

In part due to the Israel lobby, and its insistence that all enemies of Israel must also be enemies of the USA, it is likely that future Democratic administrations too will pursue a policy of hostility to many of the major states and forces in the Muslim world, rather than seeking serious compromises.

Moreover, when it comes to pursuing a new, 'softer', less militarized, and more flexible strategy in the global war on terror, the Democrats are also heavily influenced by two wider and interlinked factors: the enduring memory of how eventual Democratic opposition to the Vietnam War supposedly led to a patriotic backlash against the party which continues to this day; and the fact that many leading Democratic politicians, like Richard Holbrooke and Senator Joe Biden, are extremely hawkish in their basic attitudes.

So too are many leading Democratic foreign policy intellectuals, like Will Marshall, head of the Progressive Policy Institute (the think tank of the Democratic Leadership Council), and Michael O'Hanlon of the Brookings Institution (Kagan and O'Hanlon 2007). These views are reflected in the apparent consensus among many leading Democrats as of the spring of 2007 that the USA should not withdraw all its troops from Iraq, but should keep 20,000 or so in order to continue the fight against al-Qaeda, while somehow extricating itself from involvement in Iraq's civil war.

The ideas of being able to do both these things simultaneously in Iraq seems on the face of it absurd. Elsewhere, in the short to medium term at least the USA will not necessarily suffer any really shattering defeats as a result of this strategy, such as outright military catastrophe, an Islamist revolution, or another massive attack on the USA itself. All of these scenarios are possible and even probable at some time in the future, but it may be a long time, unless the USA itself precipitates a disaster by another military attack on a major state.

More likely however seems to be a kind of long-term holding action, in which the USA will suffer a constant drain on its manpower, resources, and international prestige, without coming under the kind of pressure that will force it from the region altogether, or draw it into a general regional war. The USA will not suffer too badly from the eventual withdrawal from Iraq, because the conflict between Shi'a and Sunni there will divide the Muslim countries of the Middle East and create a situation in which the USA can successfully play games of 'divide and rule'. Afghanistan will remain a running sore, but the

Taliban will never be able to gain strength enough to inflict really serious defeats on the US military, let alone chase them from the country. Disastrous scenarios—like a US war with Iran or intervention in Pakistan—do however exist, and will be examined briefly at the end of this section.

For the further future, one critical question for US strategy in the Middle East is whether the USA remains the only international superpower with major influence in the region, as it has been since the collapse of the Soviet Union (or even, by some estimates, since Egypt changed geopolitical sides under Anwar Sadat more than thirty years ago).

China is obviously the most likely contender for such a role, driven by thirst for oil; but India suffers the same thirst, and Russia retains a certain residual strength (especially through relations with Iran and Syria). Moscow seems to be working cautiously towards the possibility of an international gas cartel on the model of OPEC, though its ability actually to achieve this will depend on the spread of liquid natural gas technology, and a very considerable reduction in its cost as compared to the cost of fixed pipelines.

China and the Far East

If China does adopt this role, it will also have a severe impact on wider relations with the USA. By twenty years from now, these will in any case be largely shaped by competition for increasingly scarce resources, including not only oil and liquid natural gas but grain and paper.

This rivalry, and pressure from within the USA (especially on the Democratic Party) for tougher protectionist measures against Chinese imports, must be set against the strong impulse in the USA for good relations with China, the roots of which have been explored earlier in this chapter. Given the very great interdependence of the US and Chinese economies, and US fears of Chinese power, this impulse is likely to survive both of these countervailing factors, and the constant irritant of Taiwan.

In the case of North Korea, the Bush administration between 2001 and 2007 conducted what amounted to a 180-degree turn towards compromise with Pyongyang; and the key reasons for this were not only that due to the Iraq War the US military was badly overstretched, but even more importantly that the USA could in any case not conduct any successful policy vis-à-vis North Korea without the help of China.

Given the fact that militarily China appears most probably set to grow stronger and stronger over the next generation—and the possibility of a deeply provoked China backing North Korean aggression—it seems for the foreseeable future extremely unlikely that the USA would sanction a Taiwanese declaration of outright independence, or that Taiwan would make such a declaration without US sanction. Trade issues aside, hostile statements from the Democratic Party concerning China should not be taken too seriously. This is a game that both parties have played when in opposition, only pragmatically to abandon it as soon as they come to power.

By the same token, however, if US economic relations with China were to suffer really serious disruption, then latent hostilities could quickly rise to the surface. As has often been remarked, the present structure of US–Chinese economic relations creates a kind of 'Mexican stand-off', whereby neither side can seriously hurt the other without doing terrible damage to itself. If China seriously provokes the USA, then US protectionism will smash China's export economy. On the other hand, if the USA seriously provokes China, then China will cease to support the dollar and the US consumer boom, bringing the domestic US economy down in ruins.

The problem for the USA is that this equation is not stable, and whatever changes in China over time, the outcome may be unfavourable for the USA. If China continues to grow as at present, then sooner or later it will produce a class of middle-class consumers so large and prosperous that its economy will no longer depend on exports to the USA. At that point, Beijing will be able to use its ownership of US bonds and support for the dollar as a massive lever of influence.

If on the other hand China's economic growth comes to a halt as a result of some combination of domestic economic and political shocks, then equally China will no longer be able to support US finances in the same way, quite possibly leading to a deep US recession and a radical reduction in the US population's willingness to pay the costs of global hegemony. Fortunately, key officials on both sides have so far recognized the need to preserve stable relations—a striking contrast with the rhetorical bluster and immoderate ambition that characterizes US policy towards Russia and the lands of the former Soviet Union.

Russia and the former Soviet Union

So deep rooted is hostility to Russia in the US establishment that it is difficult to foresee any formal and public change of course in US strategy, for example a deal with Moscow on abandoning further NATO expansion in return for greater Russian support in the Middle East. This hostility is multifaceted, and often does not present itself, or even see itself, as hostility. The first source is of course the legacy of the Cold War, reflected not only in attitudes but also in a range of institutions with built-in antagonism to Russia and instinctive support for Russia's enemies.

These include semi-official media outlets like Radio Liberty/Radio Free Europe, and democracy promotion/propaganda outfits like Freedom House and the National Endowment for Democracy. Created to serve the struggle against the Soviet Union and its global communist agenda, these institutions have to a considerable extent simply continued this attitude since the end of the Cold War. This legacy naturally strongly affects older security figures like Vice-President Dick Cheney, whose entire being was shaped by the Cold War, but it has been passed down to younger generations. In any dispute involving Russia, no matter how distant, and no matter what its relationship to real US interests, their natural tendency is to take the other side.

Deliberate hostility to Russia, especially in the US Congress, is also encouraged by the role of east European and Baltic ethnic lobbies in shaping the attitudes and behaviour of senators and congressmen drawn from these ethnic groups, or in whose constituencies these ethnic groups are strongly represented. The disproportionate influence of ethnic and other lobbies,

due to the structure of the US political system and the apathy of the US public, has already been noted.

More unusual than this open and unremitting hostility is what might be called disappointed love, reflected in the attitudes of many US figures who genuinely see themselves as friends of Russia, like Dr Strobe Talbott, president of the Brookings Institution. This school of thought genuinely believed in the early and mid-1990s that the revolutions that had succeeded in Moscow's former satellites in eastern Europe could simply be extended to Russia itself, and that thereby Russia would at one and the same time undergo radical and successful free market reform, establish a successful democracy, and abandon its traditional ambitions for great power status to become an obedient subordinate of the USA on the international stage.

In what might be called a copulation of illusions, these beliefs were stoked by a briefly prominent collection of Russian liberal intellectuals and politicians, who succeeded in presenting themselves in the USA as the true voice of Russian democracy. Recruited into US organizations like the Brookings and the Carnegie Endowment, whether from conviction or opportunism, they told their new masters exactly what they wanted to hear, and to a considerable extent created a monopoly of 'legitimate' Russian opinion in Washington for one Russian point of view—one that was however detested by a large majority of ordinary Russians.

The combination of these factors has created a mood in the leaderships of both major parties which is very different indeed from the mood regarding China. This is to be seen in the push in 2006 for an offer of a NATO membership action plan to Ukraine, in the face of vehement Russian opposition and private threats of drastic retaliation; despite the fact that US military officials warned in private that the USA would not even be able to defend Ukraine against any future Russian aggression or internal revolution; and despite the fact that according to opinion polls, a large majority of the Ukrainian population did not even want to be part of NATO. This plan was eventually suspended, not because of opposition within the US establishment, but because of events on the ground in Ukraine, the collapse of the pro-Western 'Orange Coalition', and the return to power as prime minister of the pro-Russian Viktor Yanukovych.

The push for Ukrainian NATO membership in the middle of wars in Iraq and Afghanistan, and desperate overstretch of the US military, might seem to suggest that the US establishment is capable of any folly in its relations with Russia. However, the course of events with regard to Georgia suggests that things may not be as bad as that. So far, Washington, while unconditionally backing Georgia's position over Abkhazia and South Ossetia, and training and equipping the Georgian military, has also warned Georgia not to try to resolve the Abkhaz and Ossete disputes by force.

As Georgia, Ukraine, and Kyrgyzstan all demonstrate in their different ways, unlike in eastern Europe, America's allies in the former Soviet Union are mostly weak and badly divided internally, not least over the question of alignment with Russia or the West. In view of this, massive US distractions elsewhere, and what are likely to be the long-term effects of failure in Iraq and disappointment in Afghanistan on the US political psyche, it seems quite likely that while US rhetoric concerning Russia and its neighbours will remain hostile and ambitious, in practice US ambitions will in fact be scaled down. Rather than changing course in the former Soviet Union, the US ship of state will gradually run out of steam.

This may be the most the US political system can achieve, since any kind of 'grand bargain' with Russia (on the analogy of Nixon's and Kissinger's reconciliation with China) would be massively unpopular in the US political classes. The problem about such a future—as already noted with regard to US strategy towards Iran, Taiwan, and North Korea—is that the absence of an actual agreement with the rival power makes the relationship acutely vulnerable to shifts in perception or actions by third parties.

If the USA goes on preaching NATO enlargement, then the Russians will continue to be worried about this even if some wiser Russian analysts realize that the USA does not really mean it, and this will encourage Russian retaliation against US interests elsewhere. Moreover, there is always the risk that a desperate Georgian government will try to trap Washington into giving military support by carrying out some form of military *coup de main* against South Ossetia, in the hope that faced with Russian retaliation against Georgia, the USA will come to Georgia's aid. The USA most probably would not in fact send real military help, but nonetheless, Washington (in the shape of both party establishments) has painted itself into such a corner by its rhetorical support for Georgia that some form of harsh US response against Russia, and a deep crisis in US–Russian relations, would be inevitable.

Europe and the transatlantic relationship

Relations with Russia constitute one area of US foreign policy where the traditional transatlantic relationship with Europe continues to matter in Washington—not surprisingly, since the entire structure of transatlantic relations during the Cold War was built around the alliance against Moscow. In other areas, the real importance of relations with Europe does not necessarily correspond to the importance they are given in the language of the US media and the US political class.

In fact, economic relations and the issue of global warming aside, there is a certain degree of conscious or unconscious play-acting about certain aspects of the present—and probably future—relationship, which stem more from domestic political and even psychological needs than from objective international reality. On the European side, a mixture of factors stemming from the Second World War and Cold War continue to combine to produce a sense of dependence on the USA: memories of the self-inflicted horrors of Europe's modern history; residual (or in the case of the east Europeans, actual) fear of Russia; and acute consciousness of Europe's weakness and division. As long as the USA does not do something quite exceptionally wild, like invading Iraq, sullen European adherence can usually be taken for granted.

However, this does not add up to a willingness to make serious sacrifices for the sake of US strategy. With the partial exception of Britain, the military contributions of America's European allies in Iraq and Afghanistan have been so pathetic that one might wonder why the USA even bothered to go to the diplomatic effort of asking for them. Then again, however, it is equally true that the USA in recent years has never made a serious change of any important policy in order to win European support.

Rather, in the geopolitical and security fields (as opposed to the equally vital but at present largely separate ones of trade, international finance, and the environment), this relationship operates on both sides at the level of psychological comfort. The Europeans need America to reassure that that they have not been left alone in the wild wood of international geopolitics, from which most instinctively shrink (except for the British establishment, for its own post-colonial reasons).

The Americans (with the exception of the neo-conservatives and the ultra-nationalists of the Cheney–Rumsfeld type) need the Europeans to reassure them that they are still 'leaders of the Free World'. This is especially true in the 'liberal internationalist' school in the Democratic Party intellectual establishment, which in the run-up to the 2008 elections is doing its best to convince the American political classes (and perhaps most of all themselves) that the old centrality of the democratic West to US strategy is essentially sound and that it can be extended to strategy in the Middle East—and indeed to the whole world, through the idea of a global 'alliance of democracies'. In truth, Europe is practically worthless to the USA in the critical area of the Muslim world.

For a long time to come, therefore, US–European relations will be characterized by a version of an old Soviet joke: the Americans will pretend to listen to the Europeans, and the Europeans will pretend to work for the Americans. The transatlantic alliance will not collapse completely, but neither will it amount to anything much in real geopolitical terms. If, as seems likely, Afghanistan remains permanently unsettled, then sooner or later most European forces will be withdrawn, and NATO will have lost its last *raison d'être* other than hostility to Russia and job creation for otherwise unemployable military bureaucrats and staff officers.

Catastrophic scenarios

Most of the scenarios set out in this chapter have envisaged drift, overstretch, and relatively slow decline rather than disaster. However, in many areas of the international scene the potential for disaster does exist; and if in every individual case the odds are against this happening, if you add all of these possibilities together, then the chances of the USA avoiding all of them begin to seem much less promising. Yet, as noted, it seems impossible for the US establishment as at present configured to take the radical action which would be necessary to extricate the USA from any one of these potentially disastrous entanglements.

The potential disasters can be broken down into three main groups: actions by the USA itself; actions by third parties, with the USA drawn in; and global economic crisis, crippling US power and leading to the triumph of radical chauvinist and anti-American forces in key countries of the world. Of these, the greatest danger may come from what could be called the 1914 scenario: a situation in which the USA has committed itself rhetorically to some local state (Georgia, Taiwan, and above all Israel) which then carries out some highly provocative action, leading to a regional war in which the USA is forced to intervene on its behalf, just as Russia came to Serbia's help against Austria in July–August 1914.

The chief specific possibilities are the following:

- A US attack on Iran, leading to a drastic intensification of attacks on US troops in Iraq; the ruin of any hope for the stabilization of Afghanistan; a withdrawal of European and British forces from both countries, and a radical growth in the extent and effectiveness of anti-US terrorism;

- Another major terrorist attack against the continental United States, leading to a savage and indiscriminate US response that further radicalizes much of the Muslim world. Only such an attack could lead the USA voluntarily to embark on the invasion of another major Muslim state (as opposed to being eventually dragged into such an invasion as a result of the unintended consequences of more limited US actions; and only such an attack could lead to an atmosphere in which the US Congress and public would be prepared to accept the reintroduction of conscription;

- The internal collapse of a major Muslim state (such as Pakistan), leading to US intervention and another disastrous war of occupation;

- A new war between Israel and some or all of its neighbours, leading to Islamist revolution across the region;

- A Taiwanese declaration of independence, leading to a localized but economically horribly disruptive military conflict between the USA and China;

- A Georgian attack on South Ossetia, leading to Russian military retaliation, a severe crisis in US–Russian relations, and intensified Russian support for enemies of the USA elsewhere in the world;

- A global economic crisis, leading to a collapse of the US–Chinese economic relationship, and a surge in mutual hostility.

Conclusion

Any of the above scenarios would be capable of severely shaking, and even possibly shattering, the existing global order, and bringing US global power to an early end. Assuming that none of them takes place, then what we are likely to see instead will be a slower decline in US power. Afghanistan on top of Iraq will emphasize the limitations on US military power, and more states will therefore feel able to defy the USA without fearing US invasion. The Middle East will remain deeply troubled, and a constant drain on US resources and attention, but without any regional eruption dedicated to throwing the USA out altogether, and destroying Israel.

The rise of China will mean that more and more states in the developing world will look to China, rather than the USA, as their key partner. Russia will consolidate its predominance—though not outright control—in the area of the former Soviet Union, without the USA being able to do much about this. Europe, crippled by internal divisions, will make mostly impotent noises from the sidelines, neither really challenging nor really supporting US strategies.

If this is the future, then the USA may be able to handle the gradual decline of US hegemony without disastrous convulsions. The USA will never formally abandon its hegemonic ambitions, but over time will be drawn more and more to treat with other leading powers on a footing of equality. Increasing disasters as a result of global warming will make many of the seemingly vital problems of today seem less and less important, and will push major states towards closer cooperation.

This is the benign version of the decline of US hegemony and the future of US foreign policy. It must be said, however, that history offers few encouraging examples when it comes to the decline of empires. Most such experiences have been bloody and disastrous in the extreme, with the declining powers launching wars in an effort to re-establish their global or local predominance. This is true even if one takes the west European empires of Britain and France, ruled by west European democracies and with self-assigned civilizing missions not dissimilar to that of the United States. The Dutch and Belgian empires also came to an end amidst great bloodshed.

The end of all these empires involved terrible wars and convulsions; and only took place at all because all the countries concerned had previously been crippled by two world wars which exhausted the will of their metropolitan populations to pay or fight for empire, and undermined the entire claim of Europe to civilizational and racial superiority.

> **KEY QUOTES 22.1:** United States in a dangerous world

To protect our Nation and honor our values, the United States seeks to extend freedom across the globe by leading an international effort to end tyranny and to promote effective democracy.

(National Security Strategy 2006)

The characteristic American adjustment to the current foreign and domestic enigmas that confound our national myths has not been to abandon the myths but to reaffirm them.

(C. Vann Woodward)

It is possible to speak of a body of political ideas that constitutes 'Americanism' in a sense in which one can never speak of 'Britishism', 'Frenchism', 'Germanism', or Japaneseism'.

(Samuel Huntington)

America is becoming more cautious without becoming wiser.

(Anatol Lieven)

Iraq: Victory is not an option.

(Lt.-General (retd.) William Odom)

The [US] military is grossly under-resourced. It's a flippin' disaster . . . Their equipment is shot. It's coming apart. We are in a position of enormous strategic peril. What happens if the other shoe drops [in Iran or North Korea]?

(General (retd.) Barry McCaffrey)

The USA may do better, given its own anti-imperialist traditions, the even greater unwillingness of its population to fight, and the fact that with rare exceptions it is not trying to maintain a territorial empire in which it rules directly over other people. However, Israel—perceived by the Muslim world as identical to the USA—fulfils that bitterly unpopular and dangerous role on America's behalf; and while most Americans may not believe that they possess an empire, belief in America's preordained right to lead humanity is so deeply rooted in the culture of the establishment and most of the population as easily to match the popular imperialism of Europe in the past. Drifting along, in the style of the Democrats, may not be as openly reckless as steaming full speed ahead, in the style of the Bush administration. But given the number of icebergs about, it is still extremely dangerous.

? Questions

1. What are the principal ideological forces shaping US foreign policy?
2. What are the chief domestic political forces and structures shaping US foreign policy?
3. Why is the belief in America's mission to lead the world towards freedom so strong?
4. What are America's chief strengths and weaknesses when it comes to projecting power and influence?
5. Why is US international aid so low compared to America's previous record during the Cold War?
6. What is the role of domestic ethnic lobbies in shaping US foreign policy?
7. Why is the global war on terror likely to continue?
8. What would be the possible consequences of another massive terrorist attack on the USA?
9. What are the different possible future courses of US foreign policy with regard to China?
10. What role does Europe play in the US foreign policy mentality?
11. What are some possible future disasters that could accelerate the decline of US power?

Further Reading

Bacevich, Andrew J. (2004), *American Empire: The Realities and Consequences of US Diplomacy* (Cambridge, Mass.: Harvard University Press).

Holmes, Stephen (2007), *The Matador's Cape: America's Reckless Response to Terror* (Cambridge: Cambridge University Press).

Hunt, Michael H. (1987), *Ideology and US Foreign Policy* (New Haven: Yale University Press).

Ikenberry, G. John (2004), *American Foreign Policy: Theoretical Essays* (New York: Longman).

Lieven, Anatol (2004), *America Right or Wrong: An Anatomy of American Nationalism* (London: HarperCollins).

Marshall, Will (ed.) (2006), *With All our Might: A Progressive Strategy for Defeating Jihadism and Defending Liberty* (Totowa, NJ: Rowman and Littlefield).

Perle, Richard, and Frum, David (2004), *An End to Evil: How to Win the War on Terror* (New York: Ballantine Books).

Smith, Tony, and Leone, Richard C. (1995), *America's Mission* (Princeton: Princeton University Press).

Walt, Stephen M. (2005), *Taming American Power: The Global Response to US Primacy* (New York: W. W. Norton).

Endnotes

1. Retrenchment of this kind has for example been argued for by Layne (2006) and by Lieven and Hulsman (2006).

2. For the historical background to this belief, see Tuveson (1968); Hughes (2003: 19–41). For fictional versions of America as liberating and/or modernizing redeemer, see Mark Twain, *A Connecticut Yankee in King Arthur's Court* (1889) and the original TV series of *Star Trek*. Cf. also McDougall (1997: 81 ff.); Smith (1979).

3. For a discussion of this theme, see Lieven and Hulsman (2006).

4. Speech at the New America Foundation, Washington, DC, 18 Apr. 2007.

Visit the Online Resource Centre that accompanies this book for web links to accompany each chapter, and a range of other resources: www.oxfordtextbooks.co.uk/orc/cox_stokes/

References

Chapter 1

Chomsky, N. (2004), *Hegemony or Survival: America's Quest for Global Dominance* (New York: Henry Holt and Co.).

Elman, C. (1996), 'Horses for Courses: Why Not Neorealist Theories of Foreign Policy?', *Security Studies*, 6: 7–53.

Gholz, E., Press, D., and Sapolsky, H. (1997), 'Come Home, America: The Strategy of Restraint in the Face of Temptation', in M. Brown, O. Cote, S. Lynn–Jones, and S. Miller (eds.), *America's Strategic Choices*, rev. edn. (Cambridge, Mass.: MIT Press), 55–98.

Grieco, J. (1997), 'Realist International Theory and the Study of World Politics', in M. Doyle and G. J. Ikenberry (eds.), *New Thinking in International Relations Theory* (Boulder, Colo.: Westview Press), 163–201.

Halper, S., and Clarke, J. (2004), *America Alone: The Neoconservatives and the Global Order* (Cambridge: Cambridge University Press).

Hartz, L. (1991), *The Liberal Tradition in America* (San Diego: Harcourt Brace).

Ikenberry, G. J. (2000), 'America's Liberal Grand Strategy: Democracy and National Security in the Post-War Era', in M. Cox, G. J. Ikenberry, and T. Inoguchi (eds.), *American Democracy Promotion: Impulses, Strategies, and Impacts* (Oxford: Oxford University Press), 103–26.

—— (2002), 'Democracy, Institutions, and American Restraint', in G. J. Ikenberry (ed.), *America Unrivaled: The Future of the Balance of Power* (Ithaca, NY: Cornell University Press), 213–38.

Jervis, R. (1978), 'Cooperation under the Security Dilemma', *World Politics*, 30: 167–214.

Kennan, G. (1984), *American Diplomacy*, expanded edn. (Chicago: University of Chicago Press).

Kolko, G. (1969), *The Roots of American Foreign Policy: An Analysis of Power and Purpose* (Boston: Beacon Press).

Layne, C. (1994), 'Kant or Cant? The Myth of the Democratic Peace', *International Security*, 19: 5–49.

—— (2006), *The Peace of Illusions: American Grand Strategy from 1940 to the Present* (Ithaca, NY: Cornell University Press).

Lynn-Jones, S. (1995), 'Offense–Defense Theory and its Critics', *Security Studies*, 4: 660–91.

Mearsheimer, J. (2001), *The Tragedy of Great Power Politics* (New York: W. W. Norton).

Nau, H. (2002), *At Home and Abroad: Identity and Power in American Foreign Policy* (Ithaca, NY: Cornell University Press).

Pape, R. (2005), 'Soft Balancing against the United States', *International Security*, 30: 7–45.

Rose, G. (1998), 'Neoclassical Realism and Theories of Foreign Policy', *World Politics*, 51: 144–72.

Rosenau, J. (1971), *The Scientific Study of Foreign Policy* (New York: The Free Press).

Russett, B. (1993), *Grasping the Democratic Peace: Principles for a Post-Cold War World* (Princeton: Princeton University Press).

Smith, T. (1994), *America's Mission: The United States and the Worldwide Struggle for Democracy in the Twentieth Century* (Princeton: Princeton University Press).

Snyder, J. (1991), *Myth of Empire: Domestic Politics and International Ambition* (Ithaca, NY: Cornell University Press).

Walt, S. (2002), 'The Enduring Relevance of the Realist Tradition', in I. Katznelson and H. V. Milner (eds.), *Political Science: The State of the Discipline* (New York: W. W. Norton), 199–230.

Waltz, K. (1979), *Theory of International Politics* (New York: Random House).

—— (1996), 'International Politics is Not Foreign Policy', *Security Studies*, 6: 54–7.

Wendt, A. (1992), 'Anarchy is what States Make of it: The Social Construction of Power Politics', *International Organization*, 46/2: 391–425.

White House (1995), *A National Security Strategy of Engagement and Enlargement* (Washington, DC: The White House).

Williams, W. (1972), *The Tragedy of American Diplomacy* (London: W. W. Norton).

Wohlforth, W. (2002), 'US Strategy in a Unipolar World', in G. John Ikenberry (ed.), *America Unrivaled: The Future of the Balance of Power* (Ithaca, NY: Cornell University Press), 98–118.

Zakaria, F. (1992), 'Realism and Domestic Politics: A Review Essay', *International Security*, 17: 177–98.

Chapter 2

Deudney, D. (1995), 'The Philadelphian System: Sovereignty, Arms Control, and Balance of Power in the American States Union, ca.1787–1861', *International Organization*, 49/2 (Spring): 191–228.

—— (2007), *Bounding Power: Republican Security Theory from the Polis to the Global Village* (Princeton: Princeton University Press).

Hartz, L. (1991), *The Liberal Tradition in America: An Interpretation of American Political Thought since the Revolution*, 2nd Harvest/HBJ edn. (San Diego: Harcourt Brace Jovanovich).

Hendrickson, D. C. (2003), *Peace Pact: The Lost World of the American Founding* (Lawrence, Kan.: University Press of Kansas).

Huntington, S. P. (2004), *Who Are We? The Challenges to America's National Identity* (New York: Simon & Schuster).

Johnson, C. (2004), *The Sorrows of Empire: Militarism, Secrecy, and the End of the Republic* (New York: Henry Holt).

Katzenstein, P., and Keohane, R. O. (2007), *Anti-Americanism in World Politics* (Ithaca, NY: Cornell University Press).

Kinzer, S. (2006), *Overthrow: America's Century of Regime Change from Hawaii to Iraq* (New York: Times Books).

Kramer, P. A. (2006), 'Race-Making and Colonial Violence in the US Empire: The Philippine–American War as Race War', *Diplomatic History*, 30/2: 169–210.

LaFeber, W. (1963), *The New Empire: An Interpretation of American Expansion, 1860–1898* (Ithaca, NY: Cornell University Press).

Lieven, A. (2004), *America Right or Wrong: An Anatomy of American Nationalism* (New York: Oxford University Press).

Lipset, S. M. (1996), *American Exceptionalism: A Double-Edged Sword* (New York: W. W. Norton).

Mead, W. R. (2001), *Special Providence: American Foreign Policy and How it Changed the World* (New York: Routledge).

Morone, J. A. (2003), *Hellfire Nation: The Politics of Sin in American History* (New Haven: Yale University Press).

Tocqueville, A. de (1988), *Democracy in America*, trans. G. Lawrence, 1st Perennial Library edn. (New York: Harper & Row).

Chapter 3

Adams, B. (1902), *The New Empire* (London: Macmillan).

Ferguson, N. (2004), *Colossus: The Price of America's Empire* (New York: Penguin Press).

Gardner, L. (1984), *Safe for Democracy: The Anglo-American Response to Revolution, 1913–1923* (New York: Oxford University Press).

——et al. (1976), *Creation of the American Empire*, 2 vols. (Chicago: Rand McNally College Publishing Co.).

Jefferson, T. (1903), *The Writings of Thomas Jefferson*, ed. A. A. Lipscomb, 20 vols. (Washington, DC: US Government Printing Office).

Johnson, C. (2004), *The Sorrows of Empire: Militarism, Secrecy, and the End of the Republic* (New York: Metropolitan Books).

Record, J. (2006), *The Specter of Munich: Reconsidering the Lessons of Appeasing Hitler* (Dulles, Va.: Potomac Books).

Sherwin, M. (1975), *A World Destroyed* (New York: Alfred K. Knopf).

Stimson, H. L., and Bundy, M. (1949), *On Active Service in Peace and War* (New York: Scribner's).

Tocqueville, A. de (1948), *Democracy in America*, 2 vols. (New York: Alfred A. Knopf).

Van Alstyne, R. (1960), *The Rising American Empire* (Chicago: Quadrangle Books).

Chapter 4

Ambrose, S., and Brinkley, D. (1997), *Rise to Globalism: American Foreign Policy since 1938*, 8th edn. (Harmondsworth: Penguin).

Barnet, R. (1972), *Intervention and Revolution: The United States in the Third World* (New York: New American Library).

Campbell, D. (1998), *Writing Security: United States Foreign Policy and the Politics of Identity* (Manchester: Manchester University Press).

Carew, A. (1987), *Labour under the Marshall Plan: The Politics of Productivity and the Marketing of Management Science* (Manchester: Manchester University Press).

Colás, A., and Saull, R. G. (eds.) (2005), *The War on Terrorism and the American 'Empire' after the Cold War* (London: Routledge).

Cox, M. (1984), 'Western Capitalism and the Cold War System', in M. Shaw (ed.), *War, State and Society* (London: Macmillan).

Cox, R. (1987), *Production, Power, and World Order: Social Forces in the Making of History* (New York: Columbia University Press).

Crockatt, R. (1995), *The Fifty Years War: The United States in World Politics, 1941–1991* (London: Routledge).

Cumings, B. (1981/1990), *The Origins of the Korean War*, 2 vols. (Princeton: Princeton University Press).

Feis, H. (1967), *Churchill, Roosevelt, Stalin: The War They Waged and the Peace They Sought* (Princeton: Princeton University Press; 1st pub. 1957).

——(1970), *From Trust to Terror: The Onset of the Cold War, 1945–1950* (London: Blond).

Gaddis, J. L. (1987), *The Long Peace: Enquiries into the History of the Cold War* (New York: Oxford University Press).

——(1997), *We Now Know: Rethinking Cold War History* (Oxford: Clarendon Press).

Halliday, F. (1986), *The Making of the Second Cold War* (London: Verso).

——(1994), *Rethinking International Relations* (Basingstoke: Macmillan).

Horowitz, D. (1967), *From Yalta to Vietnam: American Foreign Policy in the Cold War* (Harmondsworth: Penguin).

——(1969), *Imperialism and Revolution* (London: Allen Lane).

Kennan, G. (1947), 'The Sources of Soviet Conduct', *Foreign Affairs*, 25/4 (July): 566–82.

——(1967), *Memoirs, 1925–1950* (New York: Pantheon Books).

——(1984), *American Diplomacy* (Chicago: University of Chicago Press).

Kissinger, H. (1961), *The Necessity for Choice: Prospects of American Foreign Policy* (New York: Harper and Brothers).

——(1994), *Diplomacy* (New York: Simon & Schuster).

Kolko, G. (1969), *The Roots of American Foreign Policy: An Analysis of Power and Purpose* (Boston: Beacon Press).

——and Kolko, J. (1972), *The Limits of Power: The World and United States Foreign Policy* (New York: Harper and Row).

LaFeber, W. (1989), *The American Age: US Foreign Policy at Home and Abroad—1750 to the Present* (New York: W. W. Norton).

Lebow, R. N. (1994), 'The Long Peace, the End of the Cold War, and the Failure of Realism', *International Organization*, 48/2: 249–77.

Leffler, M. (1994), *The Specter of Communism: The United States and the Origins of the Cold War, 1917–1953* (New York: Hill & Wang).

——and Painter, D. (eds.) (1994), *Origins of the Cold War: An International History* (London: Routledge).

Lippman, W. (1947), *The Cold War: A Study in US Foreign Policy* (London: Hamilton).

Lundestad, G. (1998), *'Empire' by Invitation: The United States and European Integration, 1945–1997* (Oxford: Oxford University Press).

Mearsheimer, J. (2001), *The Tragedy of Great Power Politics* (New York: W. W. Norton).

Morgenthau, H. (1951), *In Defense of the National Interest* (New York: Alfred A. Knopf).

——(1969), *A New Foreign Policy for the United States* (New York: Frederick A. Praeger).

Paterson, T. (1988), *Meeting the Communist Threat: Truman to Reagan* (New York: Oxford University Press).

Prados, J. (2004), '40th Anniversary of the Gulf of Tonkin Incident', *National Security Archive* (August), available at www.gwu.edu/~nsarchiv/NSAEBB/NSAEBB132/essay.htm.

Public Papers of the Presidents of the United States: Harry S. Truman, 1947 (1963) (Washington, DC: Government Printing Office).

Risse-Kappen, T. (1991–2), 'Did "Peace through Strength" End the Cold War?', *International Organization*, 16/1: 162–88.

Rupert, M. (1995), *Producing Hegemony: The Politics of Mass Production and American Global Power* (Cambridge: Cambridge University Press).

Saull, R. G. (2001), *Rethinking Theory and History in the Cold War* (London: Frank Cass).

——(2007), *The Cold War and After* (London: Pluto Press).

Schlesinger, A. Jr. (1967), 'Origins of the Cold War', *Foreign Affairs*, 46: 22–52.

Sheehan, N. (1971), *The 'Pentagon Papers': As Published by the New York Times* (London: Routledge Kegan Paul).

Waltz, K. (1979), *Theory of International Politics* (Reading, Mass.: Addison-Wesley).

Weinberger, C. (1990), *Fighting for Peace: Seven Critical Years in the Pentagon* (New York: Michael Joseph).

Young, M. (1991), *The Vietnam Wars, 1945–1990* (New York: HarperCollins).

Chapter 5

Albright. M. (2003), *Madam Secretary: A Memoir* (London: Macmillan).

Asmus, R. (2002), *Opening NATO's Door: How the Alliance Remade Itself for a New Era* (New York: Columbia University Press).

Bacevich, A. J. (1996), 'The Impact of the New Populism', *Orbis*, 40: 31–43.

Berger, S. R. (1998), 'Challenges Approaching the Twenty-First Century', in R. L. Hutchings (ed.), *At the End of the American Century: America's Role in the Post-Cold War World* (Washington, DC: Woodrow Wilson Center Press).

Bert, W. (1997), *The Reluctant Superpower: United States Policy in Bosnia, 1991–95* (Basingstoke: Macmillan).

Beschloss, M. R., and Talbott, S. (1993), *At the Highest Levels: The Inside Story of the End of the Cold War* (Boston: Little, Brown).

Brinkley, D. (1997), 'Democratic Enlargement: The Clinton Doctrine', *Foreign Policy*, 106: 111–27.

Brown, S. (1994), *The Faces of Power* (New York: Columbia University Press).

Bush, G. and Scowcroft, B. (1998), *A World Transformed* (New York: Alfred A. Knopf).

Chomsky, N. (1994), *World Orders, Old and New* (London: Pluto Press).

Christopher, W. (1995), 'America's Leadership, America's Opportunity', *Foreign Policy*, 98: 6–28.

Clark, I. (2001), *The Post-Cold War Order: The Spoils of Peace* (Oxford: Oxford University Press).

Clinton, W. J. (2005), *My Life* (London: Arrow Books).

Crabb, C. V., Sarieddine, L. S., and Antizzo, G. J. (2001), *Charting a New Diplomatic Course: Alternative Approaches to America's Post-Cold War Foreign Policy* (Baton Rouge, La.: Louisiana State University Press).

Daalder, I. H. (1996), 'Knowing When to Say No: the Development of US Policy for Peacekeeping', in W. Durch (ed.), *UN Peacekeeping, American Policy, and the Uncivil Wars of the 1990s* (New York: St Martin's Press).

DiPrizio, R. C. (2002), *Armed Humanitarians: US Interventions from Northern Iraq to Kosovo* (Baltimore: Johns Hopkins University Press).

Doyle, M. W. (1995), 'On the Democratic Peace', *International Security*, 19: 164–84.

Dumbrell, J. W. (2002), 'Was there a Clinton Doctrine? President Clinton's Foreign Policy Reconsidered', *Diplomacy and Statecraft*, 13: 43–56.

Fisher, L. (1995), *Presidential War Power* (Lawrence, Kan.: University Press of Kansas).

Freedman, L., and Karsh, E. (1994), *The Gulf Conflict, 1990–91: Diplomacy and War in the New World Order* (London: Faber and Faber).

Fukuyama, F. (1989), 'The End of History', *National Interest*, 16: 61–84.

Gray, J. (1998), 'Global Utopias and Clashing Civilizations: Misunderstanding the Present', *International Affairs*, 74: 149–64.

Halberstam, D. (2003), *War in a Time of Peace: Bush, Clinton and the Generals* (London: Bloomsbury).

Haney, P. J., and Vanderbush, W. (1999), 'The Role of Interest Groups in US Foreign Policy: The Case of the Cuban American National Foundation', *International Studies Quarterly*, 43: 341–61.

Hendrickson, R. C. (2002), *The Clinton Wars: The Constitution, Congress, and War Powers* (Nashville: Vanderbilt University Press).

Hoffman, S. (2002), 'Clash of Globalizations', *Foreign Affairs*, 81: 76–91.

Hunter, R. E. (1992), 'Starting at Zero: US Foreign Policy for the 1990s', in B. Roberts (ed.), *US Foreign Policy after the Cold War* (Cambridge, Mass.: MIT Press).

Hurst, S. (1999), *The Foreign Policy of the Bush Administration: In Search of a New World Order* (London: Cassell).

Jentleson, B. W. (1992), 'The Pretty Prudent Public: Post-Vietnam American Opinion on the Use of Military Force', *International Studies Quarterly*, 36: 49–74.

Kennedy, P. (1998), *The Rise and Fall of Great Powers: Economic Change and Military Conflict from 1500–2000* (Harmondsworth: Penguin).

Kiger, P. J. (1997), *Squeeze Play: The United States, Cuba and the Helms Burton Act* (Washington, DC: Center for Public Integrity).

Kirschten, R. (1995), 'Ethnics Resurging', *National Journal*, 25 Feb.: 484–6.

Kolb, C. (1994), *White House Daze* (New York: Free Press).

Krauthammer, C. (1991), 'The Unipolar Moment', *Foreign Affairs*, 70: 23–33.

Kull, S. (1995–6), 'What the Public Knows that Washington Doesn't', *Foreign Policy*, 101: 102–15.

Lake, A. (1994), 'Confronting Backlash States', *Foreign Affairs*, 73: 45–55.

McCormick, J. M. (2005), *American Foreign Policy and Process* (Belmont, Calif.: Thomson Wadsworth).

McHenry, D. F. (1994), 'Post-Cold War Foreign Policy: Toward Shared Responsibility', in D. Yankelovich and I. M. Destler (eds.), *Beyond the Beltway: Engaging the Public in US Foreign Policy* (New York: W. W. Norton).

Maclean, G. A. (2006), *Clinton's Foreign Policy in Russia: From Deterrence and Isolation to Democratization and Engagement* (Aldershot: Ashgate).

McNamara, R. S. (1989), *Out of the Cold* (New York: Pantheon).

Maechling, C. (1990), 'Washington's Illegal Invasion', *Foreign Policy*, 79: 113–31.

Marsden, L. (2005), *Lessons from Russia: Clinton and US Democracy Promotion* (Aldershot: Ashgate).

Melanson, R. A. (1996), *American Foreign Policy since the Vietnam War: The Search for Consensus from Nixon to Clinton* (Armonk, NY: M. E. Sharpe).

9/11 Commission Report (2004), *The 9/11 Commission Report: Final Report of the National Commission on the Terrorist Attacks upon the United States* (New York: W. W. Norton).

Nordlinger, E. A. (1995), *Isolationism Reconfigured* (Princeton: Princeton University Press).

Nye, J. S. (1991), *Bound to Lead: The Changing Nature of American Power* (New York: Basic Books).

Ornstein, N. J. (1994), 'Congress in the Post-Cold War World', in D. Yankelovich and I. M. Destler (eds.), *Beyond the Beltway: Engaging the Public in US Foreign Policy* (New York: W. W. Norton).

Paarlberg, R. L. (1995), *Leadership Abroad Begins at Home: US Foreign Economic Policy after the Cold War* (Washington, DC: Brookings Institution).

Petras, J., and Morley, M. (1995), *Empire or Republic? American Global Power and Domestic Decay* (New York: Routledge).

Polsby, N. (1990), contribution to 'IGS Panel Assesses the Bush Administration', *Public Affairs*, Sept.

Public Papers of the Presidents of the United States: George Bush, 1992–3, book II (1993) (Washington, DC: US Government Printing Office).

Rielly, J. E. (1995), *American Public Opinion and US Foreign Policy, 1995* (Chicago: Chicago Council on Foreign Relations).

Ritter, S. (2005), *Iraq Confidential: The Untold Story of the Intelligence Conspiracy to Undermine the United Nations and Overthrow Saddam Hussein* (London: I. B. Tauris).

Rosner, J. D. (1995–6), 'The Know-Nothings Know Something', *Foreign Policy*, 101: 116–29.

Ross, D. (2004), *The Missing Peace: The Inside Story of the Fight for Middle East Peace* (New York: Farrar, Straus and Giroux).

Russett, B. (1993), *Grasping the Democratic Peace* (Princeton: Princeton University Press).

Steel, R. (1995), 'The Domestic Core of Foreign Policy', *Atlantic Monthly*, June: 85–92.

Talbott, S. (2003), *The Russia Hand: A Memoir of Presidential Diplomacy* (New York: Random House).

Tenet, G. (2007), *At the Center of the Storm: My Years at the CIA* (New York: HarperCollins).

Tucker, R. W., and Hendrickson, D. C. (1992), *The Imperial Temptation* (New York: Council on Foreign Relations).

Walt, S. (2000), 'Two Cheers for Clinton's Foreign Policy', *Foreign Affairs*, 79: 63–79.

Zelikow, P. D., and Rice, C. (1995), *Germany United and Europe Transformed: A Study in Statecraft* (Cambridge, Mass.: Harvard University Press).

Chapter 6

Amnesty International (2007), 'War on Terror', www.amnestyusa.org/waronterror/index.do.

Andrew, C. (1996), *For the President's Eyes Only: Secret Intelligence and the American Presidency from Washington to Bush* (London: HarperCollins).

Arnold, T. C. (2006), 'Executive Power, the War on Terrorism, and the Idea of Rights', *Politics & Policy*, 34/4: 670–88.

Brzezinski, M. (2005), *Fortress America: On the Front Lines of Homeland Security* (New York: Bantam).

Burns, J. M. (1973), *Presidential Government: The Crucible of Leadership* (Boston: Houghton Mifflin).

Bush, G. W. (2002), 'President Bush, President Havel Discuss Iraq, NATO', Press Conference by President Bush and President Havel of Czech Republic, 20 Nov., www.whitehouse.gov/news/releases/2002/11/20021120-1.html.

Corwin, E. S. (1957), *The President: Office and Powers 1787–1957* (New York: New York University Press).

Dahl, R. (1964), *Congress and Foreign Policy* (New York: W. W. Norton).

Fisher, L. (2003), 'Deciding on War against Iraq: Institutional Failures', *Political Science Quarterly*, 118/3: 389–410.

——(2007), 'Invoking Inherent Powers: A Primer', *Presidential Studies Quarterly*, 37/1: 1–22.

Franck, T. M., and Weisband, E. (1979), *Foreign Policy by Congress* (New York: Oxford University Press).

Gordon, M. R. (2007), *Cobra II: The Inside Story of the Invasion and Occupation of Iraq* (New York: Vintage).

Hamdan v. *Rumsfeld* (2006) 126 S. Ct 2749.

Hargrove, E. C. (1974), *The Power of the Modern Presidency* (New York: Knopf).

Hart, J. (1995), *The Presidential Branch: From Washington to Clinton*, 2nd edn. (Chatham, NJ: Chatham House).

Henkin, L. (1990), *Constitutionalism, Democracy and Foreign Affairs* (New York: Columbia University Press).

Hetherington, M. J., and Nelson, M. (2003), 'Anatomy of a Rally Effect: George W. Bush and the War on Terrorism', *PS: Political Science and Politics*, 36/1: 37–42.

Hinckley, B. (1994), *Less Than Meets the Eye: Foreign Policy Making and the Myth of the Assertive Congress* (Chicago: University of Chicago Press).

Inderfurth, K. F., and Johnson, L. (eds.) (2004), *Fateful Decisions: Inside the National Security Council* (New York: Oxford University Press).

Jeffreys-Jones, R. (1998), *The CIA and American Democracy*, 2nd edn. (New Haven: Yale University Press).

Johnson, L. (1991), *America's Secret Power: The CIA in a Democratic Society* (New York: Oxford University Press).

——(2004), 'The Contemporary Presidency: Presidents, Lawmakers, and Spies: Intelligence Accountability in the United States', *Presidential Studies Quarterly*, 34/4: 828–37.

Kernell, S. (2007), *Going Public: New Strategies of Presidential Leadership* (Washington, DC: CQ Press).

Koh, H. H. (1988), 'Why the President (Almost) Always Wins in Foreign Affairs: Lessons of the Iran-Contra Affair', *Yale Law Journal*, 97/7: 1255–342.

Lindsay, J. M. (1994), *Congress and the Politics of US Foreign Policy* (Baltimore: Johns Hopkins University Press).

McDonald, F. (1985), *Novus Ordo Seclorum: The Intellectual Origins of the Constitution* (Lawrence, Kan.: University Press of Kansas).

Mueller, J. E. (1973), *War, Presidents, and Public Opinion* (New York: John Wiley).

——(2005), 'The Iraq Syndrome', *Foreign Affairs*, 84/6: 44–54.

Nathan, J. A., and Oliver, J. K. (1987), *Foreign Policy Making and the American Political System*, 2nd edn. (Boston: Little, Brown).

Ornstein, N., and Mann, T. (eds.) (2000), *The Permanent Campaign and its Future* (Washington, DC: AEI Press).

Pious, R. M. (1979), *The American Presidency* (New York: Basic Books).

——(2007), 'Inherent War and Executive Powers and Prerogative Politics', *Presidential Studies Quarterly*, 37/1: 66–84.

Prize Cases (1862) 67 US 635.

Rakove, J. N. (1982), *The Beginnings of National Politics: An Interpretive History of the Continental Congress* (Baltimore: Johns Hopkins University Press).

——(1997), *Original Meanings: Politics and Ideas in the Making of the Constitution* (New York: Vintage).

Ricks, T. E. (2006), *Fiasco: The American Military Adventure in Iraq* (New York: Penguin).

Ripley, R. E., Lindsay, J. M., and Farrell, T. (1993), *Congress Resurgent: Foreign and Defense Policy on Capitol Hill* (Ann Arbor: University of Michigan Press).

Schlesinger, A. M., Jr. (1974), *The Imperial Presidency* (London: Andre Deutsch).

Spanier, J. (1981), 'Introduction: Congress and the Presidency: The Weakest Link in the Policy Process', in J. Spanier and J. Nogee (eds.), *Congress, the Presidency and Foreign Policy* (New York: Pergamon).

Sundquist, J. L. (1981), *The Decline and Resurgence of Congress* (Washington, DC: Brookings).

Tocqueville, Alexis de (1948), *Democracy in America* (New York: Alfred A. Knopf).

United States v. *Curtiss-Wright Export Corp.* (1936) 299 US 304.

Yoo, J. (2005), *The Powers of War and Peace* (Chicago: University of Chicago Press).

Chapter 7

BBC (2002), 'Afghan Bombing "Most Accurate Ever"', BBC News, 10 Apr., www.news.bbc.co.uk/1/hi/world/south_asia/1921614.stm.

Cowell, A. (2007), 'US Talks with Britain on Installing Missile Defense System', *New York Times*, 24 Feb.

Deutch, J. (2005), 'A Nuclear Posture for Today', *Foreign Affairs*, Jan.–Feb.: 49–60.

Gordon, M. R., and Trainor, B. E. (2007), *Cobra II: The Inside Story of the Invasion and Occupation of Iraq* (New York: Vintage).

McNamara, R. S. (2005), 'Apocalypse Soon', *Foreign Policy*, May–June: 29–35.

Powell, C. (1992–3), 'US Forces: The Challenge Ahead', *Foreign Affairs*, Winter: 32–45.

Rice, C. (2000), 'Promoting the National Interest', *Foreign Affairs*, Jan.–Feb.: 45–62.

Risen, J. (2006), *State of War: The Secret History of the CIA and the Bush Administration* (New York: Free Press).

Woodward, B. (2004), *Plan of Attack: The Definitive Account of the Decision to Invade Iraq* (New York: Simon & Schuster).

——(2006), *State of Denial: Bush at War*, Part III (New York: Simon & Schuster).

Chapter 8

Abramowitz, M. (2006), 'Bush Says "America Loses" under Democrats', *Washington Post*, 30 Oct.

Agnew, J. (1987), *The United States in the World-Economy* (Cambridge: Cambridge University Press).

Alberts, S. (2004), 'Candidates Address "Security Moms": Bush Warns Kerry would "Invite Disaster"', *The Gazette* (Montreal), 19 Oct.

Bensel, R. (1984), *Sectionalism and American Political Development, 1880–1980* (Madison: University of Wisconsin Press).

Burnham, W. D. (1970), *Critical Elections and the Mainsprings of American Politics* (New York: W. W. Norton).

Bush, G. W. (2000), acceptance speech, Republican National Convention, 3 Aug., *Washington Post*, 4 Aug.

Cook, C. (2007), 'Opinion Gulf', *National Journal*, 17 Apr., at http://nationaljournal.com/cook.htm.

Edsall, T. B. (2006), *Building Red America: The New Conservative Coalition and the Drive for Permanent Power* (New York: Basic Books).

Jacobson, G. C. (2007), *A Divider, Not a Uniter: George W. Bush and the American People* (New York: Pearson).

Key, V. O. (1964), *Politics, Parties, and Pressure Groups* (New York: Thomas Y. Crowell).

Kupchan, Charles A., and Trubowitz, Peter L. (2007), 'Grand Strategy for a Divided America', *Foreign Affairs*, 86 (July–Aug.): 71–8.

Markusen, A. (1987), *Regions: The Economics and Politics of Territory* (Totowa, NJ: Rowman & Littlefield).

Narizny, K. (2007), *The Political Economy of Grand Strategy* (Ithaca, NY: Cornell University Press).

Schattschneider, E. E. (1960), *The Semisovereign People: A Realist's View of Democracy in America* (New York: Holt, Rinehart and Winston).

Silva, M. (2006), 'Cheney Back on the Campaign Trail as GOP's "Attack Dog"', *Chicago Tribune*, 18 Aug.

Silverstone, S. A. (2004), *Divided Union: The Politics of War in the Early American Republic* (Ithaca, NY: Cornell University Press).

Trubowitz, P. (1998), *Defining the National Interest: Conflict and Change in American Foreign Policy* (Chicago: University of Chicago Press).

——and Mellow, N. (2005), 'Going Bipartisan: Politics by Other Means', *Political Science Quarterly*, 120 (Fall): 433–54.

Chapter 9

Aday, S., Livingston, S. L., and Herbert, M. (2005), 'Embedding the Truth: A Cross-cultural Analysis of Objectivity and Television Coverage of the Iraq War', *Press/Politics*, 10/1: 3–21.

Aldrich, J. H., Sullivan, J. L., and Borgida, E. (1989), 'Foreign Affairs and Issue Voting: Do Presidential Candidates "Waltz before a Blind Audience?"', *American Political Science Review*, 83: 123–41.

Almond, G. (1950), *The American People and Foreign Policy* (New York: Harcourt Brace).

Althaus, S. L. (2003), 'When News Norms Collide, Follow the Lead: New Evidence for Press Independence', *Political Communication*, 20/3: 381–414.

Baum, M. (2003), *Soft News Goes to War: Public Opinion and American Foreign Policy in the New Media Age* (Princeton: Princeton University Press).

Bennett, W. L. (1990), 'Toward a Theory of Press–State Relations in the United States', *Journal of Communication*, 40/2: 103–25.

——Lawrence, R., and Livingston, S. (2006), 'None Dare Call it Torture: Indexing and the Limits of Press Independence in the Abu Ghraib Scandal', *Journal of Communication*, 56/3: 467–85.

Cohen, B. (1973), *The Public's Impact on Foreign Policy* (Boston: Little, Brown).

Domke, D. (2004), *God Willing? Political Fundamentalism in the White House: The War on Terror and the Echoing Press* (London: Pluto Press).

Entman, R. (1991), 'Framing US Coverage of International News: Contrasts in Narratives of the KAL and Iran Air Incidents', *Journal of Communication*, 41/4: 6–27.

——(2000), 'Declarations of Independence', in B. L. Nacos, R. Y. Shapiro, and I. Isernia (eds.), *Decision-Making in a Glass House: Mass Media, Public Opinion and American and European Foreign Policy in the 21st Century* (London: Rowman and Littlefield Publishers).

——(2004), *Projections of Power: Framing News, Public Opinion and US Foreign Policy* (Chicago: University of Chicago Press).

'Forum on Chomsky' (2003), *Review of International Studies*, 29/4: 551–620.

Foyle, D. (1999), *Counting the Public In: Presidents, Public Opinion and Foreign Policy* (New York: Columbia University Press).

Gilboa, E. (1998), 'Media Diplomacy: Conceptual Divergence and Application', *Press/Politics*, 3/3: 56–75.

——(2005). 'The CNN Effect: The Search for a Communication Theory of International Relations', *Political Communication*, 22/1: 27–44.

Gowing, N. (1994), 'Real-Time Coverage of Armed Conflicts and Diplomatic Crises: Does it Pressure or Distort Foreign Policy Decisions?', working paper (Joan Shorenstein Barone Center on the Press, Politics and Public Policy at Harvard University).

Hallin, D. (1986), *The Uncensored War* (Berkeley and Los Angeles: University of California Press).

Herman, E., and Chomsky, N. (1988), *Manufacturing Consent: The Political Economy of the Mass Media* (New York: Pantheon).

Hoge, J. (1994), 'Media Pervasiveness', *Foreign Affairs*, 73: 136–44.

Holsti, O. R. (1992), 'Public Opinion and Foreign Policy: Challenges to the Almond–Lippman Consensus', *International Studies Quarterly*, 36/4: 439–66.

Iyengar, S., and Kinder, D. R. (1987), *News That Matters: Television and American Public Opinion* (Chicago: University of Chicago Press).

——and Simon, A. (1994), 'News Coverage of the Gulf Crisis and Public Opinion: A Study of Agenda-Setting, Priming and Framing', in W. L. Bennett and D. P. L. Paletz (eds.), *Taken by*

Storm: The Media, Public Opinion and US Foreign Policy in the Gulf War (Chicago: University of Chicago Press).

Kennan, G. F. (1993), 'Somalia, Through a Glass Darkly', *New York Times*, 30 Sept.

Lang, K., and Lang, G. E. (2004), 'Noam Chomsky and the Manufacture of Consent for US Foreign Policy', *Political Communication*, 21/1: 93–101.

Lawrence, R. (2000), *The Politics of Force* (Berkeley and Los Angeles: University of California Press).

Lippman, W. (1922), *Public Opinion* (New York: Free Press paperbacks; Simon & Schuster).

——(1955), *Essays in the Public Philosophy* (Boston: Little, Brown).

Livingston, S. (1997) 'Clarifying the CNN Effect: An Examination of Media Effects According to Type of Military Intervention', Research Paper R-18 June (Cambridge, Mass.: Joan Shorenstein Barone Center on the Press, Politics and Public Policy at Harvard University).

——and Bennett, W. L. (2003), 'Gatekeeping, Indexing and Live-Event News: Is Technology Altering the Construction of News?', *Political Communication*, 20/4: 363–80.

——and Riley, J. (1999), 'Television Pictures in Multilateral Policy Decision Making: An Examination of the Decision to Intervene in Eastern Zaire in 1996', paper presented at the British International Studies Annual Conference, University of Manchester, 21–3 Dec.

McCombs, M. E., and Shaw, D. L. (1972), 'The Agenda-Setting Function of the Press', *Public Opinion Quarterly*, 36: 176–87.

Mandelbaum, M. (1994), 'The Reluctance to Intervene', *Foreign Policy*, 95: 3–8.

Milbank, D., and Deane, C. (2003), 'Hussein Link Lingers in Many Minds', *Washington Post*, 6 Sept.: A01.

Mueller, J. E. (1973), *War, Presidents and Public Opinion* (New York: John Wiley).

Nixon, R. (1978), *The Memoirs* (New York: Grosset and Dunlap).

Nye, J. (1990), *Bound to Lead: The Changing Nature of American Power* (New York: Public Affairs).

——(1999), 'Redefining the National Interest', *Foreign Affairs*, 78/4: 22–35.

Robinson, P. (2002), *The CNN Effect: The Myth of News, Foreign Policy and Intervention* (London: Routledge).

Shaw, M. (1996), *Civil Society and Media in Global Crises* (London: St Martin's Press).

Taylor, P. M. (2006), 'Strategic Communications and the Relationship between Government "Information" Activities in the Post 9/11 World', *Journal of Information Warfare*, 5/3: 1–25.

Wheeler, N. (2000), *Saving Strangers: Humanitarian Intervention in International Society* (Oxford: Oxford University Press).

Wittkopf, E. R. (1990), *Faces on Internationalism: Public Opinion and American Foreign Policy* (Durham, NC: Duke University Press).

Wolfsfeld, G. (1997), *The Media and Political Conflict* (Cambridge: Cambridge University Press).

Woodward, B. (2004), *Plan of Attack* (London: Pocket Books).

Chapter 10

Agathangelou, A., and Ling, L. (2004), 'Power, Borders, Security, Wealth: Lessons of Violence and Desire from September 11', *International Studies Quarterly*, 48/3: 517–38.

Allison, G., and Zelikow, P. (1999), *Essence of Decision: Explaining the Cuban Missile Crisis*, 2nd edn. (New York: Longman).

Anderson, B. (1991), *Imagined Communities: Reflections on the Origins and Spread of Nationalism* (London: Verso).

Art, R. (1991), 'A Defensible Defense: America's Grand Strategy after the Cold War', *International Security*, 15/4: 5–53.

Aspin, L. (1992), 'An Approach to Sizing American Conventional Forces for the Post–Soviet Era', 24 Jan., memorandum.

Barkawi, T. (2004), 'On the Pedagogy of "Small Wars"', *International Affairs*, 80/1: 19–37.

Barthes, R. (1973), *Mythologies*, trans. A. Lavers (St Albans: Paladin).

BBC News (2000), 'US Rebrands its Rogues Gallery', 19 June, available at www.news.bbc.co.uk/1/hi/world/middle_east/797950.stm (accessed 13 July 2007).

Bennis, P. (2003), *Before and After: US Foreign Policy and the September 11th Crisis* (Moreton in Marsh: Arris Publishing).

Blum, W. (2003), *Killing Hope: US Military and CIA Interventions since World War II* (London: Zed Books).

Boot, M. (2002), 'The Case for American Empire: The Most Realistic Response to Terrorism is for America to Embrace its Imperial Role', *Weekly Standard*, 15 Oct., available at www.weeklystandard.com/content-public-articles-000-000-000-318qpvmc.asp (accessed 13 July 2007).

Bush, G. H. W. (1990a), 'Remarks at the Aspen Institute Symposium in Aspen Colorado', 2 Aug., repr. in *Public Papers of the Presidents of the United States: George Bush, 1990*, book II (Washington, DC: Government Printing Office, 1991).

——(1990b), 'Address before a Joint Session of the Congress on the Persian Gulf Crisis and the Federal Budget Deficit', 11 Sept., repr. in *Public Papers of the Presidents of the United States: George Bush, 1990*, book II (Washington, DC: Government Printing Office, 1991).

Bush, G. W. (2001a), 'Remarks Following a Meeting with the National Security Team', 12 Sept., *Weekly Compilation of Presidential Documents*, available at http://frwebgate.access.gpo.gov/cgi-bin/getdoc.cgi?dbname=2001_presidential_documents&docid=pd17se01_txt-16 (accessed 13 July 2007).

——(2001b), 'Remarks by the President upon Arrival', 16 Sept., available at www.whitehouse.gov/news/releases/2001/09/20010916-2.html (accessed 13 July 2007).

——(2001c), 'Address to a Joint Session of Congress and the American People', 20 Sept., White House, Office of the Press Secretary, available at www.whitehouse.gov/news/releases/2001/09/print/20010920-8.html (accessed 13 July 2007).

——(2001d), 'President Bush and Russian President Putin Discuss Progress', 21 Oct., available at www.whitehouse.gov/news/releases/2001/10/20011021-3.html (accessed 13 July 2007).

——(2001e), 'President Bush Speaks to United Nations', 10 Nov., available at www.whitehouse.gov/news/releases/2001/11/20011110-3.html (accessed 13 July 2007).

——(2002a), 'State of the Union Address', 29 Jan., available at www.whitehouse.gov/news/releases/2002/01/print/20020129-11.html (accessed 13 July 2007).

——(2002b), 'Alliance of Freedom Being Tested by "New and Terrible Dangers"', 23 Nov., available at www.whitehouse.gov/news/releases/2002/11/20021123-5.html (accessed 30 July 2007).

——(2003), 'Operation Iraqi Freedom: President Bush Addresses the Nation', 19 Mar., available at www.whitehouse.gov/news/releases/2003/03/print/20030319-17.html (accessed 23 July 2007).

——(2004), 'President's Remarks in "Focus on Education with President Bush" Event', 27 Sept., available at www.whitehouse.gov/news/releases/2004/09/20040927-4.html (accessed 13 July 2007).

——(2005a), 'President Discusses Second Term Accomplishments and Priorities', 3 Aug., available at www.whitehouse.gov/news/releases/2005/08/20050803.html (accessed 30 July 2007).

——(2005b), 'President Commemorates Veterans Day, Discusses War on Terror', 11 Nov., available at www.whitehouse.gov/news/releases/2005/11/20051111-1.html (accessed 13 July 2007).

——(2006a), 'President Discusses Global War on Terror at Kansas State University', 23 Jan., available at www.whitehouse.gov/news/releases/2006/01/20060123-4.html (accessed 13 July 2007).

——(2006b), 'President Bush Addresses American Legion National Convention', 31 Aug., available at www.whitehouse.gov/news/releases/2006/08/20060831-1.html (accessed 30 July 2007).

Campbell, D. (1998), *Writing Security: United States Foreign Policy and the Politics of Identity*, rev. edn. (Minneapolis: University of Minnesota Press).

Carter, J. (1980), 'Address to the Nation on Afghanistan', 4 Jan., available at www.millercenter.virginia.edu/scripps/digitalarchive/speeches/spe_1980_0104_carter (accessed 13 July 2007).

——(2002), 'Discourse Analysis and the "Linguistic Turn"', *European Political Science*, 2/1, available at www.essex.ac.uk/ecpr/publications/eps/onlineissues/autumn2002/research/carver.htm (accessed 13 July 2007).

Chapman, J. (2000), *License to Thrill: A Cultural History of the James Bond Films* (New York: Cornell University Press).

Chomsky, N. (1991), 'The US and the Gulf Crisis', in H. Bresheeth and N. Yuval-Davis (eds.), *The Gulf War and the New World Order* (London: Zed Books).

——(2003), *Understanding Power: The Indispensable Chomsky* (New York: Vintage).

Clinton, W. J. (1993), 'Address to the Nation on Somalia', 7 Oct., *Weekly Compilation of Presidential Documents*, available at http://frwebgate4.access.gpo.gov/cgi-bin/waisgate.cgi?WAISdocID=30452724457+0+0+0&WAISaction=retrieve (accessed 13 July 2007).

——(1999), 'Remarks by the President to the Veterans of Foreign Wars on Kosovo', 13 May, *Weekly Compilation of Presidential Documents*, available at http://frwebgate3.access.gpo.gov/cgi-bin/waisgate.cgi?WAISdocID=3047394619+3+0+0&WAISaction=retrieve (accessed 13 July 2007).

Cohn, C. (1987) 'Sex and Death in the Rational World of Defense Intellectuals', *Signs*, 12/4: 687–718.

Collins, J., and Glover, R. (2002), *Collateral Language: A User's Guide to America's New War* (New York: New York University Press).

Connolly, W. E. (1991), *Identity/Difference: Democratic Negotiations of Political Paradox* (Ithaca, NY: Cornell University Press).

Cox, M. (1984), 'Western Capitalism and the Cold War System', in M. Shaw (ed.), *War, State and Society* (New York: St Martin's Press).

Dean, R. D. (2001), *Imperial Brotherhood: Gender and the Making of Cold War Foreign Policy* (Amherst, Mass.: University of Massachusetts Press).

Doty, R. L. (1993), 'Foreign Policy as Social Construction: A Post-positivist Analysis of US Counterinsurgency Policy in the Philippines', *International Studies Quarterly*, 37/3: 297–320.

——(1996), *Imperial Encounters: The Politics of Representation in North–South Relations* (Minneapolis: University of Minnesota Press).

Drinnon, R. (1990), *Facing West: The Metaphysics of Indian Hating and Empire Building* (New York: Schocken Books).

Eisenhower, D. D. (1961), 'Farewell to the Nation', 17 Jan., reprinted in S. Melman, *Pentagon Capitalism: The Political Economy of War* (New York: McGraw-Hill, 1970).

Enloe, C. (1996), 'Margins, Silences and Bottom Rungs: How to Overcome the Underestimation of Power in the Study of International Relations', in S. Smith, K. Booth, and M. Zalewski (eds.), *International Theory: Positivism and Beyond* (Cambridge: Cambridge University Press).

Entman, R. M. (2004), *Projections of Power: Framing News, Public Opinion, and US Foreign Policy* (Chicago: University of Chicago Press).

Farmanfarmaian, A. (1992), 'Sexuality in the Gulf War: Did You Measure Up?', *Genders*, 13: 1–29.

Foucault, M. (1972), *The Archaeology of Knowledge and the Discourse on Language*, trans. A. M. Sheridan Smith (New York: Pantheon Books).

——(1980), 'Truth and Power', in C. Gordon (ed.), *Power/Knowledge: Selected Interviews and Other Writings, 1972–1977*, trans. C. Gordon, L. Marshall, J. Mepham, and K. Soper (New York: Pantheon).

Gaddis, J. L. (1982), *Strategies of Containment: A Critical Appraisal of Postwar American National Security Strategy* (Oxford: Oxford University Press).

Gans-Boriskin, R., and Tisinger, R. (2005), 'The Bushlet Administration: Terrorism and War on *The West Wing*', *Journal of American Culture*, 28/1: 100–13.

Griffin, P. (2007), 'Sexing the Economy in a Neo-liberal World: Neo-liberal Discourse and the (Re)production of Heteronormative Heterosexuality', *British Journal of Politics and International Relations*, 9/2: 220–38.

Grossberg, L. (1986), 'On Postmodernism and Articulation: An Interview with Stuart Hall', *Journal of Communication Inquiry*, 10/2: 45–60.

Hall, S. (1997a), 'Introduction', in S. Hall (ed.), *Representation: Cultural Representations and Signifying Practices* (London: SAGE Publications).

——(1997b), 'The Work of Representation', in S. Hall (ed.), *Representation: Cultural Representations and Signifying Practices* (London: SAGE Publications).

Hallin, D. (1989), *The 'Uncensored' War: The Media and Vietnam* (Berkeley and Los Angeles: University of California Press).

Hardt, M. and Negri, A., (2000), *Empire* (Cambridge, Mass.: Harvard University Press).

Hearn, J. (2004), 'From Hegemonic Masculinity to the Hegemony of Men', *Feminist Theory*, 5/1: 49–72.

Herman, E. S., and Chomsky, N. (1988), *Manufacturing Consent: The Political Economy of the Mass Media* (New York: Pantheon Books).

Herz, J. (1951), *Political Realism and Political Idealism: A Study in Theories and Realities* (Chicago: University of Chicago Press).

Hollis, M., and Smith, S. (1990), *Explaining and Understanding International Relations* (Oxford: Clarendon Press).

Hooper, C. (2001), *Manly States: Masculinities, International Relations and Gender Politics* (New York: Columbia University Press).

Horowitz, D. (2004a), 'How the Left Undermined America's Security before 9/11', 10 Sept., available at www.frontpage-mag.com/Articles/ReadArticle.asp?ID=15021 (accessed 13 July 2007).

——(2004b), 'Unholy Alliance: How the Left Supports the Terrorists at Home', 24 Sept., available at www.frontpagemag.com/Articles/ReadArticle.asp?ID=15221 (accessed 13 July 2007).

——(2006), *The Professors: The 101 Most Dangerous Academics in America* (Washington, DC: Regnery Publishing).

Huntington, S. (1993), 'The Clash of Civilizations', *Foreign Affairs*, 72/3: 22–49.

——(1996), *The Clash of Civilizations and the Remaking of World Order* (New York: Simon & Schuster).

Ignatieff, M. (2003), *Empire Lite: Nation Building in Bosnia, Kosovo, Afghanistan* (London: Vintage).

Independent (2007), 'How Brown Distances Himself from Blair' 12 July: 7.

Jackson, R. (2005), *Writing the War on Terrorism: Language, Politics and Counter-Terrorism* (Manchester: Manchester University Press).

Jeffords, S. (1986), 'The New Vietnam Films: Is the Movie Over?', *Journal of Popular Film and Television*, 13/3: 186–95.

——(1989), *The Remasculinization of America: Gender and the Vietnam War* (Bloomington, Ind.: University of Indiana Press).

Johnson, L. B. (1964), 'The Tonkin Gulf Incident', 5 Aug., *Department of State Bulletin*, available at www.pbs.org/wgbh/amex/presidents/36_1_johnson/psources/ps_tonkin.html (accessed 13 July 2007).

Kelly, J. (1995), '"Amicable Divorce" Could Turn Nasty, Experts Say', *USA Today*, 22 Nov., 12A.

Kennedy, J. F. (1961), 'Radio and Television Report to the American People on the Berlin Crisis', 25 July, available at www.jfklibrary.org/Historical+Resources/Archives/Reference+Desk/Speeches/JFK/003POF03BerlinCrisis07251961.htm (accessed 13 July 2007).

——(1962), 'Arms Quarantine of Cuba: The Soviet Military Build-up', television and radio address, 22 Oct., *Vital Speeches of the Day*, 29/3 (15 Nov.): 66–8.

Kimmel, M. (2003), 'Globalization and its Mal(e)contents: The Gendered Moral and Political Economy of Terrorism', *International Sociology*, 18/3: 603–20.

Klare, M. (1996), *Rogue States and Nuclear Outlaws: America's Search for a New Foreign Policy* (New York: Hill & Wang).

Kline, S. (2004), 'The Culture War Gone Global: "Family Values" and the Shape of US Foreign Policy', *International Relations*, 18/4: 453–66.

Laclau, E., and Mouffe, C. (1987), 'Post-Marxism without Apologies', *New Left Review*, 166, available at http://newleftreview.org/?page=article&view=817 (accessed 13 July 2007).

————(2001), *Hegemony and Socialist Strategy: Towards a Radical Democratic Politics*, 2nd edn. (London: Verso).

Laffey, M., and Weldes, J. (2004), 'Methodological Reflections on Discourse Analysis', *Qualitative Methods*, 2/1: 28–30.

Linklater, A. (1998), *The Transformation of Political Community: Ethical Foundations of the Post-Westphalian Era* (Cambridge: Polity Press).

Lutz, C. A., and Collins, J. L. (1993), *Reading National Geographic* (Chicago: University of Chicago Press).

Mair, J. (2002), 'Rewriting the "American Dream": Postmodernism and Otherness in *Independence Day*', in Z. Sardar and S. Cubitt (eds.), *Aliens R Us: The Other in Science Fiction Cinema* (London: Pluto Press).

Mallaby, S. (2002), 'The Reluctant Imperialist: Terrorism, Failed States, and the Case for American Empire', *Foreign Affairs*, 81/2: 2–7.

Mayer, J. (2007), 'Whatever it Takes', *New Yorker*, 19 Feb., available at http://newyorker.com/printables/fact/070219fa_fact_mayer (accessed 13 July 2007).

Milliken, J. (1999), 'The Study of Discourse in International Relations: A Critique of Research and Methods', *European Journal of International Relations*, 5/2: 225–54.

Morgenthau, H. J. (1993), *Politics among Nations: The Struggle for Power and Peace*, brief edn., rev. K. W. Thompson (New York: McGraw-Hill).

Nayak, M. (2006), 'Orientalism and "Saving" US State Identity after 9/11', *International Feminist Journal of Politics*, 8/1: 42–61.

Niva, S. (1998), 'Tough and Tender: New World Order Masculinity and the Gulf War', in M. Zalewski and J. Parpart (eds.), *The 'Man' Question in International Relations* (Boulder, Colo.: Westview Press).

Nixon, R. M. (1969), 'Vietnamization', 3 Nov., repr. in *Public Papers of the Presidents: Richard Nixon, 1969* (Washington, DC: Government Printing Office, 1971).

Ó Tuathail, G., and Agnew, J. (1992), 'Geopolitics and Discourse: Practical Geopolitical Reasoning in American Foreign Policy', *Political Geography*, 11/2: 192–3.

Panitch, L., and Gindin, S. (2004), 'Global Capitalism and American Empire', available at www.alternatives.ca/IMG/pdf/Panitch_Gindin,pdf (accessed 23 Nov. 2007).

Peterson, V. S. (2003), *A Critical Rewriting of the Global Political Economy: Integrating Reproductive, Productive and Virtual Economies* (London: Routledge).

——and Runyan, A. S. (1999) *Global Gender Issues* (Boulder, Colo.: Westview Press).

Project for the New American Century (n.d.), available at www.newamericancentury.org/ (accessed 30 July 2007).

Purvis, T., and Hunt, A. (1993), 'Discourse, Ideology, Discourse, Ideology, Discourse, Ideology . . .', *British Journal of Sociology*, 44/3: 473–99.

Reagan, R. (1986), 'Transcript of the President's Speech', 16 Mar., *New York Times*, 17 Mar.: A12.

Record, J. (2007) 'The Use and Abuse of History: Munich, Vietnam and Iraq', *Survival*, 49/1: 163–80.

Rice, C. (2000) 'Campaign 2000: Promoting the National Interest', *Foreign Affairs*, 79/1, available at www.foreignaffairs.org/20000101faessay5/condoleezza-rice/campaign-2000-promoting-the-national-interest.html (accessed 13 July 2007).

Rogin, M. (1987), *Ronald Reagan, the Movie and Other Episodes in Political Demonology* (Berkeley and Los Angeles: University of California Press).

——(1998), *Independence Day, or How I Learned to Stop Worrying and Love the Enola Gaye* (London: British Film Institute).

Rosenau, J. (1968), 'National Interest', in D. L. Sills (ed.), *International Encyclopedia of the Social Sciences*, vol. i (New York: Macmillan).

Rotberg, R. I. (2002), 'The New Nature of Nation-State Failure', *Washington Quarterly*, 25/3: 85–96.

Said, E. W. (1991), 'Thoughts on a War: Ignorant Armies Clash by Night', in P. Bennis and M. Moushabeck (eds.), *Beyond the Storm: A Gulf Crisis Reader* (New York: Olive Branch Press).

Shaheen, J. G. (2001), *Reel Bad Arabs: How Hollywood Vilifies a People* (New York: Olive Branch Press).

Shapiro, M. J. (1986), 'Metaphor in the Philosophy of the Social Sciences', *Cultural Critique*, 2: 191–214.

——(1992), *Reading the Postmodern Polity: Political Theory as Textual Practice* (Minneapolis: University of Minnesota Press).

Sharp, J. (2000), *Condensing the Cold War: Reader's Digest and American Identity* (Minneapolis: University of Minnesota Press).

Shepherd, L. J. (2006), 'Veiled References: Constructions of Gender in the Bush Administration Discourse on the Attacks in Afghanistan post-9/11', *International Feminist Journal of Politics*, 8/1: 19–41.

Smith, A. D. (1991), 'The Nation: Invented, Imagined, Reconstructed?', *Millennium*, 20/3: 353–68.

Stokes, D. (2005), 'The Heart of Empire? Theorising US Empire in an Era of Transnational Capitalism', *Third World Quarterly*, 26/2: 217–36.

Stuckey, M. E. (1991), *The President as Interpreter-in-Chief* (Chatham, NJ: Chatham House Publishers).

Terry, J. J. (2005), *US Foreign Policy in the Middle East: The Role of Lobbies and Special Interest Groups* (Ann Arbor: Pluto Press).

Truman, H. S. (1947), 'Address to a Joint Session of Congress', 12 Mar., available at www.hbci.com/~tgort/truman.htm (accessed 13 July 2007).

——(1950), 'Radio and Television Report to the American People on the Situation in Korea', 1 Sept., repr. in *Public Papers of the Presidents: Harry S. Truman, 1950* (Washington, DC: Government Printing Office, 1965).

Weldes, J. (1999a), *Constructing National Interests: The United States and the Cuban Missile Crisis* (Minneapolis: University of Minnesota Press).

——(1999b), 'Going Cultural: *Star Trek*, State Action and Popular Culture', *Millennium*, 28/1: 117–34.

——(1999c), 'The Cultural Production of Crises: US Identity and Missiles in Cuba', in J. Weldes, M. Laffey, H. Gusterson, and R. Duvall (eds.), *Cultures of Insecurity: States, Communities, and the Production of Danger* (Minneapolis: University of Minnesota Press).

——Laffey, M., Gusterson, H., and Duvall, R. (1999), 'Introduction: Constructing Insecurity', in J. Weldes, M. Laffey, H. Gusterson, and R. Duvall (eds.), *Cultures of Insecurity: States, Communities, and the Production of Danger* (Minneapolis: University of Minnesota Press).

Wendt, A. (1992), 'Anarchy is What States Make of It: The Social Construction of Power Politics', *International Organization*, 46/2: 391–425.

White House (2002), *The National Security Strategy of the United States of America*, available at www.whitehouse.gov/nsc/nss.pdf (accessed 13 July 2007).

Williams, W. A. (2004 [1962]), *The Tragedy of American Diplomacy*, new edited edn. (New York: W. W. Norton).

Zalewski, M. (2000), *Feminism after Postmodernism: Theorising through Practice* (London: Routledge).

Chapter 11

Bacevich, A. J. (2005), 'The Realist Persuasion', *Boston Globe*, 6 Nov., www.boston.com/news/globe/ideas/articles/2005/11/06/the_realist_persuasion/?page=full.

Bard, M. G. (1994), 'The Influence of Ethnic Interest Groups on American Middle East Policy', in E. R. Wittkopf (ed.), *The Domestic Sources of American Foreign Policy: Insights and Evidence* (New York: St Martin's Press).

Brown, L. C. (1984), *International Politics and the Middle East: Old Rules, Dangerous Game* (Princeton: Princeton University Press).

Bush, G. H. W. (1990), 'Toward a New World Order', The President Addresses a Joint Session of Congress, 11 Sept., http://se2.isn.ch/serviceengine/FileContent?serviceID=23&fileid=02FE0D5C-D6BD-7295-48EB-F1D4393A71A7&lng=en.

Bush, G. W. (2002a), 'The President's State of the Union Address', 29 Jan., www.whitehouse.gov/news/releases/2002/01/20020129-11.html.

——(2002b), *The National Security Strategy of the United States of America*, www.whitehouse.gov/nsc/nss.html.

——(2003), 'Remarks by the President of the United States at the 20th Anniversary of the National Endowment for Democracy', United States Chamber of Commerce, Washington, DC, 6 Nov.

Cox, R. (1986), 'Social Forces, States and World Orders: Beyond International Relations Theory', in R. O. Keohane (ed.), *NeoRealism and its Critics* (New York: Columbia University Press).

Dershowitz, A. (2006), 'Debunking the Newest—and Oldest—Jewish Conspiracy: A Reply to the Mearsheimer–Walt "Working Paper"', www.ksg.harvard.edu/research/working_papers/facultyresponses.htm.

Dodge, T. (2005a), *Iraq's Future: The Aftermath of Regime Change* (London: International Institute for Strategic Studies and Routledge).

——(2005b), *Inventing Iraq: The Failure of Nation Building and a History Denied* (New York: Columbia University Press).

——(2006), 'Iraq: The Contradictions of Exogenous State Building in Historical Perspective', *Third World Quarterly*, 27/1: 187–200.

——(2007), 'The Causes of US Failure in Iraq', *Survival*, 49/1: 85–106.

Gaddis, J. L. (1987), *The Long Peace: Inquiries into the History of the Cold War* (Oxford: Oxford University Press).

——(2002). 'A Grand Strategy of Transformation', *Foreign Policy*, Nov.–Dec., www.foreignpolicy.com/issue_novdec_2002/gaddis.html.

Halliday, F. (1994), *Rethinking International Relations* (Basingstoke: Macmillan).

Harvey, D. (2003), *The New Imperialism* (Oxford: Oxford University Press).

Hudson, M. (2005), 'The United States and the Middle East', in L. Fawcett (ed.), *International Relations of the Middle East* (Oxford: Oxford University Press), 283–305.

Keohane, R. O. (1986), 'Realism, NeoRealism and the Study of World Politics', in R. O. Keohane (ed.), *NeoRealism and its Critics* (New York: Columbia University Press).

Khalidi, R. (2004), *Resurrecting Empire: Western Footprints and America's Perilous Path in the Middle East* (London: I. B. Tauris).

Little, D. (2002), *American Orientalism: The United States and the Middle East since 1945* (London: I. B. Tauris).

Mamdani, M. (2004), *Good Muslim, Bad Muslim: America, the Roots of the Cold War and the Roots of Terror* (New York: Three Leaves Press).

Massing, M. (2006), 'The Storm over the Israel Lobby', *New York Review of Books*, 53/10: 1–5.

Mearsheimer, J. (2005). 'Hans Morgenthau and the Iraq War: Realism versus Neo-conservatism', www.opendemocracy.net/debates/article.jsp?id=3&debateId=77&articleId=2522.

——and Walt, S. (2006), 'The Israeli Lobby', *London Review of Books*, 28/6, 23 Mar., www.lrb.co.uk/v28/n06/mear01_.html.

Morgenthau, H. J. (1985), *Politics among Nations: The Struggle for Power and Peace* (New York: Alfred A. Knopf).

Packer, G. (2005), *Assassins' Gate: America in Iraq* (New York: Farrar, Straus and Giroux).

Ruggie, J. G. (1998), *Constructing the World Polity: Essays on International Institutionalization* (London: Routledge).

Shlaim, A. (1995), *War and Peace in the Middle East: A Concise History* (Harmondsworth: Penguin).

Wendt, A. (1999), *Social Theory of International Politics* (Cambridge: Cambridge University Press).

Westad, O. A. (2005), *The Global Cold War: Third World Interventions and the Making of our Times* (Cambridge: Cambridge University Press).

Wilson, W. (1918), 'Fourteen Point Speech', 8 Jan., http://net.lib.byu.edu/~rdh7/wwi/1918/14points.html.

Chapter 12

Albright, M. K. (1998), Statement to the North Atlantic Council, Brussels, 8 Dec.

Allen, D., and Smith, M. (1983), 'Europe, the United States and the Middle East: A Case Study in Comparative Policy-Making', *Journal of Common Market Studies*, 22/2 (Dec.): 125–46.

————(1989), 'Western Europe in the Atlantic System of the 1980s: Towards a New Identity?', in S. Gill (ed.), *Atlantic Relations: Beyond the Reagan Era* (Brighton: Harvester/Wheatsheaf).

Andrews, D. (ed.) (2005), *The Atlantic Alliance under Stress: US–European Relations after Iraq* (Cambridge: Cambridge University Press).

Baker, J. A., III (1989), Address to the Berlin Press Club, 12 Dec.

Bush, G. W. (2005), Speech in Concert Noble, Brussels, 21 Feb.

Calleo, D. (1970), *The Atlantic Fantasy: The US, NATO and Europe* (Baltimore: Johns Hopkins University Press).

——(1987), *Beyond American Hegemony: The Future of the Western Alliance* (New York: Basic Books).

Cleveland, H. van B. (1966), *The Atlantic Idea and its European Rivals* (New York: McGraw-Hill for the Council on Foreign Relations).

Cooper, R. (1968), *The Economics of Interdependence: Economic Policy in the Atlantic Community* (New York: McGraw-Hill for the Council on Foreign Relations).

Cromwell, W. (1978), 'Europe and the "Structure of Peace"', *Orbis*, 22/1: 11–36.

DePorte, A. (1986), *Europe between the Superpowers: The Enduring Balance*, 2nd edn. (New Haven: Yale University Press).

Eagleburger, L. (1984), Speech to the National Newspaper Association, Washington, DC, 7 Mar.

Fursdon, E. (1980), *The European Defence Community: A History* (London: Macmillan).

Gompert, D., and Larrabee, S. (1997), *America and Europe: A Partnership for a New Era* (Cambridge: Cambridge University Press).

Gordon, P., and Shapiro, J. (2004), *Allies at War: America, Europe, and the Crisis over Iraq* (New York: McGraw-Hill).

Grosser, A. (1982), *The Western Alliance: European–American Relations since 1945* (New York: Vintage Books).

Heller, F., and Gillingham, J. (eds.) (1996), *The United States and the Integration of Europe: Legacies of the Postwar Era* (New York: St Martin's Press).

Hocking, B., and Smith, M. (1997), *Beyond Foreign Economic Policy: The United States, the Single European Market and the Changing World Economy* (London: Pinter/Cassell).

Hoffmann, S. (1978), *Primacy or World Order: American Foreign Policy since the Cold War* (New York: McGraw-Hill).

Hogan, M. (1987), *The Marshall Plan: America, Britain, and the Reconstruction of Western Europe, 1947–1952* (Cambridge: Cambridge University Press).

Howorth, J. (2000), *European Integration and Defence: The Ultimate Challenge?* (Paris: WEU Institute for Security Studies).

——(2005), 'From Security to Defence: The Evolution of the CFSP', in C. Hill and M. Smith (eds.), *International Relations and the European Union* (Oxford: Oxford University Press).

Joffe, J. (1987), *The Limited Partnership: Europe, the United States, and the Burdens of Alliance* (Cambridge, Mass.: Ballinger).

Kagan, R. (2003), *Of Paradise and Power: America and Europe in the New World Order* (New York: Knopf).

Kennedy, John F. (1962), Address on the Goal of an Atlantic Partnership, Philadelphia, 4 July.

Kissinger, Henry A. (1973), Address to the Associated Press Annual Luncheon, New York, 23 Apr.

Krause, L. (1968), *European Economic Integration and the United States* (Washington, DC: Brookings Institution).

Lindberg, T. (ed.) (2005), *Beyond Paradise and Power: Europe, America and the Future of a Troubled Partnership* (London: Routledge).

Lindstrom, G. (ed.) (2003), *Shift or Rift? Assessing EU–US Relations after Iraq* (Paris: EU Institute for Security Studies).

Lundestad, G. (1998), *'Empire' by Integration: The United States and European Integration, 1945–1997* (Oxford: Oxford University Press).

McGuire, S., and Smith, M. (2008), *The European Union and the United States: Competition and Convergence in the World Arena* (Basingstoke: Palgrave/Macmillan).

Marshall, G. C. (1947), Address at the Commencement Exercises of Harvard University, Cambridge, Mass., 5 June.

Milward, A. (1984), *The Reconstruction of Western Europe, 1945–1951* (London: Methuen).

Peterson, J. (1996), *Europe and America in the 1990s: Prospects for Partnership*, 2nd edn. (London: Routledge).

Philippart, E., and Winand, P. (eds.) (2001), *Ever-Closer Partnership: Policy-Making in US–EU Relations* (Brussels: PIE/Peter Lang).

Pollack, M. (2003), 'Unilateral America: Multilateral Europe?', in M. Pollack and J. Peterson (eds.), *Europe, America, Bush: Transatlantic Relations in the Twenty-First Century* (London: Routledge).

——and Peterson, J. (eds.) (2003), *Europe, America, Bush: Transatlantic Relations in the Twenty-First Century* (London: Routledge).

——and Shaffer, G. (eds.) (2001), *Transatlantic Governance in the Global Economy* (Lanham, Md.: Rowman and Littlefield).

Rees, G. W. (2006), *Transatlantic Counter-Terrorism Cooperation: The New Imperative* (London: Routledge).

Rosecrance, R. (ed.) (1976), *America as an Ordinary Country: US Foreign Policy and the Future* (Ithaca, NY: Cornell University Press).

Rumsfeld, D. H. (2003), Briefing at the Foreign Press Center, Washington, DC, 22 Jan.

Sloan, S. (2005), *NATO, the European Union, and the Atlantic Community: The Transatlantic Bargain Challenged*, 2nd edn. (Lanham, Md.: Rowman and Littlefield).

Smith, M. (2000), 'The United States and Western Europe: Empire, Alliance and Interdependence', in A. McGrew (ed.), *The United States in the Twentieth Century: Empire* (London: Hodder and Stoughton).

——(2004), 'Between Two Worlds? The European Union, the United States and World Order', *International Politics*, 41/1: 96–117.

——(2007), 'The European Union and International Order: European and Global Dimensions', *European Foreign Affairs Review*, 12/4: 437–56.

——and Woolcock, S. (1993), *The United States and the European Community in a Transformed World* (London: Pinter for the Royal Institute of International Affairs).

————(1994), 'Learning to Cooperate: The Clinton Administration and the European Union', *International Affairs*, 70/3: 459–76.

Steffenson, B. (2005), *Managing EU–US Relations: Actors, Institutions and the New Transatlantic Agenda* (Manchester: Manchester University Press).

Treverton, G. (1985), *Making the Alliance Work: The United States and Western Europe* (London: Macmillan).

——(ed.) (1992), *The Shape of the New Europe* (New York: Council on Foreign Relations).

Winand, P. (1993), *Eisenhower, Kennedy and the United States of Europe* (London: Macmillan).

Zaborowski, M. (ed.) (2006), *Friends Again? EU–US Relations after the Crisis* (Paris: EU Institute for Security Studies).

Zielonka, J. (2006), *Europe as Empire* (Oxford: Oxford University Press).

Chapter 13

Council on Foreign Relations Task Force (2006), *Russia's Wrong Direction: What the United States Can and Should Do*, March.

Goldgeier, J., and McFaul, M. (2003), *Power and Purpose: US Policy Toward Russia After the Cold War* (Washington, DC: Brookings Institution).

Kanet, R. (ed.) (2007), *Russia: Re-emerging Great Power* (London: Palgrave).

Rice, C. (2000), 'Campaign 2000: Promoting the National Interest', *Foreign Affairs*, Jan./Feb.

Simes, D. K., (2007), 'Losing Russia: The Costs of Renewed Confrontation', *Foreign Affairs*, Nov./Dec.

Talbott, S. (2002), *The Russia Hand* (New York: Random House).

Chapter 14

Berger, T. (2000), 'Set for Stability? Prospects for Conflict and Cooperation in East Asia', *Review of International Studies*, 26/3: 405–28.

Calder, K. E. (2006), 'China and Japan's Simmering Rivalry', *Foreign Affairs*, Mar.–Apr.: 129–39.

Carter, J. (2006), 'Solving the Korean Stalemate, One Step at a Time', *New York Times*, 11 Oct.

Cha, V. D. (2007), 'Winning Asia; Washington's Untold Success Story', *Foreign Affairs*, Nov.–Dec.: 98–113.

Foot, R., and Walter, A. (1999), 'Whatever Happened to the Pacific Century?', *Review of International Studies*, 25/5: 245–69.

Friedberg, A. L. (1993–4), 'Ripe for Rivalry: Prospects for Peace in Multipolar Asia', *International Security*, 18/3: 5–33.

Friedman, T. L. (2005), *The World is Flat: A Brief History of the Globalized World in the Twenty-First Century* (London: Allen Lane).

Gregg, D. (2006), 'Bush's Blunder in North Korea', 9 Oct., available at http://newsweek.washingtonpost.com/postglobal/needtoknow/2006/10/bushs_blunder_in_north_korea.html.

Moltz, J. C., and Quinones, C. K. (2004), 'Getting Serious about a Multilateral Approach to North Korea', *Nonproliferation Review*, Spring.

Zissis, C. (2007), 'Crafting a US Policy on Asia', Council on Foreign Relations Backgrounder, 10 Apr., available at www.cfr.org/publication/13022/crafting_a_us_policy_on_asia.html#2.

Chapter 15

Bulmer-Thomas, V., and Dunkerley, J. (1999), *The United States and Latin America: The New Agenda* (Cambridge, Mass.: David Rockefeller Center for Latin American Studies/Institute of Latin American Studies, University of London).

Grandin, G. (2006), *Empire's Workshop: Latin America, the United States, and the Rise of the New Imperialism* (New York: Metropolitan Books).

Huntington, S. (2004), *Who Are We?* (New York: Simon & Schuster).

Kirkpatrick, J. (1979), 'Dictatorships and Double Standards', *Commentary*, 68 (Nov.): 34–45.

LaFeber, W. (1983), *Inevitable Revolutions: The United States in Central America* (New York: W. W. Norton).

Reagan, R. (1983), *Public Papers of the Presidents of the United States: Ronald Reagan* (Washington, DC: US Government Printing Office).

Reid, M. (2007), *Forgotten Continent: The Battle for Latin America's Soul* (New Haven: Yale University Press).

Schoultz, L. (1998), *Beneath the United States: A History of US Policy toward Latin America* (Cambridge, Mass.: Harvard University Press).

Shifter, M. (2002), 'A Shaken Agenda: Bush and Latin America', *Current History*, Feb.

Chapter 16

Aljazeera.Net (2006), 'Somalia Unrest Worries Bush', 8 June, available at http://english.Aljazeera.net/English/archive/archive?Achiveld+23427 (accessed 13 Apr. 2007).

Bolton, J. R. (1994), 'Wrong Turn in Somalia', *Foreign Affairs*, 73/1: 56–66.

Brzezinski, Z. (1983), *Power and Principle* (London: Weidenfeld and Nicolson).

Bush, G. W. (2002), *The National Security of the United States of America*, available at www.whitehouse.gov.nsc.nss.pdf (accessed 16 Feb. 2007).

Cameron, F (2002), *US Foreign Policy after the Cold War: Global Hegemon or Reluctant Sheriff?* (London: Routledge).

Carmody, P. (2005), 'Transforming Globalization and Security: Africa and America Post-9/11', *Africa Today*, 52/1: 97–120.

Cheru, F. (2006), 'Aid and Trade Policies: Shifting the Debate', in D. Rothchild and E. J. Keller (eds.), *Africa–US Relations: Strategic Encounters* (Boulder, Colo.: Lynne Rienner Publishers), 217–44.

CNN.Com (2002), 'Study Explores High Cost of HIV/AIDS Care in US', 10 July, available at http://archives.cnn.com/2002/HEALTH/conditions/07/10/aids.costs/ (accessed 27 July 2007).

Cobb, C. (2006), 'Diplomacy's Odd Couple', *Mail & Guardian*, 18 Dec., available at www.mg.co.za/articlePage.aspx?articleid=293674&area=/insight/insight_comment_and_analysis/ (accessed 13 May 2007).

Copson, R. (2004), 'Africa: US Foreign Assistance Issues', *CRS Issue Brief for Congress*, 9 Dec.

Dagne, T. S. (1991), 'Ethiopia: New Thinking in US Policy', *CRS Report for Congress*, 91–489F.

Howe, H. M. (2001), *Ambiguous Order* (Boulder, Colo.: Lynne Rienner).

International Commission on Intervention and State Sovereignty (2001), *The Responsibility to Protect* (Ottawa: International Development Research Centre), available at www.iciss.ca/pdf/Commission-Report.pdf (accessed 27 July 2007).

Johnston, H., and Dagne, T. (1997), 'Congress and the Somalia Crisis', in Walter Clarke and Jeffrey Herbst (eds.), *Learning from Somalia: The Lessons of Armed Humanitarian Intervention* (Boulder, Colo.: Westview).

Keller, E. J. (2006), 'Africa and the United States: Meeting the Challenges of Globalization', in D. Rothchild and E. J. Keller (eds.), *Africa–US Relations: Strategic Encounters* (Boulder, Colo.: Lynne Rienner Publishers).

Lawson, L. (2007), 'US Africa Policy since the Cold War', *Strategic Insights*, 6/1, available at http://www.ccc.nps.navy.mil/si/2007/Jan/lawsonJan07.pdf (accessed 22 Mar. 2007).

Malan, M. (1999), 'Leaner and Meaner? The Future of Peacekeeping in Africa', *African Security Review*, 8/4, available at www.iss.co.za/pubs/ASR/8No4/Malan.html (accessed 1 June 2007).

——(2002), 'The Post 9/11 Security Agenda and Peacekeeping in Africa', *African Security Review*, 11/3, available at www.iss.co.za/pubs/ASR/11No3/Malan.html (accessed 1 June 2007).

Office of the US Global AIDS Coordinator (2007), *The United States President's Emergency Plan for AIDS Relief*, available at www.pepfar.gov/press/87565.htm#ogac (accessed 6 July 2007).

Office of Trade and Industry Information (OTII), Manufacturing and Services, International Trade Administration, US Department of Commerce (n.d.), *Data Sources from OTII*, available at www.ita.doc.gov/td/industry/otea/OTII/OTII-index.html (accessed 6 July 2007).

Patman, R. G. (1990), *The Soviet Union in the Horn of Africa: The Diplomacy of Intervention and Disengagement* (Cambridge: Cambridge University Press).

——(2001), 'Beyond "the Mogadishu Line": Some Australian Lessons for Managing Intra-State Conflicts', *Small Wars & Insurgencies*, 12/1: 59–75.

——(2007), 'Somalis Test Bush's Anti-Terror Strategy', *Dominion Post*, 22 June.

Rothchild, D. (2006), 'Trends in US–Africa Relations: Implications for the Future', in D. Rothchild and E. J. Keller (eds.), *Africa–US Relations: Strategic Encounters* (Boulder, Colo.: Lynne Rienner Publishers).

Saunders, P. C. (2006), 'China's Global Activism: Strategy, Drivers, and Tools', *Institute for National Strategic Studies*, Occasional Paper 4: 38–54.

Schabas, W. (1999), 'The Genocide Convention at Fifty', Special Report, United States Institute of Peace.

Schraeder, P. J. (1993), 'Reviewing the Study of US Policy towards Africa from Intellectual "Backwater" to Theory Construction', *Third World Quarterly*, 14/4: 775–86.

——(1994), *United States Foreign Policy toward Africa: Incrementalism, Crisis and Change* (Cambridge: Cambridge University Press).

Sloan, S. R. (1991), 'The US Role in a New World Order: Prospects for George Bush's Global Vision', *CRS Report for Congress*, 91–294 RCO.

——(2002), *President Proposes $5 Billion Plan to Help Developing Nations*, available at http://www.whitehouse.gov/news/releases/2002/03/20020314-7.html (accessed 23 Apr. 2007).

Thürer, D. (1999), *The 'Failed State' and International Law*, available at http://www.icrc.org/Web/eng/siteeng0.nsf/html/57JQ6U (accessed 27 July 2007).

UNAIDS (2006), *2006 Report on the Global AIDS Pandemic*, available at www.unaids.org/en/HIV_data/2006GlobalReport/default.asp (accessed 27 July 2007).

United Nations Development Programme (1994), *Human Development Report 1994* (Oxford: Oxford University Press).

Ward, George (1994), 'Peacekeeping: An Essential Tool', *New Zealand International Review*, 19/3: 23–5.

White House (2002), 'President Proposes $5 Billion Plan to Help Developing Nations', White House News Release, www.whitehouse.gov/news/release/2002/03/20020314-7.html.

Chapter 17

Bairoch, P. (1993), *Economics and World History: Myths and Paradoxes* (New York: Harvester Wheatsheaf).

Baldwin, D. A. (1985), *Economic Statecraft* (Princeton: Princeton University Press).

BEA (Bureau of Economic Analysis) (2007), *National Economic Accounts, 2007* (Washington, DC: Bureau of Economic Analysis).

Bhagwati, J. N. (2001), *Wind of the Hundred Days: How Washington Mismanaged Globalization* (Cambridge, Mass.: MIT Press).

——and Patrick, H. T. (eds.) (1990), *Aggressive Unilateralism: America's 301 Trade Policy and the World Trading System* (Ann Arbor: University of Michigan Press).

Bichler, S., Rowley, R., and Nitzan, J. (1989), 'The Armadollar–Petrodollar Coalition: Demise or New Order?', Working Paper 11/89 (Montreal: Department of Economics, McGill University), 1–63.

Bobbitt, P. (2002), *The Shield of Achilles: War, Peace and the Course of History* (New York: Knopf).

Cox, R. (1996), 'Gramsci, Hegemony and International Relations: An Essay in Method', in R. Cox with T. J. Sinclair (eds.), *Approaches to World Order* (Cambridge: Cambridge University Press).

Cox, R. W., and Skidmore-Hess, D. (1999), *US Politics and the Global Economy: Corporate Power, Conservative Shift* (Boulder, Colo.: Lynne Rienner).

Davis, M. (1984), 'The Political Economy of Late-Imperial America', *New Left Review*, 1/143 (Jan.–Feb.): 6–38.

Giles, C. (2006), 'A Productivity Prescription: How the US has Pulled Away from Europe and Japan', *Financial Times*, 25 Jan.: 19.

Goldstein, J. (1988), 'Ideas, Institutions and American Trade Policy', *International Organisation*, 42/1 (Winter): 178–218.

Gramsci, A. (1971), *Selections from the Prison Notebooks*, ed. and trans. Q. Hoare and G. Nowell Smith (London: Lawrence and Wishart).

Hathaway, R. (1984), '1933–1945: Economic Diplomacy in a Time of Crisis', in W. H. Becker and S. Wells, Jr. (eds.),

Economics and World Power: An Assessment of American Diplomacy since 1789 (New York: Columbia University Press).

Hogan, M. (2004), 'The "Next Big Thing": The Future of Diplomatic History in a Global Age', *Diplomatic History*, 28/1 (Jan.): 1–21.

Huntington, S. P. (1973), 'Transnational Organisations in World Politics', *World Politics*, 25/3: 333–68.

Isaacson, W., and Thomas, E. (1986), *The Wise Men: Six Friends and the World They Made* (New York: Simon & Schuster).

Jorgenson, D. W., and Khuong V. (2006), *Information Technology and the World Growth Resurgence*, Hitotsubashi University Research Unit for Statistical Analysis in Social Sciences Discussion Paper Series No. 181, Aug.

Kolko, G. (1976), *Main Currents in Modern American History* (New York: Harper and Row).

Krugman, P. (1994), 'Competitiveness: A Dangerous Obsession', in Foreign Affairs, *Competitiveness: An International Economics Reader* (New York: Council on Foreign Relations).

Lawrence, R. Z., and Schultze, C. L. (eds.) (1990), *An American Trade Strategy: Options for the 1990s* (Washington, DC: Brookings Institution).

Low, P. (1993), *Trading Free: The GATT and US Trade Policy* (New York: The 20th Century Fund Press).

McGuckin, R. H., III, and Van Ark, B. (2005), *Performance 2005: Productivity, Employment and Income in the World's Economies*, Report R-1364-05 RR, May (New York: The Conference Board).

Meunier, S. (2005), *Trading Voices: The European Union in International Commercial Negotiations* (Princeton: Princeton University Press).

Negri, A., and Hardt, M. (2000), *Empire* (Cambridge, Mass.: Harvard University Press).

Nitze, P. H. (1959), 'Coalition Policy and the Concept of World Order', in A. Wolfers, *Alliance Policy in the Cold War* (Baltimore: Johns Hopkins University Press).

Odell, J. S. (2000), *Negotiating the World Economy* (Ithaca, NY: Cornell University Press).

Pastor, R. A. (1980), *Congress and the Politics of US Foreign Economic Policy* (Berkeley and Los Angeles: University of California Press).

Schumpeter, J. A. (1934), *The Theory of Economic Development* (New York: Knopf).

Sheikh, A., and Tomak, E. A. (1994), *Measuring the Wealth of Nations: The Political Economy of National Accounts* (Cambridge: Cambridge University Press).

Skarstein, R. (2005), 'Economic Development by Means of Free Trade?', in G. Chaloupek, A. Heisse, G. Matzner-Holzer, and W. Roth, *Sisyphus als Optimist* (Hamburg: VSA Verlag).

Spiro, D. E. (1999), *The Hidden Hand of American Hegemony: Petrodollar Recycling and International Markets* (Ithaca, NY: Cornell University Press).

Verdier, D. (1994), *Democracy and International Trade* (Princeton: Princeton University Press).

Wade, R., and Veneroso, F. (1998), 'The Asian Crisis: The High Debt Model Versus the Wall Street–Treasury–IMF Complex', *New Left Review*, 1/228 (Mar.–Apr.): 3–22.

Williams, W. A. (1970), *The Roots of the Modern American Empire* (London: Anthony Blond).

——(1972), *The Tragedy of American Diplomacy* (New York: Dell Publishing).

Williamson, J., and Milner, C. (1991), *The World Economy* (New York: Harvester Wheatsheaf).

Wolf, M. (2004), *Why Globalisation Works* (New Haven: Yale University Press).

Wright-Mills, C. (1959), *The Power Elite* (Oxford: Oxford University Press).

Chapter 18

Bello, W. (2001), 'Endless War', Focus on the Global South, Manila, Philippines, Sept., available at www.focusweb.org/publications/2001/endless_war.html (accessed 25 May 2007).

Bush, G. W. (2002), State of the Union Address, Jan., available at www.whitehouse.gov/stateofhteunion/2002/ (accessed 25 May 2007).

Wardlaw, G. (1982), *Political Terrorism: Theory, Tactics and Countermeasures* (Cambridge: Cambridge University Press).

Chapter 19

Barkdull, J., and Harris, P. (2002), 'Environmental Change and Foreign Policy: A Survey of Theory', *Global Environmental Politics*, 2/2: 63–91.

Barnett, J. (2001), 'Environmental Security and US Foreign Policy: A Critical Examination', in P. G. Harris, *The Environment, International Relations, and US Foreign Policy* (Washington, DC: Georgetown University Press).

Benedick, R. (1991), *Ozone Diplomacy: New Directions in Safeguarding the Planet* (Cambridge, Mass.: Harvard University Press).

Boal, Iain, Clark, T. J., Matthews, J., and Watts, M. (2005), 'Blood for Oil?', *London Review of Books*, 27/8 (21 Apr.), review, available at http://bnarchiv es.yorku.ca/168/02/050421_Boal_et_al_Blood_for_oil_(print).htm.

Boykoff, M., and Boykoff, J. M. (2004), 'Balance as Bias: Global Warming and the US Prestige Press', *Global Environmental Change*, 14: 125–36.

Broder, J. (2007), 'Energy Bill Adopted by House Requires Utilities to Use Renewable Power Sources', *New York Times*, 5 Aug.

Bromley, S. (1991), *American Hegemony and World Oil* (Cambridge: Cambridge University Press).

——(2005), 'The United States and the Control of World Oil', *Government and Opposition*, 40/2: 225–55.

Brown, L. (1991), *State of the World 1991* (Washington, DC: WRI).

Bush, G. (2006), 'State of the Union Address' (The White House), available at www.whitehouse.gov/stateoftheunion/2006/ (accessed 19 Apr. 2007).

——(2007), 'State of the Union Address' (The White House). available at www.whitehouse.gov/stateoftheunion/2007/index.html (accessed 19 Apr. 2007).

Carter, J. (1979), 'The Crisis of Confidence Speech', PBS American Experience, available at www.pbs.org/wgbh/amex/carter/filmmore/ps_crisis.html.

Christoff, P. (1996), 'Ecological Modernisation, Ecological Modernities', *Environmental Politics*, 5/3: 476–500.

——and Eckersley, R. (2007) ,'The Kyoto Protocol and the Asia Pacific Partnership on Clean Development and Climate', paper presented at the 'Climate Law in Australia' Conference held at the National Museum of Australia, 12–13 Apr.

Christopher, W. (1998), *In the Stream of History: Shaping Foreign Policy for a New Era* (Stanford, Calif.: Stanford University Press).

CNA Corporation (2007), *National Security and the Threat of Climate Change* (Alexandria, Va.: CNA Corporation), available at http://securityandclimate.cna.org/ (accessed 19 Apr. 2007).

Council on Environmental Quality (CEQ) and Department of State (DoS) (1980), *The Global 2000 Report to President of the US: Entering the 21st Century the US President* (New York: Pergamon Press).

Depledge, J. (2005), 'Against the Grain: The United States and the Global Climate Change Regime', *Global Change, Peace and Security*, 17/1: 11–27.

DeSombre, E. (2000), *The Domestic Sources of International Environmental Policy: Industry, Environmentalists and US Power* (Cambridge, Mass.: MIT Press).

——(2005), 'Understanding United States Unilateralism: Domestic Sources of US International Environmental Policy', in R. Axelrod, D. Downie, and N. Vig (eds.), *The Global Environment: Institutions, Law and Policy* (Washington, DC: Congressional Quarterly Press).

Donnelly, J. (2007), 'Bush Calls for Rules to Reduce Emissions: In Reversal, Order EPA to Target Climate Change', *Boston Global*, 15 May.

Dryzek, J., Downes, D., Hunold, C., and Schlosberg, D. (2003), *Green States and Social Movements: Environmentalism in the United States, United Kingdom, Germany and Norway* (Oxford: Oxford University Press).

Eckersley, R. (2004), *The Green State: Rethinking Democracy and Sovereignty* (Cambridge, Mass.: MIT Press).

EurActiv.com (2007), 'EU Energy Blueprint Puts Onus on Climate Change and Renewables', 11 Jan., available at www.euractiv.com/en/energy/eu-energy-blueprint-puts-onus-climate-change-renewables/article-160805 (accessed 19 Apr. 2007).

Falkner, R. (2001), 'Business Conflict and US International Environmental Policy: Ozone, Climate and Biodiversity', in P. G. Harris, *The Environment, International Relations, and US Foreign Policy* (Washington, DC: Georgetown University Press).

——(2005), 'American Hegemony and the Global Environment', *International Studies Review*, 7: 585–99.

——(2007), 'International Cooperation against the Hegemon: The Cartagena Protocol on Biosafety', in R. Falkner (ed.), *The International Politics of Genetically Modified Food* (London: Palgrave).

Friedman, T. (2007), 'The Power of Green', *New York Times Magazine*, 15 Apr., available at www.nytimes.com/2007/04/15/magazine/15green.t.html?ex=1334289600&en=77253fdf8f321a95&ei=5088&partner=rssnyt&emc=rss.

Goel, R. (2004), 'A Bargain Born of Paradox: The Oil Industry's Role in American Domestic and Foreign Policy', *New Political Economy*, 9/4: 467–91.

Hartmann, T. (2003), 'Creating a World in Balance, Instead of an Empire of Oil', *Garlic and Grass: A Grassroots Journal of America's Political Soul*, 4 (June), available at www.garlicandgrass.org/index04.cfm (accessed 4 Apr. 2007).

Hopgood, S. (1998), *American Environmental Foreign Policy and the Power of the State* (New York: Oxford University Press).

Intergovernmental Panel on Climate Change (IPCC) (2007), *Climate Change 2007: Impacts. Adaptation and Vulnerability: Summary for Policy Makers* (Geneva: IPCC Secretariat), www.ipcc.ch/SPM13apr07.pdf (accessed 19 Apr. 2007).

International Energy Agency (IEA) (2005), *World Energy Outlook 2005*, available at www.worldenergyoutlook.org/2005.asp (accessed 19 Apr. 2007).

Keohane, R. (1984), *After Hegemony* (Princeton: Princeton University Press).

Klare, M. (2004), *Blood and Oil: The Dangers and Consequences of America's Growing Petroleum Dependency* (New York: Metropolitan Books).

Kolk, A., and Levy, D. (2001), 'Winds of Change: Corporate Strategy, Climate Change and Oil Multinationals', *European Management Journal*, 19/5: 501–9.

Levidow, L. (2007), 'The Transatlantic Agbiotech Conflict as a Problem and Opportunity for EU Regulatory Policies', in R. Falkner (ed.), *The International Politics of Genetically Modified Food* (London: Palgrave).

Lisowski, M. (2002), 'Playing the Two-Level Game: US President Bush's Decision to Repudiate the Kyoto Protocol', *Environmental Politics*, 11/4: 101–19.

Long, C., Cabral, M., and Vandivort, B. (1999), 'The Chief Environmental Diplomat: An Evolving Arena of Foreign Policy', in D. Soden (ed.), *The Environmental Presidency* (Albany, NY: State University of New York Press).

McCright, A. M., and Dunlap, R. (2003), 'Defeating Kyoto: The Conservative Movement's Impact on US Climate Change Policy', *Social Problems*, 50/3: 348–73.

McGee, J., and Taplin, R. (2006), 'The Asia-Pacific Partnership on Clean Development and Climate: A Complement or Competitor to the Kyoto Protocol?', *Global Change, Peace and Security*, 18/3: 173–92.

Newell, P., and Paterson, M. (1998), 'A Climate for Business: Global Warming, the State and Capital', *Review of International Political Economy*, 5/4: 679–703.

Oberthur, S., and Ott, H. (1999), *The Kyoto Protocol: International Climate Policy for the 21st Century* (Berlin: Springer-Verlag).

Paarlberg, R. (1999), 'Lapsed Leadership: US International Environmental Policy since Rio', in N. Vig and R. Axelrod (eds.), *The Global Environment: Institutions, Law and Policy* (Washington, DC: Congressional Quarterly).

Rabe, B. (2003), *From Statehouse to Greenhouse: The Emerging Politics of American Climate Change Policy* (Washington, DC: Brookings Institute Press).

Schellenberger, M., and Nordhaus, T. (2004), *The Death of Environmentalism: Global Warming Politics in a Post-Environmental World*, available at www.thebreakthrough.org/images/Death_of_Environmentalism.pdf (accessed 19 Apr. 2007).

Sitaraman, S. (2001), 'The Evolution of the Ozone Regime: Local, National, and International Influences', in P. G. Harris, *The Environment, International Relations, and US Foreign Policy* (Washington, DC: Georgetown University Press).

Smith, S. (1993), 'The Environment on the Periphery of International Relations', *Environmental Politics*, 2/4: 28–45.

Soden, D., and Steel, B. (1999), 'Evaluating the Environmental Presidency', in D. Soden (ed.), *The Environmental Presidency* (Albany, NY: State University of New York Press).

Sprinz, D., and Vaahtoranta, T. (1994), 'The Interest-Based Explanation of International Environmental Policy', *International Organization*, 48/1: 77–105.

Stern, N. (2007), *The Economics of Climate Change: The Stern Review* (Cambridge: Cambridge University Press).

Sunstein, C. (2007), 'On the Divergent American Reactions to Terrorism and Climate Change', *Columbia Law Review*, 107: 503–58.

Supreme Court of the United States, *Massachusetts et al. v. Environmental Protection Agency et al.* 548 US (2007); No. 5 1120, decided 2 Apr. 2007, available at www.supremecourtus.gov/opinions/06pdf/05-1120.pdf.

United Nations Environment Program (UNEP) (2005a), *Millennium Ecosystem Assessment Synthesis Reports* (UNEP), available at www.maweb.org/en/Synthesis.aspx (accessed 19 Apr. 2007).

——(2005b), *Register of International Treaties and Other Agreements in the Field of the Environment*, available at www.unep.org/law/PDF/register_Int_treaties_contents.pdf (accessed 24 Aug. 2007).

United States Department of State (USDS) (1998), *Environment Diplomacy: The Environment and US Foreign Policy,* First Annnual Report, available at www.state.gov/www/global/oes/earth.html (accessed 19 Apr. 2007).

Vig, N. (2006), 'Presidential Leadership and the Environment', in N. Vig and M. Kraft (eds.), *Environmental Policy: New Directions for the Twenty-First Century* (Washington, DC: Congressional Quarterly).

White House (1996), *National Security Strategy of Engagement and Enlargement*, Feb. (Washington, DC: White House), available at www.dtic.mil/doctrine/jel/research_pubs/nss.pdf (accessed 19 Apr. 2007).

——(2002), *Global Climate Change Policy Book* (Washington, DC), available at http://whitehouse.gov/news/releases/2002/02/climatechange.html (accessed 19 Apr. 2007).

——(2006), *A Realistic, Growth-Oriented Approach to Global Climate Change: A Synopsis*, available at http://whitehouse.gov/infocus/environment/index-cont.html (accessed 19 Apr. 2007).

World Bank (2007), *Little Green Data Book*, available at http://siteresources.worldbank.org/INTDATASTA/64199955-1178226923002/21322619/LGDB2007.pdf.

World Commission on Environment and Development (WCED) (1987), *Our Common Future: The Report of the World Commission on Environment and Development* (Oxford: Oxford University Press).

World Resources Institute (WRI) (2001), 'CO2 Emission Per Capita', http://earthtrends.wri.org/searchable_db/index.php?theme=3&variable_ID=666&action=select_countries (accessed 25 Mar. 2006).

World Watch Institute (2007), *State of the World Report 2007: Our Urban Future* (Washington, DC: WRI), available at www.worldwatch.org/ (accessed 19 Apr. 2007).

Chapter 20

Albright, M. (2004), *Madame Secretary: A Memoir* (London: Pan).

Amis, M. (2002), *Kobra the Dread Laughter and the Twenty Million* (London: Jonathan Cape).

Booth, K., and Dunne, T. (eds.) (2002), *Worlds in Collision: Terror and the Future of Global Order* (London: Palgrave).

Burleigh, M. (2004), *Earthly Powers* (New York: Harper Collins).

——(2006), *Sacred Causes* (New York: Harper Collins).

Chan, S. (2004), *Out of Evil* (London: Hurst).

Chomsky, N. (2003), *Hegemony or Survival: America's Quest for Global Dominance* (London: Penguin).

Fawn, R., and Buckley, M. (eds.) (2003), *Global Responses to Terrorism: 9/11, Afghanistan and beyond* (London: Routledge).

Gaddis, John Lewis (2002), *The Landscape of History: How Historians Map the Past* (Oxford: Oxford University Press).

——(2004), *Surprise, Security and the American Experience* (New Haven: Yale University Press).

Gray, C. S. (2005), *Another Bloody Century: Future Warfare* (London: Weidenfeld & Nicolson).

Halbestam, D. (2003), *War in a Time of Peace* (London: Bloomsbury).

Hansen, V. D. (2002), *An Autumn of War* (New York: Anchor Books).

Holbrooke, R. (1999), *To End a War* (New York: Modern Library).

Huntington, S. P. (2002), *The Clash of Civilizations and the Remaking of World Order* (New York: Free Press).

Isacson, W. (1996), *Kissinger* (New York: Touchstone).

Johnson, C. (2002), *Blowback* (New York: Time Warner).

Kagan, R. (2003), *Paradise & Power: America and Europe in the New World Order* (New York: Knopf).

Kennedy-Pipe, C., and Rengger, N. (2006), 'Apocalypse Now? Continuities and Disjunctions in World Politics after 9/11', *International Affairs*, 82/3: 539–53.

Keohane, R., and Nye, J. (2000), *Power and Interdependence*, 3rd edn. revised and expanded, World Politics in Transition (Boston: Little, Brown).

Keppel, G. (2005), *The Roots of Radical Islam* (Paris: Saqi Books).

Kissinger, H. (1982), *Years of Upheaval* (Boston: Little, Brown).

—— (1994), *Diplomacy* (New York: Simon & Schuster).

Mann, J. (2004), *The Rise of the Vulcans* (London: Penguin).

Mueller, J. (1989), *Retreat from Doomsday? The Obsolescence of Major War* (New York: Simon & Schuster).

—— (2004), *The Remnants of War* (Ithaca, NY: Cornell University Press).

Nye, J. S., Jr. (1992), 'What New World Order', *Foreign Affairs*, Spring: 83–96.

Rashid, A. (2001), *Taliban* (New Haven: Yale University Press).

Rice, C. (2000), 'Campaign 2000: Promoting the National Interest in Foreign Affairs', Jan.–Feb., 79/1, available at www.foreignaffairs.

Stelzer, I. (2005), *NeoConservatism* (London: Atlantic Books).

Thomas, S. (2005), *The Global Resurgence of Religion and the Transformation of International Relations* (London: Palgrave).

Woodward, B. (2004), *Plan of Attack* (New York: Simon & Schuster).

Wright, L. (2006), *The Looming Tower: Al Qaeda and the Road to 9/11* (New York: Knopf).

Chapter 21

Cooper, R. (2005), 'Imperial Liberalism', *National Interest*, Spring: 25–34.

Deller, N., Makhijani, A., and Burroughs, J. (eds.) (2003), *Rule of Power or Rule of Law: An Assessment of US Policies and Actions Regarding Security-Related Treaties* (New York: Apex Press).

Gaddis, J. L. (2003), *Surprise, Security and the American Experience* (Cambridge, Mass.: Harvard University Press).

Haass, R. (2003), 'Sovereignty: Existing Rights, Evolving Responsibilities', lecture at Georgetown University, 14 Jan..

Jervis, R. (2006), 'The Remaking of a Unipolar World', *Washington Quarterly*, 29/3 (Summer): 7–19.

Kagan, R. (2004), 'America's Crisis of Legitimacy', *Foreign Affairs*, 83/2 (Mar.): 2. Gaddis (2003: 66–7).

Rice, C. (2006), 'Transformational Diplomacy', speech at Georgetown University, 18 Jan.

Chapter 22

Bacevich, A. J. (2002), *American Empire: The Realities and Consequences of US Diplomacy* (Cambridge, Mass.: Harvard University Press).

Cobb, W. J., Jr. (1998), *The American Foundation Myth in Vietnam: Reigning Paradigms and Raining Bombs* (New York: University Press of America).

Hartz, L. (1955), *The Liberal Tradition in America* (New York: Harcourt Brace Jovanovich).

Hughes, R. (2003), *Myths America Lives By* (Urbana, Ill.: University of Illinois Press).

Huntington, S. (1981), *American Politics: The Promise of Disharmony* (Cambridge, Mass.: Harvard University Press).

Kagan, F., and O'Hanlon, M. (2007), 'The Case for Larger Ground Forces', Stanley Foundation series *Bridging the Foreign Policy Divide*, Apr.

Layne, C. (2006), 'Impotent Power?', *National Interest*, 85 (Sept.–Oct.): 41–7.

Lieven, A., and Hulsman, J. (2006), *Ethical Realism: A Vision for America's Role in the World* (London: Pantheon).

McDougall, W. A. (1997), *Promised Land, Crusader State: The American Encounter with the World since 1776* (Boston: Houghton Mifflin).

National Security Strategy (2006), http://www.whitehouse.gov/nsc/nss/2006/.

Nye, R. (1966), *This Almost Chosen People: Essays in the History of American Ideas* (East Lansing, Mich.: Michigan State University Press).

Peters, R. (2006), *Never Quit the Fight* (Mechanicsburg, Pa.: Stackpole Books).

Robberson, T. (2007), ' "US in Strategic Peril", US General Warns', *Dallas Morning News*, 4 Dec.

Sharp, J. M. (2005), 'The Middle East Partnership Initiative: An Overview', Congressional Research Service Report for Congress, 8 Feb.

Smith, T. L. (1979), 'Righteousness and Hope: Christian Holiness and the Millennial Vision in America, 1880–1900', *American Quarterly*, 31/1 (Spring): 21–45.

Snyder, J. (1991), *Myths of Empire* (Ithaca, NY: Cornell University Press).

Tuveson, E. L. (1968), *Redeemer Nation: The Idea of America's Millennial Role* (Chicago: University of Chicago Press).

Wittes, T. C., and Yerkes, S. E. (2004), 'The Middle East Partnership Initiative: Progress, Problems and Prospects', Saban Center Middle East memo no. 5, 29 Nov.

Woodward, C. V. (1968), *The Burden of Southern History* (Baton Rouge, La.: Louisiana State University Press).

Index